SEL

Studies in ENGLISH LITERATURE 1500-1900

The English Renaissance

VOLUME 27 WINTER 1987 NUMBER 1

Studies in English Literature 1500 - 1900

VOLUME 27 WINTER 1987 NUMBER 1

PUBLISHED BY RICE UNIVERSITY

CONTENTS

Allusive Coherence in Sidney's *Apology for Poetry* — John Hunt — 1

The Meaning of "Grace" and "Courtesy": Book Six of *The Faerie Queene* — Mark Archer — 17

"Words cannot knytt": Language and Desire in Ralegh's *The Ocean to Cynthia* — Robert E. Stillman — 35

The Arrangement of Ben Jonson's *Epigrammes* — James A. Riddell — 53

Expanding "The Poem Itself": Reading George Herbert's Revisions — Janis Lull — 71

The Fellowship of the Mystery: Emergent and Exploratory Metaphor in Vaughan — Harold Skulsky — 89

Milton and the Idea of the Restoration of the Jews — N. I. Matar — 109

The Muting of Satan: Language and Redemption in *Paradise Regained* — Steven Goldsmith — 125

Recent Studies in the English Renaissance — A. Leigh DeNeef — 141

U.S. Postal Service

STATEMENT OF OWNERSHIP, MANAGEMENT AND CIRCULATION

Required by 39 U.S.C. 3685)

1A. TITLE OF PUBLICATION	1B. PUBLICATION NO.	2. DATE OF FILING
Studies in English Literature, 1500-1900	0 0 3 9 3 6 5 7	9/18/86

3. FREQUENCY OF ISSUE	3A. NO. OF ISSUES PUBLISHED ANNUALLY	3B. ANNUAL SUBSCRIPTION PRICE
Quarterly	Four	U.S.: $20.00 Foreign: $25.00

4. COMPLETE MAILING ADDRESS OF KNOWN OFFICE OF PUBLICATION *(Street, City, County, State and ZIP+4 Code) (Not printers)*

SEL, Rice University, P.O. Box 1892, Houston TX 77251-1892

5. COMPLETE MAILING ADDRESS OF THE HEADQUARTERS OF GENERAL BUSINESS OFFICES OF THE PUBLISHER *(Not printer)*

Same

6. FULL NAMES AND COMPLETE MAILING ADDRESS OF PUBLISHER, EDITOR, AND MANAGING EDITOR *(This item MUST NOT be blank)*

PUBLISHER *(Name and Complete Mailing Address)*

William Marsh Rice University, P.O. Box 1892, Houston TX 77251-1892

EDITOR *(Name and Complete Mailing Address)*

Edward Doughtie, SEL, Rice University, P.O. Box 1892, Houston TX 77251-1892

MANAGING EDITOR *(Name and Complete Mailing Address)*

Lynne Wilson, SEL, Rice University, P.O. Box 1892, Houston TX 77251-1892

7. OWNER *(If owned by a corporation, its name and address must be stated and also immediately thereunder the names and addresses of stockholders owning or holding 1 percent or more of total amount of stock. If not owned by a corporation, the names and addresses of the individual owners must be given. If owned by a partnership or other unincorporated firm, its name and address, as well as that of each individual must be given. If the publication is published by a nonprofit organization, its name and address must be stated.) (Item must be completed.)*

FULL NAME	COMPLETE MAILING ADDRESS
William Marsh Rice University	P.O. Box 1892
	Houston TX 77251
	or
	6100 Main Street
	Houston TX 77005

8. KNOWN BONDHOLDERS, MORTGAGEES, AND OTHER SECURITY HOLDERS OWNING OR HOLDING 1 PERCENT OR MORE OF TOTAL AMOUNT OF BONDS, MORTGAGES OR OTHER SECURITIES *(If there are none, so state)*

FULL NAME	COMPLETE MAILING ADDRESS
There are none	

9. FOR COMPLETION BY NONPROFIT ORGANIZATIONS AUTHORIZED TO MAIL AT SPECIAL RATES *(Section 423.12 DMM only)*
The purpose, function, and nonprofit status of this organization and the exempt status for Federal income tax purposes *(Check one)*

[X] (1) HAS NOT CHANGED DURING PRECEDING 12 MONTHS

[ ] (2) HAS CHANGED DURING PRECEDING 12 MONTHS

(If changed, publisher must submit explanation of change with this statement.)

10. EXTENT AND NATURE OF CIRCULATION *(See instructions on reverse side)*	AVERAGE NO. COPIES EACH ISSUE DURING PRECEDING 12 MONTHS	ACTUAL NO. COPIES OF SINGLE ISSUE PUBLISHED NEAREST TO FILING DATE
A. TOTAL NO. COPIES *(Net Press Run)*	2147	2144
B. PAID AND/OR REQUESTED CIRCULATION 1. Sales through dealers and carriers, street vendors and counter sales	0	0
2. Mail Subscription *(Paid and/or requested)*	1784	1802
C. TOTAL PAID AND/OR REQUESTED CIRCULATION *(Sum of 10B1 and 10B2)*	1784	1802
D. FREE DISTRIBUTION BY MAIL, CARRIER OR OTHER MEANS SAMPLES, COMPLIMENTARY, AND OTHER FREE COPIES	90	90
E. TOTAL DISTRIBUTION *(Sum of C and D)*	1874	1892
F. COPIES NOT DISTRIBUTED 1. Office use, left over, unaccounted, spoiled after printing	273	252
2. Return from News Agents	0	0
G. TOTAL *(Sum of E, F1 and 2—should equal net press run shown in A)*	2147	2144

11. **I certify that the statements made by me above are correct and complete**

SIGNATURE AND TITLE OF EDITOR, PUBLISHER, BUSINESS MANAGER, OR OWNER

Lynne Wilson

Lynne Wilson, Business Manager

PS Form 3526, July 1984

(See instruction on reverse)

Studies in English Literature 1500 - 1900

PUBLISHED BY RICE UNIVERSITY

Studies in English Literature is a quarterly journal of historical and critical studies. Each issue will be devoted to one of four fields:

WINTER: The English Renaissance
SPRING: Elizabethan and Jacobean Drama
SUMMER: Restoration and Eighteenth Century
AUTUMN: The Nineteenth Century

SEL: Studies in English Literature, 1500–1900 (ISSN: 0039-3657) is published quarterly (February, May, August, and November) at $15.00 per year for individuals, $20.00 per year for U.S. institutions, $25.00 per year for foreign institutions, and $6.00 per single issue, by Rice University, 6100 South Main Street, P.O. Box 1892, Houston, Texas 77251. Second-class postage paid at Houston, Texas. **Postmaster:** Send address changes to the Business Manager, *SEL*, Rice University, P.O. Box 1892, Houston, TX 77251.

Studies in English Literature invites historical and critical essays of moderate length (ten to twenty-five pages) that contribute significantly to the understanding of English Literature, 1500-1900. Typescripts should be double-spaced throughout and prepared in conformity with the Chicago Manual of Style. Clean photocopy on uncoated paper is acceptable in place of the ribbon copy. We will not consider articles being simultaneously submitted elsewhere, nor will we print essays to appear in a book published within a year of scheduled publication of *SEL*. Those wishing to omit their identities from manuscripts may do so, but should include a covering letter.

Manuscripts submitted for publication should be addressed to the Editor, *Studies in English Literature,* Rice University, P.O. Box 1892, Houston, TX 77251. They must be accompanied by a sufficient number of unattached stamps for return. Receipt of manuscripts will be acknowledged by postcard. Editorial decisions usually take a minimum of three months.

Annual subscription rates: $15.00 for individuals, $20.00 for U. S. institutions, $25.00 for foreign institutions, $6.00 per issue for partial subscriptions and single copies. Regular subscriptions may be obtained for any or all quarterly issues. Remittance should accompany subscription requests. Notice of non-receipt of an issue must be made within ninety (90) days following the publication of that issue. No refunds or cancellations. Business communications should be addressed to Business Manager, *Studies in English Literature,* Rice University, P. O. Box 1892, Houston, TX 77251.

Microfilms of previous volumes (Vols. 1-26) may be obtained from University Microfilms, Inc., 300 N. Zeeb Road, Ann Arbor, Michigan 48106; xerox copies of individual articles may be ordered by calling (800) 521-0600 (toll free). Copies of articles are also available from ISI's The Genuine Article service, 3501 Market Street, Philadelphia, PA 19104; phone (800) 523-1850; telex 84-5305; electronic mail through CLASS; or facsimile transmission via FAXPAX.

Volumes 1 through 3 and 5 through 10 of *Studies in English Literature* are available from Johnson Reprint Corporation, 111 Fifth Avenue, New York, N. Y. 10003, or Berkeley Square House, London W. 1, England.

SEL 27 (1987)
ISSN 0039-3657

Allusive Coherence in Sidney's *Apology for Poetry*

JOHN HUNT

Anyone who tries to track down Philip Sidney's aesthetic speculations pursues an elusive prey. Criticism of the *Apology for Poetry* in this century has discovered ever more sources of influence on the work, from the poetic theory of Aristotle and his followers in the Italian Renaissance, to rhetorical theory of antiquity and later periods, and still farther afield to borrowings from ethics, politics, visual aesthetics, epistemology, and religion. These many perspectives on the literary fiction complicate Sidney's argument. So too does the philosophical eclecticism which he shares with many sixteenth-century writers. For four decades, the critical consensus that the *Apology* is a fundamentally Aristotelian work has been tested by recognition of its many Platonic elements and its extensive use of Stoic, Neoplatonic, and Christian ideas. A critic who comes to terms with Sidney's eclecticism and his wideranging intellectual curiosity has still more ground to cover. He must also allow for the man's willingness to take refuge equally in speculative ideals of morality and art and pragmatic ones. Private and public standards of accountability, contemplative enlightenment and active virtue, appeals to reason and to will, metaphysical justifications of the poetic fiction and emphasis on its empirical efficacy, praise for the artist's subjective freedom of invention and objective prescriptions for his craft—in each of these related oppositions, Sidney confounds logical tidiness by maintaining both sides of the argument. Finally, there is the inaccessibility produced by casual presentation: intellectual sources are alluded to in perfunctory or misleading ways, or not at all, and ideas expressed obscurely in the *Apology* are sometimes developed more clearly in one or another of the fictions.[1] Confronted with all these difficulties, even the most canny and persistent reader

---

After receiving his Ph.D. from Stanford University, John Hunt was a postdoctoral fellow at the University of Rochester, and now teaches English at Tufts University. He is completing a study of the psychological basis of Sidney's aesthetics, and has an article on Joyce's *Ulysses* forthcoming in *MLQ*.

can go astray as he tries to infer from the eloquence on the page the processes of reasoning that it represents.

As a result there is no consensus, not only about what Sidney thought on some important points, but even about what kind of a thinker he was. At least three distinct approaches have been pursued. After the extent of his debt to the Italian Aristotelians was first recognized, Sidney was typically regarded as an unoriginal transmitter of the ideas of other men. Later discoveries of the breadth of his reading, his extraordinary eclecticism, and his keenly critical treatment of received ideas forced a modification of this view, but did not completely erase the impression that he is either an unaccomplished amateur or a cautious humanist scholar, more the scribe than the author of his ideas.[2] A view of Sidney more prominent in the last two decades acknowledges the diversity of his borrowings but sees a powerfully original and coherent intelligence modifying, juxtaposing, and synthesizing ideas according to a systematic plan of its own. Explaining the connections among utterances not self-evidently consistent with each other, holders of this view sketch the outlines of the particular theoretical rationale which they believe Sidney had in mind as he wrote.[3] Still another appraisal of Sidney, adumbrated but seldom explicitly stated in past decades, and now suddenly attractive with the rise of deconstruction and kindred literary theories, identifies outright conceptual disjunctions in his thought as evidence of a deeply ironic and skeptical sensibility. By this reading, Sidney raises expectations of a theoretical union of opposites only to subvert them; placing more confidence in the strength and subtlety of his wit than in its access to universal criteria of significance, he deliberately confronts us with a breakdown of coherence, a liberation from systematic thinking.[4]

I will argue here for the second of these positions (and implicitly against the other two) by examining a crucial passage of the *Apology*, its discussion of the "final end" of learning. Conclusions about one passage studied in isolation cannot support any general argument about Sidney's intellectual method. But they may carry some suggestive weight, given the importance of this passage in his total argument and the degree to which it involves radical oppositions of sources and concepts. Prior to arguing that poetry represents a valuable and effective form of moral teaching, Sidney requires of himself a definition of the purpose of moral understanding. His answer is provocative in its ambiguity. After introducing a distinction between the immediate and ultimate "ends" of human knowledge, the passage identifies three very different ultimate ends and defines them by allusion to three different philosophical sources. Neither the "ends" of learning nor the texts which have inspired them are related to each other in any immediately apparent way. Specifying the contexts and implications of Sidney's allusions brings the passage into focus, revealing much about how he organizes multiplicity and balances oppositions—that is to say, about how he thinks.

In the first section of the passage, Sidney maintains that the ultimate goal of all knowledge is religious: to restore to the soul as much of its lost perfection as is possible. He proceeds to define a state of contemplative enlightenment in which the soul, aspiring to the condition of "felicity," is "lifted up" from the limitations of mortal consciousness:

> learning, under what name soever it come forth, or to what immediate end soever it be directed, the final end is to lead and draw us to as high a perfection as our degenerate souls, made worse by their clayey lodgings, can be capable of. This, according to the inclination of the man, bred many formed impressions. For some that thought this felicity principally to be gotten by knowledge, and no knowledge to be so high and heavenly as acquaintance with the stars, gave themselves to Astronomy; others, persuading themselves to be demigods if they knew the causes of things, became natural and supernatural philosophers; some an admirable delight drew to Music; and some the certainty of demonstration to the Mathematics. But all, one and other, having this scope—to know, and by knowledge to lift up the mind from the dungeon of the body to the enjoying his own divine essence.[5]

The second section introduces a pair of earthly scales into these high reveries, deflating the *O altitudo!* with a consideration of mundane human depravity:

> But when by the balance of experience it was found that the astronomer looking to the stars might fall into a ditch, that the inquiring philosopher might be blind in himself, and the mathematician might draw forth a straight line with a crooked heart, then lo, did proof, the overruler of opinions, make manifest that all these are but serving sciences, which, as they have each a private end in themselves, so yet are they all directed to the highest end of the mistress-knowledge, by the Greeks called *architectonike,* which stands (as I think) in the knowledge of a man's self.

The third section is introduced by the subtlest of transitions—an apposition of prepositional phrases—but it changes the subject significantly, from the imperfect state of the human soul to the accomplishment of various practical actions in the physical world:

> which stands (as I think) in the knowledge of a man's self, in the ethic and politic consideration, with the end of well-doing and not of well-knowing only: even as the saddler's next end is to make a good saddle, but his farther end to serve a nobler faculty, which is horsemanship, so the horseman's to soldiery, and the soldier not only to have the skill, but to perform the practice of a soldier. So that, the ending end of all earthly learning being virtuous action, those skills, that most serve to bring forth that, have a most just title to be princes over all the rest.

Clearly the impulse behind each of these three valuations of knowledge is moral: each concerns itself with how man can best realize his capacity for goodness. But moral excellence has a very different character in each instance.

In the first case, it is inspired by what the Christian Renaissance called Platonism: an enthusiastic response to the strict dualistic oppositions of Plato's middle dialogues (mind and body, thought and sensation, intelligible and visible objects) colored by various Neoplatonic concepts. One Neoplatonic idea in particular stands out in this instance, adding some theoretical precision to the stirring but vague talk of raising the mind from the dungeon of the body, inspired by Plato's *Phaedo* and *Republic*. It originated with the ancient Neoplatonists and found its way into the works of St. Augustine, most prominently in a passage at the beginning of the *De Doctrina Christiana*. Some things, Augustine says there, are to be enjoyed, and others used. The former are those which we embrace with love for their own sake, and which "make us blessed"; the latter are things which, though not cherished of themselves, we take advantage of in pursuit of what we love, and which "sustain us as we move toward blessedness" (1.3-4).[6] Augustine proceeds to describe the entire created world as something to be used on the way to the soul's enjoyment of the invisible things of God: "in this mortal life, wandering from God, if we wish to return to our native country where we can be blessed we should use this world and not enjoy it . . . so that by means of corporal and temporal things we may comprehend the eternal and spiritual" (1.4). One thing on earth escapes the wrath of Augustine's profound *contemptus mundi:* man's rational soul, which was made in the image of God and which retains vestiges of its original nature, though darkened and diminished by Adam's sin. In a passage from the *De Trinitate,* Augustine applies the concept of enjoyment to the mind's effort to recover its nature:

> What then can be the purport of the injunction, Know thyself? I suppose it is that the mind should reflect upon itself, and live in accordance with its nature: that is to say, strive to be ordered according to its nature, under him whom it should be set under, and over all that it should stand over. . . . It sees beauties of the inward realm, belonging to that transcendent reality which is God. Its duty is to stand fast for the enjoyment of them.
>
> (10.7)[7]

Clinging with love to the spiritual nature that he finds evidence of within his own rational soul, man finds himself in a proper relationship both to God and to the inferior things of this world.

Augustine is always quick to point out that if man ascribes this insight into spiritual beauty to his own power instead of to God, he loses that which he presumes to possess. In the *Confessions,* he makes proud astronomers symbolic of an intellect enamored of itself. These men, he says, "think themselves to be lifted up to the stars and to be shining lights, and lo, they plunge down to earth, 'and their foolish heart is darkened over' "(5.3).[8] The astronomer who, according to Sidney, falls in a ditch while pursuing his "high and heavenly" knowledge, the philosopher who is "blind in himself," mistakenly think themselves "demi-gods" because of their intellectual power. They do not recognize the source of what Astrophil calls the "inward light" or "heavenly part" through which we pilgrims "should in soul up to our country move."[9] The ultimate purpose of human knowledge, according to the first section of Sidney's analysis of moral ends, is to "lift up the mind" from earthly concerns and set it moving toward its native country, by properly "enjoying" its own heavenly nature.[10]

In the second section of the passage, the distinction between immediate and final ends of knowledge is cast metaphorically as a division of disciplines into "serving sciences" and "the mistress-knowledge." Here Sidney echoes the 88th of Seneca's *Epistulae Morales,* whose subject is the liberal arts. With his characteristic pessimism about the efficacy of intellectual endeavor, Seneca subverts the phrase *artes liberales,* which for a Roman meant those disciplines which were suitable for a free-born man, as opposed to the mechanical arts of slaves. Such arts cannot in truth be called "liberal," says Seneca, for they do not liberate men from the ignorance and depravity which miserably enslave them. They are instead mere preparations (in Sidney's language, "serving sciences") for the only truly liberating study, moral philosophy, which educates men in good and evil. Like other Stoics of antiquity, Seneca believed that all moral rectitude began in a correctly attuned individual psyche and spread outward, like concentric rings on water, to the social groups in which the individual was involved. (Sidney alludes to this belief when, at the end of a portrait of the moral philosopher in the *Apology* that has much of the stern Stoic about it, he says that virtue "extendeth itself out of the limits of a man's own little world to the government of families, and maintaining of public societies.")[11] Thus the 88th *Epistle* describes the transition from ordinary intellectual disciplines to moral philosophy as a turning inward, from the great physical cosmos to the little world of the psyche. Sidney's vignettes of the earthbound astronomer, the blind philosopher, and the morally irregular mathematician recall larger sketches such as these in Seneca's letter:

> Do you raise the question, "Through what regions did Ulysses stray?" instead of trying to prevent ourselves from going astray at all times? We have no leisure to hear lectures on the question whether he was tost between Italy and Sicily, or outside our known world. . . . we ourselves encounter storms of the spirit, which toss us daily, and our depravity drives us into all the ills which troubled Ulysses.
>
> O what marvellous skill! You know how to measure the circle; you find the square of any shape which is set before you; you compute the distances between the stars; there is nothing which does not come within the scope of your calculations. But if you are a real master of your profession, measure me the mind of man! Tell me how great it is, or how puny! You know what a straight line is; but how does it benefit you if you do not know what is straight in this life of ours?[12]

The ultimate purpose of learning, according to the second of Sidney's definitions, is "knowledge of a man's self"—a knowledge which turns away from the relatively unimportant study of physical nature and sounds the depths of the psyche, seeking to fathom its treacherous passions.

Finally, Sidney turns his attention to the field of "virtuous action." At the beginning of the *Nicomachaean Ethics,* Aristotle introduces his subject by observing that all disciplines, methods, and crafts have some good at which they aim, and that in many cases the immediate good is subordinate to some further, and higher, good—as harness-making is subordinate to horsemanship, and horsemanship to military strategy. If there is some good which is desired only for its own sake and toward which all subordinate goods are directed, it must, he argues, be the Supreme Good of human life, and the art or science which has it for its object will be an "architectonic" or controlling art, the master of other disciplines. Sidney repeats these observations almost verbatim, and implies that the ultimate aim of knowledge is the ethical "practice," or behavior, of a good man. Reinforcing this claim, he adds to Aristotle's remarks about the master-art another Aristotelian distinction, one which is mentioned in the opening paragraphs of the *Ethics* but developed more precisely in Book 6. Aristotle divides rational disciplines into the theoretical speculation of the philosopher, the skilled craftsmanship of the artist, and the prudential action of the politician or moralist—in short, into knowing, making, and doing. Of these three types of rational discipline, the last two differ from the first in that they have some end outside of the mere act of thinking; their excellence consists primarily in the object which they produce or the action which they perform, and not in the process of reasoning by which the object or action has been brought into being. For Aristotle, such arts are not superior to theoretical knowledge for having this attribute; in fact, he argues at the end of the *Ethics* that theoretical learning is the noblest and most fulfilling form of intellectual activity. But Sidney uses the distinction to reinforce the ideal of virtuous action which he finds in Aristotle. The function of a soldier, he says in the last section of the passage, is "not only to have the skill, but to perform the practice of a soldier." He summarizes this ideal of practical action informed by rational skill in his third statement of the final end of learning: "the ethic and politic consideration, with the end of well-doing and not of well-knowing only."

Thus the passage from the *Apology* offers three distinctly different answers to the question which it has posed, answers suggested by at least three different philosophical sources. The end of learning is consistently defined as moral, but in one case moral virtue is described as a contemplative familiarity with the divine source of understanding, in another as a mature mastery of the soul's passions, and in still another as a standard of action which unites and governs all other pragmatic standards. The logic of this seemingly disjointed passage reveals itself when one examines the order in which Sidney has constructed it and the resemblances between the materials which he has juxtaposed. Of the three kinds of virtue, he presents two as virtual synonyms: intertwining descriptions of the knowledge of the psyche associated with Seneca's letter and of the ethical science envisaged by Aristotle, he speaks of a "mistress-knowledge, by the Greeks called *architectonike,* which stands (as I think) in the knowledge of a man's self, in the ethic and politic consideration." His rationale in doing so is not hard to construe, for if all other disciplines of production and action are subordinate to the ethical and political discipline which sets standards for man's behavior in general, and if man's behavior in general is determined by his desires, capabilities, and dispositions, then knowledge of these psychological conditions will be the ultimate object of study in any effort to correct action. As Seneca pithily says in one of the sentences of his letter, one which Sidney might well have added to Aristotle's example of disciplines associated with horsemanship, "For what good does it do us to guide a horse and control his speed with the curb and then find that our own passions, utterly uncurbed, bolt with us?"[13] A knowledge of passion, in this view, is the inevitable and necessary completion of the knowledge of making bridles, the knowledge of governing horses, and so forth. Aristotle in fact develops just such a view in the *Ethics,* by defining the supreme good as happiness, which is an "activity of the soul"; by observing that some theoretical psychology must underlie any system of ethics, and consequently supplying a brief summary of his own; and by offering as his principal contribution to the study of ethics an analysis of the various passions in the human soul and the principles of moderation according to which man should dispose them.

The "knowledge of a man's self" also shares one important quality with the knowledge of divinity discussed earlier in the passage: both are introspective. Seneca's intention to direct the mind's gaze in upon itself, past the distractions of worldly concerns, accords with Sidney's notion of contemplation, expressed in a letter to Hubert Languet, as a chance for the mind to "turn its powers inward for thorough self-examination; to which employment no labour that men can undertake is any way to be compared."[14] It accords as well, in this one respect, with Augustine's notion of enjoyment and use.[15] And if the soul as conceived by a Christian Neoplatonist has at its center some kinship with the divine, this affinity would seem to be the source of whatever moral improvement man achieves when, obeying Seneca's dictates, he grapples with the forces of passion within himself. Here again Sidney seems to have juxtaposed essentially compatible philosophical materials, for Seneca's confidence in the efficacy of moral knowledge depends on just such a line of reasoning. The Stoics held that man's own *logos* or *ratio* was a recapitulation in miniature of the universal Reason responsible for the organization of the cosmos (Sidney's letter to Languet, alluding to this Stoic belief, calls the mind a "particle of the divine mind"), and they argued that by investigating his own mind man could attune himself to, and to some degree incorporate, the order of the cosmos. The participation of the mind in the rational principles structuring the universe, and the possibility of enacting those principles in the thought and actions of the individual, give Seneca whatever hope he has that human life is salvageable.

Thus the most opposed terms in Sidney's equation—the identifications of moral virtue as contemplative and as active—meet through the agency of a middle term which has affinities with both. Sidney also apparently intended that these opposed terms should be related in terms of their own theoretical formulae. If "enjoyment" in the Augustinian framework refers to a contemplative state in which the mind clings inwardly to its consciousness of divinity, "use" should denote the active, worldly virtue which is practiced in pursuit of that contemplative state and which helps to sustain the soul in it. Aristotle's disciplines of practical activity could, in this view, be seen as tools whose proper use would help foster and confirm the more perfect insights of contemplation. Sidney does not make clear this implication of the two terms in the *Apology,* though he implies something very much like it in a passage of the *Arcadia.*[16] The *Apology* does, however, attempt the rapprochement from the other direction by appropriating a term from the discussions of practical virtue in Aristotle's *Ethics* and applying it to the activity of contemplation. All intellectual disciplines, Sidney says, have "this scope—to know, and by knowledge to lift up the mind to the enjoying his own divine essence." The Greek word *skopos* means target, and Aristotle uses it at the beginning of the *Ethics* to describe the supreme good toward which all subordinate goods are directed:

> Will not then a knowledge of the Supreme Good be also of great practical importance for the conduct of life? Will it not better enable us to attain what is fitting, like archers having a target (*skopon*) to aim at? If this be so, we ought to make an attempt to determine at all events in outline what exactly this Supreme Good is, and of which of the theoretical or practical sciences it is the object.
>
> (1.2.2-3)[17]

The word is also used later in the *Ethics* (6.1.1) to describe the intellectual principles on which the ethical man fixes his gaze when he seeks an appropriate middle state between contrary extremes of passion. Here, in Book 1, Aristotle associates it with knowledge of the supreme good, identifies the supreme good as happiness or personal well-being (*eudaimonia*), and implies that such well-being is the object particularly of the practical sciences of ethics and politics, which he distinguishes from the life of contemplation or theory. At the end of the *Ethics*, however, he argues in his famous praise of contemplation that theoretical activity is what makes man most happy. Moral life "is happy only in a secondary degree," he says there, "for the moral activities are purely human" (10.8.1). God is supremely happy or blessed, and his activity is contemplation, not the banal business of repaying debts and regulating bothersome passions. Man has the capacity to be like God through the speculative use of his intellect (*nous*), which is something "divine," a "ruling part" or "true self" which surpasses man's mortal nature in excellence, and whose activity is "divine in comparison with human life"; man should therefore assimilate himself as far as possible to the immortal nature of the divine (10.7.8-9). Thus Aristotle seems to be saying in the *Ethics* that the condition of well-being which is essential for tempering desires and managing practical problems is acquired most fully in the comparatively disinterested contemplation of Mind. By saying, with Aristotle, that all branches of human knowledge have some "scope" at which they aim, and by associating it with Augustine's contemplative knowledge of the mind's divine essence, Sidney indicates his awareness of the ambiguity in the argument of the *Ethics* and follows out its implications, suggesting that practical actions pursue a standard of perfection discovered in contemplation.[18]

Bearing in mind these rather intricate contextual relations implied by Sidney's pattern of argument and allusion, the passage with its three answers to the same question makes some sense, better sense than Sidney goes out of his way to explain. Its thought might be rendered as follows: "The purpose of thinking is to make man as much like God as he is capable of becoming, by raising his mind above mundane concerns and increasing its godlike power of understanding. But experience shows that many intellectual endeavors miss this mark, for their practitioners, far from appearing divine, turn out not even to be good men. This is because they do not seek the divine resemblance where it lies, within themselves, obscured by misguided desire. Seeking perfection there, men will indeed find enlightenment, and at the same time they will re-lay the foundations of their lives and reform their behavior." Sidney could have made the same argument in the opposite direction: "The end of knowledge is to improve the world which we inhabit. But all considerations of practical accomplishment must culminate in an understanding of what man should desire and what he does desire; not until the latter is approximated to the former will any beneficial change of behavior result. When a man looks within himself at the passions and desires which determine his actions, he comes to realize how imperfectly they correspond to the image of God in which he was made; seeking to change them, he cultivates the intellectual power still dimly present in his soul. Thus he reforms his outward actions by contemplating the divine image within himself."[19]

Either way that the argument is made, the essential aim of Sidney's ethical speculation in this passage is the same: to present poetry as a discipline which can unify fundamental oppositions in human life by illuminating and ordering the contents of the soul. Self-knowledge as suggested by Seneca's letter and related to the moral programs of Aristotle and Augustine means the cultivation of an internal balance through which the contemplative impulse can be channelled into its proper outlet, virtuous action, and action perfected by the insights of contemplation.[20] Sidney sketches the outlines of this model for ethical life by selective allusion to some concepts and phrases from works of ancient philosophy—suppressing, in the process, contexts whose description would make the juxtaposition of those phrases and concepts intelligible.

He may have suppressed not only the contexts of allusions, but entire sources as well. Digressing for a moment from firmly based conjecture to sheer speculation, it is interesting to note that all the ideas of this passage recapitulate ideals of psychic unity-in-multiplicity established in Plato's *Republic*, a work which Sidney seems to have known fairly well.[21] Asserting the need for philosophers to return to the world of appearances (and politics), Plato argued that the blessed flight of Soul to Idea is, by itself, no more adequate a condition for the guardian of the state than is the benighted pragmatism of the cave-dweller:

> neither could men who are uneducated and inexperienced in truth ever adequately preside over a state, nor could those who had been permitted to linger on to the end in the pursuit of culture—the one because they have no single aim and purpose in life to which all their actions, public and private, must be directed, and the others, because they will not voluntarily engage in action, believing that while still living they have been transported to the Islands of the Blessed. (519C)[22]

The good not only of the state, but of the individual as well, urges that man should not simply cultivate the insights of reason, but seek to join their influence to those elements of the soul that more directly promote action. Once a man knows the Good, argues Plato, he can enact in himself a harmonious balancing of the three forces (intelligence, spiritedness, and appetite) that constitute his own being. And once he has fostered such a condition within himself, he can turn to virtuous action:

> having harmonized these three principles . . . and bound all three together and made of himself a unit, one man instead of many, self-controlled and in unison, he should then and then only turn to practice if he find aught to do either in the getting of wealth or the tendance of the body or it may be in political action or private business—in all such doings believing and naming the just and honorable action to be that which preserves and helps to produce this condition of soul.
>
> (443E)

Such a state of internal harmony, informed by vision and confirmed by practice, uniting the most disparate aspects of human inclination, is implied by Sidney's patchwork model of how ethical imperatives are organized.

The intricate conceptual connections in Sidney's analysis of moral ends suggest that, far from being a mere sifter of other men's ideas, he is very much in control of his opposition of theory and practice—and that rather than suggesting the impossibility of mediating the opposed terms, he intends a theoretical reconciliation of them. Still, it is strange that he makes so little effort to communicate the processes of his reasoning to his reader. Why juxtapose pieces from Aristotelian, Stoic, and Christian Neoplatonic works in order to describe a pattern for human life that could more easily and efficiently have been elicited from any one of them, or from a Platonic work? And why omit any explanation of how the pieces fit together?

A plausible answer to the first question is that Sidney's eclecticism indicates no lack of intellectual strength and originality, but, to the contrary, shows an aristocratic mind determined to be in control of the intellectual tradition, rather than subservient to it. By not expounding some version of Platonism, or Aristotelianism, or Augustinianism, or Senecanism, Sidney declares that he has his own vision to enact and will not rely on any one man's ideas to do it for him. The second question can be answered by observing that

Sidney's allusive procedures resemble in their abstruse intricacy the methods of artists like Donne and Joyce. Employing the mental rigor and difficulty of philosophy to engage a deep and intractable division in himself between contemplative and pragmatic impulses, he declines to trivialize either the personal dilemma or the philosophy by reducing them to a simple program for self-help. This determination not to tell the laity his love should complicate our assessment of the gallant Elizabethan courtier. Sidney's famous *sprezzatura,* his concealment of difficulty according to the principle *ars celare artem,* his attitude of wishing to divert his good readers rather than torture them with thought, conceals (as such genial postures do in, say, the poetry of Frost) a far more bristly mix of self-assertion and self-protection. Superiority to the average reader is implied by his inventing such theoretical intricacy only to bury it out of common sight; the reader may obtain some of my meaning by a casual perusal, the procedure implies, but if he wants it all he must work as hard to achieve it as I have. Like the "image" which is the centerpiece of its poetic theory, the *Apology for Poetry* delights its audience with seductive rhetorical grace, while reserving for those with the intelligence and will to discover it a sober purpose.

NOTES

[1]Geoffrey Shepherd, whose admirable edition of *An Apology for Poetry* (London: Nelson, 1965) has gone farther than any other in identifying the work's sources and contexts, expresses something close to consternation when he notes that Sidney's praise of the poet as maker of "another nature" follows the argumentative outlines of a brief passage in Scaliger's *Poetics,* but makes of the borrowing something very different from what Scaliger said or meant. Shepherd says of Sidney, p. 61: "It is highly characteristic of his easy power of assimilation—though troublesome to an editor—that he should borrow from one obvious author material with which to expound a different type of theory which he must have known about from other theorists who are left unnamed."

[2]Cornell March Dowlin long ago objected to the notion of Sidney as an epitomizer and popularizer of others' ideas that followed upon the work of Spingarn and Myrick, in "Sidney and Other Men's Thought," *RES* 20 (1944): 257-71. While Sidney has never since been read as a blank page, he has been implicated in subtler forms of intellectual passivity. Dorothy Connell's *Sir Philip Sidney: The Maker's Mind* (Oxford: Oxford Univ. Press, 1977), describes a man who, weighing ideas by "the balance of experience" (a phrase from the section of the *Apology* discussed in this essay), finds consistency among them less important than awareness of their limited applicability to the human condition. In "A Hybrid Growth: Sidney's Theory of Poetry in *An Apology for Poetry,*" *ELR* 10 (1980): 183-201, D. H. Craig explores the more sophisticated view of Sidney as a scholar picking out what he finds best in various traditions of

thought. Craig intelligently demonstrates that Sidney's theory cannot be adequately accounted for in terms of Mannerism (as Shepherd argues), or of Neoplatonism (John P. McIntyre, "Sidney's 'Golden World,'" *CL* 14 [1962]: 356-65), or of Calvinism (Andrew D. Weiner, *Sir Philip Sidney and the Poetics of Protestantism* [Minneapolis: Univ. of Minnesota Press, 1978]), but must be regarded as a humanist hybrid. Craig's own descriptions of Sidney's theory are persuasive, but are developed by contrast with its many sources and analogues, and not in terms of a coherent principle of organization.

[3]The danger in this approach lies in reading Sidney too systematically, assigning to him ideas which he cannot persuasively be shown to have held. This complaint can with justice be lodged against Forrest G. Robinson's *The Shape of Things Known: Sidney's Apology in its Philosophical Tradition* (Cambridge, Mass.: Harvard Univ. Press, 1972), which advances a coherent rationale for Sidney's borrowings but consistently declines to demonstrate its applicability to particular passages. More scrupulous interpretations of Sidney as an original synthesizer of critical ideas have been made in two studies each of which embraces several Renaissance literary theorists: Robert L. Montgomery, *The Reader's Eye: Studies in Didactic Literary Theory from Dante to Tasso* (Berkeley: Univ. of California Press, 1979), and Margaret W. Ferguson, *Trials of Desire: Renaissance Defenses of Poetry* (New Haven: Yale Univ. Press, 1983). In a recent addition to the old debate about Platonic and Aristotelian influences, "'The Poets Only Deliver': Sidney's Conception of *Mimesis*," *SLitI* 15 (1982): 67-84, John C. Ulreich, Jr., attempts to show how Sidney achieves theoretical coherence by synthesizing opposite but compatible conceptions of literary form.

[4]The best known proponent of this view is Ronald Levao, in "Sidney's Feigned *Apology*," *PMLA* 94 (1979): 223-33, and in his recently published book, *Renaissance Minds and their Fictions* (Berkeley: Univ. of California Press, 1985). Levao takes his point of departure particularly from an early essay by Jakob Bronowski in *The Poet's Defence* (Cambridge: Cambridge Univ. Press, 1939), which finds contradictory Sidney's belief that poetry can envision and constitute an ideal world and his opposite conviction that poetry shapes virtuous behavior in this world. An argument comparable to Levao's has been advanced in this journal by Martin N. Raitiere, "The Unity of Sidney's *Apology for Poetry*," *SEL* 21 (1981): 37-57. Taking his inspiration especially from O. B. Hardison, Jr., "The Two Voices of Sidney's *Apology for Poetry*," *ELR* 2 (1972): 83-99, Raitiere describes the inconsistency between Sidney's praise for the poet's "high flying liberty of conceit" and his judgment that the poet is an Icarus who needs a Dedalus to guide him.

[5]*Apology*, ed. Shepherd, p. 104.

[6]*On Christian Doctrine,* trans. D. W. Robertson, Jr. (Indianapolis: Bobbs-Merrill, 1958).

[7]Quoted from *Augustine: Later Works,* trans. John Burnaby (Philadelphia: Westminster, 1955).

[8]*The Confessions of St. Augustine,* trans. John K. Ryan (New York: Doubleday, 1960).

[9]*Astrophil and Stella* 5, lines 2 and 12-13, from *Poems,* ed. William A. Ringler, Jr. (Oxford: Clarendon Press, 1962).

[10]Sidney uses the concept of enjoyment several times in the *Arcadia* to refer to a state in which the soul is drawn inward in communion with its own uncorrupt nature, or with another soul, or with divinity. Thus Musidorus praises Pamela in an apostrophe to the "happy gods, which by inward assumption / Enjoy her fair soul, in body's fair possession" (*The Countess of Pembroke's Arcadia,* ed.

Maurice Evans [Harmondsworth, Middlesex: Penguin, 1977], pp. 184-85). After eloping, the two lovers pass an interlude of "virtuous wantonness, suffering their minds to descend to each tender enjoying their united thoughts" (p. 652). And when Philoclea sleeps through the approach of danger, the narrator says that her "innocent soul now enjoying his own goodness did little know the danger of his even fair, then sleeping harbor [i.e., body]" (pp. 737-38). *Enjoyment* also had the meaning of sexual possession in Elizabethan English, and at other points in the *Arcadia* Sidney playfully confuses the two meanings, suggesting how closely contemplative and sexual delectation are related in the erotic imagination. Thus Pyrocles-Zelmane crushes the unhappy Basilius by affecting to misunderstand his intention of "enjoying those your excellencies wherein my life is upheld": "'Enjoying,' quoth you! Now little joy come to them that yield to such enjoying" (p. 324). Defending his love for Philoclea, Pyrocles is challenged by Musidorus to identify its "end," and answers, with a deep sigh, "Enjoying"—a response which Musidorus takes for evidence of the baseness of erotic passion, until Pyrocles insists that he has been misunderstood (p. 137).

[11]*Apology*, p. 105.

[12]*Ad Lucilium Epistulae Morales*, trans. Richard M. Gummere, 3 vols. (London: W. Heinemann, 1917-1925), 1: 353, 357.

[13]Ibid., p. 361.

[14]*The Correspondence of Sir Philip Sidney and Hubert Languet*, ed. and trans. Steuart A. Pears (London: W. Pickering, 1845), p. 143. Sidney asks Languet, "For to what purpose should our thoughts be directed to various kinds of knowledge, unless room be afforded for putting it into practice, so that public advantage may be the result, which in a corrupt age we cannot hope for?" He continues, "Do you not see that I am cleverly playing the Stoic? yea and I shall be a cynic too, unless you reclaim me." Compare the embittered rejection of action in this letter with the more harmonious statement of its subservience to contemplation in the passage quoted in note 16.

[15]One could almost mistake Augustine's criticism of the astronomers in *Confessions* 5.3 (quoted earlier in this essay) for one of Seneca's portraits of the useful arts: "you are not found by the proud, not even if they could number with curious skill the stars and the sands, and measure the constellations, and plot the courses of the planets. . . . So early can they foresee a coming eclipse of the sun, but their own present eclipse they do not see, for they do not seek with a devout mind whence it is that they possess this skill by which they seek out these things" (trans. Ryan).

[16]Defending contemplative *otium* against an intolerant assertion of the demands of active virtue—in a debate with Musidorus which he eventually wins, after a fashion, when his opponent also succumbs to amatory languor—Pyrocles argues that the practical "knowledges, which you call the bettering of my mind . . . as they are of good use, so are they not all the mind may stretch itself unto. Who knows whether I feed not my mind with higher thoughts? . . . the workings of the mind I find much more infinite than can be led unto by the eye, or imagined by any that distract their thoughts without themselves. . . . Condemn not therefore my mind sometimes to enjoy itself, nor blame not the taking of such times as serve most fit for it" (*Arcadia*, p. 111). Pyrocles' characterization of active virtue as something "of good use" which must sometimes give way to the higher good of contemplative enjoyment describes a reconciliation of the two impulses which is at the heart of the *New Arcadia*.

[17]*The Nicomachaean Ethics*, trans. H. Rackham, 2nd edn. (Cambridge, Mass.: Harvard Univ. Press, 1934).

[18]It could be objected that this reading is overly ingenious. But Sidney's study of Greek, as expressed in letters to Languet, extended at the very least to a happy absorption of vocabulary (evidenced in this passage in his use of Aristotle's word *architektonike*). And his interest in the *Ethics* was more than casual. In a letter to a young acquaintance he recommends it as the single most important work of moral philosophy for a man to read, and warns that Aristotle's argument "is something dark and hath need of a logical examination" (quoted from James M. Osborn, *Young Philip Sidney: 1572-1577* [New Haven: Yale Univ. Press, 1972], p. 538).

[19]Sidney conceives of virtue as an inward condition that establishes man in correct relation to things outside himself: the mundane world in which he acts, and the divinity glimpsed within (but not identical with) his intellect. A perverse inversion of this conception is described in Cecropia's education of Artesia: she "taught her to think that there is no wisdom but in including both heaven and earth in oneself; and that . . . virtues are rather to be taken on than taken in oneself" (*Arcadia,* p. 154).

[20]Levao describes this theoretical strategy well, prior to arguing that in practice Sidney short-circuits it: "What is striking about this defense is that Sidney seeks to justify poetry by turning toward the two extremes it mediates, first to its source in the poet's 'Idea' and then to the moral effect it has on the reader's world; it becomes a conduit, leading the ideal to flow into the actual" ("Sidney's Feigned *Apology*," p. 223).

[21]Some of the principal argumentative strategies in the *Apology* clearly evolved in response to Plato's criticisms of imitative art in *Republic* 10, and incidental references to other parts of that work suggest Sidney's familiarity with it: see for instance his mention of the story of Gyges' ring early in the *Apology,* and the echo of the story of the Cave at the beginning of the *New Arcadia,* when Claius repeats Plato's metaphor of looking at the sun's reflections in water rather than directly at it. Sidney's division of ethical problems into "matters of public policy or private government" (*Apology,* p. 107) is similar to the "political action or private business" quoted below from the *Republic.*

[22]*The Republic*, trans. Paul Shorey, 2 vols. (Cambridge, Mass.: Harvard Univ. Press, 1930-1935).

SEL 27 (1987)
ISSN 0039-3657

The Meaning of "Grace" and "Courtesy": Book VI of *The Faerie Queene*

MARK ARCHER

Amidst critical discussion of the texts which are thought best to provide a gloss for the meaning of "grace" and "courtesy" in Book VI of *The Faerie Queene* there has been little detailed study of the possible influence upon Spenser's thought of the writings of Cicero and Seneca.[1] I hope to show that an appreciation of Seneca's *De Beneficiis* and Cicero's *De Officiis* helps to illumine the ideas of Book VI at a much more important thematic level than has previously been assumed. Both texts were available to Spenser in translation;[2] indeed, Arthur Golding's translation of Seneca's *De Beneficiis*, entitled *The woorke of the excellent Philosopher Lucius Annaeus Seneca concerning Benefyting, that is too say the dooing, receyving, and requyting of good turnes* (London, 1578),[3] suggests itself as a particularly appropriate source for many of the ideas Spenser explores in the Legend of Courtesy. Spenser and his audience are very likely to have known this work. Although Cicero seems to have been more widely read than Seneca in the grammar schools in England in the sixteenth century,[4] a fashion for reading Seneca at court may have been encouraged by the Queen's own translations, which seem to have been generally known and praised.[5] Arthur Golding (1536-1606) was no stranger to courtly circles. His sister had married John de Vere, the sixteenth earl of Oxford, and Golding served as tutor to his nephew Edward, the seventeenth earl, during the years in which he was a ward of court to Lord Burghley at Cecil House.[6] Golding was already more widely known, of course, as the translator of Ovid's *Metamorphoses*. Golding's translation of Seneca provides particularly illuminating support for the meaning of, and for the relationship between, grace and courtesy in Spenser's poem. In the dedication to Christopher Hatton (Hatton is also

Mark Archer is a graduate of Gonville and Caius College, Cambridge. His doctoral dissertation is entitled "Shakespeare and the Ethics of Honour."

among those to whom *The Faerie Queene* is dedicated), Golding explains that he considers the work "nor yet unexpedient to comme in Courtyers handes," for reasons which anticipate Spenser's own courteous ideal as embodied in Calidore. Courtiers, Golding writes, "shalbe the greater ornament too themselves, and to the place whereof they take their name, as their Courtesies and Benefytes bee mo and greater towardes others." "Of Court it seems, men Courtesie doe call," but as both Spenser and Golding realize, its roots can lie deeper than the court.

Any attempt to understand and elucidate Spenser's virtue of courtesy must begin with the meaning of the Graces. These "Goddesses of al bountie and comelines," in the words of E.K.'s gloss to the April eclogue in *The Shepheardes Calender,* show how "men first ought to be gracious and bountiful to other freely, then to receive benefits at other mens handes curteously, and thirdly to requite them thankfully: which are three sundry Actions in liberalitye."[7] "What is a benefite then?" asks Seneca; "It is a frendly good deede, giving gladnesse and taking pleasure in giving, foreward and redie of it owne accord, too doo the thing that it dooth" (I.vi, p. 6).

In the first example of discourtesy that Calidore encounters in Book VI, the perilous nature of the route past Briana's castle which ought to provide her with the opportunity for performing a "friendly good deede" to those who "needs must passe that way" (VI.i.13.6)[8] is in fact made the ground for exacting a shameful toll from knights and their ladies. This discourtesy towards others proceeds from the covetousness underpinning her relationship with Crudor. Crudor's refusal to reciprocate Briana's love, "through high disdaine / And proud despight of his selfe pleasing mynd" (VI.i.15.1), makes him like those "unthankfull folk" that Seneca describes, who "refuse good turnes, not bycause they cannot find in their hartes too have them, but bycause they cannot find in their hartes too bee beholden for them" (VI.xxv, p. 95). It is a token of his pride that he sets Briana conditions which she must fulfil before he will bestow his love. She must gather the mantle of knights' beards and ladies' hair. Setting conditions like this offends against that spirit of free and voluntary reciprocity which is at the heart of the meaning of the Graces. It implies that, by complying in a certain way with his demands, Briana will finally be able to "purchase" Crudor's love, just as Crudor's pride makes him want to think that his love can eventually be "bought." A genuine benefit, however, must be "foreward and redie of it owne accord," not the result of a contract, but bestowed freely and as the result of deliberate choice.

Hence, the "gifts" which Crudor and Briana do exchange, she "a ring of gould, / A privy token," he, foolishly, his own "basenet," "that of him she mote assured stand" (VI.i.29.2,31.7,8), are a parodic inversion of the true spirit of courtesy which consists in the "friendly offices that bynde" later symbolized by the Graces (VI.x.23.5). Their exchange of gifts mimics that courtesy which is genuinely and responsibly considered. It merely sets the seal upon a mutually advantageous arrangement to which they are each "bound" but to which, in terms of a "free" assent, they are scarcely "beholden." The "dooing of good turnes, and the rendering of thankfulnesse," writes Seneca, "are things too bee desyred for themselves," because "vertue is neyther allured with gayne, nor frayed away with losse, and is so farre from brybing any man with profers or promises, that she willeth men too spend uppon hir, and is commonly with them that give themselves freely unto hir" (IV.i, p. 47). Crudor and Briana's pseudo-courtesy is based upon "profers" and "promises." And yet the inability of Crudor and Briana to practice genuine courtesy in and for themselves is also, we begin to sense, bound up with their inability to come into full and genuine possession of themselves. Crudor's pride, for example, demands a mantle for his "self pleasing mynd" to be satisfied; Briana's insecurity requires the pledge of his "basenet," "that of him she mote assured stand." The couple's self-centeredness appears rather hollow. They confuse a belief in themselves for these "tokens" of themselves. They prefer, in Seneca's words, "the thyng that is seene with the eye, and delivered with the hande, and held in possession," "not a benefite, but the signe and token of a benefite," to "the thyng that is deere and precious" (I.v, p. 6).

We encounter this motif throughout the book. It is one in which a certain kind of covetousness not only offends against courtesy. More significantly, it implies that an inability to be courteous is to suffer a diminishment in individual character; it is a failure genuinely to come into possession of oneself and those "graces" which are truly one's own, and which make one oneself. Montaigne, following Cicero, describes it as the inability on the part of a man "to enjoy his being loyally."[9] The nameless knight, for instance, whom Tristram kills in the following canto, also envies "the thyng that is seene with the eye" and "held in possession," when he intrudes upon the love between Aladine and Priscilla, and hopes that he might appropriate some of the other knight's pleasure for himself: "He inly gan her lover to envy, / And wish, that he part of his spoyle might share" (VI.ii.17.2).

The nameless knight's indiscriminate and undiscriminating envy not only makes him an enemy to courtesy; it also makes his actions another manifestation of the Blatant Beast, which Envy had partly sired (V.xii.31-37). Envy is a natural concomitant of pride. The proud man is not practicing courtesy from a love or knowledge of the virtue for its own sake, and hence genuinely and "freely." His pride rather expresses the assumption that some reward or acknowledgement ought to be owed him on account of what he does. He offends against courtesy not just because, in Seneca's words, "vertue is neyther allured with gaine," nor with "profers or promises"; he is also not genuinely inhabiting himself. He is being made a continual hostage to the mark he hopes to make. His life is lived at the behest of some future gain and reward enviously anticipated, but one which cannot be presently enjoyed, in the way that practicing virtue for the love of itself is its own reward.

Meliboe, for instance, remembers how the "pride of youth" meant that he "disdain'd" to follow sheep with his "equall peares." Consequently, he went to court, where "I did sell my selfe for yearely hire" (VI.ix.24.2-3,7). The "forward pryde" of the two knights who sell their services to Turpine for the promise of "goodly meede" embodies the same assumption: "life [is] for hyre to sell" (VI.vii.6.5,4.9,15.3). In Montaigne's words, these ambitions belong to those men "which indeed passe their time: they overpasse the present and that which they possesse, thereby to serve their hopes with shadowes and vaine images, which fancy sets before them" (III.xiii, p. 662). Meliboe afterwards learns to appreciate what is properly his own: "I from thenceforth have learn'd to love more deare / This lowly quiet life, which I inherite here" (VI.ix.25.8). Montaigne likewise concludes: "I cheerefully and thankfully, and with a good heart, accept what nature hath created for me; and am there with well pleased, and am proud of it" (III.xiii, p. 663). The presence of Cicero is felt particularly strongly in these last few pages of Montaigne's final essay "Of Experience," especially his discussion in the *De Officiis* of the "gifts" which belong to a man's individual character. It is a relationship which is also central to the meaning of Spenser's idea of courtesy:

> everie mans owne gifts, not such as bee faultie, but naturall, are earnestlie to be maintayned, whereby the surer may the comelinesse be kept which wee doe seeke. . . . In briefe, if ought be comely, of truth there is nothing more seemely, than an evennesse in all mans life, and every of his dooings: which you cannot keepe, if you counterfayte anothers nature, and let passe your owne. . . . Which diversities when we behold, it shall be necessary to weigh what each man hath of his owne, and to order those gifts, and

> not to have a minde to try, how other mens graces would become him. For that becommeth each man, which is moste of all his owne. Let everie man therefore know his own disposition: and let him make himselfe a sharp judge both of his vice and of his vertues.
>
> (I, pp. 48-50)

Excessive pride, Meliboe's "pride of youth," or the two knights' "forward" pride, paradoxically set genuine self-possession for "hyre"; the realization of "everie mans owne gifts," in Cicero's words, in and for themselves, is thereby postponed. The disservice is not just to courtesy understood as the free and reciprocal exchange of benefits ("It is the propertie of a noble and vertuous minde," Seneca reminds us, "not to respect the profit of welldooing, but the welldooing itself")(I.i, p. 2). It is simultaneously a failure to "accept" and "receive" one's particular benefits, or graces, freely: "For that becommeth each man, which is moste of all his owne." It is to "passe the time," in Montaigne's phrase, and hence pass over those "gifts" constitutive of one's individual self. To confuse the "profit of welldooing" with "welldooing itself" carries a psychological corollary as significant as its ethical consequence. It is to chase after illusory gains at the expense of the pleasure which the knowledge and practice of virtue provides in itself. It is to suffer a type of self-estrangement.

The figure of Disdain, for example, who waits on Mirabella, gathers up symbolically many of the book's preoccupations with pride. His looks are meant to seem terrifying, "as if his enemies / He scorned in his overweening pryde" (VI.vii.42.3). But this is because there is in fact nothing substantial to his pride in himself at all; it is all based on show and intimidation: "He gaz'd about, and stared horrible, / As if he with his lookes would all men terrifie" (VI.vii.42.8). Disdain's display of pride is all geared to producing an effect upon other people. He possesses nothing "of his owne." Spenser's pointed repetitions of "As if" cleverly enact the insubstantiality of this character's self-identity: "As if he never had received fall," "As if he would have daunted him withall," "As if such pride the other could apall" (VI.viii.26.2,4,7). Seneca also thought pride the chief enemy of courtesy: "In dooing good turnes, nothing is too be eschewed so much as pryde. What needeth anye high looks? What needeth anye greate woords? The thing itself advaunceth thee" (II.xi, p. 16). Mirabella's "dispiteous pride" (VI.vii.38.7) likewise prevented her from being able to "weigh of worthiness aright" (VI.vii.29.6), including, of course, her own "worthiness." Although "deckt with wondrous giftes of natures grace," she nonetheless believed that, like Disdain, her "proud looks would make her praysed more" (VI.vii.28.5,30.2). She believed her own courteous part consisted of a God-like power simply to give or withhold benefits, regardless of the circumstances she was in: "She could or save, or spill, whom she would hight. / What could the Gods doe more, but doe it more aright" (VI.vii.31.8).

But the true virtue of benefiting, as Seneca emphasizes, demands that a person pay precise and scrupulous attention to the particular circumstances belonging to the individuals whom the benefits assist:

> For nothing becommeth any man, in respecte of himselfe alone. The respectes that make it comly, are what, too whom, when, why, where, and suche other, without whiche there is no reason in dooing. Proude Peacocke, if it becomme not him too receive it, neither becommeth it thee too give it. There is a proportionable respect of persones and degrees. And seeing that on either side, the vertew is the meane, as well is that a fault that overreacheth, as that which commeth too short.
>
> (II.xvi, pp. 18-19)

The true "skill" demanded by the practice of courtesy, therefore, consists of this "proportionable respect of persones and degrees." It is this capacity for subtle ethical discrimination, this ability to appreciate what is most particular about individuals and their circumstances,[10] which is implicit in Spenser's definition of courtesy at the start of canto two, even though he is often understood as recommending no more than a knowledge of the respect which is proper to each social class:[11]

> What vertue is so fitting for a knight,
> Or for a Ladie, whom a knight should love,
> As Curtesie, to beare themselves aright
> To all of each degree, as doth behove?
> For whether they be placed high above,
> Or low beneath, yet ought they well to know
> Their good, that none them rightly may reprove
> Of rudenesse, for not yeelding what they owe:
> Great skill it is such duties timely to bestow.
>
> (VI.ii.1)

The exercise of courtesy transcends the formal divisions derived merely from social position. Men "ought . . . well to know / Their good" for the same reasons Cicero thought "everie mans owne gifts" ought "earnestlie to bee maintayned, whereby the surer may the comelinesse be kept which wee doe seeke." According to Cicero, there is "no dutye more necessary than requiting of kindenesse," because such duties underpin that "common fellowship . . . which groweth of benefits to and fro, given and taken" (I, pp. 22, 26). Hence, "it skilles not of what calling the man bee that dooeth the good turne," writes Seneca, "but of what mynde he is. Vertue is forstalled from no man: She is set open for all men. She admitteth all menne: She allureth all men" (III.xvii, p. 36).

Throughout the book, Calidore's courtesy is characterized by his ability to weigh each new situation he confronts not merely in terms of the general principles most appropriate to it, but also, most significantly, in terms of the particular circumstances which uniquely define it. While acknowledging, for instance, that Crudor and Briana practice a "shameful" custom, his request that the Squire tied up by Maleffort also inform him "by what meanes did they at first it reare, / And for what cause" (VI.i.14.1,3), reveals his habit of always determining his actions by as complete a knowledge of the relevant circumstances as possible. It is likewise this same perceptive intelligence and sensitive discrimination that enables Calidore to "weigh of worthiness aright" in relation to Tristram. Although his first impression of the scene in which Tristram kills the nameless knight is one which, he believes, "armes impugneth plaine" (VI.ii.7.5), he is careful to listen to both the testimonies available to him, and to take all the possible circumstances belonging to the incident into account, before making a judgment upon it. His decisions are always measured and deliberate. He scrutinizes Tristram attentively, speaking to him only after "a while well having vewed" (VI.ii.7.1) his appearance. Calidore's careful judgment enables him to recognize how all the "graces" of Tristram's character "did so goodly fit" (VI.ii.24.7). In Cicero's words, his scrutiny of Tristram enables him to appreciate what in him is "moste of all his owne" and so to "order those gifts" which belong to him. After, again, "he long had him beholding stood" (VI.ii.24.8), he delivers an address which is in fact courteously designed to elicit an account from Tristram of who he is (its tact is suggested by the line, "But should it not displease thee it to tell") (VI.ii.26.1). Calidore's address to Tristram has been called "a conscious literary version of a hunter's life;"[12] however, it is not the "literariness" of Calidore's speech that we should notice, but rather how tactfully appropriate to Tristram's circumstances Calidore intends it to be. This is why he chooses the words "as to him seemed good" (VI.ii.24.9). In fact, Calidore's polite address serves to win

Tristram's trust ("sith ye so courteous seemed late, / To you I will not feare it to relate") (VI.ii.27.4), just as earlier Briana had been "All overcome with infinite affect, / For his exceeding courtesie" (VI.i.45.2). This is the particular "gift" of Calidore's life and character: "For some so goodly gratious are by kind, / That every action doth them much commend" (VI.ii.2.2). Cicero calls it "decorum," when "all the parts with a certaine grace agree together: right so this comelynesse that shineth abroade in our lyfe, winneth theyr lyking wyth whom we live by an order, steadfastnesse, and measurablenesse in all our woordes and deedes" (I, p. 44).[13]

The moral necessity for the kind of careful and fastidious attention to individual circumstances that Calidore practices is one of the principal themes of *Positions,* the educational treatise written by Spenser's teacher at the Merchant Taylors' school, Richard Mulcaster. The moral art is no different in this respect from the discipline of a schoolteacher, or "trayner." Although a man may "see and embrace the worthiness of his subject," he must nonetheless possess "discretion how to apply it according unto that, which is most fit to the verie meanest not bowghes and branches, but even the twigges and sprigges of the petiest circumstances."[14]

Attention to the "twigges and sprigges of the petiest circumstances" is indeed the great strength of Calidore's courtesy. The sturdy independence of his own presence of mind ensures he is not thrown off balance by each new set of circumstances; it makes him capable of considering them in full and dispassionately. He is "*hominem quadratum,* a square man."[15] In his help to Aladine and Priscilla, he was "fearlesse," Spenser tells us, "who ought did thinke, or ought did say, / Sith his own thought he knew most cleare from wite" (VI.iii.16.5). Calidore's self-possession is not set "for hyre." It is the strength and independence of his own integrity which frees him from practising courtesy either for the sake of working off some passion or for some advantage of which he stands in need. His independence of mind allows him to attend most "objectively" to the particular circumstances of others. What distinguishes his attitude from obstinacy or pride is that he keeps to his judgment because he has rigorously questioned it and has become persuaded that it is the right one, and not because it answers merely to his self-esteem. Just as Montaigne thought that "we especially . . . ought in our hearts [to] establish a touch-stone [un patron au dedans],[16] and there to touch our deedes and try our actions" (III.ii, p. 486), Calidore's own integrity likewise suggests how a genuine understanding of courtesy is itself the expression of what is most unique and particular, what is "moste of all his owne," about the character who practices it. It is this integrity which best equips Calidore to resist the attacks of the Blatant Beast, and finally to defeat it. The Beast is most likely to attack those who lack this type of self-possession, this informed particularity or (in Montaigne's phrase) this inner "patron."[17]

Timias's excessive devotion to honor, for example, makes him especially vulnerable, for it barely masks the fragile self-esteem propelling him in his quest for renown, the precariousness of which is continually forcing him to have to try and "prove" himself. His belief in himself, unlike Calidore's integrity, seems externally mediated through the opinion of others. When he "did stand againe assured" of the "grace" and "favour" of Belphoebe, "he was full high uprear'd" (VI.v.12.2-4). He thereafter grows enboldened, "secure," "of perill nought adrad," "Ne skilfull of the uncouth jeopardy" (VI.v.16.9,3-4). The strength of Belphoebe's good opinion of him is not only Timias's main ally in his fight against Defetto, Decetto, and Despetto, fellow conspirators with the Blatant Beast (just as Detraction had helped to breed it) (V.xii.35); his urgent need to depend upon it makes him paradoxically most vulnerable to their assult. Insofar as his honor can be won and lost, his self-possession is correspondingly precarious. On the two occasions that he meets Arthur in Book VI, he is shamed into silence (VI.v.24 and VI.viii.5), and we can guess that it is partly the shame of his imminent defeat which hastens his capitulation to Disdain:

> when he up did looke,
> And saw him selfe captiv'd, he was dismayd,
> Ne powre had to withstand, ne hope of any ayd.
> (VI.vii.48. 7-9)

Disdain, the terrible specter of disgrace, easily cows the man who is not, like Calidore, "fearlesse who ought did thinke or ought did say" because "his own thought," he knows, is "most cleare from wite." When Briana, for example, cries "shame" upon Calidore, he is momentarily "abashed" (VI.i.26.1); the shame of this reproach, however, does not drain him of all his self-possession, but neither does it automatically incite him to the defence of his reputation, as Maleffort unreasonably reacts to Calidore's challenge merely "for those words sake" (VI.i.19.4). He possesses sufficient presence of mind to take stock of himself, to "aske consideration counsell," in Mulcaster's phrase (p. 107), and thus answer her charge reasonably and in his own voice. This self-possession belongs to one who has "learnd him selfe first to subdew" (VI.i.41.6), which is the Hermit's lesson to Calepine and Serena (VI.vi.7). Subdue but not suppress, however, for Spenser's point about disdain, or over-weening confidence, is that its complementary opposite condition is almost always "selfe despight," or the debilitating incapacity adequately to believe in oneself. Enias suffers the same fate as Timias, and for the same reasons, when he too rushes to help Mirabella and is overcome as much by his own disdain; "with his owne handes might," we are told, he was "rebeaten backe upon him selfe againe," and "driven was to ground in selfe-despight" (VI.viii.10.5). Enias's passion for honor, Spenser is suggesting, is commensurate with an equally intense self-contempt; his attitude scarcely reflects Cicero's belief that "that becommeth each man, which is moste of all his owne." Like the nobly vicious "heroic enthusiast" described by Cicada in Bruno's *Gli Eroici Furori*, because "he is not in the temperance of indifference," that "evennesse," in Cicero's words, "in all mans life, and every of his dooings," "but in the excess of contraries, his soul [is] in discord."[18]

In contrast to the way Calidore focuses his self most acutely upon the circumstances which confront him, we can compare Serena's behavior at the moment we see her captured by the Blatant Beast. Calidore attends to circumstances; Serena seems much more aimlessly driven by them, "loosely wandring here and there" (VI.iii.24.3), "as liking led / Her wavering lust after her wandring sight" (VI.iii.23.6). Her dependence on "precept," or the appearance of courtesy, thereby empties her private pleasure of that focused presence of mind which an inward grasp of courtesy instills in Calidore. The lack of a distinctive edge to her self-possession means she can be easily accommodated in the Beast's "wide great mouth" (VI.iii.24.4), because his indiscriminate assaults naturally only threaten those who equally fail to discriminate about what "each . . . hath of his owne." Her passivity makes her discourteously blame Calepine at one point for being "th' onely author of her wofull tine" (VI.viii.33.3); such an evasion of at least some responsibility for her own "good" is, symbolically perhaps, not unconnected with the way she thence immediately becomes a helpless "object" for the savages' gratification. It is as much fear for her reputation, as fear for herself, which makes her flee the sight of Mirabella, "afeard / Of villany to be to her inferd" (VI.viii.31.4), "inferd" signifying her desire to escape any imputation of shameful conduct as well as actual injury. Serena lacks the kind of inward "patron" which Calidore possesses, which would not only give a distinctive and balanced expression to her life, but would also mean she had genuinely grasped the principles of courtesy for herself. Her unhelpful bouts of guilt and shame are the expression of this self-estrangement, such as when they render her touchingly incapable of returning thanks to Calepine for his good turn in rescuing her from the savages (VI.viii.51).

Outwardly to obey the principles of courtesy is only half a man's responsibility; to take refuge merely in the spotlessness of reputation is to trust to an "outward salve" (VI.vi.13.4). The Blatant Beast will always seek to implant "reproch, or secrete shame" (VI.vi.12.9). One solution, as Montaigne explains in his essay "Of Repenting," is not exclusively to "ground the recompense of vertuous actions upon the approbation of others"; it is equally necessary, Montaigne says, recalling Cicero again, that "within, and in bosome" we "keepe a due rule or formall decorum, that's the point." Hence, this is "to be so in ones owne home, and in his ordinary actions, whereof we are to give accoumpt to no body: wherein is no study nor art." A man should be "such inwardly by himselfe, as he is outwardly, for feare of the lawes, and respect of mens speaches" (III.ii, p. 486). Excessive shame and guilt, "reproch, or secrete shame," are not just the signs of an attack by, as much as a vulnerability to, the Blatant Beast; they are also the sign of a personality not in its "owne home," and hence not "at home" with itself,[19] or appreciative and cognizant of its own "gifts" and "grace." "For that becommeth each man, which is moste of all his owne." "For everie thing, to which one is inclin'd, / Doth best become, and greatest grace doth gaine" (VI.ii.2. 7-8).

Calepine's experiences also illustrate how true courtesy demands more of its practitioner than merely a passive trust in its rules and principles. His own helplessness is often the result of too complacent a trust that these rules ought to be obeyed by everyone, or of too rash and affronted a reaction when he discovers that, on the contrary, they are not universally binding. When Calepine's request for help is snubbed by Turpine, the kind of self-possession which would have informed Calidore's response leaves him; he becomes "inly wroth" against the knight, and as if to "prove" a point, impulsively crosses the stream on foot, "As in despight to be so fowle abused / Of a rude churle" (VI.iii.33.1,4). All that Calepine's pride enables him to see is the personal affront he has suffered. The "lewd words and deedes" with which he threatens Turpine only exacerbate his difficulties, for they make that villain even more eager to exact a "sore vengeance" on him (VI.iii.48.5-6). Calepine's nagging urge to "avenge that vile despight" (VI.iii.45.7) in fact curiously mirrors the obsessive hatred Turpine has nurtured, which has made him indiscriminately work off a grudge (and so "prove" himself) against "every errant knight" because of one who, long ago, "wrought him fowle despight" (VI.iii.40.5). Indeed, Calepine's passion at this point makes him neglect the "twigges and sprigges of the petiest circumstances" upon which Seneca had said true benefitting depends. His fit of pique leads him to refuse Blandina's offer to have her horse bear the injured Serena, which, however unlikely its source, is a sensible suggestion in these rather desperate circumstances. Calepine is always liable to be overcome with shame and scorn at failing to realize his best intentions. When he finds himself lost later on, he falls to complaining how "he his love lucklesse now had lost" and "On the cold ground, maugre himselfe he threw, / For fell despight, to be so sorely crost" (VI.iv.40.2-4).

Like Enias's "selfe despight," there is a sense here in which Calepine's frustration with his own inadequacies puts him beside himself. A moment before, for instance, Matilde had offered him important practical help for his having presented her with a child. She:

> offred him, his courtesie to requite,
> Both horse and armes, and what so else to lend,
> Yet he them all refused, though thankt her as a frend.
> (VI.iv.39.7-9)

But as in his response to Blandina's offer of help, Calepine is possibly too self-occupied properly to appreciate its practical implications. He is, of course, acting magnanimously like Calidore, who would not accept any "hyre of his good deede" (VI.i.47.2), but we are perhaps meant to understand that in these altered and rather more desperate circumstances, such a gesture is not quite so appropriate. Instead of acting, Calepine turns to "vowing":

> that never he in bed againe
> His limbes would rest, ne lig in ease embost,
> Till that his Ladies sight he mote attaine.
> (VI.iv.40.6-8)

The theme of "vows" and "vowing" appears frequently in the course of the book of courtesy. Calidore's own "vow and high beheast" (VI.x.1.3) to Gloriana to capture the Blatant Beast is no less urgent, or pressing, an obligation than it has been for the other knights whose adventures in the service of Gloriana give the poem its structure. It is a vow which Calidore is in danger of shamefully neglecting by his sojourn among the shepherds. Nevertheless, Spenser also suggests that the relationship of "vows" to the proper exercise of courtesy can be particularly fraught, and is one which must be subject to some unavoidable tension. Insofar as courtesy is a virtue which must cooperate with those chance circumstances which fortune throws up, the "twigges and sprigges of the petiest circumstances," if it is to have the greatest practical benefit, a strict and unyielding obedience to vows over and above experience would be to try and preempt those unforeseeable contingencies upon which courtesy depends for its operation. In this respect, "vows" are potentially as foolish as those made by the Lords of Navarre in *Love's Labours Lost;* glossing this episode in that play, Dr. Johnson reasons that "the folly of vows" is that "they are made without sufficient regard to the variations of life, and are therefore broken by some unforeseen necessity. They proceed commonly from a presumptuous confidence, and a false estimate of human power."[20]

They are "fooles therefore," Meliboe tells Calidore, "which fortunes doe by vowes devize." Nevertheless, his belief that "each unto himselfe his life may fortunize" (VI.ix.30.8) is itself proved wrong by the malevolence of his later fortunes. Meliboe's self-sufficiency, while claiming not to "devize" fortune, is yet passively dependent upon it. At the other extreme, it is typical of Arthur's chivalric impulses that, when "sore moved" by Serena's account of her misfortune, he "there avowd / . . . He would avenge th'abuses of that proud / And shameful Knight" (VI.v.34.1-4). But Arthur's "vow" of "revenge" presupposes the strict application of retributive justice, balancing ill for ill, exacting a punishment as though it were a "debt" owed by the criminal. The "grace" we see Calidore exhibit, in relation to Crudor and Briana for instance, foregoes such exactitude; it is a bestowing and not an exacting, because, in Seneca's words, "wilfull goodnesse overcommeth evill men" (VII.xxx, p. 120). Hence, "it is no point of a noble courage too give and loze, but to loze and give" (VII.xxxii, p. 121). The true spirit of the Graces, and so of benefits, transcends the law: "No lawe defineth what an unthankfull persone is" (III.vii, p. 32). Likewise, the pressure of intrusive circumstances which means that Calidore can hardly get started on his quest shows how courtesy is not a virtue that can be pursued with the single-mindedness of a "vow." Courtesy's very dependence upon "unforeseen necessity" implies its practice cannot depend upon a preordained rule or "precept." The "reason is," Mulcaster explains,

> art weyeth the matter abstracte, and free from circumstance, and therefore having the whole object at commaundement, she may set down her precept, according to that perfitnes, which she doth conceive: but the execution being chekt with a number of accidentarie occurences, which art cannot

> comprehend, as being to infinite to collect, must have one eye to her precept, and an other to her power, and aske consideration counsell, how to performe that with a number of lettes, and thwartings which, art did prescribe, eyther without any, or at the lest, with not so many.
>
> (p. 107)

The dance of the Graces represents an ideal of courteous "perfitnes," of a free and virtuous reciprocity of benefits, which it has been Calidore's magnanimity to try and imitate, but which, Spenser constantly reminds us, the imperfection of men and of the world is scarcely able to allow. The early episodes in the book have shown, as far as they can, the beauty of Calidore's courtesy and the benefits it is capable of bestowing; but they have also ultimately had to show its limitations, how it cannot be expected to operate as a general save-all, conjuring up solutions to every particular problem. Appropriately, therefore, several of these episodes end inconclusively; the future prospects of Aladine and Priscilla have the same uncertain "finish" about them as we sense is intimated in the Shakespearean silence which the nameless lady keeps when she rides off with Tristram (VI.ii.39). The outcome of these episodes depends upon many more circumstances than are discoverable, for the moment at least, from the episodes themselves. This same interrelatedness of her self with her circumstances causes Mirabella to warn Arthur not to attack the figure of Scorn who is punishing her, "for more on him then doth him selfe depend" (VI.viii.17.8). Arthur wishes to do her a benefit, but a complete appreciation of all the particular circumstances relevant to the scene before him is not available to him, nor could we expect it to be. In Mulcaster's words, they would be "to infinite to collect." It is significant that we next hear Mirabella's phrase used to describe the ordered pattern of the Graces, or "Venus Damzels":

> They all are Graces, which on her depend,
> Besides a thousand more, which ready bee
> Her to adorne, when so she forth doth wend.
>
> (VI.x.21.6-8)

The harmonious and decorous order of the Graces is a symbol of the divinely-patterned unity which God's love providentially gives to those circumstances in earthly life which seem fragmented, unconnected, and inconclusive. "Fate," Tansillo explains in Bruno's *Gli Eroici Furori,* "is called blind and even guilty not of itself, for it is the very number and measured order of the universe; but with respect to its subjects it is called blind and is blind because it renders them blind to its view by being itself most uncertain" (I.i, p. 92).

The image of heavenly perfection expressed by the dance of the Graces, or by the stars encircling Ariadne (VI.x.13), can be glimpsed occasionally on earth in the circle of knights around Gloriana at court, or in the circle of "lasses" and "shepheard swaynes" whom Calidore first sees gathered around Pastorella (VI.ix.8.4); its promise of concord can also be parodied in the ring of bloodthirsty savages who encircle Serena (VI.viii.39). Equally significant, however, is the way in which Calidore's interruption of the Graces is part of a larger theme in Book VI in which numerous moments of poised and balanced courtesy, of individual human happiness, are disrupted by unpredictable force of circumstance.[21] The nature of experience in this penultimate book appropriately anticipates the subsequent two cantos on mutability. Appreciation of the mutability in human experience is not merely daunting; it is a knowledge which consequently graces each circumstance of real human happiness with unique significance. A "thousand sowres" become "tempred with one sweet, / To make it seeme more deare and dainty, as is meet" (VI.xi.1.8-9).

Calidore's own experience of love is instructive in bringing him maturely to admit the force of a personally-felt happiness, and so its mutability, in a way his previous innocence had occasionally suggested he had not been capable of appreciating fully. The early cantos have shown Calidore assisting characters whose own hearts, for better or for worse, but generally for worse, have been invaded by love's passion. In comparison, some of his own advice has sometimes sounded too newly-minted, as though it were simply "courteous lore" (VI.i.27.8), as Briana contemptuously calls it at one point, or the "lip-wisdome, which wants experience," which Musidorus is made to rue in Sidney's *Arcadia.*[22] His advice to Briana to gain "glory" for herself, instead of Crudor's "love" (VI.i.27.4), implies an easily-resolved choice which is far from easy for Calidore to resolve when his time comes to love Pastorella. Likewise, the sanguine assurance which enables him to deal mercifully with Crudor, "What haps to day to me, to morrow may to you" (VI.i.41.9), momentarily deserts him in the fit of despair which overtakes him on discovering Pastorella's disappearance ("even his hart for very fell despight, / And his owne flesh he readie was to teare"—VI.xi.25.5-6).

By his sojourn in the pastoral world, Calidore manages to cope with the experience of love more successfully than any of the characters whom he had encountered previous to arriving there, and whom love, in varying degrees, had tended to debilitate. Love is the greatest test to Calidore's self-possession, to the confidence that he has indeed "him selfe first subdewed." Nevertheless, Spenser like Sidney is careful not to disavow the dependence of love upon an awareness of man's "infected will."[23] Calidore's very capacity to love, however graciously, is a symptom of his fallen state, and of an "infected will" which requires constant vigilance. From the moment he "falls" for Pastorella, examples such as the disingenuousness of his replies to Meliboe or his shrewd treatment of Coridon, suggest how courtesy, when in the service of love, and however outwardly decorous, can thenceforth never be wholly altruistic. After interrupting the Graces, his love's wound even then prevents him from listening for too long to Colin's explanation of the vision he has just been granted. The harmonious dance of the Graces to which Colin pipes represents one of those "morall images, and Examples" which it is the artist's gift to show forth "as directing threads" to other men.[24] They are patterns of the divine perfection itself, fashioned by imitators of "this world's great workmaister."[25] Nevertheless, visions such as the one bestowed on Calidore cannot take the place of the individual's effort to recreate this ordered pattern in his own life.

To expect more of literature than this would be to confuse two importantly divided spheres; it would be to treat literature itself as a medium equivalent to those vain "showes" that Spenser denigrates in his prefatory letter to Raleigh, in which lessons are delivered "plainly in way of precepts, or sermoned at large," instead of being woven by the reader's understanding into the unique and individual texture of his own life. Likewise, when Calidore's thoughts turn again to "his first quest" and the "losse of so much loos and fame" (VI.xii.12.2,8), the maturation which his character has undergone as a result of his experience of love means he has achieved the balance between the inward and the outward man which Montaigne, following Cicero, recommended; there is no risk now of his being dependent upon those tokens as if they were "shadowes vaine" (VI.x.2.7). When the reader takes leave of Spenser's book, it is assumed that he too will have then cultivated a correspondingly independent presence of mind to be able to afford the poem the kind of courteous regard which we have seen Calidore grant to others; in so doing, he will protect it from the Blatant Beast, who "rends without regard of person or of time" (VI.xii.40.9). What the reader finally takes from the poem is what the poem has subliminally taught him to bring to it: the satisfaction of knowing his own mind through the courteous activity of attending to Spenser's.

NOTES

[1]D. T. Starnes, "Spenser and The Graces," *PQ* 21 (1942):268-82, includes Seneca's *De Beneficiis* among the sources which contain a description of the Graces, but he argues that Renaissance dictionaries were the source for Spenser's specific portrayal of them. Edgar Wind, *Pagan Mysteries in the Renaissance* (London: Faber and Faber, 1958), includes Seneca and Spenser in his chapter on the inconographic history of the Graces. James Nohrnberg, *The Analogy of "The Faerie Queene"* (Princeton: Princeton Univ. Press, 1976), p. 684, discusses Seneca's Graces in relation to the theme of truth and sincerity and in many ways his argument anticipates my own. The Variorum editors make a brief comparison between "courtesy" and Cicero's *honestas. The Works of Edmund Spenser. A Variorum Edition*, ed. E. Greenlaw, C. G. Osgood, F. M. Padelford and others, 10 vols. (Baltimore: John Hopkins Press, 1932-1949), 6:336. Dorothy Woodward Culp, "Courtesy and Moral Virtue," *SEL* 11 (1971):37-51 relates "courtesy" to the moral duty of Cicero's *De Officiis*, but she argues finally that there was no "clearly formulated theory" of courtesy available in Renaissance books on the gentleman (p. 39). While I agree substantially with her view of Spenser's courtesy as a skill requiring a knowledge of circumstances, I also suggest that the *De Beneficiis*, translated by Golding explicitly for courtiers, embodies just such a theory.

[2]The *De Officiis* was translated by Robert Whittington, *The thre bookes of Tullyes offyces* (London, 1534), and by Nicholas Grimald, *Marcus Tullius Ciceroes three bookes of duties to Marcus his sonne* (London, 1553). References are to the 1596 edition of Grimald's translation and are subsequently given in parentheses in the text, cited by book and page.

[3]All references to this work are given in parentheses in the text, cited by book, chapter, and page.

[4]T. W. Baldwin, *William Shakespere's Small Latine & Lesse Greeke*, 2 vols. (Urbana: Univ. of Illinois Press, 1944), 2:581-98.

[5]Eric St. J. Brooks, *Sir Christopher Hatton: Queen Elizabeth's Favourite* (London: Jonathan Cape, 1947), p. 140. The first English translation of Epictetus (*The Manuell*, trans. James Sanford, London, 1567) was dedicated to Elizabeth.

[6]Louis Thorn Golding, *An Elizabethan Puritan: Arthur Golding the translator of Ovid's "Metamorphoses" and John Calvin's "Sermons"* (New York: Richard R. Smith, 1937), p. 32.

[7]Edmund Spenser, *Poetical Works*, ed. J. C. Smith and E. De Selincourt, 23rd edn. (Oxford: Oxford Univ. Press, 1966), p. 434.

[8]Edmund Spenser, *The Faerie Queene*, ed. A. C. Hamilton, 3rd edn. (London and New York: Longman Annotated English Poets Series, 1984). All references to *The Faerie Queene* are to this edition, cited by book, canto, stanza, and line.

[9]Michel de Montaigne, *Essayes*, trans. John Florio (London, 1603), III. xiii, p. 664. Further references to this edition are given in parentheses in the text, cited by book, chapter, and page.

[10]"Perfected courtesy . . . takes all elements of a situation into consideration before deciding what action, in each particular instance, will really help the individuals involved," Culp, p. 50.

[11]"Courtesy . . . has much to do with the recognition of one's proper place in the social order, and recognizing that both one's superior and one's inferior each has his rights in his proper place." Arnold Williams, *Flower on a Lowly Stalk:*

the sixth book of "The Faerie Queene" (East Lansing: Michigan State Univ. Press, 1967), p. 42 .

[12]Kathleen Williams, *Spenser's Faerie Queene: The World of Glass* (London: Routledge & Kegan Paul, 1966), p. 198 .

[13]Cf. Ronald Arthur Horton, *The Unity of "The Faerie Queene"* (Athens: Univ. of Georgia Press, 1978), p. 95 .

[14]Richard Mulcaster, *Positions* (London, 1581), pp. 130-31 . Further references to this work are given in parentheses in the text.

[15]"The Prince of Philosophers, in his first booke of the Ethicks, termeth a constant minded man even egal and direct on all sides, and not easily overthrowne by every litle adversitie, *hominem quadratum,* a square man," George Puttenham, *The Arte of English Poesie,* ed. Gladys Doidge Willcock and Alice Walker, 2nd edn. (Cambridge: Cambridge Univ. Press, 1970), p. 100.

[16]*Les Essais de Michel de Montaigne,* ed. P. Villey and V-L. Saulnier, 2 vols. (Paris: Presses Universitaires de France, 1965), III. ii, p. 807.

[17]"That unique inwardness of person, the source of name and style, which is *our* only reality." Harry Berger, Jr., "The Prospect of Imagination: Spenser and the Limits of Poetry" *SEL* 1 (1961):93-120, 106. "Courtesy is shown in the respect accorded to another person's determination upon inward possession," Nohrnberg, p. 662.

[18]Giordano Bruno's *The Heroic Frenzies,* trans. Paul Eugene Memmo, Jr., (Univ. of North Carolina Studies in the Romance Languages and Literatures, 50, 1965), I. ii, p. 101. Further references to this work are given in parentheses in the text, cited by book, chapter, and page.

[19]For the importance to Montaigne of the self's "dwelling at home," see M. A. Screech, *Montaigne & Melancholy: The Wisdom of the Essays* (London: Duckworth, 1983), p. 111. For the importance of the idea to Ben Jonson, see Thomas M. Greene, "Ben Jonson and the Centered Self," *SEL* 10 (1970): 325-48.

[20]*Johnson on Shakespeare,* ed. Arthur Sherbo, vol. 7 of *The Works of Samuel Johnson,* 15 vols. (New Haven: Yale Univ. Press, 1968), p. 267.

[21]The "covert glade" (VI.ii.16.3) sheltering Aladine and Priscilla is broken in upon by the nameless knight; Calidore interrupts the "solace" enjoyed by Calepine and Serena in their "covert shade" (VI.iii.20.3); Pastorella is stolen away from Calidore by the brigands, and they lay waste to the pastoral world in which he had looked to enjoy "happy peace" and "perfect pleasure" (VI.x.3.4).

[22]*The Countesse of Pembrokes Acadia,* in *The Complete Works of Sir Philip Sidney,* ed. Albert Feuillerat, 4 vols. (Cambridge: Cambridge Univ. Press, 1939), 1:18, 113.

[23]Sir Philip Sidney, *An Apology for Poetry or The Defence of Poesy,* ed. Geoffrey Shepherd, 4th edn. (Manchester: Manchester Univ. Press, 1979), p. 101.

[24]Fulke Greville, First Baron Brooke, *Life of Sir Philip Sidney,* ed. Nowell Smith (Oxford: Clarendon Press, 1907), p. 223.

[25]Edmund Spenser, *An Hymne in Honour of Beautie,* line 29, *Poetical Works,* p. 590.

SEL 27 (1987)
ISSN 0039-3657

"Words cannot knytt": Language and Desire in Ralegh's *The Ocean to Cynthia*

ROBERT E. STILLMAN

> Every mode of thought is bestowed on us, like a gift, with some new principle of symbolic expression. It has a logical development, which is simply the exploitation of all the uses to which that symbolism lends itself; and when these uses are exhausted, the mental activity in question has found its limit. Either it serves its purpose and becomes truistic, like our orientation in 'Euclidean space' or our appreciation of objects and their accidents (on the pattern of language structure significantly called 'logic'); or it is superseded by some more powerful symbolic mode which opens new avenues of thought.[1]

Susanne Langer supplies in this passage a model for analyzing the transformation of one symbolic mode to another. Her account of the exhaustion of older symbols and their replacement by new, more powerful means of symbolizing experience presents a clearly optimistic paradigm for cultural change. Symbols that no longer work make room for symbols that work better; knowledge advances; culture marches on. Langer provides one version of the old story. It is a version that offers, nonetheless, a useful if unexpected introduction to Ralegh's poetic practice in *The 21th: and last booke of the Ocean to Scinthia.* For Ralegh, too, has a strong interest in the exhaustion of the symbolic order (to use Langer's terms) or in what Ralegh himself might otherwise describe as "fancy's tragedy," the discovery that the mythology surrounding a queen whom one worships is mere mystification and that time leads all things to decay, including love and language.

The Ocean to Cynthia is an extended complaint for the loss of Queen Elizabeth's favors. Ralegh writes as a courtier in disgrace,

---

Robert E. Stillman is an Assistant Professor in the English Department at The University of Tennessee, Knoxville. This article will be part of a forthcoming book on Renaissance language theory.

whether on account of his secret marriage to Elizabeth Throckmorton or some other indiscretion, and in apparent hope of a return to favor.[2] The subject of the poem is the frustration of desire. In losing Elizabeth, Ralegh makes clear, he has been subjected to multiple losses that the uniformly elegaic tone of the complaint renders nearly equivalent in importance. He has been deprived of a love that deserved requiting, of a well-merited place at court, and of a near-religious faith in what can only be called the cultic status of the Queen. Cynthia assumes a special kind of importance in *The Ocean* because of the significance attached to Elizabeth as the reigning deity of a national cult. It is useful to remember that the Queen was the center of a symbolic order whose existence helped to consolidate and perpetuate the power of the Tudor state. Virgin Queen, heavenly Venus, triumphant Diana, returned Astraea—these are only a few of the roles that Elizabeth played in a national mythology providing aesthetic, religious, and philosophical legitimacy to her sovereignty. The coherence of what used to be called the Elizabethan world picture was founded upon the order of symbols surrounding the Queen.[3]

It is useful to remember the Queen's cultic status because Ralegh reminds us repeatedly in *The Ocean* that he had been instrumental in its creation. Like so many other poets, he had once celebrated Elizabeth as "natures wonder, Vertues choyse," "Th' Idea remayning of thos golden ages."[4] As Shepherd of the Ocean, Ralegh gives every indication that he believed in his symbolism, that the Queen and the cultic images surrounding her were one. The loss of her love changed all that, however, depriving him of everything that he had formerly valued in those symbols, and more disastrous still, of the capacity to believe in the validity of the symbols themselves and the activity of mind which produced them. After his loss, Ralegh writes, "A Queen shee was to mee, no more Belphebe" (327). She has been demythologized. The once-loving cult goddess descends from benefactress to tormentor, from a sustaining symbol to one more especially painful part of his fragmented reality. Even the golden-age symbolism that Ralegh had earlier applied to Elizabeth is now dismissed as a deceitful fiction that "worthless worlds but play onn stages" (350).

Ralegh's poem, then, represents as a personal tragedy exactly that process of symbolic exhaustion that Langer describes at the level of cultural change. His complaint is more than a courtier's lament for the loss of a queen's favors, amorous or professional. The loss that Ralegh has suffered—or so he represents it—is the exhaustion of a whole order of symbolism upon whose existence his status at court, his identity, and the coherence of his world depended. Elizabeth had been more than his beloved or his sovereign. She was the repository of all that was valuable in the world. The striking disproportion between the event reported—a courtier's loss of his queen's favors, and the terms in which it is represented—the demise of the symbolic order, is responsible for much of the poem's extraordinary melodrama and, strangely, for much of its conceptual interest.

The Ocean to Cynthia emerges, then, from the absence created by the now exhausted order of symbols with which Ralegh had once surrounded the Queen. His poem is an extended attempt to discover what Langer might call "some more powerful symbolic mode" to replace the older order of discarded symbolism. This does not mean that we can read Ralegh's lament with Langer's optimism about the ease with which one more effective form of symbolism replaces another. There is nothing easy about the task that Ralegh undertakes; his failure is sufficient proof of that. Ralegh does not discover in *The Ocean to Cynthia* the more powerful symbols for which he is in search. The strange ebb and flow of the poem's fragmented imagery does not finally rescue from love, time, and fortune, the poet's primary antagonists, any values of transcendent importance. But Ralegh's poem does explore the reasons for his failure, for the insufficiency of all modes of symbolizing, and this clarification is significant both in itself and for an understanding of attitudes toward language in Elizabethan culture as a whole.

When Ralegh comments upon his art in *The Ocean to Cynthia,* he compares his labors, significantly enough, to those of a historian. Overwhelmed by the enormity of his loss and the impossibility of fully measuring its extent, Ralegh describes his poetic task as if it were an attempt "when after Phebus is dessended . . . To write the story of all ages past / And end the same before th'aprochinge night" (97, 102-103). (We think ahead, inevitably, to his unfinished *History of the World.*) His analogy is telling. Ralegh looks to history with its parade of mutability for an understanding of his own decline, and he represents his decline as if it were a microcosmic version of the decay of the world. In good pastoral fashion, the complex is incorporated into the simple. The analogy is typical of Ralegh as a self-aggrandizing effort to lend pathos to his sufferings, and it is certainly characteristic of the Ralegh who has come to dominate contemporary critical thinking; Greenblatt has written a fine study of the courtier's lifelong devotion to theatrical self-presentation.[5] Ralegh's urge for self-aggrandizement is apparent, but the form in which that urge finds expression, as the poet bemoans the frustration of his desires, remains puzzling and problematic. Why do complaints about frustrated desire appear so frequently in *The Ocean to Cynthia* in conjunction with laments about the inadequacies and failures of language? How does an event so personal (the loss of love) come to be associated with an issue so seemingly abstract (linguistic adequacy)? When Ralegh draws the analogy between his attempt to write the story of his fall and an effort to record all history on a single evening before the world's decay, he comments not just about the extent of his desires, but about the failures of writing. His poem is not so much unfinished as unfinishable, since in Ralegh's view language lacks the resources to allow him adequately to express the greatness of his loss. When he complains that he "Writes in the dust as onn that could no more"(91), he laments the ineffectuality and impermanence of words. Words fail to satisfy desire, since mutability rules both love and language; the connection among these terms needs further exploration.

Ralegh is only one among many Renaissance writers who lament mutability's sway over language.[6] The increased historical awareness and philological sophistication of the Renaissance brought with it a greater consciousness of linguistic change, but without the intellectual structures with which to interpret change in language as something other than decadence or decay, the new learning also carried a new sense of linguistic crisis. Because words change form and meaning, because they lose currency over time, they cannot be trusted. Abraham Fraunce echoes Horace when he writes "Woordes are lyke leaves . . . : leaves spring before Summer, and fall before Winter; and the same inconstancy is in words."[7] When William Drummond illustrates "The Instabilitie of Mortall Glorie," "what wee write to keepe our Name" takes its place alongside triumphant arches and proud obelisks destined to be "made the sport of Dayes."[8] At the end of his *Defence of Ryme,* Samuel Daniel warns his contemporaries against importing foreign words into English, only to conclude in near-desperation: "But this is but a Character of that perpetuall revolution which wee see to be in all things that never remaine the same, and we must heerein be content to submit our selves to the law of time, which in few yeeres will make al that, for which we now contend, *Nothing.*"[9] Castiglione notes that all words in the course of time "come to their end, because at the last both wee and whatsoever is ours, are mortall."[10] There is real sadness here over the decay of words, but clearly much of that sadness derives from what words stand for; so often in the Renaissance the mutability of language comes to represent synecdochally human mortality and sometimes even the decay of the world.

In this context, Ralegh's lament for the decline of language and the world's decay becomes more comprehensible as the expression of a larger cultural crisis, but the sadness of his lament derives, as we have seen, from something more specific than a consciousness of mutability. The failure of language is intimately linked in *The Ocean to Cynthia* to the frustration of desire. There is an important cultural context for this linkage as well. Ralegh's dark pastoral takes its place among a large body of English Renaissance poems in which an erotic occasion provides the context for direct and pointed complaints about linguistic inadequacies. An obscure but fascinating pastoral lyric incorporated into *England's Helicon* (1600), Edmund Bolton's "Theorello. A Shepherd's Idillion," provides a paradigm for these complaints. The lyric dramatizes the love of Theorello (a rather intellectual-sounding shepherd) for Cosma (the world) as an allegory of the poet's effort to seduce nature into satisfying his desires. This is pastoral turned metaphysics. The poet woos nature as a lover woos his mistress. As the lover seduces his beloved by flattery, so the poet pays tribute to the beauties of a divinely inspired cosmos by naming them aright: "Yet hath the world no better name than she: [Bolton puns] / And then the world, no better thing can be."[11] However, the desire to fix words properly is frustrated by the fact that "names her beauty show not" (31). Language is not adequate to the task of naming the world correctly. Bolton's frustration over the failure of words finds expression in Theorello's unsatisfied and unsatisfiable desire for Cosma.

The same connection between frustrated desire and the inadequacies of language is repeatedly employed by Sidney in *The Old Arcadia* as a warning against the dangers of the impassioned imagination. When Philisides, a lovesick shepherd exiled from court, bemoans the loss of Mira's favors in the second eclogues, he sings an echo poem that reflects upon the causes of his frustrations:

> But when I first did fall, what brought most fall
> to my heart? Art.
> Art? What can be that art which thou dost mean
> by thy speech? Speech.
> What be the fruits of speaking art? What grows
> by the words? Words.
> O much more than words: those words served more
> to me bless. Less.[12]

Nature contradicts the logic of passion. What Sidney comically portrays in these lines is the consternation of the romantically idealizing poet upon discovering that his words, far from satisfying his desires, have actually compounded his sufferings. Words deceive, the sarcastic nymph reminds Philisides. They load the mind with corrupt and insatiable passions that turn men into fools. Sidney is inclined to treat comically the failures of language and the frustrations of desire that are for John Donne (to cite one more example) primary sources of tragedy. In the disintegrating universe that Donne describes in *The First Anniversary,* the death of a loved woman, Elizabeth Hardwicke, is made symbolic of a lost cosmic coherence; nature is out of joint, fragmented, and that fragmentation is identified in the poem with the failure of language to contain experience and observation, to build causeways over the abyss. Elizabeth is the world's "name," now fatally divorced from it. Donne addresses his decaying world:

> thou art speechlesse growne.
> Thou hast forgot thy name, thou hadst; thou wast
> Nothing but she, and her thou hast o'rpast.
> . . . .
> Her name defin'd thee, gave thee forme and frame,
> And thou forgetst to celebrate thy name.[13]

He, too, laments the mutability of the world as a matter of mutable words. In Donne, as in Sidney, Bolton, and Ralegh, the loss of a desired woman is connected with the failure of language. I do not mean to suggest that the theme of desire and the inadequacy of language is in any sense unique to the texts in question. Desire and the failure of words to serve that desire haunt Sidney's Astrophil as he attempts to make Stella "pity the tale of me," just as the persona of Shakespeare's *Sonnets* must struggle against "all-oblivious enmity" to secure his love and language against the ravages of time. The subject is one of broad cultural importance in late Elizabethan and Jacobean society, and it remains so throughout the seventeenth century. When midway through the century, John Webster envisions the creation of a universal language to make words adequate tools for expressing things, he makes the revealing argument that the discovery of this new Adamic language would serve "*to marry the world*, that is, fitly and duly to join and connex agents to their patients, masculines to faeminines, superious [sic] to inferiours, Caelestials to Terrestials, that thereby nature may act out her hidden and latent power."[14] A perfect language is the fulfillment of desire: it is the marriage of man to nature.

In an effort to account for the persistence with which language and desire are "married" in these works, it is useful to remember that they appear in the context of a Renaissance critical tradition which acknowledges, at times in surprisingly current terms, the force of that connection. Joachim Du Bellay's *Defence and Illustration of the French Language* begins, as an explanation of the diversity of languages, with a telling rationalization of the myth of Babel:

> If nature . . . had given to men a common will or consent, besides the innumerable commodities which would thereby have resulted, human inconstancy would not have needed to forge for itself so many manners of speaking. Which diversity and confusion can rightly be called the Tower of Babel. For languages are not born of themselves after the fashion of herbs, roots, or trees: . . . all their virtue is born in the desire and will of mortals. That (it seems to me) is a great reason why one should not thus praise one language and blame the other; since they all come from a single source and origin, that is from the caprice of men.[15]

Language springs from the restlessness of human desire; it is a product of what Sidney would call will, not wit. Du Bellay's insistence upon the origins of language in desire is less commonplace in Renaissance criticism than an emphasis upon speech as the expression of human reason, but it is scarcely idiosyncratic; this passage follows closely one in Speroni. In any case, Du Bellay's insistence is significant because it helps to clarify the poetic practice of Sidney, Donne, and most important for my purposes, of Ralegh. For if language is a function of desire, whether that entails in a poetic context the seduction of a queen or the wooing of a shepherdess, then the frustration of desire presents a natural occasion for a lament over the inadequacy of words. The Renaissance critical tradition brings more clarity to Ralegh's poetic practice, even as it suggests by means of the very terms it highlights—language and desire—that Ralegh's poetry can usefully be understood in light of contemporary critical theory.

"Language is an operational superstructure on an erotic base": Norman O. Brown's formula has become axiomatic in much contemporary criticism for the analysis of discursive practices.[16] For semioticians like Barthes and Kristeva, "there is no other primary *significatum* in literary works than a certain desire: to write is a mode of Eros";[17] for neo-Freudians like Ricoeur and Lacan, speech is demand, and the desire that motivates demand is both the cause and "perpetual effect of symbolic articulation."[18] The connection between language and desire that is thematized so frequently and explicitly in Renaissance poetic texts occupies in these contemporary critical schools the central place in investigating not just all literary, but all linguistic acts. In light of such criticism, texts like those of Sidney,

Donne, and Ralegh acquire particular interest because they are self-conscious explorations of the dynamic that semiotics and psychoanalysis locate at the foundations of discourse. In turn, a theoretical perspective of this kind—and I am thinking particularly of Ricoeur's—provides an intellectual framework in which to analyze how these texts function.

In Ricoeur's words, "what makes desire speak [is] namely, the *absence* inherent in instincts and the connection between lost objects and symbolization" (p. 503n.).[19] Language is an effort to recover or to compensate for what has been given up in the past; its function is determined etiologically by its origins in the individual's development. In some of the most influential pages from *Beyond the Pleasure Principle,* Freud locates the genesis of signs in a child's game of "*fort*" ["gone"] "*da*" ["there"]. In the absence of the mother, the child whom Freud observes devises a simple game by which he makes his toys disappear and reappear. His playing reenacts the mother's departure as a necessary preliminary to the pleasure of her return, and in this way he compensates himself for the "renunciation of the instinctual satisfaction which he had made in allowing his mother to go away without protesting."[20] What this game defines is the institution of signs, which are universally a giving up of what Ricoeur calls "brute presence and an intending of presence in absence" (p. 385).

The child's game functions, it is important to recognize, not as a passive response to loss, but as an active effort to achieve mastery over privation. A similar function has been claimed, at times usefully it seems to me, for the more sophisticated games of art. Ralegh's lament in *The Ocean to Cynthia* for the loss of Queen Elizabeth's favors is suffused with familiar pastoral nostalgia for a golden age of requited love; at the same time, the poem strives to achieve mastery over that loss (as I will show) by the creation of new, more powerful symbols to replace the now exhausted order of symbolism surrounding the Queen. *The Ocean to Cynthia* can be read, then, as an elaborate game of "*fort-da,*" with some crucial differences. Ralegh's "game" endlessly reenacts in memory the painful loss of love, but it concludes not with the restoration of the Queen's favors, a goal deemed hopeless, or even with the creation of more powerful, sustaining symbols, a task specifically abandoned, but with a sobering awareness of the inevitability of frustrated desire and linguistic failure. In the process of bringing the unconscious toward consciousness, of making explicit the interconnection between desire and language, the poet can *reflect* upon what the child can only *enact*. In this way, as Norman O. Brown writes, "consciousness in the artistic use of language is subversive of its own instrument" (p. 73). Language, the instrument of desire, functions to unmask the futility both of itself and the master who drives it. This is art in the service of the reality, not the pleasure principle—or so it seems.

Language is replete with mystifications: "In and through man desires advance masked" (Ricoeur, p. 162). This is a point worth making here, because before Ralegh is too quickly enlisted as a servant of the reality principle (after all, this is a courtier who devoted a lifetime to the pursuit of visionary projects), it is important to recognize that his desperation over the fate of love and language can itself be interpreted as simply one more function of desire. The very act of writing is a continued demand for royal favors, favors that are the object of Ralegh's erotic and political aims. His desire for Elizabeth's love is both a sexual desire and a desire for the power that she represents, though his rhetoric so closely associates the two that it seems impossible to distinguish between them. The difficulty in making that distinction works, of course, to Ralegh's advantage, since it allows him to negotiate under cover of a plea for love what is also a ploy for power. When Ralegh points at the opening of his poem to "The broken monuments of [his] great desires," he both reflects upon the frustration of desire in preparation for an analysis of its hopelessness and manifests desire in the hope of being restored to favor. These are indeed great desires, and they lead to great contradictions. The construction of Ralegh's poem is governed by the unresolvable tension between a wish to expose the futility of passion and an urge to find satisfaction for it, whether in substitute symbols or in the favors of the Queen.

In the attempt to clarify how an event so personal (frustrated love) comes to be associated with an issue so seemingly abstract (linguistic adequacy), I have invoked several large contexts in which to situate *The Ocean to Cynthia:* a network of poems in the English Renaissance in which the failure of desire is explicitly associated with linguistic inadequacies; a sixteenth-century critical tradition that posits the origins of language in desire; and contemporary psychoanalytic theory that represents all discourse as an operation motivated by eros to recover or to compensate for what has been lost in the past. These contexts in turn should now help to shed light on how desire speaks in and through *The Ocean to Cynthia* as Ralegh struggles with his problems of symbolic expression.

The 21th: and last booke of the Ocean to Scinthia begins in a sea of confusion. As Ralegh struggles to make sense out of his loss, the reader struggles with him, astonished, even overawed, by his capacity to endure emotional agony. For all of the poem's pastoral trappings, this speaker intones against fate with a distinctly heroic voice. Who can believe, while reading, that there could have been twenty previous books like this one? (And who, if the truth be told, is not slightly relieved at having been spared them?) Ralegh dates his loss from "when first my fancy erred" (3). "Fancy" is an important word in the poem and needs clarification here. In the faculty psychology that Renaissance writers inherited from the classical tradition, the term has a specific and clearly defined meaning; it is the mind's ability to represent images to itself in the absence of sense perception.[21] As neutral and unambiguous as such a description might appear, fancy is a mental faculty loaded with equivocal moral potential. A recognition of the faculty's ambiguity is apparent in Sidney's *Apology for Poetry*. Sidney writes: "Man's wit may make poesy (which should be *eikastike,* which some learned have defined, figuring forth good things) to be *phantastike,* which doth contrariwise infect the fancy with unworthy objects."[22] The kind of infection that concerns Sidney, as well as many of his contemporaries, is the seduction of the fancy by desire. If the good painter portrays "Judith killing Holofernes, David fighting with Goliath," the artist controlled by fantasy "please[s] an ill-pleased eye with wanton show of better hidden matters" (Sidney, pp. 59-60). It is desire's complicity with the imagination that makes art vulnerable to criticism, a point that Bacon later enforces in an extremist argument about poetry and the dangers of fancy. Poetry operates, Bacon writes, "by submitting the shows of things to the desires of the mind."[23] Given this cultural background, and the repeated association of desire and "fancy" in Renaissance critical theory, Ralegh's use of the word in *The Ocean* becomes more comprehensible; fancy refers in his poem to the imagination and those passions inextricably connected with it. The term provides a ready vehicle for relating the poet's desires to the image-making faculty by which he attempts to satisfy those desires.

Ralegh's effort to date his loss from "when first my fancy erred" is less an attempt to explain his error than it is to find some fixed point in time from which he can make meaningful divisions in his experience. (How did his fancy err? He fails to say.) As Ralegh drives a wedge between his past and his present, isolating the "happy then" of his courtship of Elizabeth from the woes that he suffers now, he strives to rescue from that "golden age" something of value for his present (31). Time, however, is a more difficult antagonist than Ralegh anticipates. In the wild ebb and flow of the poem's imagery, past and present refuse to remain separate, as every attempt to idealize the "happy then" of Elizabeth's love ends in frustration. If she is remembered as "The seat of joyes, and loves abundance,"

Ralegh is unable to forget the "great worlds of woes" that he endured under her sovereignty (44, 50). (Petrarchan metaphor has a terrifying literalness for a courtier in love with his queen.) Cynthia not only "apeased," she "wounded"; she not only "gave," she "tooke" (56). If Ralegh recalls "The honor of her love," he is also reminded that her love forced him "to leve great honors thought" (57, 65). His sorrows did not begin with fancy's error. They were present all along. Nothing illustrates this point better than the swift transition which takes place between Ralegh's praise of the "force" which her "angellike aparance had / To master distance, tyme, or crueltye" (112-13), and his bitter recognition that:

> Twelve yeares intire I wasted in this warr,
> Twelve yeares of my most happy younger dayes,
> Butt I in them, and they now wasted ar,
> Of all which past the sorrow only stayes.
>
> (120-23)

What lends this illustration such power is that Ralegh makes us aware in the very next line ("So wrate I once"), that these verses are themselves the product of his earlier years, the flotsam and jetsam cast ashore by some previous agonizing undulations of the ocean. No small part of Ralegh's tragedy consists, then, in the fact that his experience has been far less discontinuous than he would like to believe. The sorrows of his past are a piece with those of his present. To date his woes from "when first my fancy erred" is simply to make another error in fancy since the past contains no golden age from which value can be rescued for the present.

The further that Ralegh extends our awareness of the sorrows which he endured in the past, the clearer it becomes both to himself and to us that his love for Cynthia was doomed from the first to frustration. As he recalls a queen "Whose Love outflew the fastest fliinge tyme" (182), Ralegh confronts the symbolism of Elizabeth's cult in its most idealizing form. He remembers admiring her as

> A springe of bewties which tyme ripeth not
> Tyme that butt workes onn frayle mortallety,
> A sweetness which woes wronges outwipeth not,
> Whom love hath chose for his devinnitye.
>
> (185-88)

Even as Ralegh gives, he takes away; he has acquired one of his sovereign's tricks. Time does not ripen Cynthia's beauties. But if Cynthia's beauties are unripe, are they also imperfect? Some doubt is cast upon her store of "frayle mortallety." More telling still is the evidence which Ralegh marshalls from "strong reason" (173) to undermine her status outside of time. The mythology of Elizabeth's cult is subjected to historical critique as the poet holds before his eyes

The Images, and formes of worlds past
Teachinge the cause why all thos flames that rize
From formes externall, cann no longer last,

Then that thos seeminge bewties hold in pryme
Loves ground, his essence, and his emperye,
All slaves to age, and vassalls unto tyme
Of which repentance writes the tragedye.

(174-80)

Mutability rules both world and self. A queen's love will decay just as certainly as her empire. History and suffering replace an exhausted mythology, as the poetic argument turns from exalting Cynthia's love above time to acknowledging time's power over her, to identifying, finally and tragically, her love with the power of time itself. As mutable as the moon, the Queen is a heavenly body whose absence has blighted his mental landscape:

But as the feildes clothed with leves and floures
The bancks of roses smellinge pretious sweet
Have but ther bewties date, and tymely hores,
And then defast by winters cold, and sleet,

So farr as neather frute nor forme of floure
Stayes for a wittnes what such branches bare,
Butt as tyme gave, tyme did agayne devoure
And chandge our risinge joy to fallinge care;

So of affection which our youth presented,
When shee that from the soonn reves poure and light
Did but decline her beames as discontented
Convertinge sweetest dayes to saddest night.

(241-52)

Ralegh's is a dark pastoralism. By associating Cynthia's love with the order of nature's decay, he imparts a strong sense of inevitability to his sufferings. It is the nature of a moon to change. The Queen has come to embody devouring time itself.

Ralegh's love was doomed to frustration, it is important to recognize, more because of the way in which he conceived the Queen than because of any attributes that she in fact possessed. Fancy's error plays a greater role in his tragedy than either the poet or the reader at first suspects. For what becomes increasingly evident as the poem proceeds is that the Cynthia at whose feet Ralegh worshipped is a construct of his own imagination. She is, as he tells us, "my object, and invention," a "princely forme, my fancies adamande" (37, 41). As one more especially ardent devotee of her cult, Ralegh transformed an imperfect, time-bound Elizabeth into Cynthia, a symbol of transcending perfections, thereby setting "the stage of fancies tragedye" (144). History is raised to mythology with drastic consequences. For as Ralegh makes plain, "thos marvelous perfections" which he bestowed upon the Queen became "The parents of my sorrow and my envy" (193-94). His fancy—the imagination driven by desire—gave her a symbolic significance too weighty to bear, and with her inevitable collapse from the timeless Cynthia to the mutable Elizabeth, Ralegh found himself in love with a fiction of his own creation, tormented by the loss of an ideal which had no existence outside of his imagination. He laments his "Unlastinge passion, soune outworne consayte / Whereon I built, and onn so dureless trust!" (295-96). Once more Ralegh associates the frustration of his desires with linguistic failure. In the midst of his loss, he rejects not only the exhausted symbols with which he had once surrounded the Queen, as he again and again disables their idealizing significance, but the very principle that had generated them. Fancy errs in attributing transcendent value to the persons and objects of a time-bound world.

Fancy's error produces fancy's tragedy; this is the blunt logic at the heart of *The Ocean to Cynthia*. There is no single consequence of his fall from the Queen's favor that Ralegh details more painstakingly than the effects of that fall upon his imagination. In the "happy then" of Cynthia's love, his thoughts had been "confinde" (or so he hoped) by a central object for his inventions (32). With her loss, the floodgates of his imagination burst open, inundating the fancy with a sea of chaotic images. As Ralegh writes, "Then furious madness wher trew reason lackt / Wrate what it would, and scurgde myne owne consayte" (145-46). No small part of the poet's loss is his weakened ability to repair it. His images no longer cohere. In an attempt to discover some new center in which to confine his fancy, Ralegh undertakes an important change of direction midway through his complaint.

Cynthia has already been demythologized as "A Queen . . . , no more Belphebe"; her influence over the poet has been identified with time's devouring power. In her place, Ralegh attempts to substitute a new symbolic order whose center is the transcendent power of his own love. It is no longer Cynthia who survives time, but the poet's adoration of her, as Ralegh exclaims in a new, more assertive tone of voice: "My love is not of tyme, or bound to date" (301). Ralegh here follows the near-obligatory pattern of the Petrarchan poet, who, denied the possibility of erotic satisfaction in his mistress because of her loss or death, seeks fulfillment in the substitute gratifications of poetic composition. It is well to remember, however, that the fulfillment he seeks goes beyond what is typical of the Petrarchan writer in the self-consciousness of Ralegh's search for a new set of sustaining symbols to replace those that have been exhausted. Almost immediately, as if hesitating to take the leap, he retreats from his new-found theme into increasingly somber laments for the loss of Cynthia and increasingly bitter attacks upon the golden-world mythology which he had once applied to her. His past praises for the Queen seem "now an Idell labor, and a tale / Tolde out of tyme that dulls the heerers eares; / A marchandise whereof ther is no sale" (357-59). In the midst of tragic posturing that looks ahead to Macbeth's, the poet complains once more that the old symbols have lost their value, metaphysical and professional. In full awareness of this fact, Ralegh returns to his new theme with an increased decisiveness. Once again, he exalts his love as a power "Too great and stronge for tymes Jawes to devour" (383). But now, instead of retreating into laments or remonstrations, Ralegh proceeds to attribute to his love qualities which he had formerly reserved for the Queen. As he had once done for Cynthia, he exalts his passion above "age" and "natures overthrow," "honors bayte" and "worlds fame" (401, 406). What he praises is an "essentiall love, of no frayle parts cumpounded" (410). As a new center of imaginative and emotional coherence, "Thes thoughts, knitt up by fayth, shall ever last, / Thes, tyme assayes, butt never can untye" (391-92). Ralegh's metaphor is important. The faith of his essential love provides a tool for "knitting" together the broken threads of the old symbolic order.

In the flux of the Ocean's mental turmoil, new confidence quickly gives way to new despair. The very memory of his essential love creates "a relapps of passion" (414), as the poet is driven back into his consuming woe. In search of a cure for his "minds long deseas"(421), Ralegh stumbles upon one of *The Ocean*'s greatest ironies. His long pursuit to rescue something of value from time itself appears exhausted, as he turns to his single most powerful antagonist for the mental relief that he is unable to discover elsewhere: "Externall fancy tyme alone recurethe / All whose effects do weare away with ease" (422-23). Fancy is now time's patient, not its conqueror. Ralegh appears permanently trapped in history, with no sustaining mythology to turn to. It is precisely this understanding, one suspects, that motivates the poet's final desperate attempt to exalt his love above time. All the stops are pulled out, as Ralegh likens his love to a first principle of nature, as a cosmic power equally fundamental to his being, "As water to the fyshe, to men as ayre, / As heat to fier, as light unto the soonn" (434-35). Love is the new "Center" of his imaginative life, the new prime "mover" of his being (442, 455). A timeless abstraction seems somehow more secure as the foundation for a sustaining order of symbols than the time-bound Elizabeth.

Security, however, is not one of the strong points of Ralegh's world. With the recognition that love has destroyed the "better part" (461) of his being, he abandons any further attempt to discover a fixed order of transcendent values. Ralegh rejects as merely one more error of mythmaking fancy the effort to idealize his own love.

> But what of thos, or thes, or what of ought
> Of that which was, or that which is, to treat?
> What I possess is butt the same I sought;
> My love was falce, my labors weare desayte.
>
> (462-65)

The complete flatness of his diction is a measure of his frustration, but how do we allow our understanding of his emotional state to guide our interpretation of the final line? Is Ralegh convinced that his love was false, or is he mimicking Cynthia's estimation of its value?

The very fact that he allows us to pose such questions, without caring to resolve them, indicates the hopelessness of his condition. For it simply no longer matters whether his love was true or false. All that now concerns Ralegh is that he has been victimized, partially by love, partially by time, and partially by his own fancy. He understands, at last, that "Words cannot knytt, or waylings make a new" (481). Trapped in a time-bound landscape, amidst the outworn conceits of a disabled symbolic order and the imagery of a natural world that itself perpetually decays, the poet has available to him no linguistic resources for discovering symbols of transcendent value.

NOTES

[1]Susanne K. Langer, *Philosophy in a New Key: A Study in the Symbolism of Reason, Rite, and Art* (Cambridge, Mass.: Harvard Univ. Press, 1960), p. 201.

[2]For studies of the biographical circumstances surrounding the poem's composition, see Katherine Duncan-Jones, "The Date of Ralegh's, '21th: and Last booke of the Ocean to Scinthia'," *RES*, n.s. 21 (1970): 143-58; Philip Edwards, *Sir Walter Ralegh* (London: Longmans, Green, 1953), pp. 90-96; Stephen Greenblatt, *Sir Walter Ralegh: The Renaissance Man and His Roles* (New Haven and London: Yale Univ. Press, 1973), pp. 59-98; Pierre Lefranc, *Sir Walter Ralegh, écrivain* (Paris: Librairie Armand Colin, 1968), pp. 99-132.

[3]Two recent informative studies of Elizabeth's cult are Helen Cooper's *Pastoral: Medieval into Renaissance* (Totowa, N.J.: Rowman and Littlefield, 1977), pp. 193-213, and Louis Adrian Montrose's "'Eliza, Queene of Shepheardes,' and the Pastoral of Power," *ELR* 10 (1980): 153-82.

[4]*The Poems of Sir Walter Ralegh,* ed. Agnes M. C. Latham (Cambridge, Mass.: Harvard Univ. Press, 1951), pp. 25-43, lines 344, 348. All further citations from *The Ocean* are documented in the text by line number.

[5]Greenblatt's arguments (pp. 76-98) are cogent and often persuasive, but they do not reckon with Ralegh's equally important concerns with the Queen's symbolic status and with the nature of symbolic expression. See also Donald Davie, "A Reading of *The Ocean's Love to Cynthia,*" in *Elizabethan Poetry* (New York: St. Martin's Press, 1960), Stratford-upon-Avon Studies 2, pp. 71-90; Michael L. Johnson, "Some Problems of Unity in Sir Walter Ralegh's *The Ocean's Love to Cynthia,*" *SEL* 14 (1974): 17-30; and A. D. Cousins, "The Coming of Mannerism: The Later Ralegh and the Early Donne," *ELR* 9 (1979): 86-107.

[6]See also Thomas M. Greene, *The Light in Troy: Imitation and Discovery in Renaissance Poetry* (New Haven and London: Yale Univ. Press, 1982), pp. 4-27; and Jane Donawerth, *Shakespeare and the Sixteenth-Century Study of Language* (Urbana and Chicago: Univ. of Illinois Press, 1984), pp. 13-55.

[7]Abraham Fraunce, *The Lawier's Logicke* (London: W. How for T. Newman and T. Gribbin, 1588), *STC* 11345, sig. 2^r.

[8]*William Drummond of Hawthornden: Poems and Prose* , ed. Robert H. Macdonald (Edinburgh: Scottish Academic Press, 1976), p. 88.

[9]Samuel Daniel, *A Defence of Ryme* in *Poems and A Defence of Ryme,* ed. Arthur Colby Sprague (Cambridge, Mass.: Harvard Univ. Press, 1930), p. 158.

[10]Baldassare Castiglione, *The Book of the Courtier, trans. Sir Thomas Hoby* (London: J. M. Dent; New York: E. P. Dutton, 1928), p. 60.

[11]*England's Helicon, 1600, 1614,* ed. Hyder E. Rollins, 2 vols. (Cambridge, Mass.: Harvard Univ. Press, 1935), 1:9, lines 32-33.

[12]Sir Philip Sidney, *The Countess of Pembrokes Arcadia* (The Old Arcadia), ed. Jean Robertson (Oxford: Clarendon Press, 1973), p. 161.

[13]*The First Anniversarie* in *The Complete Poetry of John Donne,* ed. John T. Shawcross (Garden City, N.Y.: Anchor Books, 1967), lines 30-32, 37-38.

[14]John Webster, *Academiarum Examen, or the Examination of Academies* in Allen G. Debus, *Science and Education in the Seventeenth Century: The Webster-Ward Debate* (London: Macdonald; New York: American Elsevier, 1970), p. 152.

[15]Joachim Du Bellay, *The Defence and Illustration of the French Language,* trans. Gladys M. Turquet (London: J. M. Dent, 1939), p. 21.

[16]Norman O. Brown, *Life Against Death. The Psychoanalytical Meaning of History* (Middletown, Conn.: Wesleyan Univ. Press, 1959), p. 69.

[17]Roland Barthes, *Critical Essays,* trans. Richard Howard (Evanston: Northwestern Univ. Press, 1972), p. xvi.

[18]Jacques Lacan, *Écrits: A Selection,* trans. Alan Sheridan (New York: W. W. Norton, 1977), p. viii.

[19]Paul Ricoeur, *Freud and Philosophy: An Essay on Interpretation,* trans. Denis Savage (New Haven and London: Yale Univ. Press, 1970), p. 503n.

[20]Sigmund Freud, *Beyond the Pleasure Principle,* trans. James Strachey (New York: Bantam Books, 1967), p. 34.

[21]For an excellent discussion of imagination in Renaissance critical theory, see John Guillory, *Poetic Authority: Spenser, Milton, and Literary History* (New York: Columbia Univ. Press, 1983), pp. 1-22.

[22]Sir Philip Sidney, *An Apology for Poetry,* ed. Forrest G. Robinson (Indianapolis: Bobbs-Merrill, 1970), p. 59.

[23]Sir Francis Bacon, *The Advancement of Learning* in *The Works of Francis Bacon,* ed. James Spedding et al, 14 vols. (New York: Garrett Press, 1870), 2:343.

SEL 27 (1987)
ISSN 0039-3657

The Arrangement of Ben Jonson's *Epigrammes*

JAMES A. RIDDELL

Ben Jonson's *Epigram* 131, the third-to-last in the collection, is addressed to Alfonso Ferrabosco. It was written as a commendatory poem, "To My Excellent Friend, Alfonso Ferrabosco," for Ferrabosco's *Lessons for 1. 2. and 3. Viols* (1609), and was reprinted in the *Epigrammes* immediately following a commendatory poem for another of Ferrabosco's books, *Ayres* (also 1609). In 131, Jonson deals with a topic that is dear to him, the relation between an artist and his audience. He tells Ferrabosco that a large portion of his audience are fools, bound to favor an artist inferior to Ferrabosco:

> Say, this, or that man they to thee preferre;
> Even those for whom they doe this, know they erre:
> And would (being ask'd the truth) ashamed say,
> They were not to be nam'd on the same day.[1]

Although the topic is a common one in Jonson, his treatment of it here is uncommon. His observation that an author of an inferior work would be shamed by misplaced praise (and know it) gives more credit to such an author than one would expect, for Jonson can usually be relied upon to hold that such an author would be too dim to realize that the work he had written was inferior.[2] I think that Jonson places the poem with its somewhat unusual observation at just this position in the *Epigrammes* for a purpose, and that an examination of *Epig.* 131 and of epigrams immediately before and after it will lead not only to an understanding of that purpose, but also to a general understanding of the organization of the entire "book."

Epig. 131 is the final one that we are to take as a straightforward statement. *Epig.* 132 is the commendatory poem that Jonson wrote

---

James A. Riddell, Professor of English at California State University, Dominguez Hills, has published articles on English lexicography and on Jonson and Shakespeare. He is currently pursuing a bibliographical study of the Jonson folio of 1616.

for Joshua Sylvester's translation of du Bartas's *Divine Weekes and Workes* first published in 1605, and it is probably true that Jonson grew to regret that he had praised Sylvester.[3] If Jonson did regret praising him, he apparently did not regret having written the poem or he would not have included it in his book. Aside from his merely liking the poem, can Jonson have had a purpose in including it, and, furthermore, a purpose in placing it where he did? If one takes seriously Jonson's assertion that "Who e're is rais'd, / For worth he has not, He is tax'd, not prais'd" (*Epig*. 65), it does make sense to find a poem for Sylvester following hard upon poems for Ferrabosco. The first two not only explain the presence of the third, but also help to explain its location. One finds well-placed praise for Ferrabosco in two poems, along with a warning about the implications of misplaced praise. The warning, in turn, is followed by what may be considered an example of misplaced praise. If this is indeed the case, the three poems form a kind of introduction to the final poem in the book, "On The Famous Voyage," which defines epigrams in somewhat the same way that the piece for Sylvester defines poems of praise: it shows the opposite of what the thing ought to be. Jonson's opinion was that an epigram could not be a narrative, rather it must relate one incident that is capped by an ending neither "obvious or otiose" (H & S, 2:351). Bruce R. Smith contends that "Jonson's mock-epic . . . stretches the definition of epigram beyond recognition"; Peter E. Medine goes somewhat further and says that Jonson, following, in his own terms, "the old way and the true," marks in "The Famous Voyage" a "deliberate departure from that 'way.' It is thus a final irony of Jonson's satire that in concluding his volume with a mock epic on his age, he writes what to him was a veritably *modern* epigram."[4] I think that Smith makes a good deal of sense, and that Medine makes even more, but I wish to take the argument still one more step in my consideration of the general pattern of the *Epigrammes* and in the smaller patterns, or "clusters,"[5] of poems within the general one.

"On The Famous Voyage" in being a "modern epigram" denies virtually everything that an epigram should be, and as it does so denies what a poem should be. But, as Jonson demonstrates in his masques, an absolute denial constitutes one kind of affirmation.[6] So when we find in a collection of epigrams a poem which is indisputably narrative, has "bombard-stile" (line 46), considerable length (196 lines, some of which are given over to mere diversions such as that in lines 31-36), no epigrammatic "point," and has an ending that is both obvious and otiose,[7] we have in fact a good definition of what an epigram should not be. Thus, the final four poems in the *Epigrammes* are closely related,[8] and, taken together, demonstrate what praise should and should not be, what an epigram should and should not be, and, with these two considerations in mind, what poetry should and should not be. I intend to demonstrate in this paper that there is a pattern to the group of poems at the conclusion of the *Epigrammes,* a pattern, moreover, that recurs throughout the book and, in large part, determines the arrangement of the poems in it.

At the end of his collection, Jonson catches up topics with which he begins it. Of the first nine epigrams, some deal with those whom Jonson would have members of his audience (1, "To the Reader" and 3, "To my Booke-seller"), with what the nature of an epigram is and is not (2, "To my Booke" and 9, "To all, to whom I write"), with two particularly appropriate subjects for praise (4, "To King James" and 5, "On the Union"), and with three subjects for blame (6, "To Alchymists"; 7, "On the new Hot-house"; and 8, "On a robbery"). In these poems the instruction is, fittingly, much more direct than it is in those at the end of the book; the reader is being introduced to the topics. There is no ironic demonstration of someone's being falsely praised, and the qualities of an epigram are directly explained, not defined by way of an anti-epigram. Nonetheless, essentially the same issues are being dealt with in the two places, which suggests that Jonson intended that the collection have a kind of symmetry.

Evidence that the symmetry is not merely fortuitous can be found through consulting some poems at the middle, almost the exact center of the *Epigrammes, Epig.* 65 ("To my Muse") and the epigrams that are immediately before and after it. In "To my Muse," Jonson tells how a subject of praise is made more lustrous *or* is condemned (by the self-same words), depending not upon the poem's merits but upon his own. For fourteen lines Jonson berates his muse for betraying him "to a worthlesse lord; / Made me commit most fierce idolatrie / To a great image through thy luxurie." The final two lines, in an abrupt turn, provide the epigrammatic point:

> But I repent me: Stay. Who e're is rais'd,
> For worth he has not, He is tax'd, not prais'd.

This poem, coming as it does after two poems to the Earl of Salisbury (*Epigs.* 63 and 64), has caused several observers to suggest that Jonson may have had Salisbury in mind.[9] Drummond recorded that Jonson came to have a low opinion of Salisbury. If he did, the opinion was apparently not much different from that of many of his countrymen, at least after Salisbury's death in 1612.[10]

Jonson slightly altered *Epig.* 63 from an earlier manuscript version when he prepared it for the printer; the effect of the alteration is to link 63 to 65 by removing the poet himself as the one responsible for praising Salisbury and substituting the poet's muse, to whom, of course, 65 is addressed. In a holograph copy of the poem preserved at Hatfield House, the final couplet of 63 is:

> Curst be my voyce, if it lye dumbe, or hid
> To such true worth, though thou thy self forbid.[11]

This appears in the printed version,with the changed words here enclosed in brackets:

> Curst be [his *Muse*, that could] lye dumbe, or hid
> To [so] true worth, though thou thy selfe forbid.

Jonson not only transfers the onus from himself to his muse, but, through the slight change in the last line, he also introduces a new possibility: "such" tends to be an absolute intensive, whereas "so" is an intensive of uncertain or even of ambivalent force and could as well mean "little" as "much." If, as I believe he is, Jonson is using the two poems to Salisbury as examples, the meanings of which are explained in a poem immediately adjacent, the pattern is just that of the last three poems in the *Epigrammes,* and is consistent with the pattern of the first ones. The congruency of these three groups of poems becomes more evident when two more poems are taken into account.

Epigs. 66 and 67 are to Sir Henry Cary and to Thomas, Earl of Suffolk. No poems in the collection deal more explicitly with the meaning of praise and its distinction from flattery than do these.

> THat neither fame, nor love might wanting be
> To greatnesse, CARY, I sing that, and thee,

Jonson begins in 66, and then goes on to extol Cary's extraordinary bravery on a field of battle. But however brave Cary has been, Jonson's interest is not in the action itself but in the moral underpinning of it. He concludes:

> Though every fortitude deserves applause,
> It may be much, or little, in the cause.
> Hee's valiant'st, that dares fight, and not for pay;
> That vertuous is, when the reward's away.

As Herford and Simpson point out in their notes to the *Epigrammes* (11:12), the final line is almost the same as one in *Cataline* ("So few are vertuous, when the reward's away" [III. 480]) that is spoken by Cicero as he deplores the fallen condition of Roman society, and the observation in *Cataline* echoes one in Juvenal's Tenth Satire (lines 141-42). Jonson also deplores the "sloth of this our time," and against the generally contemptible conduct of mankind, which, in effect, has existed throughout history, he sets his praise of Cary, whose virtue is as notable for its rarity as for its excellence. A similar point of view prevails in the first part of *Epig.* 67, "To Thomas Earle of Suffolke":

> Since men have left to doe praise-worthy things,
> Most thinke all praises flatteries. But truth brings
> That sound, and that authoritie with her name,
> As, to be rais'd by her, is onely fame.

That which is begun with the poems to Salisbury and explained in "To my Muse" is completed in the poem to Suffolk, who is described by Jonson as being, like Cary, an ideal figure, "design'd to be the same thou art, / Before thou wert it, in each good mans heart."[12] At the beginning, the middle, and the end of the collection are groups of poems which both describe and demonstrate Jonson's concept of the epigram. Appropriate topics include the deplorable condition of mankind, the possibility of there being good men, and the quality of true fame. How the poet treats these topics is a topic itself, and the "how" can be demonstrated by showing the thing itself or by showing its antithesis.

II

The poems at the middle of the *Epigrammes*, as Edward Partridge has remarked, stand as a kind of introduction to the second part of the book, in which poems of praise prevail. I agree with his general assessment of the purpose of a certain group of poems at nearly the exact center (to mark the place "where the book moves away from censure to praise" [p. 171]), but I disagree with his analysis of the structure of that group. This must be the case, for he does not consider as part of his argument that the epigrams for Salisbury are examples of false praise, and there is no reason for him to include them as a part of this group of poems. The difference is an important one because I find that often groups of poems throughout the book reflect the arrangement of those at the beginning, the middle, and the end. Many groups, I suggest, comprise poems that deal with praiseworthy and blameworthy exemplars of a particular topic. I have not found it possible to be certain about the precise arrangement of groups, and I have no doubt that Jonson ordered his poems in such a way that the whole cannot be reduced into simple patterns. In the following discusion of several groups of poems I shall try to avoid oversimplifying Jonson's scheme.

Epigrammes 23 to 26 constitute a group in which one can see Jonson's deepest admiration and his sharpest outrage; all deal with good and corruption, both public and private. In *Epig*. 23, "To John Donne," Jonson praises the good poet (public figure) and the good man (private figure). Jonson's well-known opinion that the good poet must be first a good man lies behind his professed inability to praise Donne adequately, Donne being so extraordinarily good as both. Donne, we are told, not only possesses a great wit, but also:

> To it, thy language, letters, arts, best life,
> Which might with halfe mankind maintayne a strife.
> All which I meant to praise, and, yet, I would;
> But leave, because I cannot as I should!

This is followed by an outburst against public corruption, a distich "To the Parliament," and then by two poems (25 and 26), both of which are on "Sir Voluptuous Beast." *Epig*. 25 is bitter enough, 26 is pure acid. Beast's private corruption is particularly disgusting because it results not merely in his being reduced to something less than human, but beyond that results in the defiling of his "faire, and innocent wife." Both reason and religion are denied.

ON SIR VOLUPTUOUS BEAST

> WHile BEAST instructs his faire, and innocent wife,
> In the past pleasures of his sensual life,
> Telling the motions of each petticote,
> And how his GANIMEDE mov'd, and how his goate,
> And now, her (hourely) her owne cucqueane makes,
> In varied shapes, which for his lust shee takes:
> What doth he else, but say, leave to be chast,
> Just wife, and, to change me, make womans hast?

ON THE SAME BEAST

> THen his chast wife, though BEAST now know no more,
> He adulters still: his thoughts lye with a whore.[13]

The second poem alludes to a passage in Seneca,[14] but, as is so often the case, Jonson compounds the matter that he takes from his source. Seneca's general argument is that the intention of commiting a crime is crucial, not whether the crime is accomplished. In the relevant passage, Seneca is giving an example: "It is possible for one to become a wrongdoer, although he may not have done a wrong. If a man lies with his wife as if she were another man's wife, he will be an adulterer, though she will not be an adultress." Jonson transmutes this by saying that even though Beast no longer knows any woman other than his chaste wife he still commits adultery, because the whore (not just another man's wife, who may herself be innocent) with whom his thoughts lie is his wife. In *Epig.* 25, the pun which inheres in "hourely"[15] (to which the parentheses invite particular attention) gives support to the reading. It is, of course, possible that "whore" means other than his wife; however there is more outrage in the idea of his having made her a whore in his own mind. And this is perfectly in keeping with the Senecan notion that "he will be an adulterer, although she will not be an adulteress," for she is still, after all, his "chast wife." Though he cannot make her an adulteress, Beast does make her a whore, the one with whom he commits adultery.[16] The many turns of depravity that Jonson packs into this brief poem provide a measure of his outrage. John Donne's wit, "language, letters, arts, best life" are at one pole, Beast's depravities at the other.

There are several other groups of poems in which Jonson treats poets and their opposites, that is, bad men (or women). *Epigs.* 110 and 111, addressed to Clement Edmondes, are reprintings of commendatory poems which were prefixed to the 1609 edition of his *Observations on Caesars Commentaries.* Strictly speaking, Edmondes is not a poet; he is a historian. But just as Jonson praises Alfonso Ferrabosco's art and in his praise discusses true and false fame, so he does with Edmondes. Jonson explains how Edmondes has rescued Caesar's words from near oblivion in books "whose good / How few have read! how fewer understood!" Jonson's description of Edmondes's achievement is the description of what a good poet should do:

> Thy learned hand, and true *Promethean* art
> (As by a new creation) part by part,
> In every counsell, stratageme, designe,
> Action, or engine, worth a note of thine,
> T[o] 'all future time, not onely doth restore
> His life, but makes, that he can dye no more.

In *Epig.* 111 Jonson goes on to talk about the reception of Edmondes's work in much the same manner as he talks about the reception of Ferrabosco's:

> Yet thou, perhaps, shalt meet some tongues will grutch,
> That to the world thou should'st reveale so much,
> And thence, deprave thee, and thy worke. To those
> CAESAR stands up, as from his urne late rose,
> By thy great helpe: and doth proclaime by mee,
> They murder him againe, that envie thee.

The next epigram is "To a Weake Gamster in Poetry" (112), followed by one "To Sir Thomas Overbury." The first of these is about a poetaster who tries to emulate Jonson; the second, like the poem to Joshua Sylvester (and, it would seem, the two to Salisbury), to a man whom Jonson came to regret having praised, perhaps doubly regret because Jonson had associated Overbury's name with poetry ("SO PHOEBUS makes me worthy of his bayes, / As but to speake thee, OVERBURY, is praise"). The pattern of this group of poems seems to be a reasonably complete one, but in a sense it is not, for it has links with what follows. The next poem is addressed to Mistress Philip Sidney, whose name is that of a true poet ("I Must beleeve some miracles still bee, / When SYDNYES name I heare, or face I see"), so that the poem to her is related to the Overbury poem in being virtually its opposite. The Sidney poem is about the congruity of her virtue, beauty, and name. The opposite of this congruity is found in *Epig.* 115, on the "Townes honest Man," who is anything but honest.

> YOu wonder, who this is! and, why I name
> Him not, aloud, that boasts so good a fame:
> Naming so many, too! But, this is one,
> Suffers no name, but a description:
> Being no vitious person, but the vice
> About the towne.

The irony of calling him "honest Man" is manifold. Neither "honest" nor "man" (he is referred to throughout the poem as "it"), he is also the antithesis of the subjects of the previous poem and of the following one. In *Epig.* 116, Sir William Jephson is described as being a man whose name deserves all praise—and his merit is greater even than his name; Jephson is a throwback to better days, when "bloud not mindes, but mindes did bloud adorne: / And to live great, was better, then great borne." *Epigs.* 114, 115, and 116 form a triad in which the meaning of names is explored, including the meaning that inheres in Jonson's refusal to name one at all. Because of one of Jonson's concerns in 114 (Mrs. Philip Sidney's having the same name as her uncle), that poem is related to the antecedent group of 110-13, poems which deal with the meaning of "poetry." This sort of complex association helps to provide a continuity for sections of the book but also makes it impossible always to separate the poems into conveniently discrete groups that can be arranged under categories.

Edward Partridge notices the same phenomenon, as when he sees a connection between *Epigs.* 90 and 91 on the one hand and among 91, 92, and 93 on the other. In the first two, says Partridge, "Mill, a servant, who came to court and learned vice contrasts sharply with Sir Horace Vere [91], . . . an aristocrat who practices virtue"; and then, "between Vere and Sir John Radcliffe [93], both statesmen and soldiers, Jonson places an epigram satirizing the amateur politicians who pretend to a knowledge of statecraft they do not have" (p. 174). Partridge does not speculate on a reason for Jonson's arranging groups of poems to overlap in this manner, but I shall: I think that Jonson intended that readers not be able to say something to the effect of "*this* is the pattern of the collection," any more than he wanted "none, whose scatter'd names honor my booke, / For strict degrees of ranke, or title look" (*Epig.* 9). To make it convenient for the reader so to reduce the entire collection of epigrams (in either way) is possibly to tease him away from what he should be attending, the meanings of the poems themselves; that would be "'gainst the manners of an *Epigram.*"

Ironically, then, to the extent that I have correctly assessed Jonson's intention, whatever claim I might make about the structure of his book is bound to be somewhat undermined. Let me suggest one example of the way poems may be divided, not so much into groups that overlap as into groups that interlock, that is, into groups (comprising the same poems) that can be perceived in quite different ways. Of *Epigs.* 1 through 36, I have already discussed two groups, 1 through 9 (audience, subjects for praise, definitions of epigram) and 23 through 26 (good, corruption). A different division of the poems cuts across the former of these groups and subsumes the latter; the result is a small group and a very large one, the first composed of the first three epigrams (to reader, to book, and to bookseller) and the second composed of *Epigs.* 4 through 36. In *Epig.* 4, Jonson addresses his monarch as both a ruler and a poet and in 5 he celebrates the union of the kingdom. After a number of epigrams in which he examines the best and worst in the realm, in *Epig.* 35 he returns to praise James and to express gratitude for the preservation of his monarch and "the whole land." In 36, "To the Ghost of Martial," he alludes to the greatness of a classical poet he imitates, but asserts that his own "royall subject" ennobles Jonson's verses because "Thou flattered'st thine, mine cannot flatter'd bee." James's greatness not only is worthy of great praise, but also assures that the poet cannot betray himself into flattery. The relation between poet and king which begins the large group also rounds it off. There are, of course, other ways of grouping the various poems in *Epigs.* 1 to 36, and one of them (1 to 5) I shall touch on shortly. My intention here has been to suggest the most important pattern to be found in the arrangement of the *Epigrammes* (thesis and antithesis) and to suggest other patterns that may also be relevant, but not to provide a catalogue of them, which, if I am correct, would in any case be a goal impossible of achievement. What remains is to list a few examples of additional groups of poems in the book (the listing is not meant to be exhaustive) and to look at a couple of possible antecedent collections of epigrams that seem to be echoed in Jonson.

III

I wish to turn briefly to three of the groups, or clusters, of epigrams that Edward Partridge has identified. All three are pairs of poems, two of which are rather obvious: 17 and 18 (true and false critics) and 107 and 108 (false and true soldiers). The third is less obvious: 44 is on the death of Chuffe, a particularly worthless man; 45 is the elegy "On My First Sonne." Thus, observes Partridge, the "vast democracy of death welcomes Jonson's beloved son even as it had Chuffe, the churl."[17] Each of the pairs illustrates in the briefest possible way the kind of contrariety that I see as the essential quality of Jonson's principle of order in the *Epigrammes.* Although, as I noted before, Partridge's interest is not specifically in this aspect of the poems' arrangement, he does mention these examples. The difference between his approach and mine can be seen in another instance of poems we see as composing one group. Partridge describes: "Lovely dead Margaret Ratcliffe . . . caught between Old Colt, an ex-lecher, and Gypsee, an ex-whore" (p. 173). If I am right, these three epigrams (39-41) are much more closely connected than Partridge suggests, because the topics in them are specifically antithetical: fidelity and infidelity; true and false passion. Margaret, who died of grief for the deaths of her brothers, praised for her "wit, feature, and true passion," is contrasted with the faithless Colt, guilty of "night-sinnes, with others wives, unknowne," and with Gypsee, who, whore turned bawd, is in either of her callings a dealer in false passion.

There are other groups of poems with antithetical balance in which Jonson not only explains but also illustrates what a certain quality should and should not be. All of these have patterns which are consistent with those of the groups at the beginning, middle, and end of the book. A coupling of poems which is similar to that of 44 and 45 is to be found in 21 and 22. *Epig.* 21 is on the gamester who is reformed, by way of whipping, into a Puritan, which provokes Jonson's caustic observation: "What severall wayes men to their calling have! / The bodies stripes, I see, the soule may save"; 22 is on the death of his first daughter, whose soul is saved quite another way, by virtue of her innocence. Two groups, 52 through 56 and 58 through 61, are chiefly concerned with Jonson himself and with his work. In contrast to a handful of poetasters and ignorant critics who cannot understand him (52, 53, 54, 56, 58, 61) is Francis Beaumont (55), praised for his poetry and thanked for his appreciation of Jonson's poetry.[18] Spies (59), those who were sent to betray Jonson (H & S, 11:11), are placed next to Lord Mounteagle (60), whom for his service in thwarting the Gunpowder Plot Jonson calls "saver of my countrey."

In *Epig.* 97 Jonson dwells upon the utter superficialty of "The New Motion," a man who is not substantial enough even to be a pimp or a purveyor of low entertainments or a favorite. In the manner of gallants who wear a fashion "only to shew their braines,"[19] New Motion's entire form and stature are no more than his bloated clothing. In 98 and 99 Thomas Roe is celebrated for his solidity:

> He that is round within himselfe, and streight,
> Need seeke no other strength, no other height:
> Fortune upon him breakes her selfe, if ill,
> And what would hurt his vertue makes it still.[20]

Roe, like Jephson, is greater than his name, perhaps greater than the greatest of names: "Well, though thy name lesse then our great ones bee, / Thy fact is more" (*Epig.* 99). Entirely self-contained, Roe is absolutely the antithesis of the puppet-like New Motion.

A different kind of antithesis, but just as absolute, lies in the view of women in *Epigs.* 83 and 84. Although both epigrams are jocular, in subject matter they are as dissimilar as possible. In the former, Jonson suggests that "whore" and "woman" are approximately synonyms; in the latter, he gently appeals to the generosity of Lucy, Countess of Bedford, whom he esteemed highly, so highly that the name, as he explains in another epigram, amounts to a description of womanhood idealized. The epigram in which Jonson invokes the Countess of Bedford's name is 76; it and 77 also constitute an antithetical pair. In 76, Jonson explains that his intention was to describe an ideal woman, a "creature I could most desire, / To honor, serve, and love; as *Poets* use." Then, after a dozen lines in which he describes the qualities of ideal woman, he concludes: "Such when I meant to faine, and wish'd to see, / My *Muse* bad, *Bedford* write, and that was shee." The name itself is the poem. In *Epig.* 77 the absence of a name is the poem:

To ONE THAT DESIRED ME NOT TO
NAME HIM.

BE safe, nor feare thy selfe so good a fame,
That, any way, my booke should speake thy name:
For, if thou shame, ranck'd with my friends, to goe,
I'am more asham'd to have thee thought my foe.

The group 125-29 is similar, not only in having to do with names, but also in structure, as the first four epigrams are about ideal figures (with genuine names) and the fifth is about a false figure (with a mock name) whose character is antithetical to those of the first four. *Epig.* 125 is to Sir William Uvedale, "a man / Made for what *Nature* could, or *Vertue* can." The next is to Mistress Carey, who in Jonson's poem is beloved by Phoebus. *Epig.* 127 contains Jonson's expression of gratitude to Lord Aubigny, and 128 is to William Roe, who, because of the completeness of his own character, is perfectly suited to gain everything and lose nothing in a journey abroad. After the epigrams to these, ideal man, ideal subject of a poem, ideal patron, ideal traveler, *Epig.* 129, "To Mime," has for its subject a man whose company is sought not that he may be admired but that he may be laughed at. He is a false wit, false man (a mime, only an imitation of a man), and even, in the penultimate line of the poem, a traveler who out-zanies Thomas Coryate, whose account of his journey was known by all for its foolishness. Herford and Simpson identify Mime as Inigo Jones, calling the association with Coryate "decisive for Inigo's identity with Mime" (11:28). It is also decisive for confirming that Mime is the very opposite of the last of Jonson's ideal figures, William Roe.

IV

Two collections of epigrams seem particularly to have been in Jonson's mind as he established the form of his own book. The general influence of Martial was well set out some time ago by T. K.

Whipple, who describes the "definite parallels from the work of the two men" and the "general resemblances . . . in subject matter and . . . form."[21]

Insofar as a specific structural connection between the collections is concerned, Kathryn Anderson McEuen points out similarities in the beginnings of Martial's and Jonson's books.[22] In his dedication to the Earl of Pembroke, Jonson, like Martial, talks about the propriety of his epigrams and the implications of a Cato judging them. But whereas Martial in his preface to Book I defiantly proclaims, "non intret Cato theatrum meum aut, si intraverit, spectet,"[23] Jonson, significantly varying Martial's meaning[24] claims that in his "*Theater* . . . *Cato* if he liv'd, might enter without scandall." This is not the place to go into the implications of Jonson's alterations;[25] that Jonson had Martial's introductory note in mind when he wrote his own is indisputable. Of the first four epigrams, McEuen further observes: "Both poets address the reader in number I; in number II, Jonson addresses his book, while Martial addresses his reader, telling from what bookseller his book may be purchased; in number III, Jonson addresses his bookseller, while Martial apostrophizes his book; and in number IV, both poets write to their respective rulers" (p. 17).

Another significant, but hitherto undiscussed, antecedent of Jonson's *Epigrammes* is the Latin epigrams of Sir Thomas More. The two collections have enough points in common that mere coincidence could scarcely account for them all. More's collection seems particularly to have affected Jonson's imagination when he fashioned the beginning and the ending of his book.[26] More's first four epigrams are addressed to or are about King Henry, so it is perhaps only accident that More's fourth epigram, like Martial's and Jonson's, should be addressed to his ruler. In the subject matter of their fifth epigrams, however, More and Jonson embrace a topic different from Martial's and in a strikingly similar fashion. Martial's fifth epigram is a brief, self-mocking jest. More's fifth epigram is on the union of the red rose and the white; Jonson's is on the union of Scotland and England. One additional point in common between More and Jonson may be mentioned here; in their fourth epigrams (and elsewhere) More and Jonson are similar in the way that they write about their monarchs' actions. Bradner and Lynch point out that "among [More's] topics, the most original for an epigrammatist was kingship. In fact, we know of no other sixteenth-century poet who used this theme for short poems."[27] In the early seventeenth century, so far as I am aware, it was still far from common for short poems to be written on the theme. Bradner and Lynch go on to say that More's "favorite concern [was] for the difference between a good king and a tyrant," which is just the topic of Jonson's epigrams 35 and 36.

An interesting, if complex, relationship of Jonson's and More's epigrams lies in the subject matter and placement of Jonson's final epigram, the scatological "On The Famous Voyage," and perhaps in the structure of the poem itself. As has been noted, one reason that "On The Famous Voyage" may be considered as being a kind of anti-epigram lies in its structure; it is a lengthy narrative. If Jonson thought that such a structure would disqualify a poem from being an epigram, he would have been constrained to judge that the first poem in More's collection was no epigram. A commentary on Henry VII's character, his early achievements as a monarch, and his wife, it is a narrative of 190 lines. "On The Famous Voyage" is almost the same length; it has 196 lines. As Jonson was distinctly willing to judge the bad as well as the good in anything that came to his attention, it is tempting, and even reasonable, to consider that one of the long "non-epigrams" that Jonson was parodying was the first in More's collection.

A more compelling and more substantial argument can be made about the subject matter and the placement of "On The Famous Voyage" as they are related to More's epigrams, even though there will remain (inevitably, it would seem) a certain amount of uncertainty about what precisely Jonson's intentions were. In *The Metamorphosis of Ajax,* Sir John Harington describes antecedents for his study of a stale subject; one of the antecedents is More. Harington says:

> Among Sir Thomas Mores Epigrams, that flie over all Europe for their wit and conceit, the very last (to make a sweet conclusion) is this:
>
> *Sectile ne teros porrum tibi spiret odores;*
> *Protinus à porro fac mihi cepe vores;*
> *Denuo foetorem si vis depellere cepe:*
> *Hoc facile efficient allia mansa tibi:*
> *Spirtus at si post etiam gravis allia restat;*
> *Aut nihil, aut tantum, tollere merda potest.*
>
> Which for their sakes that love garlicke, I have taken some paines with, though it went against my stomache once or twise.

If leeks you leeke, but do their smell disleeke,
Eat onions, and you shall not smell the leeke:
If you of onions would the sent expell,
Eat garlick, that shal drown the onions smell;
But against garlikes savour, at one word.
I know but one receipt. whats that? go looke.[28]

Elizabeth Story Donno points out that the spelling of *cepe* offers a clue as to which edition of More Harington consulted: the 1520 or the 1563 edition (p. 99n.). The word is spelled *cepe* in both the 1518 and the 1520 editions, but "1563" is a slip. In the 1563 edition (printed at Basel), the spelling is *cepae*. In the 1565-1566 edition (printed at Louvain), however, the spelling is *cepe*. Much more important, but also consistent with the *cepe* spelling, is Harington's identifying this epigram as "the very last." Of the several editions to which Harington could have had access, no two are the same. They vary in the number of epigrams they contain and in arrangement of epigrams. The only one that has More's scatological jest as its concluding epigram is the Louvain edition.[29]

In the last couplet of "On The Famous Voyage," Jonson says of his two heroes:

And I could wish for their eterniz'd sakes,
My *Muse* had plough'd with his, that sung A-JAX.

No one has doubted that Jonson had Harington in mind in these lines. Whether he knew, or cared about, which edition of More's epigrams Harington referred to may be impossible to tell. That he was unaware of Harington's reference to More is virtually impossible to believe. Although it may be the case that Jonson wanted to twit Harington, because, having seen an edition of More which was not that of 1565-1566, Jonson "knew" that Harington had erred in using the term "very last," it is much more likely that he took Harington's reference to More at face value. In either case, Jonson would have had a kind of tradition to exploit, the tradition of ending a collection of epigrams with one that is scatalogical, which had, after all, been brought to the public's attention by no less an authority than the man whose Muse had sung *A-jax*.

NOTES

[1]C. H. Herford and Percy and Evelyn Simpson, *Ben Jonson,* 11 vols. (Oxford: Clarendon Pess, 1925-1952), 8:83. Unless otherwise noted, all citations of Jonson are from this edition; however, here and throughout, I have regularized i/j and u/v to conform with modern practice. The edition is referred to as H & S.

[2]See, for instance, *Epigs.* 56 and 112.

[3]"Conversations with William Drummond of Hawthorndon," lines 29-31 (H & S, 1:133). Although it is difficult to know how accurate Drummond's account is at all points, he seems at least to have Jonson's language correct here. Drummond reports of the translation that "[Jonson] wrote his Verses befor it err he understood to conferr." In the commendatory poem Jonson says of his limited ability to assess Sylvester's work: "How can I speake of thy great paines, but erre? / Since they can only judge, that can conferre" (lines 5-6).

[4]Bruce R. Smith, "Ben Jonson's *Epigrammes:* Portrait Gallery, Theater, Commonwealth," *SEL* 14 (1974):109; Peter E. Medine, "Object and Intent in Jonson's "Famous Voyage" *SEL* 15 (1975):110.

[5]The term is Edward Partridge's, taken from his very useful essay "Jonson's *Epigrammes:* The Named and the Nameless," *SLitI* 6, 1 (April 1973):153-98. My indebtedness to his article will be apparent throughout.

[6]For a succinct treatment, see Thomas M. Greene, "Ben Jonson and the Centered Self," *SEL* 10 (1970):326-28.

[7]In lines 31-36 Jonson inserts in parentheses several kinds of travel the "heroes" of the poem quite apparently did *not* take into consideration; at the end of the narrative itself (line 192), the heroes, having concluded nothing, "went bravely backe, without protraction."

[8]An additional relation is pointed out by Wesley Trimpi: a portion of "On The Famous Voyage" is a parody of a passage in Sylvester's translation of Du Bartas (*Ben Jonson's Poems: A Study of the Plain Style* [Stanford: Stanford Univ. Press, 1962], pp. 98-99).

[9]Ian Donaldson, for instance, says: "Jonson's placing of this epigram raises the suspicion that Salisbury may be the lord in question" (Donaldson, ed., *Ben Jonson: Poems* [Oxford: Oxford Univ. Press, 1975], p. 35n). B. N. De Luna claims quite a bit more for the Jonson-Salisbury connection (*Jonson's Romish Plot: A Study of "Cataline" and Its Historical Context* [Oxford: Clarendon Press, 1967], pp. 67-73).

[10]According to Drummond, Jonson's opinion was that "Salisbury never cared for any man longer nor he could make use of him" ("Conversations," lines 353-54 [H & S,1:142]).

Only three days after Salisbury's death (27 May 1612), John Chamberlain wrote to Dudley Carleton that he "never knew so great a man so soone and so generally censured" (*The Letters of John Chamberlain,* ed. N. E. McClure, *MAPS* 12, pt. 1 [1939]:351). See also a letter of 26 May 1612 from the Earl of Northampton to the Viscount Rochester, in which Salisbury's death is described as an occasion "for which so many rejoice, and so few even seem to be sorry, except Pembroke, Hay, and Cope" (*Calendar of State Papers, Domestic,* 1611-1618).

[11]See H & S, 8:7-8, 47n.

[12]The last two lines of the poem are:

> Which, by no lesse confirm'd, then thy kings choice,
> Proves, that is gods, which was the peoples voice.

If Whalley's conjecture is correct (Peter Whalley, ed. *The Works of Ben. Jonson,* 7 vols. [London, 1756], 6:246), that these last two lines refer to Suffolk's appointment as Lord Treasurer, there is one more association in this group of poems. Suffolk was Salisbury's direct successor in office, as in the interval between the death of Salisbury and the appointment of Suffolk in 1614 the Treasury was presided over not by one man but by Royal Commissions.

[13]Donaldson's notes on the first of these two poems are particularly good, and in the first line of the second poem his changing of "Then" to "Than" for modern readers is instructive: the phrase means, "other than his chast wife."

[14]*De Constantia,* VII, 4 (H & S, 11:5). The translation by John W. Bashore is from the Loeb edition (London: Heinemann, 1928).

[15]So glossed by W. B. Hunter, ed., *The Complete Poetry of Ben Jonson.* The Stuart Editions (New York: New York Univ. Press, 1963), p. 13n.

[16]Donaldson also cites Matt. 5: 27-28, which is cogent insofar as Beast's adultery is concerned.

[17]Partridge, p. 173. See also pp. 172, 175.

[18]*Epig.* 55 is a reply to Beaumont's "Letter from the Country to Jonson" (reproduced in H & S, 11:374-77).

[19]From "In Authorem," Jonson's commendatory poem for Nicholas Breton's *Melancholike Humours* of 1600 (H & S, *Ungathered Verse* 2).

[20]This image is discussed in some detail by Richard S. Peterson, *Imitation and Praise in the Poems of Ben Jonson* (New Haven and London: Yale Univ. Press, 1981), pp. 46-48. See also Greene, "Ben Jonson and the Centered Self," particularly pp. 330-31.

[21]Thomas King Whipple, *Martial and the English Epigram from Sir Thomas Wyatt to Ben Jonson, UCPMP* (Berkeley: Univ. of California Press, 1925), p. 387. See also: Smith, "Ben Jonson's *Epigrammes,*" pp. 91-109; and David McPherson, "Ben Jonson, Martial, and the Bawdy Epigram," *Res Publica Literarum* 2(1979):217-28.

[22]Katherine Anderson McEuen, *Classical Influence upon the Tribe of Ben* (Cedar Rapids: Torch Press, 1939), p. 17. See also, Smith, p. 101.

[23]"Let no Cato enter my theatre, or if he enters, let him look on." Loeb Library, trans. Walter C. A. Ker (London: Heinemann; New York: Putnam, 1919).

[24]Donaldson makes this point in his edition of Jonson's poems (p. 6n.).

[25]See McPherson's essay, especially pp. 220-25.

[26]In at least one other place Jonson incorporates one of More's epigrams. In *Every Man In His Humour,* Jonson adapts More's Epigram 144 (*The Complete Works of St. Thomas More,* ed. Clarence H. Miller, Leicester Bradner, Charles A. Lynch, and Revilo P. Oliver, 14 vols. [New Haven and London: Yale Univ. Press 1984], 3, pt. 2), which deals with the man who does not punish one who has wronged him because the cozener "confesses." *EMI:* quarto, II.iii.135-77; folio, 111.i.145-92 (H & S, 3). This is noticed on p. 724 of the Yale edn. of More.

[27]*The Complete Works of St. Thomas More,* vol. 3, pt. 2:62.

[28]Sir John Harington, *A New Discourse of a Stale Subject, Called the Metamorphosis of Ajax,* ed. Elizabeth Story Donno (London: Routledge & Kegan Paul, 1962), p. 99.

[29]The Basel edition is titled *Lucubrationes* and the Louvain *Opera.* "The *Lucubrationes* . . . and the *Opera* . . . represent two different traditions, the first fostered by the disciples of Erasmus and the second by the pious English Catholic refugees, who removed all references to their hero's most famous friend.

A comparison of the text of the epigrams in these two editions shows that the Basel editors used *1520,* with occasional reference to *1518* . . . . The Louvain edition, on the other hand, based as it is on *1518*. . . . contains the three pieces omitted by More from the 1520 edition . . . but lacks the corrections made by More for *1520* and the eleven poems added by More to that edition . . . . The Louvain edition, furthermore, omits material found in *1518*. The sexually indelicate epigrams . . . and the poems in praise of Erasmus' work on the New Testament . . . are missing" (Bradner and Lynch, Yale edn., vol. 3, pt. 2:9). In view of the efforts to purify More's epigrams it is ironic that Harington should have called the attention he did to the final poem in this edition.

SEL 27 (1987)
ISSN 0039-3657

Expanding "The Poem Itself": Reading George Herbert's Revisions

JANIS LULL

Authorial intention, long the subject of controversy in literary criticism, remains an important if unacknowledged source of critical authority for recent readers of George Herbert's poetry. Stanley Fish, for example, although he is associated with reader-response theory, implicitly relies on something like what Michael Hancher has referred to as "final intention"—"an intention to *cause* an effect of one sort or another"—as one criterion for understanding Herbert's major English work.[1] According to Fish, Herbert intended *The Temple* to lead its readers through self-examination to revelation, and therefore the book "should be regarded as a strategy rather than as an object."[2] But when he attempts to deal with what Hancher would call "active intentions," ("the actions that the author, at the time he finishes his text, understands himself to be performing in that text" [p. 830]), Fish abandons the literal temporality that makes his critical method so useful for tracing the moment-to-moment responses of readers. To avoid convicting Herbert of the "sin of playing God" by believing that he could create meaning on his own, Fish appeals to predestination. Since all the poems in *The Temple* have already been pre-written by God, they are not the intentional constructs they seem to be. "The order in the poetry can be explained by attributing to the poet a conscious aesthetic strategy (to drive the reader to a deep and dark point of religion), but since the strategy is one for which he finally cannot claim responsibility, the explanation dissolves into a mystery (the driving behind the driving)" (p. 168). Herbert clearly stated his final intention in "The Church-porch": "A verse may finde him, who a sermon flies, / And turn delight into a sacrifice."[3] But at the moment of writing, did he understand his poems (and therefore, according to Hancher, intend for others to understand them) as personal struggles of spiritual discovery, or was he interested only in his final intention, only in the goal of

Janis Lull is an Assistant Professor of English at the University of Alaska at Fairbanks. This article is part of a book-length study of Herbert's revisions.

constructing meditational heuristics to "rhyme" his readers to God? For Fish, the question cannot be answered because it depends on "a relationship—between the poet and God—whose dynamics are unavailable to rational analysis" (p. 168). The appeal to God as preemptive author, while it undoubtedly reflects Herbert's own beliefs, allows Fish to ignore the possibility that the actual moment-to-moment behavior of writers, like the behavior of readers, may be relevant to the study of literature. Just when he might have been expected to propose a correspondence between the intentional acts of writers and the interpretative acts of readers, Fish's analysis jumps from the literal level—where Herbert's intentions are regarded as human actions that took place in real time—to a figurative level on which the poet's textual intentions are equated with his religious beliefs.

Nor is Fish alone in his confusion over the uses of real time and intentionality in interpreting *The Temple.* Here is how Helen Vendler, for example, describes Herbert's "provisional quality": "His poems are ready at any moment to change direction or to modify attitudes. Even between the title and the first line, Herbert may rethink his position. There are lines in which the nominal experiences or subjects have suffered a sea change, so that the poem we think we are reading turns into something quite other."[4] In the space of three sentences, Vendler has suggested that the experiences of a poem by Herbert belong to its readers, the poet, and the poem itself. This way of writing about poems, as if a text, its writing, and its reading were all events taking place in the immediate present, derives from the admirable urge to keep literature alive and "happening" now. But, like Fish's identification of God as the author of Herbert's poems, Vendler's shifting attribution of the poetic experience represents a retreat from the literal facts. A critic may well describe reading, especially a first reading, as a series of guesses, decisions, doubts, and modified attitudes unfolding through present time (though even this is a convenient fiction, unless the critic can read a poem and write about it simultaneously). But when critics ascribe these reading events to anyone but the reader—to the poet, to the text, or even to God—they seek the authority of intentionality while trying to avoid the notorious difficulties of talking about intention directly.

Although she manages not to discuss Herbert's active intentions, however, Vendler still finds it necessary to refer to the poet's final intentions, as well as to what Hancher has called "programmatic" intention, "the author's intention to make something or other" (Hancher, p. 829). Like Fish, Vendler seems to feel that to convict

Herbert of writing *The Temple* as a "conscious aesthetic strategy" would be to lessen its value as a work of art. She agrees with Rosemond Tuve that sincerity can be opposed to design in interpreting and evaluating Herbert's poems of spiritual conflict.[5] Quoting Tuve ("Herbert and *Caritas*"), Vendler concurs that "There is something unlike Herbert in the picture of a poet manipulating tensions to a predetermined end. Herbert was a great artist, perhaps because he nursed no tensions he could foreknow the resolution of; they were sins to him, keeping his Saviour on the rack. A 'picture of [a] spiritual Conflict' *is* written after not during it, yet truth to an experience which led to an end is not the same as drawing conflicting elements with steady hand toward a known end" (Vendler, p. 233). Both Tuve and Vendler assume (and Fish's discussion also implies) that Herbert's poems are too finely wrought to have been written during his actual devotional experiences. Yet all three critics suggest that the poems are somehow better if they were intended primarily as records of such experiences rather than as constructions of a certain type designed to have certain effects on their readers. What none of the these critics considers is a possibility implied by Hancher's threefold distinction and supported by a close reading of Herbert's drafts: that the poet wrote his verses as aesthetic strategies, personal histories, and active devotions, all at once.

Vendler follows her discussion of Herbert's sincerity with analyses of some of his revisions, including "Church-musick," "The H. Communion," "Whitsunday," and "The Elixir." Although she does not relate this evidence of the poet's composing process to the question of what actions he understood himself to be performing as he composed, the use of the drafts here and in other interpretative criticism implies the connection: drafts are intentional evidence. Perhaps critics like Vendler and Fish, trained in New Critical methods, do not make the connection explicit because they distrust hermeneutic evidence from "outside" the poem. Such suspicion is often seen as part of the legacy of W. K. Wimsatt and Monroe Beardsley's "The Intentional Fallacy,"[6] even though, as E. D. Hirsch has pointed out, that essay drew careful distinctions between acceptable and unacceptable kinds of intentional evidence, distinctions that have "now vanished in the popular version which consists in the false and facile dogma that what an author intended is irrelevant to the meaning of his text."[7] One remembers that Wimsatt and Beardsley accepted only "internal" evidence for a poem's meaning and forgets that they included "the biography of an author, his use of a word, and the associations which the word had for *him*"

(Wimsatt, p. 10) as parts of the public (hence "internal") body of facts that could legitimately be applied to interpretation.

Whatever their critical legacies, few recent writers on Herbert have depended entirely on the supposed "poem itself"—the received text divorced from all traces of its evolution. Although they seldom use the vocabulary of intentionality, Herbert's critics tacitly recognize his revisions as intentional evidence, relevant to interpretation not in the sense of displacing the final version as the poet chose to present it, but as essential clues to how he meant (and re-meant) his text as he wrote it. But in spite of comments such as Arnold Stein's that the evidence of Herbert's revisions "has not yet been given enough attention," there has been no systematic study of the drafts as aids to interpretation.[8] If writing is conceived as an evolutionary intentional process analogous to the tentative and provisional processes of reading, Herbert's drafts emerge as the very traces of intention. (This conception of active intention stresses temporal process more than Hancher's, in which "the author's active intention for the whole of a just-completed text will in most cases be simply a summary or integration" of intentions for each of the parts) (Hancher, p. 831, n. 10). For readers interested in how Herbert understood his own work—and this appears to include most Herbert scholars today—his drafts offer essential help, both in choosing between conflicting interpretations and in generating new readings.[9]

Many of Herbert's revisions of the poems in the Williams manuscript (W) show the poet deciding what he did *not* want a poem to mean, discriminating against undesirable readings rather than generalizing to make new ones.[10] In revising "Deniall," for instance, he concentrated on finding exactly the right words for the final two lines. He changed the last stanza twice, the first time as indicated in square brackets below (all references to W are from the facsimile):

Deniall (W)

When my devotions could not peirce
Thy silent eares,
Then was my Hart broken as was my verse
My Brest was full of feares
And disorder.

My bent thoughts like a brittle bow
Did fly asunder:
Each took his way: some would to pleasures goe
Some to the warres & thunder
Of Alarmes.

As good goe any-where, they say:
As to benumm
Both hart & knees, in crying night & day,
Come, come my God, O come
But no hearing.

O that thou shouldst give dust a tongue
To cry to thee,
And then not heare it crying; All day long
My hart was in my knee,
Yet no hearing.

Therefore my soule lay out of sight
Vntun'd, vnstrung:
My feeble spirit, vnable to look right,
Like a nipt blossome, hung
Discontented.

O cheere and tune my hartless brest,
Deferr no time:
That so thy favours granting my request,
They & my [hart] soule may chime
And meet my ryme.

In the Bodleian or B manuscript, Herbert made several more alterations, including replacing "soule" with "mind," and changing "meet" to "mend" in the last stanza (all references to B are from the facsimile):

Deniall (B)

When my Devotions could not peirce
Thy silent eares;
Then was my heart broken, as was my verse:
My brest was full of feares
And disorder.

My bent thoughts, like a brittle bow,
Did fly asunder.
Each tooke his way, some would to pleasures goe,
Some to ye warres and thunder
Of Alarmes.

As good goe any where, they say,
As to benumme

Both knees & heart, in crying night & day,
Come, come, my God, O come,
But no hearing.

Oh that thou shouldst giue dust a tongue
To cry to thee,
And then not heare it crying: all day long
My heart was in my knee,
But no hearing.

Therefore my soule lay out of sight,
Vntun'd, vnstrung:
My feeble spirit, vnable to looke right,
Like a nipt blossome, hung
Discontented.

O cheere, & tune my hartles brest,
Deferre no time.
That so thy fauors granting my request,
They & my mind may chime,
And mend my rime.

Vendler comments on the changes to the penultimate line (from "hart" to "soule" to "mind") that "Herbert is so fragmented in this poem that he could not decide, literally, which portion of himself was having the experience described in it" (p. 296, n. 9). But the progression of changes here recalls a biblical injunction that Herbert echoed elsewhere (in "A true Hymne"), "Thou shalt love the Lord thy God with all thy heart, and with all thy soul, and with all thy mind" (Matt. 22:37). All three of the "portions of himself" Herbert used in revising this stanza are faculties for carrying out the First Commandment, and as such, potentially interchangeable. It seems likely that the first revision, from "hart" to "soule," was made because the speaker has just prayed for God to "tune my hartles breast," his heart having been in his knee "All day long." Rather than complicate an already difficult metaphor, Herbert substituted for "hart" the synonym "soule." He later changed "soule" to another synonym, "mind," possibly because the poem describes his soul as "out of sight," but also for "mind's" more complex musical "chiming" with both "rime" and "mend."

The last two lines of the final version, the poem's only rhymed couplet, are often read as what J. L. Austin in *How to Do Things With Words* called a "performative"—a speech act in which the utterance itself performs the action it mentions.[11] According to

Joseph Summers, for example, "the final stanza, with its establishment of the normal pattern of cadence and rhyme, is the symbol of reconstructed order, of the manner in which men (and the poem) function when God grants the request."[12] Similarly, Diana Benet says that "the finally regularized rhyming in 'Deniall' is an indication of God's presence."[13] A stanza form that had been "broken" in the poem's other verses by failures of meter and rhyme is healed in the last line. But Richard Strier argues against the suggestion that Herbert intended to perform the act of spiritual mending by mending his verse form.[14] According to Strier, "my ryme" does not refer to "Deniall" at all, but to a hoped-for future "chiming" of the speaker's soul with the will of God. Strier rejects the idea that Herbert believed he could mend himself by mending his poem, as well as Stein's charge that "by the standard of Herbert's best poems the conclusion is a piece of arbitrary wit" (p. 16).

Did Herbert believe that restoring order to his verse in "Deniall" could in any way achieve a spiritual reordering? One does not have to go as far as Heather Asals, who regards Herbert's attitude toward his poetry as ontological, even sacramental, to recognize that Herbert saw the poetic process as analogous to the sacraments.[15] As he wrote in "The Quidditie" (originally titled "poetry"), verse is "that which while I use / I am with thee" (lines 11-12). This definition clearly privileges the composing process over the product, implying that revising was a devotional act for Herbert, not just an aesthetic strategy.

In the first version of "Deniall," the speaker prays that God's favors and his own desires will join together and "meet my ryme." In a verbally similar passage in the W version of "H. Baptisme (I)," the speaker prays that the waters of infant baptism and the tears of the sinful adult will "still meet in my brest / And mend as rising starres & rivers doe." Here "mend" is primarily intransitive, meaning not to restore (something) but to join or converge: "Let the workings of baptism and tears not only meet in me but blend and become one with me." But the context suggests the transitive sense, too: "let these influences come together to mend me." "Meet" in the first version of "Deniall" calls for the blending without the mending—God's will and the speaker's becoming one and blending with his "ryme," his poetic activity. The substitution of "mend" for "meet" in this poem redirects the emphasis from reciprocity to a need to fix the "rhyming" process. "Meet" suggested that God should meet the speaker halfway; "mend" speaks unequivocally of self-correction.

Although Asals believes Herbert thought he could institute a new sacrament of language—"Herbert *breaks the host of language* itself;

he *breaks* the Word itself" (p. 11)—her approach assumes a pride that is inconsistent with this revision of "Deniall," which moves toward increased humility, and with the authorial persona evident everywhere in *The Temple*. Yet neither is "my rime" merely a metaphor for, as Strier puts it, "a state of harmony ('chiming') between God's will and the poet's" (p. 191). As his careful revising here and elsewhere demonstrates, Herbert did not retain a word if he didn't accept all its connotations in context. He wrote "rime" and he meant "rime," using the word and the couplet itself as synechdoches for the poetic-devotional process, "which while I use / I am with thee." "My rime" does refer to lines themselves—"this rhyme that you've just read"—but also to the process of poetic writing generally, during which, if only for a moment, Herbert sometimes felt that God was present.

But something in this particular rhyme kept it from piercing God's "silent eares." This startling catechresis in stanza 1 shows that the poet, unlike his speaker, knew from the start where the trouble lay. Ears are not silent; voices are silent, or rather apparently silenced by the limitations of speakers. As Herbert said in the W version of "Church-lock and key" (titled "Prayer"), "I know it is my sinn, wch stops thine eares." In "Prayer (II)," he was even more emphatic: "Thou canst no more not heare, then thou canst die" (line 6). God hears. If the supplicant doesn't know it, it is not because the "eares" need mending, but because the devotional process is flawed.

Acknowledging that the speaker makes no real progress in this poem (because God heard all along), Mark Taylor claims that the repetition of "But no hearing" in lines 15 and 20 "tend [s] to reverse the direction of the poem's second half, forming a kind of structural chiasmus that leads us back to where we began. In a much more subtle way, 'Deniall' is operating on the mirroring principle of 'Easter-wings'."[16] Like the word "mend," chiasmic form ties the end of the poem to its beginning; and like "mend," the repeated line was introduced during the revising process. In the first version, line 15 read "But no hearing," and line 20, "Yet no hearing." Taylor seems to be right about the effects of this structural chiasmus. By changing "Yet" to "But" in line 20 and substituting "mend" for "meet" in line 30, Herbert transformed a conventional temporal progression (suggested by the "when . . . then" frame in stanza 1 and the change from past to present tense in stanza 5) to a temporal circle. Like many of his poems, the revised version of "Deniall" almost forces a second reading, drawing attention back to the first verse and to the title, which, as Taylor observes, "refers not only to God's apparent denial of man's pleas, but also to Herbert's denial that such an appearance can be real" (p. 83).

The drafts of "Deniall," then, offer some new answers to critical questions about the poem. Was Herbert so "fragmented" that he couldn't decide which part of him was experiencing the poem? No, although he took considerable care in deciding which faculty for loving God would work best in this complex metaphorical representation of a fragmented speaker. Did Herbert mean for the last two words to refer to the poem itself or to his spiritual state? Both, because the poetic process was also a devotional process for him. Did he think he could call down God's grace by "mending" his poem? No. The change from "meet" to "mend" clarifies Herbert's meaning: silence is a property of "rime" and not of "eares." Grace is always present but a fragmented worshiper may not perceive it. Should the repeated line be read as a suggestion of chiasmic form that helps direct attention back to the beginning of the poem? Probably. Herbert created the repetition at the same time that he added "mend," a word that also associates the poem's end with its beginning.

In spite of occasional comments such as Vendler's on the drafts of "Deniall," critical interest in Herbert's revisions has focused primarily on "The Elixir." This poem, often regarded as "one of the most beautiful and meaningful of all Herbert's poems,"[17] and even "the key to his entire *Temple*,"[18] was revised more than any other lyric in the Williams manuscript, where it was initially called "Perfection":

Perfection

Lord teach mee to referr
All things I doe to thee
That I not onely may not erre
But allso pleasing bee.

A man that looks on glass
On it may stay his eye:
Or if he pleaseth, through it pass
And then the Heau'en espy.

He that does ought for thee,
Marketh y[t] deed for thine:
And when the Divel shakes y[e] tree,
Thou saist, this fruit is mine.

All may of thee pertake:
Nothing can be so low,
W^{ch} wth his tincture (for thy sake)
Will not to Heauen grow.

A servant, wth this clause,
Makes drudgery, divine.
Who sweeps a chamber, for thy lawes,
Makes that, and th'action fine.

But these are high perfections:
Happy are they that dare
Lett in the light to all their actions
And show them as they are.

The second draft, revised in Herbert's hand in W, includes the first two stanzas as above, eliminates stanza 3, and ends with the three verses below. Herbert also added a new title, "The Elixir," but did not cross out "Perfection":

All may of thee pertake:
Nothing can be so meane,
W^{ch} wth his tincture (for thy sake)
Will not grow bright & cleane.

A servant, wth this clause,
Makes drudgery divine.
Who sweeps a roome, as for thy lawes,
Makes that, and th'action fine.

This is ye famous stone
That turneth all to gold
For y^{t} wch God doth touch & owne
Can not for less be told.

A third draft, titled "The Elixer" and later corrected to "The Elixir" appears in the Bodleian manuscript:

The Elixir

Teach mee, my God & King,
In all things thee to see,
And what I doe in any thing
To doe it, as for thee.

Not rudely, as a Beast,
To runne into an action:
But still to make thee prepossesst,
And giue it his perfection.

A man, y^{t} lookes on glasse,
On it may stay his eye;
Or if he pleaseth, through it passe,
And then ye heauen espy.

All may of thee partake:
Nothing can be so meane,
W^{ch} with his Tincture (for thy sake)
Will not grow bright & cleane

A servant wth this clause
Makes drudgery divine
Who sweeps a roome, as for thy laws
Makes that & th'action fine

This is ye famous stone
That turneth all to gold
For that, wch God doth touch & owne
Cannot for lesse be told.

"Though without knowing which came first," writes Stein, "we may observe that this new image [the "famous stone"] is related to Herbert's turning from the imagery of tree, fruit, and organic growth in the canceled fourth [sic] stanza to the different kind of growth implied by the 'tincture'" (p. 141, n. 2). But Stein's own analysis shows which came first. As Mary Ellen Rickey observes, the alchemical connotations were present all along in the word "tincture."[19] By removing the old last stanza, Herbert reduced the organic suggestions of "tincture" and expanded the alchemical and transcendental ones. In a parallel rejection of vegetable imagery in stanza 2, he replaced "to Heauen grow" with "grow bright & cleane," substituting for a transformation characteristic of living things one more appropriate to the inorganic vehicles of his emerging major metaphors, glass and gold. Herbert elsewhere tends to distrust his own images of organic growth. Commenting on "The Flower," Vendler says, "We cannot miss the tentative sexuality of his 'budding' and 'shooting up' and later 'swelling'—one question the poem puts is whether such self-assertion can ever be guiltless" (p. 51). Strier adds, "Herbert views his erected wit with alarm" (p. 39, n. 30).

In any case, as Hutchinson saw, the new title stresses the inorganic and, "was, no doubt, chosen after he had added the new last verse" (p. 184).

But Herbert did not cancel the old title when he added the new one. "Perfection," echoed in the original last verse by "high perfections," suggests a state of being—with an implied comparison to high stained-glass windows (another meaning of "tincture" is a dye or stain)—that "Lett[s] in the light" of heaven. The revised ending focuses instead on the "famous stone" and, as Stein says, "all that it symbolizes of human endeavor, the whole history of the search for 'perfection.'" But by leaving both titles, Herbert explicitly linked the search process, the active principle of the elixir, to its end result. Charles Molesworth calls the rewriting of this poem "revision toward action," a shift from "an emphasis on appearance (how one looks in the sight of God) to an emphasis on action (how one fulfills the law of God")."[20] Strier, on the other hand, says the revision transforms the poem from one "about actually doing things well" to one about "the transforming power of a fiction—or, more accurately, of an attitude" (p. 207). Does the revised "Elixir" discriminate in favor of action or attitude, process or stasis? The double title of the second draft leaves the issue in doubt.

The two titles imply that as he worked on "The Elixir," Herbert was consciously comparing action and perfection (two words that probably "chimed" perfectly in the seventeenth century). "Action" was a cue word for at least one of his other changes. In the new fourth stanza, "Who sweeps a chamber, for thy lawes" becomes "Who sweeps a roome, as for thy lawes." While modern readers may assume, as Molesworth does, that "roome" is a more humble word than "chamber," this was not necessarily so in Herbert's time, when "chamber" suggested a private room or bed chamber, usually one of the simpler rooms of the house. Rather than being an instance of Herbert's moving to the "homely" diction he is often said to prefer, this revision aims at logical and theological precision; the important word is "as," and not "roome." ("Roome" replaces "chamber" mainly for the meter.) To act *as if* for God's laws differs from acting *for* them as the New Dispensation differs from the Old. The revision responds to the Pauline distinction between the letter and the spirit of the law, "for the letter killeth, but the spirit giveth life" (2 Cor. 3:6). As Tuve says, "considerations of God as Law or rigorous Justice and God as Love are thematic not haphazard in his work."[21] The "action" in this stanza is not only the act of sweeping. Perhaps originally suggested by "lawes" just above it, "action" also connotes legal action, and "fine" is a complex pun reflecting both "the tincture" that makes base things fine and the sacrifice of Christ that "puts fine" to the action (for debt) brought against humanity by the Old Testament God. This is the reason for the counting figure that ends the poem in the second and third drafts. Only "gold" will pay the debt—Tuve cites the Song of Solomon as a source of the convention of Christ as gold (p. 143)—and God "tells" as gold everything transmuted by the "famous stone."

Just as "a man that looks on glass" may read only its reflecting surface, a reader of "The Elixir" may see the phrase "for thy sake" as a human utterance that makes even menial work fine enough for God. But if the reader goes deeper, to "th'action" against sinners canceled by the Crucifixion, it becomes clear that "for thy sake" must also be the utterance of Christ. As a merely mortal utterance, the "clause" cannot alter fallen nature. Only as spoken by God of his sacrifice does "for thy sake" become the transforming elixir. If, as Strier persuasively argues, Herbert was deeply committed to the doctrine of salvation by grace alone, Christ is necessarily the real speaker of "for thy sake." Mortals cannot mend by their own actions, whether humble or grand. Only God can mend them. Although the "hidden" speaker was present in the poem from the first draft, the change from "for thy lawes" to "as for thy lawes" reinforces this second level of meaning.

In his last draft, Herbert finally eliminated "Perfection" from the title and substituted two new stanzas for the old first one. Of this portion of the poem, Helen White remarks that "'As for Thee' says all there is any need of saying. The essential thing is there. One is almost sorry not to rest with that" (p. 182). But Vendler's reaction to the first four lines is strongly negative: "I cannot think of any beginning of a great poem in English so unpromising as the first stanza of *The Elixir*, which is pure versified catechism, with banal rhymes, an awkward repetition of 'things—thing,' and an infantile vocabulary" (p. 270). Herbert, of course, often insisted on the poetic excellence of scriptural and liturgical language: "Nor let them punish me with losse of rime, / Who plainly say, *My God, My King*" ("Jordan" (I)). But he usually employed such plain language, as both Stanley Fish and Barbara Leah Harman have pointed out, at the ends of poems that begin more ambitiously. In such poems, Herbert's "versified catechism" sounds like a renunciation of literary individualism in favor of the language of religious ritual. But "The Elixir," instead of ending with familiar formulas, begins with them. Vendler sees in this "banal" and "awkward" language attitudes that need—and receive—correction. Herbert, she says, introduced the "complacent tonal echo of the Pharisee" (p. 270) in the first stanza and "overintellectuality" in the second (p. 271) to illustrate "the passage from self-consciousness to service [that] guarantees a divine response" (p. 272).

This interpretation, which has Herbert advocating the efficacy of human works—the right attitude "guarantees" a response—may be right, of course, and Strier may be wrong about Herbert's devotion to the doctrine of justification by faith. But the sequence of Herbert's composing process here argues against Vendler's reading. The plain, formulaic beginning of "The Elixir" was really its ending—not for readers, as in "Jordan" (I)—but for Herbert. He wrote the beginning last, after he had fine-tuned the rest of the poem to stress the unhuman (alchemical, inorganic, divinely instigated) nature of the transmutation. It would be strange if he then decided to reemphasize human agency, constructing a speaker-persona whose attitudes needed correction. The earlier versions do not suggest such a persona. The original first stanza might be called hymnlike, but not infantile, and the new "over-intellectualized" second stanza has no counterpart in previous drafts. The canceled third stanza ("He that does ought for thee / Marketh y[t] deed for thine") does not resemble the final version's second one, though it hints at prepossession in the image of the "tree," always associated with the cross in Herbert. Vendler says this stanza was canceled because it was too "gloomy" (p. 235), especially in its conjuring of the devil. Instead, it may have been too active, failing to point toward the mystery of prepossession because it stressed human agency too strongly.

The revised beginning of "The Elixir" resembles the "borrowed" biblical and catechistical language that concludes poems like "Jordan" (I) and "Antiphon" (I) (where "My God and King" is the repeating refrain) because for Herbert, these words came at the end of the poetic process. He was adept at finding "rest" for his verses in scriptural language (and, as Harman shows, in scriptural stories). If the first two stanzas of "The Elixir," as White sensed, have a ring of finality, it is because they *were* final for Herbert. As his earlier revisions had made clear, only Christ's payment of human debt makes deeds acceptable to God. "Referr" is rejected in favor of a prayer to "see" what is already there, just as actions are now done *as for*, but not *for God*. Merely desiring to act "for thy sake" is enough, not because of any power or merit in human will, but because "his tincture" (this tincture, but also *his* tincture, Christ's own attitude and words infused into the speaker) has already transformed the unworthy to "gold."

For Herbert, writing "The Elixir" became a process of discrimination in which he discovered that certain connotations of the word "tincture"—a physical growth principle, a stain or dye—spoke too strongly of earthly transformations. Eliminating these connotations, he added lines that stressed the transcendental nature of "the elixir" and the mysterious double perspective from which actions apparently in the process of becoming "fine" in human time are, through Christ, debts already paid ("made fine") in eternity. Actions "as they are" are worthy neither in themselves nor for the motives that inform them, but only by God's grace. In the second revision, Herbert added two new stanzas suggesting in their measured finality that what seems to be in the future for the speaker—God's prepossession of all acts—has already been granted. Faith consists in "seeing" this truth rather than in doing anything. In the poem's second verse, the last one that Herbert wrote, he used "still" with all the force of both its meanings. The opposite of a beast that "runne[s] into an action" is "still to make thee prepossesst"—always to recognize that it is God who acts, and as a result, to be still.

Herbert stopped writing at the end of line 8, ending where he had started, with the word "perfection." While his revisions to "Deniall" encourages readers to associate the poem's end with its beginning through semantic and formal structures, "The Elixir" became a recursive process for its author. For readers, understanding this process helps explain how the finished poem manages to encompass both the human sense of time as "the whole history of the search for 'perfection'" and the non-time of God, in which perfection is not past or future but fact. The reader who sees the received version of "The Elixir" as a poem about fulfilling God's law through correct action does not read deeply enough. Nor is it a poem about serving God with an attitude that "guarantees a divine response." In the final version of the poem, "for thy sake" still signifies a commendable human attitude toward action. But at a different level of spiritual understanding, God speaks the words "for thy sake," addressing humanity at large and each individual, transmuting their unworthiness and hopeless debt to "gold." Every element of the finished poem gestures toward this double perspective, from the visual metaphor that stresses two ways of seeing, to the sound-collocation of "action" and "perfection," to the legal puns that underscore the difference between God's mysterious fulfilling of divine requirements and humanity's acting "as if" it could satisfy God's law.

"The Elixir" is a "deep and dark" meditation, a poem whose best meanings the reader construes not so much by reversing initial interpretations as by going beyond them and viewing them from an altogether different perspective. The hermeneutic danger here lies not so much in misinterpretation as in underinterpretation. It is a small danger where Herbert's final intention is concerned, for even a superficial reading will help "rhyme" the reader to good, as "The Church-porch" implies. But Herbert's own care with his drafts urges the interpreter to go further, to wonder about such things as why the poet was slow to commit himself to a new title that Rickey and others have praised as "infinitely superior" to the old one, or why "as for thy lawes" struck him as better than "for thy lawes." The resulting insights suggest not only how intensely and immediately Herbert's devotional intentions were involved in the process of writing poetry, but also how profoundly he expected his readers to contemplate the finished poems. The drafts leave little doubt that the poetic process often engaged Herbert simultaneously in "aesthetic strategies" (final intentions), in "picturing" past conflicts (programmatic intentions), and in active spiritual and intellectual struggles. By showing the progress of all three kinds of intention, the revisions of poems such as "Deniall" and "The Elixir" provide just the kind of "internal" intentional evidence that Wimsatt and Beardsley had in mind, the kind that helps critical readers match their active *reading* intentions to the poet's writing intentions. In this sense, if not in the narrower one that regards only the final version as relevant for interpretation, the drafts are part of "the poem itself."

NOTES

[1]Michael Hancher, "Three Kinds of Intention," *MLN* 87 (1972): 834.

[2]Stanley E. Fish, *The Living Temple: George Herbert and Catechizing* (Berkeley: Univ. of California Press, 1978), p. 171.

[3]George Herbert, *The Works of George Herbert,* ed. F. E. Hutchinson, corr. edn. (Oxford: Oxford Univ. Press, 1945), p. 6. All quotations of Herbert's works other than those from the manuscript facsimiles are from this edition.

[4]Helen Vendler, *The Poetry of George Herbert* (Cambridge, Mass.: Harvard Univ. Press, 1975), p. 25.

[5]See Rosemond Tuve, "George Herbert and *Caritas,*" *Essays by Rosemond Tuve,* ed. Thomas P. Roche (Princeton: Princeton Univ. Press, 1970), pp. 167-206.

[6]W. K. Wimsatt, Jr., and Monroe C. Beardsley, "The Intentional Fallacy," *Sewanee Review* 3 (1946): 468-88. Rpt. in Wimsatt, *The Verbal Icon* (Lexington, Ky.: Univ. of Kentucky Press, 1954).

[7]E. D. Hirsch, Jr., *Validity in Interpretation* (Hew Haven: Yale Univ. Press, 1967), pp. 11-12.

[8]Arnold Stein, *George Herbert's Lyrics* (Baltimore: Johns Hopkins, 1968), p. 141, n. 2.

[9]In a collection of related poems such as Herbert's, the evidence of revision can also be applied to readings of the unrevised poems. See for example, Janis Lull, "George Herbert's Revisions in 'The Church' and the Carnality of 'Love' (III)," *George Herbert Journal* 9 (1985): 1-16.

[10]For the use of the terms "generalization" and "discrimination" in the analysis of revision, see Janis Lull, "Past Texts: Shakespeare, Herbert, and the Revising Process," *Style* 19 (1985): 326-40.

[11]J. L. Austin, *How to Do Things With Words* (Cambridge, Mass.: Harvard Univ. Press, 1962).

[12]Joseph H. Summers, *George Herbert: His Religion and Art,* 1954 (rpt. Binghamton, New York: Center for Medieval and Early Renaissance Studies, 1981), p. 136.

[13]Diana Benet, *Secretary of Praise: The Poetic Vocation of George Herbert* (Columbia, Mo.: Univ. of Missouri Press, 1984), p. 48.

[14]Richard Strier, *Love Known: Theology and Experience in George Herbert's Poetry* (Chicago: Univ. of Chicago Press, 1983).

[15]See Heather A. R. Asals, *Equivocal Predication: George Herbert's Way to God* (Toronto: Univ. of Toronto Press, 1981).

[16]Mark Taylor, *The Soul in Paraphrase: George Herbert's Poetics* (The Hague: Mouton, 1974), pp. 82-83.

[17]Helen C. White, *The Metaphysical Poets: A Study in Religious Experience* (New York: Macmillan, 1936. Rpt. New York: Collier, 1962), p. 177.

[18]Louis L. Martz, *The Poetry of Meditation: A Study in English Literature of the Seventeenth Century* (New Haven: Yale Univ. Press, 954), p. 257.

[19]Mary Ellen Rickey, *Utmost Art: Complexity in the Verse of George Herbert* (Lexington, Ky.: Univ. of Kentucky Press, 1966), p. 120.

[20]Charles Molesworth, "Herbert's 'The Elixir': Revision Towards Action," *Concerning Poetry* 5 (1972): 18.

[21]Rosemond Tuve, *A Reading of George Herbert* (Chicago: Univ. of Chicago Press, 1952, Midway Reprint, 1982), p. 123.

[22]See Barbara Leah Harman, *Costly Monuments: Representations of the Self in George Herbert's Poetry* (Cambridge, Mass.: Harvard Univ. Press, 1982).

SEL 27 (1987)
ISSN 0039-3657

The Fellowship of the Mystery: Emergent and Exploratory Metaphor in Vaughan

HAROLD SKULSKY

A metaphor need not be carried directly by a particular word or phrase. It may emerge gradually, as the hovering implication of a *series* of metaphors that begin to cluster in the mind, helped along by the unfolding argument. The emergent metaphor is to the poem what sadness is to a sad face: it supervenes on the whole instead of inhering in any part. Vaughan is good at it, and it says something about his personality as a writer that he is. In fact, there is a particular emergent metaphor that occurs tellingly in four of his best poems. I will be tracing it through them in what follows.

The metaphor captures very well, in all their ambivalence, the frustrated gnostic yearnings that underlie a lot of Vaughan's devotional poetry. And the general strategy of metaphoric emergence, as I will argue later, is just the sort of thing we might expect of a poet who cherishes his privacy and yet wants somehow to confide in his reader. But what chiefly interests me here is the kind of reading Vaughan's figurative idiom is designed to elicit. Even in so comparatively undramatic and unconversational a devotional poet, metaphor turns out to be best understood as a move in a game of dialogue—in this case, a double game: with George Herbert, Vaughan engages in a kind of repartee or *antanaclasis*, in which one player volleys back the other's terms, but with a twist in the sense; with the reader, Vaughan plays a semantic version of hide-and-seek subtly controlled by metaphoric emergence itself. Neither transaction, it seems to me, is a zero-sum game in which one player wins only if another loses;

Harold Skulsky is Professor of English at Smith College. The distinctions drawn in the present essay are part of a transactional theory of figurative language that the author sets out and defends in "Metaphorese." *NOUS* 20, 3 (1986). Other applications of the same theory will be found in "*Upon Appleton House:* Marvell's Comedy of Discourse," *ELH* 52 (1985):591-620, and in a book-length study of the seventeenth-century theory and practice of metaphor that will be completed in a few years.

both are plus-sum games of coordination, or (as Vaughan might prefer to put it) of charity, in which somebody winds up ahead only if everybody does. Solitary as this devotional poet or his speaker appears to be, he is engaged in an enterprise that is deeply and intricately social. It seems to be essential to acts of speaking and construing figuratively that this should be so.

The two games in which Vaughan's metaphor is caught up are vivid examples of literary phenomena that have been widely discussed in recent years: intertextuality and the guidance of reader response. The first turns out, on the view recommended here, to be precisely *allusion*, in the classic sense: utterance that *plays* on and off what precedes it. The second turns out to be a refinement of the sort of conversational listening in which, by moving intently from cue to cue, one achieves as much rapport as the speaker invites or allows. In what follows, I will concentrate on playing the second; but I must begin by watching Vaughan play the first, and here we will need to look carefully at the relevant Herbert poem, "Vanitie (I)."[1]

When the fleet Astronomer threads the spheres in his quick-piercing mind, cosmographical meridians and parallels are presumably being drawn through them on a mental chart. But what is it to walk from door to door, looking them over, dances and all, as if one "design'd to make a purchase"? What is it to do this with a familiarity that lets one tell just when to expect a "full-ey'd" look, and when a "secret glance"? Take all this literally, in a cluster, and you have a connoisseur of the stews on a shopping visit, even though each detail taken separately is a metaphor for something chastely astronomical—or lewdly astronomical; for the point of the emergent metaphor is that stargazing is prurient in its own way.

The Diver of Herbert's next example is also looking for something better hidden, and in fact something "God did hide / On purpose from the ventrous wretch." But the notion of prurient looking and searching comes back in the portrayal of the subtle Chymick who can "devest / And strip the creature naked." On a literal reading of the whole phrase, "the creature" is a contemptuous way of referring to the person being stripped. But of course the creature (in a usage rather archaic even in Herbert's day) is the material creation, whose clothes are simply the appearances that obscure causes, elements, or principles. The Chymick is skilled in dispelling appearances and disclosing principles, which (in the next metaphor) are nestlings still without their feathers: they are potentialities at the savant's (perhaps predatory) disposal. But the next metaphor brings a correction: the principles are great lords of whom the Chymick is the favorite suitor—the one who is allowed to "impart" his "minde" in the bedchamber while ordinary suitors have to wait at the door until the great man has finished the ceremony of dressing for the levee. The elements will not change their nature for the asking, but they will favor the projects of someone who is privy to that nature; laymen (ordinary suitors) know them only by their dress (their observable effects). In this metaphorical development, the rapist has vanished, to be replaced by an ironic picture of a successful parasite.

Herbert's poem turns out to be a homily on Paul's exhortation not to "walk" in the vanity of the mind (Eph. 4:17). The idea of implicating scientists in this offense is perfectly traditional; Herbert's astronomer is simply Jerome's "tenacious inquirer into nature who sends his eyes across heaven."[2] As for the sexual metaphors, the eyes have their own kind of lust (1 John 2:16), and the lust for empirical inquiry is merely a sophistication of this desire "to see with thine eyes the things that are secret" (Ecclus. 3:22-23). In Herbert's treatment the Pauline metaphor of walking about comes to describe a perverse response to the promise "Seek and ye shall find" (Matt. 7:7): "What hath not man sought out and found, / But his deare God?" God is not to be found by walking about. He is waiting in the "glorious law" that he "embosomes in us."

Vaughan's narrative in "Vanity of Spirit"[3] is a retort, in the classic sense, on Herbert's emergent metaphors of rape and voyeurism: the metaphors in the retort alter only slightly the literal sense of the ones they challenge, but pointedly differ in figurative sense. Again a sequence of distinct metaphors generates still another, this time by being grammatically coordinated or "mixed":

> I summon'd nature: peirc'd through all her store,
> Broke up some seales, which none had touch'd before,
>   Her wombe, her bosome, and her head
>   Where all her secrets lay a bed
>   I rifled quite.
>
> (9-13)

Taking the metaphors separately, we have a speaker calling nature to mind ("summoning" her), going through an inventory of natural things ("peircing" her "store"), forcing access to some secrets of nature, and inquiring intrusively ("rifling") into others hidden in parts of the organic system of the world. Taking the terms together as if they jointly supplied the literal sense of a single composite metaphor, we have a self-confessed rapist and voyeur.

A passage in Vaughan's brother Thomas's work has Vaughan's notion of seal-breaking and Herbert's of stripping, and can serve as a gloss at least on Herbert: "Me thinks Nature complaines of a

Prostitution, that I goe about to diminish her Majesty, having allmost broken her Seale and exposed her naked to the world, and now I must recall my selfe: For there is a necessity of reserving as well as publishing some things."[4] This is a little incoherent; if Thomas is reserving (keeping) nature's secret, he already knows it, and has broken her seal; otherwise he is at most letting her keep her own secret. If not prostitution, there is at least a suspicious ménage a deux.

But unlike Thomas, or the paradigmatic savants in Herbert, Vaughan's speaker is not after the scientific discoveries that are the by-products of his search. He is after the "name" of the Creator (7). He wants to "descry"—to glimpse from a distance—"some part" of the Creator's "great light." And the last of the creatures he searches—with no noticeable change in attitude—is himself; the rifler-voyeur has simply turned his attentions inward, as called for by his plan of "peircing" through all of nature. He is in effect acting on the promise of Herbert's preacher, or of Jeremiah (31:33), that God's law is to be found inscribed in the bosom or in the "inward parts." But his faint inner light goes out before he manages to piece together the broken letters he finds there. Unlike the speaker of Herbert's "Jesu," who manages to reconstruct the divine name engraved on pieces of his broken heart, Vaughan's spiritual prowler fails to get a peek at a "mystery" (27) into which he has yet to be initiated. To approach God, he will need to strip the creature once again: he will need to die, and hence to "disapparell" his eye of the "veyls" that eclipse and benight it (29-34).[5]

The speaker's effort to know God, or know of him, is no surprise. What is a little surprising is the failure of that effort when it turns in the right direction; this is half of the retort on Herbert's preacher in "Vanitie (1)." And what is more surprising is the metaphor (of sexual violation and spying) that emerges as the effort is described—just the kind of metaphor that the preacher reserved for describing a misdirected search; this is the other half of the retort. It seems that one may escape from vanity of mind only to be trapped in vanity of spirit: the futile attempt to spy out God's secrets in this life. These include God's "name" because, true to the spirit of retort, Vaughan is giving back Herbert's metaphors with a difference. The faithful heart in Herbert is inscribed with its own assurance—with the name of God in His capacity as *Savior* ("Jesus," Matt. 1:21). Vaughan's spy, by contrast, isn't lusting after a sign of his Election. The name he is trying in vain to decipher, from its hieroglyphic traces in his creaturehood (16, 23), is the secret name or nature of his Creator, the

God that hides Himself (Isaiah 45: 15). Same vehicle, new tenor: introspection has made way for espionage.

A recognizable variant of the same metaphor emerges as we follow the narrative in "I walkt the other day."[6] Because of winter, says the narrator, he missed finding a "gallant flowre" where he had last seen it among others as "curious" (rare? arousing curiosity? the latter will be confirmed a bit further on). He consoled himself with the argument that

> there might be other springs
> Besides this here
> Which, like cold friends, sees us but once a year,
> And so the flowre
> Might have some other bowre.
>
> (10-14)

So far there is no pressing reason to suspect a metaphor—only a bit of stretching—in "springs" and "flowre": the Bermudan equivalent of the spring season, for example, is no "cold friend," like the spring "here" (in England), but "sees" the Bermudans all year round; maybe the flower (species, that is) can be found growing there right now. The argument seems to be a justification for looking elsewhere, or giving up, especially since the narrator introduces it by insisting that his search "lov'd not to peep and peer / I'th' face of things" (8-9). On the other hand, why this disclaimer, out of the blue? Who would have *thought* him a peeper (busybody? voyeur?) just because he wanted to have a second look at a species of flower he found magnificent (which is what "gallant" ought to mean on a literal reading of "flowre")? And the disclaimer has a little catch in it anyhow: it is hard to see how an addict of peeping and peering could get a thrill out of looking at the *face* of things, which is as available to a "full-ey'd" look as to a "secret glance."

These suspicions are confirmed by what the speaker says he did next: rather than give up his search for a specimen of the "gallant" flower, or decide to carry on in a "bowre" that enjoys a friendlier spring, the speaker took up the nearest thing he could "spie" (in the circumstances, "spie" is rather ironic) and "digg'd about / That place where I had seen him to grow out" (17). The plant is now a "him," in fact a "warm Recluse," still alive, though "of us unseen" (18-21). Where does this leave us? It is still just possible to take "flowre" literally, though the sudden personification is pointless, and the blind digging an odd way of showing solicitude for a plant. And why the earlier talk of other climates that might support the species, if this particular specimen was what really mattered? The alternative is to take "flowre" figuratively, and "him" and "Recluse" literally, as implying that the victim of the speaker's prying is a person. But then in what figurative sense is a living person said to be lying buried, or a buried person said to be alive? There is a metaphor here somewhere. The task remains to say just where. In this particular narrative, so far, the branching possibilities that build suspense are not narrated events but textual meanings. The one *donnée* is the emerging figure of the forlorn busybody, compulsively "digging" (in a sense yet to be determined) for sights otherwise denied him.

The speaker had invaded the privacy of the "Recluse"; now (he recalls) he tried to "extort" (etymologically: twist away) answers to "many a question Intricate and rare" (24, 22). What is it to coerce a flower into answering questions? Perhaps, to twist the facts about it into a spurious confirmation of what one believes. Given the arbitrary personal pronoun, this just barely saves the literal reading of "flowre," though that reading is accommodated by the only answer the speaker managed to "extort":

he now
Did there repair
Such losses as befel him in this air
And would e'r long
Come forth most fair and young.

(24-28)

If a personified root is talking about itself, then with a little straining we can find here a description of the winter dormancy of the plant—though "repair" is an odd way of describing the replacement of last year's flower (lost in "this air") with a new one. If the occupant of a grave is doing the talking, then "he" has somehow been forced to give an assurance of his own resurrection, with the accompanying repair of his body and soul, which will be rid of the nastiness they picked up in "this air." (The climate in which spring is a "cold friend" will be the fallen world's and not England's.) This glosses more details, but has the unpleasant effect of suggesting a desire to invade privacy that extends to violating graves and harassing their occupants. And on this reading the spy doesn't know an important secret when he finds it; first-hand testimony to a fundamental Christian hope gets dismissed as "all I could extort" (24).

What follows seems to confirm that "flowre" is euphemistic. In imagination at least, a grave was violated after all:

This past, I threw the Clothes quite o'r his head,
And stung with fear
Of my own frailty dropt down many a tear
Upon his bed,
Then sighing whisper'd, *Happy are the dead!*
What peace doth now
Rock him asleep below?

(29-35)

The movement to restore the privacy he invaded—stripped, in fact—has a panicky disproportion: throwing the grave-clothes over the uncovered head. He was, he explains, terrified (stung with fear) of his own frailty; and the tears that followed were evidently remorse as well as grief. (His summary remark about the happiness of the dead is another indication, by the way, that he has missed the point. As he goes on to say, his informant was a "poor root" without "wings / To raise it to the truth and light of things" [37-40]. He appreciates the "root" was a source of "doctrine" even though its "winglessness" will let few believe this [36-42]. But the doctrine itself seems to have escaped him.)

At the same time, these lines subvert the reading again. Necromancy in Vaughan's day was believed in, surely, by more than a few; and unless the grave in question is unmarked and situated in an open field, the assumption that the loved one is "still trod / by ev'ry wandring clod" (41-42) is a little alarmist. If the subject is really a root, these absurdities dissolve. The speaker's concluding prayer explains that what he has caught sight of is one of the "Masques and shadows" of an omnipresent Creator—an instance of what Vaughan elsewhere calls "*prolusions* and strong *proofs* of our *restoration* laid out in *nature*."[7] ("Prolusion" is introductory play—here presumably edifying play.)

"Flowre" and "root" are to be taken literally after all, and the person-predicates figuratively; the speaker has been describing a merely botanical invasion of privacy. But he has also been describing a divine masque in which he has been the principal actor. The semantic rule of the masque is that expressions that apply innocuously to performers and properties (a root exposed) apply momentously to objects in the fiction being acted out (a body partly exhumed); the hidden greenness of the root would go without saying if it weren't for what is being said in the same breath: that even in dissolution the body of the beloved is somehow being prepared for its resurrection.[8] It is in the masque scenario that values get partly reversed: a *figurative* root being stripped of his *literal* clothes. But in its main action the masque (like other masques) is clearly figurative:

the wish whose fulfilment the speaker was acting out is hardly a wish to learn of the body's metaphysical status by literally peeping under a shroud, with or without the aid of the black arts. The violation of the grave is an emergent metaphor for the penetration of the grave's secrets by less desperate means—by trying to find analogues of resurrection hidden in nature by God. In the concluding prayer the cemetery spy is replaced by a hunter who "tracks" the steps of God in pursuit of his "hid ascents."[9] The hunter, like the spy, wants to be shown things hidden—above all,

> hid in thee, shew me his life again
> At whose dumbe urne
> Thus all the year I mourn.
>
> (61-63)

The emblematic message of life in the root was evidently not enough; and neither was the elegiac masque that the speaker had woven around the act of digging for it. Whether one plays with emblems or masques, a "prolusion" apparently won't do duty for a "proof."

If his concluding prayer is granted, things hidden will be gradually revealed to a speaker who, despite his disclaimer, loves to peep and peer into the face of things. The storytelling itself mimics this pattern by only gradually resolving its ambiguities, forcing the reader into the role of semantic spy or hunter. In the process the metaphorical notion of an invader of graves, carried by no single word or phrase, has emerged and eventually declared its figurativeness. The process is a lot more complex than its counterpart in "Vanity of Spirit," but in both poems an emergent metaphor that literally describes sneaky and illicit looking is used as a figurative description of the struggle for illumination.

To judge by his use of pronouns and demonstratives, the speaker of "They are all gone into the world of light" is registering various objects in his thoughts and surroundings for the benefit of nobody in particular. He is a soliloquist, sitting (2) on or near a hill (7), perhaps at dusk (8). (This last detail will depend on whether the tense of "is" in "those faint beams in which this hill is drest" [7] is the present or the habitual, with "every evening" understood.) The speaker is trying out responses to his belief that his dead friends are in heaven.

The first is envy, faint resentment, and impatience: in going on ahead, they have left him alone, and he is merely "lingring" (2); survival is a kind of hanging around stranded while one's friends are all happy elsewhere. But the speaker checks himself immediately: even remembering his friends (not to mention being with them) brightens his "cloudy brest" as starlight does a gloomy grove or "faint beams" a hill after sunset. This, of course, is a very feeble retraction; it would take more than starlight to relieve the gloom of a grove. And the sequence of ideas is revealing: the memory of his friends

> glows and glitters in my cloudy brest
> Like stars upon some gloomy grove,
> Or those faint beams in which this hill is drest,
> After the Sun's remove.
>
> (5-8)

The conviction pumped up by "glows and glitters" subsides along with the candlepower of the speaker's analogies, and with the alliterative diminuendo of "glows," "glitters," "gloom." What was troubling him, anyhow, was the vision of his friends' present and future happiness, not his memory of their friendship; a momentary change of subject is serving as a change of attitude.

The attitude persists with the vision's return; he is thinking again of the world of light—now an "Air of glory" in which his friends are "walking" (9). As they *walk*, the light of glory (as if to join them in triumphing) "doth *trample* on my days" (10; my emphasis). The semantic illusion of gloating complicity here results only from the fact that "trampling" literally understood describes a kind of walking; the speaker has chosen an expression of bitter envy that he can disavow as an ineptitude, an accident of mixed metaphor. But he can disavow only the bitterness, not the envy. The figurative sense is that the light surpasses his days—if one can call them days (here a reduplication introduces a revision): surpassing this kind of daylight argues no special brightness! The point once again is the light that surrounds the others and excludes him, and (equivalently) the gloom he has been left in.

What follows is another attempt to get beyond envy, this time by a reinterpretation of the notion of walking. The "walks" he has been contemplating are not only those of his friends; they are also the "walks" of hope and humility (13). Envy or "cold love" (16) has no place there. *Whose* hope and humility? Presumably his own, among others. If one reads literally again, heaven has somehow already welcomed the speaker's surrogates; he is virtually there by proxy. But again the perverse suggestion is only the literal sense of a metaphor: heaven is par excellence what hope and humility "walk" in, dwell on, contemplate. It is what they have "shew'd" the speaker (15), presumably in the sense that being humble and hopeful has enabled him to see it. Unfortunately, the speaker's mounting vehemence carries him pell mell into an admission that he has been enabled to do no such thing. Death is "the Jewel of the Just, / Shining nowhere, but in the dark" (17-18). The Elect will be able to see their jewel shine only when they are with it—in the dark. Such mysteries "lie beyond thy dust" (19), and hence beyond the range of the speaker's vision; death is a "mark" man cannot "outlook" (20). It's easy enough to know by a look at the body-nest that the soul-bird has flown (21-22); but we don't know "what fair Well, or Grove he sings in now" (23). The speaker presumes that there is a grove for the bird—fair and not gloomy like the speaker's breast-grove (6); but the rest is ignorance. So much for the visionary claims of a few moments before.

Despite those claims the speaker is (metaphorically) a person who craves a look at sights denied him—enjoyments from which he is excluded. He can't add to the range of his vision by taking thought. But maybe what he can't take he will be given—provided that "some strange thoughts transcend our wonted theams, / And into glory peep" (26-27). As the revelation portentously delayed (and promised) by all the fanfare of suspensive grammar, the anticlimax of "peep" is almost comic, but revealing all the same. The forlorn peeping of the speaker's predecessors in "Vanity of Spirit" and "I walkt the other day" is now (by wishful thinking) somehow licensed; but it remains an outsider's furtive look.[10] This is once again to take it literally, of course; taken together with the whole complex of details that have led up to it, it is really a metaphor, or rather part of an emergent metaphor.

Earlier the speaker compared his "brest" (state of mind) to a "gloomy grove" under a starry sky. The stars corresponded to his remembered friends, the objects of his confused love and envy. But why should one star envy another? Now he too is a star, a "captive" star "lockt up" in a tomb. The "star" is shut out of a glory into which she can do no more than peep (9, 28). But she herself is one of God's "created glories" (34). When her jailer sets her free, she won't go into the world of light so much as light up the world, or at least the part of the world in her charge (29-32). Sense can be made of this rodomontade in Platonic and Hermetic terms,[11] but this doesn't keep it from being rodomontade, or from earning its keep by treating if not curing the speaker's *invidia,* which for him at least is the lust of the eye by another name.[12]

The apparent setting of these reflections is a hill, perhaps just after sunset (7-8). What is the speaker doing there? If, like the speaker of "I walkt the other day," he is enacting a solitary masque, then what he says he is doing is literally as well as figuratively true. He prays for the scattering of the passing mists that are blocking his telescope: either remove *them*, or remove *him* "unto that hill, / Where I shall need no glass" (40). What is relevantly blocked, in the attempt to penetrate death, is the speculative intellect; but is this situation being emblematically mimed? Masque property or not, the "glass" is a final telling detail in the emergent metaphor of the outsider looking in, this time as an ineffectual spy on the hidden joys that Paul describes as "the fellowship of the mystery" (Eph. 3:9).[13]

In "The Night" that fellowship is represented by Nicodemus, who saw the divinity of Christ (his "light") through the shrine-veil covering the full force (the "noon") of his divinity. The body of Christ is God's tent or dwelling (Heb. 9:11, Exod. 25:8), and the flesh of Christ is the veil over the holiest place (Exod. 26:33, Heb. 10:19-20).[14] These are the inevitable typological metaphors; but the sequence of ideas is the speaker's: first we get, with some elaboration, the limits on the "blest believer's" privilege, and only then the privilege. Even Nicodemus must content himself with peeping into glory:

> Through that pure *Virgin-shrine*,
> That sacred vail drawn o'r thy glorious noon
> That men might look and live as Glo-worms shine,
> And face the Moon:
> Wise *Nicodemus* saw such light
> As made him know his God by night.
>
> (1-6)

The veil lets one *look at God* and live, in spite of the warning (Exod. 33:20), just as the moon lets the glowworms *face the moon* and *shine* (hence survive) even though the light they are facing would snuff them out if it were coming straight from the source.

Can we let it go at that? The reading is a bit too charitable. It doesn't register the fact that the speaker has violated the logic of his own analogy by putting "shine" before "face the moon": when the listener arrives at "shine," he finds no counterpart of "look" and has no reason to recognize a counterpart of "live." The result is the illusion of an alternative parsing, with men being permitted two actions by the veil: (a) looking and living as glowworms shine; (b) facing the moon. This is almost nonsensical, but not quite; on its face, it implies that the effect of the veil is not to save lives but to blight them by reducing them to the wan glimmer of a glowworm in the moonlight. The impression won't outlast the reader's second thought, but he isn't to blame for the first. He has been given false cues. Are they merely a lapse? Or will we find that they have provided rhetorical immunity for feelings that will be vented less discreetly later on?

We haven't quite exhausted the difficulties of this first sentence. Doing so will introduce us to a central difficulty of the poem itself for a student of metaphor: underlying the process of emergence we are tracing, there are other processes involving clusters of metaphors, some of them rather subtle. For example, there is apparently (and characteristically) a metaphor lurking in the emphatic "night" of the claim that Nicodemus "saw such light / As made him know his God by night." Of course it was literally night at the time, but that doesn't explain "such light." In what kind of night does God need to be more luminous than he would by day to be recognized? Presumably, a metaphorical "night" compatible with metaphorical "noon," just as, in a later pseudoparadox, the metaphorical "Sun" Nicodemus spoke with needs no miracle to be seen at midnight (10). In both cases, the night that interests the speaker is the metaphorical equivalent of "darkness and blinde eyes" (8) in a hieratic speech that is, among other things, a pattern of metaphorical equivalences.

In fact metaphorical equivalence functions as a kind of contemplative discipline. Take the three metaphorical notions we've started with: veil, tent, light-darkness (or day-night). The winged sun of Mal. 4:20 that is played on next (9-12) recapitulates two of them: the sun corresponds to the noon of the opening, and the wings whose sight Nicodemus is "blest" with (9) are the veil (Christ's visible flesh) once again. A little further on we have a recapitulation of all three notions, in the flower "within whose sacred leafs did lie / The fulness of the Deity" (17-18): the leaves (petals) are the incarnational wings or veil once again; "fulness" coincides with the "noon" of God's presence; and the flower is the place par excellence where the fulness of the Godhead "lies" or dwells (Col. 2:19). Night-darkness-blindness; noon-sun-fulness; veil-wings-petals; tabernacle-flower. Each series of coreferential metaphors circles its own object of passionate concentration. The string of metaphorical descriptions of night (25-36) is only the most explicit and passionate of these series.[15]

But there is a countercurrent to this metaphorical concentration, a pattern of exploration in which a metaphorical term keeps on shifting its sense or reference. This exploration of meaning, or possible meaning, continually redefines the object of the speaker's frustrated searching, and ends by filling out an emergent metaphor like the ones we've been considering. "O who will tell me, where / He found thee?" (13). The answer is, not in a tabernacle, much less a temple (19-20), but in Christ's own "living works" (21). These were not only his "lodge" or tent (22) but timid spectators that "did watch and peep / And wonder" (23-24). Like Nicodemus, their privilege is qualified; their way of looking has a bit of the furtiveness of the outsider who is imagining and envying them. But the upshot is that the tent now in question need not be peeped into—by him, at least; he is already in it, and Christ is in it no longer. The speaker has arrived too late.

He is aware, from the chapter of Canticles he quotes (5:2) in his metaphorical encirclement of night, that the soul itself is a dwelling at whose door Christ calls and knocks (32-35).[16] But in that chapter the soul opens too late, and its predicament becomes an analogue of the speaker's: "I sought him, but I could not find him" (Cant. 5:6). The remedy offered by Christ himself, of course, is perseverance: "Seek and ye shall find; knock, and it shall be opened unto you" (Matt. 7:7). The story in Canticles leads (by way of the Gospel) from the soul's tent back to God's. But these hints are not very enlightening to the frustrated speaker: "O who will tell me, where / He found thee?" In the meantime, night is not only the soul's silent vigil for her opportunity to "catch" her "fair kinred" Christ (35-36); it is also a benignly dark "Tent" equal to heaven (38). As the notion of the tent has shifted its figurative sense in this last case, so have those of night and darkness. "Night" has virtually become a name for contemplation, "this worlds defeat" (25), the soul's "calm retreat" (27); and "dark" a way of describing a contemplative solitude, "calm and unhaunted" (38).

"Sun" and "light" have been redefined to match. The sun that keeps all things awake to "mix and tyre / Themselves and others" (44-45) is no longer the sun of righteousness, but it isn't the creaturely sun either; a sinner's "mixing and tyring" don't respect curfews any more than a saint's "defeat" of the world ends at daybreak. What is it, then? The rhetoricians recognize a trope in which "out of one improper term issues by signification another, then out of that improper term perhaps another, and so on, until one comes to the proper term."[17] This is the path laid down for us here, as if we too, in a semantic dimension, were groping our way toward a hidden interior:

I consent and run
To ev'ry myre,
And by this worlds ill-guiding light,
Erre more than I can do by night.

(45-48)

(a) The light that leads people astray into mires is foolish fire, the will-o'-the-wisp. (b) But there *is* no cosmic will-o'-the-wisp, unless one takes this notion figuratively, as a contemptuous reference to the sun. (c) But the sun literally so called doesn't light one's way to moral error or confusion; so by metonymy the notion of sun stands in turn for the worldliness that dominates people's waking lives. The emergent figure of the outsider longing for a peep into the holy of holies has been embellished by a suggestion of his tragicomic encounters with puddles in the moral darkness that Nicodemus enviably escaped.

The outsider is even willing to consider hearsay, if it promises to gratify his forlorn curiosity: "O who will tell me where?" And hearsay is what he concludes with:

> There is in God (some say)
> A deep, but dazling darkness; As men here
> Say it is late and dusky, because they
> See not all clear;
> O for that night! where I in him
> Might live invisible and dim.
>
> (49-54)

There is a parallel between people who speak of a darkness in God and men who say it is dusk here when it isn't: neither party can see its object clearly. But there is also a difference: the purblind men don't speak of a *dazzling* dusk. Unlike them, the theologians have qualified their epithet so as to mark it as figurative; what is infinitely bright is dark only in the metonymic sense that it darkens the sense of the finite seer. Herbert's parallel extension of "dark" is more explicit:

> If that bee dark we can not see,
> The sunn is darker then a Tree,
> And thou more dark then either.[18]

But here again we have reached an improper term—God's effect on the eye. We need another step to reach the proper term, the semantic interior: God's fullness of being registers as a blank on the mind, which can grasp only what it can analyze. Inside the tent, as at the outset, it is still noon.

But now the tent is God, who has an interior (49) that the speaker is longing to enter and live in (54). *God* is now the coveted dwelling place. If the speaker asks here only for the right to be "invisible and dim," this is not because his desires have suddenly become modest. "Dim" is in effect a qualifying gloss on "invisible": the speaker is praying for a degree, however imperfect, of the divine splendor we have already been taught to call darkness. Dimness is a step toward darkness, and in the semantic revaluation of the last stanza this implies that the speaker is praying for angelic brightness or fullness of being. But he is still outside the tent, stumbling in mire, still recognizably the thwarted voyeur of the poems we have already considered.

That thwarted voyeur doesn't play a major role in other devotional poems of Vaughan, but the yearning for revelation, for a glimpse of secret truth unveiled, surely does. It distinguishes the accent of Vaughan's Protestantism from that of Herbert's. What is mainly at issue in Vaughan is whether the already justified speaker can hope before he dies to be regenerated fully enough to enjoy a visiting "Ray" of the Johannine light or (equivalently) a breath of the Pentecostal wind that blows where it pleases ("Regeneration," 68-71, 80; John 3:8; Acts 2:2), whether he will be allowed the privilege of "th'Inlightned spirit" ("The Retreate," 25)—or else, as seems unfortunately more likely, must resign himself to a long delay of his "invisible estate" and "glorious liberty, still late!" ("The Water-fall," 37-38). The central issue is not love, but light.

As for the strategy of metaphoric emergence, with its attendant devices of concentration and exploration, Vaughan has perfected in "The Night" his own highly contrapuntal version of the Metaphysical approach to the transaction between writer and reader. These devices are just right for putting maximal pressure on the etiquette of cooperation, or benefit of the doubt, or patience, or "humanity," or "sophisticated charity," that we could hardly do without even in ordinary conversation: we forbear to take the figurative speaker at his word, or rather to take him at ours; we allow him to build up his own idiom, and we do the best we can to learn it patiently as he and we go along. Even for Vaughan, as for less reticent and saturnine Metaphysicals, a critic could do worse than to heed the lessons of such modern theorists of talk and uptake as Paul Grice, Donald Davidson, Richard Grandy, and David Lewis.[19] I've tried to heed those lessons by treating the study of metaphoric emergence as a complex exercise in hermeneutic patience—in waiting for the poet to teach us his idiom, by contextual cue and gesture, as he goes along.

What such theorists have to contribute to a treatment of complex metaphor are not their views on the nature of figurative sense (Davidson, for one, debunks the notion),[20] but their recognition of the essential role in conversation of the presumption of reasonableness, and (not less essential) the role of the subtle inferential moves that go into the fair interpretation of sentences that are false, absurd, nonsensical, or pointless on a literal reading. These moves amount to a protocol of conversational response. Of course, in most conversations one can elicit a clarification by getting the speaker to respond to one's responses. But not all conversations are two-way; constraints of status or ceremony sometimes leave one to one's own interpretative devices, or rather to conventional devices one can apply on one's own. Reading is a special case of such one-way conversation. The repertoire of uptake that one falls back on in such emergencies is the staple of one's negotiations with a text, and especially with a figurative text. Reading, in this perspective, is a steady state of conversational emergency—steadiest and most demanding when what is emerging is a metaphor.

One further conjectural point needs to be made about Vaughan's choice of strategy. It has to do with the possibility that its effect on the reader is itself emblematically significant. There is an analogy between the general effect of the emergent metaphor and the subject matter of the particular one we have been tracing. Vaughan warns the readers of *Silex* that "you will (peradventure) observe some *passages*, whose history or *reason* may seem something *remote*; but were they brought *nearer*, and plainly exposed to your view, (though that (perhaps) might quiet your *curiosity*) yet would it not conduce much to your greater *advantage*."[21] The emergent metaphor suits this poetic of privacy very well. It leaves the reader in a position like that of Vaughan's metaphorical figure, peering at a meaning close enough to be just made out, far enough away to exclude him from the fellowship of the mystery.

NOTES

[1]*The Works of George Herbert,* ed. F. E. Hutchinson (Oxford: Clarendon Press, 1954), pp. 85-86, cited hereafter as Hutchinson.

[2]Migne, *PL* 26: col. 537, sect. 621. Jerome goes on to say that the *physicus perscrutator* "dives beyond the earth's depth and the void, as it were, of the abyss." Herbert gives us a mercenary diver. With Jerome, compare Augustine's discussion of *experiendi noscendique libido, Conf.* 10.35. See *Augustini Confessionum libri XIII,* ed. P. Knoll (Leipzig: G. Freytag, 1896).

[3]*The Works of Henry Vaughan,* ed. L. C. Martin (Oxford: Clarendon Press, 1957), pp. 417-19), cited hereafter as Martin. Poems are cited by line numbers.

[4]*Anima Magica Abscondita* by Eugenius Philalethes (London: T. W., 1650), p. 13, cited hereafter as *Anima Magica.*

[5]For disappareling in the same sense, see Plotinus 5.3.17. The notion of the mind's clothing is an ancient commonplace, but the Hermetics dignify it with an essential role in their theory of embodiment. See, for example, the Hermetic tractate *Poimandres* 10.1618, and *Reallexicon für Antike und Christentum* (Stuttgart: Hiersemann, 1927), 10 s. v. *Gewand [der Seele],* esp. cols. 955-58.

[6]Martin, pp. 478-79. James D. Simmonds, in *Masques of God: Form and Theme in the Poetry of Henry Vaughan* (Pittsburgh: Univ. of Pittsburgh Press, 1972), pp. 185-89, also finds a "symbolic exhumation" in the poem and identifies the root as an emblem, and hence as one of Vaughan's divine "prolusions and strong proofs." But Simmonds misses the crucial point that the "exhumation" is a ritual-histrionic act. He doesn't supply a clear account of the alleged distinction between emblem and symbol. There is no recognition of the conflicting cues the poem supplies in a gradual and uneven process of self-clarification. And above all, merely saying that the exhumation is symbolic simply finesses the prior question of how the exhumation-*language* applies to whatever it is describing. My answer, in brief: (a) figuratively, to the root-digging; (b) literally, to a fictitious exhumation the root-digging is used to act out; (c) figuratively, again, to an effort of the actor's speculative imagination. These meanings aren't a motionless array, the poem only gradually lets us see how they fit together. That process of semantic forthcoming is a crucial part of what the poem as a whole has to say.

[7]Martin, p. 177.

[8]Cf. *Poimandres* 12.6: "The dissolution [of bodies] is not death but the dissolution of a mixture. Bodies decay, not to be destroyed, but to become young." Ficino's version embroiders this a bit: "soluitur autem vnio [mistionis], non vt ea, quae sunt, intereant, sed vt vetera iuuenescant" (*Iamblichi de mysteriis liber* [*et alia opuscula*] [Lyons: Ioannes Tornaesius, 1570], p. 473; hereafter *Pimander*. The Greek edition from which I am translating is A. D. Nock's in *Corpus Hermeticum* 1 (Paris: Société d'édition "Les Belles Lettres," 1945), with A.-J. Festugiere's French version. With Vaughan's thought compare also his own version of Nollius's *Chymists Key:* "Nothing can be animated and borne, unlesse it first suffer corruption, putrefaction, and mortification, saith Raymond Lullie in his testament" (Martin, p. 604). Cf. also *Anima Magica,* pp. 13-14: "everything in the world is directed for [Man's] preservation by a *spice* or *touch* of the *first Intellect.*" "Everything" will include the remains of the dead.

[9]Ficino says that a particular Hermetic dialogue "hunts God from the center, the pole, place, and the forms of things" (*Pimander,* p. 388).

[10]E. C. Pettet, *Of Paradise and Light: A Study of Vaughan's "Silex Scintillans"* (Cambridge: Cambridge Univ. Press, 1960), p. 165, suggests that "in the middle of the seventeenth century ['peep'] was entirely, or relatively, free of furtive, prurient, and comic associations." This is mistaken. It has acquired this complex of associations at least by the time of Shakespeare and Spenser. "Why pry'st thou through my window? Leave thy peeping" (*Lucrece,* line 1089). As the speaker of the *Epithalamion* enjoys his wedding night he asks playfully "who is the same, which at my window peepes" (line 372). In a similar vein of whimsy the speaker of Shakespeare's Sonnet 24 mentions "windows to my breast, wherethrough the sun / Delights to peep." Whimsy or not, the common thread here is a stealthy invasion of privacy, including sexual privacy.

[11]The notion that the soul is astral in substance is ancient and ubiquitous. See Franz Cumont, *Lux Perpetua* (Paris: P. Geuthner, 1949). The adage that the body is a tomb (*Gorgias* 493[a]) is also familiar in various forms. It is a little more enterprising for the speaker to claim that on dying his inner star will irradiate the universe. He can claim Hermetic endorsement: man in his disembodied essence has power over everything (*Poimandres* 1.15). In the Neoplatonic scheme the human soul is at the same level of the cosmic hierarchy as the world

soul, with which it potentially shares control of the universe. See Ficino's comment on Plotinus 4.4.16, reproduced in *Plotini Enneades,* ed. F. Creuzer and G. H. Moser (Paris: Firmin Didot, 1855). Hereafter *Plotini Enneades.*

[12]*Invidia,* at its most primitive, is the evil eye. See Catullus 5.12, where the act of *invidere* is associated with spying on lovers. Cf. Isidore of Seville, *Etymologiae* 10.34: "Inuidus dictus ab intuendo felicitatem alterius." See *Etymologiarum libri XX,* ed. W. M. Lindsay (Oxford: Clarendon Press, 1911). Spenser, *Faerie Queene* I.iv.31, seems to be playing with this traditional etymology when he makes envy a perverse response to seeing "good," and includes among Enuie's personifying attributes a kirtle "ypainted full of eyes."

[13]The glass one sees God through darkly is canonically a mirror, of course (*esoptron,* 1 Cor. 13:12). There is also a familiar Latin pun submerged in the notion of a "hill [*specula,* vantage point], / Where I shall need no glass [*speculum*]." "Speculation" is a kind of intellectual spying that the chosen soul is destined to rise above. Cp. Ficino's kindred though distinct use of the pun: "In mundo sequente, praecedentem gradatim velut *speculo* speculabere, atque vicissim ex superiore inferiorem tamquam ex *specula* contemplabere" (*Plotini Enneades* 5.3.9; my emphasis). The speaker is engaging in some serious play—to use Vaughan's term, in a "prolusion."

[14]Alan Rudrum's case for a Hermetic and Boehmian reading in "'The Night': Some Hermetic Notes," *MLR* 64 (1969):11-19, depends on a rigorous program of taking things out of context. To accept it, we have to abandon the notion that in verbal communication meaning is constrained by ongoing argument. This is a high price to pay. But if we don't pay it, then we gain nothing by bloating the glossary with esoteric usages that the logic of the text won't let apply. The "virginity" of Christ's flesh, for example ("The Night," 1), can hardly express a mystical bisexuality unless there is some defect in the standard alternative meaning *inviolate* (supported by "pure" immediately preceding). There is something obvious that Christ's flesh *literally* has in common with virgins; so we have been given no reason to cast about for something (femaleness) that it only *figuratively* has in common with them. Having to invoke a notion of unsignalled or unmotivated figurativeness, once again, is a high price to pay for an esoteric reading.

[15]Vaughan is playing, of course, on the familiar virtuoso *topos* of spinning out alternative definitions of something. The sub-*topos* involving Sleep (as in *Macbeth* II.ii.33-37) is especially relevant. Praise sleep highly enough (to outdo the opposition) and you will end up suggesting a contemplative state. Thus, in Drummond's sonnet, Sleep is "silence' child," and "Prince whose approach peace to all mortals brings." This hardly takes much revision to become a real rather than a mock prayer. In Vaughan's retort on the *topos,* the "care-charmer sleep" of secular poetry meets its pointed antithesis, the sacred vigil that is (without flattery this time) "cares check and curb."

[16]The body is also a tent, 2 Cor. 5:1, 4—*corporis nostri tabernaculum,* Calvin, *Inst.* 3.9.5. See *Ioannis Calvini Institutio Christianae Religionis,* ed. A. Tholuck (Berlin: Eichler, 1834).

[17]I am translating from Charles Butler, *Rhetoricae libri duo* (London: William Bentley for John Williams, 1649), pp. 7-8. Cf. Gerard Vossius, *Rhetorices contractae libri quinque* (Leyden: Ioannes Maire, 1640), p. 353.

[18]"Euen-song" 14-16, Hutchinson, p. 203. In Dionysian terms, God is without essence (*an-ousion*) and hence beyond predication or rational understanding.

Union with God yields "a knowledge, beyond mind, of Nothing." See Pseudo-Dionysius, *De divinis nominibus,* in Migne, *PG* 3:1001/2A.

[19]H. P. Grice, "Logic and Conversation," in *Syntax and Semantics,* ed. Peter Cole and Jerry Morgan (New York: Academic Press, 1975); pp. 41-58, Donald Davidson, "Semantics for Natural Languages," in *On Noam Chomsky: Critical Essays,* pp. 242-52, esp. 250; Richard E. Grandy, "Reference, Meaning, and Belief," *Journal of Philosophy* 70 (1973): 439-52; David Lewis, "Radical Interpretation," *Synthèse* 23 (1974): 331-44.

[20]See "What Metaphors Mean," in *On Metaphor,* ed. Sheldon Sacks (Chicago: Univ. of Chicago Press, 1978); "A Nice Derangement of Epitaphs," in *Truth and Interpretation,* ed. Ernest LePore (Oxford: Blackwell, 1986).

[21]Martin, p. 239.

In his defense of a topical reading of "The Night" in *Henry Vaughan: The Unfolding Vision* (Princeton: Princeton Univ. Press, 1982), pp. 203-204, Jonathan F.S. Post ignores both Vaughan's warning and the text of the poem. "That land of darkness and blinde eyes" is supposed to draw an "explicit" parallel between Nicodemus's and Vaughan's reasons for seeking Christ at night: both "blest believers" are avoiding persecution, whether from Nicodemus's fellow council members or from the Puritan enemies of Welsh Anglicanism. But stanza 2 doesn't even say this implicitly, much less explicitly. And security from persecution doesn't fit in with the advantages of night prayer actually listed in stanzas 5-6; the common denominator here is simply freedom from the distractions of the workaday world.

In fact Vaughan would have *needed* to be fairly "explicit" to carry off any such implication; there is no single authoritative reading of Nicodemus's motive that Vaughan could count on his audience to take for granted. Luther thinks the night visit was dictated by fear of persecution, but Calvin opts for personal vanity: Nicodemus was too vain about his prowess as a teacher to risk being caught playing pupil to anybody. (See *Luther's Works,* ed. Jaroslav Pelikan, 54 vols. [Saint Louis:. Concordia, 1957], 22:276; *Commentary on the Gospel according to John by John Calvin,* trans. William Pringle, 2 vols. [Grand Rapids: Eerdmans, 1956], 1:105.)

In Vaughan's last stanza Post finds still another reference to church troubles in Wales, as well as a millenarian hint that world history is growing "late" and is about to end (p. 209). But "lateness" comes into the speaker's actual line of thought only as a subjective *appearance,* not as a fact. See my analysis above.

SEL 27 (1987)
ISSN 0039-3657

Milton and the Idea of the Restoration of the Jews

N. I. MATAR

In Book III of *Paradise Regained,* Satan urges Jesus to use force towards the establishment of the messianic kingdom. The means needed to fulfil such a goal, he adds, are armed struggle against the Romans and the liberation of the ten lost tribes of Israel from the Medes. Only by "conquest or by league," he concludes, will Jesus be able to rule in "David's royal seat" (lines 370, 373).[1]

Jesus opposes the militaristic zeal of Satan. He declares that the appointed time of this kingdom "is not yet come" and impresses upon Satan the weakness of using "politic maxims" and "fragile arms" in such a cause (lines 397, 400, 388). Although he recognizes that his kingdom cannot be established until after the Restoration of the Jews, Jesus rejects Satan's urgency and affirms that the Restoration is a divine act to be implemented by God alone in his own due time:

> Yet he at length, time to himself best known,
> Rememb'ring Abraham, by some wondrous call
> May bring them back repentant and sincere,
> And at their passing cleave the Assyrian flood,
> While to their native land with joy they haste
> As the Red Sea and Jordan once he cleft,
> When to the Promised Land their fathers passed;
> To his due time and providence I leave them.
>
> (lines 433-40)

This passage has been viewed by critics as an echo of the Isaianic prophecy, specifically relevant to Milton apropos of the publication of Manasseh Ben Israel's *The Hope of Israel* in 1650, and of the Sabbatai Sevi commotion in the mid-1660s.[2] Such criticism is

---

Nabil Matar is Associate Professor of English and Civilization Sequence at the American University of Beirut. He has just completed an edition of select writings from Peter Sterry (1613-1672) and is writing on the controversy over the Restoration of the Jews in English Protestant thought.

supported by the available historical data about Milton and reflects his awareness of the Jewish issue in those years. But what is more significant than the circumstantial source of the above passage from *Paradise Regained* is Milton's theological position regarding it: for the idea of the Restoration of the Jews, much as it was discussed in the 1650s and 1660s, was not a theological principle on which all Englishmen agreed. Although a cursory look at the literature of the seventeenth century shows how popular the idea was, it also reveals how seriously it was opposed by numerous theologians and polemicists. Indeed, since its appearance on the theological scene in the Reformation, the idea of Restoration had been a bone of constant contention between Restorationists and anti-Restorationists. Three factors were instrumental in generating this novel principle in English thought: the military Turko-Catholic threat to Protestant Christendom; the Puritan millenarian speculations between 1640 and 1660; and England's moral responsibility to the Jews. During the sixteenth and seventeenth centuries, the fear of Catholic and Turkish military power led English theologians to the view that the Jews' conquest of Palestine would necessarily be preceded by victory over Islam and Catholicism—Protestantism's two main enemies. And although they had never met a Jew in their lives, English theologians supported the Restoration as a means to their religio-national end. Moreover, they believed that the Restoration of the Jews would lead to the fulfilment of the Pauline expectation of the millennial kingdom, and the inauguration of England's messianic age. Finally, and by concentrating on Romans 11, some English evangelists felt that they owed the Jews a debt which they could repay only by converting them to Christianity and then restoring them to Palestine. This became the Englishman's burden of responsibility to the Jews whose rejection of Christ in the first century had allowed the salvation of the Gentiles.[3]

The fact that at the publication of *Paradise Regained* Milton supported the idea of the Jews' Restoration suggests that, theologically, he had opted for the Restorationist stand. Although Milton did not become involved in the debate on the settlement of the Jews in England in the mid-1650s, he eagerly took a stand on the Restoration—a highly controversial issue then. Indeed, by putting lines 433-40 into Jesus' mouth, Milton was not echoing a standard biblical view but positing a highly polemical interpretation of the Isaianic prophecy. That the Jesus of *Paradise Regained* upheld the Restorationist position towards the Jews indicates that he was not only opposing Satan, but some of Milton's contemporary theologians who rejected the Restoration and its varied theological implications—

namely those regarding its relationship to Christ's second coming and the millennial kingdom. The questions that loom large at this point are the following: why did Milton support the Restorationist position, and how does that position clarify his views on the Jews and on their relationship to Christ's messianic kingdom in England? Furthermore, and as Milton's name is conspicuously missing from the list of Cromwell's supporters on the project of the Jews' admission in 1655, is it possible to shed light on the causes of his nonparticipation in the Conference after examining his view on the Restoration?

II

Although *Paradise Regained* was published in 1671, the date of its composition is far from certain. Critical opinions vary on whether Milton had written some of the Jesus-Satan debate between 1646-1648, or in the early or mid-1650s and then grafted the passages into the short epic completed after the publication of *Paradise Lost*.[4] When the Restoration lines (433-40) were written cannot be exactly determined, but that they belong to the immediately pre-Interregnum or to the Interregnum periods would not be surprising, since many in Milton's circle then were Independents who fully supported the idea: Thomas Goodwin, John Owen, Peter Sterry, and Henry Jessey were chaplains and aides to Cromwell with whom Milton is known to have communicated in meetings and convocations, and with whose preaching he was familiar. Thomas Goodwin, whose sermons Milton had attended in Cambridge during the 1630s, advocated in 1639 the Restoration and directly linked it to the advent of the messianic kingdom in England. Less than a decade later and in a sermon preached before the House of Commons, John Owen proclaimed with reference to the Books of Isaiah and of Revelation "that the Promises of the Restauration of God's people into a glorious condition after all their suffering, is perpetually in the Scripture held out," and that the "time is come, yea the full time is come [for] the King the Lord Christ" to appear. On 5 November 1649 Peter Sterry echoed Owen's sermon, and because he believed that the Restoration of the Jews had already started ("to which, perhaps the Affairs of Constantinople, as they now stand, may make way"), he identified 1652 as the year of England's millennial kingdom. Sterry repeated his calculations with more detail in his 1651 sermon, "Before the Supreme Authority of this Nation," and again pointed to the Jews' Restoration as the signal to the Messianic event. By the early 1650s, the idea of the Restoration was so theologically established in revolutionary circles that it was noted as the official Protestant interpretation of Romans 11:11-18 in the *Annotations*.[5]

Goodwin, Sterry, Owen, and others of Cromwell's circle, including the Lord Protector himself, were instrumental in crystalizing Milton's theology of the Restoration.[6] This is not to underestimate the influence of Milton's Cambridge tutor, Joseph Mede, whose writings about the Jews were extremely influential. Milton was familiar with the corpus of this Restorationist, specifically "The Mystery of S. Paul's Conversion: or, The Type of the Calling of the Jews." So must he have been familiar with the work of Thomas Brightman, as influential on seventeenth-century eschatology as was Mede, and equally supportive of the Jews' Restoration.[7] Furthermore, between 1647 and 1653, the prospect of the Jews' Restoration was bandied about among visionaries and millenarians, scholars and preachers: from Mary Cary and John Robins, to Theuravjohn Tany, Samuel Gott, George Foster/Jacob Israel, Nathaniel Homes, John Canne, Moses Wall, Henry Oldenburgh, and Henry Jessey. Milton knew in person, and is known to have shared opinions with, a number of these writers.[8]

Clearly, there was enough contextual influence on Milton to align him with the idea of the Restoration. Furthermore, like all supporters of the idea, Milton viewed the Restoration as a signal of the inauguration of the messianic kingdom. The early 1640s witnessed in England the beginning of the political and military confrontation between king and parliament, and between Canterbury Anglicans and London and Edinburgh Puritans. Such tension led opposition theologians to interpret the times as eschatological: the kingdom of Christ was imminent and King Jesus would soon descend to England to wrench his promised monarchy from the papistical king and his archbishop. Between 1641 and 1643, writers of Puritan leanings like Thomas Goodwin, John Archer, Nathaniel Homes, John Cotton, Robert Lord Brooke, Edward Calamy, and William Bridge all expressed their anticipation of Christ's second coming: "the Time is at hand"; "Yet but for a little while"; "It is but one hour and the work is done."[9] Like these contemporaries in opposition Milton was also waiting for King Jesus, and in his *Animadversions,* declared that God had "manifestly come downe among us" (*Prose,* 1:703). He then turned to the Book of Revelation to support his plea to Jesus whose "Kingdom is now at hand:" "Come forth out of thy Royall Chambers, O Prince of all the Kings of the earth, put on the visible roabes of thy imperiall Majesty, take up that unlimited Scepter which thy Almighty Father hath bequeath'd thee" (*Prose* 1:707).

Like numerous preachers after the outbreak of the civil wars in 1642, Milton recognized the crucial role of England in the drama of Christian reformation. This "*Britannick Empire* . . . with all her Daughter Ilands" was at the center of opposition to the Popish anti-Christ, and to all the forces of Catholicism (*Prose* 1:614). With imagery that derived from Ezekiel and the Book of Revelation, Milton joined the opposition chorus which associated the Great Whore with the Catholic church, and anticipated the destruction of the Papacy just before "the shortly-expected King" ruled over the earth (*Prose* 1:616). Also in the strain of Brightman and others, he criticized the English church as Laodicean—a reference to its lukewarm reformatory zeal (*Prose* 1:690).[10]

Although Milton's language was consonant with the messianic mood of the Puritan opposition in the 1640s, his expectations of Christ's kingdom did not lead him to speculations about dates, to clamors for war, nor to a Fifth Monarchy position. Much as he became imbued with the apocalyptic imagery of confrontation with the Catholics and with the English monarch (*Prose* 1: 496-97) he did not develop millenarian schemes to justify contemporary historical changes. But like his Cromwellian colleagues who had associated Christ's coming with the Restoration of the Jews, Milton supported the principle that the kingdom of Christ was predicated on the Jews' Restoration from their captivity. Since the appearance of Brightman's *The Revelation of Saint John* and Mede's *Clavis Apocrafica,* the Jews' Restoration had been viewed—although not unanimously—as the signal for Christ's second coming. This theological position proliferated widely after the early 1640s and became a favored position for the Puritan opposition. In 1647 this view was consolidated among Cromwellian and pro-Cromwellian theologians as a result of propitious news that had reached London about the Jews' movement in "Illyria, Brithania and Cappadocia for the conquering of the Holy Land."[11] Preachers both at Westminster and on street pulpits responded to the news as a confirmation of the Brightman/Mede interpretation of the Book of Revelation and the imminent advent of King Jesus to England. The Jews' Restoration, it was believed, was the signal for England's revolution of the saints. In 1649, Peter Sterry preached in celebration of Cromwell's victory in Ireland. He was certain that the news about the Jews and the massacre of Drogheda heralded the much-awaited "Comings Forth of Christ": "But such Calamities, and Confusions, as the World never saw to this day, must follow, when once Jesus Christ shall begin to appeare for His People, and the Return of the Jewes. . . . The Late Providence of God in this Island and Ireland seem to give a Rise to the fulfilling of this part of the Revelation." A few years later, John Canne repeated the same principle in a sermon addressed to Cromwell: "As the time of the end is neerer at hand [the year 1655 will mark the] . . . time designated for the rising and beginning of the Jewes, after their long dispersion [and] . . . entring into the Land of Judea."[12] It was in this context that Milton composed lines 433-40 in *Paradise Regained*: Jesus informs Satan, and Milton the anti-Cromwellian opposition, that once the Restoration of the Jews is completed, Christ's Kingdom will be inaugurated in England. At the writing of *Christian Doctrine*, Milton affirmed his creed in Christ's kingdom and the idea of the Restoration:

> The special signs are extreme carelessness and impiety, and almost universal rebellion. . . .
> Secondly, the revelation of antichrist, and his destruction through the spirit of Christ's mouth. . . .
> Some authorities think that a further portent will herald this event, namely, the calling of the entire nation not only of the Jews but also of the Israelites.
>
> (*Prose* 6: 616-17)[13]

The reference to "some authorities" in the above passage points to the Restorationist theologians with whom Milton was closely involved during the Interregnum and to the lay preachers and authors who had supported that position. That it is a doctrine which only "some" accept indicates Milton's familiarity with the anti-Restorationist argument and with the polemics surrounding the whole issue. That it was to be a Restoration of all the twelve tribes shows Milton's accord with the near-to-unanimous aspirations of Restorationists. But Milton's concern with the Restoration was not confined to its connection with the millennium: given the association which preachers had established between Christ's kingdom and the Jews, Milton recognized the contemporary relevance of the Restoration to the English revolutionaries. Throughout the late 1640s and early 1650s, Cromwell and his theologians had described their military victories as miraculously ordained, and had treated their upheaval against the king as a preparation for the advent of Christ. Consequently, they learnt to appreciate the significance of the fulfilment of the Jews' Restoration—a prophecy that had been associated with the second coming. The Cromwellians needed concrete proof from biblical history to demonstrate that their messianic expectations in England were being realized: as they pointed to the execution of the king and to the declaration of the commonwealth as heralds of the second coming, they concluded that the Restoration of the Jews would historically confirm their messianic anticipations. Because the Jews were physically being restored, then the messianic kingdom was physically being inaugurated. In this respect, the Jews' Restoration retroactively justified the Independents' revolution and their eschatological view of events. Owen preached in 1652: "Look what Kingdome soever, the Lord Christ will advance in the World, and exercise amongst his holy Ones, the beginning of it must be with the Jewes."[14] Thus to be a Restorationist towards the Jews meant to support the messianic interpretation of the civil upheavals against Charles, the "little horne," and the Papacy, the "great whore." The theological position towards the Jews indicated a political position towards the revolution of the saints. For Milton, at the center of Whitehall strategy, it was only consistent that he affirm the Restoration of the Jews as a signal of the messianic kingdom in England. If the Jesus of *Paradise Regained* had said otherwise than what he did in lines 433-40, Milton would have demonstrated his opposition to the Cromwellian regime.

Understandably, criticism of the idea of the Restoration came from those who neither viewed Cromwell's ascendancy to power as divinely legitimized, nor identified Interregnum England with the shortly-expected kingdom of Christ. Specifically, Presbyterians in the Assembly of Divines were hostile to Cromwell's regime and to the whole millenarian heresy on which the justification of the civil wars, Pride's Purge, the regicide and Cromwellian dictatorship rested. As early as 1644 Robert Baillie had condemned the millenarian politics of the Independents and of the Army. And so had Thomas Hayne, John Lightfoot, William Gouge, and many others.[15] As millenarianism was linked with the idea of the Restoration of the Jews, the English and Scottish Presbyterians opposed the latter idea, and treated it as a revolutionary slogan. Equally hostile to millenarianism were the Anglicans who had seen their church and monarch destroyed by Christ-expecting fanatics. In 1653, Henry Hammond published his *Paraphrase, and Annotations Upon all the Books of the New Testament* in which he violently attacked Thomas Brightman and the whole allegorical method of interpretation. Implicit to Hammond's emphasis on the historical reading of the apocalyptic texts rather than the prophetic was a rejection of millenarian theories and prospects of Jewish Restoration.[16] By opposing Cromwell, Presbyterians and Anglicans rejected all the theological arguments which he and his aides used to justify their revolutionary and sectarian actions—specifically the argument of the Jews' Restoration.

By defending the idea of the Restoration, as he does in lines 433-40 of *Paradise Regained,* Milton was defending theologically the

Interregnum politics of the saints. At the writing of the Jesus-Satan debate, Milton was not echoing ideas picked from his contemporary readings, but was proposing a polemical position against the anti-Restorationists who were anti-Independents. As he had defended the Cromwellian upheaval against European critics, so would he support it against its Presbyterian and Anglican enemies. The Restoration of the Jews proved England's messianic role, and pointed to the coming of Christ. In advocating that position towards the Jews, Milton was not only justifying his and Cromwell's and the Independents' actions in the past decade, but their expectations of Christian history which was to end, and to begin anew among them, the English Zion.

If we turn to 1671, the date of the publication of *Paradise Regained,* the situation had changed. The Cromwellian hopes had failed, monarchy had returned, and England had gone back to "Egypt." Milton, however, kept lines 433-40 and probably sharpened them in light of the implications of the idea of Restoration on the defeated saints. Although the idea could not have kept its earlier Cromwellian associations, it was still relevant to the view which nonconformists held of themselves. The question that must be addressed at this point is the following: what does the idea of the Restoration of the Jews in lines 433-40 signify to Milton in 1671, at a time completely different from when he had composed the dialogue between Jesus and Satan?

The 1660s constituted a period of trial and extreme hardship to nonconformists as a whole, and to Milton in particular. From the political involvements of the Interregnum, Milton found himself in a condition of incapacitation and mortal danger. He was now confined to his house, and like other ex-Cromwellians and nonconformists, ostracized from the intellectual life of London and of the universities. The shock of England's return to monarchy, the repression of the Cavalier Parliament, and the restrictions of the various acts impressed upon Milton a sense of defeat: in meeting with friends of the Interregnum, Milton could not but have wondered about God's ways with the saints, and about the once-promised kingdom that had never come. It was in this period of trial that he completed *Paradise Lost* and *Paradise Regained.*

The retention of the lines on the Restoration of the Jews in *Paradise Regained* fits with the prevailing theological attitude of nonconformists between 1660-1671. It is no coincidence that all the writers who supported the idea of the Restoration in these eleven years were nonconformists: John Eliot, Arise Evans, Increase Mather, Edward Bagshaw, William Sherwin, and the anonymous author of *The Restauration of the Jews* (1665). All these figures shared in the opposition to the Anglican establishment and also in a Restorationist position toward the Jews. Whether Quaker, Congregational, or Presbyterian, with or without previous Cromwellian association, nonconformists reaffirmed the Restorationist position; and so did Milton. Although the major surviving Restorationists of the past decades were no longer addressing the issue—Sterry, for instance, or Goodwin—others were keeping it alive, and a curious assembly of nonconformists it was: John Eliot, the missionary to the Indians; Increase Mather, the Congregationalist in Boston; Vavasor Powell, a Welsh millenarian; Arise Evans, a self-proclaimed prophet; and the author of *The Restauration*, one among many who wrote apropos of the Sabbatai Sevi commotion.[17] Evidently, they all recognized the relevance of this idea to their own cause: the Jews' Restoration was still a polemical issue, now between the nonconformists and the Anglicans, as earlier between the Cromwellians and the Presbyterians. No wonder that Sir Paul Rycaut and John Evelyn, both staunch Anglicans, blamed the millennial craze of 1666 and the enthusiasm for the Restoration of the Jews on "the heads of Fanatical Enthusiasts."[18] The Restoration of the Jews, they seemed to suggest, was not a doctrine to which respectable and law-abiding churchgoers subscribed. For orthodox members of the Church of England, the idea was firmly associated with an anti-establishmentarian stand: and Milton, who was still hopeful that God would justify His way to the saints, reaffirmed his anti-Anglican antimonarchical attitude by allowing lines 433-40 to stand as written.

The reason why nonconformists clung to the idea of the Restoration as a slogan of opposition rested on their enduring eschatological expectations: especially in their private meditations and sermons, nonconformists still awaited Christ's coming, although they no longer attached millennial or politically subversive implications to that advent. The Quakers internalized eschatology, while others like Sterry and Owen continued to await the advent albeit without calculations or militaristic threats.[19] In similar fashion, Milton expected the kingdom: as he put lines 433-40 into Jesus' mouth he emphatically associated the Restoration with the messianic kingdom and specified the conditions under which such a Restoration would be carried out. Only when the conditions were divinely sanctioned would the Restoration take place and serve as God's sign for the inauguration of Christ's kingdom on earth. Milton did not wish to misinterpret God's plan for the English Zion, as perhaps it had been in the early 1650s. The Restoration was no simple event which anybody could speculate about; by 1671, Milton believed, the Restoration had not taken place because theologians had failed to identify its distinctive characteristics. A Restoration with no divine sanction, like that proposed by George Foster or attempted by Sabbatai Sevi was not the fulfilment of biblical prophecy, but merely a false endeavor which stemmed from a false interpretation of the Isaianic verses. Consequently, Milton tried to identify the true Restoration because that alone would herald the true messianic kingdom.

Although there is little in Milton's 1670s writings to define his attitude to the Jews, it is very probable that he continued to view the Restoration as an act of divine confirmation: if he and other nonconformists could witness before them the fulfilment of the Isaianic prophecies, then they would possess tangible proof that God was still pursuing His goal among the saints. This use of the Restoration as proof of divine power had long before been established by Thomas Brightman: "the Jewes shall be here gathered together who now live as exiles, and out of their owne Country . . . [so] that the admirable goodnesse of God might openly appeare unto all men, now againe, pitying his people whom he had estranged from himself, with so long a divorce."[20] Over half a century later, Brightman's view was still gaining ground, especially among nonconformist Restorationists. If the God who restored Israel from Babylon would now restore the Jews to Palestine, then He was preparing that Restoration as a sign of the saints' own return from the Babylonish captivity of Anglicanism. If God could be seen to fulfill His Isaianic promises to the Jews, then He would certainly not forget the promises made to the once-victorious but now defeated saints. Like the Jews, the nonconformists viewed themselves as theological exiles awaiting God's divine and supreme intercession. The Restoration of the Jews now would demonstrate that God was preparing a similarly victorious restoration of the saints to their messianic kingdom. Only a Restoration under such conditions was truly God's action and was preparatory for Christ's true kingdom. In light of such convictions, Milton must have felt the urgency of lines 433-40: a decade after the failure of the Puritan trial in England, a few years after the Sevi fiasco, Milton hoped to correct the previous mistakes of the Restorationists. Only after a Restoration with the following four distinctions would Christ's messianic kingdom be truly proclaimed:

1. The Restoration of the Jews was to be effected "by some wondrous call." Milton urged that the Restoration was a miraculous act initiated by God, not a migration of a purely social nature. "This

is a mighty wonder," wrote Increase Mather in 1669.[21] In this corrective, Milton was completely opposed to the English Protestants who had earlier proposed—and attempted—themselves to lead the Jews on their journey. Tany declared in 1650: "Now unto ye Jewes, my Brethren, am I sent to proclaime from the Lord of Hosts, the God of Israel, your Returne from your Captivity in what Nation soever ye are Scattered. From thence ye shall be Gathered into your own Land: and JERUSALEM shall be built in Glory, in her owne Land."[22] In contrast to the above, Milton adopted the standard position of Mede, Brightman, and Archer which treated the Restoration as an act of God, not of self-proclaimed prophets or fanatics. Only after God effected the Restoration would Christ's kingdom be proclaimed. A Restoration under any other leadership was null and void, and signified nothing about the kingdom: God was the restorer of the Jews, not man.

2. The Restoration would take place after the conversion of the Jews, "repentant and sincere." The issue of the Jews' conversion was always associated with their Restoration: no sixteenth- or seventeenth-century English theologian was willing to condone the Jews' Restoration to Palestine without their prior conversion to Christianity. That the Restoration was associated with conversion was unanimously accepted, and the debate among writers was not as to whether the Jews would give up their Judaism for Christianity, but as to the timing of their conversion: would it precede or succeed their Restoration? Unlike Thomas Cooper and Increase Mather, and in the tradition of Mede, Brightman, Archer, and Sterry, Milton affirmed the safer theological position:[23] only after the Jews converted would they be restored. This was the "safer" position because it completely disqualified the false messianic claims of any Jew who might proclaim himself king of the Jews before converting: Sabbatai Sevi was clearly for Milton the notorious case in point.

3. The Restoration of the Jews was to take place across the "Assyrian flood," the river Euphrates. This is an ambiguous passage only because its interpretation in seventeenth-century commentary took on either of two possibilities: the Euphrates could mean the river in Mesopotamia which identified the Restoration in its Isaianic sense as a return of the ten lost tribes from Babylon. This was the prevalent interpretation. Brightman wrote: "the Euphrates must be drawne drie . . . [so] that the Jewes may have nothing to hinder them, when they returne into their Countrey againe." And Bagshaw explained: "When the sixth Vial is poured out, which I take to be the time when the Jews (who are called the Kings from the East) shall have their way prepared for them over Euphrates to return into their own

Land, at which time Christ himself shall appear at the Head of them."[24]

Alternatively, however, the Euphrates could be understood "mystically" to refer to the whole "Pontifician hierarchy" of the Catholic church or to the Papacy and the Turks together. In this case, the drying up of the Euphrates meant the destruction of both these powers—an event that necessarily preceded the inauguration of Christ's kingdom.[25]

Milton's position regarding the interpretation of the "Assyrian flood" is clear: his reference two lines later to "the Red Sea and Jordan" in a literal-historical sense suggests that he was in favor of the first view. Milton's Jesus did not favor the allegorical interpretation of the Isaianic prophecies: the Restoration of the Jews addressed a concrete situation that would take place among the tribes in Babylon, across the Euphrates which separated them from Palestine.

4. Finally, that the Restoration will take place in "God's due time and providence" and by implication, that the messianic kingdom, which is to succeed the Restoration, will be in God's appointed time is the central thesis in Jesus' whole argument against Satan. As Satan had started the debate by tempting Jesus to proclaim the kingdom and restore the Jews, he now receives from Jesus a crushing defeat: Jesus refuses to seize the kingdom either at the wrong time or by the wrong means.[26] This affirmation draws Milton's Jesus close to the Restorationists who admitted the Restoration of the Jews and the advent of Christ as mysteries known only to God. Although at the height of the Cromwellian revolution theologians rashly ventured with dates and threats, in the period after 1660 Restorationists were satisfied to renege on their earlier proclamations and to leave the whole matter to God's providence. Milton's Jesus was confirming New Testamental orthodoxy: the Restoration of the Jews is a mystery, which, like the messianic kingdom, is foreknown only to God.

Lines 433-40 situate Milton at the center of a theological debate about the Restoration of the Jews. Whether in the Interregnum or in 1671, the passage in *Paradise Regained* points to a polemical position that Milton had taken, one which specified his religio-political allegiance. To be a Restorationist in the late 1640s or in the 1650s pointed to a pro-Cromwellian interpretation of the messianic kingdom in England; to be a Restorationist in 1671, at the publication of *Paradise Regained,* meant expectation of tangible proof of God's continued involvement in the history of his previously chosen people, the Jews, and his presently chosen Zion, the nonconformists. In both periods, the Restorationist position clarified Milton's view of contemporary events, whether towards the revolution under Cromwell, or towards the continued messianic expectations of nonconformists during the period of the "great persecution."

III

As was noted above, Milton did not contribute to the debate on the settlement of the Jews in England—an issue that busied Cromwell and many of his theologians in the 1650s. That silence, Don M. Wolfe correctly maintains, stemmed from Milton's limits of toleration which did not extend to Catholics or to unconverted Jews.[27] Not surprisingly, Milton's support for the Restorationist position in the early 1650s confirms this view: like many of his mentors and contemporaries, Milton did not view the Jews as a community with an individual history and religion, but as delayed Christians. And because he hoped for the Jews' conversion he showed interest in their Restoration: for the Restoration was to be necessarily subsequent upon their conversion. Unconverted Jews, however, like the ones pleading for settlement in 1655 did not interest him. Manasseh Ben Israel, who was conducting the negotiations with Cromwell and author of *The Hope of Israel,* mentioned nothing, to Milton's dismay, about the forthcoming conversion of the Jews before or once they arrived in England. Milton thus showed no concern for these Jews. Not surprisingly and in that same year, Milton lamented the Protestant Piedmontese in a Hebraic tone, comparing their suffering with the Babylonian exile, but he ignored the contemporary Jews in London for not accepting Christ.[28]

NOTES

[1]All poetry references are to Douglas Bush, ed., *Milton: Poetical Works* (Oxford: Oxford Univ. Press, 1969). The prose passages are from the *Complete Prose Works,* gen. ed. Don M. Wolfe, 8 vols. (New Haven and London: Yale Univ. Press, 1953-1983).

[2]See Michael Fixler, *Milton and the Kingdoms of God* (Evanston: Northwestern Univ. Press, 1964), pp. 237-40; Barbara Lewalski, *Milton's Brief Epic* (Providence: Brown Univ. Press, 1966), pp. 271-73.

[3]See my "The Idea of the Restoration of the Jews in English Protestant Theology: From the Reformation until 1660," *DUJ* 78 (1985):23-36.

[4]See John T. Shawcross, "The Chronology of Milton's Major Poems," *PMLA* 76 (September 1961):345-58. See also William R. Parker, *Milton*, 2 vols. (Oxford: Oxford Univ. Press, 1965), 2:1140.

[5]Thomas Goodwin, *An Exposition of the Revelation* (1639), in *The Works of Thomas Goodwin,* Nichol's Series of Standard Divines, 28 vols. (Edinburgh, 1861-1865), 3:62ff., and Parker, 1:42.

See also T.G. [Thomas Goodwin?], *A glimpse of Syons glory* (London, 1641), passim; John Owen, *The Shaking and Translating of Heaven and Earth. A Sermon Preached to the Honorable House of Commons, April 19, 1649* (London, 1649), pp. 12, 40; Peter Sterry, *The Comings Forth of Christ In the Power of His Death* (London, 1650), pp. 11ff., and *England's Deliverance from the Northern Presbytery* (London, 1652, preached on 5 November 1651), pp. 33ff.; Henry Jessey, *An Information Concerning the Present State of the Jewish Nation in Europe and Judea* (London, 1655); *Annotations Upon all the Books of the Old and New Testament By the Labour of certain Learned Divines,* 2 vols. (London, 1651), 2, on Rom. 11:11-18. For a study of Milton's interaction with these writers, see ch. 12 of Arthur E. Barker, *Milton and the Puritan Dilemma, 1641-1660* (Toronto: Univ. of Toronto Press, 1942).

[6]For Cromwell and Milton, see Antonia Fraser, *Cromwell our Chief of Men* (London: Panther, 1975), pp. 87, 391, 455-86; Austin Woolrych, "Milton and Cromwell, 'A Short but Scandalous Night of Interruption'?" in Michael Lieb and John T. Shawcross, eds., *Achievements of the Left Hand* (Amherst: Univ. of Massachusetts Press, 1974), pp. 185-218.

[7]For Milton and Mede, see Marjorie Nicolson, "Milton's 'Old Damoetas'," *MLN* 41 (May 1926):293-300, and the various references in Michael Lieb, *Poetics of the Holy* (Chapel Hill: Univ. of North Carolina Press, 1951). For Mede's and Brightman's influence on Milton and others, see Peter Toon, ed., *Puritans, the Millennium and the Future of Israel. Puritan Eschatology, 1600-1660* (Cambridge and London: James Clarke, 1970), pp. 26ff. and 60ff. See also R. Clouse, "The Influence of John Henry Alsted on English Millenarian Thought in the Seventeenth Century" (Ph.D. Diss., State Univ. of Iowa, 1963), ch. 2; Frederick Plotkin, "Sighs from Zion: A Study of Radical Puritan Eschatology in England, 1640-1660" (Ph. D. Diss., Columbia Univ., 1966), ch. 2.

[8]Mary Cary, *The Little Horns Doom and Downfall* (London, 1651), pp. 139ff., John Robins, *The Declaration of John Robins the false Prophet* (London, 1651), p. 5; Joanna and Ebenezer Cartwright, *The Petition of the Jewes for the Repealing of the Act of Parliament for their banishment out of England* (London: 1649); Theauravjohn Tany, *I Proclaime from the Lord of Hosts the Returne of the Jewes from their Captivity* (London, 1650); Samuel Gott, *Nova Solyma, the Ideal City,* ed. Walter Begley, 2 vols. (London: John Murray, 1902, first pub. 1649), 2:89ff. For possible Gott-Milton contact, see Christopher Hill, *Milton and the English Revolution* (London: Faber and Faber, 1977), p. 147; George Foster, *The Pouring Forth of the Seventh and Last Viall* (London, 1650), pp. 63ff.; Nathaniel Homes, *The Resurrection—Revealed, Raised* (London, 1661), pp. 52, 97, 101, 154-55, 195, 217-20. Homes was closely associated with the Cromwell regime and Nathan Paget, Milton's doctor, owned MSS by him. See Hill, *Milton*, p. 494; John Canne, *A Second Voyce from the Temple to the Higher Powers* (London: 1653), pp. 25-31. For the Canne-Milton contact, see George Wesley Whiting, *Milton's Literary Milieu* (New York: Russell and Russell, 1964), pp. 311-23. Moses Wall, "Considerations Upon the Point of the Conversion of the Jewes," cited in Lucien Wolfe, *Menasseh Ben Israel's Mission to Oliver Cromwell* (London: Macmillan, 1901), pp. 55-61. For the Milton-Wall contact, see the letter by Wall in *Prose*, 7:510-13. Milton and Oldenburgh were friends and correspondents; see *Prose*, 7:489-92, 495-96, 498-500, 502-505, 513-15, and Fixler, pp. 243-44. For general studies on this issue, see Christopher Hill, *Antichrist in Seventeenth-Century England* (London and

New York: Oxford Univ. Press, 1971), pp. 114ff. and 179ff.; and Bryan W. Ball, *A Great Expectation* (Leiden: E. J. Brill, 1975), ch. 3.

[9]T. G., *A glimpse*, p. 31; Robert Lord Brooke, *A Discourse Opening The Nature of That Episcopacie Which Is Exercised in England* (London, 1642), p. 63; William Bridge, *Works*, 5 vols. (London, 1845), 4:345. The sermon was preached on 29 November 1643.

[10]Thomas Brightman, *The Revelation of Saint John* (Amsterdam, 1644, first pub. 1609), p. 41; Samuel Gibson, *The Ruine of the Authors and Formentors of Civill Warres* (London, 1645), p. 33; see also Sterry's use in *England's Deliverance*, p. 40. For studies on Milton's eschatology, see Hill, *Milton*, ch. 21; Barker, ch. 12; and Paul Christianson, *Reformers and Babylon* (Toronto: Univ. of Toronto Press, 1978), pp. 193-95.

[11]*Doomes-day: or, The Great Day of the Lords Judgement, proved by Scripture* (London, 1647), p. 2. See also Alan Macfarlane, ed., *The Diary of Ralph Josselin 1616-1683* (London: Oxford Univ. Press, 1976), pp. 219, 227.

[12]Sterry, *The Comings Forth*, pp. 11-13; Canne, pp. 9, 26-27.

[13]In *Prose*, 7:617, n. 9, the editor draws attention to Wollebius, *Compendium Theologiae Christianae*, I, xxxiv , p. 170, and to Zanchius, "De Fine," *Operum Theologicorum*, vol. 3, tome vii, col. 88 as possible sources.

[14]*A Sermon Preached to the Parliament, Octob. 13. 1652* (Oxford, 1652), p. 16.

[15]Robert Baillie, *A Dissuasive from the Errours of the Time* (London, 1645), ch. 11; see also his sermon on *Errours and Induration* (London, 1645); Thomas Hayne, *Christs Kingdome on Earth Opened according to the Scriptures* (London, 1645); John Lightfoot, *A Sermon Preached Before the Honorable House of Commons . . . 26 Aug. 1645* (London, 1645); William Gouge, *The Progresse of Divine Providence* (London, 1645), pp. 29ff.; Thomas Edwards, *The First and Second Part of Gangraena* (London, 1646), p. 19. John Frederick Wilson, in *Pulpit in Parliament: Puritanism during the English Civil War, 1640-1648* (Princeton: Princeton Univ. Press, 1969), maintains that millenarianism was one of the distinctions that separated the Independents from the Presbyterians. For a study of the transformation of eschatology in the late 1640s and the 1650s, see Tai Liu, *Discord in Zion* (The Hague: Martinus Nijhoff, 1973).

[16]Henry Hammond, *A Paraphrase and Annotations Upon all the Books of the New Testament*, in *The Miscellaneous Theological Works of H.H.*, 3rd edn., 3 vols. (Oxford, 1847-1850), 4:502.

[17]*The Learned Conjectures of Reverend Mr. John Eliot* in *Jews in America*, by Thomas Thorowgood (London, 1652), pp. 1, 20; Increase Mather, *The Mystery of Israel's Salvation* (London, 1669), passim; Vavasor Powell, *A New and Useful Concordance to the Holy Bible* (London, 1671), "A Collection of the Prophesies which concern the Calling of the Jews, and the glory that shall be in the latter days"; and *The Life and Death of Mr. Vavasor Powell* (London, 1671), pp. 44-45; Rhys (Arise) Evans, *Light for the Jews* (London, 1665); William Sherwin, *Λογοξ περυ λογου: or the vvord vvritten. Concerning the World Everlasting* (London, 1670), pp. 5-13, and *A Paper shewing that the great Conversion and Restauration of all Israel and Judah will be fulfilled at Christs second coming* (London, 1674).

[18]Sir Paul Rycaut, *The Turkish History*, 3 vols. (London, first pub. 1668, 6th edn. 1687), 2:174; John Evelyn in 1669 included Rycaut's account of Sevi in his *The History of the Three late Famous Imposters* (London, 1669), pp. 42ff.

[19]See John Owen, *Works*, ed. William Goold, 6 vols. (London and Edinburgh, 1851), 9:322, 489, 506, 510. It is surprising to find Christopher Hill commenting

on Owen and Milton that "they became less certain that the Second Coming was imminent," *Milton*, p. 284. As late as 1676, Owen was warning about "these last days." See also Sterry, MS III, catalogue no. 292 in Emmanuel College Library, Cambridge, pp. 149-50. See my "Peter Sterry, the Millennium and Oliver Cromwell" in *The Journal of the United Reformed Church History Society* 2 (October 1982):334-43. Nathaniel Homes, *The Resurrection—Revealed, Raised, Above Doubts, and Difficulties* (London, 1661), "The First Exercitation." William Bridge, 5:352-57; the sermon was preached in 1668. See also Bernard Capp, *The Fifth Monarchy Men* (London: Faber and Faber, 1972), pp. 203, 215-23.

[20]Brightman, p. 314.

[21]Mather, p. 82.

[22]Tany, *I proclaime from the Lord of Hosts the return of the Jews from their Captivity* (London, 1650), broadsheet.

[23]Thomas Cooper *The Blessing of Japheth* (London 1615) p. 53; Mather, p. 97; Brightman, p. 267; Mede, *The Works of Joseph Mede* (London, 3rd edn., 1672), p. 891, and Bk. V, ch. 11; John Archer, *The Personall Raigne of Christ upon Earth* (London, 1642), p. 52; Sterry, *The Comings Forth*, pp. 11ff.

[24]Joseph Mede, *Clavis Apocraphica*, trans. R. Bransby Cooper (London, 1833), pp. 427-31; Brightman, p. 357; Goodwin quotes Brightman in *Exposition*, pp. 62-63; Bagshaw, p. 31; Jessey, p. 7; Henry Finch, *The Worlds Great Restauration* (London, 1621), passim.

[25]Hugh Broughton, *The Seven Vialls* (London, 1628), p. 48; John Cotton, *The Pouring Out of the Seven Vialls* (London, 1642), vial 6, pp. 30ff.; see also Thomas Matthews, *Clavis Apocalyptica* (London, 1651), p. 111, and Sterry, *England's Deliverance*, pp. 38-39.

[26]Lewalski, p. 265.

[27]Don M. Wolfe, "Limits of Milton's Toleration," *JEPG* 60 (October 1961):834-46. For perceptive analyses of Milton's attitude to the Jews and Judaism, see Samuel S. Stollman, "Milton's Dichotomy of 'Judaism' and 'Hebraism'," *PMLA* 89 (January 1974):105-12, and "Milton's Understanding of the 'Hebraic' in *Samson Agonistes*," *SP* 69 (July 1972):334-47.

[28]Charles E. Goldstein, "The Hebrew Element in Milton's Sonnet XVIII," *MiltonQ* 9 (December 1975):111-14.

SEL 26 (1986)
ISSN 0039-3657

The Muting of Satan: Language and Redemption in *Paradise Regained*

STEVEN GOLDSMITH

So much has been made of Jesus' passivity in *Paradise Regained* that few readers recognize the action he takes decisively and takes often. To stress the interiority of the poem, the psychological drama of Jesus' free choice not to engage in action as Satan presents it, is to lose sight of the fact that Milton deliberately places the reader outside of Jesus' consciousness and thus outside of such drama. After Satan's arrival in the wilderness, when the conflict properly begins, Milton provides only sixteen lines of the Son's interior monologue; our assessment of Jesus depends entirely upon his external behavior, his willingness to act in the normal sense of the word and to adopt means that may at first seem earthly and tainted—namely, his willingness to speak. Stanley Fish has noted that speech is an action,[1] but he assumes that Jesus must therefore eradicate speech on his way toward a perfect passivity and obedience embodied in silence. Exactly the opposite is the case. Although his style remains temperate and succinct, the Son steadily speaks at greater length and in the process of debate consistently renders Satan mute until the adversary's final silence is the emblem of nonexistence, spiritual substancelessness. What happens in the desert, which the narrative commentary celebrates again and again, serves to differentiate the divine word from the fallen word and so redeem language as the means by which the Son can go about his Father's business. Jesus enters the wilderness not to discover his identity, but to learn how he may best execute his office as Messiah; by the time he leaves, he has demonstrated the spiritual efficacy of an action previously immersed in corruption. The Son enters the desert "obscure, / Unmarked, unknown,"[2] and though he returns to his mother's house in "private," he is ready to embark on his public ministry.[3]

Steven Goldsmith is an Assistant Professor of English at the University of California, Berkeley. He is currently working on a study of prophecy, apocalypse, and British Romanticism.

The events of *Paradise Regained* consist almost uniformly of the Son's unswerving response to temptation and do not lend themselves to the dramatic conflict that typically propels narrative.[4] Jesus' absolute invulnerability suggests the extent to which he and Satan inhabit antithetical and exclusive realms, eliminating the possibility of conflict that arises from mutual interaction. In a very real sense the two characters talk past one another. One source of tension, however, resides in the poem's very condition of debate; despite Jesus' overwhelming triumph, he shares his opponent's medium of verbal warfare. When the Son relates his private history in Book I, we applaud his childhood rejection of the "heroic acts" (I, 216) with which Satan will endlessly confront him. He has already made good Michael's assertion in *Paradise Lost* that Messianic victory will not come by the "local wounds" of a physical "duel" (XII, 387). Yet the apparently superior alternative—"By winning words to conquer willing hearts, / And make persuasion do the work of fear" (I, 222-23)—should stir a note of suspicion. After all, Satan is the master of "persuasive rhetoric" (IV, 4), and readers of both *Paradise Lost* and *Paradise Regained* delight in exposing the artful techniques behind his all too "winning words."[5] Although Jesus refuses to wield a material weapon that would reduce him to the level of Satan, he is willing to adopt the language corrupted by Satan.[6] In a cunning temptation, couched in the appeal to Greek literature, Satan senses Jesus' need for language in order to achieve his mission:

> And with the Gentiles much thou must converse,
> Ruling them by persuasion as thou mean'st.
>
> (IV, 229-30)

Camouflaged by the foolish suggestion that Jesus "Be famous then / By wisdom" (IV, 221-22) is the penetrating implication that persuasion for whatever end requires fallen means. Should Jesus accept that he participates in the same system of discourse as Satan, the gap between the divine and the demonic will have been vitally narrowed.

That Jesus' speech runs any risk of conflation with "persuasive rhetoric" reveals a central problem of Milton's epic: the Word Incarnate enters a world where language has so fallen that all manifestations of it are equivocal. Although, as Joan Webber asserts, "the poem is suffused with the language of doubt,"[7] Milton counters this necessary impact of the Fall with an equally thorough emphasis on "proof," the renewed certainty of the word through which paradise will be regained. The doubt/proof motif is established early, Milton praising in his invocation the Spirit that led Jesus into the desert and "brought'st him thence / By proof the undoubted Son of God" (I, 10-11). Not only will the Son emerge certain of his identity (*if* that was ever in question), but we as readers will trust his verbal repulse of Satan. It is the burden of *Paradise Regained* to affirm continuously that confidence in speech.

Two passages from *Paradise Lost* point to the peculiar, linguistic difficulty Jesus faces in *Paradise Regained*. The first involves the problem inherent in the shift from a language of presence, where word and referent are intrinsically bound, to a language of absence, where reference depends upon the mediation of an intervening sign. Told he must abandon the garden, Adam most laments being severed from direct discourse with the divine source.

> This most afflicts me, that departing hence,
> As from his face I shall be hid, deprived
> His blessed countenance; here I could frequent,
> With worship, place by place where he vouchsafed
> Presence divine, and to my sons relate;
> On this mount he appeared; under this tree
> Stood visible, among these pines his voice
> I heard, here with him at this fountain talked.
>
> (XI, 315-22)

Adam's contact with God had been immediate and direct; he relishes the specific locations—mount, tree, pine, fountain—where deity itself actually appeared. Because of the Fall, Adam's sons will never apprehend the face of divinity, but must content themselves with the expression of that face through "many a sign" (XI, 351). Even though Michael reassures Adam that such signs will follow him when he leaves the garden, language has been punctured critically and the gap between signifier and signified becomes an immediate source of doubt in the fallen world.

The second important gloss on postlapsarian language provided by *Paradise Lost* portrays the confusion of tongues at Babel, where the influence of the Adamic language is forfeited. Well into the seventeenth century, certain linguists contended that our corrupt state of language variation represented the fragmentation, at Babel, of Adam's original unfallen speech, in which "perfect harmony [existed] between word and thing."[8] Milton's description of the Old Testament punishment, emphasizing the loss of "native language," reflects contemporary thought. Michael explains to Adam how God

> in derision sets
> Upon their tongues a various spirit to raze

Quite out their native language, and instead
To sow a jangling noise of words unknown.

(XII, 52-55)

The effect is to remove man even further from a language of presence by rendering arbitrary the link between sound and referent. When Adam named the animals in Eden, "words could not merely be accidental";[9] instead, the names corresponded to perfect knowledge of nature itself. The events at Babel disrupted the ideal bond between language and epistemology, and though the original sounds of Adam's speech remained, they (and the knowledge they represented) became the pieces of an unsolvable puzzle. Even toward the end of the Renaissance, mystical etymologists continued to hope that they could unscramble the Babylonian confusion in order to learn the ontological essence the original word of Adam revealed.

No wonder, given the problematic nature of language with which *Paradise Regained* begins, that the heavenly pronouncement at the Messiah's baptism should be met by varying degrees of doubt. The responses of the new baptized, Mary, and Satan reflect the necessary uncertainty of minds divorced from direct access to truth, and firmly establish the fallen condition Jesus and Milton must overcome. Even in the first description of the baptism scene, Milton begins to counteract doubt; Jesus is identified by progressively more valid means of communication. John the Baptist's public recognition of the Messiah cannot suffice, for the "great proclaimer" (I, 18) speaks the corrupt tongue descended from Babel. Further proof is needed, and drawing upon scriptural narrative, Milton obliges:

nor was long
His [John's] witness unconfirmed: on him baptized
Heaven opened, and in the likeness of a dove
The Spirit descended, while the Father's voice
From heaven pronounced him his beloved Son.

(I, 28-32)

Although both events occur simultaneously, the verse first provides a sign, the mediating appearance of the Dove, and then reveals the immediate presence of the Father's voice. The force of this "voice divine" is so great that Satan is "Nigh thunderstruck" (I, 35-36); in the first instance of what will become the recurring pattern, he is rendered momentarily silent. To find a seed of doubt with which he can initiate his assault, Satan turns away from the voice of presence to the equivocal nature of the intervening sign ("A perfect dove . . . , whate'er it meant" [I, 83]), and more importantly, to the inherent ambiguity of the verbal medium itself. Son of God, he tells the Messiah in Book IV, "bears no single sense" (IV, 517). Jesus, on the other hand, in his effort to interpret the same events, relies foremost on the immediate contact with God.

> And last the sum of all, my Father's voice,
> Audibly heard from heaven, pronounced me his.
>
> (I, 283-84)

"Audibly heard" is no redundancy. Jesus stresses the actual, physical perception of divine presence so that we cannot mistake it for the symbolic or mediated perception characteristic of the fallen world.

The antithetical responses of Satan and Jesus to the baptism pronouncement should not surprise us; they reflect opposing approaches to language. Jesus finds in the "divine voice" a model for the original language of presence by which he can express the private wisdom he derives from access to the Father. "What concerns my knowledge God reveals" (I, 293), he says, and so concludes the meditation some critics see as the expression of identity crisis. Satan, cut off permanently from such revelation, seizes upon the mediatory function of language created by the fall into absence, created by the removal of verbal beings from direct contact with the divine presence that guaranteed undeflected communication. It is by exploiting the gap between signifier and signified that he is able to multiply doubt and falsehood. These two notions of language permeate the debate of *Paradise Regained,* as Satan tries to compromise Jesus through his language of doubt only to be thwarted by Jesus' ability to communicate truth directly through speech. The Son emerges from this interaction as the Logos, an expression of divinity where no discrepancy exists between vehicle and tenor. At the same time, he identifies Satan as the lie. The adversary's speech actually proves the negation of speech—a vehicle empty of substance, a void.

The effort to instill incertitude underlies nearly every temptation, and Satan weaves doubt into the very fabric of his discourse. Sometimes he employs a syntax that implicates Jesus in uncertainty, as in the banquet temptation, when he asks, "What doubts the Son of God to sit and eat?" (II, 365), and moments later, "What doubt'st thou Son of God? Sit down and eat" (II, 377). More often, Satan subtly urges Jesus to accept the arbitrary link between name and thing that would weaken the significance of the title, Son of God. Careful never to award him any special, intrinsic status, Satan always contends that Jesus has been merely "called . . . Son / Of God" (I, 329-30) or "Declared the Son of God" (I, 385), the enjambment of the former quotation indicating Satan's implicit attempt to drive a wedge between the Son and actual godhead.

Jesus consistently sees through such temptation and manifests throughout the epic his awareness that the disruption between name and thing common to the fallen word belongs to Satan's influence, not God's. That earthly conquerors who "swell with pride" must be "titled gods" (III, 81), that verbal glory is most often "false glory" (III, 69), that courtiers typically vent "hollow compliments" (IV, 124) indicates no inherent flaw in the word—rather, a demonic inversion that drains the word of its truth. Thus Jesus remains essentially unafflicted by the storms Satan wreaks upon him in Book IV. "As signs" (IV, 489) they have no efficacy, for like Satan's words, they are superficial emblems without matter, "false portents, not sent from God" (IV, 491). As early as their first encounter Jesus knows as much, telling Satan he is "composed of lies / From the beginning, and in lies wilt end" (I, 407-408). The words echo the opening of the Gospel according to John and clearly establish Satan as the linguistic anti-christ. The Messiah lives by "each word / Proceeding from the mouth of God" (I, 349-50), the language of presence wherein true force resides, but "lying" is Satan's "sustenance" (I, 429). Jesus faces Satan's lies unmoved, but as Fish points out, Satan reacts to Jesus' speech as if struck by a material blow.[10] Such is the difference between language as presence and absence, language as truth and lie. By the end of the temptation of bread Satan has confessed that falsehood serves his purpose best and he characterizes his use of speech in a revealing manner. The adversary chooses "to lie, / *Say and unsay,* feign, flatter, or abjure" (my emphasis, I, 473-74). As positive and negative digits balance at zero, so words cancel words and the sum of Satan's verbal warfare is nothing.

For Jesus to expose that nothingness, that void which lies beneath Satan's surface manipulation of signs—for Jesus, in other words, to make Satan's sound conform to his substance—he must render his opponent mute. But he cannot do so by remaining silent himself. Arnold Stein asserts that "It is not enough for the protagonist to refuse offers; he must answer, and fully."[11] As Jesus' voice emerges and proves overwhelming, Satan's voice inevitably recedes; in the process Jesus not only discovers his enemy's true identity, but he also resurrects the language needed to communicate divine knowledge to fallen man. The debate provides the Messiah with the means he seeks to bring about redemption and so fuels his transition from private to public life.[12] Although this epic ends with his return "unobserved" and "private" (IV, 638-39) to his mother's house, we cannot forget that the next significant biblical event is the Sermon on the Mount.

Appropriately, Jesus' first silencing of Satan is to put an end to the adversary's public voice:

> henceforth oracles are ceased,
> And thou no more with pomp and sacrifice
> Shalt be inquired at Delphos or elsewhere,
> At least in vain, for they shall find thee mute.
>
> (I, 456-59)

Jesus then announces the direction his own mission will take as the "living oracle" sent "to teach" (I, 460-61) the will of God. With the public voice of Satan quelled and that of Jesus presently taking shape, the remainder of the poem focuses on the integral linguistic power-struggle between two individuals, contending for mankind.

The next of several mutings of Satan occurs in the extraordinary gap between Books II and III, the precise center of the epic. What may appear to be a structural defect represents brilliant formal strategy on Milton's part. Culminating in Jesus' fifty-three line dissertation on the proper role of the political ruler, Book II ends abruptly with the final word of Jesus' speech. No authorial comment, no reply from Satan follows. The startling effect is to render everything but Jesus' word insignificant; all else disappears but the resonance of the Messiah's wisdom. By the time the distance between books has been traveled, Satan still has not recovered his voice. Book III must begin just as Book II ended, with Jesus still in the act of speech (now by narrative description) and Satan dissolved in silence.

> So spake the Son of God, and Satan stood
> A while as mute confounded what to say,
> What to reply, confuted and convinced
> Of his weak arguing, and fallacious drift;
> At length collecting all his serpent wiles,
> With soothing words renewed, him thus accosts.
>
> (III, 1-6)

The enjambment from lines three to four is effective; Satan is first convinced of the potency of Jesus' word, which then compels him to recognize the weakness of his own. Milton also places a good deal of weight on "At length," deliberately stretching the time needed for Satan to recover, and when at last he does revive, his only recourse is a return to the same tactics, the same "wiles," the same "soothing words" that must surely meet an identical fate.

Before Satan renews his assault, however, he ironically provides the epic's most explicit description of Jesus' unique linguistic strength. With the awe of his blow still lingering, he cannot help but explain aloud the secret his foe has always known.

> I see thou know'st what is of use to know,
> What best to say canst say, to do canst do;
> Thy actions to thy words accord, thy words
> To thy large heart give utterance due, thy heart
> Contains of good, wise, just, the perfect shape.
>
> (III, 7-11)

The monosyllabic plainness of the first two lines suggests that Satan has not yet fully recovered his latinate wiles, and consequently, he expresses a rare truth. For Jesus, knowledge, language, and action are synonymous. No rupture exists between external and internal; signifier and signified are identical. Before Satan even knows what he says, he verifies Jesus' status as the Logos, an act equivalent to linguistic concession. The perfect goodness, wisdom, and justice contained in Jesus' heart, the inheritance of his heavenly birth, will not remain uncommunicated because soiled by the inadequacy of fallen language and action. Fish claims that language in *Paradise Regained* is "identified not only with the false values (wealth, power, earthly kingship) that are the basis of Satan's appeal but also with the overruling temptation they always represent, the temptation to value (and therefore to assert) the self."[13] This accurate description of Satan's corrupt speech, however, cannot apply to the language of presence Jesus restores. Far from asserting selfhood, the Son's word is the immediate expression of the divine, that presence incarnate which is least connected to earthly self. The Messiah makes his mother's perhaps misguided encouragement—"By matchless deeds express thy matchless sire" (I, 233)—innocently and literally come true. The matchless deed becomes speech, not military action, and most importantly, speech not as a vehicle for self-expression but for God-expression. Stein is right; the Messiah must answer fully; it is his obligation, as an obedient Son of God, to convey as comprehensively as possible the glory of the Father he feels within his breast. Fish's understanding of the relationship between silence and expression thus proves misleading. "On the verbal level," he writes, "there is a progressive diminishing, first of the complexity of language and then of its volubility, until finally as the relationship between the self and God is specified, there is only silence."[14] It is Satan, not Jesus, whose true state is silence, and such silence indicates but one thing; Satan has nothing to express.[15]

To ask why Satan then continues the debate beyond the pivotal transition from Books II to III is to ask why *Paradise Regained* lacks traditional dramatic conflict. Thoroughly defeated, Satan must tempt again and be muted again. Thoroughly triumphant, Jesus must still be alert, though it is outside of his nature to be otherwise. The temptation is the same at every moment and it never ends. Even the pinnacle confrontation provides no real finale; the outcome is firmly established, but the battle will continue to the end of time.[16] In a recent article, Stuart Curran argues that "However distinct the forms it takes, there is essentially one temptation in *Paradise Regained*, that of narrowing one's spiritual and psychological range to accord with an already structured and external pattern."[17] The temptation in *Paradise Regained* is to choose a path, and by doing so limit oneself to the identity forged by that particular path. Resisting such restriction, Jesus allies himself with the infinite potential of godhead. Yet that infinite potential cannot remain the private property of silence; to extend it to mankind, and thus begin the office of Messiah, it must be made public. At a certain point, the disguise in which the one temptation is garbed ceases to interest us, but with each verbal rejection our ability to distinguish the Word from the word, and therefore our confidence in Jesus' language, grows greater.

Within the first hundred and fifty lines of Book III, Jesus again silences Satan, and while Milton does not dwell on the incident as formerly, it proves critical in the process of differentiation between the language of Satan and that of the Messiah. After Jesus exposes the emptiness of earthly reputation, Satan, "murmuring" (III, 108), cautions Jesus not to demean glory, which, according to the fiend, God "requires" (III, 113) from all creation almost as a form of despotic rent. The readers who wish to argue for the static nature of this epic's narrative typically cite the redundant "unmoved" that often prefaces Jesus' speech, but they do not account for the present response of the Son, the emotion of which may seem out of character.

> To whom our Saviour fervently replied.
> And reason; since his word all things produced,
> Though chiefly not for glory as prime end,
> But to show forth his goodness, and impart
> His good communicable to every soul
> Freely.
>
> (III, 121-26)

To understand the propriety of this response, one must realize first that Jesus' "fervently replied" stands in opposition to Satan's "murmuring," and secondly, that the subject at hand is God's glory. Jesus argues that man's praise of divinity marks the proper use of language because it reciprocally manifests the goodness of soul God has already communicated through the act of creation. Jesus' emotion does not reveal a lack of composure; by defending the Father with such passion he parallels the Father's own desire "to show forth his goodness." Milton makes effective use of the Latin root for fervently—*ferveo, fervere,* "to glow." Satan, on the other hand, already half the distance toward silence, can introduce the topic of divine glory only in a low murmur. As early as Book I, Jesus explains that Heaven's "bliss" is "no more communicable" (I, 419) to Satan, a significant comment on the adversary's present lack of volubility. Satan *cannot* praise; his only form of speech is "obloquy" (III, 131), a perverse negation of true communication that reveals the absence of a soul. After Jesus' defense, Satan loses even that, and is, of course, struck dumb.

> So spake the Son of God; and here again
> Satan had not to answer, but stood struck
> With guilt of his own sin.
>
> (III, 145-47)

One might be tempted at this point to interpret the sequence of mutings as a series of preliminary triumphs that foreshadow the climactic pinnacle scene, but I have no intention that this essay encourage readers to see the pattern as a narrative structure that allows for progression. In his most recent work on *Paradise Regained,* Fish chastises those critics who impose plot upon Milton's intentionally plotless epic. "The difficulty, for both Milton and his reader," Fish asserts, "is the writing of poetry, and of narrative poetry, that in no way relies upon crisis, climax, change, development, and suspense but makes them the vehicles of temptation."[18] Every one of Satan's mutings is fundamentally identical, and while some, like that above, are given less emphasis, all share in the astonishing realization that radiates not from a concluding climax, but from the epic's spiritual and physical center—the interlude between Books II and III. Frozen in that instant is the relationship between Satan and Jesus that adheres at every moment of the poem. Thus Milton repeats nearly the same strategy in the passage from Books III to IV, though the cumulative effect allows him to be more explicit about the lesson that pertains equally well to the previous mutings. In this case, Book III does not end with Jesus' word, but with the following authorial comment:

> So spake Israel's true King, and to the Fiend
> Made answer meet, that made void all his wiles.
> So fares it when with truth falsehood contends.
>
> (III, 441-43)

Just as before, an actual void in the text follows the exposure of Satan's spiritual and linguistic void, the space between books filled, if at all, by Milton's almost reductive assessment of the difference between words Jesus all along has stressed. Book IV then begins just as Book III began, with Satan still silenced.

> Perplexed and troubled at his bad success
> The tempter stood, nor had what to reply,
> Discovered in his fraud, thrown from his hope,
> So oft, and the persuasive rhetoric
> That sleeked his tongue, and won so much on Eve,
> So little here, nay lost.
>
> (IV, 1-6)

The only advancement that takes place from book to book occurs in the understanding of the reader, who increasingly recognizes that the rhetoric of Satan, "to shameful silence brought" (IV, 22), has no essence. The potential confusion between Satan's persuasion and Jesus' persuasion, the tension with which *we* began, has been eliminated. For Jesus and Satan, it never actually existed.

Despite a last attempt by Satan to blur the distinction between words, the concluding pinnacle scene results in a muting not substantially different from those earlier. Lee Sheridan Cox observes that Milton adheres to the narratives of Matthew and Luke by having Jesus quote Scripture in response to each of the three Satanic temptations, but in the third he deviates by allowing Satan to appropriate Scripture.[19] Urging Jesus to leap from the pinnacle, Satan echoes the biblical precedence Jesus has relied upon in his rejections:

> For it is written, He will give command
> Concerning thee to his angels.
>
> (IV, 556-57)

As always, Satan fires blanks. Because he speaks "in scorn" (IV, 550), he severs the spirit of the word from the letter, rendering it ineffective. When spirit and letter coincide, the word proves the same invulnerable weapon we witness in every one of Satan's mutings. Citing the Bible himself, Jesus removes Scripture from Satan's corruption, adding it to the general restoration of language that has taken place throughout the poem.

> To whom thus Jesus: Also it is written,
> Tempt not the Lord thy God, he said and stood.
> But Satan smitten with amazement fell.
>
> (IV, 560-62)

The paradoxical fulness of the sparse phrase "he said and stood" resonates in several directions. The near simultaneity of saying and standing recalls the instantaneous bond between language and action characteristic of the original act of speech, that of the Father in Genesis: God said, . . . and there was. At the same time, it mirrors several of Satan's mutings, holding up, as it were, an emblem of the essential linguistic contrast *Paradise Regained* as a whole has sought to effect. Compare, for example,

> Satan stood
> A while as mute confounded what to say,
>
> (III, 1-2)

or

> Satan had not to answer, but stood struck
> With guilt of his own sin,
>
> (III, 146-47)

or

> The Tempter stood, nor had what to reply.
>
> (IV, 2)

Jesus stands by an act of verbal expression; Satan can only stand mute, the linguistic equivalent of the fall we see materially only after the pinnacle temptation. Both characters, in this posture so important to Milton as a sign of obedience, reveal their final nature.

Milton significantly concludes *Paradise Regained* with "heavenly anthems" sung by "angelic choirs" (IV, 593-94) in praise of Jesus. These songs do more than permit Milton tactfully to avoid "shameful silence" until the poem's final four lines, in which he sends the Son home "private" to his mother. They end by reminding us that the real battle is yet to commence:

> Queller of Satan, on thy glorious work
> Now enter, and begin to save mankind.
>
> (IV, 634-35)

But such announcement is made only after the angels assure us of both the means and the end of victory. Jesus has delivered the decisive blow not to Satan, but to doubt; the process of verification that is the purpose of *Paradise Regained* has been accomplished. We remember God's explanation to the angels, early in Book I, for leading Jesus into the desert.

> Gabriel this day by proof thou shalt behold,
> Thou and all angels conversant on earth
> With man or men's affairs, how I begin
> To verify that solemn message late,
> On which I sent thee to the virgin pure.
>
> (I, 130-34)

Milton, by publishing deeds "unrecorded left through many an age" (I, 16), allows the reader the privilege of beholding what is meant for angels, and when the debate concludes, the reader shares in the angelic affirmation. Authority now rests secure, for we have witnessed "proof" (IV, 621) that Jesus "all unarmed / Shall chase [Satan] with the terror of his voice" (IV, 626-27).

Beyond the theology of the Logos, the triumph of voice over silence becomes for Milton a triumph of his own poetry; indeed, *Paradise Regained* takes on the subtle significance of a personal defense of poetry. By making language the active vehicle of redemption, and expression the very nature of the redeemer, Milton justifies the palpable text of his own creation. For the poet as well as his protagonist, words cannot be hindrances that get in the way, products of the Fall blocking access to divine reality. The Logos redeems the body of poetry precisely because it is simultaneously both truth and expression; the two cannot be severed despite Satan's efforts to corrupt. Such is the idealizing premise necessary for the writing of sacred verse, though Milton suggests in his invocation the real precariousness of the all too human poet, tenuously poised on the line between song and silence, expression and void. Aware from the start of the linguistic problems central to his epic, Milton asks the Holy Spirit to "inspire, / As thou art wont, my prompted song else mute" (I, 11-12). To surrender the self to the prompting of higher truth, Milton asserts, is to assure access to the means of expressing that truth. Without such access, poetic fate must be Satan's fate of silence. Before the process of linguistic differentiation and verification even begins, the language of presence that Christ resurrects Milton appropriates as his own.

NOTES

[1]Stanley Fish, "Inaction and Silence: The Reader in *Paradise Regained*," in *Calm of Mind: Tercentenary Essays on "Paradise Regained" and "Samson Agonistes" in Honor of John S. Diekhoff*, ed. Joseph Anthony Wittreich, Jr. (Cleveland: The Press of Case Western Reserve Univ., 1971), p. 38.

[2]John Milton, *Paradise Regained*, in *The Poems of John Milton*, ed. John Carey and Alastair Fowler (London: Longmans, Green, 1968), Book I, lines 24-25. All subsequent references are to this text, cited by book and line.

[3]Shortly after this essay was completed, Leonard Mustazza's closely related "Language as Weapon in Milton's *Paradise Regained*" appeared in *MiltonS* 18 (1983):195-216. On the most general level, Mustazza independently confirmed my sense that Milton's poem is a self-reflexive consideration of language—that "the epic 'conflict' concerns the nature and the uses of language itself. Clearly, the epic battle in this poem, unlike that of any other epic, brief or diffuse, is fought almost exclusively with words" (p. 195). The affinity deteriorates, however, as Mustazza vindicates Fish's conception of silence, which he too sees as both the inexorable destination of the poem and the proper representation of Jesus' unearthly obedience. Although I could not concur more fully that Jesus "is in effect redeeming words" (p. 199), I find it incongruous that such linguistic redemption would finally yield to linguistic absence, the silence that nullifies the power of the restored word. Why redeem language if it is then to be abandoned? For Mustazza, *Paradise Regained* ends with Satan and Jesus in an antithetical silence: "whereas Satan's word-weapons are all spent, Christ no longer has need for his" (p. 214). And yet Jesus' "need" for words in fact begins only here, after the linguistic differentiation in the desert has secured him the means of his public ministry, and thus the means of restoring mankind. Moreover, by enacting a validation of words, the poem in turn attempts to validate its own medium, the verbal triumph of Jesus substantiating the integrity of language (the verbal body of the poem itself). Silence, put simply, is antithetical to poetry.

[4]Almost all writers on *Paradise Regained* have something to say about the issue of dramatic conflict in the poem, and I will let two prominent critics represent the opposing camps here. Barbara Lewalski, contending that Jesus "is genuinely subject to temptation, able to fall, and capable of growth in understanding" (p. 323), sees the poem as a "dramatic account of the hero's progress toward complete self-realization" (p. 322). Joan Webber, closer to my own position, asserts that "it is difficult to use accurate language with regard to what occurs in Jesus' mind in this poem. This is not a bildungsroman; there is no character development, yet he is in the wilderness for a reason" (p. 199). Lewalski, "Theme and Action in *Paradise Regained*," in *Milton's Epic Poetry: Essays on "Paradise Lost" and "Paradise Regained,"*, ed. C. A. Patrides (Baltimore: Penguin Books, 1967), and Joan Mallory Webber, *Milton and His Epic Tradition* (Seattle: Univ. of Washington Press, 1979).

[5]Two recent articles that explore the Renaissance techniques of Satan's rhetoric are William E. McCarron, "The 'persuasive Rhetoric' of *Paradise Regained*," *MiltonQ* 10 (1976):15-20, and Douglas Wurtele, "'Persuasive

Rhetoric': The Techniques of Milton's Archetypal Sophist," *ESC* 3 (1977):18-33. Several critics have observed more generally the stylistic opposition that informs the debate—Jesus' "ground-style" subduing Satan's "high oratorical style" (Martz, p. 256)—but none have considered the tension generated by both characters' use of the same linguistic raw material and both for the end of persuasion. Stylistic opposition presupposes a shared medium. For discussion of the rhetorical differences involved, see the following: Louis Martz, *Poet of Exile* (New Haven: Yale Univ. Press, 1980), especially pp. 256-57; Northrop Frye, "The Typology of *Paradise Regained*," in *Milton's Epic Poetry*; and most recently, Henry J. Laskowsky, "A Pinnacle of the Sublime: Christ's Victory of Style in *Paradise Regained*", *MiltonQ* 15 (March 1981):10-13.

[6]Mustazza notes that "Satan and Christ go about their work in exactly the same way," "Language as Weapon in Milton's *Paradise Regained*," p. 199.

[7]Webber, p. 171.

[8]Hans Aarsleff, *From Locke to Saussure* (Minneapolis: Univ. of Minnesota Press, 1982), p. 281. Belief in the Adamic language, though still current in some religious and popular circles, largely faded in light of the seventeenth-century rational inquiry into language. The same concern with referentiality became the central issue in a new emphasis on linguistic reformation, largely in the form of the famous debate between *Res* and *Verba*. Theorists such as Hobbes and Bishop Sprat sought to curb the excesses of rhetoric by urging a use of language that clearly and directly expressed only things, not abstractions. As becomes clearer in *Paradise Regained*, Milton needed to place himself between the opposite poles of *Res* and *Verba* in a position that transcended the double bind of this dialectic. The turn away from ornate figuration toward the plain style, clearly reflected in *Paradise Regained*, if pushed to the extreme meant the end of poetry. For Milton to protect the figurative language that was his medium, he needed to find an alternative linguistic formulation to that proposed by the generation that brought on the Royal Society; he did so by implicit recourse to the older, outdated concept of the Adamic language, both literal and figurative, which, as we will see, is redeemed from Babel only through Christ's incarnation. For a brief overview of the word/thing debate in the seventeenth century, see A. C. Howell, "*Res et Verba:* Words and Things," in *Seventeenth-Century Prose: Modern Essays in Criticism*, ed. Stanley Fish (New York: Oxford Univ. Press, 1971), pp. 187-99.

[9]Aarsleff, p. 281.

[10]"Fish, "Things and Actions Indifferent: The Temptation of Plot in *Paradise Regained*," *MiltonS* 17 (1983):165.

[11]Arnold Stein, *Heroic Knowledge* (Hamden, CT: Archon Books, 1965), p. 10. For a similar point of view, see Irene Samuel, who argues that Jesus' "exemplary answers are also detailed. In Milton's version Jesus never merely says NO, much less dismisses what Satan has said as not worth answering because it is Satan who said it"—"The Regaining of Paradise," in *The Prison and the Pinnacle*, ed. Balachandra Rajan (Toronto: Univ. of Toronto Press, 1973), p. 122.

[12]C. A. Patrides, in *Milton and the Christian Tradition* (Oxford: Clarendon Press, 1966), notes that the "common sentiment" of Milton's contemporaries was that the wilderness encounter marked the transition from Christ's private life to the execution of his office (pp. 145-46).

[13]Fish, "Inaction and Silence: The Reader in *Paradise Regained*," p. 39.

[14]Ibid., p. 27.

[15]There is a Christian tradition that links silence to direct, immediate contact with divine reality. Well before the anti-oratorical debate between *Res* and *Verba* in the seventeenth century, Augustine, as Joseph Anthony Mazzeo puts it, advocated that "we must pass, as it were, from the voices of man to the silent voice of God's creation"—"from words to silence, from signs to realities," *Renaissance and Seventeenth-Century Studies* (New York: Columbia Univ. Press, 1964), p. 9. As a poet, Milton clearly cannot defend such a position without self-defeat. By making silence Satan's true verbal nature and expression that of Jesus, he attempts to fuse word and thing in a language of presence that, however tenuous, is necessary for salvaging a medium for action for Jesus in the fallen world, and of equal importance, Milton's own medium.

[16]See the end of Webber's chapter on *Paradise Regained* for an eloquent description of exactly this paradox.

[17]Stuart Curran, "*Paradise Regained:* Implications of Epic," *MiltonS* 17 (1983): 218.

[18]Fish, "Things and Actions Indifferent: The Temptation of Plot in *Paradise Regained*," p. 166.

[19]Lee Sheridan Cox, "Food-Word Imagery in *Paradise Regained*," *ELH* 28(1961):225.

SEL 27 (1987)
ISSN 0039-3657

Recent Studies in the English Renaissance

A. LEIGH DeNEEF

I. Collections

With a few exceptions, 1986 has been dominated by collections proposing a single aim—rewriting the Renaissance. The most obvious advantages of the collection as a medium—the capacity to offer a wide range of often brilliant readings of particular problems and to suggest the variety of ways that theory and practice embrace and contest—may also signal a potential weakness—an inability to sustain rigorous self-analysis. Since the following pages concentrate mainly upon the strengths of the collections, I shall begin with what I sense as their limitations.

Volume 16 of *English Literary Renaissance* marks a turning point: the New Historicism has now been officially entered into scholarly canonicity. Were there any lingering doubts about the power of works by Stephen Greenblatt, Louis Montrose, Richard Helgerson, Jonathan Goldberg, Leah Marcus, and others radically to change the course of Renaissance studies, this issue of *ELR* should resolve them. At the same time, the volume poses two strong challenges. The first appears in Montrose's reflections on "Renaissance Literary Studies and the Subject of History." Montrose argues, after Frank Lentricchia, that the New Historicism is committed to a "multiplicity of 'histories' characterized by 'forces of heterogeneity, contradiction, fragmentation, and difference'" (p. 5). The essays of the year's collections confirm this assertion: they are themselves fragments of a massive revisioning of the Renaissance, and in their various attempts to shatter the myths of a stable world picture or a stable literary canon they also willingly relinquish the desire to replace those structural totalities with any other single "background." To this extent, the short essay would seem the appropriate theoretical form to emphasize

Leigh DeNeef is Associate Professor of English and Associate Dean of the Graduate School at Duke University. He has written *"This Poetick Liturgie"* and *Spenser and the Motives of Metaphor,* as well as a recently completed study, *Traherne in Dialogue: Heidegger, Lacan, and Derrida.*

discontinuity, culture-specific practices, and individual negotiations. But Montrose identifies a second dimension to the New Historical project: "a realization . . . that the critic's own text is as fully implicated in such an interplay [of historical pressures] as are the texts under study" (p. 7). Here again the current collections support Montrose's point: the complexities of gender/power relations, the fearfulness of historical recovery itself, and a skepticism about "literature" as a privileged and autonomous discourse are all marks of our own historical position. And yet these contemporary pressures appear covertly rather than overtly in the various essays. Rewriting the past, it seems, must marginalize historicizing the present.

This point is raised most tellingly in Montrose's distinction between the American practitioners "whose emphasis has been almost exclusively upon a refiguring of the sociocultural field in which Renaissance texts were *originally* produced" and the British practitioners, who have put "a relatively greater emphasis upon the uses to which the *present* has put its versions of the past" (p. 7). It is reiterated by Jean E. Howard, who asks why the New Historicism has been so successful in Renaissance studies. If criticism has grown weary of "teaching texts as ethereal entities floating above the urgencies and contradictions of history" (p. 15), then the resituating of those texts in a problematized, contextualized set of "histories" recovers for the modern critic a paradoxically comfortable image of his own socioliterary condition—his "sense of the exhilaration and fearfulness of living inside a gap in history, when the paradigms that structured the past seem facile and new paradigms uncertain" (p. 17). The failure of New Historicists generally to confront that sympathetic identification with the historical burdens of their Renaissance others may be, to Howard, symptomatic of a deeper evasion: "if literature [now] refers to no ground extrinsic to itself, what can be the nature of its relationship to a historical context or to material reality? In fact, if one accepts certain tendencies in poststructuralist thought, is the possibility of a historical criticism even conceivable?" (pp. 18-19). Both of Howard's charges are serious and they will lead me, in the conclusion, to a further question: are the authority and the power of the current revisions necessarily dependent upon an evasion of, or a certain blindness to, the conditions that enable them? More specifically, would the claims of recovering specific historical enactments be sustained or subverted by fuller engagement with the theoretical and practical pressures upon the contemporary critic? I will return to these issues shortly, but let me turn now to the successes of the new readings.

Rewriting the Renaissance, edited by Margaret Ferguson, Maureen Quilligan, and Nancy Vickers, is the most ambitious and provocative of the year's collections. Divided into three parts, "The Politics of Patriarchy," "The Rhetorics of Marginalization," and "The Works of Women," the volume offers "a dazzling array" of Renaissance discourses of sexual difference. In part one, Jonathan Goldberg reviews a series of family portraits to suggest how patriarchal rhetoric mystifies the gap between nature and power by converting domestic images into ideological metaphors. Although fatherly authority reigns supreme in these figurations, the fissure upon which it builds is itself exposed by the discourses of the various others it must appropriate—wives, daughters, mothers, mortality, bodies. Richard Halperin explores the ways in which the "ghost of maenadism"—a Dionysian revolt of cultural otherness, a gender threat to masculine identity, and a sign of the primary contradictions within the patriarchal puritan family structure—subverts the sexual and political ideology of Milton's *Mask.* Who controls, owns, or deploys feminine sexuality; under what conditions are religious freedom and wifely propriety conflictual; and in what ways are virginity and promiscuity not antitheses but doubles? For Halperin, these tensions arise from "historically specific" class and gender struggles, and they mark the site of the ideological triumph of the *Mask* as Milton forges a domestic, patriarchal, and imperial refiguring of the "home." John Guillory's analysis of the sexual and political divisions of labor in *Samson Agonistes* feeds on and into Halperin's essay. The projection of divorce onto the biblical narrative recontextualizes the sexual difference of Samson and Dalilah as a conflict between two ideological institutions, vocation and marriage. As prototype of bourgeois career drama, *Samson* offers the tragic agon of masculine and feminine bodies over control of both "home" and "civilization" at large.

The middle section of the volume, focused on particular marginalizing consequences of the age's dominant patriarchy, is not as strong as the other two. Carla Freccero sets the polemical tone of the section against modern phallocentric criticism by revealing how blindly it has misread the *impresa* on Gargantua's medallion as a spiritualized and narcissistic androgyne rather than as a monstrous and sexually doubled hermaphrodite. Merry Wiesner and Judith Brown offer more strictly historical recoveries (of spinners and weavers in sixteenth-century Germany; of urban and rural women's work in Tuscany) in order to question both the Marxist models that have been used to explain women's economic status and the general conclusions of earlier feminist studies. Their essays point to the need for the more precise historical research that is attempted in the final section.

Part three tries to articulate specific instances of women both constrained by and subverting the patriarchal dominance. Sheila ffoliott sensitively analyzes how Catherine de' Medici figures herself as Artemisia in order to assume political power in a period of extreme monarchial conflict; Clark Hulse convincingly repositions Stella as a feminine, readerly figure of superior authority in *Astrophil and Stella*; Francois Rigolot explicates Louise Labe's appropriation of authority by an ungrammatical subversion of the male dominated grammar of love; and Ann Jones compares Labe's subversion of the humanist celebrations of poetry as a strictly masculine preserve with Veronica Franco's more dramatic subversion of a masculine rhetoric to announce, affirm, and present her own strident sexuality. These four essays are the real fruit of the volume. Dramatically and specifically, they demonstrate the theoretical and practical achievements of the feminist agenda—both then and now.

Women in the Middle Ages and the Renaissance, edited by Mary Beth Rose, is not as theoretically self-conscious as the previous volume, but it begins its own feminist critique at the same point—Joan Kelly-Gadol's question of whether women had a Renaissance—and it attempts the same kind of historical recovery: by cataloging the defensive strategies that enabled women to participate in public life (Merry Wiesner), by articulating the complex heroics of virginity (Jane Schulenburg), by investigating women accused and punished by branches of the Roman Inquisition (William Monter), and by charting the literary gestures by which women tried to achieve a new sense of selfhood through autobiography and authorship (Janel Mueller). The strongest essays in the volume are by Leah Marcus, Mary Ellen Lamb, Tilde Sankovitch, and Rose herself. Building upon the earlier work of Goldberg, Montrose, Schleiner, and Tennenhouse, Marcus extends the relations between an Elizabeth figured by and within an androgynous sexual rhetoric and the political implications of such layering of gendered self-presentations. She applies these relations to the composite comic heroines of Shakespeare and defines the ways in which the playwright both embodies and sets limits upon the androgyne. Together with Freccero's essay in *Rewriting the Renaissance,* Marcus's helps us reimagine the broader scenario of the complex sexual/political androgyne in the period.

Reiterated scenes of the noble deaths of virtuous women and the act of translating works inscribing those scenes offered a model of heroism that Renaissance women might adopt without seriously challenging the dominant patriarchal ideology. Mary Ellen Lamb pursues this thesis by following the career of Mary Sidney. Paradoxically self-effacing and self-presenting, the Countess's translations of Mornay, Garnier, and Petrarch both capitulate to the sexist culture of the age and promulgate a model of intellectual self-assertiveness that challenges that very capitulation. Like Marcus's essay, Lamb's contributes to a broader project and should be read in conjunction with those by Bornstein, Hannay, and Fisken in the collection I will take up shortly, *Silent But for the Word*.

Tilde Sankovitch compares two French poets, Madeleine and Catheine des Roches, in order to analyze the gestures by which women writers, explicitly alienated from a masculine literary tradition, appropriate authority by reinventing a mythic origin. Whether such invention takes the form of rewriting traditional myths or establishing new ones, both mother and daughter adapt the mythological terms to their own sexual realities and suffer the fragmentation of self made inevitable by the challenge they try to mount.

The kind of tension Sankovitch reveals in the poetry of the Dames des Roches reappears in Rose's essay on the autobiographies of Mary Cavendish, Lady Halkett, Lady Fanshawe, and Alice Thornton. Rose's analysis assumes that the civil war upset, for these royalist ladies, the sexual and political hegemony of their previously male-dominated world, and that despite the moral injunctions against feminine self-expression, the developing genre of secular autobiography provided a perfect form for the women to dramatize and attempt to overcome the conflicting aspects of their historical situation. Adopting Elaine Showalter's notion of women's writing as a "double-voiced discourse," Rose tries to disclose the dominant and muted strains of the autobiographies her four women have written. Their failures to reconcile those strains produce the dilemmas and negotiations that will come to characterize this particular genre.

Silent But for the Word, edited by Margaret P. Hannay, also focuses on the problematic scene of Renaissance women writers. The book's theoretical challenge is set by its concluding essay, Gary F. Waller's "Struggling into Discourse: The Emergence of Renaissance Women's Writing." Waller's thesis is that most of the work done on women remains trapped within the dominant critical paradigms of a masculine profession. "The insistence that we analyze what is in the words of the text, the valorization of the perceivable, the pictorial, the 'images' of women" are all indications of this entrapment. Waller calls, therefore, for more attention to absences, silences, and constraints, to the suppression of opposing voices, to the struggle to articulate a new sexuality. What is it like, Waller asks us to ask, "to read and be read, to write and be written, as a woman" (p. 256)?

On the whole, the essays of the volume do not measure up to Waller's idealistic program. Most are more narrowly (old?) historicist even as they seek to revise conventional historical accounts. An exception to this generalization is Anne Lake Prescott's sensitive interpretation of Marguerite de Navarre's *Miroir* as translated by the young Elizabeth and presented to her stepmother, Catherine Parr. Prescott's account, which ranges from the Erasmian and Reformist reinforcement that Catherine and her circle would have seen in the translation, to the diplomatic uses to which Marguerite herself might be put by the Tudor court, and to Elizabeth's puzzling and at times startling deviations from Marguerite's text, offers tantalizing glimpses into the psychological pressures of Elizabeth's youth.

Equally provocative is Elaine V. Beilin's study of "Anne Askew's Self-Portrait" in the two *Examinations* which recount her imprisonment and interrogation by the Henrician counter-reformists. By reading Askew's own *Examinations* against John Bale's interlinear "Elucydacyon," Beilin is able to compare the way a mid-century woman fashioned herself and the way a sympathetic propagandist refashioned her. Her conclusion—that Askew's own conflicts in being both a supposedly weak, silent, and domestic woman and a courageous, disputatious, and strong martyr are consistently flattened or unproblematized by Bale—is at once a historical illustration of the constraints Renaissance patriarchy imposed upon women and a forceful transhistorical dramatization of the failure of masculine criticism to hear the authentic voice of its other.

The most aggressive essay in the volume is Mary Ellen Lamb's study of the four daughters of Anthony Cooke. With the exceptions of Queen Elizabeth and the Countess of Pembroke, these sisters were the most prolific women writers of the time. Lamb examines, therefore, the several translations they undertook and, as she had in the essay on Mary Sidney already noted, how deeply translation itself was fractured by simultaneously licensing the feminine voice and marginalizing it as derivative, imitative, secondary. The misogyny Lamb uncovers is seen best in Florio's remark that "all translations are reputed femalls" and consequently "defective." The feminist writing in these three collections is a clear rebuttal to any remaining Florios.

In comparison with *Rewriting the Renaissance,* Patricia Parker and David Quint's *Literary Theory/Renaissance Texts* is not as successful. Not because the essays here are weaker, but because the volume seems split in half. John Freccero, Eugenio Donato, Thomas

Greene, Terence Cave, Rene Girard are all perceptive and sophisticated critics who have set the stage for the current critical scene; but they are not the protagonists of this scene. Stephen Greenblatt, Richard Halperin, Derek Attridge, Louis Montrose, Mary Nyquist, and Victoria Kahn have stolen the play. Their writing here is consistently more interesting and more provocative, more capable, I think, of establishing the future direction of Renaissance studies.

In "Psychoanalysis and Renaissance Culture," Greenblatt returns to his now familiar notion of "the social fabrication of identity," but with a vigorous twist: the bafflement of psychoanalysis by texts that at once invite and elude the method. Greenblatt's test case is *The Return of Martin Guerre,* which he deploys in a cogent attempt to re-historicize psychoanalysis itself. Derek Attridge's "Puttenham's Perplexity: Nature, Art, and the Supplement in Renaissance Poetic Theory" and Patricia Parker's further explorations of "Deferral, Dilation, and Differance" are part of a broader deconstructionist project. Whether they are treating the problematics of "decorum" in Puttenham or narrative dilation in Shakespeare, both are making crucial steps towards a pragmatic application of one of the most profound insights of Jacques Derrida. Montrose's "The Elizabethan Subject and the Spenserian Text" is, like all of his recent essays, richly suggestive, convincing as far as it goes, and frustrating in its self-prescribed limits. Montrose's explications of the collective discourses produced by and producing the images of royal power are among the most brilliant being written today. Here he shows how Spenser's text both represents the Queen and foregrounds its own act of doing so. Montrose thus reopens questions of the subject and his subjection, the acceptance of subjection as the necessary but anxious ground of subjectivity itself, and the "paradoxical celebrations of power that, in making the poem serve the queen, make the queen serve the poem" (p. 332).

The final two essays in the volume, by Mary Nyquist and Victoria Kahn, are specific challenges to modern criticism. Nyquist uses the history of (male) criticism of Milton's Dalilah as an illustration of a normative misogyny which tradition transmits through literary history. Kahn, working between early humanists like Castiglione and Erasmus and modern followers like Paul de Man, argues that a deep-seated resistance to literary theory and the attempt to avoid theory by commitment to practice is a complex transhistorical evasion involving Renaissance author and modern interpreter.

With Barbara Kiefer Lewalski's collection on *Renaissance Genres* we seem to shift methodological ground. Although Earl Miner opens this volume by questioning the appropriateness of various generic terms, for the most part the essays here rechart familiar territory. I do not mean that the essays are unrewarding: Mary Crane's reinterpretation of the epigram in terms of its appropriations of authority, Janel Mueller's study of how Milton politicizes the sonnet, and Annabel Patterson's shrewd analysis of the ideological tensions embedded in Virgilian quotations and allusions are incisive and convincing readings. What I do mean is that the terms which have motivated genre criticism for the last fifty or sixty years reappear here with an unexamined predictability. There is, of course, no theoretical reason why genre study should not contribute to the tasks of contemporary practice, yet such historical problematizing of genre as we tend to do seems largely grounded in a naive faith in historical recovery and in a mode of analysis which privileges both determinate text and determinate context.

Two other collections merit more attention than I can give them. *The Vulnerable Text* brings together a series of important essays published over the last sixteen years by Thomas Greene. The collection offers a unique perspective on how one of our most perceptive and wide-ranging Renaissance scholars has developed in response to new theories, new conceptions of the burdens of history, and new sophistication in charting Renaissance intertextualities. The same point could be made about Volumes Two and Three of *The Collected Essays of Christopher Hill.* The sheer number of citations to Hill's landmark historical work in all the volumes published this year testifies to the tremendous influence he has had and continues to have on contemporary historical/literary study. With these volumes, the reissue of Hill's essays is complete and offers a marvelous survey of his persistent exploration of the counterforces of the period. No scholar writing today can afford to remain unfamiliar with this work.

II. Sixteenth-Century Studies

The mere appearance of Gary Waller's *English Poetry of the Sixteenth Century* should shock most readers into realizing that we have not seen a general history of the period in over thirty years (Smith's *Elizabethan Poetry* appeared in 1952; Evans's *English Poetry in the Sixteenth Century* in 1955). The changes in both historical perceptions and critical vocabularies that have occurred in those years will be apparent to anyone who rereads the opening chapters of Evans's study against those of Waller's. Where Evans emphasized the idealism and optimism of the age's sundry humanists and the successful fusions of its great poets, Waller stresses dislocations and disruptions, the private anxieties and the ideological struggles that continuously fracture various texts. Where Evans sees in the poetry a steady progress of philosophical, moral, and literary authority, Waller sees a "promiscuous riot of *ecriture*" being steadily marginalized and restricted by other modes of discourse.

What the two histories share, of course, is the need to make sixteenth-century poetry relevant to the dominant critical vocabularies of the day. Waller is frank about this intent, aligning his history with the concurrent work of Sinfield, Dollimore, Goldberg, Greenblatt, and Montrose, as well as with Jameson, Eagleton, Althusser, and Foucault. The result is a lively, challenging, and fairly sweeping revision of preceding histories and a general application of New Historicist concerns to the entire period. There are a number of provocative insights throughout the individual chapters Waller devotes to the lyric, to four representative court poets, to three Sidneys, to Spenser's *Faerie Queene*, and to Shakespeare and early Donne. While the constraints of writing a history place severe limits on the details Waller has time to marshal, he does manage to summarize those questions that modern criticism has found most useful and to extend their implications across the century. That very extension, of course, pays a certain price: more often than not, arguments about the cultural dynamics of the poetry derive from a predetermined critical objective rather than the texts under question. And this tendency toward generalization is at times surprisingly blind to its own assumptions. "One important function of the literary text—perhaps . . . what constitutes 'greatness' in a work—is that of bringing out the multiplicity, contradictions, and tensions that a dominant ideology tries to ignore or cover over" (p. 11); "the most interesting poetry of the whole period is written in the last twenty years of the century precisely because it is torn among conflicting ideological pressures that fracture its apparent serenity" (p. 29). "Precisely because" is the mark of *our* appropriation.

If appropriation is inescapable in any literary history, the more crucial question is whether such histories identify the major areas of critical concern and provide their readers with appropriate vocabularies to conduct further study. In these terms Waller's history is long overdue and extremely successful. To the extent that it becomes required reading for classes on the Renaissance, our own courses will be saved a considerable amount of "background" preparation and should be able to expect a much fuller sophistication.

Peter Ruppert's *Reader in a Strange Land* tries to bring contemporary theory to bear upon Utopian literature generally and More's work in particular. This literature, he assumes, must be reclaimed from widespread scholarly disdain and reinvested with the power to disturb and defamiliarize the reader's sense of his world. Utopian literature, then, must be seen as dialogic in nature, forcing the reader to recognize the contradictions between what is and what might be, between historical necessity and social possibility. Behind Ruppert's generalizations lies Iser's notions of reader response, but the readerly model gives rise to some strange consequences. If "each reading imposes its own interests and priorities and relates the text to its own framework of significance" (p. 79), Utopia would seem necessarily deprived of any power to defamiliarize. Similarly, if the apparent inconsistencies and contradictions of social constructs are intensified rather than resolved by genuine Utopian literature, Ruppert's reader seems to respond to this awareness not by political or historical action but by imagining fictive Utopian alternatives. To argue that "the reader becomes the strategic site at which the political and fictional forms of discourse converge" (p. 89) is fair enough, but Ruppert has not sufficiently mapped the relations between that reader's dialectical relation to the text and his ability to project that relation forward to his own political future.

To the extent that Donne has been accepted as the model of an energetic and radical Renaissance lyricism, criticism has tended to favor Wyatt over Surrey. In an attempt to reclaim for Surrey his due regard as an innovator and experimenter, William A. Sessions's *Henry Howard, Earl of Surrey* offers a brief analysis of every poem we can be sure Surrey wrote. The strategy, I think, has serious flaws, for *explication de texte,* while gesturing occasionally towards a given poem's intertextual confrontation with tradition and its embeddedness in the complex personal history of Surrey himself, cannot recover adequately the vitality Sessions sees here. If, as Sessions argues, Surrey's art develops from "a special awareness of self operating in time and history" and therefore illustrates a textual "interplay between his life, his self-perception, and the formal resources of the communal language he is reshaping" (pp. 20-21), then it merits a more comprehensive account than Sessions has time to provide.

In the sixteen years since Walter Davis's *Idea and Act in Elizabethan Fiction,* our understanding of the issues and complexities of Renaissance rhetorical theory has increased dramatically. So too has our sense of the deep conflicts scarring the entire humanist project. No one, however, has attempted to bring these new awarenesses to bear upon the fascinating line of prose fiction from More to Nashe and Lodge. Arthur F. Kinney's *Humanist Poetics,* therefore, answers to a real scholarly need by offering a massive revision of the development of Renaissance fiction. Kinney has long been one of the most outspoken proponents of a specifically humanist poetic. Radically and at the same time nervously committed to a rhetoric of persuasion, that poetic both articulates the age's most idealistic reformative hopes and establishes the intellectual conditions of its most troubling fears. In the present set of perceptive, often brilliant, readings of the period's major prose works, Kinney delivers the fuller demonstration of his argument. His history, therefore, is actually two: of the central conflicts within rhetorical theory that were initially submerged within an optimistic programme of humanistic education and reform only to reappear with an urgency that brought its practitioners to doubt and despair; of the central anxieties within fiction itself that both enabled its sudden emergence in the sixteenth century and led, by the century's close, to its demise. Although Kinney's own eloquent and learned wit will certainly revitalize the study and the teaching of this prose, I am not as optimistic about his larger project of reclaiming for the fiction a central place in the literary canon of the period. Certainly More and Sidney will continue to hold their own, but I doubt that Gascoigne, Lyly, Greene, Nashe, or Lodge can be retrieved on Kinney's terms. The grounds of the argument are too academic, too abstract, and not as socially specific as competing reclamations.

Jonathan Crewe argued some time ago that Thomas Nashe reflects a late Elizabethan crisis in which rhetoric loses faith in itself. Stephen Hilliard's *The Singularity of Thomas Nashe* tries to resituate that insight (now corroborated by Kinney) within the historical contexts and the conflicting ideological pressures of the 1590s. Caught between a desire to champion the ideals of court humanism and a compulsion to expose the social discontents of the alienated, Nashe's "singularity" is at once an ironic literary defense and a self-defeating rhetorical stance. Hilliard's analysis of all Nashe's work is important and compelling: it offers another dramatic illustration of the conflicts at work in even the marginal literature of the period.

Few Renaissance scholars would deny the intricate relations between music and poetry in the period, but far fewer have been able to analyze those relations in any precise way. What are the general features of each art that come into play when they are joined in song? What distinctive resources of each art must be sacrificed in order to achieve an ideal union? How can we begin to chart the history of the initial separation of music and poetry in the sixteenth century and the compromises which reunite them at the end of that century and into the next? These are some of the issues, both practical and theoretical, that Edward Doughtie tries to clarify in *English Renaissance Song*. The study represents an important supplement to Doughtie's earlier work and a reminder of how much remains to be done in this complex and difficult field. Doughtie poses crisply and efficiently the significant theoretical problems of assessing the sometimes conflicting, sometimes cooperating demands of each art upon the other, and his treatments of Whythorne, Byrd, Morley, Dowland, and Campion should serve as models for any such analysis.

III. Sidney, Spenser, Shakespeare, and Milton

Sidney studies are well served by publication of two books, Arthur F. Kinney's collection of *Essential Articles* and Robert E. Stillman's *Sidney's Poetic Justice*. Although Kinney, like previous editors of this useful series, laments the restrictions space imposes upon his choices, he has managed to bring together a fully representative survey of modern approaches to Sidney. From Hardison to Barnes on the *Defence*, from Stillinger and Hamilton to Williamson on *Astrophil and Stella*; from Greenlaw to Sinfield on the *Arcadia*, the volume not only defines the "essential" grounds of traditional Sidneian criticism, but allows the reader to follow the opening of Sidney's texts to newer, often conflicting interpretive models. My only reservations are two: that the more radical deconstructive approaches to the *Defence* have been omitted (Ferguson's and Levao's, for example), and that the section on *Astrophil and Stella* does not capture the intensity of the interpretive debate this sequence continues to evoke.

Robert Stillman shares with much recent criticism the belief that Sidney sought in his fiction deliberate remedies for the misfortunes of life in a corrupt age; he disagrees, however, with most of that criticism that the fiction fails to provide what the poet seeks. In Stillman's view, the *Old Arcadia* dramatizes distinct versions of the idle pastoral life and, largely through the eclogues, shapes a moral and aesthetic performance of intellectual judgment which erects a contented foundation for happy active life. The poet imitates his shepherd-critics by reinterpreting and selecting from the traditional materials of the genre the historical grounds of his own aesthetic, moral, and social values. Thus locating his own place in history, the poet makes available to the reader an equally moral and aesthetic judgment upon the necessary historical choices of *his* situation.

The middle section of Stillman's study is the fullest analysis yet of the eclogues in the *Old Arcadia* and the kinds of escape they offer from the moral dilemmas of the prose narrative. Stillman argues that the eclogues clarify, by separating out, the mental conditions of Sidney's characters; force us, by the absence of a narrator, to make our own judgments on rival points of view; and remove both characters and readers from a realm of contingent and consequential action to one of moral ideas and abstraction. As this summary might suggest, there is a fundamental contradiction between the timeless, plotless, actionless world of the eclogues and the real readerly activity Stillman wants to install there. The eclogues, he tells us, are a kind of pastoral-within-the-pastoral, "what might be called a reader's paradise" (p. 94), which releases us from the existential conflicts exposed in the narratives and presents in their place lyric images of wholeness and stability. This argument depends upon too fine a distinction between the book's prose and its verse, and too idealistic a conception of poetry itself. The prose narratives *must* fail because they are *necessarily* limited; only the poetry of the eclogues can supply "due balance." Euarchus's justice fails *because* it is constrained by a narrative plot; only the poet has the sensibility to correct it. It is difficult to see how Stillman's desire to resituate both the poet and his readers in a contemporary history can possibly survive such literary quietism.

Kenneth Gross's *Spenserian Poetics* is one of the best and most provocative books of the year. It represents a brilliant compression of a number of key insights into Spenser's complex imaginative anxieties that have been developed in recent years, and its own terms will offer, I would guess, fruitful ground for study in years to come. Gross's Spenser is profoundly antimythological and antiallegorical; deeply skeptical of the "place and power of such structures of order as myth, custom, and law" (p. 81); and intensely committed to the "master trope" of *aporia,* or "the doubtful," a figure that "entails the multiplication within a discourse of such a variety of alternative perspectives as to call into question . . . any divisive choice among those alternatives" (p. 82). Gross's task is not to find an accurate name for this displaced, diffused, and demystifying poetic, but to create a conceptual grammar by which its antithetical gestures might be analyzed. He locates that grammar in the complex relations of iconoclasm, idolatry, and magic.

If iconoclasm can stand metaphorically for the urgency of the imagination to break up and to break away from, to dismantle and to cut off, to unfix and unfigure, then idolatry forms its conceptual, grammatical other: the urge to build up and commit to, to conclude and to sew up, to refigure and define. Idolatry is, therefore, a form of false writing and false reading whereas iconoclasm is a radical hermeneutic of suspicion. And yet, as Gross's sophisticated analysis of New Testament revisionism demonstrates, the rhetoric of iconoclasm is constantly being threatened by its own drives toward remythologizing. Iconoclastic rhetoric "thus tends to sustain even as it empties out the realm of the demonic and the idolatrous" (p. 56). The third term in Gross's lexicon, magic, is less clear to me, but I take it to represent a conceptual site in which the polarities of enchantment and disenchantment, sanctity and sacrilege, grace and disgrace, prophecy and history, mythologizing and demythologizing are sustained and energized by the mysterious power of Spenser's unique poetics. Gross puts each of his three terms into play in a fascinating reading of the skeptical urgencies that run throughout *A View of the Present State of Ireland.* It is a brilliant strategy, at once grounding the remainder of the book in an otherwise underdeveloped historical context and at the same time locating in Spenser's ironic account of Ireland as a land enchanted by mythology and illusion his more personal antipathy to "structures of deception," especially to the false authorities of custom, folklore, superstition, and language itself.

The major portion of the book is devoted to selected incidents in *The Faerie Queene.* Chapter 3 deals with Orgoglio and Arthur, the former an "iconoclastic idolater," the latter a mystified demystifier; chapter 4 treats Britomart's mirror and threshold as exposing the idolatrous dynamics of the quest itself; chapter 5 focuses on the Garden of Adonis as a defense against idolatry, iconoclasm, and allegory; and chapter 6 isolates moments of special and dangerous fragility (the vision of the Graces, the escape of the Blatant Beast, the Faunus episode) in which Spenser's anxieties, his presumptions, and his self-consciousness are particularly evident.

To some readers, Gross's selection of incidents will appear purely arbitrary and scattered; others may find his analyses of literal scenes of either idolatry or iconoclasm the least impressive moments in the argument. But the argument itself and the terms Gross employs are remarkably effective in delineating the burdens of "a poet who both embraces and fears mythology, whose visionary quests come into conflict with a manifold skepticism of vision" (p. 9).

Robert F. Gleckner's *Blake and Spenser* continues the intertextual project begun in *Blake's Prelude.* Not all of this massive study will be of interest to Spenserians: the first three chapters especially are extremely difficult for anyone not thoroughly familiar with all of Blake. Gleckner's intent here is to chart the "significant allusions" to Spenser which lace the Blakean text, but that sketch is only preparatory to posing the larger questions of whether, to what extent, and on what grounds Blake saw Spenser as "redeemable." At issue is Blake's consistent antagonism toward "systems," towards any fixing of ideas in the permanent forms of mind-forged allegories. Blake finds in Spenser, of course, frequent systems and allegories, but he also discovers, according to Gleckner, a vision that needed to be freed from its allegorical entrapments. Blake thus reads Spenser against himself in order to deallegorize the allegory or "unspell" the Spenserian enchantment from its own literary fantasies.

In the fourth chapter, "Calling and Naming," Gleckner isolates the site of this Blakean move in Spenser's characters—in the fact that, to Blake, those characters were both minutely particular and at the same time constantly shifting identities. Calling and naming thus chart a dialectical process by which "character" both is and is not, assumes "substance" and resolves into "form," takes on and puts off various fleshly and verbal veils. Upon this fundamental fluidity, Gleckner erects three chapters of intensive analysis of Blake's painting, *The Characters in Spenser's "Faerie Queene."* For anyone who has tried to puzzle out the possible meanings in this difficult painting, Gleckner's treatment is dazzling. He leaves no character, accoutrement, animal, building, or shade unturned—turned, moreover, against Blake's painting of the Canterbury pilgrims, against Spenser's romance, against Blakean analogues, against alternative readings of and within the painting itself. As the cogs of Gleckner's interpretive wheel turn against the cogs of Blake's turning against the cogs of Spenser's adverse wheel, he marshals an important critique not only on traditional conceptions of Spenser's characters, but also on traditional conceptions of his allegorical technique. Such intertextual complexity may unsettle many Spenserians, but the questions Blake, and Gleckner, pose are serious ones. Where and to what extent did Spenser work against his own vision; where and to what extent is his poetic in conflict with itself; where and to what extent is his romance an "antiallegorical allegory"? Obviously these questions are similar to those posed by Gross. I take that congruence, in fact, to represent not only a surprising confirmation of Gross's project, but an affirmation that Gleckner too has much to offer the serious student of Spenser.

David R. Shore's *Spenser and the Poetics of Pastoral* shares at least one of Stillman's concerns in the *Arcadia:* the relation between pastoral contentment and judgment. They part company, however, when Shore argues that while the eclogue may dramatize conflicting moral positions, it is unable to resolve them on any authoritative moral grounds. The "moral" eclogues of *The Shepheardes Calender* consistently stage the competing claims of country and city, self and society, pleasure and duty. Just as consistently, they affirm both sides of these claims by denying any common ground between them or any reconciliation. Where resolution is achieved, it is always by virtue of an extra-pastoral mode such as the fable. To this extent, Shore absolutely reverses Stillman's argument.

If this approach seems generally driven by a version of pastoral similar to that of Andrew Ettin, it is directed against such versions as Patrick Cullen's. Shore's analysis of the "recreative" eclogues supports this impression. In each eclogue Colin must accept his lot with a stoical contentment, for to do otherwise would mean the loss of pastoral altogether. In "December," for example, Colin accepts the losses love occasions and thereby "preserves" his pastoral world. The *Calender*, in this argument, "is essentially static, the unfolding of an image rather than the development of an argument" (p. 102). There is a real pessimism at the core of this argument: Shore's pastoral succeeds only insofar as it denies the very moral choices it raises. Shore's analyses of *Colin Clout* and Book VI of *The Faerie Queene* define renunciation as the pastoral poet's characteristic act. Renunciation is not without recognition, of course, but such knowledge as pastoral offers is simply that the demands of poetry are entirely distinct from those of public life. We are a far cry here from the arguments of recent scholars, like Annabel Patterson, that pastoral is continuously fraught with ideological and political engagements.

Steven Marx, in *Youth Against Age: Generational Strife in Renaissance Poetry,* covers much the same ground as Shore, although his study is not limited to Spenser and his interests are more psychological. Pastoral, to Marx, is a rejection of middle age and the civic anxieties of procreation, custodianship, ambition, wealth, and power. Youth and old age, both marginalized by that rejection, remain to fight over control of the pastoral oasis. Each, of course, is both a positive and a negative image, with the characteristics of each side carefully balanced by antitheses on the other. Marx suggests that the medieval dialectical model such strife gives rise to—proposal, counterproposal, and rebuttals to each—remains the essential form of Elizabethan pastoral. Applying his model to *The Shepheardes Calender,* Marx argues that the poem uses the central debates of youth and age to chart the maturation of Immerito, Spenser's conception of individual growth and integrity: a self that is fashioned, over time, by assimilating and unifying the youth-age mentalities always debating within it. Like Shore's, Marx's pastoral is a highly romanticized mode; unlike Shore's, Marx's pastoral must itself be rejected in order to get on with real, historical work.

"Edmund Spenser," according to Thomas Hyde, was "the last major poet to make Cupid's theology a sustaining fiction and the one whose works comprehend nearly all the phases of Cupid's career and bring it to culmination" (p. 72). *The Poetic Theology of Love* attempts, therefore, to chart this career from the middle ages through the Renaissance and to bring its history to bear on Spenser's poetry. The task is complicated from the beginning, for Hyde is not after "the myriad of works of art in every age that use Cupid ornamentally, frivolously, or facilely," but only those in which Cupid's divinity is taken seriously. One might think that distinction difficult enough, but Hyde makes it even more problematic, for "to use Cupid's divinity seriously is . . . to question whether it is a fact, a figure of speech or a delusive fiction" (p. 20). I take this to mean that only works which question Cupid's uncertain ontology can be said to embody a theology. And yet that theology is always torn between idolatry and iconoclasm (*pace* Gross), mythologizing and demystifying. A theodicy of Cupid, in short, is a scene of literary anxiety, for both the author and the reader.

The essential stages in Cupid's career are three: Capellanus's *De amore*, by appropriating the authority of scripture, makes interpretation of Cupid a moral problem; Dante and Petrarch dramatize the internal struggle to distinguish between a Cupid fashioned by an obsessive passion deifying itself and an allegorical Cupid who represents divine reformation; Ficino makes Cupid simultaneously divine and human. In the final two chapters Hyde turns to Spenser, who, he argues, never treats Cupid as a mere passion of the mind and who tries throughout his career to erect a poetic gospel that will, paradoxically, both affirm Cupid's divinity and subsume that fiction within the religion of a real God. Unfortunately, Hyde rarely shows in his analyses of Spenser the sophistication of his treatment of, say, Dante, and while his conclusion—that Spenser's iconoclasm leads him to acknowledge that the poetic theology of love can never be anything other than a pious fiction or an enthralling idolatry (p. 175)—seems reasonable enough, these chapters do not reveal the anxiety that energizes Spenser's negotiations with the various Cupids tradition offers him.

Like the year's work on Spenser, that on Shakespeare is headed by another brilliant book, Joel Fineman's *Shakespeare's Perjured Eye*. Fineman's study begins with the assumption that Shakespeare's sonnets inherit the debts of a bankrupt poetic tradition, a Petrarchan poetics of praise which renders poetic subjectivity increasingly artificial at the same time as the sonneteering poet becomes increasingly self-conscious. It is precisely in understanding and foregrounding those debts that Shakespeare "invents" the only kind of literary subjectivity that can survive the demise of this tradition. The key strains of Fineman's argument are not easy to disentangle, but these seem to be the crucial ones: that the rhetoric of praise is paradoxical and circular, inscribing upon the ego of the praising poet the ideal ego of the praised other; that the poetic "I," insofar as it must thematize a "speaking eye," reenacts the differences between mimesis and metaphor, vision and language; and that difference as such is the "invention" of erotic desire and subjectivity. Obviously these are very large issues and they commit Fineman to a massive revisionist project which involves reconceiving the history of epideictic rhetoric, the poetic traditions of mimesis, the duplicitous otherness of language, and the inevitable fragmentations of a psychological self.

The essential ground of Fineman's analysis is a conventional division of the sonnets into two sub-sequences. Sonnets 1-126, the young man's sonnets, are shaped by historical epideixis: they tend to derive similarity out of difference; the poet's primary mode is visual; and his "I" is an idealized identification with the object of his gaze. The opening sonnets, therefore, are compelled by the motives and the language of mimesis: simulacra, eidola, reproduction, representation. Sonnets 127-54, the dark lady sonnets, derive difference and identity out of similarity. The dark lady poems are radically verbal and their language cross-couples and decouples the mimetic idealizations of the opening subsequence into paradox, difference, lying. The "I" is here a scene of the burdens of this lost ideal and identification, as well as of the generation of subjective desire. Like everything in this extremely difficult book, such distinctions do not remain as uncomplicated as summary might suggest. If Fineman initially distinguishes the young man's sonnets from the dark lady ones, it is only finally to re-complicate the rhetoric of each in the sight and language of the other. What concerns Fineman most is the way Shakespeare is able to thematize the disjunctures the two subsequences merely represent.

Chapter by frequently repetitive chapter Fineman complicates the metacritical scene. The progress of the sonnets acts out a succession of opposites which initially seems purely downward: from truth to falsity, from fair to foul, from vision to speech, from man to woman. Yet that progress is deceptive, for the young man's sonnets are already fractured by a binary indeterminacy self-conscious of its own rhetorical gestures. And the way the young man's poet consistently points to the difference between his first and second persons initiates a divided subjectivity that motivates all epideictic poetry—between, that is, a panegyric signifier and a panegyrized signified. The poet's self is this division: temporally and psychologically, that rupture both constitutes and circumscribes the poet's "I."

Fineman's analysis, then, shows what happens to poetic subjectivity when "a language of visionary presence is replaced and displaced by a language of verbal" re-presentation (p. 297). His concern is to make palpable "this sense of literary belatedness, of poetic secondariness, of literary repetition" (p. 244). In the material textuality of such losses, desire arises as "the transgressive troping or returning of traditional ideality" (p. 271). This argument, needless to say, is abstract in the extreme, but its density is everywhere grounded in the cross-coupled language of Shakespeare's text and the interpretive difficulties that criticism has always had with that text. Whether Fineman is convincing in his largest claim about the uniqueness of Shakespeare's "invention," no study of subjectivity within *any* Renaissance poet can afford to avoid his argument.

Although as aggressive and relentless as Fineman's study, Joseph Pequigney's *Such Is My Love* is of a wholly different order. The sonnets, he tells us, must be retrieved from the protectionism that has motivated traditional criticism and kept us from recognizing them as the grand masterpiece of homoerotic poetry. The primary strategy for this retrieval is a persistent quest after bawdy innuendoes licensed by the *OED*, E. A. M. Coleman, and Eric Partridge. Like its only begetters, the book is burdened by a "phallacious" logic that constantly equates "can mean" with "obviously does mean." It is not, finally, the belaboring of homosexuality that undermines Pequigney's treatment, but the fact that his analysis forecloses further discussion. Its claims are either too obviously reductive or largely irrelevant to wider critical demands. The reader should compare Pequigney's treatment of Sonnet 20 to Fineman's analysis of how an excessively developed sexualized vocabulary points to the more challenging issue of how the poet materializes and validates desire as such.

In the context of the revisionary feminism of the year's several collections, Stevie Davies's *The Feminine Reclaimed* cannot avoid seeming reactionary. Davies is herself conscious of this fact and careful to make clear that she is concerned with a humanistic, Platonic Idea of woman, not with historically situated gender conflicts. Her thesis is that in the late Renaissance, and particularly in the works of Spenser, Shakespeare, and Milton, the idea of woman is revalued upwards as "an essential constituent part of the God-reflecting universe" (p. 6). Reclamation in this sense is cognate with faith in a divine feminine principle, most often figured in an Orphic androgyne. Davies's arguments about her three poets draw on many of the Neoplatonic commonplaces of traditional criticism, but absent from them are the anxieties and fragmentations that criticism has illuminated. A particularly stunning illustration is Davies's gloss on the cancelled conclusion to *Faerie Queene* III: Amoret and Scudamore "melt into one another's nature—Herm/Aphrodite—until there are no raw edges left, but a sense of almost chemical wholeness" (p. 102). That slash, however, can hardly be read today outside the burdens of a Derridean or Lacanian differance; that Spenser himself cuts the stanzas can only problematize the "sense of . . . wholeness" Davies would have us see.

The theme of the foundling, Barbara L. Estrin argues in *The Raven and the Lark,* embraces many of the central burdens of the Renaissance: the need to know a historical ancestry in order to have a future dynasty; the need to sublimate the social guilt over wardship and apprenticeship into a fantasy of societal reform; the need to affirm the irreplaceability of the individual in an indifferent world. Estrin proposes to explore these anxieties by demonstrating how the "lost-child plot" shapes various works of Malory, Spenser, Sidney, and Shakespeare. The plot itself becomes paradigmatic: the child faces an initial shock of alienation, is rescued and nurtured in an "artistic" adoptive interlude, and is reunited with family and society in a "natural" affirmation of providence. The formulaic nature of this plot is Estrin's major problem, for the texts are too quickly forced into a constrained model. The anxieties she identifies are important ones, but the model she articulates is not adequate to exploring them.

In a version of the *humilitas* trope, Cedric C. Brown calls his study of *John Milton's Aristocratic Entertainments* a "sympathetic imaginative reconstruction" (p. 102). In fact, it is much more, for what is "reconstructed" here are the social occasions for which *Arcades* and *Comus* were originally produced and subsequently published, as well as Milton's developing sense of his political/religious/poetic vocation between 1631 and 1637. Brown argues that Milton's "entertainments are peculiarly, and in the end problematically, reformist in intent" (p. 2), that rather than merely rehearsing the social ideals of the noble class, they prescribe an idealistic reformation of that class.

The central portions of Brown's book provide the fullest account yet of the historical situations of the Dowager Countess of Derby and the Earl of Bridgewater's second visit to Ludlow as President of the Council in Wales. In addition to this historical reconstruction, Brown marshals a convincing argument that the emblematic and mythological sources usually imported to explicate difficult figures or ideas in the entertainments are not as appropriate as etymological and literary sources. The primary example is a complex of associations involving *komos* (to revel), *komazein* (revelling) and *komastes* (revellers). Beginning with the "proof-text" of Romans 13.12-13, Brown shows how the very form of the masque could be seen by even the young Milton as less a moral celebration of aristocratic virtue than a tangible symbol of aristocratic moral laxity. In both entertainments, Milton focuses on the necessity of proper spiritual education for the welfare of the nation as a whole. The voice of the true poet joins those of reformed parents and real pastors in furthering that education. In many ways Brown's study is a model of historical recovery and it makes a substantial contribution to the growing body of work on these entertainments.

Paul Stevens's *Imagination and the Presence of Shakespeare in "Paradise Lost"* is a different project, but no less successful. His primary thesis is that the educated imagination is, for Milton, the peculiar instrument of grace, "the psychological mechanism by which we come to faith" (pp. 5-6). The secondary thesis is that Milton found in Shakespeare a shadowy literary type of this truth and that the echoes and allusions in *Paradise Lost* confirm this. Stevens begins by tracing a few of the parallels between *The Tempest* and *Comus* in order to distinguish between "modes of fancy": ungoverned or governed by reason, autonomously creative or cooperatively reflective. The highest mode, he argues, is an icastic or figurative imagination which, in harmony with rather than in opposition to reason, becomes both the ground and evidence of faith. The second part of the book pursues Shakespearean allusions in order to distinguish the operations and failures of Satan's imagination from the successes of the Son's. The third part traces the implications of proper and improper, trained and unconstrained imaginations on the problems and progress of Adam and Eve. Stevens demonstrates how fantasy enables them to apprehend more than cool reason can comprehend and how they represent Milton's celebration of the grace that lifts "Human imagination to such hight/ Of Godlike Power." Stevens's argument is not so much a presentation of novel insights as a judicious marshalling of sustained and resonant echoes—not only from Shakespeare, but also from the best of previous Milton criticism.

"The language of sonship," writes Hugh MacCallum, "is pervasive in Protestantism" (p. 3) as well as in the works of John Milton. *Milton and the Sons of God* is an account of Milton's efforts to develop a coherent and original position on the controversial nature of sonship and to transform that theme into a potent and pervasive subject of his poetry. MacCallum thus situates Milton's theology in relation to the competing claims of orthodox Calvinism, the Cambridge Platonists, the Socinians, and other radical groups or heretical notions. He agrees that Milton's doctrine is clearly subordinationist, but argues that Milton makes major claims for the Son's mediational role. The bulk of MacCallum's study traces the development of the idea of sonship through the two epics, concentrating first on the depictions of the Son in *Paradise Lost* and then on the image(s) of God in man both before and after the fall. At issue here is how Milton dramatizes the growth of the Son into a merited Godhead and how that growth becomes a model by which God's "second" son can progress through the fall to a restoration of proper sonship. In the final two chapters MacCallum sketches the contrasting yet complementary treatment of sonship in *Paradise Regained.* Here, he suggests, Milton's subordinationist position created unique opportunities for the poetry, as did his notion of *kenosis.* Mediating carefully between opposing views of the Incarnation, Milton is able to forge an image of the Son who is at once both man and God, fully within history, a perfect fulfillment of the will of the Father, a perfect fulfilling of the capabilities of man. As in the earlier chapters, MacCallum's argument here is helpful and clear, sensitive at the same time to the contexts of Reformed theology and the demands of Milton's poetic project.

Situating his own work somewhere between Harold Bloom's theory of influence as anxiety and Thomas Greene's notion of influence as dialectic imitation, Richard J. DuRocher argues, in *Milton and Ovid,* that "heroically and with considerable risk, Milton exposes his Christian epic to the potential contamination, fragmentation, and multivocality of Ovid's metamorphic epic" (pp. 9-10). He does so, DuRocher suggests, because of "the insufficiency of scripture and Judeo-Christian culture generally to supply images and material for his poem" (p. 10). That, of course, is a rather bold claim and DuRocher immediately modifies it: the Ovidian matter "expands and revitalizes" the new Christian epic. This is still a large claim since the allegorized Virgil and Spenser's *Faerie Queene,* more familiar Miltonic sources, had already done much of that work. What makes Ovid's epic crucial to Milton's are its nonlinear narrative structure and its universal argument of mythic and psychological change. DuRocher centers attention, then, on how Milton transforms and transvalues Ovidian material to heighten the dramatic and moral conflicts of his poem.

In the main body of the book DuRocher shows how allusions to Proserpina, Echo, Pomona, and Medea help Milton compose Eve's character; how strategies and tropes from the *Metamorphoses* both uphold and undermine Satan's heroism; how Milton's broader dialogue with Ovid effects a revision of the epic by rejecting external force in favor of interiorized psychology, by expanding the role of the narrator, and by developing a narrative strategy which reinscribes universal patterns in personal, imaginative history. As DuRocher frequently notes, none of these Miltonic effects can be assigned a specific literary origin and the claim of a unique presence of Ovid must negotiate with the competing presences of Virgil and Spenser. Only in the final chapter, however, does DuRocher attempt this further task. As a result, and despite the useful analyses of particular allusions, I do not think the study will support its largest claims.

Charles Martindale is also concerned with *John Milton and the Transformation of Ancient Epic,* although his focus is at once wider and less precise than DuRocher's. Martindale offers helpful chapters on Milton's transvaluations of Homer, Virgil, Ovid, and Lucan. What the book sacrifices in charting particular resonances and allusive revisions it makes up for in providing a fuller sense of the comprehensiveness of Milton's engagements with the classics.

Thomas Merrill's *Epic God-Talk* attempts to apply the linguistic model of John Maquarrie to Milton's epic. Although there is much discussion here about how God-talk is semantically eccentric and aggressively performative, the book's major effect is to disjoin the *literary* from the *religious* in ways its argument simply will not support. Merrill wants, I guess, to talk about the ontological and epistemological weight of Milton's language, but he bases that argument on an extremely questionable theory of verbal presence.

In *The Wall of Paradise,* John M. Steadman brings his thorough knowledge of things Miltonic to bear upon the question of Milton's poetic. Situating Milton's scattered assertions about poetry in the contexts of Renaissance rhetorical theory, Aristotelian and Horatian dicta, and the actual demands of Milton's practice, Steadman tries to show that the poet does have a consistent poetic theory and that it is carefully accommodated to the often conflicting demands of art and religion. Although his conclusions are hardly novel, the book does offer an elegant overview of a rich and complex subject.

The best of the year's Milton studies is Joseph Wittreich's *Interpreting "Samson Agonistes."* As the title implies, it is a study that seeks actively to politicize both the Samson story itself and the ideological appropriations to which it has been subjected—by historical doctrinal controversy as well as modern criticism. My only quibble with this intent is that it seems somewhat blind to the predictability of its own conclusions: "*Samson Agonistes* is not a representation of this or that tradition but an embodiment of both.... In this way, *Samson* may be seen as a poem about the interpretive conflicts it has spawned, about the ideological rifts they have opened; it does not proselytize or propagandize but instead exposes ideological differences and mediates the space between them" (p. 52). Deconstructing interpretations of *Samson* in order to reconstruct *Samson* as the deconstruction of interpretation—one could hardly imagine a more sophisticated contemporary appropriation.

That caveat aside, Wittreich's argument is thorough and masterful. It begins with a reconsideration of how the appropriation of the Samson legend as it appears in the Book of Judges to the ideological and canonical constraints of Hebrews smooths over many of the tensions in the earlier story. And Wittreich suggests, provocatively, that Milton's departures from the text of Judges are "fictions deployed against the falsehoods of superstition and tradition that over the ages have tainted the Word" (p. 63). This writing against the letter of the text in order to reconstruct its historical truth is analogous, Wittreich suggests, to refusing to let the Judges narrative be subsumed in the larger, comic vision of the Bible as a whole. The Judges text is a tragedy—in particular, the tragedy of the nation of Israel. In order to reawaken that sense of the story, Milton must strip from Samson the retrospective sanctions his various choices later evoked. That he does so in a narrative that is itself retrospective suggests that the poem is "calling in for review all interpretations and reinterpretations of the Samson story" (p. 121).

In chapters 4 and 5, Wittreich reviews a number of Renaissance political and literary typologies of Samson in order to show that "what Milton would have understood as being the real issue is that typology, becoming increasingly independent of the biblical text and, in the process, muffling awareness of it, was subverting biblical narrative as narrative, was silencing the particularities of a history" within a programmatic new mythology (p. 177). Wittreich's historical sketch shows how the Samson story consistently evokes competing claims; how in the 1640s he became virtually the patron saint of the revolutionaries of the New Model Army; and how in the 1650s both Puritans and royalists redeploy the story in order to anatomize the failures of the Revolution. To situate Milton's poem in this context, then, is to emphasize anew the historical and national tragedy of Judges: a would-be deliverer of his people who, in doing to the Philistines what they have done to him, not only compromises his own moral position but also makes it impossible to distinguish faithful from faithless, victim from victimizer. Samson's failure, in short, is that "by employing force, he perpetuates the very patterns of history that he would reverse" (p. 284). And this, Wittreich goes on to argue, is Milton's critique of the revolution he himself was shaped by and helped to shape.

In the final two chapters Wittreich returns to *Samson* itself, now recontextualized in relation to its companion, *Paradise Regained.* It is finally that relation which retrieves the story from the historical allegories wrought by overzealous ideologies and transforms it into a typological model of interpretation itself. Although Wittreich has suggested the general lines of this argument before, its fuller development is comprehensive and impressive.

IV. Seventeenth-Century Studies

Arthur F. Marotti's *John Donne, Coterie Poet* begins with as fine a discussion of the necessity of reconceiving Donne's socioliterary and biographical contexts as has yet been written. His polemic against earlier Donne criticism—that it has dislocated the poems from these contexts and thereby blinded us to their rhetorical or situational "enactment of the author's relationships to peers and superiors through the conflicting styles of egalitarian assertion, social iconoclasm, and deferential politeness" (p. xi)—is both powerful and convincing. The corrective, he argues, is to recognize that the medium of literary communication was the manuscript. Of course, Donne's poems exist in and were collected by any number of manuscripts, so Marotti suggests we need to determine the "stages" of their circulation. A telling example is Rosenbach MS 243/4, in which poems of Donne that had circulated in an earlier manuscript are now "decontextualized" from their original circumstance and "recontextualized" within the narrative anthology of many poets by the Rosenbach compiler. Further gatherings of certain poems, like the Satires or the Elegies, and whether by Donne himself or by friends or contemporaries, constitute yet other stages.

If the present task, therefore, is to reconstruct the conditions under which Donne's poems served as coterie social transactions, as products "of a series of social relationships" (p. 24), then Marotti's initial decision to base his study upon modern editions must surely strike the reader as curious. Why does he not pursue the enactment stages of the various or at least groups of various manuscripts? Would that not be the methodological consequence of his own theoretical position? And would not such a study offer a unique opportunity to display the complex and changing social conditions of self-fashioning and refashioning? This disjuncture between Marotti's major socioliterary insights and his actual critical practice only widens as the book progresses, leaving a reader convinced by the former frustrated with the self-imposed constraints upon the latter.

The remainder of Marotti's study consists of three chapters in which he sketches the main cultural environments of Donne's early life—Inns of Court, the realm of fashion and Elizabethan courtiership, social exile and Jacobean courtiership—and then "reads" the poems as gestures toward and with these disparate "worlds." Building upon the biographies of Cary and Bald, as well as upon the work of Finkelpearl, Montrose, and others, the socioliterary sketches of Donne's milieu are useful and provocative. Unfortunately, they do not always produce the kind of reinterpretation of the poetry we expect. Marotti generally devotes one or two pages to each poem, but the readings are pretty conventional. What is most distressing about Marotti's attempts to contextualize the poems is that they result not in more situation-specific interpretations, but in questionable generalizations. The Inns of Court poems are characterized by an irreverent wit, as if such wit were unique to that isolatable coterie. Because certain poems play self-consciously on Ann's last name, she *must* be their primary audience. More frequently than not, rhetorical enactment is supplanted by an ungrounded psychoanalysis. Many of the poems, we are told, are either compensations for "the way things were" (p. 136) or sublimations of repressed guilts or fears. Donne's notorious onlookers reenact "the voyeur in the primal scene fantasy," "a father figure connected with both social disapproval and personal guilt" (p. 156), and thus constitute threatened acts of symbolic castration. This "psychoanalysis" reaches its most outrageous level in the treatment of "Batter my heart." Simultaneously masochistic and sadistic, the poem "homoerotically sexualize[s] salvation" in order to address "male-male patron client transactions generally" and the Jacobean courtier-King relationships specifically (p. 259). Donne's psychology, of course, has fascinated critics for most of this century, but it is not the project Marotti set upon and to that extent the important book his own historicist principles demand remains to be written.

Marotti's study is supplemented by Claude J. Summers and Ted-Larry Pebworth's collection *The Eagle and the Dove*. The fifteen essays offer a variety of modern approaches to Donne, although genre criticism predominates, and seek to reevaluate a number of his works—both the more celebrated and the neglected.

Ernest B. Gilman's *Iconoclasm and Poetry in the English Reformation* is a challenging and perceptive companion to Gross's *Spenserian*

Poetics. I emphasize the connection because brilliant as each book is on its own terms, together they mount a significant assault upon unproblematized conceptions of the relation between *pictura* and *poesis* (see also Fineman) and sketch the essential dynamics of what Gilman calls the scene of poetic iconoclasm. Although Gross's study is a more theoretical and sustained analysis of the iconoclastic/ idolatrous impulses of a single poet, Gilman's is more historically grounded in the controversies of the age and more suggestive of the range of poets those controversies affected.

Gilman defines the essential anxieties that burden a literary iconoclasm: "the scene of such writing is set at the crossroads where a lively tradition of image-making confronts a militantly logocentric theology armed not only with an overt hostility to 'images' in worship but with a deep suspicion of the idolatrous potential of the fallen mind and its fallen language" (p. 11). His first two chapters trace a few of the theological roots of this debate (Roman versus reformist apologists, Lutheran versus Calvinistic emphases) in order to suggest how the argument against external sacred imagery becomes relocated as a mental and spiritual agon within the individual Christian. So resituated, the controversy raises an anxiety it cannot resolve: are the images of the mind (or the text) marks of spiritual illumination or a residual depravity? For poetry, Gilman argues, this anxiety is creative as poets as diverse as Sidney, Chapman, Jonson, and Herbert begin to dramatize their own dilemmas in acts of literary self-censorship.

Gilman's subsequent chapters explore this drama in the works of Spenser, Quarles, Donne, and Milton. Spenser's poetry, he suggests like Gross, continuously drives below the surfaces of the imagery it erects in order to disclose "a tangle of desire and repudiation" from which that poetry cannot extricate itself. Drawing strength from what it abhors, creating ornaments in order to deface them, Spenser's poetic is not iconographical but an agonistic battle with its own pictorialism. The chapter on Quarles is a sharper delineation of the strains between *pictura* and *poesis.* Although earlier Protestant emblem books had responded to the pressures of the iconoclastic controversy, Quarles's *Emblemes* is more deeply divided. His task, Gilman argues, is to defuse the potential visual idolatry inherent in the Jesuit emblems that were his sources by focusing, in his poems, on the problems of vision itself. The tension between the need to see and the intellectual/spiritual perils of sight complicates every stage of Quarles's book. This paradox makes most of the emblems emblematic of their own traps: "the [Jesuit] image is reconceived as an emblem of its own opacity" (p. 107).

Gilman's discussion of Donne opens with a provocative account of his own picture galleries in the rooms at St. Paul's and the Catholic/Protestant split consciousness those rooms betray. The subsequent survey of telling passages in both the poetry and the prose suggests the extent to which the making and breaking of images is a deeply charged manifestation of Donne's personal conflicts. Milton too is trapped within this interiorized agon, although in Gilman's view his solution is stabler than Donne's and can be seen in the decisive stylistic turn in Book XII of *Paradise Lost* and the two subsequent poems. The most dramatic of Gilman's Miltonic "scenes," however, is his destruction, in *Eikonoklastes,* of Marshall's reclamation of the emblem tradition as the frontispiece for *Eikon Basilike.* Within the larger frame of this idolatrous/iconoclastic agon—Jesuit emblems to Whitney and Quarles to Marshall to Milton—we can glimpse the persistent power of the forces Gilman is exploring here.

To Charles Whitney, Bacon is both a test case for conflicting views of modernity and a modern whose own conflicts are especially pertinent today. Thus the "and" in *Francis Bacon and Modernity* does not designate any naive attempt to appropriate Bacon to a contemporary legitimization of knowledge-as-power or to ground modernity in a privileged point of origin. Both Bacon and modernity are in equal question here: what Bacon's own unresolved modernity implies, to Whitney, is a confirmation of the deconstructive gestures and discontinuities which both constrain and empower any historical self-consciousness.

So summarized, Whitney's project may sound more committed to contemporary theory than it is. The bulk of the study centers upon the paradoxes embedded in Bacon's privileged term, *instauratio.* Part I sketches the implications of instauration as reform: a re-edification of knowledge; a displacing and dismantling of cultural, literary, and religious idols in order to replace them with a discourse of secular prophecy; and a reinterpretation of received ideologies in order to validate a transfer of political power. Part II sketches the antithetical implications of instauration as revolution: the claims about priority and originality; the devaluing of authority; the assertion of absolute discontinuity with previous events or ideas; an insistence that this distinctiveness be actualized. In both parts, however, Whitney shows how the discontinuities between tradition and innovation, historical progress and ahistorical immediacy entangle Bacon constantly in radically conflicting impulses and gestures. As a reading of the urgencies and the designs of Bacon's major work, Whitney's study is a demanding and substantial contribution. As a challenge to contemporary criticism of Bacon and to contemporary debates about modernity and postmodernism, it is an intelligent focusing of some of our more compelling burdens.

It is appropriate that a year devoted to so much self-conscious historicism should also present a survey of six prominent seventeenth-century authors confronting their own historicity. The volume in question is Achsah Guibbory's *The Map of Time,* which traces the "three major conceptions of the shape of history: the idea of decay; the cyclical view of history; and the idea of progress" (p. 5). In the opening chapter Guibbory defines each of these conceptions and identifies their major exponents. Subsequent chapters address both details of imagery and language as well as the scopes and purposes of the writings of Bacon, Donne, Jonson, Herrick, Milton, and Dryden. Much of Guibbory's narrative confirms oft stated assumptions: that Bacon's history is linear and progressive (but compare Whitney); that Donne is obsessed with decay; that Jonson's and Herrick's views are cyclical; that Milton begins, like Bacon, with a sense of history as progress, but ends with one of man caught in cyclic error; that Dryden plays all three conceptions against one another. The strongest chapter is that on Jonson: Guibbory is right, I think, about the powerful antihistorical impulse in his work. Somewhat surprisingly she does not see the same impulse in Herrick. The usefulness of Guibbory's study does not reside in the perceptions of individual chapters but rather in the intelligent and comparative deployment of the ideas of history across the century. Her *Map* gives us the general pattern of historical patterns; it does not reveal the contradictions and the anxieties either inherent in or created by those patterns.

Outside of Mitchell's *English Pulpit Oratory* and a small resurgence of interest in the early 1970s, Renaissance sermons have never commanded the kind of critical attention they deserve. Horton Davies tries to rectify that blindness in *Like Angels from a Cloud,* a survey of metaphysical preachers from 1588 to 1645. Davies first tries to distinguish his forty-one metaphysicals from alternative sermon modes, the Catholic and the Puritan, and then to demonstrate the doctrinal range within the metaphysicals themselves, from unyielding Calvinists like Brownrig and Prideaux to outstanding Arminians like Andrewes, Donne, and Laud. The bulk of the study attempts to clarify what Horton sees as the eleven characteristics of the metaphysical sermon style. Since most, if not all, of these features derive from previous studies, Horton's chapters provide additional illustrative analogies rather than new or challenging material. Of more interest, I think, is his larger thesis that "almost every sermon in town and country church was an official statement of government policy" (p. 10). The historical details that support this view should open a new avenue into the complex relations between church and state as well as those between an important literary mode and the political situation in which it is forced to work.

Michael O'Connell's *Robert Burton* and Robert Wilcher's *Andrew Marvell* are useful introductions. Wilcher is more narrowly concerned with defining thematic contexts and with offering general "readings" of most of Marvell's poems. O'Connell's argument concerns "the melancholy of the printed book." Burton's compulsions to repeat, summarize, arrange, and master everything that entered his prodigious library provide a revealing glimpse of the copia of Renaissance humanism being overwhelmed by the proliferation of learning.

I confess I am unable to characterize Harold Toliver's *Lyric Provinces in the English Renaissance.* Toliver's intent, I think, is to chart the transactions between a number of poets and their representations or conceptions of "place"—local and social, natural and supernatural, interiorized and externalized. Behind the project lies the imposing figure of Heidegger and the difficulties of phenomenological "placements." The lyric of the period, Toliver argues, constantly brings into question what place signifies and how one is to respond to, control, take inventory of it, or negotiate crossings to alternative spaces. Although the individual chapters contain a number of fascinating observations, the book as a whole seems confused and unfocused.

I have saved *Voice Terminal Echo* for last, primarily because it subverts all reviewing categories. Is it a book or a text? Does it have a subject or is it a reverie on subjectivity? Who speaks: Marvell, Spenser, Shakespeare's characters, Herbert, Milton, Lacan, Derrida, or "Jonathan Goldberg"? Is it historicist or antihistoricist, provocative or subversive, compelling or self-indulgent? These are not trivial questions, although I expect many readers will not stay for the answers. For those who do, both Goldberg's irreverence and his intelligence will offer a challenging and demanding test of their fundamental assumptions about Renaissance texts.

But the book is more. I would describe it, hesitantly, as a sustained exploration of the grain of voice, of voice as an inscribed and transcribed intertextual scene of absence, an elegiac locus of echo and loss. It begins with Marvell's "Nymph" and stories of Sylvio/Sylvia (Virgil's, Ovid's, Spenser's: A *Silvae* or anthology of poems). It progresses through dispersed voices in Spenser, figurative voices in Shakespeare, other voices in Herbert, preventive voices in Milton. To trace the grain of such voices, of voice itself, is to follow transumptive iterations of loss continuously reinscribing themselves as writings, as dead letters to and of Echo. "In a certain way, these pages could . . . be read as an account of the fortunes of Ovid in the English Renaissance, or as some further versions of pastoral, particularly in its elegiac voice" (p. 5). They could also be read as a radical extension of the second part of *Endlesse Worke* or as a deconstruction of the more conventional methodology of *James I*. They cannot be read dispassionately.

As I suggested earlier, the essay, singly or collected, has become the favored medium of the New Historicism. There is wisdom and logic in that choice: the essay requires efficient delineation of a specific socioliterary problem and dramatizes an equally efficient revision. Generally surprising, frequently stunning, sometimes brilliant, the year's essays light up many corners of our period. But they also pay a price for this success: they rarely put either their authors or the methodology at risk and they rarely allow any sustained questioning of either the critic's own historical pressures or the important divisions within New Historicism itself. In the work of Fineman, Goldberg, Gross, and Whitney the risks are clear and considerable; but so too are the rewards. This work refuses to let us settle into any comfortable sense that we finally have a handle on this fascinating and troubling literature. As a counterforce to the increasingly dominant new mode, it keeps our options open.

BOOKS RECEIVED

I should like to apologize to all authors whose work appears below but not in the review itself. My selection of works to discuss was driven by the usual constraints of private time and public space, not by prejudgments about interest or merit.

Bacon, Sir Francis. *The Essayes or Counsels, Civill and Morall.* Ed. Michael Kiernan. Cambridge, Mass.: Harvard Univ. Press, 1985. Pp. cxviii + 339. $30.00. ISBN 0-674-31740-8.

Bietenholz, Peter G., ed. *Contemporaries of Erasmus: A Biographical Register of The Renaissance and Reformation*, vol. 2: F-M. Toronto and London: Univ. of Toronto Press, 1986. Pp. 490. $75.00. ISBN 0-8020-2571-4.

Brown, Cedric C. *John Milton's Aristocratic Entertainments.* Cambridge and New York: Cambridge Univ. Press, 1985. Pp. xii + 210. $34.50. ISBN 0-521-30440-7.

Cook, Elizabeth. *Seeing Through Words: The Scope of Late Renaissance Poetry.* New Haven and London: Yale Univ. Press, 1986. Pp. viii + 180. $20.00. ISBN 0-300-03675-2.

Crupi, Charles W. *Robert Greene.* Boston: Twayne, 1986. Pp. 182. $21.95. ISBN 0-8057-6905-6.

Davies, Horton. *Like Angels From a Cloud: The English Metaphysical Preachers 1588-1645.* San Marino: Huntington Library, 1986. Pp. ix + 503. $38.00. ISBN 0-87328-088-1.

Davies, Stevie. *The Feminine Reclaimed:. The Idea of Woman in Spenser, Shakespeare, and Milton.* Lexington: Univ. Press of Kentucky, 1986. Pp. xii + 273. $25.00. ISBN 0-8131-1589-2.

Diehl, Huston. *An Index of Icons in English Emblem Books.* Norman and London: Univ. of Oklahoma Press, 1986. Pp. xiii + 258. $35.00. ISBN 0-8061-1989-6.

Doughtie, Edward. *English Renaissance Song.* Boston: Twayne, 1986. Pp. 185. $19.95. ISBN 0-8057-6915-3.

DuRocher, Richard J. *Milton and Ovid.* Ithaca and London: Cornell Univ. Press, 1985. Pp. 241. $27.50. ISBN 0-8014-1812-7.

Erasmus, Desiderius. *Collected Works of Erasmus.* Ed. J. K. Sowards, vols. 25 and 26: Literary and Educational Writings. Toronto: Univ. of Toronto Press, 1985. Pp. lix + 289 (vol. 25); 292-678 (vol. 26). $95.00 the set. ISBN 0-8020-5521-4.

Estrin, Barbara. *The Raven and the Lark: Lost Children in Literature of the English Renaissance.* Lewisburg: Bucknell Univ. Press, and London and Toronto: Associated Univ. Presses, 1985. Pp. 228. $29.50. ISBN 0-8386-5075-3.

Ferguson, Margaret W., Quilligan, Maureen, and Vickers, Nancy J., eds. *Rewriting the Renaissance: The Discourses of Sexual Difference in Early Modern Europe.* Chicago and London: Univ. of Chicago Press, 1986. Pp. xxxi + 426. $50.00 cloth, ISBN 0-226-24313-3. $15.95 paper, ISBN 0-226-24314-1.

Fineman, Joel. *Shakespeare's Perjured Eye: The Invention of Poetic Subjectivity in the Sonnets.* Berkeley and London: Univ. of California Press, 1986. Pp. ix + 365. $35.00. ISBN 0-520-05486-5.

Gilman, Ernest B. *Iconoclasm and Poetry in the English Reformation: Down Went Dagon.* Chicago and London: Univ. of Chicago Press, 1986. Pp. xi + 227. $19.00. ISBN 0-226-29382-3.

Gleckner, Robert F. *Blake and Spenser.* Baltimore and London: Johns Hopkins Univ. Press, 1986. Pp. xi + I 403. $29.50. ISBN 0-8018-2521-0.

Goldberg, Jonathan. *Voice Terminal Echo: Postmodernism and English Renaissance Texts.* New York and London: Methuen, 1986. Pp. x + 195. $13.95. ISBN 0416-42200-4.

Gottlieb, Sidney, ed. *George Herbert Journal* 8:2 (Spring 1986) and 9:1 (1986). Bridgeport: Sacred Heart Univ. Pp. 60 and 57. $7.00 annually. ISSN 0161-7435.

Greene, Thomas M. *The Vulnerable Text: Essays on Renaissance Literature.* New York: Columbia Univ. Press, 1986. Pp. xx + 250. $32.50. ISBN 0-231-06246-X.

Griffin, Dustin. *Regaining Paradise:. Milton and the Eighteenth Century.* New York: Cambridge Univ. Press, 1986. Pp. xi + 299. $29.95. ISBN 0-521-30913-1.

Gross, Kenneth. *Spenserian Poetics:. Idolatry, Iconoclasm, and Magic.* Ithaca and London: Cornell Univ. Press, 1986. Pp. 271. $24.95. ISBN 0-8014-1805-4.

Guibbory, Achsah. *The Map of Time: Seventeenth-Century English Literature and Ideas of Pattern in History.* Chicago: Univ. of Illinois Press, 1986. Pp. 284. $24.95. ISBN 0-252-01264-X.

Haigh, Christopher, ed. *The Reign of Elizabeth I.* Athens: Univ. of Georgia Press, 1985. Pp. vi + 301. $27.50. ISBN 0-8203-0757-2.

Hannay, Margaret P., ed. *Silent But for the Word: Tudor Women as Patrons, Translators, and Writers of Religious Works.* Kent: Kent State Univ. Press, 1985. Pp. ix + 304. $27.50. ISBN 0-87338-315-X.

Harris, Barbara J. *Edward Stafford, Third Duke of Buckingham, 1478-1521.* Stanford: Stanford Univ. Press, 1986. Pp. ix + 334. $37.50. ISBN 08047-1316-2.

Hawkins, Anne Hunsaker. *Archetypes of Conversion: The Autobiographies of Augustine, Bunyan, and Merton.* Lewisburg: Bucknell Univ. Press, and London and Toronto: Associated Univ. Presses, 1985. Pp. 191. $25.00. ISBN 0-8387-5079-6.

Haynes, Jonathan. *The Humanist as Traveler: George Sandys's "Relation of a Journey begun An. Dom. 1610."* Rutherford, NJ: Fairleigh Dickinson Univ. Press, and London and Toronto: Associated Univ. Presses, 1986. Pp. 159. $26.50. ISBN 0-8386-3240-8.

Hill, Christopher. *The Collected Essays of Christopher Hill,* vol. 2: Religion and Politics in 17th Century England. Amherst: Univ. of Massachusetts Press, 1986. Pp. xi + 356. $25.00. ISBN 0-87023-503-6.

Hill, Christopher. *The Collected Essays,* vol. 3:. People and Ideas in 17th Century England. Amherst: Univ. of Massachusetts Press, 1986. Pp. xi + 340. $27.50. ISBN 0-87023-550-8.

Hilliard, Stephen S. *The Singularity of Thomas Nashe.* Lincoln and London: Univ. of Nebraska Press, 1986. Pp. ix + 260. $22.50. ISBN 0-8032-2326-9.

Hunter, William B., intro., and Shawcross, John T., bibliog. *Milton's English Poetry: Being Entries from "A Milton Encyclopedia."* Lewisburg: Bucknell Univ. Press, and London and Toronto: Associated Univ. Presses, 1986. Pp. 248. $29.50. ISBN 0-8387-5096-6.

Hyde, Thomas. *The Poetic Theology of Love: Cupid in Renaissance Literature.* Newark: Univ. of Delaware Press, and London and Toronto: Associated Univ. Presses, 1986. Pp. 212. $29.50. ISBN 0-87413-273-8.

Kibbey, Ann. *The Interpretation of Material Shapes in Puritanism: A Study of Rhetoric, Prejudice, and Violence.* Cambridge and New York: Cambridge Univ. Press, 1986. Pp. xi + 203. $27.95. ISBN 0-521-26509-6.

Kinney, Arthur F., ed. *English Literary Renaissance* 16:1 (Special Issue on Studies in Renaissance Historicism). Amherst: Univ. of Massachusetts Press, 1986. Pp. 268. $6.00 per issue. ISSN 0013-8312.

Kinney, Arthur F., ed. *Essential Articles For the Study of Sir Philip Sidney.* Hamden, Conn.: Archon Books, 1986. Pp. xvii + 458. $49.50. ISBN 0-208-02085-3.

Kinney, Arthur F. *Humanist Poetics: Thought, Rhetoric, and Fiction in Sixteenth-Century England.* Amherst: Univ. of Massachusetts Press, 1986. Pp. 507. $35.00. ISBN 0-87023-485-4.

Kupersmith, William. *Roman Satirists in Seventeenth-Century England.* Lincoln: Univ. of Nebraska Press, 1985. Pp. xii + 193. $19.95. ISBN 0-80322710-8.

Lewalski, Barbara Kiefer, ed. *Renaissance Genres: Essays on Theory, History, and Interpretation.* Cambridge, Mass., and London: Harvard Univ. Press, 1986. Pp. 498. $8.95. ISBN 0-674-76041-7.

MacCallum, Hugh. *Milton and the Sons of God: The Divine Image in Milton's Epic Poetry.* Toronto, Buffalo, and London: Univ. of Toronto Press, 1986. Pp. x 325. $35.00. ISBN 0-8020-5679-2.

Marotti, Arthur. *John Donne, Coterie Poet.* Madison: Univ. of Wisconsin Press, 1986. Pp. xviii + 369. $35.00. ISBN 0-299-10490-7.

Martindale, Charles. *John Milton and the Transformation of Ancient Epic.* Totowa: Barnes and Noble, 1986. Pp. 239. $28.50. ISBN 0-389-20624-5.

Martines, Lauro. *Society and History in English Renaissance Verse.* Oxford and New York: Basil Blackwell, 1985. Pp. viii + 191. $24.95. ISBN 0631-14115-4.

Marx, Steven. *Youth Against Age: Generational Strife in Renaissance Poetry.* New York and Berne: Peter Lang, 1985. Pp. xiii + 252. $27.70. ISBN 0-8204-0183-8.

McKeen, David. *A Memory of Honour: The Life of William Brooke, Lord Cobham.* Salzburg: Universität Salzburg, 1986. 2 vols. Pp. iv + 762.

Merrill, Thomas. *Epic God-Talk: "Paradise Lost" and the Grammar of Religious Language.* Jefferson, NC, and London: McFarland & Co., 1986. Pp. vii + 132. $18.95. ISBN 0-89950-194-X.

Milton, John. *Selected Prose.* New and rev. edn. Ed. C.A. Patrides. Columbia: Univ. of Missouri Press, 1985. Pp. 463. $8.50. ISBN 0-82620484-8.

More, St. Thomas. *The Yale Edition of the Complete Works of St. Thomas More, Volume II.* Answer to a Poisoned Book, ed. Stephen Merriam Foley and Clarence H. Miller. New Haven: Yale Univ. Press, 1985. Pp. xcii + 424. $60.00. ISBN 0-300-03129-7.

O'Connell, Michael. *Robert Burton.* Boston: Twayne, 1986. Pp. 130. $18.95. ISBN 0-8057-6919-6.

Ogilvie-Thomson, S.J., ed. *Walter Hilton's "Mixed Life" Edited From Lambeth Palace MS 472.* Salzburg: Universität Salzburg, 1986. Pp. 69.

Parker, Patricia, and Quint, David, eds. *Literary Theory/Renaissance Texts.* Baltimore and London: Johns Hopkins Univ. Press, 1986. Pp. vii + 399. $30.00 cloth, ISBN 0-8018-3294-2. $12.95 paper, ISBN 0-8018-3295-0.

Pequigney, Joseph. *Such Is My Love: A Study of Shakespeare's Sonnets.* Chicago and London: Univ. of Chicago Press, 1985. Pp. ix 249. $19.95. ISBN 0226-65563-6.

Rose, Mary Beth, ed. *Women in the Middle Ages and the Renaissance: Literary and Historical Perspectives.* Syracuse: Syracuse Univ. Press, 1986. Pp. xxviii + 288. $12.50. ISBN 0-8156-2352-6.

Rowse, A. L., ed. *Shakespeare's Self Portrait: Passages from his Work.* Lanham: Univ. Press of America, 1985. Pp. vi + 187. $17.95. ISBN 0-8191-4220-4.

Ruppert, Peter. *Reader in a Strange Land: The Activity of Reading Literary Utopias.* Athens and London: Univ. of Georgia Press, 1986. Pp. xiv + 193. $19.00. ISBN 0-8203-0821-8.

Scheps, Walter, and Looney, J. Anna. *Middle Scots Poets: A Reference Guide to James I of Scotland, Robert Henryson, William Dunbar, and Gavin Douglas.* Boston: G. K. Hall, 1986. Pp. xvi + 292. $55.00. ISBN 0-81618356-2.

Sessions, William A. *Henry Howard, Earl of Surrey.* Boston: Twayne, 1986. Pp. 172. $19.95. ISBN 0-8057-6920-X.

Shore, David R. *Spenser and the Poetics of Pastoral: A Study of the World of Colin Clout.* Montreal: McGill-Queen's Univ. Press, 1985. Pp. 191. $25.00. ISBN 0-7735-0577-6.

Simmonds, James D., ed. *Milton Studies 21.* Pittsburgh, PA: Univ. of Pittsburgh Press, 1986. Pp. 227. $24.95. ISBN 0-8229-3524-4.

Spearing, A.C. *Medieval to Renaissance in English Poetry.* Cambridge and London: Cambridge Univ. Press, 1985. Pp. viii + 369. $44.50. ISBN 0521-24769-1.

Steadman, John M. *The Wall of Paradise: Essays on Milton's Poetics.* Baton Rouge and London: Louisiana State Univ. Press, 1985. Pp. 156. $20.00. ISBN 0-8071-1230-5.

Sterne, Laurence, and Kollmeier, Harold H., gen. eds. *A Concordance to the English Prose of John Milton.* Medieval & Renaissance Texts & Studies, vol. 35. Binghamton, NY: Center for Medieval & Renaissance Texts & Studies, 1985. Pp. xvii + 1491. $96.00. ISBN 0-86698-068-7.

Stevens, Paul. *Imagination and the Presence of Shakespeare in "Paradise Lost."* Madison: Univ. of Wisconsin Press, 1985. Pp. 270. $32.50. ISBN 0-29910420-6.

Stillman, Robert E. *Sidney's Poetic Justice: "The Old Arcadia," Its Eclogues, and Renaissance Pastoral Traditions.* Lewisburg, PA: Bucknell Univ. Press, and London and Toronto: Associated Univ. Presses, 1986. Pp. 277. $35.00. ISBN 0-8387-5085-0.

Summers, Claude J., and Pebworth, Ted-Larry, eds. *The Eagle and the Dove: Reassessing John Donne. Essays in Seventeenth-Century Literature 1.* Columbia: Univ. of Missouri Press, 1986. Pp. xv + 220. $24.00. ISBN 0-8262-0489-9.

Toliver, Harold. *Lyric Provinces in the English Renaissance.* Columbus: Ohio State Univ. Press, 1986. Pp. xii + 247. $25.00. ISBN 0-8142-0391-4.

Waller, Gary. *English Poetry of the Sixteenth Century.* New York: Longman, 1986. Pp. xiv + 315. $29.95. ISBN 0-582-49248-3.

Whitney, Charles. *Francis Bacon and Modernity.* New Haven and London: Yale Univ. Press, 1986. Pp. x + 234. $18.50. ISBN 0-300-03585-3.

Wilcher, Robert. *Andrew Marvell.* Cambridge and New York: Cambridge Univ. Press, 1975. Pp. xi + 191. $34.50. ISBN 0-521-258197.

Willmott, Richard, ed. *Four Metaphysical Poets: An Anthology of Poetry by Donne, Herbert, Marvell and Vaughan.* Cambridge: Cambridge Univ. Press, 1985. Pp. 184. $12.95. ISBN 0-521-27758-2.

Wittreich, Joseph. *Interpreting "Samson Agonistes."* Princeton: Princeton Univ. Press, 1986. Pp. xxx + 394. $42.50. ISBN 0-691-06671-X.

SEL

Studies in ENGLISH LITERATURE 1500-1900

Elizabethan and Jacobean Drama

VOLUME 27 SPRING 1987 NUMBER 2

Studies in English Literature 1500 - 1900

VOLUME 27 SPRING 1987 NUMBER 2

PUBLISHED BY RICE UNIVERSITY

CONTENTS

Gammer Gurton's Needle and the Concept of Humanist Parody — Douglas Duncan 177

Falstaff and the Art of Dying — Paul M. Cubeta 197

Comfort in *Measure for Measure* — Maurice Hunt 213

Jonson's Jacobean Masques and the Moral Imagination — Nathaniel Strout 233

Play-making, Domestic Conduct, and the Multiple Plot in *The Roaring Girl* — Viviana Comensoli 249

"Great Women of Pleasure": Main Plot and Subplot in *The Duchess of Malfi* — Christina Luckyj 267

John Fletcher as Spenserian Playwright: *The Faithful Shepherdess* and *The Island Princess* — Philip J. Finkelpearl 285

Women Beware Women and the Economy of Rape — Anthony Dawson 303

Recent Studies in Elizabethan and Jacobean Drama — Jean E. Howard 321

Studies in English Literature
1500 - 1900

PUBLISHED BY RICE UNIVERSITY

Studies in English Literature is a quarterly journal of historical and critical studies. Each issue will be devoted to one of four fields:

WINTER: The English Renaissance
SPRING: Elizabethan and Jacobean Drama
SUMMER: Restoration and Eighteenth Century
AUTUMN: The Nineteenth Century

SEL: Studies in English Literature, 1500–1900 (ISSN: 0039-3657) is published quarterly (February, May, August, and November) at $15.00 per year for individuals, $20.00 per year for U.S. institutions, $25.00 per year for foreign institutions, and $6.00 per single issue, by Rice University, 6100 South Main Street, P.O. Box 1892, Houston, Texas 77251. Second-class postage paid at Houston, Texas. **Postmaster:** Send address changes to the Business Manager, *SEL*, Rice University, P.O. Box 1892, Houston, TX 77251.

Studies in English Literature invites historical and critical essays of moderate length (ten to twenty-five pages) that contribute significantly to the understanding of English Literature, 1500-1900. Typescripts should be double-spaced throughout and prepared in conformity with the Chicago Manual of Style. Clean photocopy on uncoated paper is acceptable in place of the ribbon copy. We will not consider articles being simultaneously submitted elsewhere, nor will we print essays to appear in a book published within a year of scheduled publication of *SEL*. Those wishing to omit their identities from manuscripts may do so, but should include a covering letter.

Manuscripts submitted for publication should be addressed to the Editor, *Studies in English Literature,* Rice University, P.O. Box 1892, Houston, TX 77251. They must be accompanied by a sufficient number of unattached stamps for return. Receipt of manuscripts will be acknowledged by postcard. Editorial decisions usually take a minimum of three months.

Annual subscription rates: $15.00 for individuals, $20.00 for U. S. institutions, $25.00 for foreign institutions, $6.00 per issue for partial subscriptions and single copies. Regular subscriptions may be obtained for any or all quarterly issues. Remittance should accompany subscription requests. Notice of non-receipt of an issue must be made within ninety (90) days following the publication of that issue. No refunds or cancellations. Business communications should be addressed to Business Manager, *Studies in English Literature,* Rice University, P. O. Box 1892, Houston, TX 77251.

Microfilms of previous volumes (Vols. 1-26) may be obtained from University Microfilms, Inc., 300 N. Zeeb Road, Ann Arbor, Michigan 48106; xerox copies of individual articles may be ordered by calling (800) 521-0600 (toll free). Copies of articles are also available from ISI's The Genuine Article service, 3501 Market Street, Philadelphia, PA 19104; phone (800) 523-1850; telex 84-5305; electronic mail through CLASS; or facsimile transmission via FAXPAX.

Volumes 1 through 3 and 5 through 10 of *Studies in English Literature* are available from Johnson Reprint Corporation, 111 Fifth Avenue, New York, N. Y. 10003, or Berkeley Square House, London W. 1, England.

SEL 27 (1987)
ISSN 0039-3657

Gammer Gurton's Needle and the Concept of Humanist Parody

DOUGLAS DUNCAN

Because its primitive content was rashly equated with primitive art, *Gammer Gurton's Needle* was for long a victim of primitive critical error. Even today one finds it jokingly used as a touchstone of unsophistication,[1] and its title alone can raise condescending smiles, as anyone who has worked on it knows. In obvious ways it invites such treatment, as though daring critics to make fools of themselves by taking it solemnly. Its merits, however, are now clearly perceived.[2] Well-constructed, lively, funny, actable, and even intelligent, its status as good comedy is no longer in question and has been confirmed by two recent editions.[3] Yet even the most appreciative comments leave doubt as to whether it is being read in the spirit that its author writ, and whether its place in the history of English comedy has been accurately gauged. These two concerns, both strikingly unfashionable, will be addressed in turn in the present essay, which attempts to set *Gammer Gurton's Needle* in the context of humanist saturnalian parody.[4]

Much of the learned discussion of the play concerns problems of authorship and date.[5] Since none of the candidates or dates proposed invalidate the view offered here, it will be convenient to accept the majority verdict that it was written in the early 1550s by William Stevenson, Master of Arts, Fellow of Christ's College, Cambridge, to be performed in hall by the college students (and presumably the college cat). Whether earlier or later than Nicholas Udall's *Roister Doister,* it shares with that play the distinction of being the earliest surviving comedy in English to use Roman comic form. And since,

---

Douglas Duncan is Professor of English at McMaster University, Hamilton, Ontario. His continuing interest in how humanist modes of wit impinge on English comedy has been expressed in *Ben Jonson and the Lucianic Tradition* (Cambridge Univ. Press, 1979) and "Mythic Parody in *The Country Wife,*" *EIC* 31 (1981).

in content, it is the less indebted to Roman models, Stevenson is credited with having pushed English comedy a step or two further toward independence.

One must question whether that was his aim. The impulse to naturalize Roman models as a means of enriching the vernaculars is one of the best-accredited features of humanist writing, comedy included, but that it was always operative cannot be assumed. Both *Roister Doister* and *Gammer Gurton's Needle* were conditioned by other factors, long familiar to scholars, which have not been sufficiently linked and applied to them in criticism. One of these is the prominence accorded in Tudor schools and colleges to Roman comedy and especially the plays of Terence, studied in relation to a large body of comic theory, almost wholly based on Terence, which commended his usefulness for teaching good Latin and good morals.[6] We can deduce how Terence was taught in England, not only from the the prescriptions of Erasmus and Wolsey,[7] but also from the material which kept being reprinted in the numerous early-sixteenth-century editions of his work: the essays on comedy attributed to Donatus, the preface to Servius's commentary, rhetorical and moral explications of his text by Melanchthon and lesser-known humanists. The other relevant factor is that mid-century college plays, which were usually in Latin but sometimes in Greek, were most commonly presented during times of licence, often under the auspices of a Christmas lord or lord of misrule.[8] The plays so performed were not necessarily or normally saturnalian themselves; it was the acting of them which marked a concession to holiday, and college statutes which required the practice justified it on sober educational grounds.[9] None the less, it seems reasonable to surmise that the first dons or schoolmasters who offered comedies in English, the discouraged vernacular—applying strict Roman form to absurd English matter—did so in a spirit of holiday indecorum, more intent on upsetting the dignity of the curriculum than on furthering the development of native drama.

Udall and Stevenson were probably at one in regarding their versions of Roman comedy as something of a saturnalian joke, but in their practice of imitation they differ significantly. Imitation could be "straight" or "mock." *Faceta imitatio* (witty imitation) is how humanists described mock writing: a mock epic such as the *Batrachomyomachia* or a mock encomium like *The Praise of Folly*.[10] In the case of comedy, where the imitated genre is already inherently unpretentious and amusing, it becomes tricky to distinguish the mock from the straight and thus to determine the spirit of the writing. But a clue can be found in the attitudes which comic writers display toward the native elements they embody in their plays. Are these being welcomed in the inclusive spirit of straight imitation, uniting Roman and English humor? Or are they being treated with sardonic irony, as though to stress the incongruity of their appearance in a Roman genre? The first attitude is primarily Udall's. Roister Doister himself, though a mock-heroic figure, is essentially an anglicization in terms of mock chivalry of *milites gloriosi* who were already mock-heroic in Plautus and Terence. Udall shares with his students the straightforward fun of seeing classroom comedy adapted to an English idiom, and it is generally agreed that the charm of his play owes much to his openness in embracing English traits of character, humor, and folksong. Stevenson's design is more secretive. Life-like and funny as his treatment of country life is, there is an intellectual edge to it which suggests mock pastoral: the college man's "use" of rustic characters as a reference-point for his college audience. Seeming to flout learned theory, he continually and humorously recalls it. Working through the medium of curricular parody, he achieves something ultimately more serious than Udall attempted, a radical saturnalian inversion of what humanist educators normally stressed.

An appropriate way of supporting these assertions will be by analyzing *Gammer Gurton's Needle* as Stevenson's pupils were trained to analyze Terence. That means approaching it under the traditional rhetorical headings of invention, disposition, and style; noting how it illustrates Donatus and Servius on comedy and Aristotle and Cicero on the sources of laughter; glancing at its usefulness for the study of rhetoric; and finally harvesting its golden fruit, its "sentence" or moral.

With regard to invention, or choice of subject, the story and setting of the play must have struck Tudor students as like nothing in Roman comedy. It is true that the main character Diccon, in his opening lines, recalls the parasite in his quest for free dinners, and his scheming at times recalls the Plautine slave, but these echoes turn out to be deceptive. They are signs which define him by misdirection, serving to show that he is something quite other: a Bedlam vagabond apart from society, a spirit of mischief depending on no one and serving no master. So also with the street-scene before two houses—the Roman convention serves only to stress that the squalid lodgings of Gurton and Chat are far from being straightforward English counterparts to the middle-class Greek homes in Plautus and Terence. The plot spun out of the loss of a needle could be a *fabliau* told by Chaucer or Heywood but bears no resemblance to anything classical. How do we account for the basic invention? Why a needle? Even then the thing was proverbially hard to find,[11] but that tells us little. In vulgar parlance it may already have been phallic,[12] and there are moments in the play which suggest an allusion to some bawdy folk-song or Villonesque *chanson de regret*, an old woman regretting the instrument of her former pleasures.[13] But that echo, too, if it is one, is a decoy, since the play is not bawdy. The source of the invention is more plausibly traced to a common-room wager: the challenge of writing a five-act comedy about something insignificant or worthless, another proverbial facet of needles.[14] Into that we can read a little more. First of all, as a trifle, or *nugae,* which is to be treated with learned wit and ultimate seriousness, the needle is a reminder of Erasmus's famous defence of *nugae* in his preface to *Folly*.[15] That reminder points to the mode in which Stevenson wrote. Secondly, as the trifle which occasions such a stir in the play, the needle recalls the reductive terms in which the earliest commentators had described comedy: Servius called its subject-matter "paltry" (*vilis*) and Donatus said it dealt with "petty disturbances" (*parvi impetus periculorum*).[16] This indicates the level where we shall find Stevenson "mocking" his textbook authorities. But his parodic design was also larger. Around the search for the needle he built a moral fable which humorously recalls the edifying lessons extracted from Terence by his humanist interpreters. When Hodge makes his first mud-bespattered appearance from "dabbling in the dirt" (I.ii.1), a biblical resonance is instantly evoked. Hodge, like Adam, emerges from the clay, and ditchers (as Shakespeare's gravedigger knew) were "of Adam's profession." And in the Genesis story the needle (though unmentioned) played a major role, becoming the archetype of necessary art in the history of man. Even before Adam resorted to his spade, it was the first tool needed by our fallen parents to conceal their shame when they "sewed fig leaves together, and made themselves aprons" (or "breeches" in the Geneva Bible of 1560). So Gammer Gurton's needle is required to hold together Hodge's breeches and preserve his modesty. How Stevenson used that aspect of his invention will be explained in relation to his "sentence."

It seems fair to assume that Stevenson's originality was perceived in his day in terms of incongruity: the deliberate mismatching of content and form, low nature and high art, primitive invention indecorously at odds with highly sophisticated disposition, or treatment. The discrepancy was to be noticed, not only in performance, but also on the printed page, as we have it in Colwell's text of

1575. With its scrupulous division into acts and scenes, and the names of characters massed at the head of each scene they appear in, the aim was to make the text look as much as possible like a printing of Plautus or Terence. Stevenson's awareness of the difference between a printed text and a text for performance is suggested at the start in his choice of prologue. Donatus had listed four types of prologue, the two main ones being the *prologus commendativus,* spoken on behalf of the poet or his play (as found in *Roister Doister*) and the *prologus argumentativus,* a synopsis of the story (as memorably parodied in *A Midsummer Night's Dream*). Prologues of the latter type—now recognized as late accretions to the manuscript tradition and not strictly prologues at all—were written in a compressed narrative style which made no pretence to audience-address. By choosing to write such a prologue—whether or not he meant it to be spoken—Stevenson was highlighting an undramatic feature of Roman texts which annihilated suspense more effectively than Brecht could have wished.[17] His reason for doing so was to give exaggerated comic emphasis to an important pedagogical distinction made by Horace, and expounded by the commentators, between the "natural" order of events in a story and the "artificial" order of events as presented by the poet.[18] His prologue tells the story *ab ovo,* as Horace puts it, and so starts with a clear statement of where Gammer Gurton put the needle, the very last fact which the artificial order will reveal. The play itself then hastens *in medias res* and imitates a favorite Terentian technique whereby the audience is introduced to a strange state of affairs, subsequently explained through the rhetorical device of *narratio.* Diccon in scene i, Hodge in scene ii, "marvel" at the "howling and scowling," the "sighing and sobbing" in Gammer Gurton's cottage, explained in scene iii by Tib, her maid. She "narrates" the cause of the distress: how the needle has been lost ever since her mistress, seated on her hassock, cast aside her sewing in alarm on seeing Gib, the cat, "over head and ears" in the milkpan. When we perceive that Tib's ludicrous speech faithfully adheres to the six-part division of the *narratio* recommended by a much-used textbook, the *Progymnasmata Rhetorica* of Aphthonius,[19] we begin to suspect that here, as in the Prologue, we are dealing not with straight imitation but with a scholarly send-up of rhetorical concepts treated solemnly in class.

In considering the play's structure it has to be remembered that the structural principles behind Roman comedy were hotly debated in Stevenson's time. The earliest editors had had to divide the plays into acts and scenes, since no such divisions had been marked in the manuscripts, and a much larger problem was to reconcile Horace's reference to five acts with the tripartite division of the action by Donatus into protasis, epitasis, and catastrophe.[20] In his structural analysis of *Gammer Gurton's Needle* T. W. Baldwin argued that it shows familiarity with the particular solution of that problem propounded by Iodochus Willichius in his commentary on the *Ars Poetica* (1539) and his edition of Terence (1550).[21] Where Donatus had equated the protasis with Act I, Willichius made it cover the second act as well. Stevenson clearly marks the end of his protasis at the end of Act II where Diccon tells the audience, "here will the sport begin," having set up a quarrel by telling Gammer Gurton that her neighbor Dame Chat has stolen the needle and by telling Dame Chat that Gurton accuses her of having stolen her cock. The term *epitasis,* which Donatus had applied loosely to the whole complication of plot between protasis and catastrophe, was applied by Willichius to a particular stage in the plot and located in Act III. So in Stevenson's third act the epitasis is the battle, the violent exchange of words and blows between the two women. Since the catastrophe had to occur in Act V, scholars were unsure how to describe Act IV. Most called it simply the *summa epitasis,* but Willichius defined it more specifically as an attempt to remedy the conflict in Act III, preparing the way for the catastrophe. As Baldwin shows, this fits our play well. Dr. Rat, the curate, arrives at the start of Act IV to sort out the women's dispute, but is diverted by Diccon into searching for the needle by breaking into Dame Chat's alehouse through a hole in the ground, where he gets his head broken with a doorbar. His attempted remedy, having made matters worse, prepares for the catastrophe because he sends for the law in the person of Master Bailly, whose fifth-act judicial enquiry ultimately, though not directly, leads to the final solution.

It is certain that an up-to-date knowledge of structural theory helped Stevenson to create, years ahead of his rivals, one of the best plots in English sixteenth-century drama, remarkably tight in terms of logic and motivation—what the commentators called *paraskeue.* Whether Baldwin was right in thinking that he followed Willichius would need to be decided by a scholar with an equally comprehensive knowledge of the theorists. But the sad flaw in Baldwin's account is his failure to consider the spirit in which Stevenson exercised his structural mastery. We can sense that spirit most clearly in the catastrophe, where the presence of parody has been detected by earlier critics.[22] All commentators agreed with Donatus that the catastrophe should be brought about by a *cognitio,* a recognition or discovery. Stevenson's is caused by the discovery, not of a long-lost child, but of a long-lost needle in Hodge's backside. This makes a fitting conclusion to the playful guying of comic conventions which marks the whole work. To praise its author, as Baldwin and others have done, for having perfectly transposed Roman comedy into English terms is to recognize his achievement more exactly than his aim.

From invention and disposition the sixteenth-century analyst turned to style. The variety of styles employed in the play might repay investigation, and it would certainly be useful to relate its prosody to that of Plautus and Terence, which was exhaustively studied in Renaissance editions. But for our purposes here it is sufficient to note that the play's most memorable style—that of Gurton and her household who use the guttural first person singular—is an attempt to render the low style, or *genus humile*, which Servius thought appropriate to comedy.[23] This brings us back to a point made earlier, that in choosing as his subject a vulgar commotion about not very much Stevenson was making a joking allusion to authoritative definitions of comedy, "low" definitions in terms of style (*humile*) and matter (*vile, parvum*) to which commentators had been led by their invariable practice of contrasting comedy and tragedy. A problem which must have arisen in the classroom was how such definitions were to be squared with the reverence accorded to Terence in the humanist curriculum on account of the purity of his language, his mastery of rhetoric, the serious lessons of moral conduct to be drawn from his matter. Stevenson makes fun of this evident anomaly by taking the low definitions literally and pushing them to absurd extremes. One might of course argue that the play was not written with reference to Terence but was meant to be Plautine: M. C. Bradbrook, for example, so defines it.[24] It is indeed closer to Plautus than to Terence and has many Plautine features: violence on stage, rough language, sacrilegious oaths, disrespect for authority, frequent audience-address. Moreover it is full of the Plautine *vis comica* which Caesar had famously denied to Terence. But resemblances to Plautus really strengthen the case being made here. The humanists' praise of Terence was conventionally accompanied by relative dispraise of Plautus; many of the characteristics just listed were singled out for disapproval by commentators from Donatus onward. Since Terence was the approved model for comedy in the early sixteenth-century—the master on whose example Erasmus, Melanchthon, and the rest had raised the temple of humanist comic theory[25]—one way of "mocking" this near-apotheosis was through reminders of the lower comic level on which the less respectable (and probably more popular) dramatist had worked.

A more specific matter on which Stevenson jests is the etymology of the word "comedy" itself. All commentators discussed this, struggling to reconcile contradictory derivations furnished by Donatus as well as by Aristotle. Explaining that comedy had its origin in country festivals, Donatus declared that the word could either mean a song of revelry (from Greek *komos*) or a village-song (from Greek *komē*). Servius preferred the second derivation. Most of the humanists preferred the first—comedy for Melanchthon is *convivale carmen*—but they were characteristically reluctant to throw either away. Donatus had asserted that comic characters live in villages because they cannot, like tragic characters, afford to live in palaces.[26] Stevenson makes his characters live where Donatus, in the teeth of almost all the surviving classical evidence, said that they did live. He also manages to allude to the first derivation, in that Act II opens with a song of revelry emanating from Dame Chat's alehouse, which later forms a convenient rendezvous for the convivial conclusion.

To uncover this kind of joking innuendo between author and audience after four hundred years may seem a desperate enterprise, but in dealing with this type of writing we have no option but to try. Another joke bears more closely on lowness of humor, the topic which Victorian critics of the play found offensive. Some might explain this by supposing that, in order to amuse sixteenth-century undergraduates, if one couldn't be bawdy, one had to be shitty. But for this, too, a learnedly mischievous justification was available. Already by the mid-century theorists were showing interest in the sources of comic laughter. Whether or not Stevenson knew Aristotle's *Poetics,* or the commentaries on it of Robertellus (1548) or Madius (1550), he certainly knew the outline of the Aristotelian theory of laughter as transmitted through Cicero and Quintilian,[27] and alluded to by Victor Faustus in an essay on comedy (1511) which was often reprinted in editions of Terence. This was that laughter arose from the painless perception of *to aischron,* Latin *turpe,* something ugly, deformed, base, or shameful. Madius's essay *De Ridiculis,* printed with his commentary and reported on by Marvin T. Herrick,[28] shows how the concept of risible turpitude could be interpreted in Stevenson's day. It could be of the body, or of the mind, or of things extrinsic; it could be true or feigned. An example of true turpitude of the body would be bandy legs, of feigned turpitude, an affected limp. Of the mind, true turpitude is natural ignorance or

stupidity, feigned is a deceitful craftiness. What leads one to associate this theory with *Gammer Gurton's Needle* is not so much Hodge's ignorance and Diccon's craft—these, after all, are commonplace in comedy—but a feature of the play which no one forgets, that astonishing accumulation of images of extrinsic turpitude, especially in the early scenes, to stress the darkness, filth, and poverty in which the characters live. Gurton's cottage is filled with smoke, there are cat's turds and hen's turds on the ground. Needing light for her search, she sends her boy Cock to grope for an inch of candle in an old shoe behind an old brass pan—and so forth. This squalid background is pointedly linked to the characters' mental attributes. When Hodge, in his superstitious fear of the devil, beshits himself on stage, turpitude of mind and body are at one. Like other aspects of the play which still need to be considered, the humor of that episode must strike us as crude. Yet it has an erudite base; here again a learned concept, that of risible turpitude, is being pushed to the limit of absurdity.

The last and most pervasive of these jokes depends on the conspicuous application to vernacular farce of dignified rhetorical techniques. Chaucer, of course, had made this joke familiar, but here it was freshly appropriate because so much emphasis was placed on rhetoric in the study of Terence. Fun must have been had in noting how Stevenson transfers to the vernacular, and grotesquely exaggerates, "flowers" of rhetoric which students of Terence were trained to observe and label. Diccon's opening speech, for instance, begins with a five-part anaphora and offers prominent examples of enargia, congeries, onomatopoeia, and epangelia. But rhetorical analysis was not merely a matter of labelling figures of speech. Whole plays and parts of plays were normally categorized according to which of the three types of oratory they mainly employed.[29] Acts I, II, and IV of our play would have been classed as deliberative rhetoric, since they mainly debate what has happened to the needle and what to do about its loss. In Act III, the great flyting between Gurton and Chat is a striking display of epideictic rhetoric, with liberal distribution of blame. And the fifth act, Bailly's judicial investigation, is obviously forensic. Here logic and rhetoric unite, and it is logic, or rather the breakdown of logic, which provides the humor. Charging Dame Chat with attempted murder, Dr. Rat offers the "proof" (V.ii.22) of his broken head. Defending her innocence, Dame Chat argues, "Because thy head is broken, was it I that it broke?" In terms of logic, both advance enthymemes which fall some way short of syllogistic validity. Rat's enthymeme is strong *de facto* but weak on evidence of intention, whereas Chat's is just the opposite: she meant to hit Hodge, whom Diccon had told her to expect, and so she assumes that she cannot have hit Rat. The darkness in which the mishap occurred becomes a potent symbol of ignorance and error, and before all the errors can be traced to Diccon, Bailly is bewildered by yet more accusations: Hodge and Gurton charge Dame Chat with theft of the now-almost-forgotten needle, and Chat charges Gurton with slander, not on this count only, but also in the matter of the cock. This confusion of charges and countercharges, proofs and disproofs, marks Act V as a hilarious comment on the way Terence's comedies were studied as textbooks of forensic skill.

That last point has been implied by Joel B. Altman, the only recent critic to have approached *Gammer Gurton's Needle* through the Terentian commentators.[30] Noting especially the emphasis on darkness, Altman reads the play as a "recreation *ad absurdum* of the subjective world of Roman comedy," where characters blindly pursue their separate obsessions in ignorance of the true state of affairs. The reading is fair, but it does not preclude the more morally "sententious" one that was earlier promised. The play is a warning against pride, aimed quite precisely at an audience for whom pride of mind was an occupational hazard. The curricular parodies we have been looking at, which upset for the moment the dignity of a literary ideal, form part of a larger saturnalian vision in which the whole positive thrust of humanist idealism is put into reverse. Instead of stressing what education can lead one to achieve, the play is a reminder to scholars of the perils of ignoring their essential, abysmal limitations as men.

Diccon is an appropriate hero for academic saturnalia because his natural wit owes nothing to book-learning and has no higher object than survival and sport. The "Bedlam" label does not mark him as the lowest of the low, as it does Poor Tom: he never uses rustic speech. Rather it serves to mark him off from the other characters, much as motley separates the Shakespearean fool. Lacking a place of his own in society, he is thereby licensed to perpetrate mischief, as Bailly's indulgent treatment of him shows, and to invert the hierarchies of birth and education, as we see when he walks off declaiming the proverb, "As proud comes behind, they say, as any goes before" (V.ii.329). He does claim a personal triumph at the end, but is mainly used—again like the fool—to expose and comment on the follies of others, and so to bring the meaning of the author's fable indirectly home to the audience. His most significant victims are

Hodge and Rat, *rusticus* and *clericus* respectively. The former, "sossing and possing in the dirt still from day to day" (I.iv.26), is a type of the ignorant clod-hopping peasant on whom the aspiring student tends to turn his back, while the latter, the "man esteemed wise" (III.iii.59), is what the same student might all too easily become: a lazy, greedy, drunken village priest, deserving an animal name. The contrast between these two is a matter of humility and pride. Stevenson, as we would expect from his treatment of the *genus humile,* makes play with the concept of *humilitas,* or closeness to the ground. The first act ends with what amounts to a visual pun on the concept. Gammer Gurton directs her household to go "Down, Tib, on thy knees, I say! Down, Cock, to the ground!" in prayer to God and good Saint Anne—a tableau of spiritual humility (I.v.41-44). While on their knees, though, they rake for the needle in the dirt and Hodge tears a cat's turd in pieces. Hodge is so persistently associated with dirt that he cannot be mistaken for a portrait of *sancta simplicitas,* yet by the end of the play, and chiefly through the contrast with Rat, his humility has been tacitly approved: the slow-dawning delight he shares with his mistress when the needle is found endears him to the audience. Rat, though he poses as the poor man who fell among thieves, is criticized throughout for his self-esteem. He is the last to learn the Christian lesson of forgiveness, which Bailly reminds him he should teach (V.ii.240, 254). Diccon's plan "to lay the Rat in the dust" (IV.iii.4), and so to bring him down to Hodge's level, is provoked by a linguistic manifestation of the doctor's pride: he alone addresses Diccon in the contemptuous second person singular.[31]

Rat's pride is shamed when he symbolically lays aside his gown and thrusts his head through the hole in the ground. There, in the darkness, where a rat belongs, he has no right to claim respectful treatment as a "learned clerk" (V.i.15). As Bailly observes, "I am sure your learning shines not out at your nose." Rat's act of folly here neatly counterpoints the words with which Hodge first lamented the state of his breeches: "By the mass, here is a gash, a shameful hole indeed; / And one stitch tear further, a man may thrust in his head!" (I.ii.7-8). Here we can see how the needle's archetypal function has been morally applied. Acknowledging his shame, the rustic seeks the emblem of necessary art to cover his nakedness, while the cleric with the learned arts at his disposal needs to have his shame brought home to him. It is a fable which would have satisfied Vives. But the image of the shameful hole is not limited to those two examples. In "The Aesthetics of Scatology in *Gammer Gurton's Needle*" William B.

Toole lists further instances of anal and excremental imagery.[32] Apart from the omnipresent shit, there is the "token" of Tom Tankard's cow with a swarm of bees in her arse, and the threatened "raking" of the cat by Hodge. The hole through which Rat meets his nemesis must perforce be on the "back side" of Dame Chat's house; the needle must be found where Hodge had disgraced himself. One must grant that all this was presumably funnier then than now, but it did have some point beyond risible turpitude. Missed by Toole, it would not have been missed by Rabelais or Jonson or Swift or Pope, for whom scatology's uses were more moral than aesthetic. It was one of Terence's characters who remarked that, as a man, he found nothing in humanity alien. Searching for the truth, aspiring to the light, the scholar above others requires to be reminded of his links with the earth.

But that sober moral is not pointed directly, either by Stevenson or (except rarely) by the greater humanists whose approach to dirt and darkness he shared. The scatology of *Gammer Gurton's Needle* has been well described as "gleeful,"[33] a word which also fits the celebration of London sewage in "On the Famous Voyage" or *MacFlecknoe* or *The Dunciad.* Far from being an expression of schoolboy humor, this gleeful scatology typified the zest with which humanist wits launched their *mises-en-abîme* of humanist aspirations. Another of Stevenson's levelling images, pointing more clearly to the mode in which he wrote, occurs in the celebrated drinking-song. Ale, which the song links discreetly to sex, is not only a leveller (II.i.7-8) but a comforter too, and the song says it brings men to "bliss" (37). There most plainly, but also throughout, from the first speech of Diccon to the final madcap verdicts of Bailly, the play presents a world ruled under the wide-spreading aegis of Folly. Stevenson treats that medieval world in a manner pioneered by Erasmus, wittily linking its reversed priorities to the classical practice of parodic imitation, controlling its release of anarchic energies with discipline of form and hidden intelligence, turning trifling nonsense to the service of spiritual sense, and (as the master put it) praising folly in a way not totally foolish.

If this linkage of a rough-and-tumble English comedy to the mode of a supersubtle Latin oration cannot fail to seem absurd, it is because the "original spirit" of the play evaporated a long time ago. Today, though it still acts well, and though its levelling moral retains some point, its curricular parodies have lost all meaning, since the students who act it or see it performed know nothing of

Terentian theory. Even in 1592, when Robert Browne took it with his travelling troupe to the autumn fair in Frankfurt,[34] he presumably chose it simply on its merits as a visually effective farce. But that a play first conceived in the spirit of humanist parody could also win popular success on other terms need not be surprising if we see how it anticipates *The Alchemist* and *Bartholomew Fair*. The rest of this essay must justify that placing of the play in English comic tradition. And to do this means facing two larger questions which have already been implicitly raised. What were the defining characteristics of humanist saturnalian parody? And how did it come to impinge on English comedy exactly as it did?

Even with our present definition of "humanist" it can be difficult to decide which vernacular authors deserve the label, and the problem increases with "humanist saturnalian parody." But by recalling undisputed nondramatic examples—*The Praise of Folly*, the works of Rabelais, and *The Dunciad*—and by relating *Gammer Gurton's Needle* not only to those but also to the Jonson plays mentioned, we can find in most or all of them a number of features which are associated with the humanism of the authors concerned and which set their works apart within the broader stream of saturnalian writing in general. (To argue that such a distinction can be made has a certain urgency,[35] which may excuse some simplification of the issue and some inevitably reductive comments on individual works in what follows.)

1. The inverted vision of the saturnalian mode is expressed by humanists through systematic inversion or breaching of classical principles of literary decorum. Rabelais carries this practice to the extreme of abandoning classical compositional principles entirely. More commonly it takes the form of point-by-point mock imitation of genre, as in the mock encomium and the mock epic. In the comedies what we find is not so much mock imitation of comic features (although we have found this in Stevenson, and Jonson practises it on Shakespearean comedy in *Bartholomew Fair*) as a calculated degradation of the genre itself to a point well below its "proper" level. As Stevenson sinks Terence to the level of barnyard farce, so Jonson fixes the level of *The Alchemist* in its opening lines or insists on the decorum of the pigbooth. In all of these practices the humanist author remains conscious of the classical principles he subverts, shows a trained awareness of stylistic levels, and (except in the case of Rabelais) gives a high degree of formal artistic ordering to his expression of saturnalian chaos. In Erasmus, Stevenson, and

Jonson, especially, elaborate structure is the clearest sign given of the erudite art being lavished on low matter.

2. Literary allusiveness of an esoteric, often classical, nature underlies and pervades texts in which the humanist author pretends to be modifying his exclusive standards and establishing common ground with the ignorant. These allusions require extensive annotation which the writer may authorize (Erasmus) or provide (Pope). The subtext of learned joking which we have detected in Stevenson is akin to what editors have long discovered in Rabelais and Jonson.

3. Although signs of erudition may lead one to suspect that the author's jesting is not without serious purpose, the tone of the writing suggests no such purpose but rather a virtuoso display of wit. Humanists classified this type of writing as epideictic, following Aristotle's definition of epideictic rhetoric as meant, not to persuade, but to compel delighted admiration for the orator's skill.[36] Hence the effect of self-conscious brilliance, of an amazing performance, which all these works convey, although *The Dunciad,* with its increasingly somber moral tone, illustrates this less well than would *The Rape of the Lock.* To appreciate this effect in *Gammer Gurton* one must imagine its impact on its original academic audience.

4. The objects of parody in the text reflect the situation and interests of the humanists themselves. The particular hierarchy they tend to invert is the educational one in which they fancied themselves at the top; the ideals they question are those they most cherish, like the benefits of the learned arts, rational discipline, principled morality. Mocking their own values, they dwell with mock relish on the hazards of their profession: how the scholar becomes a pedant, the artist a charlatan, the moralist a sham; how the "man esteemed wise" falls a victim to pride and isolates himself from humanity. And from this preoccupation with their own concerns stems a tendency toward self-parody, where the author (sometimes quite clearly identifying himself) appears to ridicule stances or statements with which his public associate him. This is the feature which, in terms of content, most closely binds the Jonson plays to Erasmus's oration, and *Gammer Gurton's Needle* to both.

5. The texts imply, but do not show openly, their authors' commitment to parodied ideals. This is the most doubtful of the features here listed, since the degree of commitment concealed by irony can be hard to ascertain. It is easy to infer that Pope's Dullness and Stevenson's Rat precisely invert what their authors most cared about, or that Stevenson respected Terentian comic theory much as Pope revered epic. It is harder to find fidelity to humanist ideals in

Rabelais, *The Alchemist,* or *Bartholomew Fair,* and this is not the place to try to convert those who don't. Those willing, however, can find it by analogy with Erasmus's claim (which needs broad interpretation) that *Folly* restated his positive beliefs "obliquely . . . in the form of a wit-game."[37] The idea advanced here, over-schematic but possibly useful, is that a combination of secretiveness and commitment serves to distinguish the humanist parodist both from those whose commitment to the parodied ideal can be said to be proclaimed and from those who use parody to suggest, not commitment at all, but ambivalence. "Proclaimed" commitment is generally a characteristic of medieval parody, where the total context draws attention to the truth that is being turned upside down. In the mystery cycles the ideals inverted by Lucifer, Noah's Wife, or Mak are personified and proclaimed in the text. Even when *The Miller's Tale* burlesques the Annunciation, Chaucer has already identified the teller as a diabolic, carnival type. Blasphemous parody was permitted in medieval art so long as it was shown and understood to be blasphemous parody.[38] At the opposite extreme we have Shakespeare's ambivalent use of carnival parody, as in *1 Henry IV* or *Twelfth Night,* where the conflict between celebratory and judgmental responses is never quite resolved, and the total context finally leaves us actively contemplating alternative attitudes to life. But when Samuel Johnson, as a latter-day humanist, objected to Shakespeare's lack of moral purpose, he was showing how hard it was for humanists to accept such an unresolved conflict, being trained to believe that human betterment lay in striving after difficult ideals and that it was the writer's duty to express that belief. So for them, as for medieval Christian writers, a condition of practising saturnalian parody was ultimate allegiance to the ideals inverted. Their portrayal of ignorance and folly and moral compromise implied respect for learning and wisdom and moral absolutes; their downward vision of human animality recalled man's higher goals.[39] Their reasons for constantly concealing their commitment were, first, their sense of the need to sustain the decorum of an oblique and witty mode and, second, their habitual (and in Jonson's case provocatively unwarranted) assumption of an educated public supposedly qualified to grasp the point unaided—theoretically, the didactic function of humanist wit-writing lay in training and testing the wit of the recipient.

If humanist saturnalian parody can be defined in those ways, and if the three plays considered can be assigned to the mode, we are left finally with a simpler historical question: how did this mode come to affect English comedy in the 1550s, and then not until Jonson? It is well to recall that parody and comedy have had a long but intermittent and changing relationship. Aristotle aligned them in *Poetics,* 2, as forms of imitation which show men as worse than they are. With the example of Aristophanes before him he had reason to do so. Old Comedy plainly enjoyed a sort of carnival licence, not only to parody the style of tragedy and its solemn treatment of sacrifices and oracles, but also to invert tragedy's belittling assumptions about man in relation to the gods.[40] In the context of the religious festivals, and using a dramatic form so similar to the tragic, Old Comedy must have been experienced comparably to the true *paroidia,* mock epic. But as tragedy and religion declined, so parody in that sense vanished from the Greek New Comedy. It reappeared in Plautus in a different guise, as a simple celebration of irresponsibility, a holiday protest against workaday standards of *gravitas.*[41] But the purer revival of New Comedy by Terence diminished parody again; he established comedy on its own modest level with no implied reference to "higher things." And it was on Terence that the commentators built their theory, a temple too large for its god. So it followed that the main line of humanist comedy was never parodic at all. The writers of *commedia erudita* in early sixteenth-century Italy and France practised "straight" imitation in the sense that, however much they altered their Roman models to mirror their own times and suit modern tastes, they were conscious of practising a legitimate genre in their own legitimate languages, evoking comic values which did not need to be measured in relation to higher ones. Why Stevenson resorted to the "mock" mode may be explained by a combination of factors in Cambridge in the 1550s: on the one hand, the much lower status accorded to vernacular writing, so that both he and Udall thought of Terence-in-English as something of a joke; on the other, the lingering spirit of Erasmian *lusus,* whereby humanist wit was infused into the still-flourishing medieval tradition of inverting hierarchy during times of licence. But as an example of humanist parodic comedy *Gammer Gurton's Needle* could well have had no successors. Erasmian wit became discredited amid the religious fervors of the 1560s and 1570s, and when the humanist Lyly revived English comedy he did so with an assured sense of the worth of English and the value of his plays to the court. The next generation of comic dramatists was still less inhibited by classical example. Saturnalian parody, as is very well known, made a strong contribution to the popular comedies of Greene and his successors, but always as an element in a larger whole, located in a subplot or particular characters, never as a mode which could be said to define a whole play. It was the accident of Jonson's position as a self-conscious humanist frustrated in his attempts to reform the comic stage which led him initially, in the play which opens with Volpone's mock encomium, to take up the secretive stance of the Erasmian parodist testing his public's response to false values, and in subsequent plays to push parodic comedy to a further extreme, not just depicting the shockingly false, but seeming positively to commend more specious and plausible evasions of truth, as though comedy were itself—as he may have thought it had been for Aristophanes and Aristotle—an inherently parodic mode, an ironic celebration of mankind's failure to pursue its proper goals.

In spite of appearances, it has not been the purpose of this essay to boost the worth of *Gammer Gurton's Needle* by linking it to much greater works; it swims in this setting like a lively minnow among sportive whales. Nor has it been said to have influenced Jonson, though it possibly did. The aim has been to recognize generic affinities, and in particular to recognize a type of parodic comedy which should be firmly segregated from the saturnalian comedy of Shakespeare. It is a type which has its later as well as earlier analogues, since in all manifestations of "intellectual farce" parody is likely to be present: not only in the recognized tradition of burlesque but in comedies as various as *The Country Wife* and *The Importance of Being Earnest*, and in plays by Beckett, Ionesco, and Pinter. But in these plays the objects and function of parody have changed. The parody we have been concerned with sprang from the application of humanist wit to humanist ideals in terms of the habit of upside-down thinking which was already in decline in the seventeenth century, though hierarchically-minded Tories in the age of Pope could revive it at will. It was Jonson's infusion of such parody into drama that led to his most brilliant and controversial comedies. It is the historical significance of Stevenson's small masterpiece that it illuminates what Jonson did.[42]

NOTES

[1]J. A. Burrow, in "What is Remembered," *EIC* 35 (1985):76, postulates an elaborate essay on the play by Henry James to illustrate "a critic too clever for his subject."

[2]Respectful references to the play in recent criticism are too numerous to cite. See esp. R. W. Ingram, "*Gammer Gurton's Needle:* Comedy Not Quite of the Lowest Order?" *SEL* 7 (1967):257-68; J. W. Robinson, "The Art and Meaning of *Gammer Gurton's Needle,*" *RenD* n. s. 14 (1983):45-77.

[3]In *Three Sixteenth-Century Comedies,* ed. C. W. Whitworth, The New Mermaids (London: Benn, New York: Norton, 1984); *Four Tudor Comedies,* ed. William Tydeman (Harmondsworth and New York: Penguin, 1984).

[4]This concept is defined toward the end of the essay. "Humanist" refers here to authors whose approach to writing was primarily determined by classical training and loyalty to classical literary principles. "Parody" is more controversial. I accept the common metaphorical extension of the term by which the object of parody can be an ideal as well as a text, and especially its use in relation to the "upside-down world," the temporary inversion of hierarchies associated with saturnalia and carnival. Historical justification for this use can be found in J. C. Scaliger, *Poetices libri septem* (Lyon, 1561), p. 46: "When the rhapsodes took a break in their recitals, others would come forward to provide comic relief by turning what they had heard upside down. These were called parodes because alongside the serious matter they would introduce something comically different. Parody therefore is inverted rhapsody, a change of words making the sense ridiculous. . . . I myself once wrote something of the kind among my drinking-companions in Carnival time" (my translation). Plainly Scaliger saw his parody of a text ("Proela merumque cano") as related to the carnival concept. But we should be clear that he was reintroducing from Aristotle's *Poetics* a rhetorical term which had dropped out of view since Quintilian; the authors discussed in this essay did not use it in the metaphorical sense used here, and even in its root-sense of burlesque poem it did not enter the vernaculars until the later sixteenth century. Present-day theorists, while extending the term to cover other kinds of intertextuality, similarly tend to restrict its object to another "work of art or . . . form of coded discourse" (see Linda Hutcheon, *A Theory of Parody: The Teaching of Twentieth-Century Art Forms* [New York and London: Methuen, 1985], p. 16).

[5]William D. Wolf, "Recent Studies in Early Tudor Drama: *Gammer Gurton's Needle* and *Cambises,*" *ELR* 8 (1978):113-19.

[6]For the Terentian comic theory of the Renaissance I am heavily indebted to T. W. Baldwin, *Shakspere's Five-Act Structure: Shakspere's early plays on the background of Renaissance theories of five-act structure from 1470* (Urbana: Univ. of Illinois Press, 1947), and Marvin T. Herrick, *Comic Theory in the Sixteenth Century* (Urbana: Univ. of Illinois Press, 1950; rpt. 1964). Without rivalling their research, I have examined enough sixteenth-century editions of Terence to confirm their findings with confidence.

[7]Quoted by Baldwin, pp. 162, 169.

[8]Frederick S. Boas, *University Drama in the Tudor Age* (Oxford: Clarendon Press, 1914), ch. 1; G. C. Moore Smith, *College Plays Performed in the University of Cambridge* (Cambridge: Cambridge Univ. Press, 1923), pp. 4-5, 17-23.

[9]Boas, pp. 16-17.

[10]Preface to *Folly,* n. 16, in Erasmus, *Opera Omnia,* 10 vols. (Leyden, 1703-1706), 4:402.

[11]See Plautus, *Menaechmi,* II.i.13, cited Erasmus, *Adagia* (ed. cit., 2:888); M. P. Tilley, *A Dictionary of the Proverbs in England in the Sixteenth and Seventeenth Centuries* (Ann Arbor: Univ. of Michigan Press, 1950), N97.

[12]See Robinson (n. 2 above), pp. 68-69.

[13]I.iv.4-6; II.i.43-44. The text referred to throughout is that of Whitworth (see above, n. 3).

[14]Whitworth, p. xxxii.

[15]"As nothing is more trivial than to treat serious matters with triviality, so nothing is more festive than to treat trivial matters in such a way that you appear anything but trivial" (my translation).

[16]For Servius, see Baldwin, p. 66; Herrick, p. 60. For the Donatus passage, see Evanthius, *De Fabula,* IV, 2, in *Donati Commentum Terenti,* ed. P. Wessner (Leipzig: Teubner, 1902), I. The *De Fabula* was attributed to Donatus in the sixteenth century.

[17]Tydeman (see n. 3 above) assumes that the prologue was spoken and cites medieval banns as evidence that audiences did not mind being told the outcome in advance (p. 399). But banns used direct audience-address, addressed a different kind of audience, and introduced a different kind of play. A better parallel are the acrostic "Arguments" prefixed to *Volpone* and *The Alchemist,* which Jonson clearly regarded as part of the conventional paraphernalia of a printed text.

[18]Horace, *Ars Poetica,* lines 146-52; Herrick, pp. 99-101.

[19]See Herrick, pp. 117-18, who cites an analysis of a Terentian *narratio* on this plan from the edition of Iodochus Willichius (Zurich, 1550). The Aphthonian six parts are the person (Gammer Gurton), the deed (lost her needle), the way of doing (cast aside her sewing), the cause (the cat in the milkpan), the place and time (when she was sitting on her hassock).

[20]See Baldwin, pp. 228-51.

[21]Baldwin, pp. 409-10.

[22]See Lois Potter, *The Revels History of Drama in English,* 8 vols. (London and New York: Methuen, 1975-), 2(1980):230; Tydeman, p. 28.

[23]Baldwin, p. 66; Herrick, p. 60.

[24]M. C. Bradbrook, *The Growth and Structure of Elizabethan Comedy* (London: Chatto & Windus, 1955), p. 66.

[25]The metaphor is suggested by Herrick's frontispiece, taken from an edition printed at Venice in 1504, which shows Terence, laurelled and magisterial, standing at a lectern in a temple-like setting, with the commentators sitting at his feet.

[26]*Donati Commentum Terenti, De Comoedia,* V, 2.

[27]Cicero, *De Oratore,* 2.58.236; Quintilian, *Institutio Oratoria,* 6.3.7.

[28]Herrick, pp. 41-52.

[29]Herrick, pp. 13-17.

[30]Joel B. Altman, *The Tudor Play of Mind: Rhetorical Inquiry and the Development of Elizabethan Drama* (Berkeley and London: Univ. of California Press, 1978), pp. 152-58.

[31]This point is emphasized at IV.ii.44, where Rat inadvertently addresses Diccon as "you". Diccon at once responds by equating Rat and himself in "degree" (line 49).

[32]William B. Toole, "The Aesthetics of Scatology in *Gammer Gurton's Needle,*" *ELN* 10 (1973):252-58.

[33]Whitworth, p. xxxi.

[34]E. K. Chambers, *The Elizabethan Stage,* 4 vols. (Oxford: Clarendon Press, 1923), 2:247.

[35]For example, Anne Barton's discovery of a Shakespearean phase in Jonson's later career (*Ben Jonson, Dramatist* [Cambridge: Cambridge Univ. Press, 1984], pp. 258-59) threatens to obscure these authors' fundamentally different concepts of saturnalian or "festive" comedy. For the suggestion that *Bartholomew Fair* upholds as well as mocks Shakespeare's saturnalian pattern, see Thomas Cartelli, "*Bartholomew Fair* as Urban Arcadia: Jonson responds to Shakespeare," *RenD* n.s. 14 (1983):151-72. I find this lively article more persuasive on the mocking than on the upholding.

[36]*Rhetoric,* I.3.2.

[37]*Epistola Apologetica ad Martinum Dorpium, Opera Omnia,* ed. cit., 9, 3 (my translation).

[38]The point is strongly made in Umberto Eco's novel, *The Name of the Rose* (New York: Warner Books edn., 1984, pp. 578-79), where anticipation of how later humanists like Erasmus and Rabelais would conceal their commitment to truth through baffling wit contributes to Jorge's motive for suppressing Aristotle on comedy.

[39]This is not to suggest that their parodies were simplistic reversals of "truth." They explore, not only the dangers and difficulties, but also the ultimate value of pursuing high ideals. Thus Erasmus, Rabelais, and Jonson like to emphasize the qualities of those who can live without them, as Stevenson is indulgent to Hodge and Diccon. My point is that humanists could not live without them, because a commitment to ideals was imposed on them by their education. Stevenson's pupils might learn something through Hodge and Diccon, but could not find them relevant to their own situation. Shakespeare, less tied to this segregated viewpoint, could be more objective, less condescending. So the Bakhtinian concept of "ambivalence" is in fact less applicable to the saturnalian writing of Rabelais and other humanists than it is to Shakespeare, whose Falstaff, "larding the lean earth as he walks along," shows a deeper and more sympathetic appreciation of carnival's "regenerative" function than do Rabelais's giants or Erasmus's heroine or Jonson's Ursula, "watering the ground as she goes like a great garden pot."

[40]See K. J. Dover, *Aristophanic Comedy* (London: Batsford, 1972), pp. 31-41, 72-77.

[41]See Erich Segal, *Roman Laughter: The Comedy of Plautus,* Harvard Studies in Comparative Literature 29 (Cambridge, Mass.: Harvard Univ. Press, 1968), *passim.*

[42]This essay is a modified version of papers given at the Conference of the Association of Canadian University Teachers of English, Vancouver, 1983, and a symposium on the Renaissance, University College, University of Toronto, 1982.

SEL 27 (1987)
ISSN 0039-3657

Falstaff and the Art of Dying

PAUL M. CUBETA

Once the historical myths and dramatic concerns of *The Henriad* served by Falstaff's comic vision have been resolved by his legendary repudiation, Falstaff the character can no longer exist: "Reply not to me with a foolborn jest" (Shakespeare, *2H4* V.v.55).[1] On that command to silence, the newly crowned king has destroyed his fool and jester. Falstaff could undergo a mock-magical death and resurrection at the end of *1 Henry IV,* and he essentially "dies of a sweat" at the end of *2 Henry IV,* when he races recklessly to Westminster Abbey "to stand stain'd with travel, and sweating with desire to see" Hal newly crowned (V.v.24-25). But Falstaff the man cannot be dismissed or lie forgotten in Fleet Prison, abandoned by king and playwright. The Shakespearean investment in the saving grace of that comic spirit in his Lancastrian world has been too great. And so in *Henry V* he redeems Epilogue's promise in *2 Henry IV* to continue the story "with Sir John in it" (Epi., 28) with a vividly realized, yet non-existent death scene, both comic and pathetic, private and demonstrated, dedicated to the spirit of Falstaff the man.

Never allowed securely to grasp this protean giant even when his comic imagination and ironic vision die, the audience participates in the immediacy and intensity of the deathbed scene but not by observing those who stand at Falstaff's bedside. Simultaneously the audience is kept at double distance from the mystery of Falstaff's dying thoughts. Instead of a sentimental farewell in the cold, pragmatic Lancastrian world, Shakespeare seeks instead a resolution in which tragedy and comedy, doubt and belief, clarity and confusion are bound in a manner historically appropriate, morally satisfying, and psychologically dazzling. The theatrical gamble of creating a character by not creating him, of giving him life by destroying him yields the most memorable scene of the play.

Paul M. Cubeta, who is College Professor of Humanities and Director of the Bread Loaf School of English at Middlebury College, has published articles on Jonson, Marlowe, and Frost, written a chapter in *Teaching Shakespeare,* and edited *Twentieth Century Interpretations of Richard II.*

To achieve the dense texture of this recollected deathbed scene, Shakespeare does not turn to his usual source for things even vaguely Falstaffian in *The Henriad—The Famous Victories of Henry V* (1598). In the life of Falstaff, Shakespeare has embodied rituals, folk tales, conventions, festivals as familiar to an Elizabethan audience as those he may now be suggestively recalling in the medieval and Renaissance tradition of *ars moriendi*, or the art of dying. To design a coherent structure and meaning to Falstaff's dying moments of introspection and memory, which appear as merely broken, delirious fragments, Shakespeare may also give Falstaff the occasion to attempt a private meditation on his life in the manner of a Renaissance meditation for Wednesday night.

Reported in an intensely moving yet uncertain retelling, Falstaff's mode of dying is as mysterious and as hauntingly perplexing as any circumstance in his life. The only words directly attributed to him, the great inventor of language, are "God, God, God!" (*H5* II.iii.19). But what this punster, this parodist and unparalleled player with the rhythms of spoken language means or what tone the repetitions are spoken in is not ours to hear. The challenger of the moral, social, political, and religious values on which civilization rests dies with a word, the Word, on which pun cannot prevail. Like his heart, which Pistol avers, was "fracted and corroborate" (II.i.124), the scene recollecting Falstaff's death is a kind of transitory memorial moment, broken, unfocused, contradictory, unchronological and impossible to recreate for even their listeners by his bedside mourners, who are then about to be swept up into events in France and propelled to their own deaths.

For the old man's allegedly delirious dying moments as told by a grieving companion whose control of the English language was never firm, Shakespeare needed some kind of intelligible inner structure not available to him in the limited theatrical possibilities of an undramatic scene of dubious recollection. All that is really necessary to complete the exposition of the Falstaff story is Pistol's opening declaration and exhortation, "for Falstaff he is dead, / And we must ern therefore" (*H5* II.iii. 5-6). The flexible strategies of the meditative exercises on *ars moriendi* allow Shakespeare the undergirding of a coherent traditional structure familiar to a Renaissance audience, with its fascination for deathbed scenes. Thus he can both shape rhetorically the dramatized design of the brief scene of companionable reminiscence and give meaning to the interior monologue and meditation of the dying Falstaff. Not rheumatic, as the Hostess suggests, he is also not incoherent, only seeming so in her narrative. In this shaky account, Shakespeare illuminates for his theater audience thoughts and intentions which even in happier times Falstaff could not always share with these companions. Yet Falstaff's voice must now be the Hostess's, hopelessly literal-minded and completely antithetical to his own.

Falstaff's mocking pledges of repentance, comically counter-pointing Lancastrian political guilt, may at the hour of his death, no longer counterfeited, be transformed into another attempt at reformation. But this one is more ambiguous than those extending from Hal's first soliloquy promising to redeem the time to his father's dying plea for divine forgiveness: "How I came by the crown O God forgive" (*2H4* IV.v.218).[2] By prince or whore Falstaff is constantly reproached to repent, to remember his day of reckoning. His friends often sound as though they were repeating the conventional pieties of Thomas Lupset in his *Waye of Dyenge Well* (1541) or Robert Parsons's *The First Booke of the Christian Exercise, Appertayning to Resolution* (1582), in which chapter 8 is entitled "The daye of deathe Of what opinion and feelinge we shalbe, touchinge these matters, at the tyme of our deathe,"[3] or Gaspar Loarte's *The Exercise of a Christian Life* (1579). The moral exhortations Loarte insistently makes are typical:

> take then a zelous and feruent desire to liue a new here after, and striue to get other new behauiours, & to liue far otherwise than thou hast done tofore. . . . Eschewe al occasions of sinne, especially the companie of wicked men, but muche more of women, such as may prouoke thee to noughtines, and geue thee loose and lewd example. . . . Thou must flye suche places where God is customably offended, as be dising houses, tauernes, dauncing schooles, and such like. . . . Thou must take hede of al excesse in eating, drinking, sleping and clothing, and indeuour thy self to obserue a mediocritie and temperance in eche of them.[4]

These books of Renaissance meditation, among others, Catholic and Protestant, published in numerous editions in fifteenth- and sixteenth-century England, all explored like good-conduct books the ways in which the devout or those whose faith was more fragile should prepare for a final reckoning.[5] The admonitions of sin, death, and judgment were so common as Renaissance homilies that an English audience could have warned Falstaff as well as Hal or Doll. "Live now as you will wish to have lived when you come to that sorrowful day" is the kind of exhortation that runs through Parsons's

First Book. He would find a curious moral ally in Doll: "when wilt thou leave fighting a' days and foining a' nights, and begin to patch up thine old body for heaven?" (*2H4* II.iv.231-33). Hal, newly crowned, is only more austerely puritanical in chastising the Falstaff he abandons: "Leave gormandizing, know the grave doth gape / For thee thrice wider than for other men" (V.v.53-54).

For Falstaff, playing the penitent is a subject for infinite amusement. In plays which find their moral center in redeeming the time, repentance, reformation, and reckoning, Hal and Falstaff can counterpoint their pledges. "I'll so offend, to make offense a skill, / Redeeming time when men think least I will" (*1H4* I.ii.216-17) is Hal's first promise to himself and to the audience as he rationalizes his manipulation of his tavern friends both to learn about the potential corruption of fleshly indulgence and to prepare for a public apotheosis in good time. The language may be spiritual, but the hours of study, more active than contemplative, are more for his brilliant political future than for the salvation necessary for his eternal life. For Falstaff, on the other hand, the language of moral reformation in *1* and *2 Henry IV* carries economic, not political or spiritual ambiguities. Hal, ironically amused, notes the rapidity with which Falstaff transforms his pledge to "give over this life, . . . and I do not, I am a villain, I'll be damned for never a king's son in Christendom" (*1H4* I.ii.95-97) into a plan to take purses at Gadshill: "I see a good amendment of life in thee, from praying to pursetaking" (102-103). Falstaff's instant moral defense is that it is "no sin for a man to labor in his vocation" (104-105). His pun on *vocation* as profession and religious conversion is echoed at Shrewsbury when Hal tells Falstaff to prepare for battle and say his prayers, for he "owest God a death" (V.i.126). Falstaff's rejoinder picks up the homophonic pun on *debt*, as he is determined that this is not the day to prepare to die well or at all: "'Tis not due yet. I would be loath to pay him before his day" (127-28). Let those who value honor do so. "A trim reckoning" (135). Playful language then can redeem all moral questions.

One of the deliberately unresolved mysteries of *The Henriad* is whether Falstaff does finally make a good end, for we have only the Hostess's not unbiased judgment that "'A made a finer end, and went away and it had been any christom child" (*H5* II.iii.10-12). An audience comes to this scene after another one of public confession and repentance so carefully orchestrated that the broken and uncertain fragments of Falstaff's only private meditation are made more resonantly convincing. Scroop, Cambridge, and Gray, trapped into confessing their treason and sentencing themselves to death, seem relieved that they have been caught. Each in turn thanks God for "the discovery of most dangerous treason" (II.ii.162), asks for divine and monarchial forgiveness, and seem almost to parody the assertion of Lupset and others that in *ars moriendi* "this dyenge well is in effecte to dye gladlye":[6]

> Cam[bridge:] But God be thanked for prevention,
> Which [I] in sufferance heartily will rejoice,
> Beseeching God, and you, to pardon me.
> (158-60)

The traitors, "poor miserable wretches" (178), are borne off to their execution at the moment when Falstaff also dies, betrayed by his king, who, says the Hostess, "kill'd his heart" (II.i.88). The perspectives of betrayer betrayed, parodied and balanced, continue as a Lancastrian legacy from the time of Bolingbroke and Northumberland in *Richard II*.

For a brief interlude, almost outside the time of *Henry V*, as Henry dispatches his traitors and exultantly moves to France "to busy giddy minds / With foreign quarrels" (*2H4* IV.v.213-14), Shakespeare elusively distances the dramatic scene of Falstaff's death by recessing it into an interior moment, a scene-within-a-scene and then within that a memory-within-a-memory. Those last friends of Falstaff—Hostess, Boy, Pistol, Nym, and Bardolph—try to recapture Falstaff's deathbed hour as a last memory. But so equivocal is their disagreement that an audience cannot even be sure who was there besides the Hostess, the Boy, and Bardolph. Nym has heard another account of Falstaff's death: "They say he cried out of sack" (II.iii.27). But who are these anonymous bedside witnesses whose story is as quickly challenged as are the contradictory reports of those who now botch the telling of their witnessed accounts? The distorted perspective of each seems finally to return the memory of Falstaff only to the security of the theater audience which can only intuit the manner of his death.

The design of the scene that is played is constructed from ambiguities of time, imagery, and theme inherent in the history plays: order/disorder, bawdy/sentimental, innocence/experience, youth/age, physical/spiritual, salvation/damnation, time/sea, life/death. Falstaff's dying like his living remains beyond precise description or adequate dramatization, imbedded in the structure of its telling. The Hostess, as the primary witness, does not herself understand the import of her account. In the confusion, distancing, and failure of Falstaff's last story lies its dramatic achievement.

To the extent that there are facts, they suggest that an emaciated Falstaff developed a sudden sweat and a high fever and died shortly after midnight. Although delirious, he seemed aware that he was on his deathbed. He apparently saw a flea on Bardolph's nose and said it was a black soul burning in hell. He inveighed against sack and prostitutes whom he called devils incarnate. He talked about the Whore of Babylon. He fumbled with his sheets, smiled at his fingertips, apparently mumbled something about green fields, called out "God" three or four times. As his feet grew cold, he asked the Hostess for more bedclothes and died.

If Falstaff is making a determined effort to die well by attempting a deathbed repentance, it is one only his Maker could be sure of. No character has been advised more insistently to remember his end, nor promised more persistently to do so when the time was right. Yet at the moment of Falstaff's dying the Hostess urges upon him as a dubious theological comfort not to think of God: "I hop'd there was no need to trouble himself with such thoughts yet" (II.iii.21-22). Her words express Falstaff's long-standing determination to postpone any day of spiritual reckoning. Nonetheless, Falstaff may be attempting a meditation in the Renaissance manner of *ars moriendi*, perhaps as broken and as incomplete as the narrated account of it. Whether spiritually efficacious or not remains beyond the limits of the play. But the dramatic, ritualistic, and psychological appropriateness of such a spiritual moment fulfills the design of Falstaff's creation and existence.

The paradoxical symmetry of Falstaff's life has always been mythic, not realistic,[7] as it embodies rituals, folk tales, and festivals. For a man who lives out of all time, the hours of his birth and death are recorded as nowhere else in Shakespeare. As he tells the Chief Justice, "My Lord, I was born about three of the clock in the afternoon, with a white head and something a round belly" (*2H4* I.ii.187-89). Born allegedly an old, fat man, he dies "ev'n just between twelve and one, ev'n at the turning o' th' tide" (*H5* II.iii.12-13) like a "christom child," newly christened and now shrouded in his white baptismal clothes. From corrupted old age he moves in death to appearing as an innocent child, even as the play returns to the first time an audience saw Falstaff as he emerged at noon from bed in *1 Henry IV*. The first mythic definition of Falstaff is reenforced in his death scene. It is, as Hal says, superfluous to ask Falstaff the time of day, for he has nothing to do with these symbols of order, political responsibility, or personal self-discipline. It is also superfluous to ask the Hostess how she could have been certain when high tide occurred on the Thames that last night. Like the fertility festival and the ritual games of the purged scapegoat, this moment is haunted by an aura of folklore and superstition. It was an old English belief, according to Sir James Frazer, held along the east coast of England that most deaths occur as the tide ebbs, a natural "melancholy emblem of failure, of weakness, and of death."[8] An audience would not have known which turning of the tide, or which twelve and one without a sense of the symbolic rightness that would remove the verbal ambiguity of the Hostess's sense of time and tide. The death of the dubiously legitimate king, Henry IV, who dies repentant in the Jerusalem Chamber as the Thames "thrice flowed, no ebb between" (*2H4* IV.iv.125) parallels that of player-king Falstaff, who once mocked him for Hal's amusement in Eastcheap and now dies in Eastcheap no longer playing penitent. These balanced moments suggest again Christian rituals intertwined with folk tales, from the death of newly christened babies to those of kings and errant knights.[9]

If the Hostess, forgiving soul, believes that Falstaff is in Arthur's bosom, she is secure in her belief that Falstaff has not been judged and damned. It makes little difference whether she means the Christian heaven of Abraham's bosom as defined in Luke 16:22 or the pagan heaven of King Arthur's Avalon. And if Henry IV's belief in the prophecy that he would die in Jerusalem on his "voyage to the Holy Land, / To wash this blood off from my guilty hand" (*R2* V.vi.49-50) can be accommodated by a quibble on Jerusalem Chamber, the Hostess's malapropism should be no less certain in its intent. Falstaff has always been more a practitioner of his view of *ars vivendi* than *ars moriendi,* so if the conduct of his life has been at best morally ambiguous, then its appropriate ending would be spiritually uncertain. Medieval and Renaissance meditative rituals serve both arts for him. At Shrewsbury he prefers catechisms on honor and comic resurrections that leave the body intact; rather than the grinning honor of dead Sir Walter Blunt, he declares, "Give me life, which if I can save, so" (*1H4* V.iii.59-60). Salvation is a matter of preserving the body in time present. When at Eastcheap he promises, "I must give over this life, and I will give it over" (I.ii.95-96), the words would suit a Puritan preacher better than does their context in the midst of battle. "But to counterfeit dying, when a man thereby liveth, is to be no counterfeit, but the true and perfect image of life indeed" (V.iv.117-19).

One of Falstaff's most agile verbal games is that in his profane parody of the language of *ars vivendi* he plays a secular *ars moriendi*. As Hal tells Poins, "He will give the devil his due" (I.ii.119). He constantly protests his fear of damnation, of being corrupted by Hal even if he were a saint; he delights in refuting the charge that he is "that villainous abominable misleader of youth, Falstaff, that old white-bearded Sathan" (II.iv.462-64). He wishes, he says, that he could have been a puritan weaver so he could sing penitential psalms. He declares to the Chief Justice that he lost his voice "hallowing and singing of anthems" (*2H4* I.ii.189-90). Whether he is playing Lord of Misrule, Antic, Miles Gloriosus, Comic Satan, or Corrupter of Youth, his archetypal roles make a travesty of the traditional posture of the penitent who must think of his sins and prepare for the hour of his dying. Robert Parsons indeed writes his *First Booke of the Christian Exercise* for readers "so carelesse, or so carnallie geeuen" that like Falstaff they would hardly do more than glance at his opening pages. He asks, therefore, only for their patience while he tries to persuade them of the error of their ways and so to move them to the "necessarie resolution, of leauinge vanities to serue God."[10] Falstaff knows Parsons's text—and Lupset's, Bunny's, and Luis de Granada's—and quotes them as liberally and as cavalierly as he does Scripture, whenever they accommodate his chameleon-like purposes of serving himself while pleasing a prince in whose earthly kingdom he has hopes of long-lasting reward. He will paraphrase a meditative counselor like Parsons to share a moment of self-mockery with his prince: "What are thow the better now to haue liued in credit with the world? in fauour of princes? exalted of men?"[11] No Renaissance leader of devotional meditation would have had the imagination to concoct for a deathbed repentance the moral inventory available to Falstaff: lying, cowardice, avarice, vanity, gluttony, drunkenness, sloth, thievery, misusing the king's press, fornication. But their ponderous spiritual guides would also have neglected to point out the love and loyalty, the wit and imagination, and the comic genius that redeem Falstaff's living.

If Falstaff's deathbed scene were simply to conclude a dissolute life as Hal, his brothers, or the Chief Justice would have it, Falstaff would fall to his prayers and seek the grace Henry urges in his repudiation of him—"How ill white hairs becomes a fool and jester!" (*2H4* V.v.48). What for Luis de Granada is a metaphor of consequence for a wasted life has been Falstaff's whole reality in Eastcheap, but the Shakespearean dramatic moment of Falstaff's dying will not yield transparent spiritual conclusions to Luis de Granada's easy rhetorical questions:

> If a waiefaringe man, hauinge but one farthinge in his purse, shoulde enter into an inne, and placinge him selfe downe at the table, shoulde require of the host to bringe in Partridges, Capons, Phesauntes, and all other delicates, that maie be founde in the howse, and shoulde suppe with verie great pleasure, and contentation, neuer remembringe that at the last there must come a time of accompt: who woulde not take this fellowe, either for a iester, or for a verie foole? Now what greater folie or madnes can be deuised, than for men to geue them selues so looselye to all kindes of vices, and to sleepe so sowndlie in them, without euer remembringe, that shortly after at their departinge out of their Inne, there shall be required of them a verie strayt and particular accompte of all their dissolute and wicked lyfe?[12]

If Falstaff denies Luis de Granada's economic and moral premises, which are also at the heart of the Lancastrian political enterprises, his dying moments are brilliantly poised between accepting and rejecting those spiritual conclusions.

The undramatized scene of Falstaff's death has been ruthlessly anticipated in *2 Henry IV* as his voice modulates from robust, zesty parody to a genuine fear of encroaching death—"Peace, good Doll, do not speak like a death's head, do not bid me remember mine end" (*2H4* II.iv.234-35). At his end he appears to be a shrunken, dying old man, no longer the maker and embodiment of vital language and consummate comic actor. No longer wittily supporting his role-playing as the devil incarnate, his language, incoherent and disconnected, is reduced to conventional religious platitudes, traditional pieties, and pleas for more blankets. No longer able to hide behind the fantasies of invented language, he cannot counterfeit kings of England nor play Lord of Misrule. He cannot turn diseases to self-serving commodity or spiritual utility. And he is no longer "the cause that wit is in other men" (I.ii.10).

As a great performer in need of an audience, Falstaff has never before had an introspective or meditative moment which might be called personal. His soliloquies on honor in *1 Henry IV* or on sack in *2 Henry IV* are essentially public moments, the comedian indulging himself with the theater audience rather than his stage audience. Only in a play in which he does not exist and on his deathbed does Falstaff have a ritualistic moment of meditation in which he is only partly aware of those around him and in which his mind turns inward and backward in memory.

Just before his death Falstaff may meditatively engage what Ignatius Loyola calls "seeing the spot," recalling the scene upon which one is meditating with the immediacy of actually being present in it.[13] This conventional "composition of place," which begins a meditation, would invoke the first of the "three powers of the soul"—memory, understanding, and will.[14] Falstaff may remember a romantic moment when he picked flowers in a green meadow, although the text remains as brilliantly insecure as the telling of the babbling. That lost innocence bears no resemblance to other memories recollected in Shallow's orchard of those nights when old classmates recall having heard the chimes at midnight. Other reminiscences are also unambiguous emblems of his life—sack and women; but those memories seem now touched with the recognition of some kind of moral or spiritual understanding, the second stage of the meditative process. Now Falstaff no longer cries out for sack but against it, and he calls the women of Eastcheap "dev'ls incarnate" (*H5* II.iii.31-32). The Hostess's well-meaning denial, based on the fact that he "could never abide carnation" (33), was repudiated from the first when Falstaff admits that he would enjoy the sun only if it were "a fair hot wench in flame-color'd taffata" (*1H4* I.ii.9-10). The identification of his whores with the Whore of Babylon may suggest that Falstaff is thinking of the Apocalypse in Rev.17:3-6: "and I saw a woman sit upon a scarlet colored beast. . . . And the woman was arrayed in purple and scarlet colour." Or perhaps as a dubiously reformed Puritan he is attacking the Catholic Church, as Edmund Bunny would have him do in his meditation. The Hostess's possible pun on "rheum" for Rome—"but then he was rheumatic" (*H5* II.iii.38)—may reinforce the allusion without clarifying Falstaff's "understanding." Seeing a flea land on Bardolph's nose may be only the last flicker of the endless jokes at his expense—"his face is Lucifer's privy kitchen" (*2H4* II.iv.333)—or a deathbed prophecy of Bardolph's impending sacrilege and punishment.

Is Falstaff like Hal seeking a reformation that will glitter o'er his fault as he tries without parody to redeem the time? The fragmented and disconnected structure of his last words, the ambiguity of his observations, and the malapropisms of the Hostess deny resolution as Falstaff may drift to the third and final step in the meditative process, the engaging of the affections, or the will, which traditionally concludes with a colloquy. A meditation on *ars moriendi* would appropriately end in an invocation or prayer to God. And Falstaff calls out to God. But what does he mean? Is this only a feverish cry of fear? Is he trying to make an act of contrition and asking for divine forgiveness? Is this the cry of a man who believes that he has been abandoned by God—as by friend and king—in his last hour? Is one perhaps to hear an elusive echo of Christ's last words on the Cross, a moment Renaissance spiritual advisors urged for deathbed meditations; as, for example, Thomas More in *Four Last Things*: "But whan the poynt approched in which his sacred soule shold depart out of his blessed bodye, at that pointe he cryed loude once or twice to his father in heuen"?[15] Luis de Granada in his *ars moriendi* exercise for Wednesday night would be secure in his spiritual interpretation of this colloquy, but Shakespeare's audience is denied that certainty:

> And as well herein, as in the other thinges, thou hast to consider what great greiffe and anguishe of mynde the sycke person shall then abide in callinge to minde his wicked and synfull life: and how gladly he wishethe at that time that he had taken a better waie: and what an awstere kinde of lyfe he woulde then determine to leade, if he might haue time to doe the same: and how fayne he woulde then enforce himselfe to call vpon almightie God, and to desier him of helpe and succour. Howbeit the verie paine, greife, and continuall increasinge of his sickenes and death will scarcely permitte him so to doe.[16]

The Hostess is equally certain that she knows, but she urges Falstaff to get his mind off death and an afterlife. This, the only time any one tells Falstaff not to worry about his end, physical or spiritual, would be an ironic comfort, indeed, if Luis de Granada's precepts were attended to:

> The first stroke wherewith death is wont to strike, is the feare of death. Suerlie this is a very great anguishe vnto him that is in loue with his lyfe: and this forewarninge is such a great greife vnto a man, that oftentimes his carnall friendes doe vse to dissemble it, and will not haue the sicke man to beleue it, least it shoulde vexe and disquiet him: and this they will doe sometimes although it be to the preiudice and destruction of his miserable sowle.[17]

The Hostess's spiritual purposes may be a miscalculation, but this is her finest moment, not just in the innocence of her double entendres, the humor of her verbal blunders, or her sentimental recollecting of Falstaff's death. If ever there was a woman who had been sorely abused and put upon and "borne, and . . . been fubb'd off" (*2H4* II.i.34), it is she who has been victimized by Falstaff, who has indeed "handled" her most outrageously. Yet at the end she loves and comforts, forgives by forgetting. There is in her a Christian charity starkly missing in Falstaff's monarch. Her ministrations may also be reminiscent of those of Socrates' friends at the onset of the death of their companion, condemned as another alleged villainous, abominable misleader of youth and a threat to the established political order: "I put my hand into the bed and felt them, and they were as cold as any stone; then I felt to his knees, and so up'ard and up'ard, and all was as cold as any stone" (*H5* II.iii.23-26). At the beginning of his "Remembrance of Death" in *Four Last Things,* Thomas More recalls Plato's account of Socrates' death in the *Phaedo*—"For some of the olde famous philosophers, whan thei wer demaunded what facultie philosophy was, answerd that it was the meditacion or exercise of death"—and then urges us to "fantasy" our own death in a detailed vision that may bear resemblance to some of the Hostess's recollection: "lying in thy bedde, . . . thy nose sharping, thy legges coling, thy fingers fimbling, . . . and thy death drawyng on." Even if Shakespeare is recalling More, the unintended bawdy is characteristically the Hostess's own in gesture and simile. Falstaff's stones are cold. Desire no longer outlives performance, as Poins once ridiculed the old man. And his nose, now as sharp as a pen, makes Falstaff's gloriously hyperbolic epithets of Hal—"you starveling, you [eel]skin, you dried neat's tongue, you bull's pizzle, you stock-fish" (*1H4* II.iv. 244-45)—an inverted echo mocked by death, which has finally dethroned surrogate king and father.

The Hostess's vivid recollection of the approaching coldness of death suggests the unrelenting descriptions constantly set out by Loarte, Parsons, Bunny, and Luis de Granada as they urge one to meditate on the moment of dying with a calculatedly precise enumeration. If Shakespeare had their admonitions in mind, he has transformed the macabre and morbid into a bittersweet and humorous account worthy of Falstaff's vital comic spirit. He has detached the spiritual implications and left instead only the poignant corporeal reality, as the scene moves from meditation and remembrance to those who witness or learn of the event with limited understanding and qualified affection. As Parsons lugubriously imagines the inevitable moment:

> Imagine, what the violent mortyfiinge of all the partes together will doe. For we see that first the sowle is driuen by death to leaue the extreamest partes, as the toes, feete and fyngers: then the legges and armes, and so consequentlye one parte dyeth after an other, vntill lyfe be restrained onlye to the harte, which holdeth out longest as the principall parte, but yet must finallye be constrained to render it selve.[19]

Not so, however, with Falstaff. His heart was fracted and corroborate and killed first.

This final creating of a character thematically and dramatically dead at the end of *2 Henry IV* is thus theatrically and structurally achieved through a transformation of an *ars moriendi* meditation composed of the fragments of the disintegrating comic world of *The Henriad.* It is a memorial to a real and mythic character whose essential ambiguity remains as mysteriously allusive in dying as in living. The Shakespearean mode of dramatization is far more affective in its indirectness than any threatening exhortation of a Renaissance spiritual counselor. For us who are invited to meditate on Falstaff the loss of Falstaffian life leads to a diminution of theatrical richness. Consolation is not to be found in any recognition that Falstaff tried to die well.

In the Hostess's disjointed narrative it is possible that some in Shakespeare's audience might recall some of the popular block wood cuts of the *Ars Moriendi* that circulated in hundreds of editions and unknown numbers of copies throughout the fifteenth and sixteenth centuries.[20] In the Editio Princeps an emaciated Moriens lies naked in bed with a blanket pulled up to his waist and his arms extended over it. He is variously surrounded by friends, family, servants, doctors, and nurses as well as grotesque little demons.[21] Such an engraving precedes Luis de Granada's Wednesday night meditation on *ars moriendi* in *Of Prayer, and Meditation.* To a Renaissance audience the realistic and the symbolic, the mythic or the allegorical could co-exist in art and could perhaps be recalled in this traditional mode as a model for the moment that Shakespeare is dramatizing through narration. The Hostess is surely an attentive nurse; Boy, a loyal young servant. Bardolph would have made a good devil; he has been advised of that often enough. Possibly at the end the shrunken Falstaff might, in addition to all his other mythic and traditional roles, unwittingly adopt that of Moriens. But whereas Moriens is shown to have died well as his soul, a young child, leaves his mouth and ascends, we are left only with the Hostess's sentimental assurance of Falstaff's "finer end."

The Hostess's lament brings only a brief truce to erstwhile companions who were at swordpoints earlier that evening. Falstaff's memory now yields to their economic self-serving calculation and suspicion even before the scene is over. By the day of Agincourt his name is forgotten. Swept up in the nationalistic fervor of war against France, this ironic band of brothers shogs off to turn a profit in a world where thievery and whoring have at least moral and mortal consequences. Nym and Bardolph are hanged by order of the King, and Nell dies disease-ridden "i' the spittle / Of a malady of France" (V.i.82-83). And there is none to mourn their passing who would argue that they died well.

NOTES

[1]Quotations are taken from *The Riverside Shakespeare*, ed. G. Blakemore Evans (Boston: Houghton Mifflin, 1974).

[2]For a persuasive exploration of the parallelisms in the *Henry IV* plays and the two historical tetralogies, see Sherman H. Hawkins, "*Henry IV:* The Structural Problem Revisited," *SQ* 33 (1982):278-301.

[3]The work of the English Jesuit Parsons was modified by the Puritan Edmund Bunny in *A Book of Christian Exercise* (1584), but with his admonitions on the Christian necessity for repentance in preparation for death virtually unchanged.

[4]Gaspar Loarte, *The Exercise of a Christian Life,* trans. James Sancer (pseudo. Stephen Brinkley), (Rheims, 1584), pp. 8-10.

[5]When Caxton translated in 1490 the early fifteenth-century anonymous Latin *Tractus* as the *Ars Moriendi*, or the *Crafte of Dying Well,* he was making available a text that was to become immensely popular over the next two centuries. For a full discussion of the tradition of *Ars Moriendi* in England during the sixteenth century, see Nancy Lee Beatty, *The Craft of Dying: A Study in the Literary Tradition of the 'Ars Moriendi' in England* (New Haven: Yale Univ. Press, 1970), chs. 2 and 4. See also Louis L. Martz, *The Poetry of Meditation* (New Haven: Yale Univ. Press, 1954), pp. 135-44, and Sister Mary Catharine O'Connor, *The Art of Dying Well: The Development of the Ars Moriendi* (New York: Columbia Univ. Press, 1942).

[6]Thomas Lupset, *The Waye of Dyenge Well* (London, 1541), fol. 11^{v}.

[7]*Morgann's Essay on the Dramatic Character of Sir John Falstaff,* ed. William Arthur Gill (London, 1912), p. 184.

[8]Sir James Frazer, *The Golden Bough* (New York: Macmillan, 1942), abridged edn., pp. 34-35. Noted in J. I. M. Stewart, *Character and Motive in Shakespeare* (London: Longman, Green, 1949), p. 137.

[9]Philip Williams, "The Birth and Death of Falstaff Reconsidered," *SQ* 8 (1957):362.

[10]Robert Parsons, *The First Booke of the Christian Exercise* (Rouen, 1582), pp. 8, 9, 14, 25, and passim.

[11]Parsons, p. 107.

[12]Luis de Granada, *Of Prayer, and Meditation,* trans. Richard Hopkins (Paris, 1582), fol. 188^{r}. An English edition was published in London in 1592.

[13]"Thou must understand, that they are in such wise to be meditated, as though they happed euen in that instant before thine eyes, in the selfe same place where thou art, or within thy soule: or otherwise imagining thou were in the very places where suche thinges happed, if haply this waies thou shalt feele better deuotion" (Loarte, p. 67).

[14]W. H. Longridge, *The Spiritual Exercises of Saint Ignatius of Loyola* (London: Robert Scott, 1919), pp. 52-57.

[15]*The Workes of Thomas More . . . wrytten by him in the Englysh tonge,* ed. William Rastell (London, 1557), p. 78.

[16]Luis de Granada, fols. 183^{v}-84^{r}.

[17]Luis de Granada, fol. 190^{r}.

[18]Rastell, pp. 77-78.

[19]Parsons, p. 102. Edmund Bunny's account (*A Book of Christian Exercise,* [London, 1584], p. 90) is essentially the same. Luis de Granada (fol. 184^{r}) is no less explicit in his urging our attention:

> Consider then also those last accidentes, and panges of the sicknes, (which be as it were messingers of death) how fearfull and terrible they be. How at that time the sicke mans breast panteth: his voyce waxeth hoarce: his feete begynnge to die: his knees to waxe colde, and stiffe: his nostrels ronne out: his eies sincke into his head: his countenace looketh pale and wanne: his tonge faultereth, and is not able to doe his office; finally by reason of the hast of the departure awaye of the sowle out of the bodie, all his senses are sore vexed, and troubled, and they doe vtterlie leese their force, and virtue.

[20]O'Connor, pp. 114-71. Of nearly 300 extant copies of block books, Sister Mary Catharine saw sixty-one of the *Ars Moriendi* in twenty-one printings from thirteen distinct sets of blocks. The series of eleven block prints depicting Moriens's deathbed temptations were printed in England by Wynkyn de Worde in the early sixteenth century and were copied and modeled with many adaptations in costume and character until Shakespeare's day, but always, as in the Wednesday night illustration in Luis de Granada's *Of Prayer, and Meditation,* with Moriens at the heart of each print in each set.

[21]In block cut I a demon with a long nose hooked upward leans menacingly over Moriens. In VIII there is a representation of the mouth of hell, signified by flames with three figures writhing in agony. In IX the long-nosed demon appears with another devil pointing to a cellar where a boy is stealing a jug of wine from one of four casks—memories of past pleasures now to be forsaken? In X a man extends a scroll to Moriens "Ne intendas amicis"—"Do not concern yourself with your friends," *The Ars Moriendi*, ed. W. Harry Rylands (London: Wyman and Sons, 1881).

SEL 27 (1987)
ISSN 0039-3657

Comfort in *Measure for Measure*

MAURICE HUNT

"Pax vobiscum"—versions of the time-honored words of spiritual comfort repeatedly echo in *Measure for Measure,* especially in the language of Vincentio and Isabella, the disguised Friar Lodowick and the aspiring nun. "Peace be with you" Vincentio exclaims at the end of Act III, when Escalus announces that he will visit condemned Claudio, whom Vincentio has attempted to comfort through a vision of the hollowness of earthly life. Earlier in the play, Lucio travesties the familiar blessing when, upon entering the nunnery of Saint Clare, he presumptuously shouts, "Hoa! Peace be in this place!" (I. iv.6).[1] "Peace and prosperity!" Isabella understandably replies; if comfort exists anywhere, it ought to live in a convent. These greetings of comfort help constitute the approximately twenty expressions of comfort in *Measure for Measure,* a total higher than that for any other appearance of the word or its derivatives in Shakespearean comedy. That fact alone suggests that comfort may be an important idea in this dark comedy. At the center of the play stands a scene in which comfort is first offered, then lost, only to be finally refound. Positioned thus in the play, the scene, in retrospect, offers itself as a model of the movement of the drama as a whole. An analysis of Act III, scene i of *Measure for Measure* reveals Shakespeare's understanding—at least his 1602-1604 understanding—of the complex relationship between love and the ability to give and receive comfort. The despair of Claudio, who desperately loves life, indicates that the key to the relationship does not simply involve one's relative capacity for love. Rather, as the character of Mariana suggests, the redemptively mixed quality and aim of one's love determines a life of comfort for others, if not necessarily for oneself, during a stormy earthly pilgrimage. Identifying the special make-up and goal of Mariana's love thus becomes crucial for

An Assistant Professor at Baylor University, Maurice Hunt has published widely on Shakespeare in journals such as *SEL* (1982), *SQ, TSLL, ELWIU, Bucknell Review,* and *CollL.*

understanding the source of comfort in Shakespeare's Vienna—not only in the events of Act III but in those of Act V as well. And yet that wellspring of comforting love flows in Act V only when Providence helps arrange dramatic events so that Vincentio can tap it. Both virtuous Isabella and philosophical Vincentio discover in the course of the play that they have some truths to learn about love and comfort, truths crystallized in the haunting figure from the moated grange.

Analysis begins with the conclusion of Act II. There, Isabella, shocked by Angelo's threat to draw out tortuously her brother's death because of her refusal to yield to his lust, resolves to reveal to Claudio the extent of her propositioner's vice:

> Then, Isabel live chaste, and brother, die:
> More than our brother is our chastity.
> I'll tell him yet of Angelo's request,
> And fit his mind to death, for his soul's rest.
>
> (II.iv.183-86)

In her capacity as nun rather than natural sister, Isabella seemingly plans to use Angelo's outrageous demand as an example of corruption that makes any worldly life, including Claudio's, not worth living. The comfort of dying that Isabella intends to offer Claudio, however, quickly becomes Vincentio's subject during the opening of Act III. As Friar Lodowick, Vincentio, in a bravura oration ("Be absolute for death"), argues that feverish, self-tormenting life is only a breath that "none but fools would keep" (III.i.8). Powerfully "proving" that life is death's fool, Vincentio claims that mundane existence is an ignoble, cowardly, insubstantial, unhappy, uncertain, impoverished, friendless, teasing affair:

> what's yet in this
> That bears the name of life? Yet in this life
> Lie hid moe thousand deaths; yet death we fear
> That makes these odds all even.
>
> (III.i.38-41)

Doomed Claudio appears to find comfort in the Friar's compelling portrayal of the endless discomfort of this world:

> I humbly thank you.
> To sue to live, I find I seek to die,
> And seeking death, find life. Let it come on.
>
> (III.i.41-43)

At the midpoint of the play, the question of consolation appears to have been quite easily and definitely settled.

Because Vincentio has been a "man of comfort" for some time, his apparently effective consoling of Claudio is not surprising. When the Duke, disguised as Friar Lodowick, approaches Mariana, who is listening to a boy's plaintive song, she exclaims:

> Break off thy song, and haste thee quick away;
> Here comes a man of comfort, whose advice
> Hath often still'd my brawling discontent.
>
> (IV.i.7-9)

Paradoxically, the character who gradually emerges as the wellspring of comfort in the play confesses her repeated need for consolation. Moreover, Mariana's comment implies a time frame for Vincentio-as-Lodowick much larger than we had imagined; as a "man of comfort," Friar Lodowick has successfully consoled Mariana, bereft of her brother Frederick, on many occasions. Apparently Vincentio's request that Friar Thomas supply him with a religious habit and instruct him how he "may formally in person bear / Like a true friar" (I.iii.47-48) antedates Mariana's remark by much more time than we had supposed.[2] Rather than implying double-time in *Measure for Measure*, Mariana's comment firmly establishes Vincentio's character as a man of comfort. The Duke has, after all, been portrayed by reliable Escalus as "a gentleman of all temperance"—high praise within the dramatic context of *Hamlet,* whose protagonist regards the virtue as the source of composure amidst a sea of troubles.

Immediately after Vincentio's consolation of Claudio, Isabella's saintly *pax vobiscum* is heard—"What hoa! Peace here; grace and good company!"—a benediction of comfort ironically extended to a young man who has seemingly just attained spiritual relief. Responsive to Isabella's greeting, Claudio pointedly says, "Now, sister, what's the comfort?" (III.i.53). Isabella replies:

> Why,
> As all comforts are: most good, most good indeed.
> Lord Angelo, having affairs to heaven,
> Intends you for his swift ambassador,
> Where you shall be an everlasting leiger.
> Therefore your best appointment make with speed;
> Tomorrow you set on.
>
> (III.i.54-60)

During the series of questions and answers which follows, Claudio discovers that he might live if Isabella would give up her virginity. His outburst over her refusal reveals that he has not, in fact, been comforted by Friar Lodowick's *contemptus mundi* argument:

> Ay, but to die, and go we know not where;
> To lie in cold obstruction, and to rot;
> This sensible warm motion to become
> A kneaded clod; and the delighted spirit
> To bath in fiery floods, or to reside
> In thrilling region of thick-ribbed ice;
> To be imprison'd in the viewless winds
> And blown with restless violence round about
> The pendent world: or to be worse than worst
> Of those that lawless and incertain thought
> Imagine howling,—'tis too horrible.
> The weariest and most loathed worldly life
> That age, ache, penury and imprisonment
> Can lay on nature, is a paradise
> To what we fear of death.
>
> (III.i.117-31)

In retrospect, Vincentio's lack of success with Claudio is predicted by his similar failure to console Juliet. After leading a penitent Juliet to embracing the "shame" of her pregnancy "with joy," a satisfied Vincentio exits with the blessing "Benedicite," only to leave the audience to hear the mother's words of torment:

> O injurious love,
> That respites me a life, whose very comfort
> Is still a dying horror!
>
> (II.iii.40-42)

Even as Claudio's "comfort" thinly masks the terror of dying, so Juliet's "content" hides a horror at the imminent execution of the father of her unborn child. In each case, Vincentio not only overestimates the power of his consolation but underestimates the human frailty of his subject as well.

When attempting to account for Vincentio's notable lack of success in comforting Claudio, critics sometimes refer to the Duke's conspicuous omission of any reference to the joys of a Christian afterlife.[3] In their view, a morbid Vincentio paints only one panel—the somber one—of the traditional diptych of *contemptus mundi*.[4]

The Duke's omission is even more striking in light of his apparent belief in Christian Providence; Vincentio's later allusion to the unfolding star that calls up the shepherd, resonant with overtones of the Nativity, reflects a hope that an otherworldly providence abets his own faltering efforts at redemption.[5] And yet we should not expect that any mortal, regardless of spiritual qualifications, can fully comfort another condemned to a possibly unjust death. While we have no reason to doubt the reality of the generally temperate life that Escalus ascribes to the Duke, Vincentio has, on at least one occasion, been an intemperate ruler of Vienna. That is simply to say that he is a man—a creature unable to conform to his own idealistic account of the wise ruler drawn in tetrameter couplets at the end of Act III.[6] Vincentio's lapse in enforcing unpleasant laws has allowed Viennese vice to grow unchecked to the degree that the painful and deceptive measures which form the play's subject matter are necessary. An early version of the retiring Prospero, Vincentio has been too comfortable in his lax withdrawal from his people, from the hurly-burly required for political strength. He has, through his license, made his subjects too comfortable with such an illegal act as fornication. Vincentio tells Friar Thomas that his "secret harbour hath a purpose / More grave and wrinkled than the aims and ends / Of burning youth" (I.iii.4-6). Almost certainly an older man, the Duke perhaps takes unjustifiable pride in having a "complete bosom" that the "dribbling dart of love" cannot pierce (I.iii.1-3). Though not a "burning youth," Vincentio later falls in love with Isabella. While he has ever strived to know himself, the Duke, on at least one count, has not fully acquired self-knowledge.

Thus it is not surprising that imperfect Vincentio cannot convert Claudio. In a figure who, like Hamlet, can admire balance and reasonable moderation but never precisely attain them, the omission—for whatever reason—of the crucial heavenly half of the diptych of *contemptus mundi* nicely reveals the inner disproportion of an ethical character who would seem to be perfect.[7] Claudio's speech implies that no lasting comfort can be found for mortals for whom death is the undiscovered country from which no traveler returns. Through the centuries, audiences have responded more warmly to Claudio's poetic cry of the heart than they have to the Duke's set piece on the empty promise of this world, primarily because Claudio's rich imagination triggers the spectator's instinctive love of life. Shakespeare validates Claudio's outburst through the character of the convict Barnardine, who ironically is so comfortable in the most wretched circumstances that he feels no need to seek or receive

Vincentio's spiritual comfort. And yet, unlike Claudio, Barnardine does not cling to misery because he fears death. Still, Barnardine's attitude, regarded in the light of his "loathed worldly life," underscores Claudio's protest; a rooted and (in Claudio) somewhat attractive love for admittedly miserable life may qualify the impact of spiritual comfort in *Measure for Measure*.[8]

In keeping with the impasse between earthly love and spiritual comfort, Isabella extends no comfort to the brother who would cling to a life which he loves, if for no other reason than Juliet's and his unborn child's welfare. It is clear, as critics of the play often emphasize, that any dislike we feel for Isabella derives, in large part, from her resolve—so much like Olivia's in *Twelfth Night*—to remove herself from those warm realities that make life worth living. After all, it takes a degree of emotional detachment to pun upon the words "ambassador" and "leiger" while telling a brother that a vicious judge will send him, via bloody execution, to another world. Moreover, once Isabella hears Claudio's compromising proposal, she lashes out so unnecessarily that countless audiences have been pained by her words:

> Take my defiance,
> Die, perish! Might but my bending down
> Reprieve thee from thy fate, it should proceed.
> I'll pray a thousand prayers for thy death;
> No word to save thee.
>
> (III.i.142-46)

At this point, the eavesdropping Duke intercedes, unaccountably excusing Angelo, who Vincentio claims is "testing" his judgment of human nature by making an odd trial of Isabella's virtue. The Duke then, without any attempt at rhetorical persuasion, baldly proclaims that Claudio must be absolute for death on the morrow, even though he has heard his philosophy fail in Claudio's horror at the loss of all sensation. A second time in the scene Claudio admits to having received comfort, although in this case the deceptively genuine ring of his words issues from the blackest of moods. "Let me ask my sister pardon. I am so out of love with life that I will sue to be rid of it" (III.i.170-71). Vincentio has not persuaded Claudio of life's worthlessness; nor has Claudio silently shed his natural fear of death. The utter despair that should be heard in the actor's tone of voice reveals that the cruelest resignation, rather than positive insight, motivates Claudio's willingness to die.

In summary, the positive comfort promised at the beginning of this scene is never truly felt by its intended object. Alone with Isabella, Vincentio proposes his trick of substituting Mariana for Isabella in a dark meeting with Angelo, thus preserving Claudio's bartered life and Isabella's virginity. "The doubleness of the benefit defends the deceit from reproof" (III.i.258-59). Or so Vincentio argues. Isabella's reaction to Vincentio's scheme predicts a comic resolution for the play: "The image of it gives me content already, and I trust it will grow to a most prosperous perfection" (III.i.260-61). The comfort announced in this remarkable scene's beginning is fulfilled in its closing lines, although in a sense initially unintended. "I thank you for this comfort," Isabella exclaims, referring to Vincentio's morally ambiguous bed-trick; "fare you well, good father" (III.i.269-70). Paradoxically, the positive comfort promised for Claudio is felt by the uncomforting Isabella; strangely, comfort has been found not in the other world but in the machinations of this morally muddy one.

Vincentio's final promise of comfort relies upon the wholehearted cooperation of Mariana. The comfort recovered at the end of III.i in fact radiates from this enigmatic character, isolated by the moated grange—the reduced green world of this perplexing comedy.[9] As part of his scheme, Vincentio explains to Isabella that Mariana has known extreme worldly loss in her brother Frederick's death by drowning, the sea-swallowing of her marriage dowry, and in rejection by her betrothed Angelo. "Did Angelo so leave her?" Isabella incredulously asks. "Left her in her tears," Vincentio affirms, "and dried not one of them with his comfort" (III.i.224-26). Isabella's angry reaction focuses the solution offered by dying: "What a merit were it in death to take this poor maid from the world! What corruption in this life, that it will let this man live!" (III.i.231-33). In *Measure for Measure,* ideas meant for one character often make a striking impression upon a character who has no need for them. It is as though the life-denying Isabella has heard Vincentio's "be-absolute-for-death" speech and been truly persuaded by it. Like Angelo, who later sues for death rather than mercy, Isabella strikes the viewer as a rather brittle character who has never loved life, or as one who has never found anything lovable in life. Thus she stands amazed at Mariana's desire to embrace not only this often sorrowful life but also the man who has so basely wronged her. Obviously Isabella cannot imagine herself doing so. Vincentio patiently explains: "This forenamed maid hath yet in her the continuance of her first affection. His unjust unkindness, that in all reason should have quenched her love, hath, like an impediment in the current, made it more violent and unruly" (III.i.239-43).

Hearing these words, we may briefly recall Helena's masochistic love for Demetrius, the unhealthy affection in *A Midsummer Night's Dream* that grows stronger with each of Demetrius's insults.[10] Yet this context from the earlier comedy, if remembered at all, is not an appropriate one for judging Mariana's affection. In the later comedy, a more positive frame of reference emerges. By saying that Mariana's love for Angelo has strangely grown out of his betrayal, Vincentio touches upon the mystery of self-denying, spiritual love. "Violent and unruly," part of Mariana's love for Angelo is strongly passionate; at first glance, the loves of Mariana and Juliet seem to be similar in their turbulence. The pregnant Juliet has cried out against the lacerating love that saves her life—for her child's sake—and yet condemns the child's father (II.iii.40-42). Unlike Juliet, however, Mariana understands that passionate love, rather than being injurious, can be the key to salvation for herself as well as for others. It does, after all, urge her to play the potentially redemptive role Vincentio writes for her when reason and personal honor would dictate otherwise. And yet directing Mariana's erotic feeling is the greater part of her love—her love against all sense for her enemy.[11] Graciously bestowed where undeserved, Mariana's secular agape condenses the "Mary" of her name.[12] Her self-sacrificial devotion to Angelo does make her an intercessor for mankind in the fallen world of the play. Ironically, it is the Catholic novice Isabella who can least appreciate this greater love of Mariana's.

Shakespeare comments upon the staging of comfort in III.i in the comic episode following it. Richard Levin has explained how Shakespearean comedy often acts as either a foil to or a parody of ideas seriously presented in a play.[13] Often a comic episode functions simultaneously as foil and parody.[14] Such is the case in III.ii of *Measure for Measure*. The scenario in question begins when Pompey, arrested for being a pimp, is about to be hauled off to jail; straightway, he sees his salvation in Lucio: "I spy comfort, I cry bail! Here's a gentleman, and a friend of mine" (III.ii.40-41). In other words, Pompey resembles Claudio needing comfort while Lucio takes the place of the comforter Vincentio. Pompey's word "bail" crystallizes what was latent in the preceding scene; the ghostly father Lodowick's initial comfort—"be absolute for death"—implies Christian redemption. Christ was the bail for mankind, just as Christ's vicar, the Friar, ought to be. However, as depraved and ridiculous foils, Pompey and Lucio heighten the genuine dilemma of Claudio and the well-meant if ineffective counsel of Vincentio. Cruelly baiting Pompey, Lucio certainly is no savior. "I hope, sir, your good worship will be my bail?" (III.ii.70), Pompey entreats. "No, indeed will I not, Pompey," Lucio replies, "it is not the wear. I will pray, Pompey, to increase your bondage; if you take it not patiently, why, your mettle is the more!" (III.ii.71-73). "You will not bail me then, sir?" (III.ii.78), Pompey asks plaintively a third time. "Then, Pompey, nor now," Lucio coldly responds. Shakespeare now appears to be parodying Isabella's icy refusal to bail Claudio once she learns that he would embrace life at the price of her virginity. Like Claudio, Pompey receives no true comfort. In the longer speech quoted above, a certain malice creeps into Lucio's wish that Pompey's bondage be increased—not abated. The parallel focuses and accentuates the cruelty latent in Isabella's desire that Claudio die quickly. "I'll pray a thousand prayers for thy death," Isabella has asserted, "no word to save thee" (III.i.145-46).[15] In short, Pompey's and Lucio's dialogue causes the viewer to realize that Vincentio's bed-trick depends upon sacrificial bail rather than a legally complicated rationale for what constitutes Elizabethan marriage.[16] More precisely, Vincentio's bed-trick is possible only because in Act III, the still-loving Mariana is a sacrificial bail for Claudio and Isabella, intending to save his life and her virtue. Through the comic episode, Shakespeare stresses by contrast (or by default) the indispensability and admirable nature of Mariana's sacrifice, causing us to realize that such an act, beyond the grasp of reason, can give desperately-needed comfort.

After listening carefully to the dialogue of Act III, a question forms itself in the mind of the theater audience. Does Vincentio, a character who has denigrated romantic love ("the dribbling dart"), possess an adequate understanding of how love can lead to comfort?[17] While the passionately loving Mariana's role in his bed-trick would indirectly indicate that he does, his somewhat cold and unsuccessful attempt to comfort Claudio casts doubt upon the question. Moreover, while Vincentio at one point says "I love the people," he quickly adds "But do not like to stage me to their eyes" (I.i.67-68). His attitude appears to stem from a disdain for popular enthusiasm:

> Though it do well, I do not relish well
> Their loud applause and *Aves* vehement;
> Nor do I think the man of safe discretion
> That does affect it.
>
> (I.i.69-72)

Yet Shakespeare later suggests that Vincentio misreads his people's affection for him. Stung by his lust for Isabella, Angelo creates an elaborate simile of how his blood rushes to his heart, incapacitating him:

> So play the foolish throngs with one that swounds,
> Come all to help him, and so stop the air
> By which he should revive; and even so
> The general subject of a well-wish'd king
> Quit their own part, and in obsequious fondness
> Crowd to his presence, where their untaught love
> Must needs appear offence.
>
> (II.iv.24-30)

Angelo's poetry implies that Vincentio may be mistaken in his appraisal of his subjects' energetic reaction to his royal presence. Ironically, the Deputy bitten by lust has an insight into "untaught" love perhaps unavailable to the virtuous, self-congratulating Duke. Unfortunately Vincentio may never understand how much his people love him.

Considered in the light of his dubious appreciation of love, Vincentio's response to Lucio's libel of him is startling. Critics of *Measure for Measure* often misread Lucio's slanderous portrait of Vincentio as a secretive whoremonger because they miss the greater meaning of the Duke's rejoinder:

> *Duke.* Therefore you speak unskilfully: or, if your knowledge be more, it is much darkened in your malice.
> *Lucio.* Sir, I know him and I love him.
> *Duke.* Love talks with better knowledge, and knowledge with dearer love.
>
> (III.ii.142-47)

A ring of conviction in Lucio's utterance—"Come, sir, I know what I know"—has misled some commentators into claiming that Vincentio is, in truth, a far cry from the divine deputy sketched by G. Wilson Knight and other critics.[18] Yet the Duke's remark about the expressive interaction between love and knowledge detects not only Lucio's slander but also the latter character's pitiless refusal moments earlier to be Pompey's bail. James P. Driscoll has argued that in *Measure for Measure* Shakespeare "anatomizes the illusions of those who believe they can possess knowledge of themselves, others, and moral law without loving."[19] Earlier possessed of a bosom so "complete" that love could not pierce it, Vincentio has apparently learned the necessity of loving while overhearing the unloving quality of Isabella's words to her wretched brother. On the verge of withdrawing into the religious artifice of eternity, Isabella implicitly endorses a view of mankind as perfectable. Thus it is not surprising that she cannot speak in dear love "with better knowledge" to her flawed brother. The better knowledge issuing in loving speech is generally experiential in nature, composed of the belief that mankind will err by necessity but that forgiveness should rule, because all are cut from the same patched cloth. The Duke of Act I, protective of his perfectable self-image, has given way to the Vincentio of Act III, a character who, in his deceptive bed-trick, plans to forgive the unforgivable Angelo because, eavesdropping, he has been struck by the absolute need for empathetic love as part of the better knowledge leading to mankind's comfort.

Speaking in the better knowledge of forgiving love and offering to sacrifice oneself for another thus become the road to enduring comfort in *Measure for Measure*. Still, unforeseen events in this often frustrating play intrude between loving attempts to comfort and a prosperous ending.[20] As Claudio exits in Act IV, seemingly to meet his death, the Provost exclaims, "Heaven give your spirits comfort!" (IV.ii.68). Appropriately, the character knocking loudly at the door as Claudio exits is the man of comfort—Friar Lodowick. "What comfort is for Claudio?" the Provost eagerly asks. "There's some in hope," Vincentio replies, confident that Mariana's bed-trick and Angelo's imagined promise have gained Claudio's pardon. Yet when that pardon never arrives the exasperated Duke must quick-wittedly resort to another means of redemption. Learning that the dissolute and manifestly guilty Barnardine is scheduled for execution that afternoon, Vincentio proposes to the jailer that the criminal's head be substituted for Claudio's. In order to save Claudio, Vincentio at this moment must reveal to the surprised Provost that Claudio is no more guilty than Angelo and that this truth will be known within four days.[21] As surety for this startling claim, Vincentio offers to lay himself in hazard (IV.ii.155). Perhaps impressed by Mariana's example, the Duke takes the first step toward offering himself as bail for fallen mankind, even though his sacrifice in this case would not be literally physical.

And yet, maddeningly, the unshriveable Barnardine ruins Vincentio's plan for saving Claudio when the convict refuses to be executed on someone else's timetable. The unregenerate prisoner balks at supplying his cutoff head as a replacement for Claudio's. Like Mariana's, Barnardine's name evokes a Christian prototype—Saint Bernard and the Bernardine monks, the saviors of travelers near death.[22] In this case, however, the allusion points a contrast; Barnardine will not rescue Claudio by his own death.[23] As their religious-sounding names suggest, Mariana and Barnardine—the greatest and the least—are complementary figures in the world of *Measure for Measure.* In brief, Vincentio's meeting with Barnardine receives a comic turn of the screw. The Duke announces: "Sir, induced by my charity, and hearing how hastily you are to depart, I am come to advise you, comfort you, and pray with you" (IV.iii.49-51). But as was previously mentioned, Vincentio's earlier but dead-end oration against worldly life haunts him with a vengeance when Barnardine finds a godless, dungy existence somehow pleasurable. "To transport him in the mind he is in," the Duke morally concludes, "were damnable" (IV.iii.67-68).

Thus Providence, despite the best initial intentions of such spiritually knowledgeable mortals as Vincentio and Mariana, must provide—*deus ex machina*—an immediate savior for Claudio, keeping alive the purposed comfort of *Measure for Measure.* At this point, Mariana's self-sacrificing love and the Duke's better knowledge, by themselves, have not been sufficient to heal a diseased city: an actual, sacrophantic death is required. Comfort becomes attainable when the great fever on goodness in Vienna breaks. The first sweats appear when the pirate Ragozine dies of an actual fever, miraculously making available a disguisable head at the very instant that one is needed. Ragozine's hair and beard even match the color of Claudio's. "O, 'tis an accident that heaven provides" (IV.iii.76), Vincentio correctly estimates. Not Vincentio, not Barnardine—but the depraved Ragozine becomes the crucial bail for the most knotty of dramatic problems. And to comprehend the humbling and inexplicable working of Providence is, in this case, to gain the better knowledge, prompting kind, forgiving words of love. A couplet from *All's Well* aptly comments upon the dramatic situation: "He that of greatest works is finisher / Oft does them by the weakest minister" (II.i.136-37).

With Claudio preserved, Vincentio has the leisure to teach Isabella a lesson about comfort. Having failed in his consolatory efforts with Claudio, he perhaps can succeed with his sister. When she enters to learn the outcome of Vincentio's plot, he speaks the following aside:

> The tongue of Isabel. She's come to know
> If yet her brother's pardon be come hither;

> But I will keep her ignorant of her good,
> To make her heavenly comforts of despair
> When it is least expected.
>
> (IV.iii.106-10)

Strangely, Vincentio would lead Isabella to heavenly comfort by first depriving her of comfort. The Duke clearly plans to mislead Isabella concerning Claudio's preservation; in fact, he would have her think that her brother died. Still, Vincentio's concluding statement is somewhat ambiguous. His explanation of his reason for having Isabella believe that her brother has perished admits two interpretations, which are mutually exclusive. Each reading hinges upon the auditor's selection of a different referent for the pronoun "it" in the utterance "To make her heavenly comforts of despair / When it is least expected."

No doubt relying upon Shakespeare's penchant for referring to plural nouns by singular pronouns, G. Blakemore Evans glosses "it" as "comforts."[24] Vincentio will make Isabella heavenly comforts of despair when comfort is least expected. In this reading of the speech, the Duke tells the audience that Isabella's later learning of Claudio's rescue (her "good") will be a "heavenly" comfort. Vincentio has noticed that Isabella's love for her brother requires refining; he has heard love speaking without the benefit of better knowledge. Moreover, struck by Providence's hand in his plot, he perhaps also believes that he can imitate its working upon another mortal (Isabella), instructing her in its marvelous power.[25] In any event, the divine degree of Isabella's later comfort depends, in this reading of Vincentio's speech, upon the depth of her despair over Claudio's imagined death. In this interpretation, the word "of" in the phrase "heavenly comforts of despair" connotes "bred out of"—the notion being one of "a physic / That's bitter to sweet end" (IV.vi.7-8). Such a reading of Vincentio's speech causes him to resemble that other ghostly father—Friar Francis—who in *Much Ado About Nothing* tells Leonato and Benedick that maintaining the falsehood of Hero's death will spiritually educate the Claudio of that play:

> She dying, as it must be so maintain'd,
> Upon the instant that she was accus'd,
> Shall be lamented, pitied, and excus'd
> Of every hearer; for it so falls out
> That what we have we prize not to the worth
> Whiles we enjoy it, but being lack'd and lost,

Why then we rack the value; then we find
The virtue that possession would not show us
Whiles it was ours. So will it fare with Claudio:
When he shall hear she died upon his words,
Th' idea of her life shall sweetly creep
Into his study of imagination,
And every lovely organ of her life
Shall come apparell'd in more precious habit,
More moving, delicate, and full of life,
Into the eye and prospect of his soul,
Than when she liv'd indeed.

(IV.i.214-30)

Vincentio may be hoping that the report of Claudio's death will—in the language of Friar Francis—cause Isabella to lament, pity, and excuse her brother, and that, having lost him, she will "rack" (increase) Claudio's value, sweetly recreating him in her imagination. But if such a purpose is Vincentio's, Isabella shows no sign of having lovingly transformed Claudio in her mind when he is discovered at the end of the play; in fact, she is enigmatically silent in the moments after Claudio's unmuffling. Obviously Isabella to some degree loves her brother; otherwise she would not weep so bitterly upon first learning of his death.[26] Yet the quality of her love neither causes her imagination to dignify (and so excuse) the lost Claudio, nor prompts her to say that she wishes he were alive (or that she wishes he could have lived). If Isabella tersely says as late as V.i.446—"My brother had but justice"—she can scarcely be thinking at this penultimate moment that Claudio's death is the transvaluing loss that would reconstitute her imagination.[27]

Now let us address the second, more likely reading of Vincentio's statement:

But I will keep her ignorant of her good,
To make her heavenly comforts of despair
When it is least expected.

At the moment these words are spoken, Isabella, having trusted the Friar's stratagem, expects comfort; it is despair that she least expects. If the pronoun "it" refers to despair, the Duke is saying that he will make Isabella heavenly comforts of despair when despair is least expected. In this reading, Vincentio apparently believes that, by despairing of any good in this life (such as a last-minute reprieve for a brother), one becomes inclined to seek "heavenly" comforts—

comforts in a Christian afterlife. The Duke's remark, in this reading, thus becomes another extension of his "be-absolute-for-death" philosophy.

The troubling possibility exists that Vincentio, who overheard Claudio deny his philosophy, persists in believing that *contemptus mundi* provides an inclusive ethos for living all of life. Yet why Isabella should need further schooling in this doctrine of comfort escapes understanding. When she publicly begs Vincentio early in Act V to believe her charge against Angelo, she says,

> as thou believ'st
> There is another comfort than this world,
> That thou neglect me not.
>
> (V.i.51-53)

Yet such quotation is unnecessary; the would-be nun distrusted the potential comfort of a worldly life as early as Act I. Still, Vincentio's and Isabella's exchange in Act V clearly endorses this second, troublesome reading of Vincentio's suggestive speech about Isabella's comfort. After he has finally indicted Angelo, Vincentio turns to Isabella:

> Your brother's death, I know, sits at your heart:
> And you may marvel why I obscur'd myself
> Labouring to save his life, and would not rather
> Make rash remonstrance of my hidden power
> Than let him so be lost. O most kind maid,
> It was the swift celerity of his death,
> Which I did think with slower foot came on,
> That brain'd my purpose. But peace be with him.
> That life is better life, past fearing death,
> Than that which lives to fear. Make it your comfort,
> So happy is your brother.
>
> (V.i.387-97)

In this late speech, Vincentio appears to be expanding upon his earlier, ambiguously expressed purpose in concealing Claudio after Isabella's brother has been saved. The Duke's final utterance again reprises his "be-absolute-for-death" philosophy, making the heavenly comforts earlier referred to those of a Christian afterlife. Not surprisingly, Isabella's response to the Duke's speech is a quick and simple "I do, my lord" ("I do make my comfort my belief that Claudio is happy in another world").

Vincentio's fifth-act emphasis upon otherworldly comfort is puzzling in light of Shakespeare's simultaneous valuing of worldly life throughout *Measure for Measure.* This valuing is perhaps most apparent in the implicit underwriting of the sensual life occurring in overtly humorous episodes. Elbow's malapropisms concerning his great-bellied wife, Master Froth, and Mistress Overdone's "hot-house," for example, suggest not only that Christians (like Isabella) on occasion might be profane but also that a brothel might in some sense be respected. Shakespeare's indirect challenging of Vincentio's and Isabella's conventional morality prepares us for understanding why these characters finally can be classed together. In general, the characters of this dark comedy can be grouped according either to a love for earthly life or to an indifference to its possible pleasures and rewards—fruits such as Claudio's and Juliet's child (one of the traditional comforts of dramatic comedy).[28] Claudio, Lucio, and Barnardine, for example, belong in differing degrees to the first camp. Angelo and Vincentio basically belong to the second group of characters, those who either find it easy to die and relinquish this life or who place their trust in the comfort of another world. Once accused, Angelo finds craving death easier than begging for mercy (V.i.474); for him, non-existence is preferable to the painful duty of trying to find happiness in a problematic life. Isabella of course belongs in this latter group, as her ready agreement with Vincentio's advice indicates. Paradoxically, she has never needed the comfort that he planned to teach her.[29] In *Measure for Measure*, Shakespeare disturbingly creates his major characters without a strong zest for living, without, in other words, a powerful need to practice the pleasure principle that, from the time of the Greeks, has informed dramatic comedy. It is perhaps unnecessary to point out that Shakespeare does not sanction one group's view over that of the other.[30] Instead, in keeping with his mindset of complementarity, he sanctions both views at once in the mysterious figure of Mariana.

Only Mariana finds comfort both in a love for the unlovable Angelo and the hard-earned joys of this life, as well as in the faith that an afterlife redeems miseries of daily existence. Two loves she has—that for Angelo and that for the God described by Friar Lodowick. Her name, reminiscent of a heavenly mediator, links her with the Providence of *Measure for Measure* that makes double comfort possible for those who desire it. Even Isabella finally comes under her influence. Kneeling to beg for mercy for Angelo, Mariana exclaims,

sweet Isabel, take my part;
Lend me your knees, and all my life to come
I'll lend you all my life to do you service.

(V.i.428-30)

By her admonition "take my part," Mariana is asking for more than Isabella's emotional support; she is in fact entreating her to assume her role of spiritual mediator. Finally dropping to her knees to ask for Angelo's salvation, Isabella mirrors Mariana beside her, capable at last of the self-humbling, forgiving attitude required of the comforter. According to Vincentio's first-act definition of virtue, good qualities become realities not when we simply possess them but only when they "go forth of us" (I.i.34), only when they issue in actions, in "use." Through the acts of kneeling and clasping her hands, Isabella's virtue clearly materializes. Comfort finally becomes a deed rather than a consolatory word that has so often failed. Vincentio's curt dismissal of her plea for Angelo's life as "unprofitable" ought not to indict her as mediator; he simply knows that her argument is rendered irrelevant by her brother's life—a reality he hastens to reveal. Like the audience, Vincentio tacitly must be pleased with Isabella's new-found capacity for comfort. That her subsequent silence before unmuffled Claudio troubles us should not qualify the triumph of her willingness to imitate Mary's blessed intercession. Such silence coming so soon after victory simply accentuates the mingled yarn out of which the play's characters are woven. Initially offered, seemingly lost forever, refound in the figures of the praying Mariana and Isabella of Act V, comfort in *Measure for Measure* becomes an overriding value, a complex value that Shakespeare teaches us to forego in easier, more comprehensible reductions, and to admire in its mysterious incarnations. Leaving the theater we find consolation in the visual image of two kneeling women which remains imprinted in our minds.

NOTES

[1]All quotations from *Measure for Measure* are taken from the New Arden edition, J. W. Lever, ed. (1965; rpt. New York: Random House, 1967). All other Shakespearean dramatic references are to *The Riverside Shakespeare,* G. Blakemore Evans, ed. (Boston: Houghton Mifflin, 1974).

[2]This temporal discrepancy is also noticed by Richard A. Levin, "Duke Vincentio and Angelo: Would 'A Feather Turn the Scale'?" *SEL* 22 (1982):264; and by Louise Schleiner, "Providential Improvisation in *Measure for Measure,*" *PMLA* 97 (1982):232.

[3]See, for example, F. R. Leavis, "The Greatness of *Measure for Measure,*" *Scrutiny* 10 (1942):238-39; A. P. Rossiter, *Angel With Horns: and Other Shakespearean Lectures* (New York: Theatre Arts Books, 1961), pp. 165-66; Lever, p. lxxxvii; Richard P. Wheeler, *Shakespeare's Development and the Problem Comedies: Turn and Counter-Turn* (Berkeley: Univ. of California Press, 1981), pp. 116-19; and Judith Rosenheim, "The Stoic Meaning of the Friar in *Measure for Measure,*" *ShakS* 15 (1982):187-88. For an alternative account of the structure and nature of the Duke's famous speech, see Ernest Schanzer, *The Problem Plays of Shakespeare: A Study of "Julius Caesar," "Measure for Measure," "Antony and Cleopatra"* (1963; rpt. New York: Schocken, 1965), p. 80.

[4]The most interesting interpretation of Vincentio's failure is Joseph Westlund's in *Shakespeare's Reparative Comedies: A Psychoanalytic View of the Middle Plays* (Chicago: Univ. of Chicago Press, 1984), pp. 164-67. In his opinion, Vincentio purposely creates through words a valueless world so that Claudio will stop idealizing others and blaming sex and Juliet for his undoing—the young man compelled in the process to find comfort in something pragmatically real, after the Duke's devastating portrait. But if this represents Vincentio's plan for comfort, his strategy does not work; Claudio never speaks of something more real than his vital love of life.

[5]Josephine Waters Bennett, in *Measure for Measure as Royal Entertainment* (New York: Columbia Univ. Press, 1966), comments upon the Duke's "Look, th' unfolding star calls up the shepherd": "The court audience had celebrated Christmas morning just the day before, and would surely be reminded of the star and the shepherds of the Nativity story" (p. 27).

[6]Also see III.ii.179-83 and IV.i.60-65, in which Vincentio implicitly alludes to himself as a mighty king, possessed of greatness.

[7]The immoderation of *Measure for Measure* is well portrayed by W. L. Godshalk, "*Measure for Measure:* Freedom and Restraint," *ShakS* 6 (1970):137-50.

[8]Leavis asserts that an implicit criticism of Vincentio's speech is conveyed through Barnardine: "of all the attitudes concretely lived in the play, the indifference to death displayed by him comes nearest to that preached by the Friar. . . . And towards him we are left in no doubt about the attitude we are to take: 'Unfit to live or die,' says the Duke, voicing the general contempt" (p. 238).

[9]See James Trombetta, "Versions of Dying in *Measure for Measure,*" *ELR* 6 (1976):62.

[10]Helena's masochism has been described by Joan Stansbury, "Characterization of the Four Young Lovers in *A Midsummer Night's Dream,*" *ShS* 35 (1982):57-63.

[11]Darryl J. Gless, in *Measure for Measure, the Law, and the Convent* (Princeton: Princeton Univ. Press, 1979), explains that the coexistence of Mariana's passion and miraculous love finds precedence in the reconciliation of passion and piety in such Renaissance works as Spenser's *Four Hymns* and *Epithalamion* (p. 222). Gless's citing of the libertine Lucio's gracious speech on natural fertility as an analogue is also convincing.

[12]In "*Measure for Measure* and Christian Doctrine of the Atonement," Roy W. Battenhouse notes: "And Mariana, without whose gift of herself the ransom could not have been paid, and the brother must then have perished, combines in her name (meaning literally 'bitter grace') the memory of Mary the Virgin and Anna the immaculate mother," *PMLA* 61 (1946):1035.

[13]Richard Levin, *The Multiple Plot in English Renaissance Drama* (Chicago: Univ. of Chicago Press, 1971), pp. 111-24.

[14]Levin, p. 124.

[15]Concerning Isabella's turning upon Claudio, Norman Rabkin, in *Shakespeare and the Common Understanding* (New York: Macmillan, 1967), remarks that "her fault is not in what she asks, but rather in her failure to recognize the value of the sacrifice she demands. Though she is right she seems too right, acts as if what she asks of Claudio is easy to give; she is a prig" (p. 102).

[16]Critics have been hard put to find precedent in Elizabethan canonic and civil law for excusing Angelo's sexual intercourse and damning Claudio's. In "The Marriage Contracts of *Measure for Measure*: A Reconsideration," Karl Wentersdorf concludes, after a survey of Elizabethan *de facto* marriage contracts, that "in no sense does Friar Lodowick's assertion that Mariana will commit no sin in bedding Angelo ring legally true," *ShS* 32 (1979):142. Also see Schanzer, pp. 75-76. According to both Wentersdorf and Schanzer, Claudio's and Juliet's private expressed intention to wed constitutes a valid Elizabethan *per verba de praesenti* marriage. Schanzer asserts that "the marriage-contract between Angelo and Mariana seems to have been a case of sworn spousals *per verba de futuro* (in which the couple promise under oath to become husband and wife at a future date). Now any *de futuro* contract was turned into matrimony and became as indissoluble as a *de praesenti* contract as soon as cohabitation between the betrothed couple took place" (pp. 110-11). III.i.213-18 establishes the *de futuro* dimension of Angelo and Mariana's marriage contract.

[17]Vincentio's initial naiveté about "wholesome romantic love" is described by Cynthia Lewis, "'Dark Deeds Darkly Answered': Duke Vincentio and Judgment in *Measure for Measure*," *SQ* 34 (1983):279. Also see John Russell Brown, *Shakespeare and his Comedies* (1962; rpt. London: Methuen, 1968), p. 194.

[18]Like G. Wilson Knight in *The Wheel of Fire: Interpretations of Shakespearian Tragedy with Three New Essays* (1949; rpt. Cleveland: World, 1957), pp. 73-96, Bertrand Evans, for example, views Vincentio as a supreme power, wholly omniscient and omnipotent. See *Shakespeare's Comedies* (Oxford: Clarendon Press, 1960), pp. 186-219.

[19]James P. Driscoll, *Identity in Shakespearean Drama* (Lewisburg: Bucknell Univ. Press, 1983), p. 107.

[20]For the aesthetically frustrating dramaturgy of *Measure for Measure*, see Michael Goldman, "Comic Expectation in *Measure for Measure*," *Shakespeare and the Energies of Drama* (Princeton: Princeton Univ. Press, 1972), pp. 162-74; Richard Fly, *Shakespeare's Mediated World* (Amherst: Univ. of Massachusetts Press, 1976), pp. 53-83; and Jean E. Howard, "*Measure for Measure* and the Restraints of Convention," *ELWIU* 10 (1983):149-58.

[21]Vincentio's admission that Angelo is as guilty as Claudio confirms the similarity of Claudio's and Angelo's acts of fornication, and so reveals Vincentio's desire to deceive Isabella for her own good when he explains that Mariana and Angelo may copulate without sin.

[22]In n. 17 of 1:156 of *The Works of Thomas Nashe*, ed. Ronald B. McKerrow, 5 vols. (Oxford: Basil Blackwell, 1958-1966), McKerrow suggests that the name Barnardine may be "a jesting allusion to the order of St. Bernard."

[23]For other interpretations of Barnardine's name, consult James E. Ford, "Barnardine's Nominal Nature in *Measure for Measure*," *PLL* 18 (1982):77-81; and Gless, pp. 257-64.

[24]*The Riverside Shakespeare*, p. 577.

[25]However, if Vincentio wanted to teach Isabella a lesson mainly about Providence, *immediately* divulging the providential death of Ragozine, the substituting of the head, and the saving of Claudio's life would be equally if not more effective.

[26]Shakespeare stresses the intensity of Isabella's grief over Claudio's loss by calling attention to her tears on three occasions. "Nay, dry your eyes" (IV.iii.127), Vincentio first implores; then he urges Isabella to "Command these fretting waters from your eyes / With a light heart" (lines 146-47). Finally, Lucio states, "O pretty Isabella, I am pale at mine heart to see thine eyes so red" (IV. iii. 150-51). While love—not simply anger or frustration—must partly cause these tears, Isabella does not love Claudio in a way that encourages her to refrain from judging him. Her love has not led her to speak apologetically (in better knowledge) of his frailties.

[27]Another reading of the failure of Vincentio's efforts with Isabella vis-à-vis Claudio is Christopher Palmer, "Selfishness in *Measure for Measure*," *EIC* 28 (1978):199-200.

[28]For the conflict between life- and death-fulfilling desires in *Measure for Measure*, see R. A. Foakes, *Shakespeare: The Dark Comedies to the Last Plays* (Charlottesville: Univ. Press of Virginia, 1971), pp. 17-31. Also see Lawrence W. Hyman, "The Unity of *Measure for Measure*," *MLQ* 36 (1975):3-20.

[29]In *King Lear*, the failure of Edgar's educational program for comforting Gloucester (his son's ill-timed revelation literally kills him) confirms Shakespeare's skeptical Jacobean attitude toward the likelihood of consoling someone through deception. In this regard, see Philip Edwards, "Shakespeare and the Healing Power of Deceit," *ShS* 31 (1978):119-24. Alternative detailed readings of Vincentio's "education" of Isabella are given by Gless, pp. 178-213, and by Bennett, pp. 69-74.

[30]In *Measure for Measure*, Norman Rabkin describes a complementary "opposition between the Christian and the hedonistic-naturalistic views of life, so powerfully dramatized in the parallel speeches of the Duke and Claudio in III.i" (p. 104).

SEL 27 (1987)
ISSN 0039-3657

Jonson's Jacobean Masques and the Moral Imagination

NATHANIEL STROUT

In the six decades since T. S. Eliot observed of Ben Jonson's court masques that the artistry of spectacle was no longer fully appreciated, we have learned a good deal about the complexity of a genre once easy to dismiss as excessive flattery of princes who ought to have been spending time on state affairs instead of spending on entertainment money they did not have. We better understand, for example, Jonson's skillful handling of such formal restrictions as a king who stayed a spectator, and the need to include dancing. We better understand the contributions to the masque of the scenic designer Inigo Jones. And we have had traced for us the ways the structure and content of Jonson's masques generally, and in some cases specifically, reflect the political concerns of the day.[1]

That the performance of a masque was a state occasion of some importance is attested to by the frequent disputes between ambassadors to James's court over precedence at those expensive evenings. Masques were meant to demonstrate the ruler's generosity and authority, to show off the magnificence of "that great name Britannia, this blessed isle" (*Blackness* 216).[2] It is worth remembering, however, that James is praised in Jonson's masques for his virtue as well as for his power, and that to Jonson the context of a masque was moral as well as political. Looking back at over twenty years of writing for the court in the introductory remarks to his first Caroline masque, Jonson granted primary importance to the great claim of his age about the moral seriousness of literature, acknowledging the importance of royalty only in a parenthesis:

Nathaniel Strout, Assistant Professor of English at Hamilton College, has published a related article on Jonson's "A Celebration of Charis" in *TSLL*. He is currently engaged in studying John Ford's ideas of how women are to be portrayed in tragedy.

> all representations, especially those of this nature in court, public spectacles, either have been or ought to be the mirrors of man's life, whose ends, for the excellence of their exhibitors (as being the donatives of great princes to their people) ought always to carry a mixture of profit with them no less than delight.
>
> (*Love's Triumph* 2-7)

Perhaps we can no longer fully appreciate the Jonsonian masque because the current fascination with the ways literature illustrates various forms of social and cultural power leads us to discount moral claims. Besides, we also tell ourselves, authorial statements of intent do not often explain authorial practice. Nevertheless, I submit, the changing shapes of Jonson's Jacobean masques reveal his moral commitment as much as his interest in what might be termed the politics of spectacle.

The ethical import of the celebratory sections of Jonson's masques—the educating praise, the orderly dances, the harmonious voices, the scene of light—is well known.[3] I am interested, however, in the consequences for a masque as a whole of the Renaissance commonplace that literary works mirror life. In particular, if one reflects the other, then reading is the equivalent of worldly experience and, as Milton puts it in *Areopagitica,* "whatever thing we hear or see, sitting, walking, travelling, or conversing, may be fitly called our book, and is of the same effect that writings are."[4] To Jonson, the act of reading implied the active exercise of understanding and judgment; therefore he published, with extended commentary for the reader, plays like *The Staple of News* and *The New Inn* that failed to please audiences in the theater. Thus a Jonsonian masque exhorts spectators to "read" James as they "would do the book / Of all perfection" (*News* 310-11). The question, though, is whether watching a masque or a play "is of the same effect" as reading it.

In the theater the willing suspension of disbelief carries with it the potential suspension of critical judgment. Instead of judicious assessment as a prelude to virtuous action, audiences may simply rest content when their expectations of plot and character are fulfilled. And if art mirrors life, this aesthetic complacency can be paralleled by moral complacency. In *An Apology for Poetry*, Sidney ascribes to literature a superior capacity for bringing about virtuous action by placing images of virtue before "the imaginative and judging power."[5] But evident in Jonson's plays are strong doubts that the imaginative experiences offered by drama, especially the unqualified happy endings of popular comedy, encourage moral awareness. From theatergoers, as has often been noted, Jonson sought judgment over uncritical empathy, active insight over passive enjoyment.[6]

In the masquing hall the problem of audience complacency was more severe than in the theater. For one thing, writers of masques faced, as Jonas Barish has remarked, "a society not so much aspiring after as joyfully contemplating its own well-being, the possession of the blessings it considers itself to have achieved."[7] At a performance, that is, the dancing courtiers, the king sitting on a throne directly across from the stage, and the glittering audience itself could expect to be as much on display as Jonson's poetry. They could also expect to enjoy the demonstration, central to the Jonsonian masque, of how the monarch's virtue and power are both the cause of and the occasion for the triumph of harmony and order over the cacaphony of folly and vice. That the masquers descended from the performing area to join with the court in celebratory dances further reinforced the complacent notion that masques presented a dressed-up version of the actual, not a morally improving version of the ideal.

Worse still, whereas the Jacobean theater audience encountered a fundamentally verbal form, Inigo Jones's scenic designs were at least as important to the court as Jonson's words. Obviously, Jones's theatrical machines could make virtue's triumphs more immediately vivid than could words alone—a positive potential for bringing ideals alive in the minds of spectators that Jonson explored in his early masques. But Jones's stagecraft, as Stephen Orgel has shown, made increasing use of perspective settings for his special effects in the main masque.[8] As a result, a masque's idealized figures increasingly appeared less like symbolic abstractions that needed to be thought about, and more like descriptive surfaces that needed only to be looked at. The powerful immediacy of the visual experience, in turn, could readily disable "the imaginative and judging power," either by making it easier for the audience to accept the essentially passive act of seeing as an adequate substitute for the mentally active search for significance, or by making it easier for the audience to accept the vicarious as an adequate substitute for the actual.

According to Orgel, "for Jonson, one of the most compelling aspects of Jones's theater was the way it could make the stage's illusion merge with the court's reality."[9] But this formulation fails to distinguish between the reality of watching a performance in the masquing hall and the reality of performing actions in the world at large. I shall argue that Jonson's later Jacobean masques seek to remind the court that attending performances of moral fictions—no matter how visually convincing they are—is not the equivalent of attending to the actual state of one's moral well-being. Given what the court expected and what Jones was ever more able to do, Jonson's means to this end were limited in extent and success. But one is especially notable in light of the frequent recourse in Jonsonian criticism to "the distinction between things as they are and things as they should be," to "the interplay between the pure vision and the impure context."[10] In the later masques the context gradually becomes the work itself, and the vision of things as they should be becomes the responsibility of the beholders to imagine and to act on, not just of the poet to portray.

As a dramatist, said Coleridge, Shakespeare is the poet of "expectation in preference to surprize."[11] To Jonson, fulfilling expectations risks inducing moral complacency. He thus tries in the court masque to be the poet of the unexpected: "I have not seen the place could more surprise" (150), says Wonder in *The Vision of Delight* (1617), as the figure models for onlookers the proper response to the rapid change of scene that occurs in all of Jonson and Jones's collaborations. Even in *The Gypsies Metamorphosed* (1621)—in which, as Jonson's epilogue at Windsor delightedly announces, the poet was "assisted by a barber and a tailor" (1398), not Jones's machines—the perception of James as an ideal monarch comes suddenly upon the palm-reading captain of the gypsies (played by the royal favorite, the Duke of Buckingham):

> You live chaste and single, and have buried your wife,
> And mean not to marry, by the line of your life.
> Whence he that conjectures your quality learns
> You're an honest good man and have care of your bairns.
> Your Mercury's hill too a wit doth betoken,
> Some book-craft you have, and are pretty well spoken.
> But stay! in your Jupiter's mount what's here?
> A king? A monarch? What wonders appear!
> High, bountiful, just, a Jove for your parts,
> A master of men, and that reign in their hearts.
>
> (281-90)

Jonson wants the abrupt shifts of scene and rhythm in his masques both to mark and to prompt the gaining of new insight.

But relying on surprise as an artistic principle invites inappropriate responses from the audience. If, for example, the imagination is bound by conventional preconceptions, then the new may wrongly be judged wanting, as happened when the court thought *Pleasure Reconciled to Virtue* (1618), in the words of one observer, "came far short of the expectation" (quoted in H&S 10:576). On the other hand, if the new is sought uncritically, then novelty wrongly becomes valuable in itself—a foolish curiosity satirized repeatedly in Jonson's later antimasques. Further, there were limits to the surprises masques could attempt. Although "Jonson was constantly experimenting with a form that was, in large measure, his to define," he still had to include such expected elements as graceful dances, glorious spectacle, and fulsome praise of masquers and monarch.[12] In *Neptune's Triumph for the Return of Albion,* Jonson's masque for 1624, a poet complains that it is a "heavy and hard task, to satisfy Expectation, who is so severe an exactress of duties, ever a tyrannous mistress, and most times a pressing enemy" (33-35). A cook answers that the full variety of audience expectations must be met, that all palates must be satisfied, even if "they expect more than they understand" (39). The poet, in other words, implies that authors usually have to fight against audience expectations while submitting to them; the cook, that having to fit the work to what the audience expects is not a burden but an inherent part of being a poet.

Neither figure, however, argues that audience expectations can simply be ignored. Thus, whether or not the poet expresses Jonson's own frustration, whether the cook is right or just gets the last word, the discussion is a sign of Jonson's concern about the distorting effect of expectations on perception and judgment. Just as authors must consider how to adjust to the expectations of audiences without sacrificing the integrity of their artistic visions, so audiences must consider the value of holding to conventional preconceptions of art. As a figure who looks for the usual symbols of the man in the moon—"his dog at his girdle and the bush of thorns at his back" (102-103)—is told in the antimasque of *News from the New World Discovered in the Moon* (1620): "if that bush of thorns should prove a goodly grove of oaks, in what case were you and your expectation?" (104-106). Unexamined expectations, and the preconceptions on which they are based, leave us unprepared to respond intelligently to what happens, whether in a work of literature or in life itself.

It is easier, though, for us to assess a work in light of what we already think than to reassess ourselves while thinking about a work. In the first decade of James's reign, Jonson concentrated on overcoming this all-too-willing complacency through direct appeals to the imagination and judgment of masquegoers. The masques in the 1616 folio, for example, regularly make their moral points by straightforwardly celebrating the triumph of virtue, harmony, and order over their opposites. This pattern, so pervasive it can misleadingly appear normative for the Jonsonian masque in general, is perhaps most obvious in *The Masque of Queens* (1609), in which witches representing vice are instantly vanquished by the sudden appearance of Heroic Virtue and the symbolic splendor of Queen Anne and her companions seated in the House of Fame. At the end of the work, the masquers themselves are physical proof that goodness exists: "Who, Virtue, can thy power forget / That sees these live and triumph yet?" (516-17). Similarly, in *The Golden Age Restored* (1615), placed out of chronological order at the end of the folio, when the Iron Age, "calling forth the evils" (32), rebels against Jove's rule in an antimasque dance, Pallas shows her shield and freezes the dancers in a tableau of vice: "Die all that can remain of you but stone, / And that be seen awhile, and then be none" (77-78). Astraea and the Golden Age then appear, and by joining in the revels the masquers and the court both celebrate and participate in the return of the goddess of justice to earth.

In the folio masques, moreover, the final words often recall the glories of the evening, even as the masquers are being called away by day. *Oberon* (1611), for example, ends claiming that the sun is hastening to rise "lest, taken with the brightness of this night, / The world should wish it last, and never miss his light" (367-68). *Love Freed from Ignorance and Folly* (1611) closes implying that what happens in the work is more important than what happens afterwards:

> Now, now gentle Love is free, and beauty blessed
> With the sight it so much longed to see.
> Let us, the muses' priests and Graces go to rest;
> For in them our labors happy be.
>
> (325-28)

Even the satiric *Love Restored* (1612), which makes fun of those trying to get in to see a masque, concludes by reaffirming the worth of masquing.[13]

If, however, the triumph of virtue is too convincing, if the ending of a masque looks backward too longingly, an audience already prone to complacency can decide that watching and dancing sufficiently demonstrate its moral sensibility. Some of Jonson's later masques address this problem by reminding the court, in the words of the closing song of *The Vision of Delight*, that "as night to sport, day doth to action call" (229). Masquing in these works is treated as an evening of relaxation, not a morally valuable activity in its own right. Before the end of *Pleasure Reconciled,* for instance, the dances are said to be instructive both for masquers and for those watching them:

> For dancing is an exercise
>   Not only shows the mover's wit,
> But maketh the beholder wise,
>   As he hath power to rise to it.
>
> (240-43)

Yet Jonson is not as satisfied as he is in, say, *The Golden Age Restored* with the moral possibilities of dance. The final song of *Pleasure Reconciled* sends the masquers back to the paths of virtue after a night of entertainment:

> These, these are hours by Virtue spared
>   Herself, she being her own reward,
>   But she will have you know
>   That though
>   Her sports be soft, her life is hard.
>   You must return unto the hill.
>
> (297-302)

The masquers then "danced their last dance, and returned into the scene, which closed, and was a mountain again as before" (318-19).

Orgel's comment in *The Jonsonian Masque* on this last bit of stage business indicates how difficult it is to counteract the potential of a masque to give the false impression that experiencing a work is the equivalent of experience in the world: "All the masque can do, Jonson seems to say, is to offer a moment in which a vision of an ideal becomes a poetic and dramatic experience—becomes, in other words, a reality."[14] Subsequent masques, significantly, point courtiers and king more directly toward the reality experienced outside the masquing hall. In *Pan's Anniversary,* the masque for James's birthday in 1620, for example, the masquers do not return "into the scene." Instead, the same figure who promises that "surely the better part of the solemnity here will be dancing" (70-71) also reminds both masquers and audience of their regular responsibilities in a closing eight-line address that begins: "Now each return unto his charge" (240). On a larger scale, after the revels of *Time*

Vindicated to Himself and to His Honors (1623) the Chorus, singing what in an early masque would have been the last song, admires the brilliance of the masquers within the masque world:

> We hope that now these lights will know their sphere,
> And strive hereafter to shine ever here,
> Like brightest planets, still to move
> In th'eye of Time and orbs of Love.
>
> (371-74)

Unexpectedly, however, Diana enters and, in a long epilogue, calls the masquers back to virtue from the world of Sport and Cupid, the two figures who watch over the dances of the revels. The Chorus then ends the work singing praise for James that is also advice the audience can act upon only in the proper theater for moral action—the world at large:

> Follow his ample
> And just example
> That hates all chase of malice and of blood,
> And studies only ways of good
> To keep soft Peace in breath.
>
> (423-27)

We know from a contemporary observer that *Time Vindicated* set its antimasque satire of the poet George Wither before "a prospective of Whitehall, with the Banqueting House" (quoted in H&S 10:649). In this masque, in effect, the court begins outside the masquing hall and, with the closing advice, is returned there.

At the same time as the endings of Jonson's masques begin to point outward from the performance, the inner experiences the masques offer onlookers begin to change as well. "Above all," Orgel has written, "to Jonson, the audience must be made to do more than view the spectacle—they must see the significance of the symbolic figures and of the central device on which the masque depends."[15] But if "to make the spectators understanders"—the title of the preface to *Love's Triumph Through Callipolis* (1631)—was always Jonson's goal, his methods grow more attuned to likely lapses in an audience's attentiveness. In early works like *The Masque of Queens* the spectators are simply presented with straightforward embodiments of ideals that, as always with Jonson, are at once political, aesthetic, and moral. Even in *Mercury Vindicated from the Alchemists at Court,* the latest masque published in the 1616 folio, Mercury can contrast the "imperfect creatures" (161) Vulcan produces as evidence of alchemy's supposed artistry with the "excellence of the sun and Nature" (164): "Vanish, I say, that all who have but their senses may see and judge the difference between thy [Vulcan's] ridiculous monsters and his [James's] absolute features" (169-71). The difference is to be seen in the truly artful depiction of nature in the main masque, which was helped into being by Inigo Jones's stagecraft: "At which the whole scene changed to a glorious bower wherein Nature was placed with Prometheus at her feet, and the twelve masquers standing about them" (172-74). The masque then pauses so that all may be "a while viewed" (174).

In Jonson's next masque, however, just looking is not enough. Where Mercury asks nothing of spectators "but their senses," *The Vision of Delight* models for its audience an actively questioning, imaginatively engaged desire to understand what one sees. Wonder, who remains silently on stage throughout the antimasque, is moved to speech by the sight of "the bower of Zephyrus": "Wonder must speak or break: what is this? Grows / The wealth of nature here, or art?" (132-33). Wonder's enthusiasm increases when the Bower opens and the masquers are "discovered as the glories of the spring" (160-61): "what better change appears?" (163). How is it, Wonder goes on to ask, that trees and flowers are blooming, the seas and rivers are calm?

> How plays the yearling with his brow scarce broke
> Now in the open grass? and frisking lambs
> Make wanton salts about their dry-sucked dams,
> Who to repair their bags do rob the fields?
>   How is't each bough a several music yields?
> The lustly throstle, early nightingale
> Accord in tune, though vary in their tale?
> The chirping swallow called forth by the sun,
> And crested lark doth his division run?
> The yellow bees the air with murmur fill?
> The finches carol, and the turtles bill?
> Whose power is this? what god?
>
> (178-89)

In their immediate context the questions are important because the answer is the king the work is praising. But the questions are also important because in them Wonder describes a pastoral ideal that not even Jones could have fully depicted on the stage. Whereas *Mercury Vindicated* takes the visual contrast between main masque and antimasque for granted, *The Vision of Delight* implies that the audience must not only look at the set, but imagine the ideal it is meant to represent. "Only through wonder, or admiration," Eugene Waith has explained, "can the approximation of the ideal in the actual be seen."[16] I would stress that in this masque, unlike its predecessors, the approximation is the work itself, and the ideal is in the mind's eye of the beholder, albeit one on the masquing stage.

Modeling the proper sort of response to a masque in a masque is as far as Jonson could go to encourage the active mental engagement of his audience without disturbing the imaginative fabric of his fiction. But when, the year after *The Vision of Delight,* Jonson reacted to the court's initial disappointment by revising the morally coherent *Pleasure Reconciled* into the artistically disjointed *For the Honor of Wales,* he necessarily interfered with the straightforward vicarious involvement of the spectator. When the main masque of *Pleasure Reconciled* was repeated forty days after the original performance, it was preceded by an antimasque of comic Welshmen who mock the morally significant events in the first version. There, Hercules, exemplifying active virtue, scatters both the mindless pleasure seekers who adore "the voluptuous Comus, god of cheer" (164) and a group of pygmies who seek revenge for Hercules' defeat of their fellow emblem of earthly vice, Antaeus. Where pygmies dance in *Pleasure Reconciled* and, to honor Comus, there is "a tun now brought in to dance, and so many bottles about him" (62-63), *For the Honor of Wales* has the far more prosaic "dance of men" (289) and "dance of goats" (314). In between the two, a character asks rhetorically: "Is not better this now than pigmies? This is men, this is no monsters, and you mark him. Well, call forth your goats now; your ursip sall see a properly natural device come from the Welse mountains: is no tuns, nor no bottles. Stand by there, sow his ursip the hills; was drunkenry in his eyes that make that device in my mind" (295-300). "Nothing is more proper, nothing more natural," wrote Jonson in *Queens* to defend the conceptual appropriateness of placing figures from different historical eras on stage at the same time (*Complete Masques,* p. 547). (They are all alive in the eternal present of fame.) The "properly natural device" of goats, however, relies on the everyday notions of realism Jonson parries in his comments to the reader of *Queens* and in the drunken comments of Hercules' Bowl-bearer in *Pleasure Reconciled*: "Ha! You look as if you would make a problem of this. Do you see? Do you see? a problem: why bottles? and why a tun? and why a tun? and why bottles to dance? I say that men that drink hard and serve the belly in any place of quality . . . are living measures of drink, and can transform themselves, and do every day, to bottles or tuns when they please" (63-70). The Welsh goats are thus less a piece of authorial self-criticism than a further, though more indirect, response to those who weigh artistic propriety against their conventional preconceptions instead of a work's conceptual coherence.

That *For the Honor of Wales* exchanges conceptual coherence for an abrupt shift from the comic realism of the Welshmen to the symbolic world left over from *Pleasure Reconciled* can in part be explained as the result of not being able to rework in less than two months the costumes, music, dances, and scenery of the main masque. But Jonson clearly found the doubling of a moral difference by an artistic one appealing. His subsequent masques, as a disapproving Barish has complained, regularly "transplant the audience from one plane of artistic reality to another."[17] For example, in *News from the New World,* the first masque after *For the Honor of Wales,* two heralds proclaim the news of a poet's recent trip to the moon and fool others on the stage with inventive descriptions of the society the poet supposedly found there. All the while, the two acknowledge to the audience that their accounts are merely the product of "the fant'sy that begot 'em" (15). Among the creatures the heralds say live on the moon are Volatees, a strange cross of bird and man, but in contrast to the heralds' other fabrications, the Volatees appear on stage as representatives of lunar reality. Herford and Simpson have commented on the unsettling effect of this for those expecting consistent planes of imaginative experience: "we are, as it were, hitched out of the world of comic realism, where romance exists only as ludicrous make-believe, into the world of the Masque, where it is the order of the day. While we are still laughing at the yarns of the Second Herald, they suddenly come true" (H&S 2:313). Or rather, they suddenly look true. They suddenly look as substantial on the masquing stage as the foolishly credulous figures in the antimasque, the costumed courtiers in the main masque, and the embodied abstraction of Fame rising in Jones's set at the end of the work. As Orgel has noted, "a realistic scene implies that seeing—not hearing, or understanding—is believing."[18] If the heralds had been right about the world in the moon, the Volatees would be as properly natural as goats in Wales. But in this masque seeing is not believing; the visual is not the actual. The work insists that spectators stay alert to the error of accepting without question any illusion that looks real.

The masques following *News* similarly require spectators to pay attention to what they are looking at. *The Gypsies Metamorphosed,* written the year after *News,* relies, as Dale Randall has argued, on the tension between accepting the surface fiction and an indirect awareness—heightened by ironic verbal resonances—of the real courtiers who spoke the lines.[19] Undoubtedly, the much-remarked linguistic inventiveness of this masque owes a good deal to the absence of Jones's theatrical spectacle. The works Jonson composed for the new Banqueting House, though, were all subject to the problem of Jones's visually convincing images. We have seen how one of the masques, *Time Vindicated,* adopts the strategy of pointing the audience away from the performance. Others make use of a particular kind of self-referentiality. In *The Masque of Augurs* (1622), *Neptune's Triumph,* and *The Fortunate Isles and Their Union* (1625), antimasque dances are said to result from the creative efforts, such as they are, of Vangoose, "a projector of masques" (*Augurs* 101-102), of a Banqueting House cook, and of "the company of players" (*Isles* 286), respectively. All three masques, that is, contain verbal references to the reality that performances are illusions.

Although the reference is the most direct in *The Fortunate Isles,* Jonson's final Jacobean masque, it is fullest in the rehearsed but, owing to an ambassadorial dispute, never performed *Neptune's Triumph.* In that work the antimasque is a discussion, held before the audience that would have gathered in the Banqueting House to see the masque, between a cook who ostensibly works in the Banqueting House kitchens and a masque-writing poet: "A kind of a Christmas ingine, one that is used at least once a year for a trifling instrument of wit, or so" (19-21). The two talk about their attitudes toward audience expectations, about the general value of antimasques, and about the details of the Twelfth Night masque to come—a conversation, in other words, that almost completely merges the reality of the court as it awaits the performance of the main masque with the actual performance of the antimasque.

According to the cook,

> there is a palate of the understanding as well as of the senses. The taste is taken with good relishes, the sight with fair objects, the hearing with delicate sounds, the smelling with pure scents, the feeling with soft and plump bodies, but the

> understanding with all these, for all which you must begin at the kitchen. There the art of poetry was learned and found out, or nowhere, and the same day with the art of cookery. (41-47)

But the work as a whole does not bear out Orgel's contention that the idea "that poetry cannot be intellectualized" is Jonson's own.[20] Even the cook wants to hear the poet explain the "device" (83) of the main masque before experiencing it—and the explanation runs to some fifty lines. To Jonson, visual and other non-verbal effects should depend on verbal information supplied by the poet. Words, not senses, are what "make the spectators understanders."

This position is implicit in having Wonder in *The Vision of Delight* verbally describe how "every sense / Hath several objects" (170-71). Yet Wonder merely models on stage the transformation of the perceived by the imagination of the perceiver—as does the captain of the gypsies in *The Gypsies Metamorphosed.* Had there been a performance of *Neptune's Triumph,* the audience would have been prompted by the poet's prior explanation to transform for itself the immediate, predominantly visual experience of main masque spectacle into the imaginative and intellectual experience of perceiving and understanding allegory. Having been told, as it were, what to look for, the audience could not, or so Jonson hoped, take what it saw at face value.

It might be objected that my argument, like the tales of the heralds about the world in the moon, has "all this while . . . adventured to tell . . . no news" (*News* 270-71). Jonson's quarrel with Jones, after all, is well-known and its grounds, thanks especially to D. J. Gordon, well investigated.[21] But there is an important difference between Jonson's irritation with Jones for presuming creative equality between poet and architect, and his concern that Jones's theater helps the masque create a false equality between experiencing a performance and moral experience. It is this concern that leads in the later Jacobean masques to efforts to turn audiences from complacent celebrators of what looked like virtue's actual triumphs into mentally active participants in moral fictions. That the efforts were slow to develop reflects the difficulty even Jonson had in recognizing all the implications of Jones's designs. That the efforts were only partial reflects the difficulty even he had in keeping under verbal control an event the court—and his collaborator—expected to be predominantly non-verbal.

Eventually, of course, the poet would lose to history and to human nature his battle against the passivity and complacency that could be induced by a masque's structure and be reinforced by what the architect made the masque look like. Because Charles danced where his father had watched, there is essentially no imaginative gap in a Caroline masque between the noble fiction and the real nobility performing it. Just as important, the more skillful Jones became at making his special effects look natural, the more easily the court could accept simply seeing a performance as a substitute for a deeper understanding of moral responsibility. "It is probable," Una Ellis-Fermor once observed, "that Ben Jonson crippled himself as an artist by his moral imposition."[22] It could, however, be said that the court masque ultimately crippled Jonson's efforts to impose moral seriousness on the form.

NOTES

[1]Eliot's 1919 essay on Jonson is reprinted in *Elizabethan Essays* (London: Faber and Faber, 1934). Notable studies of the formal qualities of the genre include Dolora Cunningham, "The Jonsonian Masque as a Literary Form," *ELH* 22 (1955):108-24; W. Todd Furniss, "Ben Jonson's Masques," in *Three Studies in the Renaissance*, ed. B. C. Nangle (New Haven: Yale Univ. Press, 1958), pp. 89-179; and Stephen Orgel, *The Jonsonian Masque* (Cambridge, Mass.: Harvard Univ. Press, 1965). For Jones, see Orgel and Roy Strong, *Inigo Jones: The Theatre of the Stuart Court,* 2 vols. (Berkeley: Univ. of California Press, 1975), esp. 1:1-75. For the general political implications of the masque, see Orgel's *The Illusion of Power: Political Theater in the Renaissance* (Berkeley: Univ. of California Press, 1975); Eugene Waith, "Spectacles of State," *SEL* 13 (1973):317-30; and Jonathan Goldberg, *James I and the Politics of Literature: Jonson, Shakespeare, Donne, and Their Contemporaries* (Baltimore: Johns Hopkins Univ. Press, 1983). For more specific analyses, see Leah Sinanoglou Marcus, "'Present Occasions' and the Shaping of Ben Jonson's Masques," *ELH* 45 (1978):201-25; and "The Occasion of Ben Jonson's *Pleasure Reconciled to Virtue,*" *SEL* 19 (1979):271-93; and Sara Pearl, "Sounding to Present Occasions: Jonson's Masques of 1620-5," in *The Court Masque*, ed. David Lindley (Manchester: Manchester Univ. Press, 1984), pp. 60-77.

[2]The masques are quoted from Orgel's modernized *Complete Masques* (New Haven: Yale Univ. Press, 1969), and hereafter cited parenthetically by line. Where the punctuation matters to my argument, I have checked the text in *Ben Jonson*, ed. C. H. Herford and Percy and Evelyn Simpson, 11 vols. (Oxford: Clarendon Press, 1925-1952). I cite the edition hereafter as H&S, giving volume and page, and modernize spelling when quoting from it.

[3]See especially Ernest William Talbert, "The Interpretation of Jonson's Courtly Spectacles," *PMLA* 61 (1946):454-73; and John C. Meagher, *Method and Meaning in Jonson's Masques* (Notre Dame: Univ. of Notre Dame Press, 1966).

[4]*John Milton: Complete Poems and Major Prose,* ed. Merritt Y. Hughes (New York: Odyssey Press, 1957), p. 733.

[5]*An Apology for Poetry*, ed. Geoffrey Shepherd (London: Thomas Nelson, 1965), p. 107.

[6]See especially Peter Carlson, "Judging Spectators," *ELH* 44 (1977):443-57.

[7]Jonas A. Barish, *Ben Jonson and the Language of Prose Comedy* (Cambridge, Mass.: Harvard Univ. Press, 1960), p. 244.

[8]See Orgel's "To Make Boards to Speak: Inigo Jones's Stage and the Jonsonian Masque," *RenD* 1 (1968):121-52; and his introduction to *The Complete Masques.*

[9]*Complete Masques*, p. 32.

[10]Gabriele Bernhard Jackson, *Vision and Judgment in Ben Jonson's Drama* (New Haven: Yale Univ. Press, 1968), p. 1; Alexander Leggatt, *Ben Jonson: His Vision and His Art* (London: Methuen, 1981), p. 274.

[11]Samuel Taylor Coleridge, *Shakespearean Criticism,* ed. Thomas Middleton Raysor, 2 vols. (2nd edn.; London: Dent, 1960), 1:199.

[12]*Complete Masques*, p. 37.

[13]Jeffrey Fischer, "*Love Restored*: A Defense of Masquing," *RenD* 8 (1977):231-44.

[14]*The Jonsonian Masque*, p. 185.

[15]*The Jonsonian Masque*, p. 93.

[16]"Things as They Are and the World of Absolutes in Jonson's Plays and Masques, 1616-25," in *The Elizabethan Theatre IV,* ed. G. R. Hibbard (Toronto: Macmillan, 1974), p. 122.

[17]Barish, p. 256.

[18]*Complete Masques*, p. 24.

[19]Dale B. J. Randall, *Jonson's Gypsies Unmasked* (Durham: Duke Univ. Press, 1975).

[20]*The Jonsonian Masque*, p. 93.

[21]Gordon's 1949 essay, "Poet and Architect: The Intellectual Setting of the Quarrel between Ben Jonson and Inigo Jones," is conveniently reprinted in *The Renaissance Imagination: Essays and Lectures by D. J. Gordon,* ed. Orgel (Berkeley: Univ. of California Press, 1975), pp. 77-101.

[22]Una Ellis-Fermor, *The Jacobean Drama: An Interpretation* (4th edn.; rpt. New York, Vintage, 1964), p. 117.

SEL 27 (1987)
ISSN 0039-3657

Play-making, Domestic Conduct, and the Multiple Plot in *The Roaring Girl*

VIVIANA COMENSOLI

I

Moll Cutpurse, the central character of Dekker and Middleton's *The Roaring Girl* (c. 1608-1611), is based on the notorious roarer Mary Frith who frequented the Fortune Theater in man's apparel. Mary was described by a contemporary as "a very Tomrig or Rumpscuttle" who "sported only in boys' play and pastime," scorned girlish endeavors such as "sewing or stitching," and showed "rude inclinations."[1] While Moll Cutpurse does many of the things her real-life counterpart did—she wears men's clothes, carries a weapon, and mixes in taverns with members of the underworld—she also punishes lecherous gallants through her skillful sword-fighting and promotes the love-marriage of Mary Fitzallard and Sebastian Wengrave. T. S. Eliot was the first to praise *The Roaring Girl* as "one comedy which more than any other Elizabethan comedy realizes a free and noble womanhood," an achievement compensating for the play's rough plotting: "we read with toil through a mass of cheap conventional intrigue, and suddenly realize that we are . . . observing a real and unique human being."[2] Since Eliot's assessment the citizen-plot, with its commonplace motif of lusty gallants chasing citizen wives, has been largely viewed as a ponderous distraction from Moll's fascinating duality. Cyrus Hoy, for one, expresses a common sentiment when he laments the conventional comedy in the play, "with its seemingly compliant citizens' wives and the impecunious gallants who would like to seduce or live off them," but praises "the bold and often brilliantly original" portrait of Moll.[3] The Royal Shakespeare Company's 1983 production of the play, the

Viviana Comensoli is Assistant Professor of English at Wilfrid Laurier University. She is currently working on a book on the domestic drama of Thomas Dekker.

first major production since the play's première at the Fortune,[4] portrayed Moll as a commendable virago but tampered considerably with the other plots in order to bring Moll's role into sharp focus.[5]

The few critics who have commented on the play's structural merits have stressed the orthodox design of the comic action and its progression toward a society renewed by married love. In 1970 David Holmes referred to the play as a "nexus of plots with a common motif," namely "the dignity of marriage."[6] More recently, some attention has been paid to the Sebastian Wengrave-Mary Fitzallard action in connection with Moll's role in bringing about the young lovers' marriage. Patrick Cheney, analyzing Moll's dual identity, links the marriage to Moll's symbolic function: because Moll "combines in her person both feminine and masculine traits, and uses her remarkable powers to unite other couples in love," she is suggestive of Renaissance representations of the hermaphrodite-figure, "a supreme symbol of two souls becoming one—particularly within the context of married love."[7] For Larry Champion, the play is "a complex pattern of schemes and counter-schemes" set in motion by Sebastian, whose feigned passion for Moll Cutpurse prompts his father to agree to his son's marriage to Mary Fitzallard, just as in the citizen-plot the gallants "set their practice upon the citizen-wives."[8] The plots are "effectively interwoven" to sustain a comic perspective and "a continuing assurance of the ultimate success of love and right reason" leading to "a happy ending."[9] Mary Beth Rose, in her analysis of the play in the context of the *Hic Mulier/Haec-Vir* controversy, acknowledges a certain amount of ambiguity in the dramatic portrayal of Moll, but also stresses the conventional nature of the comic ending.[10] Despite the pamphlet's late date, Moll is considered a direct dramatic parallel of the transvestite in *Hic Mulier*, where "the figure of the female in male attire" inspires "simultaneous admiration, desire, abhorrence, and fear."[11] While we detect authorial sympathy with "sexual non-conformity, female independence, and equality between the sexes," the play, argues Rose, ultimately resists Moll's integration into society: "having served as the instrument who brings about the happy ending," Moll "is nevertheless excluded from the renewed comic society of married couples which forms on the stage at the end of the play."[12] The "desirable social norm in the play" is thus not Moll's transvestism but the conservative "relationship and opinions" of Sebastian and Mary.[13] A full evaluation of Moll's relation to the multiple plot, I propose, must accommodate two significant qualifications: 1) while Moll does assist in ushering in the typical comic ending, she unequivocally renounces *for herself* the conventional values embodied by Mary and Sebastian, a choice which the audience is invited to condone; 2) although Moll and her roarer-companions reject conventional behavior, they are never excluded from the reformed society sketched in the denouement; instead, their presence during the final two scenes provides a compelling alternative to the ideal marriage. Moreover, the idealistic conclusion of the Sebastian-Mary action must be considered in relation to the dramatists' cynical treatment of marriage in the citizen-plot and its realistic treatment of conjugal malaise. Both Moll's misogamy and the citizens' domestic conflicts counterpoint the Sebastian-Mary action, indicating that the ideal marriage is a possibility not wholly realized, even in a transformed society.

Taken together, the three plots convey the concern at the heart of the play with the degeneration of marriage and the family, a tension sustained in the antithesis between the household (consistently portrayed as the seat of spiritual and emotional stasis and confinement) and the city (the hub of multifariousness and freedom). The multiple-plot structure is thus loosely unified through the careful arrangement of setting, so that altogether six scenes are set within various households and five in the city streets and fields around London. The world of the money-hungry social climbers and of the sycophantic gallants and self-satisfied citizens is ruled by the single pursuit of materialistic values. These characters are invariably either in their shops (notably architectural extensions of their homes) where they accumulate wealth, or at home where deception and bawdy innuendo underscore the deterioration of domestic life. The younger generation, represented by Sebastian Wengrave and Mary Fitzallard on the one hand, and by Moll Cutpurse and her roarer-companion Jack Dapper on the other, is removed from the world of the elders. Prior to their marriage, Mary and Sebastian are associated neither with the domestic sphere nor with the city, but stand apart in their idealism. For Moll and Jack, both the world of the elders and the idealism of Mary and Sebastian represent denial and limitation. Neither Moll nor Jack has or wants a home; their space is the street, the world of thieves, beggars, and drifters. Moll's contradictory behavior attests to the play's central paradox in that the resolution upholds both the ritualized cleansing of the *domus* through Mary and Sebastian's love-marriage and the roarers' rejection of that sphere in favor of the polymorphism of the city.

In the shift from one perspective to another, the spectator participates in a process of creating a multifaceted society as varied and paradoxical as the play. The tension agrees with the dramatists' idea of playmaking as a protean activity. Fashionable plays, argues Middleton in his address "To the Comicke Play-readers, Venery, and Laughter"[14] which prefaces the quarto, cater to popular taste: likening "The fashion of play-making" to "the alteration in apparell" (lines 1-2), Middleton observes that the time now being one "of sprucenes," plays are fashioned after the folly of "our Garments, single plots, quaint conceits, letcherous iests, drest vp in hanging sleeues" (lines 6-8). Middleton advises the audience that the play he and Dekker have written goes beyond popular fashion in denying easy solutions, a sentiment echoed in the Prologue, where we are cautioned against coming to the theater expecting to view a polished work, "a booke, / Compos'd to all perfections" (lines 2-3), which will gratify our preconceived notions of experience:

> each one comes
> And brings a play in's head with him: vp he summes,
> What he would of a Roaring Girle haue writ;
> If that he findes not here, he mewes at it.
>
> (lines 3-6)

Whereas fashionable plays are neatly packaged, closed systems, *The Roaring Girl* is methectic and open-ended, its emphasis on multiplicity and variability challenging the audience's complacency.

II

The play opens upon a typical conflict in city comedy; the father, Sir Alexander Wengrave, is determined to impede his son's marriage for reasons which are purely materialistic and self-serving. A recently-dubbed knight, Wengrave scorns Sebastian's love for Mary Fitzallard, whose dowry of five thousand marks renders her "but a beggars heire" (I.i.82). While the expository details are set forth Wengrave's house forms an obtrusive setting. The direct alignment of the two scenes comprising Act I draws our attention to the house's subdivisions, a fairly recent architectural phenomenon. During the late sixteenth and early seventeenth centuries, subdivided homes became indicative of status among the gentry and yeomanry.[15] This development corresponded to the increase in domestic comfort, as evidenced by improved methods of construction favoring well-lit open spaces and terraces[16] and generating a variety of household effects including upholstered furniture, chairs, draw tables, and beds with decorated frames. The new emphasis on domestic comfort represented "an important move towards the notion of individuality and sexual privacy."[17] The design of the Wengrave household confirms Wengrave's successful climb to the landed gentry, while his status-seeking is the focus of the play's sharpest satirical attack. Scene i, where the disguised Mary Fitzallard secretly visits Sebastian, is set in the foyer, situated near the "hall" or servants' quarter (I.i.16) and the "buttry" (line 21). In scene ii we enter "Th'inner roome" (I.ii.6) of the house where Wengrave is hosting a dinner party. Proud of his possessions, Wengrave subjects his guests (and the audience) to an extensive and disquieting tour of each room. We are led from the separate dining area which, ironically, is "too close" (line 6), to the cooler "Parlour" (line 7). From there, we proceed to the "galleries" in the center of the house (line 14) where a grotesque mosaic covers the walls, intensifying the claustrophobic atmosphere—"Within one square a thousand heads are laid / So close, that all of heads, the roome seems made" (I.ii.19-20)—and where the *trompe-l'oeil* effect of the floor waving "to and fro, / . . . like a floating Iland" (lines 30-31) projects an image of a world distorted by illusion.

As the dinner-party scene unfolds, the household is depicted essentially as an extension of a money economy. The adulteration of the once sacred bond between host and guest, for instance, is underscored by Wengrave's calculating advice to Greenwit upon learning of the young man's desire to leave sooner than decorum permits: "Your loue sir, has already giuen me some time, / And if you please to trust my age with more, / It shall pay double interest: Good sir stay" (I.ii.36-38). Wengrave's metaphor from commerce is a signal to the young man of the ethic that now rules the host-guest relationship, the guest's function being to defer to the host's pride and social status in exchange for patronage. As Wengrave dispenses wine during post-dinner formalities and grandly displays the furniture, which "Cost many a faire gray groat ere it came here" (line 12), his makeshift hospitality and the guests' hypocrisy are revealed through a series of double-entendres and vicious sexual innuendoes:

> *Alex.* Pray make that stoole your pearch, good
> Maister *Goshawke.*
> *Gosh.* I stoope to your lure sir.
> . . . .

Alex. furnish maister *Laxton*
With what he wants (a stone) a stoole I would say,
A stoole.
Lax. I had rather stand sir.

(I.ii.54-60)

The image of the household as the center of concupiscence links the Wengrave action and the citizen-plot where feeding, bawdy word-play, and sexual inadequacy form a complex configuration. Wengrave's feast is directly mirrored by the citizens' equally disquieting dinner party (III.ii). The scene opens upon a domestic squabble between the hosts, Prudence and Master Gallipot, disrupting the festive mood. Prudence enters "as from supper, her husband after her" (s.d.), and inveighs against Gallipot's uxorious behavior. On the surface the exchange is farcical, but broad comedy is restrained by the urgency of the language which alerts us to the couple's emotional and sexual dissatisfaction. Prudence is angry because her husband dotes on her as an infant dotes on its mother: "I thinke the baby would haue a teate it kyes so, pray be not so fond of me, . . . I'me vext at you to see how like a calfe you come bleating after me" (III.ii.2-5). The source of Prudence's frustration is Gallipot's refusal to "vp and ride" (line 9), provoking her lusty pursuit of the gallant Laxton.[18] The couple's conjugal problems are coherently sketched through an extended pattern of food imagery. Gallipot, whose virility is dubious—"Vp and ride, nay my pretty Pru, thats farre from my thought, ducke" (lines 10-11)—importunes his termagant wife to behave more decorously toward their guests, and attempts to appease her through proverbial food lore: "thy minde is nibbling at something, whats ist, what lyes vpon thy Stomach?" (lines 11-12). Suspecting that Prudence may have a lover, Gallipot articulates his suspicion through another barrage of food imagery: "I smel a goose, a couple of capons, and a gammon of bacon from her mother out of the country" (lines 70-71). Throughout the exchange Gallipot's need for oral gratification is strongly implied.[19] His inability to distinguish between feeding and love, his persistent whining—"the baby would haue a teate it kyes so"[20]—and his dependence on non-sexual contact are the source of Prudence's strongest reproach: "your loue is all words; giue mee deeds, I cannot abide a man thats too fond ouer me, so cookish; thou dost not know how to handle a woman in her kind" (lines 22-24).

The scene culminates in Prudence and Laxton's jest, whereby the gallant poses as the wife's original suitor who has come to reclaim her. Gallipot's uneasiness over having to relinquish his source of gratification to a rival, a prospect which he equates with being deprived of a choice dish of food, is an aggressive, infantile response—"Haue you [Laxton] so beggarly an appetite / When I vpon a dainty dish haue fed / To dine vpon my scraps, my leauings? ha sir?" (III.ii.229-31). When alone with Prudence, Gallipot is passive and obsequious, but to his rival and to society at large he appears sexually potent, a lie which he fosters through bawdy metaphors: "pray sir [Laxton] weare not her, for shee's a garment / So fitting for my body, I'me loath / Another should put it on, you will vndoe both" (lines 234-36). The uneasy tone is sustained in the reconciliation scene (IV.ii) where Gallipot forgives Laxton because the gallant has not actually seduced the wife, but does not offer to forgive Prudence (IV.ii.318-20). Audiences at the Fortune Theater could compare Gallipot's behavior with that of Master Frankford, the husband-hero of Heywood's domestic tragedy *A Woman Killed With Kindness* (c. 1603), which Christianized the revenge ethic in its sympathetic portrayal of a husband who forgives rather than condemns his wife's adultery. Whereas Frankford's sacrifice preserves the conjugal ideal, Gallipot's bombast during the reconciliation scene points not only to moral lassitude but also to the continuation of conjugal strife. That the marriage will never be free of conflict is confirmed by Gallipot's bold invitation of the gallant to dinner, in which he chastises Prudence with a derogatory epithet, masking once again his sexual inadequacy: "Wee'll crowne our table with it [Laxton's jest]: wife brag no more, / Of holding out: who most brags is most whore" (lines 323-24).

The unsettling tone of the Prudence-Gallipot action is only partly attenuated by the more whitewashed marriage of Master and Mistress Openwork. The central concern in the Openwork action is the husband's exposure of Goshawk's lechery: Openwork dupes the gallant by pretending that Mistress Openwork's shrewishness has led him to keep a whore in the suburbs (II.i.272-76). Openwork's test of his wife's fidelity, which she in turn requites with a feigned desire for Goshawk, is therefore only a pretense to dupe the gallant and to teach him to "deale vpon mens wiues no more" (IV.ii.216). Once the gallant has learned the valuable lesson, the action concludes with Openwork's invitation of Goshawk to dinner, paralleling Gallipot's forgiveness of Laxton:

Maist. Open. Make my house yours sir still.
Gosh. No.
Maist. Open.. I say you shall:
Seeing (thus besieg'd) it holds out, 'twill neuer fall.
(lines 217-19)

Ostensibly preserved is the general rule of decorum in the public theaters requiring gallants who attempt the seduction of citizen-wives to "come off badly."[21] That Gallipot's "virtue" remains questionable, however, has been established by his response to Laxton's and Prudence's jest. A moral ambiguity also qualifies Openwork's behavior. Goshawk's admission of guilt prompts Openwork to muse on the world's imperfection—"On fairest cheeks, wife nothing is perfect borne. / . . . What's this whole world but a gilt rotten pill?" / . . . The world can hardly yeeld a perfect friend" (IV.ii.204-13). The remark undercuts not only the confident tone of Openwork's offer of his house to the gallant, but also the promise of social stability brought about by his hospitality.[22]

From the point of view of citizen comedy, perhaps the most disturbing element of the resolution of the citizen-plot concerns the problem of Prudence Gallipot's lascivious behavior. Unlike Mistress Openwork's feigned passion for Goshawk, Prudence's desire for Laxton is never uncovered as a pretense. In Act II we learn that the affair is not consummated because the gallant has no intention of seducing the wife (II.i.114-23); he merely desires Gallipot's money, which he lavishes on other women. While Mistress Openwork comes to appreciate her husband's virtue, Prudence merely informs us that she is "ridd" of Laxton (IV.ii.40). We are given no firm indication that she unequivocally yields to Gallipot's apparent virtue.[23] Prudence's unrepentant desire is a rare occurrence in a comedy performed in the public theater where citizen-wives were not portrayed as adulterous.[24]

III

The disturbed, unregenerate world of the citizens and the landed gentry is juxtaposed with the stable, more innocent world of the young lovers, Mary and Sebastian. Their world is suffused with an aura of sacredness manifested chiefly in their dialogue which teems with devotional imagery. The couple's secret betrothal is not a grotesque extension of eating, nor is it founded on sexual appetite; instead, it is, in Mary's words, a union sanctioned by heaven: "in one knot / Haue both our hands byt'h hands of heauen bene tyed"

(I.i.68-69). For Mary, matrimony is "a bond fast sealed, with solemne oathes, / Subscribed vnto . . . with your soule: / Deliuered as your deed in sight of heauen" (lines 51-53). Mary distinguishes between love which is "wouen sleightly" (line 29) and a nobler love which is "truely bred ith the soule" (line 31). The denouement, where Mary and Sebastian reiterate their marriage vows with the blessing of their elders and of society at large, reinforces the idea of marriage as the field where one ought to practise virtue. Indeed, the language in this scene is so transformed that it becomes epideictic. In tone and structure the final one hundred lines of the play recall the celebration of marriage in epithalamic verse. Mary, dressed as a "Bride," is brought in "twixt two noble friends" (V.ii.168), and the wedding is celebrated by all of society: the guests include lords, gentlemen, ladies, citizens and their wives, and the roarers Moll Cutpurse and Trapdoor. Having abandoned his "wilfull rashnesse" (line 193) the reformed Wengrave, like the epithalamist, "call[s] into being the ideal event which the wedding must be, the ideal as defined partly by the convention, partly by the particular society, partly by the poet."[25] Repenting his former blindness, Wengrave extols the wedding as a sacred occasion (lines 173-74) and invokes heaven's blessing of the couple (line 202). He also articulates the epithalamist's conventional praise of the bride's virtue and beauty (lines 189-95), and the familiar wish for offspring and material prosperity: "the best ioyes, / That can in worldly shapes to man betide, / Are fertill lands, and a faire fruitfull Bride" (lines 202-204). The scene ends with Wengrave's injunction, "as I am, so all goe pleas'd away" (line 266), echoing the epithalamist's command to break off the revelry so that the bedding of the couple may take place.

The stylized epithalamic cadences of the final scene enhance the conventional nature of Mary and Sebastian's union which represents the renewal, typical of New-Comic endings, of a society made barren by its obsession with mercantile values. However, before he can enjoy the benefits of his new life, Sebastian, like the prodigals of New Comedy, asks and receives his father's forgiveness for the sorrow he has caused him (V.ii.170-73).[26] Paradoxically, the strongly idealistic nature of Mary and Sebastian's marriage is tempered by the Moll Cutpurse-Jack Dapper action, where language creates a radically different kind of personal and social transformation.

IV

The central ambiguity of the multiple plot hinges on the contradictions embodied in Moll Cutpurse, who aids Sebastian in securing his father's approval of his marriage while asserting that she herself would never agree to marry (V.ii.214). Moll's rejection of marriage derives in part from the Christian ascetic tradition. In her refusal to submit not only to men but to her own physical nature, Moll associates independence with physical denial:

> shee that has wit, and spirit,
> May scorne to liue beholding to her body for meate,
> Or for apparell like your common dame,
> That makes shame get her cloathes, to couer shame.
> (III.i.133-36)

Moll expresses the traditional dichotomy between body and spirit, rejecting altogether the world of desire where identity is governed by "apparell" and where marriage is not the union of opposites but the handmaiden of lust:

> Base is that minde, that kneels vnto her body,
> As if a husband stood in awe on's wife,
> My spirit shall be Mistresse of this house,
> As long as I haue time in't.
> (lines 137-40)

Elsewhere, however, Moll confesses to Sebastian that she has renounced marriage and the pleasures of the flesh for more practical, self-serving reasons: "I haue no humor to marry, I loue to lye aboth sides ath bed my selfe; and againe ath'other side; a wife you know ought to be obedient, but I feare me I am too headstrong to obey, therefore Ile nere go about it" (II.ii.35-38). Moll rejects marriage because it denies a woman freedom to act as she pleases in the world: "I haue the head now of my selfe, and am man enough for a woman, marriage is but a chopping and changing, where a maiden looses one head, and has a worse ith place" (lines 40-43). Moll, whose sense of self is highly individualized, views marriage as a threat to a woman's identity, marriage being the exchange of one "head" for another in that a wife replaces her maidenhead (a symbol, to Moll, of independence) with the sovereignty of her husband.

At the same time that Moll chooses independence for herself, she is aware of the loss which her renunciation necessitates. As she plays on the viol for Sebastian, Moll sings of her dream at the core of which is a subtle tension between denial and desire. The first part of the dream concerns a woman who delights in "unwomanly" pastimes such as squandering money and mixing with vulgar company:

I dreame there is a Mistresse,
. . . .
Shee sayes shee went to'th Bursse for patternes,
You shall finde her at Saint Katherns,
And comes home with neuer a penny.

(IV.i.99-105)

The woman in the dream, like Moll herself, does not buy "patternes" to sew dresses, sewing being the quintessential stereotypical occupation of women; instead, she prefers to carouse in "Saint Katherns," the dockside district in London's east end, which was "notorious for its brewhouses and taverns."[27] In the second part of the dream Moll describes the sexual adventures of an adulterous woman (lines 109-19), a fantasy which gives Moll pleasure, although she is careful to distinguish between her dream-life and reality: "Hang vp the viall now sir: all this while I was in a dreame; one shall lie rudely then, but being awake, I keepe my legges together" (lines 122-24). Moll's dream suggests we are viewing neither a symbol of virtue nor the two-dimensional virago of the *Hic Mulier* pamphlet, but a complex individual whose dream/song embodies the self's ambiguous relationship to the world. Through her transvestism, Moll has adopted the more forceful male role in order to escape subordination, although she has done so by sacrificing her sexual longing, a compromise which her dream brings into relief.[28] Yet the loss for Moll is preferable to a life of wifely submission. Proud of her independence, Moll cannot tolerate the subjugation which marriage entails, a loss which, by implication, will follow even Mary Fitzallard's entrance into the *domus.*

Moll's fullness and complexity are expressed through her adaptability: she is at home both in the world of "the Temple" (III.i.164) and amid thieves and prostitutes in Chicke Lane (line 167). Her duality encompasses both her proficiency as a musician (an accomplishment which a Renaissance audience would appreciate as indicative of harmony, refinement, and felicity) and her mastery of a different kind of "music," namely thieves' cant (V.i). Throughout the play the dramatists underscore Moll's protean nature, which cannot be understood by those whose understanding is weak or who conceive of the world two-dimensionally. Moll's strangeness is disturbing and everywhere draws mistrust. To those who fear her, she is "madde Moll" (Prologue, line 30; I.i.94), a despised "flesh fly," a "scuruy woman" (I.ii.127-28), and "some Monster" (line 138). To Moll's fellow-roarer, Trapdoor, Moll's identity is confusing and unpredictable: "I like you the worse because you shift your lodging so often" (III.i.168). Even the truth-obsessed Mistress Openwork denies Moll her "house and shop" (II.i.211) on the basis of Moll's outrageous appearance.

Moll's boldly unconventional nature corresponds to the play's identity as a work of art. Just as in Moll's world clothes often make the person, play-making, we noted in Middleton's address to the audience, is frequently only a matter of catering to the current fashion. *The Roaring Girl* counters the popular trend not only because the play frustrates expectation but also because it is subject to censorship for defying a law which upholds the sanctity of appearance: "For Venus being a woman passes through the play in doublet and breeches, a braue disguise and a safe one, if the Statute vnty not her cod-peice point" ("To the Comicke Play-readers," lines 13-15). The statute in question is the law forbidding women to wear male dress, which arose from "the controversy then raging over women's role and rights, their wearing men's hats or masculine dress . . . be[ing] one of the signs of moral degeneration."[29] The purpose of art, argues Middleton, is to expose truth, even if it might not always be "fit for the Times, and the Tearmers" (line 8). Moll is never forced to renounce her choices in order to gratify what Middleton considers the unreasonable expectations of certain spectators among the large citizen audiences who frequented the Fortune playhouse. At the same time, the play's favorable portrayal of a strongly independent woman points to the dramatists' awareness of an increasingly assertive audience of city women who, as the *hic mulier* controversy attests, were demanding and gradually "getting more freedom."[30]

In the final scene Moll indirectly flouts Mary and Sebastian's wedding by prophesying she will marry only when society undergoes a seemingly impossible reformation that would see, among other things, "Honesty and truth vnslandred, / Woman man'd, but neuer pandred," and "Cheaters booted, but not coacht" (V.ii.219-21). Lord Noland's alarmed reply—"This sounds like domes-day" (line 225)—is countered by Moll with a disturbing quip: "Then were marriage best, / For if I should repent, I were soone at rest" (lines 126-27). Moll's misogamy provides a powerful alternative to the veneration of marriage and procreation that informs the epithalamic ending.

V

Dekker and Middleton's provocation of the audience, together with their opposition to unjust authority, is underscored by Moll's participation in the Jack Dapper action. That Jack functions dramatically as Moll's double is suggested by Moll's street name, "Iack" (V.ii.97-98; lines 212, 215). A profligate and a spendthrift who lives on credit, Jack Dapper lavishes his money on tobacco and wine, and associates with prostitutes and catamites (III.iii.55-64). His father Davy Dapper, who is resolved to punish Jack's profligate ways, orders his arrest and detention in Bridewell, the notorious house of correction. The farcical overtones of the arrest, however, block the audience's sympathy for the father. The search for Jack is carried out amid absurd hunting cries and references to the quest for game (lines 158-91), and is headed by Sergeant Curtilax, a blusterer whose primitive understanding renders him a disturbing defender of the law: "all that liue in the world, are but great fish and little fish, and feede vpon one another" (lines 134-35). Moll's intervention prevents the arrest. Moll forcibly rescues Jack from the sergeant's custody (lines 200-10), an offense which under Jacobean law was "very serious"[31] in that it could lead to a long imprisonment. In the aftermath, neither Moll nor Jack repents the crime; instead, Moll describes her part as her "perfect one good worke to day" (line 212). The next time we see Moll and Jack together is during the long canting episode in the final act where they mingle freely among cutpurses and delight in their knowledge of the underworld.[32]

The canting scene, which is interposed between the resolution of the citizen-plot (IV.ii) and the glorious epithalamic ending (V.ii), is crucial to the play's thematic and structural design.[33] As a prelude to the canting, Moll and her fellow-roarers join with Jack Dapper in deriding his father's unsuccessful attempt to have him imprisoned. In direct counterpoint to Sebastian's request for his own father's forgiveness (V.ii.170-72), Jack renounces repentance, declaring that not even prison would reform him: "as though a Counter, which is a parke, in which all the wilde beasts of the Citty run head by head could tame mee" (V.i.40-41). The rowdy tone of the celebration also contrasts sharply with that of the wedding feast that transpires in Wengrave's household. The roarers will celebrate Jack's freedom by carousing in the London streets and taverns, and by feasting at "Pimlico . . . that nappy land of spice-cakes" (lines 49-50), described elsewhere in Dekker as a mad world frequented by revellers and crammed with "Bawdy houses."[34] The audience, moreover, is coaxed into assenting to the roarers' adventure through Lord Noland's participation in the action. A strictly sympathetic character from the upper ranks of society, Lord Noland eagerly follows the roarers, inviting his friends to join in the celebration: "Heeres such a merry ging, I could find in my heart to saile to the worlds end with such company, come Gentlemen let's on" (V.i.51-52). After the roarers flaunt their skills in the obscurities of thieves' cant, Moll engages Tearcat in a boisterous drinking song for which they receive "two shillings sixe pence" (line 220) from Lord Noland and his friends:

> *Moll.* Come you rogue sing with me.
> A gage of ben Rom-bouse
> In a bousing ken of Rom-vile.
> *T. Cat.* Is Benar then a Caster,
> Pecke, penman, lap or popler,
> Which we mill in deuse a vile.
> *Both.* Oh I wud lib all the lightmans.
> Oh I woud lib all the darkemans,
> By the sollamon, vnder the Ruffemans.
> By the sollamon in the Hartmans.
> *T. Cat.* And scoure the Quire cramp ring,
> And couch till a pallyard docked my dell,
> So my bousy nab might skew rome bouse well.
> (V.i.194-207)

The final refrain, "Auast to the pad, let vs bing, / Auast to the pad, let vs bing" (lines 208- 209), which translates "Away to the highway, let us go,"[35] asserts Moll and Tearcat's loyalty to the open streets. In Moll's subsequent paraphrase of the song (lines 235-40), which amounts to "let's drink and be merry," we learn that we have been listening to an ode to freedom. The inscrutable nature of the argot, together with its rough and spirited cadences, balances the stylized verse in the epithalamic conclusion, bestowing on the roarers' language a similar power to please the audience.

The Moll Cutpurse-Jack Dapper action is never subordinated to the Mary-Sebastian plot. Instead, the play interweaves a pattern of divergent meanings, suspending and resuspending a firm resolution until all the characters are reunited in the final scene where society is recreated as a network of disparate structures. Central to the process of renewal is the sympathetic presentation, in the popular theater, of a heroine's desire for self-realization. *The Roaring Girl* exposes the folly of popular opinion, including in this case secular law, by demonstrating that Moll's disguise is a "safe one" ("To the Comic Play-Readers," line 14), that is, "morally sound and mentally sane" (OED). Thus by the end of the play, both Alexander Wengrave and the audience are capable of judging Moll according to her worth, realizing that the "common voyce" is the real "whore," in that it "deceiues mans opinion; mockes his trust, / Cozens his loue, and makes his heart vniust" (V.ii.248-50). While the play's epithalamic ending calls attention to the possibility of regeneration through marriage, Moll and the roarers' affirmation of another "order" upholds a strikingly different set of values, fulfilling the play's promise of complexity and multiplicity.

NOTES

[1]Letter from John Chamberlain to Dudley Carleton, 11 February 1612; quoted in A. H. Bullen, ed., *The Works of Thomas Middleton,* 8 vols. (London: J.C. Nimmo, 1885), 4:4.

[2]T. S. Eliot, *Elizabethan Essays* (New York: Haskell House, 1964), pp. 100, 89.

[3]Cyrus Hoy, *Introductions, Notes, and Commentaries to texts in "The Dramatic Works of Thomas Dekker," Edited by Fredson Bowers,* 4 vols. (Cambridge: Cambridge Univ. Press, 1980), 3:9. Norman A. Brittin also praises Moll as "an upright, goodhearted girl of great size and strength who, like a questing knight, helps her friends and whose bad reputation is undeserved," but ignores the function of the citizen-plot (*Thomas Middleton* [New York: Twayne, 1972], p. 77).

[4]The play has been performed infrequently. P. Mulholland, in "Let her roar again: *The Roaring Girl* Revived," *RORD* 18 (1985):15-27, notes that since 1951, the date of "the earliest modern production on record" (p. 15), there have been six stage productions, of which the Royal Shakespeare Company's is the "most important" (p. 19), and one radio adaptation. See also Marilyn Roberts, "A Preliminary Check-List of Productions of Thomas Middleton's Plays," *RORD* 18 (1985):37-61; 52-53.

[5]To "make the play 'slightly more deft,' " the director Barry Kyle "altered the order of some scenes in Act 1 and shifted the last half of Act 4 to the middle of Act 5" (Francesca Simon, "The Honest Cutpurse at the Play: Francesca Simon talks to Barry Kyle about the RSC's *Roaring Girl* starring Helen Mirren," *The Sunday Times,* 24 April 1983, p. 42e). The "effect," wrote one reviewer, was a strong emphasis on Moll, while the rest of the action tended toward "vertical tourism" (Irving Wardle, "Distant Echo of Jacobean Mirth," *The London Times,* 27 April 1983, p. 14). Another reviewer praised Helen Mirren's spirited portrayal of Moll, but complained of loss of "audience involvement" as a result of Kyle's "cut[ting] and patch[ing]," which made for "three or four plots awkwardly intertwined" (Russell Taylor, in *Drama: The Quarterly Theatre Review* [Autumn 1983]:40-41; 40).

[6]David M. Holmes, *The Art of Thomas Middleton: A Critical Study* (Oxford: Clarendon Press, 1970), pp. 102, 107.

[7]Patrick Cheney, "Moll Cutpurse as Hermaphrodite in Dekker and Middleton's *The Roaring Girl,*" *Ren&R* n.s. 7 (May 1983):124, 125.

[8]Larry S. Champion, *Thomas Dekker and the Traditions of English Drama* (New York: Peter Lang, 1985), p. 82.

[9]Champion, p. 85.

[10]Mary Beth Rose, "Women in Men's Clothing: Apparel and Social Stability in *The Roaring Girl*," *ELR* 14 (Autumn 1984):367-91. The literary and social contexts of the controversy over the issue of women in men's apparel, which "came to a head in 1620 with a pair of pamphlets entitled, respectively, *Hic Mulier: Or, The Man-Woman,* and *Haec-Vir: Or the Womanish-Man*" (Rose, pp. 367-88), are fully explored in Linda Woodbridge, *Women and the English Renaissance: Literature and the Nature of Womankind, 1540-1620* (Urbana and Chicago: Univ. of Illinois Press, 1984), passim. For my argument concerning the dramatic complexity and attractiveness of the central character of *The Roaring Girl,* I am indebted to Woodbridge's observation that the play not only "gives favorable treatment to a man-clothed virago" (p. 250), but also "paints an intriguing portrait of modern assertive women" (p. 262).

[11]Rose, p. 368.

[12]Rose, p. 389.

[13]Rose, p. 385.

[14]*The Dramatic Works of Thomas Dekker,* ed. Fredson Bowers, 4 vols. (Cambridge: Cambridge Univ. Press, 1953-1961), 3:11. Subsequent references to the play will be to this edition.

[15]Sheila Rowbotham, *Hidden from History: 300 Years of Women's Oppression and the Fight Against It,* 2nd edn. (London: Pluto Press, 1974), p. 3.

[16]Michel Grivelet, *Thomas Heywood et le Drame Domestique Elizabéthain* (Paris: Librairie Marcel Didier, 1957), pp. 19-20. See also Marjorie Quennell and C. H. B. Quennell, *A History of Everyday Things in England: 1500-1799,* 5th edn., vol. 2 of *A History of Everyday Things in England,* 4 vols. (London: Batsford, 1960), chs. 1 and 2; and W. G. Hoskins, "The Rebuilding of Rural England, 1570-1640," in *Provincial England: Essays in Social and Economic History* (London and New York: Macmillan and St. Martin's Press, 1963), pp. 131-48.

[17]Rowbotham, p. 3.

[18]Andor Gomme, ed., *The Roaring Girl* (London and New York: Benn and Norton, 1976), p. 64, n. 9, observes that "'Ride' was Standard English for sexual intercourse," and suggests that Mistress Gallipot might be "picking up a sexual suggestion in her husband's last word ['come'] and possibly 'hony'."

[19]Understood psychoanalytically, Gallipot's excessive passivity, his dependence on non-sexual affection, and his delight in infantile behavior are manifestations of an oral compulsion. "Because the oral phase occupies the earliest period when self and object are still not clearly differentiated," writes Norman N. Holland, the phase "establish[es] . . . our abilities to do nothing, to be passive" (*The Dynamics of Literary Response* [New York: Oxford Univ. Press], 1968, p. 36).

[20]The term "kyes," as used by Prudence Gallipot, indicates "baby-talk": in talking to her husband, she uses the language of nursemaids (Gomme, p. 63, n. 3). In this case, notes Gomme, "Master Gallipot is the baby."

[21]Alexander Leggatt, *Citizen Comedy in the Age of Shakespeare* (Toronto and Buffalo: Univ. of Toronto Press, 1973), p. 135.

[22]Critics tend to ignore the ambiguities of the reconciliation scene in the citizen-plot. For Larry Champion, "The feast that follows is . . . a commonplace symbol of reconciliation and social harmony throughout Renaissance comedy" (*Thomas Dekker and the Traditions of English Drama,* p. 84). Andor Gomme views the reconciliation as part of the play's broader message that "deception

and scheming" are "found everywhere and can always be unmasked by plain dealing" ("Introduction," *The Roaring Girl*, p. xxiv). Patrick Cheney writes that "the primary aim" of the citizen-plot "is to reunite the wives with their husbands; and the secondary aim is to expose the gallants for men of lust, and then to incorporate them as friends to the married couples" ("Moll Cutpurse as Hermaphrodite in Dekker and Middleton's *The Roaring Girl*," p. 128). Similarly, Mary Beth Rose suggests that the scene restores marital harmony, mitigating the "illicit sexuality" represented by "the seducing gallants, who . . . therefore turn out not to constitute a real threat to the social order at all" ("Women in Men's Clothing: Apparel and Social Stability in *The Roaring Girl*," p. 382). A very different view is put forth by Simon Shepherd, in *Amazons and Warrior Women: Varieties of Feminism in Seventeenth-Century Drama* (Brighton: Harvester Press, 1981): Prudence and Mistress Gallipot are pawns in "the male world" which exploits women by relegating them to "the emotional and sexual sphere" (p. 49). The citizen-plot reconciles the husbands with the gallants "to the exclusion of the women, who remain used and dissatisfied" (p. 80). Shepherd's interpretation is not entirely borne out by the text, where the women are never passive in their dealings with the men, and where the reconciliation between Openwork and Goshawk is tenuous.

[23]David Holmes notes that "Mistress Gallipot's deficiencies, deceitfulness, and proneness to corruption, contrast with Mistress Openwork's plain dealing and moral hardihood" (*The Art Of Thomas Middleton*, p. 107), but he does not substantiate the claim. The Royal Shakespeare Company's production also differentiated between the citizen-couples: "At their appearance in the final scene of the play some unease still attended the Gallipots, though balanced by the firmer relationship of the Openworks" (P. Mulholland, "Let her roar again: *The Roaring Girl* Revived," p. 23). Gomme, on the other hand, echoes a prevalent view in his suggestion that both wives "realize how much more solidly worthwhile their husbands are than the gallants whom they can, it seems, trap so easily," although he acknowledges that "the innuendoes" in the dialogue between the two women (IV.ii.40ff.) "are so broad that one cannot believe they have altogether given up the search for new delights" ("Introduction," *The Roaring Girl*, p. xxx).

[24]Alfred Harbage, *Shakespeare and the Rival Traditions* (New York: Macmillan, 1952), p. 249. Harbage notes that the "single exception" is Chapman's *Blind Beggar of Alexandria* (1598).

[25]Thomas M. Greene, "Spenser and the Epithalamic Convention," in *Edmund Spenser: Epithalamion*, ed. R. Beum (Columbus, Ohio: Charles E. Merrill, 1968), pp. 37-52; p. 43. For a comprehensive analysis of the literary conventions of epithalamic verse in European literature see Virginia Tufte, *The Poetry of Marriage: The Epithalamium in Europe and Its Development in England* (Los Angeles: Tinnon-Brown, 1970).

[26]Although George E. Rowe, Jr., in *Thomas Middleton & the New Comedy Tradition* (Lincoln and London: Univ. of Nebraska Press, 1977) does not analyze *The Roaring Girl*, attributing the play largely to Dekker (p. 23), he offers a valuable discussion of the structures of New Comedy and of Middleton's sustained critique of traditional comic values: "Middleton does not revise tradition in order to create new syntheses. . . . He revises it in order to reject it" (p. 17). I concur with Rowe's suggestion that *The Roaring Girl* harbors a comic vision that is closer to Dekker's; by upholding a synthesis of discordant elements,

I believe, the play modifies Middleton's otherwise cynical treatment of comic themes. For an account of the debate surrounding the play's authorship see Gomme, pp. xxxii-xxxv, and Champion, *Thomas Dekker and the Traditions of English Drama,* p. 173, n. 52.

[27]Cyrus Hoy, 3:46, n. 104.

[28]"Moll must dress as a man," notes Caroline L. Cherry, "to make people respect her and take her seriously" and "to express herself fully" (*The Most Unvaluedst Purchase: Women in the Plays of Thomas Middleton* [Salzburg: Universität Salzburg, 1973], pp. 104-105). Simon Shepherd observes that Moll "connects . . . chastity and . . . freedom" (*Amazons and Warrior Women,* p. 78).

[29]Margot Heinemann, *Puritanism and Theatre: Thomas Middleton and Opposition Drama Under the Early Stuarts* (Cambridge and New York: Cambridge Univ. Press, 1980), p. 100. See also Louis B. Wright, *Middle-Class Culture in Elizabethan England* (1935; rpt. Ithaca: Cornell Univ. Press, 1958), pp. 494ff.

[30]Linda Woodbridge, *Women and the English Renaissance,* p. 263.

[31]Gomme, p. 87, n. 211.

[32]In his review of the 1983 production, Irving Wardle notes that although roarers, "from Ancient Pistol and Jonson's Kastril to the roaring academy in *A Fair Quarrel*, were the much-ridiculed skinheads of their time," in *The Roaring Girl* "the sympathy is entirely on the roarer's side" ("Distant Echo of Jacobean Mirth," p. 14).

[33]Critics unanimously attribute this scene to Dekker. The canting, however, is usually considered "an almost complete irrelevance to the remainder of the play" (Gomme, p. xxx). Champion, on the other hand, argues that the canting episode "serves through its linguistic hilarity to prevent a tone of heavy sentimentality in the reconciliation scenes that both precede . . . and follow" (*Thomas Dekker and the Traditions of English Drama,* p. 85).

[34]Thomas Dekker, *Worke for Armorours* (1609), Biv; quoted in Hoy, 3:49, n. 12.

[35]Gomme, p. 126, n. 194.

SEL 27 (1987)
ISSN 0039-3657

"Great Women of Pleasure": Main Plot and Subplot in *The Duchess of Malfi*

CHRISTINA LUCKYJ

It is a commonplace to say that Webster cannot construct plays—to agree with George Rylands, who directed the 1945 revival of *The Duchess of Malfi,* that "Webster could handle a scene but he could not compass a plot."[1] Even though our notion of "plot" with regard to the Elizabethan and Jacobean dramatists has changed after the important work of Maynard Mack and Bernard Beckerman, who, among others, have illuminated the multiple, analogical nature of Shakespeare's dramatic construction, it remains acceptable to speak of the "unplotted undulations" of Webster's drama.[2] As John Russell Brown points out in his edition of *The Duchess of Malfi,* "the structure of the play is yet to be vindicated."[3] Compounding the problem of dramatic construction is one of moral interpretation. Some critics like to see the play as a cautionary tale against marrying an inferior; other critics and directors invariably treat it as melodrama with a heroic martyr at its center. Webster himself included a subplot in *The Duchess of Malfi* which, though it has received little serious critical attention, may have been intended as an interpretive key to certain aspects of the main plot. An examination of the function of the subplot in *The Duchess of Malfi* illuminates both Webster's dramatic construction and his moral emphasis in the play.

The adventures of the Cardinal's mistress that form the Julia subplot were pure invention on Webster's part. Gunnar Boklund tells us that Webster did not borrow the subplot from any source, used as he was to borrowing.[4] Nor is the subplot strictly "necessary" to the main plot, a fact which has led some critics to dismiss it as "a mere excrescence on the play."[5] Yet the structural significance of the

---

Christina Luckyj recently completed her doctorate in English at the University of Toronto. She is currently working on a full-length study of repetition in the dramaturgy of John Webster's plays.

Julia subplot need not be limited to its contribution to the linear narrative. Since Webster evidently labored to invent a rough analogy to the Duchess's situation, he presumably intended it to serve a useful dramaturgical function in the play.

William Poel's contention that Julia is "designed as a set-off to the Duchess; as an instance of unholy love in contrast to the chaste love of the Duchess,"[6] has become virtually a tradition in Webster criticism, shared by a large number of modern critics.[7] In describing the Duchess in contrast to Julia, many of these critics use language which tends to misrepresent her. The Duchess's wooing of Antonio is profound and convincing precisely because it is not "chaste," as she herself points out.

> This is flesh and blood, sir;
> 'Tis not the figure cut in alabaster
> Kneels at my husband's tomb.
>
> (I.i.453-55)

The Duchess is a woman of sexual energy and vulnerability; she appears pregnant on the stage in the following act. Theatrical critics have been quick to emphasize these important qualities. The reviewer of the 1971 Royal Shakespeare Company production for *The Listener* felt that the death scene failed because "Miss Dench retained stoic dignity but, never having shared her passion with us, now kept us at a distance."[8] Michael Billington of the *Guardian* pointed to the same essential qualities when he complained, in a review of the 1985 National Theatre production, "Even when Ms. Bron's Duchess divests herself of her wrappings, she never finds the virtuous, mettlesome, sexually-charged woman underneath."[9] By way of contrast, several critics praised Helen Mirren's portrayal of the Duchess in the 1980 Royal Exchange production—one called her "playful, lascivious and vain";[10] another alluded to "her capacity for affection and her deep sexual awareness."[11] The Duchess's intense sexuality, so vital in performance, has been downplayed by critics who wish to emphasize the differences between the Duchess and Julia. Clifford Leech claims that "the general attitudes [in the play] to Julia and the Duchess are polar opposites" (p. 32), citing the Cardinal's contempt for Julia and Pescara's reference to her as a strumpet (V.i.46), in contrast to Antonio's first idealized view of the Duchess's "divine... continence" (I.i.199). Leech's moral distinctions appear doubtful, however, when one remembers the epithets applied to the Duchess by her brothers, for whom she is a "notorious strumpet" (II.v.4). Moreover, the structural justification for this interpretation of the subplot is dubious. If Julia were intended as a foil to the Duchess, she appears utterly redundant. As Boklund comments, by the final act of the play, "reader and spectator . . . have formed definite opinions about the Duchess' conduct, and neither praise nor blame, be it open or implied, will now affect their judgment" (p. 158).

Other critics have proposed Julia as a parody of the Duchess, designed to undercut and qualify her values. Boklund suggests that "since the main action of the play is based on the consequences of a deliberate flouting of the laws guarding social decorum, the by-plot may serve to provide a commentary in word and action on the heroine's behavior."[12] Such attempts to find a "tragic flaw" in the Duchess, reflected and confirmed in Julia, are difficult to support with the text. Webster's sources, Painter and Belleforest, condemn the Duchess's actions, and Webster's deliberate deviation from them in this regard brings him closer to the spirit of the Italian original, a novella by Bandello which treats the Duchess with "tolerant understanding" and sexual pragmatism. As Boklund himself admits, in Webster "there is no case for the prosecution" (p. 102). If Julia were intended as a parody or ironic reflection of the Duchess, Webster's careful construction designed to emphasize the Duchess's virtue throughout the play would seem pointless. Some critics sound alarmingly like the hysterical Ferdinand when they claim that, "Lower in her sexual drive than 'a beast that wants discourse of reason,' the Duchess of Malfi, like Hamlet's mother, steps out of the path of duty and marries for lust."[13] As William Empson puts it, "A play intended as a warning against marrying a social inferior would have to be constructed quite differently."[14] If the Julia subplot can be explained as an integral part of the play's construction, its function must transcend that of foil or parody.

Clearly, interpretation of the Julia subplot involves moral judgment of the Duchess. Yet often that moral judgment not only fails to allow for the warm humanity of the Duchess on the stage, but also reduces the status of the play as "tragedy." Those critics who emphasize the analogies between the Duchess and Julia come perilously close to reading the play as a cautionary tale. Those who concentrate on the differences tend to exaggerate the "saintliness" of the Duchess and to read the play as melodrama. Underlying both these perspectives is another implicit moral judgment—that Julia is meant to be condemned as a wanton, promiscuous, morally reprehensible woman.

Directors of the play have also tended to impose this interpretation on the character of Julia, sometimes deliberately using stage effects to undercut the immediate import of the language to the confusion of critics and theater audiences alike. For example, in the 1960 Royal Shakespeare Company production, the scene in which Julia rejects first the Cardinal, then Delio, was reinterpreted by Donald McWhinnie's staging. What began as rejection ended in mute consent, as she knelt to kiss the Cardinal's ring (II.iv.37), and later stalked off with Delio's proffered bribe (II.iv.76).[15] Visual effects contradicted the scene's language and made Delio's bewilderment at her "wit or honesty" (II.iv.77) incomprehensible. In the final act of the same production, Julia's open lasciviousness with Bosola made her a caricature of lust that so jarred with her tragic death that one critic commented in utter confusion, "Sian Phillips did not shirk the part of the Cardinal's mistress Julia, but what can any actress today make of the last scenes?"[16] In the 1985 National Theatre production, director Philip Prowse's conception of Julia was clear from the beginning when she made a dramatic entrance in the first act on the Duchess's cue, only to turn and kneel finally before a much more modest Duchess. The invented stage moment established her clearly as the Duchess's foil as well as her servant.

Critics and directors may have ceased their moral condemnation of the Duchess and instead tended to beatify her, but their moral prejudices continue to vent themselves on Julia. Her contribution to the dramatic texture and design of the play has been largely ignored in favor of the accepted view of her as a stock Jacobean whore. It is Clifford Leech's sensitivity to the text that allows him, however briefly, to entertain a third possibility in the analogical relation between the two plots. He points out "how erroneous it would be to regard the Duchess as outside the normal sphere of sexual passion," and declares that, despite the differences between them, "there is enough resemblance between the two actions of the play to keep strongly in our minds the force of the passion that urges the Duchess to speak."[17] Leech's tentative suggestion moves toward a realistic, human view of the Duchess essential to performance, but remains a suggestion, which he does not support with close examination of the text.

In fact, few critics provide a detailed reading of the three scenes of the play in which Julia figures. Only close attention to these scenes in their dramatic context can determine their relation to the rest of the play. And such close attention makes some critical claims about Julia's character seem surprising. For Boklund, she is "guided by the two forces of lust and avarice" (p. 157); for Clifford Leech she is a "rank whore";[18] for Richard Levin she is a "flagrant adulteress" (p. 98). However, actresses who attempt to play Julia this way must find themselves working directly against the text at several points.

Before Julia appears for the first time in II.iv, the audience is prepared by Bosola for her appearance. After Bosola has picked up the horoscope and discovered that the Duchess has given birth to a son, he gleefully closes the scene (II.iii) with a couplet which carries over into the following scene.

> Though lust do mask in ne'er so strange disguise,
> She's oft found witty, but is never wise.
>
> (II.iii.76-77)

At the opening of the next scene, the Cardinal echoes Bosola's couplet when he describes Julia as a "witty false one" (II.iv.5). At first Julia appears to be a fulfillment of Bosola's and the Arragonian brothers' degraded vision of the Duchess, which has dominated the stage since the beginning of the second act.[19] The device is similar to that used by Shakespeare in *Othello,* where, as Mack points out, "Bianca . . . may be thought to supply in living form on the stage the prostitute figure that Desdemona has become in Othello's mind" (p. 30). Yet just as, in *Othello,* Iago's vision of Bianca as a "notable strumpet" (V.i.78) is cast into doubt by her loyalty to Cassio, very early in the scene Julia's words and stage actions begin to contradict the Cardinal's version of her. Her first speech, with its anxious, halting rhythm, betrays the deep inner struggle of a woman who has compromised herself for uncertain gain and finds herself the victim of a cynical and abusive man.

> You have prevail'd with me
> Beyond my strongest thoughts: I would not now
> Find you inconstant.
>
> (IV.ii.6-8)

These are hardly words that convey the "lust and avarice" of a "flagrant adulteress." On the contrary, they imply that her decision to commit adultery was a painful one, the result of an ongoing struggle between the demands of sexuality and morality. As the interview progresses, Julia defends her own constancy and integrity as the Cardinal attacks them. In the face of his cruel misogyny, she finally bursts into tears when her objections can no longer be heard.

If the scene begins as a confirmation of Bosola's degraded perspective on the Duchess, it moves away from that perspective as it continues. The scene is clearly written to overturn an audience's initial impression of Julia. The "whore" and "adulteress" cannot be quite so easily dismissed.

The Cardinal's assault on the "giddy and wild turnings" (II.iv.12) of women both echoes the satiric perspective of Bosola that dominated the previous three scenes and anticipates the crazed misogyny of Ferdinand in the following scene (II.v).[20] The scene suspends and extends the previous action—its precise form is unexpected, and it carries the audience away from the world of the Duchess. At the same time, however, it exploits the tension and energy that have been built up over the previous three scenes regarding the Duchess's escalating danger. The scene is an analogical replay of the situation between Bosola and the Duchess throughout the second act, since Julia is another woman victimized by the cruel cynicism of men. Again, the satiric vision is pitted against the vulnerability of human love and sexuality with their inherent compromises. In both cases, two voices are heard in opposition to each other[21]—the tough against the vulnerable, the deeply cynical against the merely human. As Bosola's meditation on death and decay (II.i.45-60) is set against the stage image of the pregnant Duchess, swollen with life, the Cardinal's diatribe on the inconstancy of women is contrasted with Julia's long-suffering silence. Like Bosola (and like Iago in *Othello*), the Cardinal attempts to degrade women by generalizing them and by reducing them to the level of mere animals. The Duchess and Julia both contradict this version of themselves with their stage presences.

Following the interview between the Cardinal and Julia is an exchange between Julia and Delio that has puzzled most critics. Archer simply admits that "the relevance of the passage in which Delio makes love to the Cardinal's mistress utterly escapes me."[22] Lois Potter claims that the exchange "must inevitably be confusing in performance,"[23] though she suggests that it recalls Ferdinand's bribery of Bosola in Act I and reiterates the play's "service and reward" motif. If the echo is there, it is designed to enforce a contrast; Bosola finally accepts the gold while Julia rejects it. In his edition of the play, Brown suggests that the incident is designed "to aggravate the audience's sense of a growing web of intrigue and an increasing complexity of character" (p. 62). That the exchange is designed deliberately to confuse appears a weak explanation at best. Neither critic accounts for the particular nature of the incident—another kind of exchange would presumably serve just as well to reinforce a theme or to suggest intricacy of plot. Nor does either critic examine the dramatic rhythm of the exchange. Its dramatic impact is, however, unmistakable.

The first part of the interchange between Julia and Delio centers on Julia's old husband, Castruchio, who has already appeared twice in the play. As Ferdinand's poker-faced advisor in Act I, and as an aspiring courtier and the object of Bosola's mockery in Act II, Castruchio quickly impresses an audience as a foolish old man. His marital relationship to Julia, to which Webster suddenly draws attention in this scene, appears to be the culmination of his function in the play, since he disappears completely after his mention here. A foolish, impotent old man married to an obviously desirable young woman—whom Bosola later describes as "very fair" (V.ii.177)—recalls the marriage of Camillo and Vittoria in *The White Devil.* There, the husband's inadequacy helped to exonerate the wife's adultery. Here, the first explicit identification of Julia's deceived husband with foolish old Castruchio (whose name suggests castration) shifts the scene even further in the direction of Julia's redemption in the eyes of the audience. The terse reply Julia makes to Delio's mockery of her husband—"Your laughter is my pity" (II.iv.56-57)—with its brevity betrays her suffering.

Delio then offers her his gold, drawing attention to its physical properties by mockingly treating it as an aesthetic object. Julia rejects not only the gold itself, but also the crude materialism it represents.[24] In reply, she evokes a world of positive aesthetic values and refined sensual beauty—of beautiful birds, music, and fragrance. It is a world in which the Duchess also lives, and which she conjures up most eloquently just before her death in lines like these:

> What would it pleasure me to have my throat cut
> With diamonds? Or to be smothered
> With cassia? or to be shot to death with pearls?
> (IV.ii.215-18)

The struggle between two polarized views of life, between the crudely sexual and the delicately sensual, is articulated throughout the play's main action in the characters of Ferdinand and the Duchess.[25] Here, its mere suggestion is enough to associate Julia with the Duchess's refined sensuality. Finally, Julia's categorical rejection of Delio's sexual offer, combined with the disclosure of her unhappy marriage to Castruchio, is clearly designed to capture audience sympathy for Julia. Together, they confirm the impression of abused integrity suggested in her relationship with the Cardinal at the beginning of the scene. As Julia remains in the foreground, the background shifts around her so that the vulnerable victim of the Cardinal's misogyny can exhibit self-assured integrity. The question of Delio's motives is less important than the dramatic impact of Julia's reassertion of her integrity. And that integrity is not undercut by Julia's witty reply to Delio:

> Sir, I'll go ask my husband if I shall,
> And straight return your answer.
>
> (II.iv.75-76)

On the contrary, Julia's need to rely on the outward form of conventional morality by calling on her husband illuminates its inadequacy as a standard of human behavior. The courage she displays appears more significant since the audience knows that it is unsupported by the facts of her marital relationship. Delio may wonder, "Is this her wit or honesty that speaks thus?" (II.iv.77), but an audience is left in little doubt. Because Julia, like the Duchess, is forced to exceed the bounds of respectability, her "virtue" must be judged according to another standard. One might say, in the spirit of Empson, that a scene intended to portray a "flagrant adulteress" and a clear contrast to the Duchess would have to be constructed quite differently.

Just before Julia's final dismissal of Delio's offer, a servant enters to report,

> Your husband's come,
> Hath deliver'd a letter to the Duke of Calabria,
> That, to my thinking, hath put him out of his wits.
>
> (II.iv.67-69)

The audience is suddenly reminded of what has been going on in the play's main action. Bosola's report of the birth of the Duchess's "illegitimate" child has been delivered by Castruchio to the Arragonian brothers. The servant's report briefly anticipates the following scene, with Ferdinand's reassertion of his crazed view of the Duchess as a "notorious strumpet" (II.v.4). As we are reminded of Ferdinand's distorted vision of the Duchess, Delio imposes his degraded perspective on Julia, making her a sexual offer. Julia's rejection of that offer thus has the effect of salvaging the Duchess's values by association. At this point, Julia's function in the play transcends mere analogy to anticipate the reassertion of the Duchess's integrity after Bosola's and Ferdinand's assault upon it throughout the second act.

The second act, with its opening parody of the Duchess and Antonio in the figures of the Old Lady and Castruchio, tends to modify, if not to obliterate, the delicate power of the tender wooing scene that closes the first act. While an audience may have little difficulty rejecting the Arragonian brothers' tyrannical moralism in favor of the Duchess's individualism in the first act, it finds few alternatives to Bosola's relentless cynicism in the second. Bosola takes over from Antonio as the Duchess's observer in the second act, and audience response is to some extent conditioned by his vision of life and sexuality as purely physical and subject to decay. Moreover, at both times that Julia appears, the Duchess has been absent from the stage for a prolonged period. Bosola's gift of "apricocks" to the Duchess sends her into labor in the first scene of Act II; she quickly leaves the stage and does not reappear until the following act. The only momentary reanimation of her presence is an offstage "shriek" Bosola hears at the beginning of II.iii, realistically suggesting her offstage labor, but also conveying the deeper suffering that shapes her character in preparation for the death scene. Her absence from the stage throughout most of the second act may represent this implied process of necessary psychic change, what Mack (p. 35) calls the "second phase" in the development of the tragic hero or heroine. When Julia comes onto the stage, the audience is set up to judge her as the Duchess's enemies have judged the Duchess. With this scene, however, Webster overturns the simplified prejudices of conventional morality that are inevitably part of an audience's response, a response we share with the Duchess's enemies. Webster's presentation of Julia is consistent with his portrait of Vittoria in *The White Devil* and, ultimately, with his interest in the figure of the Duchess. It allows him to draw attention to something he evidently considered very important—that "whore," a word applied by social convention to someone unchaste, does not fully exhaust the psychological reality of the woman. This is true of Vittoria, of Julia, and most of all, of the Duchess.[26] The first of Julia's scenes functions as analogical probability at a point in the play when the Duchess is most vulnerable to the attacks of her enemies because she is not present on the stage.

Bosola's cynical, satiric vision presents a challenge to the Duchess's values that intensifies them by contrast when they are reasserted. But Bosola's vision also serves another purpose in the play's dramatic construction by further humanizing and illuminating the Duchess. The Duchess is above all, as she herself makes clear, an intensely sexual woman. The "apricocks" scene (II.i) becomes, in performance, not an indictment of the Duchess, but a further confirmation of the directness and sensual delight she exhibited in the wooing scene. It is precisely this sensual Duchess that Webster wanted to capture in Julia.

When Julia appears again in the first scene of Act V to request Antonio's property from Pescara, she immediately represents those who crudely profit from the ruin of the couple. Yet the focus of the scene shifts quickly from Julia's appropriation of Antonio's land to Pescara's hypocrisy. The scene centers, not on Julia's immoral action, but on the moral turpitude of those who condemn her as a "strumpet" in order to excuse their own actions. Pescara's guilt is thinly disguised by his abuse of Julia; his own fault is greater than hers. He grants Antonio's land to the Cardinal's mistress as "salary for his [the Cardinal's] lust" (V.i.52), defending his sycophantic action with perverse self-righteousness.[27] The moral status of Julia is again made relative, since her moralizing accusers are unreliable. Her appearance here is intended to drain off possible moral condemnation from the audience in the following scene.

Julia's appearance in the following scene (V.ii), as in the second act, restages for emphasis an aspect of the Duchess's experience that threatens to disappear with her. Whereas Julia's first appearance reflects the Duchess's position as a victim of the cruel cynicism of men and anticipates the Duchess's restoration, her final appearance recalls the Duchess's fate in miniature and anticipates the futile revenge of Bosola.

Julia's wooing of Bosola in the second scene of Act V seems deliberately designed to recall the Duchess's wooing of Antonio in Act I. Webster goes to considerable lengths to establish visual and verbal parallels between the two incidents. In both cases, the woman is the wooer (I.i.442; V.ii.183) and uses roughly similar phrases to express her admiration for her man with striking directness (I.i.453-59; V.ii.167-72). In both cases, the woman puts herself at great risk for her lover. While Webster clearly did not intend the crude seduction of Bosola to be a direct echo of the tender wooing of Antonio, the parallels between the two scenes appear to be as significant as the differences, which have frequently been emphasized by critics. During performances of the play, the later scene is clearly linked to the earlier one, not by its reiterated images, but by its similar effect on an audience. The two wooing scenes are virtually the only extended actions in the play to evoke laughter and delight in an audience predisposed to expect danger. As in Act I, in the last act the play's relentless machinery of crime and revenge is suspended while we watch the digressive banter of lovers.

Noting the differences between the two wooing scenes, critics have proposed interpretations of the later scene as a foil to, or parody of, the earlier one. Yet, as has been argued earlier, the dramaturgical advantages of either at this late stage in the action are limited. A foil appears superfluous, since the stature of the Duchess is by this point fixed. She is clearly exalted beyond all the characters of the fifth act. A parody seems groundless, since it would undercut the tragic intensity of her loss. There is, however, a third possibility, consistent with Webster's treatment of Julia in the second act. Here, as there, she may be intended as a mirror for the main action, reflecting its broad outlines in simplified analogical fashion from a different moral perspective. Shakespeare uses a similar dramatic strategy in the final act of *Othello*; Bianca, falsely accused by Iago of Cassio's murder, recalls Desdemona's plight as she has also been presented as a "whore" responsible for her man's destruction.

When Julia enters, pointing a pistol at Bosola and accusing him of treachery (V.ii.151), she continues the language of violence, intrigue, and deception used by the Cardinal and Bosola in their preceding interview. Similarly, when the Duchess offers her wedding ring to Antonio, visual and verbal echoes recall Ferdinand's bribery of Bosola in the same scene, and the interview is fraught with overtones of danger. In both scenes, however, the context of love and sexuality defuses the play's threatening language. The oppressive intrigue of the court is mockingly parodied and transformed by Julia. Her wit takes Bosola and the audience by surprise, as she abruptly turns apparent aggression into playful love-making. Webster sustains a tone throughout the scene that carefully avoids both romantic and sexual cliché. When Bosola attempts to seduce Julia with a conventional line, saying

> Your bright eyes
> Carry a quiver of darts in them, sharper
> Than sunbeams
>
> (V.ii.179-81)

Julia abruptly cuts him off and asserts her own status as the wooer. When he takes the opposite tack and decides to "grow most amorously familiar" (V.ii.185) with her, Julia responds with pragmatic intelligence, again drawing the focus away from Bosola and onto her own power.

> For if I see and steal a diamond,
> The fault is not i'th' stone, but in me the thief
> That purloins it:—I am sudden with you;
> We that are great women of pleasure use to cut off
> These uncertain wishes, and unquiet longings,
> And in an instant join the sweet delight
> And the pretty excuse together.
>
> (V.ii.190-96)

While the scene verges on caricature, it develops a sustained contrast between Bosola's limited conventional attitude and Julia's strong unconventional one. The echoes of the wooing scene of Act I, however distorted or exaggerated, are nonetheless startling in performance. The entire scene is structured to highlight the energy, wit, and exuberance of Julia, glimpsed only briefly in her earlier interchange with Delio. In both wooing scenes, Webster challenges the popular antifeminist stereotype that "a harlot is full of words,"[28] and links the Duchess and Julia in their common deviation from the conventional "good" woman. In the earlier scene (II.iv), the assertion of Julia's sexual integrity was necessary to suggest by analogy the Duchess's dramatic recovery at a point when it seemed threatened. In the later scene, the "splendidly sensual" and "voluptuous"[29] Julia re-evokes by association quite a different quality in the Duchess. Again, the recollection is a timely one in the play's dramatic rhythm, since Bosola's perspective on the Duchess as "sacred innocence" (IV.ii.355) threatens to distort her by exalting her. With Julia in the final act as an analogical reassertion of the Duchess's strong sexuality, a balance is restored.

In the final act, Julia reanimates by association, not the Duchess of the recent death scene, but the Duchess of the wooing scene—playful, confident, sensual, and direct. If, as I have argued, Webster attempts to recall such qualities in the Duchess by exaggerating them in Julia, he does so at considerable risk. The success of his strategy rests finally on performance—on an actress who can play Julia in this scene as a strong, vital woman rather than as a vulgar strumpet. Such risks, however, are unavoidable for the dramatist. In this instance, Webster takes the risk of falling into crude burlesque, for the greater advantage of clarifying his tragic construction. The recollection at this point of the young, carefree, and childless Duchess of the beginning of the play leads an audience to appreciate precisely what has been lost and gained in the course of the play's tragic action. The changes that are forced upon the Duchess enrich and develop her as a character who can finally face her death with courage. Yet at the same time those changes rob her of her innocent confidence that "time will easily / Scatter the tempest" (I.i.471-72). With the appearance of Julia in the final act, the audience can measure the distance it has travelled since the wooing scene. Loss of the Duchess's youthful insouciance is balanced against the recollection of the richness of her spirit in adversity. The evocation of this simple tragic paradox is the main dramaturgical function of Julia at this stage in the play.

If the wooing of Bosola is intended as an echo of the Duchess's lighthearted wooing of Antonio, then the subsequent interview with the Cardinal plunges the audience directly into the death scene. The opposed perspectives of the play's main action—the Duchess's youthful vitality and the irrational menace of her enemies—are recalled in the confrontation between Julia and the Cardinal. Julia is still witty and playful, but the Cardinal is dangerously bitter. Comic and tragic perspectives illuminate each other in their dialogue, remaining at cross purposes until the Cardinal confesses his crime:

> By my appointment, the great Duchess of Malfi,
> And two of her young children, four nights since,
> Were strangled.
>
> (V.ii.268-70)

The Cardinal's syntax imitates the dramatic suspense of the interview, delaying the final shock until the end of the sentence, thus heightening its impact. The witty innocence of Julia's playful persuasions acts as a foil to the Cardinal's bald and horrifying declaration. His admission of guilt is directly followed by a restaging of the crime, for Julia immediately pays for her indiscretion with her death. The death of the Duchess in the fourth act is painstakingly prepared for from the play's very beginning, so that its dramatic shock is greatly mitigated. For Julia, "love" is more irresponsible, knowledge of evil more sudden, and death more abrupt than for the Duchess, yet the compressed juxtaposition of these extremes of love and death recalls the Duchess's tragic fate with new force. This simplified—almost caricatured—recollection of the Duchess's life and death clarifies the essential tragic meaning of the play's action. As T. C. Worsley summarized it in a review of the 1960 Royal

Shakespeare Company production, "As we see her first the Duchess is a woman of high natural spirits and vitality, and it is that buoyancy of heart that it is so terrible to see being desolated."[30] Julia's part in the final act is a microcosm of the main action, her cruel death a striking contrast to her strength and vitality. And, unlike Cariola—the Duchess's foil in death—Julia accepts her death with dignity, though it is undeserved.

During the final act, Bosola's role as an onlooker and accomplice during the Duchess's death is restaged. After Julia's death, he argues with the Cardinal about "reward," vows vengeance for the Duchess's murder, and drags the body off the stage, exactly as he had done at the end of Act IV. His complaint as he picks up Julia's body—"I think I shall / Shortly grow the common bier for churchyards" (V.ii.311-12)—reinforces the analogue. In the staging of the scene, Bosola's vengeful soliloquy is invariably delivered as he kneels over Julia's body, precisely as he had knelt over the Duchess's body earlier. While it keeps the memory of the Duchess alive, the repetition of the sequence of crime and revenge also suggests the futility of Bosola's attempt at vengeance, futility that is later confirmed in his botched murder of Antonio.

It would, of course, be dangerous to overstate the case for the parallels between the two plots. Certainly the two women belong to sharply contrasting worlds throughout the play, and such contrasts give the play its richly varied texture. Julia is involved in the petty, broken world of the Duchess's enemies as the Duchess herself never is, and the parallels between the two women heighten their differences. Conversely, however, Webster exploits the obvious differences between them in order to reveal surprising similarities, which serve his dramatic ends. The differences between the Duchess and Julia may emphasize the Duchess's calm self-sufficiency, but the similarities between them suggest the vulnerability of women in a hostile masculine world. The play's final emphasis falls on Julia and, by analogy, on the Duchess—not as a single, heroic individual destroyed by crazed villains, but as an ordinary, vital young woman stifled by misogyny. Rather than undercutting or further exalting the Duchess's stature in the final act, Julia restores the Duchess by analogy to the world of common humanity, to which she firmly belonged throughout the play.

In conclusion, the Julia subplot has an important dramatic function in *The Duchess of Malfi*. The presentation of Julia as a character is clearly consistent with the interest Webster displays in challenging conventional morality with his other heroines, the

Duchess and Vittoria. Close examination of the scenes in which Julia figures reveals not a "flagrant adulteress" but a woman of some integrity; not a fickle temptress, but a sexually vital woman. That integrity and sexual vitality are not incompatible is a major concern of *The Duchess of Malfi*. The Julia subplot clarifies and restates Webster's primary concerns in the play's main action. As a "glass" for events in the Duchess's life, Julia reflects their essence in compressed, sometimes caricatured, form. In a review of the 1971 Royal Shakespeare Company production of the play, one reviewer described Julia as "the most genteel whore, cooing like a dove in a cage of hawks,"[31] a description which could apply equally well to the Duchess. Like the Duchess, Julia is caged and finally killed by the predatory Arragonian brothers. And like the Duchess, Julia remains fully sexually alive to the last moment.

NOTES

[1]George Rylands, "On the Production of *The Duchess of Malfi*," *The Duchess of Malfi*, ed. G. H. W. Rylands and C. Williams (London: Sylvan, 1945), p. vi.

[2]Maynard Mack, "The Jacobean Shakespeare," *Jacobean Theatre*, ed. J. R. Brown and Bernard Harris, Stratford-upon-Avon Studies 1 (London: Edward Arnold, 1960); Bernard Beckerman, *Shakespeare at the Globe 1599-1609* (New York: Macmillan, 1962). The phrase comes from Herbert Whittaker's review of the 1971 Stratford, Ontario production in *The Globe and Mail*, 9 June 1971, p. 15.

[3]John Russell Brown, ed., *The Duchess of Malfi*, by John Webster (London: Methuen, 1964), p. 62. All citations to the play refer to this edition.

[4]Gunnar Boklund, *"The Duchess of Malfi": Sources, Themes, Characters* (Cambridge: Cambridge Univ. Press, 1962), p. 42.

[5]William Archer, "Webster, Lamb and Swinburne," *New Review* 8,44 (1893); rpt. in G. K. and S. K. Hunter, eds., *John Webster: A Critical Anthology* (Harmondsworth: Penguin, 1969), p. 85.

[6]William Poel, "A New Criticism of Webster's *Duchess of Malfi*," *Library Review* 2 (1893); rpt. in Hunter, p. 87. Poel's 1892 production of *The Duchess of Malfi* at the Opera Comique restored the Julia subplot for the first time since the seventeenth century. His interpretation of the subplot did not convince the critics, however. A review in the *Nation* complained that "the intrigue of the Cardinal with Julia apparently had no other use in the tragedy save to add one more corpse to the many strewing the stage in that indescribable fifth act" (10 November 1892; rpt. in *Webster: The Critical Heritage*, ed. Don D. Moore [London: Routledge, 1981], p. 128).

[7]See Normand Berlin, "*The Duchess of Malfi:* Act V and Genre," *Genre* 3 (1970):356; Lee Bliss, *The World's Perspective: John Webster and the Jacobean Drama* (New Brunswick, N.J.: Rutgers Univ. Press, 1983), p. 160; M. C.

Bradbrook, *John Webster: Citizen and Dramatist* (London: Weidenfeld, 1980), p. 155; Travis Bogard, *The Tragic Satire of John Webster* (Berkeley and Los Angeles: Univ. of California Press, 1955), p. 138; Clifford Leech, *Webster: "The Duchess of Malfi"* (London: Edward Arnold, 1963), p. 32; Richard Levin, *New Readings vs. Old Plays: Recent Trends in the Reinterpretation of English Renaissance Drama* (Chicago: Univ. of Chicago Press, 1979), p. 98; Jacqueline Pearson, *Tragedy and Tragicomedy in the Plays of John Webster* (Manchester: Manchester Univ. Press, 1980), p. 61.

[8]Charles Lewson, "Sick Stallion," *The Listener*, 22 July 1971, p. 125.

[9]Michael Billington, "Well-Dressed Decadence Without Relief," *The Guardian*, 6 July 1985, p. 8.

[10]Lucy Hughes-Hallett, "'The Duchess of Malfi'," *Now*, 26 September 1980.

[11]Jacqueline Pearson, "Man Bites Man," *TLS*, 26 September 1980, p. 1064.

[12]Boklund, p. 78. See also Ralph Berry, *The Art of John Webster* (Oxford: Clarendon Press, 1972), pp. 38-41; Fernand Lagarde, *John Webster*, 2 vols. (Toulouse: Association des Publications des Lettres et Sciences Humaines de Toulouse, 1968), 2:851; Clifford Leech, *John Webster: A Critical Study* (London: Hogarth Press, 1951), p. 75; J. R. Mulryne, "Webster and the Uses of Tragicomedy," in *John Webster*, ed. Brian Morris (London: Ernest Benn, 1970), p. 153; Joyce E. Peterson, *Curs'd Example: "The Duchess of Malfi" and Commonweal Tragedy* (Columbia and London: Univ. of Missouri Press, 1978), pp. 88-104.

[13]Lisa Jardine, *Still Harping on Daughters: Women and Drama in the Age of Shakespeare* (Sussex: Harvester Press, 1983), p. 71.

[14]William Empson, "Mine Eyes Dazzle," *EIC* 14 (1964); rpt. in Hunter, p. 298.

[15]Details about this production were provided by the promptbook held by the Shakespeare Birthplace Trust, Stratford-upon-Avon.

[16]Philip Hope-Wallace, "The Stratford Company Goes to Town," *Guardian*, 17 December 1960.

[17]Leech, *Webster: "The Duchess of Malfi,"* p. 33.

[18]Leech, *John Webster*, p. 75.

[19]Hereward T. Price also makes this point in "The Function of Imagery in Webster," *PMLA* 70 (September 1955); rpt. in Hunter, p. 195.

[20]There are some precise verbal echoes of Bosola in the Cardinal's speeches: both use images of glass manufacture for female sexuality (II.ii.6-10; II.iv.13-14), as well as animal imagery (II.i.47-55; II.iv.27-34).

[21]For the notion of "two voices," I am of course indebted to Mack's "The Jacobean Shakespeare," pp. 19-20.

[22]Archer, in Hunter, p. 85.

[23]Lois Potter, "Realism vs. Nightmare; Problems of Staging *The Duchess of Malfi*," in *The Triple Bond*, ed. Joseph G. Price (Univ. Park and London: Pennsylvania State Univ. Press, 1975), p. 180.

[24]I find it difficult to accept Peterson's view that Julia's refusal indicates that Delio "simply has not offered enough" (p. 93).

[25]See Roger Warren, "'The Duchess of Malfi' on the Stage," in *John Webster*, ed. Brian Morris, p. 65.

[26]Although she does not discuss the Julia subplot, Linda Woodbridge's view of Webster's manipulation of antifeminist stereotypes in his plays is similar to my own when she remarks that, in *The Duchess of Malfi,* "The question of female sexuality is precisely what Webster seems interested in exploring," and,

in *The White Devil*, "The moral ambiguity readers experience in the play stems partly from Webster's attempt to achieve sympathy for a fallen woman, to turn a whore into a hero" (*Women and the English Renaissance: Literature and the Nature of Womankind 1540-1620* [Urbana and Chicago: Univ. of Illinois Press, 1984], pp. 259-62). Furthermore, according to Woodbridge, Webster's treatment of both his minor and his major female characters reflects a general trend in plays of the second decade of the seventeenth century. As she notes, "Even the image of prostitutes underwent a face-lifting in the drama during the *hic mulier* years" (p. 261).

[27]I cannot agree with the reading of this scene proposed by Bliss, who claims: "Some courtiers, or a Julia, seek to 'fortify themselves' with others' ruin, but Pescara displays an innate sense of justice" (p. 163).

[28]Woodbridge, p. 77.

[29]D. H., "Magnificent Make-Believe," review of *The Duchess of Malfi*, Royal Shakespeare Company, Aldwych, London. *Bristol Evening Post*, 16 December 1960; Milton Shulman, "Horror Unlimited Hits the Aldwych," *Evening Standard*, 16 December 1960.

[30]" 'The Duchess of Malfi,' " *Financial Times*, 16 December 1960.

[31]P. W., "A Tidy Murder," *Sunday Mercury*, 18 July 1971.

SEL 27 (1987)
ISSN 0039-3657

John Fletcher as Spenserian Playwright: *The Faithful Shepherdess* and *The Island Princess*

PHILIP J. FINKELPEARL

I

In about 1608 the young John Fletcher mounted his first play on the London stage, *The Faithful Shepherdess.*[1] Aside from its uncharacteristic lyricism, the basic ingredients of the famous "Beaumont & Fletcher" product would already seem to be in place: the intricate, "well-made" plotting, the sensationalism, the theatricality—all that is alleged to have brought about the "decadence" of the Jacobean theater. Yet when the young John Milton adapted some passages from Fletcher's play for *Comus* in 1634 (Sabrina's speech, lines 902ff.), it must have afforded him pleasures other than those immediately apparent to us. I suspect that a decade after the author's death *The Faithful Shepherdess* would have looked like another work by one of the Spenserian Fletchers, John being the first cousin of Milton's admired Giles Jr. and Phineas.[2] Today, John Fletcher is usually regarded as a theatrical caterer to a primarily courtly, "cavalier" audience. It is forgotten that his family's affiliations and traditions were with radical Protestants, and that his only known connection with the court was his lifelong patron and friend, the Earl of Huntingdon—one of the most prominent of the "noble protectors" of Puritans and someone King James regarded as an opponent.[3] Whatever distaste Milton felt for Jacobean drama—at times quite powerful—his occasional use of Fletcher's work suggests that he put him in a special category. And if he read *The Faithful Shepherdess* and other of his plays with the emphasis I will be suggesting, perhaps he even detected a kindred spirit.[4]

The immediate impression of *The Faithful Shepherdess* is of characters from *The Shepheardes Calender*—some with identical

Philip Finkelpearl, who teaches English at Wellesley College, is working on a book on Beaumont and Fletcher.

names—placed in the world of Book III of *The Fairie Queene*. On the smaller scale that is necessary in a play, Fletcher exhibits a spectrum of lovers from the basely sensual to the purely spiritual. There is, first, the "faithful shepherdess" Clorin. Since the death of her lover she has dedicated herself to a chaste life of selfless service to humanity. Her beauty and virtue have attracted the strange, idealistic love of the shepherd Thenot who vows that as long as she remains pure, he will continue to try to win her, all the while hoping that he fails. Another lover, Perigot, in a situation derived from *The Fairie Queene*, is tricked by the shepherdess Amaryllis and her amoral helper, the Sullen Shepherd. Amaryllis gets transformed by magic into the shape of Perigot's innocent mistress Amoret and tries to seduce him, because of which the upright hero—anticipating *Philaster*—twice wounds the true, helpless, and ever-loving Amoret. Finally, in a third strand of the plot, Fletcher invents a variant on the Daphnis and Chloe story, employing their very names. Desperately dissatisfied with her virginal state and eager to take up with anyone who will relieve her of her virtue, Chloe utters the immortal line, "It is Impossible to Ravish mee, / I am so willing" (III.i.212-13).[5] She finds Daphnis loving but much too virtuous. Another shepherd, Alexas, is willing to assist her, but just as she is about to gain her desire, the lustful Sullen Shepherd interferes and poor Chloe is left with her virginity intact.

Clearly, like Milton in his Horton period, the author of *The Faithful Shepherdess* was a very literary young man, aware of the latest developments on the Continent and interested in seeing how Guarini and Spenser might be combined.[6] The experiment failed to please the audience, but if we are to believe Ben Jonson, it was not damned for the "vices" it dramatized: these the sophisticated habitués of the private theater "look'd for, and came to." Its failure, according to Jonson, came from Fletcher's excessive "Innocence."[7] If anything, the play was too moral.

Fletcher's treatment of the god Pan is symptomatic. Occasionally, it is true, he cavorts playfully through the forest, entertaining various lovely nymphs in the manner we expect of him. At other moments it is evident that Pan, as in *The Shepheardes Calender*, represents Christ. However, as we hear his values expressed through his priests, this Christ is a most repressive, Augustinian figure. For example, the hapless wounded shepherd Alexas learns that he cannot be healed

Till thou hast layed a syde all heates, desiers,
Provoking thoughts, that stirr upp lusty fiers,
Commerse with wanton Eyes: strong bloud, and will
To execute, theise must bee purg'd untill
The vayne growe Whiter: then Repent and pray
Great *Pan,* to keepe you from the like decaye,
And I shall undertake your cure with ease.

(IV.ii.109-15)

This conveys the prevailing attitude in Thessaly, and Fletcher makes no real attempt to express another point of view as Milton does in Comus's encomium on nature's bounty. Everywhere the value of chastity is unquestioningly assumed and dogmatically asserted. When a feeble justification of natural desire is offered to the Priest of Pan, it is done, significantly, by the one unreformable character, the Sullen Shepherd:

Good holynesse declare,
What had the danger bene if being bare,
I had embracd her, tell me by your Art:
What comming wonders wood that sight impart?

(V.iii.139-42)

The Priest's response is terse and unyielding: "Lust, and branded soule" (line 143). The Sullen Shepherd makes one more effort at argument, advancing a primitive version of Comus's justification:

Yet tell me more,
Hath not our Mother *Nature* for her store,
And great increase, sayd it is good and just,
And willd that every living creature must,
Beget his like?

(V.iii.143-47)

Again the Priest, plainly a representative of the prevailing viewpoint, shows no interest in dallying with such specious nonsense:

Yee are better read then I,
I must confesse in Blood and Letchery:
Now to the Bowre and bring this beast along,
Where he may suffere Pennance for his wrong.

(V.iii.147-50)

And so the Sullen Shepherd, remaining forever unenlightened, is exiled from Pan's kingdom.

These harsh simplifications are further underlined at the conclusion of this, the final scene. Every character gathered in Clorin's virginal grove is subjected to a chastity test conducted by a friendly satyr armed with a kind of magical Geiger counter. All having been "brought againe / To virgin state" (V.v.158-59), they are handed over by Clorin, fully certified as "patients full of health" (V.v.167), to the care and scrutiny of the Priest of Pan. As her valedictory, Clorin gives a heavily didactic, thirty-four line speech of advice on pastoral care to the Priest. She urges him to scrutinize the private, personal conduct of his flock in a manner reminiscent of Calvin's Geneva:

> Keepe them from after ills, be ever neere
> Unto their actions: teach them how to cleare
> The tedeous way they passe through, from suspect:
> Keepe them from wrong in others, or neglect
> Of duety in them selves, correct the bloud,
> With thrifty bitts and laboure:
> . . . .
> have a care,
> Thou man of holy life, now do not spare
> Their faults through much remissnes.
>
> (V.v.168-80)

She suggests sorting out the good shepherds from the bad, teaching "strictnes" to the young maidens in order that they may fend off sexual temptations, "banish[ing] all complement"—apparently the sort youths exchange in courtship—"but single truth" (line 187). Chapman claims in his prefatory poem that Fletcher's play creates a "golden world," but it would be a heavily policed Arcadia.[8] His chastity is a far cry from the free, open, enriching concept which Britomart represents in *The Fairie Queene* and Milton develops in *Comus*.[9]

In many ways *The Faithful Shepherdess* stands outside the mainstream of the Beaumont and Fletcher plays. That he could ever have conceived this play tells us much about the sort of person Fletcher was before Beaumont appeared. The author sounds like a young man fresh from a trip to Italy after years cloistered in a college or a remote great house or (what was indeed the case) a bishop's palace. Are we to infer that only Fletcher's union with Beaumont saved us from dramatic companion pieces to Giles Fletcher's *Christ's*

Victory and Triumph and Phineas Fletcher's *Purple Island* and that the renowned "consimility of fancy" (in John Aubrey's phrase) was born along with the collaboration?

II

In their years together Beaumont and Fletcher learned how to write dramatic dialogue that reproduced supremely well, as Dryden put it, "the conversation of gentlemen." Never again do we find the kind of overly sumptuous, closet-drama lyricism or the heavy, simplistic moralizing that mar *The Faithful Shepherdess.* Nonetheless, some years after Beaumont's death, and exploiting all the sophistication and stagecraft he had acquired, Fletcher once again tried to write a play tinged with what I will tentatively call Puritanism. In his best-known plays Fletcher's heroes, with or without Beaumont, act according to some notion of what is noble and honorable, but almost always their virtues are interwoven with—sometimes they seem to engender—vices: immodesty, intemperance, inflexibility in some, indolence or passivity in others. In one of the best and most amusing plays in the canon, *The Island Princess* (1619-1621), Fletcher shows what happens when another sort of protagonist, the embodiment of all the virtues, invades Fletcher's usual world of flawed, would-be heroes.

The hero, Armusia, acts boldly, makes love chastely, offers himself as a martyr for his religion, and at all times conducts himself humbly and courteously. He is even given a poetic eloquence which (in one speech at least) attracted Milton's attention:

> We are arriv'd among the blessed Islands,
> Where every wind that rises blowes perfumes,
> And every breath of aire is like Incence:
> The treasure of the Sun dwels here, each tree
> As if it envied the old Paradice,
> Strives to bring forth immortall fruit.
>
> (I.iii.16-21)[10]

The passage, which continues in this vein for another fifteen lines, is more than a florid setpiece. It helps to establish Armusia's noble disposition—idealistic, capable of wonder, eager to admire the spice island of Tidore on which he has just landed.

But Armusia's admiration is premature. Fletcher has placed him in a world in which it is very difficult to get one's bearings or to judge with confidence any of the inhabitants. In the opening words of the play a Portuguese captain describes the islanders as "false and desperate people" (I.i.4). The speaker Pineiro, a wit with a touch of the malcontent, is reacting to a recent event which tends to justify this harsh judgment. The King of Tidore has been treacherously abducted while sailing and is being held prisoner by the governor of the neighboring island of Ternate. Pineiro also has his suspicions about the character of the beautiful and—her complexion lacking the "tauny Livery" (I.i.62) of her countrymen—fair princess Quisara: "They that observe her close, shall find her nature, / Which I doubt mainly will not prove so excellent" (I.i.43-44).[11]

Quisara is a passionate, credulous creature easily manipulated by men. At the opening she is being courted by two kings and a governor, but she has set her heart on Ruy Dias, the commander of a Portuguese garrison on the island. The obstacle to their marriage is, obviously, their great disparity in rank. To circumvent this and justify her favor, she concocts a cunning plot to enhance his status:

> that man that would be known my lover,
> Must be known his [her brother, the King of
> Tidore's] redeemer, and must bring him
> Either alive or dead to my embraces,
> For even his bones I scorne shall feele such slavery,
> Or seeke another Mistris, 'twill be hard
> To do this, wondrous hard, a great adventure,
> Fit for a spirit of an equall greatnesse;
> But being done, the reward is worthy of it.
>
> (I.iii.148-55)

Quisara's rhetoric sounds so attractively heroic that one tends to ignore the equanimity with which she is prepared to bestow the same reward for her brother or his bones.[12]

Quisara's plot was tailor-made for Ruy Dias, but unfortunately he turns out to be an extremely circumspect hero:

> *Quisara* [*Aside*]. No stirring yet, no start into a bravery?
> *Ruy Dias* [*aside*]. Madam, it may be, but being a maine danger,
> Your Grace must give me leave to looke about me,
> And take a little time, the cause will aske it,
> Great acts require great counsells.
> *Quisara* [*aside*]. Take your pleasure,
> I fear ye Portugall.
>
> (I.iii.163-68)

Here for a time *The Island Princess* becomes satiric comedy. Ruy Dias is a subtle variant on the *miles gloriosus,* and Quisara is a wit who has outwitted herself. Fletcher presents her with sufficient detail and shading so that we can comprehend and sympathize with her plight while viewing her with amusement. She "is all pure honor" (I.iii.225), as one admirer of her performance at court says, but also a gullible, naive girl who has chosen the wrong male lead for the drama she wishes to play; she is a Jacobean version of George Eliot's Dorothea, "enamoured of intensity and greatness, and rash in embracing whatever seemed to her to have those aspects; likely to seek martyrdom." Quisara's eventual aspiration to play the Virgin Martyr (V.ii.105-10) grows naturally out of her earlier tastes and preferences.

Into this fallen world of the morally ambiguous, the confused, and the cowardly, Fletcher thrusts the heroic Armusia. New on the island, totally unknown to Quisara, he has been a quiet onlooker during her announcement. He is struck by her beauty and spirit, and his imagination is inflamed by the nature of her challenge. In no time at all—easily, bravely, inventively—he accomplishes the rescue of the king. Quisara's announcement at court occurs in the last scene of the first act; by the last scene of the second act while Quisara is still trying to goad Ruy Dias out of his "wise delayings" (II.vi.77), Armusia returns in triumph with her brother—alive, of course.

After the melodrama of Act II showing the king's noble suffering in prison and Armusia's brilliantly executed rescue, Fletcher now reverts to comedy. He even indulges in a moment of farce as each cowardly suitor assures the king that he would have accomplished the rescue if Armusia had not. The main emphasis, however, is on the bitter interplay between Quisara and Ruy Dias. Instead of joy at the release of her beloved brother, Quisara can only react with anger and self-pity at the unexpected result of her over-cunning ploy:

> Must I be given
> Unto a man I never saw, ne're spoke with,
> I know not of what Nation?
> . . . .
> Oh *Ruy Dias*
> This was your sloth, your sloth, your sloth *Ruy Dias.*
> (II.vi.85-90)

Quisara uses the passive voice as though someone else had contrived the plight she has fallen into; and when she berates her sluggish lover, her accents are the most naturalistic, at least for a heroic figure,

Fletcher ever composed. Urged now by her grateful brother into honoring her promise to marry his rescuer, the still-infuriated princess pleads for time to become acquainted with him and "*apart*" moans despairingly, "O *Ruy Dias*" (II.vi.187) as she leaves the stage. Meanwhile, as we learn from the acid Pineiro, Ruy Dias "looks as though he were sick oth' worms" (II.vi.194).

The comedy turns perceptibly darker in the third act. Ruy Dias was slow in going to the aid of the captured king. Now that honor's "mighty master" is threatened with the "everlasting losing of my worth" (III.i.72) through the ascendency of "that new thing," as he calls Armusia (III.i.43), he can act decisively. But for him "action" means the employment of someone else to act, and what he wants is the murder of his rival. In a devious and self-debasing speech Ruy Dias enlists his nephew Pineiro to "doe something here" (III.i.58). Fortunately, Pineiro is "honest" and a fervid admirer of Armusia. He pretends to accept the task in order to protect Armusia from his uncle who, Pineiro thinks, is under the influence of the devil. Fletcher treats this situation—similar to that of the later *The Changeling* (1622)—comically by placing Armusia's fate in the hands of the virtuous Pineiro, but the author doubles the bitter comedy by also making Quisara approach Pineiro for the same purpose.[13] Her language is as obscure as if she believed she were being tape-recorded:

> *Pineiro.* Dare you say I [ay] to it,
> And set me on? 'tis no matter for my Uncle,
> Or what I owe to him, dare you but wish it.
> *Quisara.* I wou'd faine—
> *Pineiro.* Have it done; say but so Lady.
> *Quisara.* Conceive it so.
>
> (III.i.214-16)

Eventually we realize that though Quisara appears to be imperious and self-willed, she is in fact molded by her lover of the moment. Under the influence of the weak and mediocre Ruy Dias, she could even have become a murderess like Middleton's Beatrice-Joanna.

Soon the Princess discovers Armusia's overwhelming virtues:

> *Quisara* [*aside*]. What a pure soul inherits here? what innocence?
> Sure I was blind when I first lov'd this fellow,
> And long'd to live in that fogg stil: how he blusters!
>
> (III.iii.122-24)

This perception alters her actions, if not her character. She abandons the plan to murder Armusia, claiming to Pineiro that she is "ashamed of my share" (IV.ii.76) in the plot. Perhaps she is, but we also recall that in the interval she has fallen in love with Armusia. At the same time, Ruy Dias is driven to what a conventional cavalier of the time would call "honorable" behavior. He admits to Pineiro that in commissioning the murder he has acted badly, that his "sicke honour [must be] cur'd the right and straight way" (IV.ii.14), that is, by a duel with Armusia. Of course he is defeated and then treated with great deference and dignity by the altogether exemplary Armusia.

The first movement in this eventful, episodic play involved the rescue of the king; the second, the problems this rescue produced in Quisara's emotional life. Act IV initiates a final movement, springing from the desire of the Governor of Ternate to avenge the public humiliations of the prince's rescue and Quisara's rejection of his marriage proposal. Disguising himself as a "Moorish Priest," he easily precipitates the sort of "generall ruine" (IV.i.80) he desires. He persuades the pliable Quisara to demand Armusia's conversion to the pagan religion of Tidore[14] in exchange for her agreement to marry him; and he arranges to have the credulous king overhear the refusal Armusia is certain to make. Under Quisara's importunities the notably temperate, somehow never priggish, hero is prodded into increasingly passionate outbursts of contempt for the islanders' religion, into ardent expressions of faith in Christianity, even into angry insults at the pagan princess. Armusia's rage is theatrically a high moment because it is a surprising but legitimate extension of his character. In the excitement of the rescue, in the melancholy induced by Quisara's indifference, in his courtly wooing, even in his responses to Ruy Dias's insults, Armusia has been a model of nearly incredible self-possession. With his faith under attack by Quisara he flies into near-insane flights of passionate rhetoric of which Fletcher was a mighty master:

> [Your face] lookes like death it selfe, to which 'twou'd lead
> me,
> Your eyes resemble pale dispaire, they fright me,
> And in their rounds, a thousand horrid ruines,
> Methinkes I see; and in your tongue heare fearefully
> The hideous murmurs of weake soules have suffer'd;
> Get from me, I despise ye, and know woman,
> That for all this trap you have laid to catch my life in,

To catch my immortall life, I hate and curse ye,
Contemne your deities, spurne at their powers,
And where I meet your maumet Gods, I'le swing 'em
Thus o're my head, and kick 'em into puddles,
Nay I will out of vengeance search your Temples,
And with those hearts that serve my God, demolish
Your shambles of wild worships.

(IV.v.105-18)

This impious outburst is enough for the king. He imprisons his heroic rescuer through the cunning plotting of his former captor.

Armusia's spectacular performance has another unexpected effect. By the time he stands in captivity, the enraptured princess says in one aside that now she hates her gods, and in another, the final words of Act IV, "Oh how I love this man, how truly honour him" (IV.v.141). She has finally found a man who conforms to the rigorous specifications enunciated to Ruy Dias in the first act, someone capable of acts "Of such an unmatcht noblenesse, that I may know / You have a power beyond ours that preserves you" (I.ii.59-60). Armusia's strength, she perceives, is as much spiritual as physical.

As we have seen, Quisara's imperious airs mask a character that, although she would be courted on bended knee, will follow the path of her lover of the moment, whether a murderer or a saint. After Armusia is led to prison, she ardently proclaims her determination to link her fate with his:

Your faith, and your religion must be like ye,
They that can shew you these, must be pure mirrours;
When the streames flow cleare and faire, what are the fountaines?
I do embrace your faith sir, and your fortune;
Go on, I will assist ye, I feele a sparkle here,
A lively sparke that kindles my affection,
And tels me it will rise to flames of glory:
Let 'em put on their angers, suffer nobly,
Shew me the way, and when I faint instruct me.

(V.ii.118-26)

About this passage William Appleton remarks: "Quisara is posturing and attitudinizing like one of Bernini's saints. . . . She is already basking in a baroque 'gloire.' Corneille's Polyeucte also seeks his 'gloire' in martyrdom, but he elects his martyrdom through reason and not through passion. Quisara's motivation is entirely a transient emotional one." Appleton concludes by condemning the "meretricious manner in which Fletcher flirts with his potentially serious theme."[15] This comment makes precisely the same assumption almost everyone does about Fletcher—that it is the playwright and not the character who is meretricious. Appleton describes Quisara's performance correctly. It is to miss the tone of the scene, however, to view it as an attempt at a religious moment. Through the example of her new love, Quisara has found a vocation worthy of her sense of drama and her heroic temperament. Religion is the vehicle onto which she can now attach her idealistic ardor. Her conversion is to be regarded with as much suspicion as her other enthusiasms. Fletcher has carefully prepared us to view this new one with amusement and suspicion—this must be my defense for such a lengthy exegesis—through the many scenes which reveal her unstable suggestibility. Clearly, she has no notion of what Christianity is, but she likes how it sounds. As Armusia raves wildly against her request that he convert, she says in an aside, "I love to heare him" (IV.v.95). His unyielding adherence to his faith is part of his simple heroism; for Quisara, Christianity affords a good acting vehicle.

In the last scene Quisara proclaims some brave words for her saint's legend, had the ending been a tragic one: "Which way you go, sir, / I must follow necessary. / One life, and one death" (V.v.41-42). These are, in fact, her last words in the play because she and Armusia are saved from a martyr's fate by the plotting of Pineiro and the newly-inspired courage of Ruy Dias. Fletcher never gives her a chance to speak again, not even words of joy and love. Armusia expresses his happiness at the outcome and, pure hero that he is, remembers to apologize for the words he uttered against the noble princess in "distemper" (V.v.73). Not surprisingly, Quisara does not choose to be comparably apologetic, nor does Ruy Dias, about the more culpable plans they had once entertained. We are left with only one unresolved concern at the end: what cause or person will Quisara take up next?

Throughout the play Fletcher intermixes the heroic, the satiric, and the farcical. The citizens of Tidore joke casually about the supposedly destructive cannonading of their town in the same manner as the citizens of Ternate did during the fire which was set to effect the king's escape. Even the villainous governor is not taken very seriously. When the Portuguese rescue the heroes at the end of the play, they "tear" at the "Moor Priest" who has acted as *agent provocateur* in all the strife; the stage direction reads, "*Pulls his*

Beard and haire off" (V.v.53). The primitive unmasking works, like Armusia's effortless commando raid on Ternate, to reduce the power of evil to the level of an ineffectual dragon in a St. George's Play and thereby to reenforce the predominantly comic tone. Similarly, the Christian motif is amusingly ignored in the concluding words by the (be it noted!) unconverted king, words that assume the continuing potency of the pagan gods of the island: "And know however subtill men dare cast, / And promise wrack, the gods give peace at last" (V.v.93).

III

From Shakespeare to Dryden, the concept of honor provided dramatists with rich and fascinating themes. At once an ethical absolute and a motive for action, it was shown as driving men to martyrdom and criminality, to the most heroic and the pettiest acts. In most of his plays Fletcher created characters who treat honor as the unquestioned, unexamined pole around which their lives revolve. The more interesting plays also reveal the abuses and perversions to which worshipers of the "idol" honor were often driven. They display brave but thin-skinned gallants obsessed almost to madness by their reputations; base cowards scheming to gain the badge of honor illegitimately; well-intentioned cavaliers forced into potentially fatal duels through a distorted sense of what honor demands. Some of his best plays concentrate on the ambiguous, unpredictable ramifications of honor's influence. There, honorable actions cause disasters, dishonorable actions save a commonwealth from destruction: the road to honor is full of traps and confusions to the unwary. Collectively, the heroes of these plays could take their motto from T. S. Eliot's *Gerontion*: "Unnatural vices / Are fathered by our heroism. Virtues / Are forced upon us by our impudent crimes." Rarely was Fletcher content simply to portray honor as a star for every virtuous bark without also subjecting it to scrutiny and analysis.

It is my sense of the complexity of Fletcher's treatment of honor that sometimes leads me to differ with Eugene Waith in his classic study, *The Pattern of Tragicomedy in Beaumont and Fletcher*. For example, Waith dismisses the religious dimension to *The Island Princess* as mere window dressing for its real concern:

> One cannot avoid the uneasy feeling that this denouement is no solution to the religious problems that have been raised. But it is a speech of Ruy Dias which gives the whole show away:

> Why what a wretch art thou to work this mischief?
> To assume this holy shape to ruine honor,
> Honor and chastity.
>
> (V.v.60-62)

> The whole pagan attack upon Christianity has masked the fundamental attack upon honor and chastity.
>
> Armusia is a hero essentially like Miranda of *The Knight of Malta* or Demetrius of *The Humorous Lieutenant,* dedicated to the ideal of honor. The preservation of the faith is part of that ideal when the hero is Christian, as Armusia and Miranda are, but it is a nonessential. The pagan Demetrius speaks and acts very much like Armusia, for the chivalric ideal of the seventeenth century has become a matter of personal integrity. . . . Armusia's honor does not become a fresh instance of Christian virtue; rather, a stereotyped Christian virtue is bundled into the concept of honor along with many other things.[16]

The Island Princess is set at a pagan court imbued with Jacobean-Italianate politics and manners. Ruy Dias and Quisara are natural denizens in that world and are immediately recognizable as direct descendents of some of Beaumont and Fletcher's most famous characters: Ruy, reminiscent of the ineffectual Philaster, of the weak Amintor of *The Maid's Tragedy,* of the blustering Arbaces of *A King and No King*; and Quisara, the latest in a populous female line starting with the glamorous but morally corrupt Evadne of *The Maid's Tragedy.* As I read the attractive, honor-driven characters to whom Professor Waith compares Armusia—Miranda in *The Knight of Malta* and Demetrius in *The Humorous Lieutenant*—they are flawed in the same ways as Ruy Dias. It is true that Miranda is represented as a virtuous and Christian gentleman, but in the portions of the play written by Fletcher, Miranda clearly has feet of clay.[17] As for Demetrius in *The Humorous Lieutenant,* throughout the play he engages in foolish, showy gestures to portray himself as a supremely honorable cavalier, and at the end of the play he loses some of his attractiveness by displaying a lack of faith in his utterly trustworthy loved one, Celia.[18]

Thus I am contending that among Fletcher's later, full-length, male characterizations, Armusia is unique in being utterly flawless. The comedy of the play (as I have tried to show) stems from how uncomprehendingly and uncomfortably the courtly world responds to his perfection. Armusia is as much an alien there as (in a different way) are the Citizens who burst onto the stage of *The Knight of the Burning Pestle*: "Honest, / Perfect, and good, chaste, blushing-chaste, and temperate, / Valiant, without vaineglory, modest, stayed," he represents the "perfect school of worth," the "temple of *true* honour" (V.ii.111-16, italics mine). His is an uncourtly, but recognizable form of honorable conduct: that of the true wayfaring Christian. At his moments of angriest zeal he even becomes an iconoclastic missionary to the heathens:

> I lookd you [Quisara] should have said,
> make me a Christian,
> Worke that great cure, for 'tis a great one woman;
> That labour truly doe performe, that venture
> The crowne of all great triall, and the fairest:
> I lookd ye should have wept and kneel'd to beg it,
> Washt off your mist of ignorance, with waters
> Pure and repentant, from those eyes; I lookt
> You should have brought me your chief god ye worship,
> He that you offer humane bloud and life to,
> And made a sacrifice of him to memorie,
> Beat downe his Altars, ruin'd his false Temples.
> (IV.v.83-93)

A figure like Armusia would have been out of place in the court of King James. Even the most learned and cultivated courtiers—figures like Sir Kenelm Digby and Lord Herbert of Cherbury—behaved remarkably like the various fools of honor in Fletcher's plays. Out of a Quixotically anachronistic commitment to knight errantry, they often acted as though they were (in King James's rapturous words describing the absurd trip Buckingham and Prince Charles took to Spain) "adventurous knights worthy to be put in a new romanso."[19] But as many recent studies of seventeenth-century English culture have made clear, there was nothing obsolete about the values of this latter-day Red Cross Knight, Armusia. Behind him is that complex of attitudes, values, and beliefs that in seventeenth-century common talk often went by the label of "country" when used in contrast to "court." "Country" refers to an Arcadia of moral purity, thrift, chastity, Protestantism, and often (but not necessarily) Puritanism; its politics were frequently inspired by the model of the Roman republic; its artistic preferences were for unsophisticated, traditional, English (as opposed to Continental) styles of art, architecture, and literature. In all these categories "Court" connoted the evil opposite.[20]

In his recent study of English education, *Scholars and Gentlemen*,[21] Hugh Kearney isolates some aspects of this polarization of English culture of particular relevance to Armusia. He traces a direct conflict between the imported, Italianate "court humanism" of Castiglione and Sir Thomas Elyot and what—alluding to Hans Baron's widely-used term "civic humanism"—Kearney labels "country humanism": there "are two contrasting ideals of what a humanist education should be, the one drawing its inspiration from the values of the Italian courts, the other from the city states of Strasburg, Geneva, Basle and Zurich. One was lay, the other clerical. One looked to the court, the other to the country. One stressed the values of display, magnificence and sexual prowess, the other the virtues of restraint and godliness" (p. 43).

Kearney illustrates this countervailing brand of "humanism" through an anti-Castiglione treatise on education by Laurence Humphrey titled *The Nobles* (1563). Humphrey, a Marian exile and "probably the most important single person at Oxford in his lifetime" (p. 43), based his position primarily on the Bible rather than the classics and directed his work to a noble, courtly audience. He urged courtiers to use as models neither Castiglione's ambitious, worldly politician nor the swashbuckling cavalier who "licentiously roams the street in ryot . . . with wavering plumes, hanged to a longside blade and pounced in silks . . . haunting plays, feats, baths and banqueting" (p. 41). Courtiers should pattern themselves after the Marian exiles or better still, the "crest, the fame and type of nobility, without whom nothing is noble in this inferior circle below the moon," Christ himself (p. 39). To Laurence Humphrey a gentleman should above all be godly. He should nurture that attribute foreign to most nobles, humility, which Humphrey places above temperance, modesty, and continence in his hierarchy of the moral virtues. This sort of emphasis was familiar enough in Puritan moral tracts for the middle class. What is noteworthy about Humphrey is his insistence on the same virtues in nobles. His direct influence on some of them to act according to such values reminds us that the appeal of Puritanism often crossed class lines, that some nobles (Fletcher's friend and patron, the Earl of Huntingdon, for example) organized their households on Puritan principles and absented themselves from court as much as possible out of moral revulsion from (in the Earl's phrase) its "glittering misery."[22]

By the time of the closing of the theaters in 1642, Puritanism virtually constituted a counter-culture, hostile to the poetry, painting, and papistry of the court of King Charles and his French

Catholic Queen. But by then (in the words of Petronius that Christopher Hill aptly quotes) "ubique naufragium est"[23]—there was shipwreck everywhere, the rift was irreparable. Referring to an earlier moment around 1630, P. W. Thomas says, "There were it seems two warring cultures. But it is more accurate to talk of a breakdown of the national culture, an erosion through the 1630's of a middle ground that men of moderation and good will had once occupied."[24] In the 1620s, however, at the end of Fletcher's career, we can still find people who held much of the Puritan viewpoint without becoming narrow-minded, vituperative Prynnes. Holding to "country" views consciously or not, they could attend court, go to the theater, even patronize playwrights (as the Earl of Huntingdon did Fletcher), and yet refuse to whore after the strange gods of Renaissance courtly magnificence.

It is with Thomas's "men of moderation" that I would place the Fletcher of his later plays. As his work progressed,[25] Fletcher's attitudes mellowed—perhaps initially under the tutelage of the astoundingly sophisticated young author of *The Knight of the Burning Pestle*—towards the sort of complex moderateness for which Falkland was immortalized by Matthew Arnold.[26] Clearly, the creation late in his career of a figure like Armusia, embodying all the moral virtues advocated by Laurence Humphrey and implicit in *The Faithful Shepherdess,* suggests that much of Fletcher's youthful ardor remained. But *The Island Princess* never degenerates into a hectoring sermon. It contains subtle shadings and nuances that distinguish religion from religiosity, heroism from heroics, but still manages to convey a quiet, amused tolerance for moral frauds like Ruy Dias and Quisara. Among Fletcher's later works, *The Island Princess* is not an isolated phenomenon. We can discern the same poised, disabused sensibility in a number of plays that deserve to be better known, notably *The Mad Lover* (1616), *The Humorous Lieutenant* (1619), and *The Wild Goose Chase* (1621). Without the presence of an explicit spokesman like Armusia, they convey harsh, "country" criticism of a corrupt civilization along with an urbane acceptance of human imperfection. Fletcher's life and the Jacobean era ended in the same year. Soon "ubique naufragium est," and the "generall ruine" desired by the Moor Priest—perhaps Fletcher's prophetic anticipation of the fanatical Archbishop Laud—ensued, in Chillingworth's words, "Publicans and Sinners on the one side, Scribes and Pharisees on the other": a world with no middle ground.

NOTES

[1]There is no reason to doubt that this is his earliest play or that it is his unaided work. There are many reasons for rejecting E. K. Chambers's view, *The Elizabethan Stage,* 4 vols. (Oxford: Clarendon Press, 1923), 3:222, that another solo Fletcher play, *The Woman's Prize,* came earlier.

[2]John even lived in the same house with his cousins and their father, the poet and diplomat Giles, Sr., after the death of his father in 1596. See my "Beaumont, Fletcher, and 'Beaumont & Fletcher': Some Distinctions," *ELR* 1 (1971):144-64, esp. 151.

[3]See my "Beaumont, Fletcher, and 'Beaumont & Fletcher'" and "The Role of the Court in the Development of Jacobean Drama," *Criticism* 24 (1982):138-58, esp. 153-55.

[4]It is interesting to find the plays of Beaumont and Fletcher in the doctrinaire-Puritan, 2000-volume library of Milton's close friend Nathan Paget. According to Christopher Hill (*Milton and the English Revolution* [New York: Penguin Books, 1979], pp. 492-95), Paget's literary taste was Spenserian and Puritan. He owned no plays by Shakespeare or Jonson.

[5]All textual citations for *The Faithful Shepherdess* are from *The Dramatic Works in the Beaumont and Fletcher Canon,* ed. Fredson Bowers, 6 vols. (Cambridge: Cambridge Univ. Press, 1966-), 3 (1976). Except as noted all other Beaumont and Fletcher citations are also from the Bowers edition.

[6]Through his brother Nathaniel, until 1606 chaplain to Sir Henry Wotton in Venice, Fletcher would have had access to the very latest literary developments in Italy.

[7]"To the worthy Author *M. John Fletcher,*" prefatory to *The Faithful Shepherdess,* lines 10, 11.

[8]"To his loving friend M. *Jo. Fletcher,*" line 28.

[9]Annabel Patterson's notion in *Censorship and Interpretation: The Conditions of Writing and Reading in Early Modern England* (Madison: Univ. of Wisconsin Press, 1984), p. 74, that *FS* might be a parody of the idea of chastity comes from reading Fletcher backward from the disabling vantage point of the much more sexually ambiguous collaborative plays. Incidentally, it is not generally realized that if we are to believe the conventional attributions for the collaborative plays, Beaumont tended to be the author of the more lubricious scenes, such as the astoundingly explicit speech in *The Captain* (IV.iv.185-97) in which a daughter insists that her father commit incest with her.

[10]All textual citations for *The Island Princess* are from vol. 5 (1982) of the Bowers edition.

[11]Fletcher's source, Bartolomé Leonardo de Argensola's *Conquista de las Islas Malucas* (1609), suggests similar suspicions about Quisara's character.

[12]Fletcher may even be suggesting that Quisara prefers him dead. If he is restored alive, she says to Ruy Dias, "then we are both servants" (II.vi.27-28).

[13]In arguing for a "Puritan" coloring to *The Changeling,* Margot Heinemann, *Puritanism and Theatre, Thomas Middleton and Opposition Drama under the Early Stuarts* (Cambridge: Cambridge Univ. Press, 1980), says about the upperclass Beatrice-Joanna's commissioning the underling De Flores to commit a murder, "The new thing here is the enhanced awareness that people of inferior status are still people, with consciences and souls to be lost, and their superiors in crime are nothing more" (p. 179).

[14]As Quisara and Armusia describe it (IV.v.36-71), the religion sounds primitive and polytheistic.

[15]William W. Appleton, *Beaumont and Fletcher, a Critical Study* (London: Allen and Unwin, 1956), pp. 66-67.

[16]Eugene M. Waith, *The Pattern of Tragicomedy in Beaumont and Fletcher* (New Haven: Yale Univ. Press, 1952), pp. 159-60, 162.

[17]In the scene ascribed to Fletcher in which Miranda attempts to seduce his Turkish servant girl Lucinda, the Christian hero eventually claims that he has merely been testing her virtue. But an aside ("Forgive me, Heaven! she says true" [in reminding him how he ought to be acting], *The Works of Beaumont and Fletcher,* ed. Alexander Dyce, 11 vols. [London, 1844], 5:172; III.i) and other similar touches show that his intentions were initially less than fully honorable. Armusia's "blushing-chaste" behavior when he invades Quisara's boudoir (III.iii) makes an obvious contrast. Even Miranda's membership in a religious order cannot be taken as a sign of deep religious commitment since he joins only after it is determined that he may not marry the woman he loves (II.v; p. 150).

[18]She is, in fact, nearer to being an idealized characterization than Demetrius. Waith's description of Celia as a "satirical trickster" (p. 154) does not seem to me justifiable. Isolated in a dangerous court, refusing jewels and even the rank of queen, with nothing in her head but love for Demetrius, she finds it insulting and degrading to have to defend herself to her lover. Celia tries to respond to Demetrius's jealous accusations playfully rather than with righteous indignation. He fails to comprehend her tone and cannot even hear her when she confesses that she has been jesting with him. Like many of Fletcher's heroes, Demetrius is made of grosser stuff than his mistress. See Clifford Leech, *The John Fletcher Plays* (Cambridge, Mass.: Harvard Univ. Press, 1962), pp. 59-75, for an appreciation of this fine play and a similar view of Celia.

[19]Quoted by G. M. Trevelyan, *England Under the Stuarts,* 10th edn. (New York: Putnam, 1922), p. 129. Buckingham's gallantry reached absurd proportions in his self-destructively mild treatment of the French garrison at the Isle of Rhe; it turned a victory into a tragic fiasco. See *The Expedition to the Isle of Rhe by Edward Lord Herbert of Cherbury,* ed. Lord Powis (London: 1860). It was, in fact, very like Demetrius's absurd "courtesy match" in III.vi of Fletcher's *The Humorous Lieutenant,* in which he tries to outdo his enemies in chivalric posturing.

[20]For an elaborate formulation of this traditional opposition, see Lawrence Stone, *The Causes of the English Revolution, 1529-1642* (New York: Harper and Row, 1972), especially pp. 105-108.

[21]Hugh Kearney, *Scholars and Gentlemen: Universities and Society in Pre-Industrial Britain, 1500-1700* (Ithaca: Cornell Univ. Press, 1962.)

[22]HMC (Hastings), IV, 333.

[23]*Milton and the English Revolution,* p. 11.

[24]"Two Cultures? Court and Country under Charles I" in *The Origins of the English Civil War,* ed. Conrad Russell (London: Macmillan, 1973), pp. 168-93.

[25]I refer primarily to the (approximately) fifteen plays Fletcher wrote alone (almost all after the collaboration with Beaumont ceased), not the (again, approximately) thirteen romantic melodramas he wrote in collaboration with Massinger.

[26]See his "Falkland" in *Mixed Essays, Irish Essays and Others* (New York: Macmillan, 1908), pp. 154-77.

SEL 27 (1987)
ISSN 0039-3657

Women Beware Women and the Economy of Rape

ANTHONY B. DAWSON

In February 1986 the Royal Court Theatre in London presented a new version of Middleton's *Women Beware Women,* reshaped and substantially rewritten by the English dramatist Howard Barker. His version ends with a rape, carried out presumably in the interests of some kind of enlightenment, a gesture which he seems to think valuable and necessary. In a violent world, only a violent act can split sex off from what drags it down and under—its linkage with money and power. Thus Barker, a male playwright, claims to bring liberation to a woman through sexual violence. As male author of this paper, I'm afraid I lack Barker's cocksureness. On the contrary, as a critic influenced by and sympathetic to feminism, but unsure whether it's really possible for a man to write feminist criticism (at least at the present juncture),[1] I tread warily in the minefield of gender, though I am aware that Middleton highlights it in both title and text. Barker, it seems, wants to split power off from gender, to let passion free, but in Middleton things are not that easy. How can the sexual dancers be liberated from the dance? Not, surely, just by following the same old steps with a different intention.

Women Beware Women examines the pressures of sexual power in a quite startling way. At its center stands a rape, presented not as a brutal motive for revenge, as in *Titus Andronicus,* nor simply as a way of impelling one element of the plot, as in *The Revenger's Tragedy,* but as an emblem of hierarchy and an image of the domination that characterizes most of the play's relationships. The Duke, accustomed to power, uses his authority to crush Bianca's

Anthony Dawson, Associate Professor of English at the University of British Columbia in Vancouver, is the author of *Indirections: Shakespeare and the Art of Illusion* (1978) and *Watching Shakespeare: A Playgoers' Guide* (forthcoming from Macmillan). He is currently working on a series of essays that focus on issues of power, gender, madness, and theatricality in Elizabethan and Jacobean drama.

resistance ("I am not here in vain. . . . I can command, / Think upon that" [II.ii.334, 362-63]). The confrontation is a variation of the old case of the master, the *seigneur,* exacting his "right": and it includes the woman's fear and inevitable submission. Let's first rid ourselves of the idea that the Duke's action constitutes a seduction (which is what virtually every critic calls it) rather than a rape. Middleton is very explicit about this. He locates the issue where it belongs—in the area of power relations—and deliberately leaves ambiguous the legal bugaboo of consent. (In fact the difference between seduction and rape, hinging on the idea of consent, is not nearly as stable as the two terms, themselves part of a male discourse, would have us believe.) Bianca is clearly frightened, and her fear results precisely from her awareness of her own social, sexual, and even physical inferiority:

> *Duke.* Do not tremble
> At fears of thine own making.
> *Bianca.* Nor, great lord,
> Make me not bold with death and deeds of ruin
> Because they fear not you; me they must fright.
> Then am I best, in health.
>
> (II.ii.349-53)[2]

Bianca's fearfulness is a mark of her social position: not only a woman, not only an inferior, but also a stranger to Florence whose wary uncertainty is one of her most consistent features.[3] Hence her need for protection, and hence also her submission to, and ultimate embracing of, the Duke. But this, at least at first, is not the same as consent. She is caught in a fierce economy of sexual exchange—she is indeed the currency of that exchange, exactly as she had been for her husband at the beginning of the play:

> View but her face [says Leantio], you may see all her dowry,
> Save that which lies locked up in hidden virtues,
> Like jewels kept in cabinets.
>
> (I.i.54-56)

The duke is more aristocratic, but equally straightforward; when Bianca protests, "Why should you seek, sir, / To take away that you can never give?" he replies,

> But I give better in exchange: wealth, honour.
> She that is fortunate in a duke's favour
> Lights on a tree that bears all women's wishes.
>
> (II.ii.369-71)

He goes on explicitly to downgrade what her husband can offer in exchange for her body—"necessities, means merely doubtful"; he offers himself as shelter from the storms of want, and concludes: "We'll walk together, / And show a thankful joy for both our fortunes" (lines 376-87).

Significantly, Bianca says nothing in response to this and the two of them exit to complete the transaction. Her silence is parallel to that of Isabella at the end of *Measure for Measure* who, like Bianca, is apparently nonplussed by an inescapable economy: for the second time in as many days, authority, in the person now of Duke Vincentio himself, not Angelo his substitute, is asking Isabella to barter her body for her brother's life.[4] Of course, Claudio has already been saved, and this is the moment of comic closure, but the difficulties of Shakespeare's ending are notorious. The fact that we are dealing in *Women Beware Women* with a different Duke and (perhaps) a rather different kind of woman (though I wouldn't want to exaggerate their differences: both are young, fearful, ardent, somewhat alienated, and uncertain how to handle their sexuality in relation to the actual world) should not blind us to the structural similarity between the two situations. In both cases the impasse that the woman finds herself in is registered by her silence, forcing an interpretation on reader or actor, so that *her* consent becomes a matter of how *we* read, and hence of our own cultural context. The text as it were withholds its consent, teasing us by its very reticence. Furthermore, recent feminist criticism has made us alert to the meaning of silence as it bespeaks powerlessness and passivity, the woman as the object of the male gaze and hence eroticized and cut off from subjectivity, desire, and action. In this play, and indeed in a good deal of Renaissance literature, this silence is tied up with Petrarchan images, where, as Nancy Vickers argues, the original male transgression of gazing and the subsequent punishment of dismemberment, figured in the Actaeon myth, are reversed and the lady is ultimately silenced while the poet sings in praise of her scattered beauties.[5] What matters here is the woman's body, how it is viewed, imaged, handled, and exchanged.

That *Women Beware Women* generates this kind of thinking emerges from a consideration of how it represents marriage. In all the play's marriages it is made crudely explicit that the woman's body is a commodity, a "purchase" or "treasure" (I.i.12, 14) to be bought (or stolen) and hoarded. (Even in the reversed situation later in the play, when Livia claims a passive Leantio, there is a close link between her sexual availability and her treasure—"You never saw the beauty of my house yet, / Nor how abundantly fortune has blessed me / In worldly treasure" [III.iii.358-60]). In Leantio's case the dominant metaphor is economic, in keeping with his job as a factor and his role in the play as chief exponent of petit bourgeois values. Sex, for him, is an economic temptation—one kind of "business" (I.i.153) undoes the other[6]—"It spoils all thrift, and indeed lies abed / To invent all the new ways for great expenses" (I.iii.11-12). For him, the "expense of spirit" is literal; he must save his wealth (sexual and monetary) and spend it "careful[ly]" (line 42). In keeping with Leantio's commercialized, debased Petrarchanism, I don't think it coincidental that Bianca first appears at a distance, that she says nothing, and that we, like the Mother, are called upon to gaze at her:

> And here's my masterpiece: do you now behold her!
> Look on her well, she's mine. Look on her better.
> Now say, if 't be not the best piece of theft
> That ever was committed.
>
> (I.i.41-44)

She is indeed his master-piece, a token that reveals his mastery, his theft.

For the Ward, the bridegroom of the sub-plot, the dominant metaphor is athletic, in particular the crude, brutally physical "sports" of tipcat and trap that he plays with Sordido. This leads to all sorts of obvious phallic puns on cat-stick, trap-stick, and shuttlecock, all dedicated to an analogous form of mastery, as well as the more pervasive and insidious pun on "game" which extends to the main plot as well. Conversely, the predominant economic metaphor of the Leantio plot is carried over into the sub-plot through the haggling and finagling over the marriage of the Ward and Isabella. Probably no scene in Jacobean drama represents so graphically the commodification of women as that in which the Ward and Sordido peer down Isabella's throat and peep under her skirts in their efforts to scan "all her parts over" (III.iv.43) before buying. As in the main plot, economics and erotics come together here in the act of speculation. Isabella is not only a valuable commodity to be ventured for, she is also a visual, erotic object to be looked at. And the numerous sexual puns throughout the scene suggest what Laura Mulvey, following Freud, calls scopophilia—an eroticism of looking. The thrust of the scene is clearly voyeuristic, and fetishistic, insofar as the woman's parts are enumerated and investigated severally. It thus parodies the Petrarchan mode. Linking psychoanalysis with feminism in a perceptive reading of film imagery, Mulvey argues that voyeurism connects not only with fear of castration and, from that, sadism, but also with the viewer's own involvement. As she bluntly puts it, "sadism demands a story"; hence, for her, the genesis of narrative.[7] Without perhaps going quite that far, we might note two peculiarities of the scene which such a theory would help explain: the comic but nonetheless real anxiety that the Ward and Sordido show in the face of the woman, and Isabella's punning allusion to ball-playing, castration, and sexual sport, "I have catched two in my lap at one game" (III.iv.91). Most commentators refuse to take the Ward seriously, seeing him as vulgar comic relief, but I think we ought to ask what exactly he is doing in the text. As I see it, he is a brutalized embodiment of the male fantasies in operation in the rest of the play—he does the same thing as Leantio and the Duke, only in a cruder way. Beyond that, as audience to the Ward's voyeurism, *we* are brought uncomfortably into the story, implicated in its processes, made to watch the watchers. This is a familiar tactic in Jacobean drama, but Middleton uses it in an unfamiliar way. He is less interested in dramatic self-reflexivity than in enacting power relations themselves.

However, in certain ways, he subverts himself and the complex moral point he is making. At the beginning of the scene under discussion, Isabella cites her own "advantage," which arises ironically through her incestuous involvement with Hippolito—"But that I have th' advantage of the fool . . . What an infernal torment 'twere to be / Thus bought and sold, and turned and pried into" (III.iv.33-36). Hence the irony cuts both ways: even as it establishes her limited options within the overall economy, it reminds us of her morally compromised position—the fact that she has already been sold to and pried into by Hippolito. The further irony of her being "really" a male actor was probably beyond even Middleton, although it could serve as an added element both erotic in itself and yet, in terms of the economy I have been discussing, distanced and alienating.[8] At any event, our sympathy with Isabella is far from simple. We perceive her status as an object and commodity; we are induced into looking, *gazing*, through the Ward's eyes; we are reminded of her/his theatrical presence; and we are not allowed to forget her incest. Significantly, she ends the scene silent, like Bianca and that other Isabella, her consent tacit and skeptical.

In his book, *Drama and Society in the Age of Jonson*, L. C. Knights scolds Middleton, finding him amoral, pragmatic, and cynical, attitudes to which the *Scrutiny* group as a whole were unsympathetic.[9] Had Knights looked a little more closely, however, he might have found a more precise perception of the social changes he was tracing than is typical of the other playwrights he discusses.[10] Characters like Allwit in *A Chaste Maid in Cheapside,* for example, survive because they know how to manipulate commodities (including the lust of aristocrats and the bodies of their own wives) for their peculiar ends, and they know when to spend and when to save. The process by which spiritual values can be and are transformed into material goods is one that Middleton was deeply interested in. Knights's problem was that he wanted his playwrights to be sharply critical of rising capitalist trends whereas Middleton was more concerned with tracing their effect on public and private experience. Leantio, in *Women Beware Women,* is a rewriting of Allwit into a darker context; when he loses Bianca to the Duke, he grudgingly accepts the latter's offer of a captainship, "a fine bit / To stay a cuckold's stomach" (III.iii.46-47). He never lets go of the mean-minded commercial attitude toward women and possession he had manifested earlier. Here is no tragic anagnorisis, simply an unsentimental picture of the bourgeois spirit, hurt but unchanged:

> Here stands the poor thief now that stole the treasure,
> And he's not thought on. Ours is near kin now
> To a twin-misery born into the world:
> First the hard-conscienced worldling, he hoards wealth up,
> Then comes the next, and he feasts all upon 't—
> One's damned for getting, th' other for spending on 't.
> (III.iii.88-93)

It is quite in keeping with this way of thinking that a little later in the same scene, Leantio, after briefly mourning Bianca's loss, sells himself to the importunate Livia, and exits with the assurance, "Troth then, I'll love enough, and take enough." The underlying values and directions of nascent capitalism are, I think, more precisely delineated in such portraits than in the extravagant caricatures of Puritan acquisitiveness in Jonson.[11] Nor is Middleton awed by the presence of old money and aristocratic generosity, which Knights sees in several Jacobean writers as an antidote to, or a bygone value threatened by, capitalism. In the clash between the Duke and Leantio over Bianca, Middleton coolly represents the ethos of aristocratic display crushing the opposing ethos of bourgeois thrift and secrecy—"feasting" vs. "hoarding" in Leantio's terms.

At the end of Act I, the Duke first sees, and gazes at, Bianca. The moment is handled with typical Middleton irony—a procession, a look, and a conversation on the balcony between Bianca and her mother-in-law:

> *Bianca.* Methought he saw us.
> *Mother.* That's ev'ry one's conceit that sees a duke;
> If he look steadfastly, he looks straight at them;
> When he perhaps, good careful gentleman,
> Never minds any, but the look he casts
> Is at his own intentions, and his object
> Only the public good.
> *Bianca.* Most likely so.
> (I.iii.105-11)

Here we have an intersection of two complementary codes, one erotic and textual, the other social. By the first, Bianca is the passive object of the male gaze, and is hence brought into the triangular narrative, made part of the story which will involve her rape.[12] By the second, she enters the aristocratic arena simply by being on public view. Once Bianca is open, at the window, on display, she becomes subject to the milieu which values *showing*; hence, later, the Duke is discovered to her as a dazzling, costly portrait, and hence too, when Leantio finds that she is *known* (that *Measure for Measure* pun), he decides to lock his "life's best treasure up" in the dark secret parlor where his father, "kept in for manslaughter" (III.ii.165-66), used to hide. He thus tries to keep her in the bourgeois world.

Despite their differences in position and style, however, there is a clear congruence in the underlying attitudes of Leantio and the Duke, which is registered in the language they use. Both, as I said, see the sexual exchange in economic terms: the woman is to trade her body for wealth, honor, protection, or whatever. There's nothing specifically remarkable in this; it's the standard fare of Jacobean drama, and reflects the dominant social practice, but Middleton seems intent on showing how similar these two characters really are. "But that I glory in: 'tis theft, but noble / As ever greatness yet shot up withal" (I.i.37-38), says Leantio of his original "theft" of Bianca; the Duke counsels her likewise to "take hold of glory" (II.ii.374). Both seek to shelter their nervous treasure from storms:

> But let storms spend their furies; now we have got
> A shelter o'er our quiet innocent loves,
> We are contented.
>
> (Leantio at I.i.51-53)

> Let storms come when they list, they find thee sheltered.
>
> (Duke at II.ii.383)

Leantio speaks of Bianca as a masterpiece; the Duke first appears to her as exactly that, the monument of Livia's art collection, and then ironically reverses the silence and passivity suggested by that pose, and turns Bianca into his masterpiece, a figure that "makes art proud to look upon her work" (II.ii.343). More effectively than Leantio, he of course enacts the mastery, both economic and phallic, that his metaphor implies. Even the language of restraint and imprisonment, so typical of Leantio's hoarding instinct, is part of the Duke's sexual vocabulary:

> Strive not to seek
> Thy liberty, and keep me still in prison.
> I' faith you shall not, till I'm released now;
> We'll be both freed together, or stay still by 't;
> So is captivity pleasant.
>
> (II.ii.329-33)

Thus do Leantio's "theft" and the Duke's rape turn out to be similar strategies carried on in the name of an identical power, even though the former is "sealed from heaven by marriage" and sanctioned by Bianca's consent. From this we can perhaps speculate that the play redefines aristocratic rape as a bourgeois act—one motivated by a spirit of possession and characterized by the deployment of a power that despite its flamboyance has a clear counterpart in middle-class marriage; indeed, the so-called "conjugal family" was marked by a distinct "reinforcement of patriarchy" during the Jacobean period.[13]

But what of the woman in this economy? According to Ian Maclean, who has done a thorough study of the Renaissance notion of woman, "Marriage is an immovable obstacle to any improvement in the theoretical or real status of woman in law, in theology, in moral and political philosophy."[14] Isabella in *Women Beware Women* puts the matter even more bleakly:

When women have their choices, commonly
They do but buy their thraldoms, and bring great portions
To men to keep 'em in subjection—
As if a fearful prisoner should bribe
The keeper to be good to him, yet lies in still,
And glad of a good usage, a good look sometimes.
By 'r Lady, no misery surmounts a woman's:
Men buy their slaves, but women buy their masters.
(I.ii.169-76)

This extraordinary statement describes the experience of powerlessness using the dominant terms of exchange and the subsidiary image of imprisonment so crucial to the depiction of sexual relations and sexual desire both in this play and in *Measure for Measure,* a text that in many ways stands behind *Women Beware Women* as a precursor.[15] But Isabella's very next lines deflate the perception she has just elaborated: "Yet honesty and love makes all this happy, / And, next to angels', the most blest estate." Either these lines are ironic, which seems unlikely, or they register an uncontrolled ambivalence, not only on Isabella's part, but on that of the play as a whole—an ambivalence parallel, I think, to that suggested by Shakespeare's rather shaky happy ending in *Measure for Measure.*

At other points in *Women Beware Women,* a similar doubleness is signalled by the combination of traditional anti-feminist clichés with unsentimental observation of either male fantasies about women or their actual social situation. The title itself shares the ambivalence; is it ironic? Does the play really ask us to take away only a simple anti-feminist message? Nowhere is the swing more noticeable than in the treatment of Bianca, in, for example, the before and after of the rape scene, and again in her final speeches. To take the second example first, the last scene blends the fervent and youthful romanticism of a Juliet with Bianca's own special, alien wariness ("What make I here? These are all strangers to me," V.ii.206), while at the same time, the two feelings are haunted by an alarmingly emblematic leprosy and accompanying moralistic fever:

Leantio, now I feel the breach of marriage
At my heart-breaking. Oh the deadly snares
That women set for women, without pity
Either to soul or honour! Learn by me
To know your foes; in this belief I die:
Like our own sex, we have no enemy, no enemy!
(V.ii.210-15)

Bianca destroys her beauty, convinced somehow that it is responsible, and dies guilty but repentant. So goes the economy: she is seen, desired, stolen (Leantio) or raped (the Duke), promoted (wife, Duchess), and killed off. In the process, her moral status declines, until it is restored by her death—she is "saved" by the very sadism that has made the story.

The clearest dramatization of what the process does to her is the aftermath of the rape scene, where the shift from modest innocence to brash experience is indecently rapid—condensed into a twenty-line speech. Anticipating the finale of the play, she first blames her beauty ("Why should I / Preserve that fair that caused the leprosy?" [II.ii.424-25]), then turns her anger, which in the early part of the speech is aimed at the Duke, on Guardiano who betrayed her, "a stranger." By the end of the speech, she is "acquainted" with sin, "no couple greater," and has embraced the treachery though she "hates the traitor." In internalizing the rape as guilt, deflecting her anger away from the Duke and coming to love him, she displays the classic pattern of the victim succumbing to and embracing the inevitability of redefined power relations.

It is remarkable, if not really surprising, how often in discussions of rape, even in a modern, legal context, the belief that women provoke rape arises. Susan Griffin argues that this attitude makes the woman's body, her desire, and hence her power, suspect:

> Does not the guilt of the one who is raped, that shame of the "victim" so often called irrational . . . does it not in this ancient woman-hating frame become reasonable? . . . The very existence of our bodies [is seen as] provocation to violence . . . How does one move about the world in this body which has the power to invoke malevolence against oneself? . . . [And] what of our own desire? What of our experience of our bodies as we are inside ourselves, not as provocation but as being? . . . Our own desire, which is inseparable from our power in the world . . . becomes the harbinger of violence, the feelings in our bodies dangerous to our bodies, we enemies of ourselves.[16]

Griffin is reacting here not only to the social scientists and legal experts, but at least implicitly to those psychoanalysts, among them prominent women like Helene Deutsch, who believe that female masochism is "natural."[17] What Griffin defines is the problem of a space for women's power, although in relying on a model of domination and victimization for her analysis, she perhaps oversimplifies the issue. Recently, some feminist critics have sought to redefine traditional power relations in terms of the woman's frequently subversive place both in the text and in the world. Power is not just a matter of domination, but in Foucault's terms, a network of force relations with, by definition, points of resistance; it is "the name that one attributes to a complex strategical situation in a particular society."[18]

The figure of Livia in the play illustrates some of these issues provocatively, with the same ambivalent swing between simplistic moral judgment and acute social observation noticeable in the cases of Bianca and Isabella. Bianca's final comment, "O the deadly snares / That women set for women," which the audience has just seen acted out in a serio-comic way in the masque,[19] expresses the prevalent view of Livia's behavior: by devious means she destroys the innocence of the young women in her orbit. True, she has some scruples about suggesting Isabella into incest, but sincere sisterly love for Hippolito (itself a little suspect) impels her. With Bianca she has no scruples at all, constructing around the central rape scene the elaborate charade of the chess match, which acts out in comic ritual the deadlier game being played on the upper stage and behind the scenes. The Bianca-Duke sequence is both surrounded by the chess game and counterpointed with it (Livia and the Mother continue their game on the lower stage as the crucial scene unfolds on the upper). This has the effect of partially reducing the seriousness of the rape scene, since we view it as something signified by and signifying a chess match. But this effect is modified by the intensity of domination and victimization dramatized in the confrontation between the Duke and Bianca. Hence a dual reading of the scene as a whole is established: from one perspective we are absorbed, or repelled, by the spectacle of male power; from the other we are intrigued by the cleverness of Livia's representation of that spectacle.

As Shakespeare had shown in *The Tempest,* and Middleton was to illustrate much more fully a few years after *Women Beware Women,* chess is a powerful theatrical symbol because it condenses and transforms conflict into game through semiotic operations akin to those of the theater.[20] Livia, a theatrical manager par excellence, is fully aware of the potential of chess to point beyond itself, that is, to signify. She improvises her game with the Mother and teasingly transforms it into an ironic sign, marked by a series of puns on "business," "game," "man," "Duke," "ducat." There are two sides to the game, power (the Duke) and craft (Livia), and they reinforce each other. As the Duke exerts political force above, he also exercises craft; as Livia marshalls her ludic skill below, she also displays power. Taken together, the various elements of the scene—the split focus, the punning, and especially Livia's ironic self-awareness—highlight the fact that one stage event stands for another. According to Keir Elam, semiosis in the theater is usually projected outward towards the depiction of a represented world;[21] here, however, the "meaning" of the chess game derives from our recognition of it as a sign of another sign.

It is thus that Livia asserts her power. In controlling the lives of Bianca and Isabella, and by transforming the chess game into a reflexive event, she defines a space for herself. Hers is a power of signification and the fabrication of meanings. Her semiosis is, or seeks to be, subversive—she, as it were, takes back language and representation from dominant figures. Her house boasts a famous picture gallery in which the Duke himself appears as a grand monument. However, when she tries to assert her desire directly, as she does later with Leantio, she loses. In moving from her game of deliberate representation into the world of sexual commerce, she both loses sympathy and undoes herself. The Duke, as it turns out, is not a chess piece after all. Livia's careful construction of meanings is unmetaphored, the Duke asserts his actual power, and Livia is crushed. So too her climactic attempt to translate symbolic forms into reality (that is, to transform the masque from a theatrical, and hence representational, event into a "real" event) backfires.

The chess game ends in mate, as the love scene does. In both cases the loser is trapped, unable to move. The pun is deftly appropriate. Sexual mating leads to checkmate, and even the strategies that the players adopt to avoid the traps that their matings set don't work. This result applies to all the couples in the play and is the source of all the ironic reversals at the end. Livia's chess strategy has collapsed, and eventually all the kings and queens, bishops and even pawns are toppled. Note, however, that the major reversals come as a result of botched attempts on the part of women to assert their desire and power in the actual world—to move out of the realm of fantasy or the symbolic and into the world of life and death.

That curious ending has elicited a good deal of comment, ranging from those who see it as sensational incompetence on Middleton's part, a hapless descent into allegory, to those who see it as dramatizing incompetence in a mocking indictment of tragedy itself, and thus as a deflation of Middleton's own project.[22] In the latter reading the moral intention is deliberately undermined, while in the former, the moral intention is clear but unsuccessfully or too obtrusively enacted. In between, we have the view, best exemplified by Mulryne, that "the scene plays itself out like a speeded-up newsreel, and produces a similar effect, at once farcical and horrible."[23] For him, the moral ironies are patent (Livia as the marriage goddess, for example), structually fitting, and paramount, while the grotesque comedy of the masque, far from being a blemish, underlines the uncertainties of life in the represented world.

I would prefer to approach the scene as the result of two coherent and independent modes of thinking and dramatizing which come into overt conflict in the concluding masque. I have been suggesting that at various times in the text a double commitment is observable: one an effort to register as precisely as possible the social position of women in relation to semiotic, economic, and sexual power; the other, in conflict with the first, a frequent tendency to reassert a conventional moral view of sexual power relations, in particular to condemn women as devious, lecherous, and corrupt. Indeed, this latter aspect was the meaning singled out by the first published critic of the play, Nathaniel Richards, who wrote in his commendatory verses printed in the first edition (1657):

> *Women Beware Women*, 'tis a true text
> Never to be forgot: drabs of state, vexed,
> Have plots, poisons, mischiefs that seldom miss,
> To murder virtue with a venom kiss
> . . . .
> he [Middleton] knew the rage,
> Madness of women crossed; and for the stage
> Fitted their humours—hell-bred malice, strife
> Acted in state, presented to the life.[24]

Even Richards softens his condemnation by inserting the participles "vexed" and "crossed" to designate the source of feminine fury, thereby admitting some ambiguity or extenuation. (It's odd, ironic, and no doubt revealing that Richards gives weight to the startling metaphor, "venom kiss," when a quick glance at Jacobean tragedy shows *men* to be literal specialists at this particular art—witness Vindice, or Brachiano and his conjuror as explicit examples, Othello or Ford's Giovanni as only slightly displaced ones. Bianca, successful where Juliet was not, uses the venom kiss to kill *herself*.)

At any rate, the vexed and crossed woman attacks with energy, and there is plenty of evidence in both the language and action of the last scene to justify Richards's interpretation. It won't do, I think, to explain it all away as ironic, or as generally moral rather than as explicitly anti-feminist. Conversely, the comedy of the final scene seems to deflate the moral posture and to do so almost inadvertently. There is at one and the same time a conventional moral rendering of the meaning of these events, made explicit by Richards, and a clear failure of dramatic commitment to that position. It is precisely the gaps opened up by the conventional reading, its failure to represent actual experience, that make the alternative, subversive reading not only possible but necessary.

The role of the Cardinal, normally taken as either straight or ironic by commentators, illustrates the strain the text is under. In the course of one powerful modern production, there was a ripple of audible relief in the audience when the Cardinal made his great fourth act denunciation.[25] From a purely theatrical point of view, condemnation at that moment of the increasingly grotesque antics of these characters seems dramatically desirable, even necessary. And Middleton provides it. But the impossibility of sustaining the critique, its theatrical impertinence later on, renders the Cardinal almost speechless in Act V, until, of course, he's allowed the conventional moral tag at the end. His capitulation marks him out not so much as an inconsistent character, still less as the voice of the playwright, but rather as an overt image of irresolvable textual contradiction. And the breakdown in the character underlines the dramatic split displayed by the masque, with its combination of moral suasion and theatrical artifice.

Nearly forty years earlier, Kyd had linked revenge and the artifice of the masque in the interests of effective closure, but even he had not escaped, or resisted, the encroachment of ambiguity and self-subversion, the possibility of mute meaninglessness and "endless tragedy" (the concluding words of the play). He too had played with comic misunderstandings on the part of his bewildered onstage audience, as Middleton does in *Women Beware Women*, and had forced upon them a retrospective reinterpretation of their theatrical experience as tragically "real." (In *The Spanish Tragedy* this technique is further complicated by the continuing presence of Andrea and Revenge as another audience.) This strategy tends to break down the boundaries between categories, whether moral or aesthetic; theater in these endings has a way of dissolving into "reality" (and vice versa) and its ontological slipperiness becomes a model for the difficulty, even impossibility, of forging unambiguous moral assertions. The masque ending produces closure with a vengeance, but that closure paradoxically opens a gap between the projected meaning of experience—what it means for both the onstage audience and for the "real" audience—and the experience itself. It thereby "threatens [as Eagleton remarks in relation to post-structuralist and Freudian theory] the ideological security of those who wish the world to be within their control, to carry its singular meaning on its face and to yield it up to them in the unblemished mirror of their language."[26] To seek ideological security in the play is to read it as Richards did.

We witness in the final scene of *Women Beware Women,* I would therefore argue, a rupture in the text wherein a moralized rendering of experience is revealed as no longer tenable. This generates contradictory critical interpretations, but neither the ironic nor the straight reading really acknowledges the textual gap. The close analysis of power relations so evident earlier in the play is at least partially revoked in the final scene, leading us to the view that there was no way for the forms available to Middleton to produce a satisfactory conclusion to that dramatic line. He falls back on the grotesque farce of the masque, not as a cop-out, but as the only way of registering the dilemma posed by the conflict he is dramatizing. The text at this point may be incoherent, but that incoherence is a sign of the divided way the play represents the experience of women (in both the subjective and objective senses of that phrase).

Howard Barker, to end where I began, wants to eliminate the incoherence and what he sees as the moralistic convention of Middleton's ending.[27] He seeks to take a critical stance against sexual domination—state power metaphorically and actually linked to sexual power and money—by bringing into play what he calls "the redemptive power of desire"; but he ends up exploiting male fantasies against and about women as a mode of resolution. Sordido, a minor character in Middleton, becomes central here, as does the Ward, no longer a fool but a clever clown-lover angling for Isabella and playing the fool to hide his despair, a "study in pain."[28] Sordido is a bitter malcontent, part idealist and part madman, very much in the Jacobean, especially Websterian, mode. Barker calls him a "model of modern youth, culturally embittered." Significantly, Barker cuts the voyeuristic scene with Isabella (III.iv) from his re-cast text (of which the first half is all Middleton, cut and spliced, and the second half all Barker); he ends his play, as I noted at the beginning, with a second rape—Sordido punishing Bianca for her acquisitive complicity in her first rape. Her "protesting mouth" against the Duke was, says Sordido, "stopped, not by a fist, but greed and glamour suffocated it."[29] So he, Livia, and the Ward plot to steal "her toy virginity" as a pseudo-political act by which "all the poor of Florence grab their rights." The Ward crows in response to this plan, "While he, immaculate rebel, among her moist wound intrudes, I'll shout out *O exquisite robbery*" (p. 31). Here we have a much more dangerous voyeurism-sadism than the Ward's in Middleton, though it may indeed be one that is prevalent in our own society. But the problem is that it is here given the full weight of the play's authority. The rape occurs in the final scene, just before the wedding, and immediately after it Bianca, who had been vain and frivolous, suddenly becomes insightful and tormented, looking for the meaning of desire and rejecting the easy link between sex and power. We thus get a kind of reversal of the degradation following the first rape. In keeping with the overall economy described earlier, Bianca's status is raised—she is once again saved by sadism, though the outcome is different. She escapes rather than dies. The Duke, wanting her to go on with the charade of the wedding, threatens to kill her when she refuses, but relents and collapses, handing over power at last to the obsessively passionate lovers Livia and Leantio. But now a wedge has been driven between these two and they are specifically enjoined, in the last words of the play, "Don't love! don't love!" (p. 36). Love *should* be more important than power, but the tragedy is that it may not be possible to sustain such a view. So sex is to be separated from power once again, power crushing and destroying passion, while rape is represented as an instrument of liberation from power and greed. The idea would be absurd if it were not so serious. Unlike Middleton, Barker seems unable to see the irony of his own position, and, doubly, the irony reflected back on sexual relationships by social hierarchies. Despite his claim for optimism over Middleton's pessimism, his imagination feels darker and less resilient. He opts for a ferocious consistency, but Middleton's ending seems, by comparison, more honest and more truthful, just because it is more confused.

In Middleton's version, an awareness of what rape means in the social and political economy, its relationship to sexual blackmail, social institutions, and political power, finds a place in the text but no effective way out of it. Barker's way out of the dilemma seems as bad as the original problem. The dramatic fiasco of the masque reveals Middleton wrestling unsuccessfully with closure and suggests the impossibility of bridging the gap between genre and an often acute perception of gender, at least within traditional ideological limits—within the limits, that is, of the "discursive practices" available to him.

NOTES

[1]On this point I agree with Stephen Heath, whose intellectual and ethical balancing act on the whole question of "male feminism" I found honest and valuable. See "Male Feminism," *Dalhousie Review* 64,2 (Summer 1984):270-301. See also Elaine Showalter's witty and fair-minded analysis of the same issue, "Critical Cross-Dressing: Male Feminists and the Woman of the Year," *Raritan* 3,2 (1983-1984):130-49.

[2]The text I have used is the Revels edition, J. R. Mulryne, ed. (1975; rev. edn. Manchester: Manchester Univ. Press, 1983).

[3]In his introduction to the Revels edition, Mulryne stresses Bianca's vulnerability and anxious sense of inferiority (pp. lxviii-lxx). See also R. B. Parker, "Middleton's Experiments with Comedy and Judgement," *Jacobean Theatre*, Stratford-upon-Avon Studies 1 (London: E. Arnold, 1960), p. 194, who points to the recurrent use of the word "stranger" in the play.

[4]Meredith Skura, *The Literary Uses of the Psychoanalytic Process* (New Haven: Yale Univ. Press, 1981), p. 254.

[5]Nancy J. Vickers, "Diana Described: Scattered Woman and Scattered Rhyme," *Writing and Sexual Difference*, ed. Elizabeth Abel (Chicago: Univ. of Chicago Press, 1982), pp. 95-110.

[6]Christopher Ricks analyzes the significance of the puns on "business," "service," and the like in "Word-Play in *Women Beware Women*," *RES*, n.s. 12 (1961):238-50.

[7]Laura Mulvey, "Visual Pleasure and Narrative Cinema," *Screen* 16,3 (Autumn 1975):6-18. As the title suggests, Mulvey seeks to show how the viewer's own pleasure is implicated in the construction of male-dominant images of women. The importance of this influential article can scarcely be overestimated. See also Teresa de Lauretis, *Alice Doesn't: Feminism, Semiotics, Cinema* (Bloomington: Indiana Univ. Press, 1984), esp. ch. 5.

[8]See Lisa Jardine, *Still Harping on Daughters* (Sussex: Harvester, 1983), ch. 1.

[9]L. C. Knights, *Drama & Society in the Age of Jonson* (London: Chatto & Windus, 1937), ch. 9.

[10]T. B. Tomlinson, writing in the *Scrutiny* tradition, does just this in *A Study of Elizabethan and Jacobean Tragedy* (Cambridge: Cambridge Univ. Press, 1964). He suggests that Middleton is interested in "exploring and commenting on the entry of . . . commercial values and modes . . . into the business of living and loving" (p. 172).

[11]Mulryne calls the portrait of Leantio "a perfect stereotype . . . of the bourgeois mind" (p. lxiii).

[12]See Mulvey, p. 14, and de Lauretis, pp. 103ff. It can readily be seen from my view of this moment and what follows from it, that I strongly disagree with the sense of the scene, and indeed the whole play, propounded by A. A. Bromham in a recent issue of this journal: "Political Meaning in *Women Beware Women*," *SEL* 26,2 (Spring 1986):319ff. Bromham ignores the ironies surrounding the word "peace" and downplays the role and position of women in the play. The use of the upper stage in this scene (and subsequently) is the subject of an interesting essay in the same issue of *SEL*, although I cannot agree with all its conclusions either: Leslie Thomson, "'Enter Above': The Staging of *Women Beware Women*," pp. 331-43.

[13]Lawrence Stone, *The Family, Sex and Marriage in England 1500-1800* (Harmondsworth: Penguin, 1982), pp. 94, 109ff.

[14]Ian Maclean, *The Renaissance Notion of Woman* (Cambridge: Cambridge Univ. Press, 1980), p. 85.

[15]Margot Heinemann, *Puritanism and Theatre* (Cambridge: Cambridge Univ. Press, 1980), comments in general: "What is new in [Middleton's] plays is not so much the sexual situations as the ability of the women to reflect on them in general terms, and the natural way in which exploitation by men is shown as contributing to aggressiveness or deceit in women" (p. 194).

[16]Susan Griffin, *Rape: The Power of Consciousness* (San Francisco: Harper & Row, 1979), pp. 54-55.

[17]See Susan Brownmiller, *Against our Will: Men, Women, and Rape* (New York: Simon and Schuster, 1975), pp. 315-25, for an extended critique of Deutsch's influential views.

[18]Michel Foucault, *The History of Sexuality*, vol. 1: *An Introduction*, trans. Robert Hurley (New York: Vintage, 1980), p. 93. On the question of redefining woman's power, see, for example, Nina Auerbach's *Woman and the Demon: The Life of a Victorian Myth* (Cambridge, MA: Harvard Univ. Press, 1982).

[19]Several critics have emphasized the grotesque comedy of the masque: Heinemann, p. 197, Mulryne, p. lvii, and Nicholas Brooke, *Horrid Laughter in Jacobean Tragedy* (London: Open Books, 1979), pp. 105ff.

[20]The precise nature of chess allegory has been the subject of some debate lately. See, for example, Paul Yachnin, "*A Game at Chess* and Chess Allegory," *SEL* 22 (Spring 1982):317-30, and Neil Taylor and Bryan Loughrey, "Middleton's Chess Strategies in *Women Beware Women*," *SEL* 24 (Spring 1984):341-54. Neither of these articles seems to me to stress hard enough the fundamental issue—that chess symbolism necessarily reduces and condenses actual conflict and hence draws attention to the semiosis itself. See my essay on *The Tempest* in Anthony B. Dawson, *Indirections: Shakespeare and the Art of Illusion* (Toronto: Univ. of Toronto Press, 1978).

[21]Keir Elam, *The Semiotics of Theatre and Drama* (London: Methuen, 1980), ch. 2.

[22]See Tomlinson, pp. 183-84, for the former point of view, and Brooke, pp. 108-10, for the latter.

[23]Mulryne, p. lvii.

[24]Revels edition, p. 3.

[25]I am indebted to Joel Kaplan for information on this production, which was presented at the Coach House Theatre, Toronto, in 1967, and directed by Brian Meeson. See also Mulryne, p. lxxviii.

[26]Terry Eagleton, *Literary Theory: an Introduction* (Oxford: Basil Blackwell, 1983), pp. 108-109.

[27]Howard Barker, "The redemptive power of desire," an imaginary dialogue between himself and Middleton, in *The Times*, 6 February 1986, p. 15.

[28]Barker, p. 15, and Michael Ratcliffe, in *The Observer*, 9 February 1986.

[29]Thomas Middleton and Howard Barker, *Women Beware Women* (London: John Calder, 1986), p. 31. Subsequent page references are given in the text.

SEL 27 (1987)
ISSN 0039-3657

Recent Studies in Elizabethan and Jacobean Drama

JEAN E. HOWARD

The crassly pragmatic purpose of an *SEL* review is—ugly phrase—"information management." Publication proceeds at such a pace that no one can possibly absorb even a fraction of what is printed on Renaissance drama in a given year. An omnibus review such as this, published soon after the books themselves are published, supposedly gives overextended scholars some basis for deciding which of these scholarly and critical texts they will actually read. Consequently, I have in part proceeded as if I were simply composing an annotated bibliography, and to some extent that seems not a misrecognition of the nature of the task. On the other hand, description is not enough, and reading all these texts ideally puts one in the position to make larger statements about the state of criticism and scholarship in the field of Renaissance drama and to identify and evaluate those books that emerge from the pack as unusually provocative, ambitious, or significant. I have tried to do as much evaluating and sense-making as I could, though I am very aware of how little of that I have been able to do and of how few of these books have received anything like a comprehensive and careful "review" in this essay. Inevitably, I have devoted the most time to—and have been most critical of—books which interested me the most. I have said nothing about periodicals, books on medieval drama, or books in which only a single chapter was devoted to Renaissance plays.

A final word—all reviewers write from positions and not from a space of Olympian neutrality. As will be clear from what follows, I see literary studies to be in a state of turmoil and controversy inviting a scrutiny of critical practices that perhaps even a decade ago would have been unnecessary. Books which are self-conscious about their

---

Jean E. Howard teaches literature and critical theory at Syracuse University. She is the author of *Shakespeare's Art of Orchestration* (Illinois Univ. Press, 1984) and co-editor, with Marion O'Connor, of *Shakespeare Reproduced: The Text in History and Ideology* (forthcoming, Methuen, 1987).

own modes of proceeding thus seem, at this moment, of particular value, especially as *they argue for,* rather than *assume,* the political and intellectual validity and urgency of what they undertake. I find valuable, as well, books which engage, rather than ignore, the challenges to traditional critical practice posed by contemporary critiques of the concept of literary autonomy, by feminism, and by a range of other discourses loosely lumped under the category of "theory." These are not the only kinds of valuable books, as I also hope the review will make clear, but they often have seemed to me the ones where learning, risk, and commitment have most profitably intermingled. They acknowledge that scholarship and criticism are not self-evident and unchanging activities, but historically specific and contestatory practices through which, in part, a culture determines what *kinds* of knowledge at any given time will be deemed legitimate and important, and surely those determinations matter.

I

I have arranged the review in sections. First I will discuss a handful of books which I consider worth singling out, in part because they speak to some of the concerns of the prior paragraph. By no means are all the "good" books of the year in this section. I am simply pointing here to a few texts that seem to open space for new work and alter the questions we ask of Renaissance drama. The first of these is Malcolm Evans's *Signifying Nothing: Truth's True Contents in Shakespeare's Texts.* Evans's project is nothing less than to provide an introduction to Shakespeare based on "contemporary theories of the subject, the sign and ideology" (p. 8). As the introduction acknowledges, the methodology is sometimes eclectic and the project too big for one book, and yet Evans is remarkably successful in conveying, in terms neither simplistic nor mystifying, some of what is involved in producing a political Shakespeare criticism which takes seriously the work of contemporary Marxists and post-structuralists such as Althusser, Jameson, Lacan, and Derrida.

As a start, Evans does not see texts as having meanings which can simply be discovered or decoded. Rather, reading is a *productive* activity, and the impossibility of permanently arresting the play of signification means that texts are sites for the ceaseless dissemination of meanings (one of Evans's bravura gestures is to demonstrate the possibility of 168 possible readings for a single line of *As You Like It*). But what keeps the book from simply being about the joys of the polysemous, rather than the unified and stable text, is Evans's clear understanding that texts do get read in *particular* ways at *particular* times, and that it matters what interests get advanced by these readings and by the epistemologies, politics, and metaphysics which underlie them. For Evans, just as there can be no "true" reading of a text, so there can be no disinterested reading. All readings, wittingly or not, are what he terms "readings-for" (p. 166), that is, readings which serve particular interests, just as there is no neutral history, only, as Levi-Strauss has argued, "history-for" (p. 83). Moreover, Evans makes a convincing case for the idea that one never comes to a pristine Shakespeare text; they are "always already 'occupied' or 'incrusted' by other critical discourses, which function within the institutions, rituals and material practices of ideology" (p. 9).

This means that the critic approaching Shakespeare is already entering a contested space, and Evans's book is marked for me as distinctively British, as opposed to American, by the urgency with which it argues the case that Shakespeare—particularly in twentieth-century British culture—has often been recruited to the service of repressive institutions and practices which it is the job of critics such as himself to challenge. Consequently, the book begins with a meditation on the significance of Queen Elizabeth II quoting Donne during the Falklands crisis, and intertwined with sections of textual analysis, Evans keeps up a running attack on targets as diverse as the ISA, the Newbolt report, British imperialism, and modern editorial practices which occupy and colonize a text. All the while, readings of *As You Like It, Love's Labors Lost, Macbeth,* and other Shakespearean texts offer critiques of the basic premises of humanist criticism: that textual meaning is stable, that selves are unified and coherent, that art mimes life, or that there is an aesthetic zone "above ideology." In short, the book is highly polemical. Even those critical practices—metadramatic criticism, liberal feminism, apolitical deconstruction—which Evans acknowledges as having paved the way for the fullblown materialist poststructuralism he advocates, are subject to critique. Of course, when one casts so many friends as John the Baptist, who plays Christ is pretty apparent.

The serious question to be asked, however, in regard to Evans's critique of other positions, is how his own contestatory criticism can avoid, in its turn, getting recuperated for conservative purposes or becoming a new version of the true and the self-evident. Is it possible to avoid reinscription within the hegemonic order and systems of mastery one wishes to contest? Evans needs to address this issue explicitly. Further, the book seems at times unduly self-congratulatory because it does not always take sufficiently seriously its own proposition that the Shakespearean text is and has been a site of struggle. While Evans discusses at length the diary of one Edward Harrison who, sent to teach English in British Honduras in 1929, vowed to arm "Caliban, 300 years later, against Prospero" (p. 20), Evans uses the material anecdotally, rather than as an occasion to theorize the production of resistance or to explore Shakespeare's appropriation for oppositional purposes. Without acknowledging Shakespeare's role in a history of resistance, as well as his recruitment to the banner of oppressive orthodoxies, Evans's own oppositional work can seem more unique than it really is.

There are other problems with the book. The fusion of Marxism and poststructuralism is more difficult to achieve than Evans acknowledges. To take just one example, Weimann's and Derrida's views on mimesis and signification are not easily reconciled, and by treating them serially, Evans avoids altogether the task of reconciliation. Nor, I think, is it unproblematic for Evans simply to offer Kristeva—without critique—as the redress to humanist feminism, while he himself produces a book in which the analysis of gender, of whatever stripe, plays so small a part.

Nonetheless, I reiterate my claim that this is an important book. It makes very clear the special way in which Shakespeare figures in the political and intellectual contests of the present moment. And it is committed, witty, and intelligent on its side of the debate. Moreover, it looks in its last chapter to the future and to the work which lies ahead in refashioning the educational apparatus, in particular, to take account of the challenges to the traditional curriculum posed by a materialist poststructuralism of the sort Evans advocates. This is a book which will stir debate; it aspires to do more: radically to alter pedagogical and critical practices.

In the opening chapter of *The Patriarchy of Shakespeare's Comedies* Marilyn Williamson vigorously argues for a feminist criticism of Shakespeare that is also a sophisticated historical criticism. One of her chief points is that patriarchal structures are historically specific and that even within the various subgenres of Shakespearean comedy written at different historical moments one sees patriarchal structures assuming discernibly different forms. Always, however, for Williamson, the comedies serve political functions; they produce and circulate those cultural languages through which the domination of one gender by another is discursively effected or, upon occasion, destabilized.

In three substantial chapters Williamson looks at the festive comedies, the problem comedies, and then the romances as each, by its particular patriarchal structures, participates in the management of discrete cultural problems. Arguing that exhaustive readings impute a false unity to texts and paper over their ideological contradictions, Williamson's critical method is to intertwine an examination of various historical contexts with relatively brief and deliberately noncomprehensive comments on particular dramatic texts. In the chapter on the high comedies, she looks at them as fantasy structures which promise to the struggling, overpopulated courtier class frustrated by Elizabeth's Petrarchan politics that it will eventually win rich and socially superior women whose subordination in marriage will signal the end of female power (though often, Williamson suggests, the plays subversively indicate that woman's power does not end with marriage).

If in this chapter on the high comedies the link between text and historical context seems underargued, Williamson's method receives convincing embodiment in the chapter on *All's Well* and *Measure for Measure.* She looks at the former as part of the subgenre of plays about enforced marriage, the latter as part of the subgenre of plays about disguised rulers, and argues that each genre, and each play, is responding to and participating in specific social problems emerging *as* problems in James's reign. These include the disposition of wardships, heightened dispute about enforced marriage, fears about an increase, or perceived increase, of bastardy among "the poor," and worries about the regulation of personal life by the strongly patriarchal monarch. Striking among her conclusions are her argument that the control of male sexual desire by a male monarch in these plays seems conditional on the prolonged and overt suffering of the female heroine, and her view that these plays repeatedly translate "social problems into sexual issues" (p. 88) so that the morality of sexual desire seems to be at issue rather than the social practices and conditions leading to late marriages, to the birth of bastards, to the increase in the numbers of poor, etc. In her final chapter Williamson explores the way the romances, with the exception of *The Tempest,* literalize James's patriarchal rhetoric by having the male monarch appropriate female generative power and by using nature to make specific social relations—between king and subjects, men and women—seem inevitable and unchangeable.

While this book is uneven in the sense that its theoretical claims are sometimes more radical than its critical practice and in the sense that the link between text and context is more convincingly forged in some chapters than in others, nonetheless it is an important contribution to an emerging feminist-historicist criticism. It convinces me that the task is no longer to argue for the necessity of such a criticism, but through collective work to make its practice as innovative and as powerful as possible.

Susan Wells's *The Dialectics of Representation* is another of the difficult and important books of the year, a book which tries to offer a new language for talking about the relationship of literary works to social life. Actually, Wells's conceptual apparatus is triadic, for she is interested in the way the writer transforms the social world in representing it, and the way the historically-situated reader, in turn, transforms the writer's representation in the act of reading. As she says: "Both the relation between the text and the world and the relation between the reader and the text are specific mediations. That is, something is being done here, material is being *worked on,* things change. The text labors over the world and transforms it by representing it; the reader transforms the text by interpreting it" (p. 17). In her first chapter she examines the work of two critics, De Man and Jameson, whom she feels slight one or the other of these recognitions, De Man ignoring the text's relationship to its social and historical world, Jameson, finally, slighting the transformative power of the reading act.

In her engagement with specific texts, Wells tries to attend to both mediating processes using the work of the Frankfurt School, in particular, to guide her efforts. Central to her theory is the idea that a text is not a *reflection* of the world, but a *representation* of it in which two registers, the typical and the indeterminate, are held in dialectical interplay. The typical means, in general, those dimensions of the text which seem transparent, which seem to need no interpretation, which include the socially constituted codes of intelligibility by which our intersubjective relation to social reality is established. The indeterminate register, by contrast, signifies those aspects of a text which point to the text's artifice and textuality, which look—not out to the world—but inward to the opacity and playfulness of language as non-referential system. Much of the book is devoted to examining the relative predominance of these two registers in Renaissance drama, but also in other texts such as Henry James's fiction and the *bildungsroman.*

Wells's book might well be titled "against radical skepticism" since while it is very sophisticated about historical difference and about the fact that there is no unmediated access to reality, she refuses to allow there to be any truly radical discontinuity between work and world, past and present. For her, intersubjective communication is possible, if complex. Her approach skirts some difficult issues, however, such as the way the divisive realities of race, gender, and class difference both problematize any theory of reading based on the idea of intersubjective norms and also raise questions about the role of exclusion and marginalization in the establishment of dominant reading practices. Readers transform texts in the reading act, but at a given historical moment not all such transformations are considered equally legitimate. Wells says too little about such matters, and in her account of reading and representation words such as *struggle* appear surprisingly infrequently. It is also true that for a book which conceives of texts as processes, and not as objects, Wells is surprisingly willing to talk about determinate textual properties, particularly those features which mark works as predominantly typical or indeterminate.

Nonetheless, I found this book quite extraordinary for its range, the careful quality of its argument, and its deft and self-reflexive movement between theory and traditional explication of texts. Moreover, some of the readings are startlingly powerful. Wells deals provocatively, for example, with Renaissance city comedy as a mediation between a notion of the marketplace as communal, festive space, and the marketplace as site for profit and governmental control. And she gives a brilliant reading of *The Duchess of Malfi* as a text which reveals the dangers of domesticity at its moment of invention, a reading which strikingly probes the significance of the play's representation of the Duchess's eroticized, private body in its difference from the idealized royal body common in so many Renaissance history plays and monarchical tragedies. Throughout the book, Wells deals skillfully with the way our contemporary notions of the family, of the body, and of the difference between public and private spheres differ from—and also overlap with—Renaissance conceptions. In short, while *The Dialectics of Representation* is neither an easy book, nor one with which I always agree, it stands out as both critically astute and theoretically ambitious.

Theodore Leinwand's *The City Staged: Jacobean Comedy, 1603-13* offers a fresh, if somewhat schematic, approach to the genre of city comedy. Specifically, Leinwand looks at how certain social groups—merchant citizens, gallants, and women (wives, whores, widows, and maids)—are portrayed in city comedy and discusses what these portrayals have to do with social relations in Jacobean London. The book is socio-historical in orientation. It assumes that plays, while not directly reflecting historical conditions, nonetheless are in complex and highly mediated ways both product and producer of the extradramatic world. He argues that the representation of merchant citizens, gallants, and women found in city comedy are *interested* representations which portray, not how these groups actually behaved, but how they were conceived of by other social groups. The book thus explores "the ways Londoners typed one another" (p. 4) and how city comedy represents a "staging of relations in the City" (p. 131). And in the first chapter Leinwand critiques earlier criticism of the genre either for treating the plays as moral statements about good and evil, rather than as political representations of social relations, or for treating them as amalgams of formal and conventional features with no relationship to the Jacobean social world.

In discussing merchant citizens, Leinwand argues, following Laura Stevenson, that in Jacobean England this social group, though rapidly gaining power, did not have as yet a highly developed class consciousness or a stable identity in the eyes of the rest of society. On the stage, the merchant citizen figure largely reveals the gentry's negative and fearful response to this increasingly powerful group. Merchants are most often presented as greedy devourers of a defenseless gentry class. Young gallants, by contrast, are represented as self-possessed and self-confident figures who do not lose their core identity even when engaged in extensive role playing. Leinwand explains that the empahsis on self-possession follows from the fact that it was the gentlemen-gallants who represented established social legitimacy, and who also formed "the class that supported and protected the theater" (p. 91). In the largest sense, the theater overtly supported the ideology of this social group. Moreover, in stressing the sexual success of the young gallant, the genre compensated for the social and financial uncertainties besetting this group in the face of the ever-more-powerful citizen-merchant. In discussing women in city comedy, Leinwand emphasizes that while, at a time of general social change and disruption, the stage offered some surprising portraits of strong women, it nonetheless could not be characterized as a feminist theater. Almost inevitably, women's power is contained by being channelled into marriage or is represented as monstrous. It was, he reminds us, not *women's* desires, but *men's* fantasies and stereotypes of women which the stage enacted during this period of gender dislocation.

In his lively discussion of how the theater stages social relations and reveals social groups' stereotypes of one another, Leinwand also argues that the theater frequently disrupts this stereotyping process by revealing the inadequacy of stereotypes. For example, merchants are sometimes portrayed as so exceedingly greedy that their greed becomes parodic and so "unbelievable." At several points Leinwand argues that the theater is a conservative social force as it produces and circulates stereotypes and a progressive force as it calls them in question and reveals their insufficiencies. For him, "mature" city comedies undermine stereotypes; "immature" ones do not. This problematic formulation seems to restore to Leinwand's criticism some of the moralism he would root out. It sounds very much like theories of defamiliarization or distantiation which argue that art, by virtue of being art, distances spectators from the ideologies encoded in the work. At least good or mature art does this.

A more promising way to understand the disruptive power of the Renaissance public stage might be through a thoroughgoing analysis of the theater as material institution and of the possible contradiction between aspects of the theatrical mode of production and the apparent ideological implications of particular plays. At several points in the book Leinwand gestures toward a consideration of the materiality of the theater: for example, he talks about the way men playing women's roles can't help affecting the gender ideology of the stage. And he talks briefly of the links between the theatricality of merchants and actors, actors and prostitutes. But these matters remain marginal to his main concerns. The subversion of conservative ideologies for him seems to occur primarily because art is art, not because the theater in Jacobean England was a certain kind of social institution with its own agents and mode of production. Nonetheless, despite wanting to argue with the author about specific points, I found this a successful and provocative book—one of the year's most interesting on non-Shakespearean drama.

Leah Marcus's *The Politics of Mirth: Jonson, Herrick, Milton, Marvell, and the Defense of Old Holiday Pastimes* is a fascinating study of why James and Charles promoted some types of rural sport and festival and of how certain literary texts participated in promoting or critiquing royal policy. Marcus's basic argument is that these Jacobean and Caroline monarchs promoted May Games, church-ales, and rural sports for a number of complex reasons. They were trying, in part, to exercise a measure of control over popular festival and to channel its potentially subversive energy, the idea being that if games were part of a Sunday ritual in the churchyards after the sermon, they were less likely to lead to excess and rebellion than if unsupervised or even officially repressed. In part, Marcus argues, monarchical support of such sports and pastimes also simply expressed disapproval of puritan attacks on these activities, and in part the pro-sport position was part of an attempt to get the aristocracy out of London and back to their country estates where a renewal of hospitality and popular festivity would supposedly heal emerging animosities between the lower orders and the aristocracy and gentry. Whatever the mix of reasons, there was a conscious royal policy to repastoralize England (p. 19) and in effect to freeze social relations into what were increasingly archaic patterns.

Marcus does not attempt to say if rural sports actually came to serve the essentially conservative ends the monarchy hoped to promote; nor does she judge just how seriously popular festivity was in decline in the early seventeenth century, nor how much it revived as a result of monarchical promotion. (Social historians and historians of popular culture such as Peter Burke, Peter Clark, and Keith Wrightson are just beginning to provide answers to such questions.) Instead, Marcus looks at how royal policy concerning holiday pastimes affected the output of various poets, dramatists, and masque writers. She argues, for example, that *Bartholomew Fair* is an unsentimental defense of popular pastimes and also a critique of their abuses, an angle of approach she also uses in reading a number of Jonsonian masques. For example, in arguing that *Pleasure Reconciled to Virtue* is a point-for-point commentary on James's trip to Scotland and the subsequent publication in 1618 of the *Book of Sports*, Marcus sees the masque celebrating the royal policy on festivity codified in that document, but also criticizing the court for its own excessive indulgence in festival pleasure. During the Civil War, Marcus asserts, Royalist poets such as Herrick and Lovelace nostalgically evoked rural pastimes as a sign of their continuing allegiance to monarchical ideology, though increasingly it was only within enclosed and protected spaces that the enacting of such festivities could be imagined. Finally, with Marvell, we get a critique both of the Royalist gesture of retreat and of the nostalgic attempt to pastoralize the countryside.

This is an important book, in part because by its very title it suggests that there is a "politics" even to pleasure. Seemingly neutral activities like dancing around a Maypole are not only subject to overt regulation, but become charged signifiers in various discursive struggles over authority and legitimacy. Will Laud's view of sport (and of the social order) prevail, or will the Puritans'? Marcus reminds us that in such struggles literature plays a part, though she is reticent in theorizing just what kind of part such texts could have and in speculating about their specific effectivity. I also, however, find the book important because it moves confidently across the boundaries separating "literary" and "non-literary" texts or separating masques, plays, and lyric poems. Marcus provocatively links texts not often studied in conjunction with one another, and she provides strong and detailed readings of those texts.

Yet the book also makes me recognize how hard it is to place texts "in history," important as that attempt is. In crossing the boundaries between one type of text and another, for example, how can one take proper account of the varying material conditions in which these texts were produced and received? Do a masque and a stage play which overtly promulgate the same ideological position produce the same ideological effect when one is enacted at Whitehall and the other at the Red Bull? Other problems, of course, bedevil contemporary historical criticism. New critics attacked old style literary historians for flattening literary texts and making them reflections of a world beyond the text. And when Marcus reads *Comus* as Milton's comment on the differences between Laud and the Earl of Bridgewater over the proper use of arts and pastimes, those old charges against historicism hover somewhere in the middle distance. The problem is not that literary texts, especially occasional forms such as the masque, never comment directly on topical issues. The problem is accounting for the way language runs in excess of intention or topicality and in accounting as much for the *gap* between word and world as for their conjunction. In their quite different ways, Williamson, Wells, and Leinwand all struggle with these issues, situating themselves as historical critics, but reflecting on the difficulties of what that may mean. It would be helpful if Marcus also more explicitly addressed the problematics of historical criticism, since she is clearly far from a naive practitioner of the craft. In the end, for its union of learning and critical acumen, *The Politics of Mirth* is an important achievement.

II

The following section discusses groups of books on similar themes or having a common purpose. The first three books are all aimed primarily at the undergraduate reader and provide "introductions" to Shakespeare. The first, Philip Edwards's *Shakespeare: A Writer's Progress* includes a chapter on Shakespeare's life; another on the themes of family, sexuality, and social relationships which Edwards believes unify the Shakespeare canon; and five generically organized chapters on the poems, comedies, histories, tragedies, and tragicomedies, in which category Edwards includes *All's Well, Measure for Measure,* the four romances, and *Two Noble Kinsmen.*

I don't think this is any longer the most useful kind of introductory text to put in students' hands. For one thing, most good one-volume editions of Shakespeare offer essays on genre, text, playhouse, and author which equal or surpass the basic background material Edwards provides. And perhaps because of space, Edwards's comments on individual plays often are little more than plot summaries or "appreciations." Moreover, students will sense little of the urgency and vitality in contemporary Shakespeare studies from this volume, partly because Edwards steers away from everything overtly polemical, historical, political, or theoretical. As a result, the study of Shakespeare appears to be a hermetically-sealed activity for which one primarily needs to cultivate good taste and aesthetic judgment. Edwards is thus put in the position of forming taste without seeming to be doing so. Occasionally, however, overtly hectoring passages appear: "we mustn't be sentimental about Falstaff, any more than about Shylock or Caliban. Be sorry for them by all means, but recognize in all three a challenge to the maintenance of established authority" (p. 121). Some fairly urgent questions are shuffled aside by these directives: what was at stake in various challenges to authority in Elizabethan England and how did theatrical representations figure in these challenges or their repression? how much does one *want* to adopt, now, a politics that identifies with established authority and finds its alternative sentimental? The same lack of self-consciousness often pervades Edwards's comments on gender. He writes that *All's Well* ends unsatisfactorily in that "Helena at the beginning of the play is an extraordinarily interesting person; at the end she has become a kind of smothering Amazon with the feeble male cowering at her feet" (p. 164): by contrast, he finds nothing disturbing about the ending of *Measure for Measure*—an ending "exuberant in its openness"—in which the coerciveness of a male ruler apparently isn't experienced as "smothering."

Clearly I disagree with some of Edwards's positions. The larger point, however, is that the overtly "objective" stance he assumes obscures the fact that a position is being taken on the text rather than a truth revealed. Acknowledging no awareness of its own politics, the book encourages none in the student reader. Providing no self-conscious discussion of critical method, it leaves the student reader thinking there is a "natural" way to read if only he or she could figure it out. By contrast, an introductory volume like this one might more usefully serve students by discussing methods for reading Shakespearean drama and outlining what is under debate and contest in contemporary Shakespeare studies, which includes everything from the status of the texts to their role in ideological reproduction. Unfortunately, *Shakespeare: A Writer's Progress* positions itself too far above the fray to serve these ends.

Germaine Greer's *Shakespeare,* written for the Past Masters series put out by Oxford University Press, is an even less satisfactory introductory text: a combination of tired scholarship and sentimental effusions about Shakespeare's exemplification of all that is best in English life. "As long as Shakespeare remains central to English cultural life, it will retain the values which make it unique in the world, namely tolerance, pluralism, the talent for viable compromise, and a profound commitment to that most wasteful form of social organization, democracy" (p. 125). The historical sleight of hand by which Shakespeare comes to be the proponent of twentieth-century English values and political arrangements (such as democracy) is remarkable.

I found myself repeatedly embarrassed by this book—embarrassed, for example, by the way it circulates as "fact" the debatable proposition that the audiences for the public and private theaters were almost totally discrete. Greer writes: "while the noisy groundlings tyrannized over the public theatre, the coterie theatre found itself in the situation of having to gratify the vanity of its most powerful patrons, who could decide what should be played and when, and what themes should be treated in new works and how" (p. 31). One is troubled, however, not only by the way Greer ignores whole dimensions of contemporary scholarship and criticism, but also by her insistence on Shakespeare's perfection. In her construction, he is patriotic without being jingoistic, Christian without being dogmatic, *and* a believer in equalitarian marriage (p. 111).

Greer's is a book in which sentiment and clichéd expression stand in the stead of analysis and engagement with contemporary scholarship. A not untypical sentence, taken at random from the page before me, reads: "he created a series of female characters who were both passionate and pure, who gave their hearts spontaneously into the keeping of the men they loved and remained true to the bargain in the face of tremendous odds" (p. 109). A writer of Harlequin romances could not top such prose. Surely the students who are the likely audience of this book (it sells in paper for $3.95) deserve an introduction to Shakespeare which does more than praise through banalities and through the ahistorical assimilation of Shakespeare to the values of contemporary bourgeois culture.

For me, Northrop Frye's *On Shakespeare* is a more useful introductory book than either of the two just mentioned. It contains edited versions of Frye's undergraduate lectures on ten of the plays, plus an introductory chapter on what we might call the principles of reading Shakespeare with profit. There is nothing here to surprise experienced readers of Frye or of Shakespeare, but much that would be of news to most of the beginning undergraduates I teach: e.g., that in Shakespearean comedy the structure of the story may be more important than theme or character, or that social behavior in Elizabethan England was first and foremost determined by issues of rank. Frye provides critical principles and background information judiciously. They are introduced as they are needed, so that we hear about New Comedy when *Midsummer Night's Dream* is the focus and Renaissance theories of monarchy when the topic is *Richard II*, and the information is delivered with economy and wit. Perhaps the most productive thing about the book, however, is its opinionated and argumentative style. This, I would propose, invites students to notice that *a case is being made* about Shakespeare, a position staked, rather than a transparent truth being given common sense articulation. Whether opining that Hal, when he thinks Falstaff is dead at Shrewsbury, gives "an obituary speech that one might make about a dog that has been run over" (p. 79) or when arguing that Shakespeare reflects "the priority of mythology to ideology" (p. 143), Frye invites rejoinder by foregrounding the polemical and interpretive dimensions of his own position. I don't want to overpraise the book. In obvious ways it is "dated," reflects positions formed in the debates of prior decades. But there is a rhetorical bite and critical intelligence on display in the work that just might help undergraduates sense that there is something more to literary study than getting either the "facts" or the moral pieties down pat.

The next three books are by British academics of the left (Malcolm Evans's book could be included here, too), and I group them together to call attention to the fact that these writers take up questions most American critics eschew, such as the political ramification of various appropriations of Shakespeare, including his use in the educational apparatus. These critics see texts as sites of social struggle and their own critical task as the creation of a politically and intellectually progressive approach to Renaissance plays. In foregrounding what is often suppressed in American criticism—i.e., the politics of reading and staging and "using" Shakespeare—their work is important.

The first of these books, Terry Eagleton's *William Shakespeare,* appears in the Rereading Literature series being published by Basil Blackwell with Eagleton as general editor. The series aims to reread the major works of the major authors of the British literary tradition in light of contemporary theoretical discourses such as semiotics, feminism, and Marxism, and thus to liberate the texts from more conservative and apolitical reading practices. Just how strongly and convincingly does Eagleton "reread" Shakespeare? It depends on where you start as a reader. The book is a kind of forced march through the canon (no play gets more than about five pages of analysis) with Marx, Lacan, and contemporary feminism guiding the way. For those familiar with contemporary theory, the conclusions Eagleton reaches probably won't be revolutionary. For those unfamiliar with these discourses, the book may be merely provoking, since it is written in a kind of shorthand which assumes prior acquaintance with the language of the poststructuralist moment.

Eagleton's basic argument is that Shakespeare is a political conservative with a strong investment in upholding a traditional feudal social order but articulating, as well, the transgressive power of sexual desire, linguistic excess, and bourgeois individualism as each fragments or disrupts the containing structures of marriage, law, and social hierarchy. Eagleton's strongest move is—however sketchily—to remind us of the historical specificity of Renaissance dramatic writing: its emergence at the moment when a nascent capitalism and a residual feudalism coincided, producing plays deeply fissured by ideological contradictions: and he works hard to expose the ways in which Shakespeare's devices of closure and containment are insufficient to control the forces threatening all structures of stability. Perhaps inevitably, Eagleton seems to privilege Shakespeare's tragedies because, for him, they most fully acknowledge the disruptive force of excessive desire: sexual, commercial, and linguistic. Macbeth, for example, becomes a figure whose aggressive bourgeois individualism breaks apart the unified self made possible—at least in theory—by accepting a socially defined role in a feudal social order. Eagleton is at his most iconoclastic when he scathingly reads Shakespeare's romances as powerful mystifications of a patriarchal social order in which inequalities of rank, gender, and property are represented as "natural" and in which the disruptive power of sexual desire is sidestepped by transposing wives into daughters and sentimentalizing, without disturbing, patriarchal authority. While there are strong and provocative moments in this book, it also seems thin and rushed, more given to strong local assertions than to sustained argument, and the threads by which Eagleton links these plays to their historical context are often very frail. It is a book that overreaches itself.

The most successful of these three books is, for me, Terence Hawkes's *That Shakespeherian Rag*. Hawkes does not provide sustained readings of plays and says very little about Shakespeare's place in Elizabethan culture, other than to argue that *The Tempest* is as much product and producer of the English enclosure movement and the work relations it spawned as it is of colonialism. Instead, the book focuses—with wit and insight—on the way, in the twentieth century, the academic use of Shakespeare by prominent British men of letters is inseparably intertwined with the nation's political and social struggles. The book is a series of case studies showing how, in specific instances, this intertwining occurred. The third chapter, covering the career of Walter Ralegh, offers a case in point. Hawkes argues that after the 1867 Second Reform Bill there was a conscious attempt to use literature within the educational system to draw the lower classes into the official national culture. Part of this initiative involved the development of the prestigious *English Men of Letters* series. Hawkes has a wonderful section describing not only the patriotic, hypermasculine picture of Shakespeare created by Walter Ralegh in his book on Shakespeare written for this series, but also looking at what happened to Ralegh's own subsequent career as, in his role as spokesman for the Bard, he acquired the first Chair of Literature at Oxford, became *Sir* Walter Ralegh, and was increasingly trotted out to talk about Shakespeare on days of great political significance, such as 4 July 1918. Other chapters deal with A. C. Bradley, T. S. Eliot, and Dover Wilson, whose work on *Hamlet* is provocatively linked to the Bolshevik revolution of 1917 and to the publication of the Newbolt report in 1921.

As a history of how "Shakespeare" gets entangled in twentieth-century British political and social life, Hawkes's book is of necessity suggestive, rather than definitive. Moreover, some sections, like the attempt to link Bradley's concern with silence and revelation in the Shakespearean text to the Oscar Wilde trials, are less persuasive than others. But the book convincingly makes the point that "the academic" is also often "the political." Further, Hawkes carries his point, I think, that in England Shakespeare is a particularly significant cultural icon, undoubtedly more so than in America, and that he has been repeatedly recruited for conservative ends.

A second purpose of Hawkes's book is to argue for an enlightened critical practice which will slough off old notions of authorial authority, textual transparency, and critical disinterestedness. As Hawkes writes in his concluding pages, American jazz offers a model for such a practice:

> we only have to step beyond the shores of Europe to encounter quite a different notion of interpretation which will allow exactly what I propose: the sense of a text as a site, or an area of conflicting and often contradictory potential interpretations, no one or group of which can claim 'intrinsic' primacy or 'inherent' authority, and all of which are always ideological in nature and subject to extrinsic political and economic determinants.
>
> The abstract model I reach for is of course that of jazz music: that black American challenge to the Eurocentric idea of the author's, or the composer's, authority.
>
> (p. 117)

The paragraph goes on further to celebrate the "unservile" and improvisational nature of American criticism. I would simply observe that in trying to envision an alternative to British critical practice, Hawkes has recycled an old idealization of America and one which specifically fails to acknowledge the marginality of blacks and black culture in America and the many ways in which the ideology Hawkes attributes to jazz is antithetical to the mainstream value system of a culture strongly committed to ownership and property. Nonetheless, if Hawkes's reading of America seems idealistic, the desire which prompts it is laudable: the wish for a critical practice less tied to ideas of authorial ownership and immanent meanings, ideas which feed the desire for authoritative versions of texts and obscure the social dimensions of the struggle over meaning. Moreover, Hawkes's book serves as an invitation for Americans to begin to consider what role "Shakespeare" has played in the politics and institutions and social struggles of this country. It will not be the same role he has played in Britain, certainly, but it is a role which invites a political analysis.

I laughed so hard reading the very witty opening pages of the third book, Simon Shepherd's *Marlowe and the Politics of the Elizabethan Theatre,* that someone came to my library carrel to tell me to be quiet. Unfortunately, the book does not entirely live up, intellectually, to the cleverness of its opening pages, but it certainly has its moments. Briefly put, Shepherd's thesis is that "the Marlowe texts could be said to take a number of the ideological truths of the Elizabethan theatre and reveal them to be discourses, and to show those discourses spoken within power relations" (p. 210). Among the "truths" Marlowe is said to reveal as fictions serving particular interests are the following: that any speaking, however plain, equates with sincere self-expression; that theatrical pleasure is ever politically innocent or outside relations of power; that the subordination of female to male is natural and right; that the homoerotic is a pathological deviation from heterosexual normalcy. In short, Marlowe becomes the spokesman for a number of important, politically progressive twentieth-century ideas. The problem comes in persuading the reader of the extent to which these are also sixteenth-century ideas and of the extent to which Marlowe is as squeaky clean, ideologically, as Shepherd would have him. There is an important sense in which the book simply uses Marlowe's plays to rehearse some modern ideas about gender, discourse, power, and subjectivity. Yet the book also gestures toward being an investigation of the relationship between the dominant Elizabethan ideologies and the historically-situated drama of the 1580s. Whitgift's attacks on Puritan preaching, the succession debates in Parliament, England's relationship with the Turks and the Spanish in the eighties and nineties—these are loosely sketched in as the context against which Marlowe's plays are best read. But I would argue that the historical analysis is pretty haphazard and half-hearted, as is the institutional analysis of the nature and social function of the theater in the 1580s. Shepherd's strong suit is his clear commitment to values which he specifies as "socialist and anti-patriarchal" (p. xviii) and which motivate his readings in ways that give them both political urgency and a healthy dash of irreverence. Notable in this regard is Shepherd's view of Shakespeare. If most of the books I am reviewing are still heavily committed to idealizing Shakespeare, Shepherd connects him with a number of evils, particularly the creation of the illusion of the unified subject and of an expressive, depoliticized theory of language. Unfortunately, Shepherd doesn't seriously explore whether it is "Shakespeare" or humanist constructions of Shakespeare to which he objects, nor does he really probe the question of whether dramatic practices between the 1580s and 1590s could be as disjunctive as he implies. The book, in short, is breezy and irreverent, but it could usefully pursue some of its lines of argument with more rigor.

Three books devoted to Shakespearean comedy appeared this year. Two, Robert Ornstein's *Shakespeare's Comedies: From Roman Farce to Romantic Mystery* and J. A. Bryant, Jr.'s *Shakespeare and the Uses of Comedy,* offer traditional close readings of most of Shakespeare's comic canon. Both eschew theory and the historical contextualizing of the plays; neither revises in a substantial way mainstream accounts of these works. Bryant is a cheerfully overt bardolator, happy to admit that, for him, to study Shakespeare is to study nature (p. 2). Ignoring the labels "problem plays," "festive comedies," "romances," Bryant treats all the works usually grouped under these rubrics simply as "comedies," and he is quick to find these works teaching lessons of forgiveness, acceptance, and humility. Perhaps the most distinctive aspect of Bryant's approach to the genre is his insistence that "Shakespeare in all his comedies managed to express a concern about the unequal treatment of the sexes throughout most of historical time" (p. 10). Consequently, he finds Shakespeare critical of the exploitative behavior of figures such as Troilus and championing the idea of female equality through figures such as Kate, Beatrice, and Portia. Bryant does not, however, directly address that increasingly large body of feminist scholarship that questions the extent to which Shakespeare's plays—even the comedies—escaped from the basic premises of Renaissance patriarchalism.

Ornstein focuses on Shakespeare's "development," charting his movement from early experiments to the full achievement of romantic comedy in *A Midsummer Night's Dream* to the rejection of the comedy of courtship after *All's Well* to the final experiments in Fletcherian tragicomedy. This is an oft-told story, though Ornstein tells it with some idiosyncratic inflections. He rejects, for example, readings of *The Taming of the Shrew* that see a benevolent Petruchio leading Kate to a marriage of mutuality, and stresses instead the brutality of Petruchio and the starkness of the play's representation of male dominance. On the other hand, his reading of another much-disputed play, *The Merchant of Venice,* is highly traditional, emphasizing, despite their flaws and insularity, the essential beauty of Belmont and the virtue of the Venetian Christians.

The third book on comedy, Richard Levin's *Love and Society in Shakespearean Comedy*, packs the greatest punch. Levin presents an iconoclastic—antiromantic is his word—reading of *Merchant of Venice, Much Ado,* and *Twelfth Night.* His intent is to eschew "melodramatic" readings of these plays which focus on the moral division of the characters into those who are good and those who are evil—with good justly triumphant. Instead, he sees the plays enacting struggles for social power and social acceptance, and argues that status and wealth, not morality, often determine the outcome. While there is a tradition of reading Portia as a manipulative schemer and the Venetians as hypocritical protectors of their privileges against the Jewish outsider, Levin's treatment of the other two plays is more unexpected. For him both Illyria and Messina are societies which produce aggressive struggles for social rewards and where the moral differences between, say, Don Pedro and Don John are not nearly as sharp as traditional criticism has assumed. In Levin's view, not only are Malvolio, Feste, and Toby rivals for power in Olivia's house, but Maria actively schemes to improve her social position by marrying Toby, and Viola calculatedly sets out to wrest Orsino from Olivia.

The book's greatest value is to direct attention away from moral evaluation of characters to a consideration of the relative status, power, and economic position of characters and the relationship between these things and the plays' politics of inclusion and exclusion. But in many ways the iconoclasm of the book is tamed by the thoroughly traditional mode of criticism employed. Levin psychologizes Shakespeare's characters with a vengeance, speculating about their "motives" and treating them at every moment as "real people," not dramatic representations. Moreover, the status and ground of these iconoclastic readings is never theoretically addressed nor historically situated. Levin admits that the plays *can* be read in the traditional way and that they *can* be read as he reads them. So what claims are being made for the readings offered? Do they reflect Shakespeare's intentions, Renaissance social realities, or Levin's own politics and historical situation? Many of the books under review beg all such questions, implying that all the things we say about Shakespeare are in some sense simply "in the text." Levin's book, by self-consciously producing readings that challenge what so many other twentieth-century critics have found "in the texts" of these plays, invites in a special way reflection on the status of interpretation, especially on the political and historical determinants of those acts of textual production/reproduction we call readings. Consequently, while Levin offers antiromantic alternatives to the content of many humanist readings of these three plays, he does not decisively break with their fundamental assumptions about the nature of interpretation as the uncovering of "what is already there." The book is vigorously written and its readings provocative, but it is ultimately less iconoclastic than it appears.

Three books this year deal at least in part with art as a theme or object of inquiry within Shakespeare's plays and sonnets. Presented as a union of metadramatic and performance criticism, Sidney Homan's *Shakespeare's Theater of Presence* remains more the former than the latter. It is firmly in the tradition of reading Shakespeare's plays as statements about—as well as enactments of—dramatic art. What interests him are the terms *presence, language, spectacle,* and *audience,* and the way the plays comment on these aspects of the theatrical experience and embody them. Much is familiar here, though the readings of nine plays are pursued with energy and wide reference to prior criticism. *Troilus and Cressida* enacts an "aesthetics of failure" (p. 49) because the correspondence of language to object has been sullied; in *Julius Caesar* both spectacle and language are untrustworthy and difficult to interpret, leading to recognition of the mystical aspect of life, "that dimension beyond the rational faculties of vision and hearing" which is "most often associated with women" (p. 95): the second tetralogy reverses Richard III's private theatrics of negativity to enact a public art and a proper union of the visual and verbal. Throughout, masculine and feminine are treated as essentialized categories, with women positively equated with nature, the life force, and a positive theatricality; men with a sterile rationality and self-alienation.

James L. Calderwood is something of the reigning monarch of such metadramatic studies of Shakespeare, and for good reason. He largely opened the field, and his several books are both insightful and conspicuously well-written. In *If It were Done: "Macbeth" and Tragic Action*, as in the recent book on Hamlet, however, Calderwood is increasingly concerned with more than metadramatic topics (the present book contains a good deal of anthropological material on sacrifice, ritual, and gift giving, for example) or raises metadramatic concerns within a decidedly deconstructive framework. To summarize an elegant argument pretty crudely, in *If It Were Done* Calderwood approaches *Macbeth* as a counter to *Hamlet*, in fact, as a counter-*Hamlet*. He argues that the play stresses action over words, the future over the past, a tight dramatic structure over a meandering one, etc. The first chapter suggestively teases out these and other oppositions between *Macbeth* and *Hamlet*. The remaining two chapters undo the clear picture of the play thus erected. It turns out that despite the play's emphasis on action and the hero's decisive orientation toward the future, actions are undone in *Macbeth* in that their consequences cannot be trammeled up nor controlled any more than Macbeth's desires can be achieved. Deferral, repetition, and undifferentiation haunt the play; they are not the exclusive property of *Hamlet*. Moreover—and here Calderwood shares territory with Harry Berger—Macbeth is not the sole origin of evil in a world of essential goodness. Rather, the violence he displays is a central feature of his culture, part of the process by which that culture erodes distinctions and remakes them by creating heroic survivors (p. 84).

Calderwood is a strong reader of the play, extremely good in talking about the endless deferral of Macbeth's desire, in discriminating between Macbeth as ritual scapegoat for his culture and as tragic victim of himself, and in thinking through the implications of the sexual language used in representing the unseen murder of Duncan. Calderwood's metadramatic concerns show themselves in his argument that the audience to the play is not only invited to watch violence, but to become complicit with it, by imagining what is not seen, most importantly, the murder of the sacred king. Moreover, Calderwood insistently links the characters' concern with action to Aristotle's concern that drama mime a complete action and wonders aloud how much the undoing of action within the play ruffles the certainty with which we regard plays as closed structures of perfect linearity, with their beginnings, middles, and definitive ends. About these matters Calderwood seems himself uncertain, unsure whether a play like *Macbeth* provides the audience the satisfactions of closure and achieved desire, or whether it undermines those satisfactions and achievements (see pp. 68-70 and also p. 119).

An equally interesting part of the book, however, may well be what I haven't yet mentioned: the preface and the "supplements" (Calderwood's own Derridean term). In the first—implicitly answering the critique that deconstruction and metadramatic work are often indifferent to politics and history—Calderwood mounts a well-mannered critique of some historical and political criticism, urging that criticism is not the best way to overthrow "national hegemonies" and urging critics to do their political work (marching and writing checks) when in their non-professional roles (p. xvi). (Of course, as any Derridean knows, when private and professional are thus opposed, the opposition is easy to deconstruct and the political function of the opposition itself then becomes the issue.) In the "supplements" which close the volume, moreover, in the middle of lots of material on gift giving and why dogs are stratified by "degree" in *Macbeth*, Calderwood includes material on Renaissance dueling, on social aspiration as a phenomenon of the period, and on violence in early seventeenth-century England. Even though, in the preface, Calderwood wanted to make clear that in chapter 3 he was "talking about manifestations of violence and power in Shakespeare's Scotland, not in King James's England" (p. xi), in the "supplements" he returns the reader, in an admittedly fragmentary fashion, to the historicist territory he vowed no intention to visit. While the body of the book overtly deals with the world of literary representations in all their self-regarding and self-contained complexity, the frame of the book looks first to the contemporary scene of criticism in which Calderwood's book is written and then back to the world in which Shakespeare's play was first composed. How criticism will negotiate among these sites, whether they all will be granted legitimacy as objects of inquiry, whether they can be held in pure separation from one another, and how the politics of criticism and teaching as social practices can be acknowledged and not trivialized—these are matters which arise on the margins of Calderwood's text and muddy its claims simply to be about the fictional world of Shakespeare's Scotland and its intertextual links to *Hamlet.*

The third book, Ekbert Faas's *Shakespeare's Poetics,* tries to deduce what Shakespeare thought about the nature and purpose of art by looking at statements about art in the plays and sonnets and by relating this material to parallel views supposedly held by Montaigne and Bacon. His conclusion is that Shakespeare is the poet of nature, as Jonson claimed. By this Faas means in part that Shakespeare was largely indifferent to formal debates about genre, made fun of overly elaborate rhetorical displays, eschewed didacticism in drama, and espoused "a psychology of spontaneous creation" over a "rationale of rhetorically calculated craftsmanship" (p. 80). Most crucially, Shakespeare is presented as sharing with Bacon and Montaigne a strong antiessentialist bias and a tendency to radical empiricism (p. xxii). Others will have to piece out exactly what these terms mean in Faas's narrative, because I, finally, could not. Sometimes Faas seems to mean that Shakespeare is simply an anti-Platonist who eschews "a hyperintellectual ascent toward the absolute" (p. 85). But while positing Shakespeare as an empiricist attempting to "capture the minute particulars of what is" (p. 80), Faas seems to locate a new (essentialist) absolute in "nature," which, however, Shakespeare is said not to be concerned to imitate, but to *enact,* through his art (p. 172). For me, from this mixture of Renaissance, romantic, and modern notions, a coherent and convincing poetics did not emerge.

Three books this year represent the posthumous publications of established Shakespeare scholars. William Empson's *Essays on Shakespeare* is the least successful of this trio. The book is a collection of miscellaneous pieces on Shakespeare, most of them written in the early fifties on issues that have lost much of their urgency. In the 1964 essay, "Hunt the Symbol," for example, Empson attacks the excesses of those who in rejecting character analysis of the Bradleyean sort, fetishize image patterns and the moral meanings supposedly conveyed by dramatic symbols. The only new essay which Empson completed for this volume before his death is a long, speculative piece on the physical features of the Globe Theater in which he argues for an inner and upper stage, for the inseparability of the tiring house from the stage, and for the particular placement of windows by which to illuminate the playing areas. By themselves, the essays don't make a very satisfying or coherent whole, and the editor, David Pirie, would have done both Empson and the reader a service by providing an introduction in which he discussed the role of Empson's Shakespeare studies in his larger critical concerns and placed these particular essays in historical context. As it stands, this scattered volume does not begin to convey the tremendous critical accomplishments of this distinguished scholar.

More coherent and finished is Clifford Leech's *Christopher Marlowe: Poet for the Stage*, capably and unobtrusively edited by Anne Lancashire, to whom Leech had entrusted his book at the time of his death in 1977. After opening chapters on Marlowe's life and the much-disputed dates of his major writings, Leech gives us the traditional march through the Marlowe canon, supplying close readings of individual texts and paying relatively little attention to extraliterary contexts. Leech seems to have had two general ends in mind: to argue for Marlowe as a highly successful and innovative theatrical craftsman and, more controversially, to argue for the essential ideological neutrality of his plays. For example, while Marlowe obviously uses morality play elements, Leech contends that Marlowe "takes out the firmly enunciated lesson which was at the heart of the moral drama and inserts in its place a question mark" (p. 49). While argued in this instance in relation to *Tamburlaine,* the point is made again in regard to *Dr. Faustus*. Both in religion and politics, Leech finds Marlowe's plays embodying an "active and deliberate neutrality" (p. 129), in effect revealing the contradictions of the age, rather than either championing or challenging its dominant orthodoxies. One question, of course, is why Marlowe has so often been received as subversive if his plays are as studiously neutral as Leech suggests. I think the strengths of the book do not lie in its case for Marlowe's "neutrality," but in its essentially formalist investigations of such matters as the effects of comedy within Marlowe's dramatic structures and the role of his plays in the evolution of particular dramatic and nondramatic genres such as tragedy or the erotic epyllion.

The most powerful of these posthumous books is C. L. Barber's *The Whole Journey: Shakespeare's Power of Development*, brought to completion by Richard P. Wheeler, who not only edited Barber's drafts, but collaboratively added to them. This unusual mode of composition attests to the remarkable loyalty and affection Barber seems to have inspired in students and friends and to his own capacity for a nonproprietary relationship to ideas.

Perhaps not surprisingly, Barber's psychoanalytic study of Shakespeare's life and works makes Shakespeare the exemplar of values Barber seems himself particularly to have honored. Essentially he argues that Shakespeare, because of his own early family situation, as an adult had the capacity for a "feminine" self-forgetfulness which allowed for cherishing, nurturing relationships with others of the sort we see in the first seventeen of his sonnets to the young man. According to Barber, Shakespeare's Oedipal confrontation with threatening male authority occurred relatively late, and is recorded in the tragedies, while the romances testify to the recovery of a sense of self based on an alliance with the feminine. As Barber writes: "The major tragedies come late because, as I see it, his sensibility is shaped by a constellation of family relationships in which, initially, female or maternal power is more important than paternal. The classic Oedipal confrontation, with its possibility of atonement by identification with the father, is postponed because for him there are alternative ways of achieving identity. After the effort to shift the prime allegiance to heroic manhood in the great tragedies, the romances again show the female as predominant; with the exception of the artist-dominated *Tempest,* male identity is lost when relationship to women is lost, and regained as their gift when relationship is recovered" (p. 3).

Obviously, this is a compelling narrative, not least because it has a happy ending, and in elaborating this narrative, Barber produces strong accounts of such things as the eruption of misogyny in the tragedies and of the relationship of the sonnets to Shakespeare's plays of the middle period. Particularly strong is his case that Shakespeare essentially inhabited a post-Christian world in which secular relationships had to bear the impossible weight of displaced transcendental investments.

The costs of telling this narrative about Shakespeare are also obvious. To me the biggest loss is history. Shakespeare's plays finally have little to do with the culture in which he lived; instead, they reflect his own personal development, and that can best be understood by recourse to the Freudian paradigm of the endlessly recurring family romance. For me the hardest moments of the book to accept occurred when Barber's investment in the idea of the author's personal history as the source of his plays led him to produce profiles of Shakespeare's mother and father and accounts of the son's early relations with them both. What we lose by such an approach is any sense of the many things that speak through an author besides the effects of early family relations, any sense of the historicity of such human institutions as the family, any sense of the material conditions under which Shakespeare's plays were produced and of the effect of those conditions on his art. Moreover, while feminists obviously owe a debt to Barber for valuing what he denominates as the feminine in culture and for taking seriously the role of gender in art, Barber nonetheless tends to essentialize the feminine and to equate female power with "subtle manipulation guided by superior understanding" (p. 7). In the end, any such fixing of gender qualities threatens to become oppressive.

Many readers will be less at odds with the book's central premises than I am. No one, I think, will find it less than a serious, daring, and provocative piece of work. Precisely by occupying a particular critical position so strongly, the book allows one to see the achievements of such a method and to understand its difference from other, competing methods of textual analysis.

III

The following section discusses, alphabetically by author's name, the remaining critical books, aside from collections of essays. I could find no meaningful way to group these books into batches, so each, like the cheese, stands alone.

The study of Shakespeare as theatrical craftsman now has a formidable history, but in *Shakespeare's Dramatic Structures* Anthony Brennan often ignores that fact. The book has no notes, but, more importantly, it often simply repeats—without significant embellishment—what has become the standard wisdom of performance criticism. He argues that Shakespeare composed with an eye to the effect of the staged performance on the audience, and the first half of the book primarily considers devices of repetition by which the enacted play is given structure. Here, many of the examples are familiar: the repetition of scenes of violence in *Romeo and Juliet*, the two wooing scenes in *Richard III*, recurring instances of kneeling in *Lear* and *Othello*. Attention to the effects upon an audience is intermittent. The second and more successful half of the book mainly investigates why Shakespeare keeps certain characters separate from one another for much of a given play. Brennan examines, for example, the effect on the audience of having Hotspur and Hal separate from one another until the final battle at Shrewsbury, considers why Cordelia is kept off stage for much of *Lear*, and explores why the characters in *Hamlet* seldom seem fully to be in the presence of one another. Although this book is clearly the product of its author's long engagement with the Shakespearean canon, it finally breaks little new ground and stands more as an appreciation of Shakespeare's theatrical talent than as a rigorous analysis of it.

In *Christopher Marlowe's Use of the Bible*, R.M. Cornelius tries to tabulate all of Marlowe's direct and indirect references to Scripture with the aim of refuting charges of Marlowe's atheism and proving that Marlowe "honors the person of Christ and the principles of Biblical Christianity but attacks the faulty practices of professing Christians" (p. 124).

How Jungian psychology illuminates Shakespeare's characters is H.R. Coursen's field of inquiry in *The Compensatory Psyche*. Implicitly equated with real people (Coursen, for example, calls Lear an "insecure little boy" who "desires stroking" [p. 132]), Shakespeare's characters are divided into the eight Jungian personality types and their receptivity to unconscious psychic material examined. Coursen argues that in comedy the positive signals of the psyche are accepted (p. 29), as when Rosalind in male disguise accepts the possibilities of androgyny; but in tragedy the compensatory energy of the psyche is rejected, as shown by the male protagonist's frequent rejection of the female principle, the *anima* (p. 63). Almost inevitably, as Coursen himself hints in his preface (p. ix), such a study turns the plays into an allegory of Jungian psychology; it also skirts the difficult issue of the historical dimensions of the construction of subjectivity, as well as the relationship of artistic representations to "real life."

Alan Dessen's *Shakespeare and the Late Moral Plays* usefully reminds us that a flourishing didactic drama was produced during the early years of Elizabeth's reign, a drama which present-day critics and present-day dramatic anthologies largely ignore. Dessen's thesis is that plays such as *Enough Is as Good as a Feast, The Trial of Treasure,* and *The Three Ladies of London* provided a repertory of dramatic options and theatrical strategies employed by many later Elizabethan playwrights, even when those later dramatists abandoned overt allegorizing. Dessen correctly argues that these sixteenth-century "moral plays" differ somewhat from such heavily anthologized fifteenth-century "moralities" as *Everyman* and *The Castle of Perseverance*. The later plays, for example, do not necessarily center all the action on a single Humanum Genorum figure torn between Vice and Virtue; instead, they often feature dual protagonists, often make the Vice the symbolic embodiment of the ills of the social body, and often display a two-part structure in which a rising tide of social ills is reversed by the triumphant emergence of a purgative agent. Dessen devotes the bulk of his book to showing how these sixteenth-century moral plays influenced Shakespeare, particularly in his construction of history plays. For example, he examines *Richard III* and *1 Henry IV* in terms of the two-phase structure of the moral plays and looks at Hal and Hotspur in *1 Henry IV* as an example of the dual protagonist convention also prominent in this earlier drama.

Though the plays' links to the sixteenth-century moral play have not before been so fully explored, I don't think Dessen's book significantly alters one's understanding of the Shakespeare canon. In the wealth of commentary on Shakespeare, most of Dessen's critical observations have already been made. It is often noted, for example, that *Richard III* has a two-part structure or that Shakespeare's characters are constructed by principles other than that of nineteenth-century realism. Moreover, Shakespeare's plays are traversed by so many traditions and conventions that focusing on one can easily seem reductive. Dessen's study doesn't entirely evade this danger. Some of his readings are schematic, even though he clearly states that he sees Shakespeare's plays as neither allegories nor sermons. Yet in discussing *1 Henry IV* he posits an utter moral contrast between Hal and Hotspur, turning the one into an all-knowing, all-controlling exemplar of civic responsibility and the latter into a personification of irascible irresponsibility. Dessen's Shakespeare thus emerges as a moral and somewhat unimaginative figure, a writer who seldom interrupts or stands on their heads the didactic impulses of the "moral" plays by which he was influenced.

The book also embodies an unintentional irony. Dessen—borrowing from Raymond Williams—talks interestingly about the way a lived culture gets reduced to a "selective tradition" as certain texts get privileged and others ignored. Part of Dessen's aim is to recover for us some understanding of the moral plays—now ignored, but immensely popular in the decades immediately before Kyd, Lyly, and Marlowe came to prominence. But instead of focusing primarily on these plays and on their place in sixteenth-century culture, Dessen uses them to direct more attention to the epitome of the selective tradition, Shakespeare. It is as if these plays still only have value as they point to and tell us more about "the bard." I, for one, would like to hear more about the conventions, social function, and relationship to other aspects of popular culture of plays such as *The Three Ladies of London,* for it is in providing a picture of what the "selective tradition" ignores that Dessen's book breaks the most new ground.

Diane Dreher's *Domination and Defiance: Fathers and Daughters in Shakespeare* does little to advance the important work of feminist scholarship. Dreher's focus is on the father-daughter bond in Shakespeare's plays, and her terms for examining this bond are largely drawn from developmental psychology. Shakespeare's characters—relentlessly treated as real people—either meet or fail to meet various "tasks" of the life cycle. Thus, for example, Ophelia, Hero, and Desdemona all fail the test of intimacy; Lear fails the test of integrity; while the androgynous heroines such as Portia, Viola, and Beatrice pass triumphantly through the difficult transition from adolescence to sexual and psychic maturity. Such assertions are both reductive and naive. In saying that the love of Desdemona and Othello fails "because they do not know who they are" (p. 93), Dreher trivializes the social issues being negotiated through Shakespeare's tragedy and makes it impossible to ask what ideological work is being performed by this particular representation of the union of a black man and a white woman. Characters are not real people, and Dreher's naive psychologizing keeps emptying her feminist critique of power. Morever, though Dreher wishes to place her discussion of the father/daughter bond in a Renaissance framework, she also flattens historical difference by seeing in the plays "our eternal drama of identity, of what it means to be a man or woman in this world, providing us with images of what we have been and the promise of what we may become" (p. 3). Predictably, for Dreher, Shakespeare is "ahead of his time" (p. 1). Her Shakespeare is on the side of the angels, castigating possessive fathers, supporting independent women, and affirming a thoroughly modern view of marriage as the cooperative, trusting relationship of equals. It is an understatement to suggest that the sexual politics of the plays are capable of less optimistic interpretations. The state of the discussion concerning Shakespeare's representation of gender has, by now, simply gone beyond the terms afforded by Dreher's analysis.

Charles Forker's *Skull Beneath the Skin: The Achievement of John Webster* is the longest (500 pages) of the books being reviewed. Its length comes from the fact that Forker gives the reader an inclusive picture, not only of the plays Webster wrote or partly wrote, but also of his life and of his posthumous reputation and influence right up to the present day. It is a work of painstaking and dedicated scholarship. Much of what Forker sets out to investigate is murky territory. For example, though something is known about Webster's family (his father was a maker and renter of coaches and carriages in the London parish of St. Sepulchre), we don't know where the playwright was educated. Forker, for good reasons, speculates that Webster went to the Merchant Taylors' School and the Inns of Court and provides full accounts of the kind of training Webster would have received at each. But that the playwright actually attended either remains uncertain. Similarly, while Webster clearly had a hand in the writing of a number of collaboratively-produced plays, just which plays and how large a hand are often unclear. Forker, however, gives the best account of these matters that we are likely to have for some time. Among other things, he convincingly argues that Webster collaborated with Middleton on *Anything for a Quiet Life* and with Fletcher, Massinger, and Ford on *The Fair Maid of the Inn*, these being plays where Webster's possible authorship has been in dispute.

As a critic of Webster's dramatic works, Forker is somewhat predictable. He takes the title of his book from Eliot's remarks on Webster, and there is a sense in which Forker is preoccupied with questions that have been well-debated in the criticism of the past several decades: are these plays decadent? what is their moral vision? are they unified? are the characters unified? Forker's chief critical argument is that it is the paradoxical proximity of love and death in Webster's work that both ties him to other playwrights of the period and gives his canon its overarching unity. This is a fairly general proposition which, to the extent it can serve to thread together the Webster canon, also serves to blur differences within that canon. Little attempt is made to link Webster's literary works to other signifying practices or to political and cultural phenomena in Jacobean society. And when contradictions in characterization are discussed, as in the case of Antonio in *The Duchess of Malfi*, these are most often attributed to "Webster's acknowledged interest in the mysterious unpredictabilities of personality and behavior" (p. 333), rather than to the contradictory nature of the literary schema from which Webster created such figures or to the contradictory ideological ends such representations served. In short, as a critic of Webster Forker is not overly adventuresome and does not move far beyond a formalist preoccupation with matters of character, theme, and aesthetic unity. There remains, then, I think, more for other scholars to do with Webster's texts, but no one, I believe, will want to undertake such work without first consulting Forker's ambitious and painstaking study.

In *Engagement with Knavery* Robert Jones examines an implied audience's changing engagement with four knaves—Richard III, the Jew of Malta, Volpone, and Vindice—during the course of performance. He asserts that these figures raise difficult questions of audience response because they all take part in morally repugnant actions. Focusing on techniques by which response is shaped, Jones examines, for example, how audience engagement with knaves increases as their knavery seems motivated more by love of sport than by love of gain (p. 10) and examines how, in the cases of Barbaras and Vindice, audience engagement increases at those times when the knave seems most in control of the sport and lessens as the knaves themselves are upstaged. While there is much—such as the historical dimensions of response—which a purely formalist approach to theatrical experience cannot encompass, within its own terms Jones's is a modest, but well-executed, project. His discussion of *Richard III* is not new, but the treatments of Volpone and Vindice are useful. In handling Barabas, Jones seems uncertain, probably because the switches in tone and point of view in Marlowe's play are unusually rapid and extreme and can only be adequately addressed—not by a formalist study such as this—but by an analysis of the social pressures and contradictory ideological forces traversing the play and disrupting both the representation of character and the management of response.

The subtitle of Stephen Kogan's *The Hieroglyphic King: Wisdom and Idolatry in the Seventeenth-Century Masque* signals his thesis. In the Jacobean period Jonson, Daniel, Chapman, and Campion made the masque a visionary vehicle for teaching a wisdom that "emanate(d) from heaven, not the court" (p. 106); in the Caroline period Townshend, Carew, and Davenant used it to promote the idolatrous worship of Charles and Maria and substituted stupifying spectacle for moral revelation. Milton's *Comus* is presented as the only exception. Useful as the book sometimes is on the moral and intellectual significance of a masque's structure and iconography, such absolute distinctions between Jacobean and Caroline practice seem questionable. Moreover, read in the light of Leah Marcus's study, *The Hieroglyphic King* also seems historically impoverished, inattentive both to the specific occasions of performance and to the specific political questions addressed through a given masque. Finally, Kogan does not convey a strong sense of the complexity of the masque as teased out by critics such as Orgel, Strong, and Goldberg: its capacity to embody contradiction, to efface and promote its creators, to praise and dispraise the monarchs it honors. In short, in pursuing his narrative of the masque's moral and aesthetic decline, Kogan makes the masques of both periods less contradictory and less politically charged than they probably were.

Jerzy Limon's *Dangerous Matter: English Drama and Politics in 1623/24* argues that in late 1623 and early 1624 Buckingham and Prince Charles orchestrated a propaganda campaign—making heavy use of theatrical productions—to celebrate the collapse of the Spanish match and to critique aspects of James's foreign policy: namely, his failure to offer military support to the Protestant cause in Europe, especially the campaign to recover the Palatinate, and his failure to break decisively with Spain. Limon gives detailed topical readings of five dramatic works—*Neptune's Triumph, The Sun's Darling, The Life of the Duchess of Suffolk, The Bondman,* and *A Game at Chesse*—to show how they allude to the contemporary political scene. Much of Limon's argument is speculative. He can offer, for example, almost no direct evidence of Buckingham and Charles's sponsorship of the plays in question or of their links to an *organized* propaganda campaign. Readings of Jonson's masque and Middleton's play belabor the obvious political references; readings of the other three works stretch to bring into view a coherent political intent. But grant Limon the truth of every one of his claims about these five plays and even of their sponsorship, and the book still would leave many important questions largely unanswered: how typical are these plays of Jacobean theatrical practice? does their staging revise our understanding of how censorship of theater operated in the period? in the Jacobean social formation, could a stage play function as propaganda *in the same way* as a news sheet or religious treatise—modes of writing to which Limon compares these plays? perhaps most crucially, does the reproduction of political propaganda on the stage in any way alter, destabilize, or transform that discourse? Topical studies often flatten dramatic works to make them simply redactions of "real world" events. Once the key to unlock the text's elaborate system of allusions has been identified, the work's "meaning" is assumed to have been exhausted and the critic's task completed. Limon's work is really no exception, though as an example of the genre it is a serious and in places a persuasive undertaking. But it suggests to me the need for further work on the whole topic of topicality and its role in a more ambitiously conceived historical and political analysis of drama.

Originally published in France in 1981 as *Le Proche et Le Lointain*, Richard Marienstras's anthropological study of Shakespeare has been translated into English by Janet Lloyd and issued under the duller title *New Perspectives on the Shakespearean World.* Drawing on the work of Mary Douglas and Claude Levi-Strauss, Marienstras examines how the Elizabethans drew boundaries between the forbidden and the acceptable, the foreigner and the citizen, the wild and the civilized, and how we find traces of those boundaries in Shakespeare's plays. There are some truly fascinating chapters in the book on things such as Edward Coke's legal decisions determining who was a subject of James I and who a foreigner, and discriminating, as well, among the *types* or categories of "the foreign" into which one could fall. This discussion precedes chapters on the foreigner in *Othello* and *The Tempest*. Similarly, a wonderful discussion of the laws governing the King's forests, demarcating its boundaries, and specifying how hunting was regulated in and near those forests, precedes a chapter on *Titus Andronicus*. Throughout, Marienstras's objective is to show how Elizabethan culture established symbolic boundaries and the consequences of transgressing those boundaries through acts of incest, regicide, cross-cultural marriage, etc.

I don't think the strength of the book is that Marienstras provides strikingly new readings of the plays he examines. We already know, for example, that good and evil don't stay completely separate in *Macbeth*, that the outlaw hero, in his function as *pharmakos*, or victim, is made to seem more foreign to his culture than is really the case. We know that in *Titus Andronicus* the juxtaposition of city and forest is part of a complex and ironic meditation on the boundary between the wild and the civilized. Still, the book for me achieved something new in the way it wove the plays into a dense web of culturally-specific signifying practices stretching far beyond the drama. From this study Shakespeare emerges less as universal genius than as the denizen of a culture that in some ways is very foreign to a modern sensibility. Two things emerging sharply from Marienstras's study are the violence—literal and symbolic—and the xenophobia of Elizabethan society. Reading the book, I repeatedly felt that for me it was "making strange" the Renaissance England that so much Shakespeare criticism manages to make cozily familiar.

In Harry Morris's *Last Things in Shakespeare* we are offered a full-scale Christianizing of the Bard. He argues that a number of plays, including the four Bradley designated as "major," as well as comedies such as *As You Like It* and histories such as *Henry IV*, are preoccupied with last things: with death, judgment, salvation, and damnation. In his hands the plays become illustrations of Christian doctrine, and Shakespeare primarily an allegorical and emblematic playwright. As a relatively belated practitioner of this type of criticism, Morris does too little by way of answering the critiques to which it has been submitted. As a practical critic, he tends to the schematic, as when he argues that Macbeth is a bad man damned,

Lear a bad man saved, Othello a good man damned, and Hamlet a good man saved (p. 13). (One of the oddest features of the book, to me, was in fact the confidence with which Morris discerned who in the plays was damned and who saved.) The book's most incongruous reading, however, occurs when Hal's encounter with Francis becomes an allegory of Paul's saving mission to the Gentiles. While Shakespeare's plays are hardly free of Christian elements, Morris's book obscures the extent to which the Renaissance stage was something other than an apparatus for the dissemination of religious doctrine.

Dale B. J. Randall's monograph, *"Theatres of Greatness": A Revisionary View of Ford's "Perkin Warbeck,"* reopens the question of the date of *Perkin Warbeck.* Randall believes the play more likely to have been composed in 1622 or 1623, before the proposed Spanish match so spectacularly fell through, than in the early 1630s, close to the play's publication date of 1634. Randall argues that the play bears the imprint of the later years of James's reign because it offers a positive treatment of a Spanish marriage for one of Henry's children, focuses on Henry VII, a figure with whom James liked to compare himself, and emphasizes themes dear to James, such as the desirability of the Union of Scotland and England and the desirability of a king being a peacemaker. In short, the play enacts a conservative praise of James by means of its flattering portrait of Henry VII. I find that portrait *less* flattering than does Randall and the politics of the play more ambiguous, but this monograph succeeds in calling in question the assumption made by many scholars that the play is definitely a product of the reign of Charles.

In *Shakespeare's Lost Play* Eric Sams revives Ephraim Everitt's suggestion that *Edmund Ironside* is an early play by Shakespeare, one written sometime around 1589, which anticipates both the later history plays and the Senecan concerns of *Titus Andronicus.* Sams bases his claims mostly on stylistic evidence, arguing that the author of *Edmund Ironside* used certain words, phrases, and image clusters characteristic of the early Shakespeare. Such evidence is notoriously inconclusive. Having read the play, I must say that I found the case for Shakespearean authorship less apparent than Sams does. Those interested in assessing his argument will find it set forth at length both in an introduction and in the copious commentary which follows the play text.

Everything in Paul Siegel's *Shakespeare's English and Roman History Plays* follows from his unproblematized adoption of Marx and Engel's statement that "the ruling ideas of each age have ever been the ideas of its ruling class" (p. 22). Consequently, while he argues that Renaissance drama was largely produced for a bourgeois audience, it expressed the ideology of the aristocracy. "Christian humanism was the ideology of the new aristocracy, the dominant ideology of 'the period of transition' under absolute monarchy, and it received expression in the great literary works of the period as well as in the drama. That it lies behind the popular drama written for predominantly middle-class audiences illustrates the ideological subjection of which Marx and Engels speak" (p. 22). Holding these views, Siegel reads Shakespeare's plays on English and Roman history as illustrations of the cultural orthodoxies outlined in Tillyard's work on the Elizabethan world picture, with the difference that for Siegel these are not an innocent set of culturally neutral beliefs, but the product of a particular class used to rationalize the social position of that class. Consequently, he sees the history and Roman plays as vehicles for disseminating the view that the hierarchical social order is natural and inevitable, that regicide is an unspeakable crime (as is the killing of Caesar), and that Providence oversees men's affairs and punishes rebels. Of course, in reading the plays, Siegel acknowledges that they are complex literary works which complicate the ideological positions they enact, but he remains committed to the idea that in essence this drama disseminates the coherent ideological views of the dominant social class.

That Elizabethan drama simply reflects a class ideology seems questionable. This is partly because the Elizabethan stage, with its mixture of popular and elite elements, was probably as much a site for ideological contestation as a site where a monolithic ideological position was simply replicated. Moreover, much contemporary work on ideology suggests that a dominant ideology is produced only through the process of social struggle (between classes, but also between other social groups) and that the resulting "dominant ideology" always bears traces of the contestatory or subversive elements it has attempted to recuperate. These traces remain as elements of volatility within the dominant position. Michael Bristol's work on traces of popular carnival in Renaissance drama indicates one way destabilizing elements appear within theatrical works. Moreover, Walter Cohen has argued that one has to pay attention, as well, to the material conditions of Renaissance theatrical production in judging its ideological effects. He argues that there is a tension between the essentially artisanal mode of Renaissance theatrical production and the aristocratic ideologies enacted in many plays and that this tension also creates ideological volatility. In short, Siegel's goal of talking about the drama in relationship to class interests and economic formations is an important one, but it is probably far too simple to argue that that drama simply reflects the coherent ideological position of a dominant aristocratic class. Viewed from that perspective, the plays themselves become remarkably free of contradictions, gaps, silences, and signs of struggle. They illustrate, instead, a unified world view which is a class view—which is why Siegel ends up arguing for the rehabilitation of Tillyard.

In *Dreams of Love and Power: On Shakespeare's Plays,* Joseph Summers focuses on seven plays which in some way treat of love and/or power and the relations between them. Thus, for example, *The Winter's Tale* is viewed as a play which explores the destructiveness of power and leads to the embrace of love. Summers asserts that he is not interested in adopting a self-consciously theoretical approach to the plays, but in working from specific dramatic cruxes or problems toward an understanding of the play as a whole. Thus, in discussing *Lear,* he focuses on the problematic ending: does Lear believe Cordelia lives? Why does it matter? In discussing *The Tempest,* he focuses on the long second scene of exposition, inquiring into its function, particularly in demonstrating Prospero's anger, which for Summers is what the play's events must exorcise. Both for the problems it explores and for its method of close reading, *Dreams of Love and Power: On Shakespeare's Plays* covers familiar ground.

Rowland Wymer's *Suicide and Despair in the Jacobean Drama* begins with approving remarks about E. D. Hirsch's theories of authorial intention, ends with a brief poke at Jonathan Dollimore's materialist analysis of divided subjectivities in the Renaissance, and in between offers a traditional history-of-ideas approach to the representation of suicide on the Renaissance stage. Wymer's chief argument is that while suicide was condemned by Christian theologians, Renaissance writers were also influenced in their depiction of suicide by the writings, in particular, of classical philosophers who in certain instances argued that suicide was a way to insure individual honor or to defy political tyranny. Moreover, the suicide of particular groups—such as women who kill themselves to protect their chastity or to wipe away the stain of rape—was in a variety of dramatic and nondramatic contexts depicted approvingly in the Renaissance. Consequently, Wymer argues, the stage depiction of suicide was often a contradictory affair, with the deed provoking sympathy even as it figured as a sign of despair or divine retribution. The plays Wymer discusses were primarily staged between 1600 and 1625 and include several of Shakespeare's tragedies and a number of works by Marston, Chapman, Middleton, Massinger, Webster, and Beaumont and Fletcher.

IV

Collections of essays on Renaissance drama proliferate like rabbits, and too many have no clear purpose. A case in point is *Drama in the Renaissance,* edited by Clifford Davidson, C. J. Gianakaris, and John H. Stroupe. The twenty essays discuss drama from Lyly to Ford and do so employing an odd mix of critical approaches ranging from a computer-based analysis of Jonson's attitudes toward various social classes to thematic studies of love in Renaissance comedy to traditional source study to a new historicist approach to the relationship between language and a changed political order in *Coriolanus.* No common purpose, problem, or approach binds the collection together; moreover, all the essays have already appeared in *Comparative Drama,* so that the volume cannot even claim to present new material. The collection seems to exist primarily so that the three-volume series on medieval, Renaissance, and modern drama of which it is a part can fulfill its obligation to "cover," however eclectically, the second of these periods.

By contrast, *Shakespeare and the Question of Theory,* edited by Patricia Parker and Geoffrey Hartman, does have a unifying purpose, which is to consider Shakespeare in relationship to the emerging debates within contemporary criticism and theory. Of course, theory isn't a monolithic entity, and it is worth noting that the volume evokes Derrida and Lacan far more often than Marx or Bakhtin to justify its undertakings. In short, deconstruction and psychoanalysis figure more prominently than more overtly political theoretical discourses. Moreover, whatever kind of theoretical model is evoked, it is put in this volume in the service of a reading of a Shakespeare text (the exception is Terence Hawkes's investigation of the cultural forces producing Dover Wilson's *What Happens in Hamlet).*

These observations lead me to my chief critique of the volume: namely, that, despite its title, it does not sufficently make a *question* of theory. It mounts no sustained arguments for either the necessity or the dangers of theory; and it is reticent in its treatment of the divisions within the "theory establishment" about the relative value of various *kinds* of theory and their political implications. Just as importantly, the volume only infrequently lets theory question traditional critical practices. In a world where "theory" has a place, is its function primarily to authorize a variety of "new readings?" Or can theory significantly alter the objects to which we attend as critics and our *modes* of attention? How will/could theory alter the form or the content of the Shakespeare classroom? These are some of the questions which this volume prompts/invites, and which it in general addresses only glancingly, rather than in a sustained fashion.

Nonetheless, these reservations don't change the fact that this is the most ambitious collection of essays on Renaissance drama published this year and the one which opens the most new territory. And if some of the essays end up being rather like old formalist readings in new language, others attain the polemical and speculative edge that at its best such an undertaking invites. Stephen Greenblatt, for example, opens his piece on Shakespeare and the exorcists by talking about how contemporary theory has changed his critical practice by subverting his ideas of the autonomy of literature, and also goes on to examine aspects of the deconstructive project. By contrast, Geoffrey Hartman, in his essay on *Twelfth Night,* carries on an oblique critique of those modes of systematic criticism, including some versions of political and historical criticism, which flatten the Shakespearean text to the contours of an external ground. And in an extremely controversial essay, Jonathan Goldberg uses a mixture of contemporary genre theory and the French feminism of Luce Irigary to call in question certain types of feminist criticism relying on essentialist and fixed notions both of gender difference and of genre, but in making his case comes perilously close to arguing that patriarchal oppression did not exist in the Renaissance. Such pieces invite argument, refutation, rejoinder. They indicate some of the consequences of theory for critical practice; they begin to indicate what is at stake, politically, in situating oneself within one theoretical discourse as opposed to another. At its best this volume invites such political and critical self-awareness and invites changed practices; at its weakest it demonstrates that theory will not automatically, by itself, change anything essential.

Shakespeare Study Today, edited by Georgianna Ziegler, is another of the collections of essays appearing this year. These papers, originally presented in 1982 to celebrate the fiftieth year of the Horace Howard Furness Memorial Library at the University of Pennsylvania, aim in a general way to assess the state of those institutions and practices by which the Shakespeare industry sustains itself in this country. The volume is interesting in that it contains no "readings." Instead, it includes pieces as diverse as O. B. Hardison, Jr.'s account of his stewardship of the Folger Library during his term as Director, and the late Bernard Beckerman's analysis of why there are at present no great American Shakespeare actors. The volume also includes an essay by Fredson Bowers and a strong one by Steven Urkowitz on the state of Shakespearean textual scholarship, and an interesting piece by Ann Cook in which she not only surveys the development of Shakespearean scholarship in this century, but begins to analyze the social factors (political, economic, and demographic) which have affected that development. The concluding biographical essay on Horace Howard Furness allows one to glimpse the quite different conditions under which the scholarship of another era was conducted. This is not a groundbreaking collection, but taken together the essays reveal just how thoroughly Shakespeare libraries, theaters, journals, conferences, and scholars are indeed part of a cultural industry in which fashion, money, and politics play as large a role as does the disinterested love of "great literature."

Another collection, *Shakespeare and His Contemporaries: Essays in Comparison*, edited by E. A. J. Honigmann, has the laudable aim of reading Shakespeare in relationship to his fellow Elizabethan dramatists. The conditions for the investigation, however, have been limited by the editorial decision to have each contributor focus on just two texts, one by Shakespeare and one by "another" dramatist, in order to see what is unique or technically inventive in the practice of each. A number of the resulting essays are narrow in focus, and a number unimaginatively use the comparative mode primarily to argue, yet again, that Shakespeare surpasses his fellows as a theatrical craftsman. A few pieces stand out as more ambitious or imaginative than the majority in the collection. Philip Edwards, discussing *The Old Wives Tale* and *The Winter's Tale*, explores the remarkable inventiveness of Peele in juxtaposing narration and dramatic enactment in ways that enabled Shakespeare's later experiments in the romances. Alexander Leggatt, comparing representations of kingship in *Richard II* and *Perkin Warbeck*, concludes by showing how the notion of a private sphere begins to emerge in the Caroline history play in ways that transform the terms of the genre. Perhaps most provocative is George Hunter's "Bourgeois Comedy: Shakespeare and Dekker" which looks at *The Shoemaker's Holiday* and *The Merry Wives of Windsor* in terms of the way citizen comedy handles, or avoids handling, the economic and class divisions which lie at its heart. Hunter's essay refreshingly opens the literary texts to the social world beyond the text and presents Shakespeare's—not as the best—but simply one of the possible responses to social and economic dislocation.

Comedy from Shakespeare to Sheridan honors Eugene Waith, a preeminent scholar of Renaissance drama and a much-esteemed teacher. The editors of the volume, A. R. Braunmuller and J. C. Bulman, have given it unity by having contributors focus on the genre of comedy in the sixteenth, seventeenth, and eighteenth centuries. While the quality of the essays varies, there are a number of good pieces ranging from George Hunter's look at the respective importance of plot and character in organizing particular types of comedy to Jonas Barish's focused examination of three Caroline plays—*The Roman Actor, The Muses' Looking-Glass,* and *The Antipodes*—which in varying and sometimes in contradictory ways offered replies to the decade's anti-theatrical polemic. Occasionally, the essays take issue with one another in interesting ways. For example, Gail Paster and Philip Edwards each examine Massinger's *A New Way to Pay Old Debts* and reach quite different conclusions about the reasons for, and the significance of, the Sir Giles Overreach character's schemes for an aristocratic marriage for his daughter. By mingling essays from scholars working on the comic drama over the course of several centuries, *Comedy from Shakespeare to Sheridan* pays tribute to the range of Waith's own interests and to the quality of the publications and the teaching by which his influence has been felt.

Two scholars have given us collections of their own essays. The first, Samuel Schoenbaum's *Shakespeare and Others*, is a fairly light affair, a gathering of essays, reviews, and occasional lectures. I was surprised at some inclusions—do we, for example, really need chatty accounts of Shakespeare conferences in exotic quarters of the globe? The stronger pieces reveal Schoenbaum's skills as a literary sleuth and master of the arcane facts of Shakespeare's life and times. The opening essay, for example, explores just how many and what kind of books would have been available to Shakespeare as he grew up in Stratford; other useful pieces assess A. L. Rowse's claims to have discovered Shakespeare's "dark lady" and examine for their probability a host of stories that grew up from the seventeenth to the twentieth century about the personal and artistic relations of Shakespeare and Ben Jonson. It is in Schoenbaum's witty exploration of such topics that readers will find the volume's greatest value.

Leo Salingar's *Dramatic Form in Shakespeare and the Jacobeans* offers meatier critical fare. Salingar states that his seven essays on Shakespeare and six on other Jacobean dramatists are bound together by a concern for dramatic form and for "the relations between Elizabethan drama and its setting" (p. vii). In practice, this often means connecting a play to its sources, as when the form of *The Revenger's Tragedy* is explained by its relationship to the medieval morality play (p. 207), or Aristophanes is evoked as the model for Jonson's principles of comic construction (p. 158). In connecting plays to their setting, Salingar also often seems to mean tracing ideas in the plays to their extradramatic origins, as when he finds bits of Harsnett and Montaigne in *Lear* (pp. 107-39), or connects Shakespeare's treatment of art in his later plays to the larger Renaissance debate over the meaning of the term (pp. 1-18). There is immense learning in this book, and much critical acumen, but often art works get treated as reflections of something antecedent to themselves rather than as agents of cultural production, and often the historical and cultural matrix or setting of Jacobean theater shrinks to mean the literary and philosophical matrix, not politics, economics, demography, or the range of social practices examined by the new historicists. And there is only so far one can go in relating a play to its cultural setting if one stays primarily in the domain of intellectual history. In several of the essays on the non-Shakespearean drama Salingar does venture onto the terrain of social history. In a particularly successful essay on *Bartholomew Fair,* for example, he looks at the changing conditions of the commercial theater in Jacobean London and at the play as Jonson's attempt to represent "London society considered as a literary or theatrical public" (p. 198), a concept which, Salingar argues, the play helped to bring into being. Most often, however, it is literary antecedents and "ideas," rather than social factors, that provide the points of reference for Salingar's analyses.

V

A number of books this year deal with the historical development of Shakespeare studies or with the staging, editing, or criticism of Renaissance drama in the eighteenth, nineteenth, and twentieth centuries. The purpose of Arthur Sherbo's *The Birth of Shakespeare Studies: Commentators from Rowe (1709) to Boswell-Malone (1821)* is to trace which particular people—many of them now largely unknown—contributed the explanatory or interpretive notes for editions of Shakespeare compiled between 1709 and 1821. The project thus described seems stupifyingly dull, but in the execution proves otherwise. Sherbo writes with wit and economy and has delivered a book which not only recovers the identities of many now-obscure annotators, but also casts light on the collaborative processes of eighteenth-century editing and provides a useful companion to the variorum editions of Shakespeare. Along the way, Sherbo records many learned and useful, and also some bizarre and funny, notes to the plays, my favorite of which is George Steevens's baroque fantasia—attributed to a probably non-existent Mr. Collins— on Thersites' use of the phrase "potato finger."

In *"One Touch of Shakespeare"* John W. Velz and Frances H. Teague provide a careful edition of a number of letters written between 1875 and 1878 by Joseph Crosby, a Shakespeare enthusiast and collector of a distinguished private library of Shakespeare materials who passed most of his adult life in the grocery business in Zanesville, Ohio. The letters were all written to Joseph Parker Norris, a Philadelphia lawyer and fellow Shakespeare enthusiast. Collectively they establish Crosby's credentials as a Shakespeare scholar (especially his philological skills and his ability to explicate difficult textual cruxes), and the obsessiveness of his dedication to Shakespeare. Not only did he, after a day of business, write thirty-page letters to Norris about the meaning of words such as "over-scutched," but he lined his meager living quarters with Shakespeare memorabilia and fantasized about the day when there would be a magazine devoted entirely to writings about Shakespeare. The correspondence also reveals much about Shakespeare's role in small-town American culture during this period. Crosby describes the Shakespeare reading clubs which formed in towns like Zanesville or Wheeling, West Virginia, and the production of comparatively cheap subscription editions of Shakespeare which brought the bard to the reading public in financially and intellectually manageable installments. In short, this well-done volume contains a good deal of useful information.

A good companion piece to the Velz and Teague volume is the lavishly illustrated *Shakespeare and the Victorian Stage*, edited by Richard Foulkes. This collection of essays covers many aspects of Victorian stage production of Shakespeare: costumes, sets, prominent actors and actresses, and their acting styles (including foreign actors such as Salvini), the nature of cuts in acting texts, music, and Shakespeare's role in provincial theater outside of London. The book reminds us of the tension between the Victorians' desire to restore a more authentic Shakespearean text and the continuing desire for stage spectacle and pictorial effects which precluded using anything but heavily cut and rearranged acting versions of the plays; and it reveals the tension between the desire for antiquarian accuracy in costume and setting and the countless ways in which Victorian productions reflect Victorian values and preoccupations. Marion

Jones, for example, describes how archeologically "correct" and "picturesque" costumes were created for the Victorian stage, but also looks at the anomalies produced when actors insisted on wearing Victorian underwear and Victorian hairstyles with their "Roman" togas or "Elizabethan" gowns. Among the stronger essays, Peter Thompson writes provocatively of how Henry Irving's acting style embodies both a display and a critique of Victorian codes of manliness and self-confidence; Gary Mazer of the link between the criminal and the actor in the career and writings of H. B. Irving, Henry's son; and Christopher Murray of why the now-forgotten playwright, James Sheridan Knowles, could for much of the Victorian period have been favorably compared with Shakespeare. Provocative, but unfinished, is Jeremy Crump's examination of how Shakespeare may have functioned in popular working class culture in the nineteenth century, both as an agent of middle class attempts to "civilize" the working class and, conversely, as an instrument for strengthening class consciousness and articulating a radical critique of middle-class culture.

Despite the obvious strengths of individual essays, the volume as a whole is weakened by the essentially descriptive cast of many of the pieces included. Often, the material that has been unearthed cries out for a more imaginative and purposeful analysis. Moreover, one wants to ask—why do this kind of theater history anyway? What motivates a concern with the Victorians? Why attend to *certain* aspects of their theatrical appropriation of Shakespeare and not to others? For the most part the volume avoids engaging such questions. In doing so, it flirts with the antiquarian fiction that the past is simply "there" for retrieval and its retrieval a self-evident good, rather than exploring and justifying the problematic and political nature of any encounter with the past.

John Crawford's *Early Shakespearean Actresses* provides impressionistic, highly romanticized accounts of the lives and careers of a handful of women who played Shakespearean roles from the seventeenth to the nineteenth centuries. The book trivializes its material.

Christine Dymkowski's *Harley Granville Barker: A Preface to Modern Shakespeare* examines some of Barker's critical and theatrical work with Shakespeare. The book has three parts: discussions of the Savoy productions of 1912-1914, of Barker's Shakespeare criticism, and of the *Prefaces* to *Lear* and the 1940 production of that play starring Gielgud and partly directed by Barker. The book rehearses the by-now-familiar story of Barker's importance to the "theatrical revolution" of the early part of the century without adding a great deal to our understanding of his contributions. Examination of Barker's importance to Shakespeare criticism is impeded by Dymkowski's failure to discuss any of the *Prefaces* except that to *Lear*. Lavishly illustrated, the book is best as a descriptive account of the actual productions with which Barker was involved.

Ejner Jensen's *Jonson's Comedies on the Modern Stage* documents Jonson's increasing popularity on the twentieth-century stage after nearly a century of theatrical neglect. Jensen recapitulates the familiar story of Jonson's unpopularity in the nineteenth century: the criticism that, unlike Shakespeare, his characters are artificial, his inventions labored, and his language marred by pedantry and obscenity. Jensen then describes—sometimes quite sketchily and usually quite unanalytically—all the professional productions of Jonson that occurred between 1899 and 1972, the 400th anniversary of the dramatist's birth. The book reads like a list, which it essentially is. Only occasionally does Jensen use prompt books and other records of production to give a fuller account of particular performances than the accounts available in the newspapers. While Jonson scholars may occasionally turn to this book for basic information about twentieth-century productions, it is not an ambitious or satisfying study.

Players of Shakespeare, edited by Philip Brockbank, offers essays by twelve distinguished actors describing how they created a role in a particular Royal Shakespeare Company production. Most of these accounts have an absorbing, you-were-there quality produced by the first person narration and by the considerable wittiness of the writers (see, for example, Roger Rees's very funny self-assessment of his career as a Shakespearean actor before being offered the part of Posthumus); and the whole is enlivened by bits of theatrical gossip such as Sinead Cusack's half-resentful, half-admiring account of John Barton's directing techniques. Besides being entertaining, the book usefully reminds academic critics that stereotypes of inarticulate or anti-intellectual actors will hardly bear scrutiny. RSC actors, at least, can write and research with the best of the academic crowd. For most, preparing a role clearly includes knowing "the criticism," finding out how others have played the part, and going in detail through a good annotated edition of the play. As a result, Shakespeare critics will feel at home with this book, largely because the RSC obviously takes the scholarship *we* produce seriously; and we return the compliment by flocking to RSC productions on our leaves and vacations. We are simply in different, but related, branches of the Shakespeare industry.

In the end, of course, the book also makes clear some of the genuine differences between the study and the stage. The writers speak often of the unpredictable aspects of performance, of the occasional difficulties with directors, and of the effects of set and costume design on an actor's performance. As Brenda Bruce archly remarks, "The first time I played Gertrude in *Hamlet* I was encased in white sheepskin. I felt and looked like a bedside rug" (p. 94). The book is full of remarks that remind one that the actor often works under very particular conditions of constraint.

While most of the essays in the volume offer interesting glimpses into the Shakespearean actor's trade—as plied in the special environment of the RSC—some do more. Tony Church's discussion of the difference in his 1965 and his 1980 portrayals of Polonius is a case in point. The essay not only describes two quite different interpretations of the role and of the play, but also shows how contemporary events in English public life spawned these two quite different productions. Other essays, such as Patrick Stewart's intelligent and probing account of playing Shylock, make clear how much any production of Shakespeare is in conversation with past productions, since one of Stewart's chief problems was how to bring a fresh understanding to a role already so strongly interpreted by prior actors.

The RSC, of course, probably looks over its shoulder more than most theatrical companies which attempt Shakespeare because it is *the* Shakespearean company of the English-speaking world. Its job, in part, is to preserve Shakespeare as a national treasure. Consequently, what we don't get in *Players of Shakespeare* are accounts of any truly iconoclastic or irreverent productions of Shakespeare, nor accounts of acting techniques which aim at anything other than a convincing enactment of characters conceived of as "real people." As Brockbank says in the introduction, it is Stanislavski, not Brecht, whose voice is heard in these accounts of acting Shakespeare. For alternative acting styles and alternative Shakespeares one will probably have to look beyond the RSC, but *Players of Shakespeare* offers an entertaining glimpse into what it was like in the 1970s and 1980s to create Shakespearean roles within that particular institutional framework.

VI

Turning now to editions of dramatic texts, one bumps first against A. L. Rowse, whose first objective in his modernized texts of

Shakespeare, now being published in inexpensive paper editions by the University Press of America, is to make Shakespeare accessible to students and other readers who have trouble with Elizabethan English. Consequently, Rowse replaces obsolete or obscure words with terms in common use today, banishes Shakespeare's *thees, thous, wouldsts* and *shouldsts,* removes "superfluous" subjunctives and most contractions, and performs a host of other "tidying up" operations on the texts.

Judged simply by how well these texts make Shakespeare accessible to use by moderns, I think they fail miserably. Put kindly, the critical introductions are extremely sketchy; and for every obscure term silently replaced, a dozen more remain unaltered and hence incomprehensible, since Rowse offers next to no explanatory material in notes. It is instructive to compare, as I did, a notoriously difficult scene, II.iv of *1 Henry IV,* in the Rowse and Penguin editions. I had no trouble deciding that if I wanted students simply to comprehend what was happening in the scene, I'd send them to the Penguin text with its copious notes rather than to Rowse's eclectic modernization.

These editions, however, not only fail their stated objectives; they are in some other important ways simply offensive. Each volume of the series begins with the essay, "Why a Contemporary Shakespeare?" Rowse's answer seems to be: because a modernized Shakespeare better enables England to maintain—if not her political—at least her cultural hegemony. Rowse unabashedly writes: "We must remember that he (Shakespeare) is our greatest asset, and that other peoples use him a great deal in learning our language. There are no Iron Curtains for him—though, during Mao's Cultural Revolution in China, he was prohibited. Now that the ban has been lifted, I learn that the Chinese in thousands flock to his plays" (p. 4). Elsewhere, explaining why he got rid of Shakeapeare's "superfluous subjunctives" he writes: "I see no point whatever in retaining them. They only add superfluous trouble in learning English, when the great appeal of our language as a world-language is precisely that it has less grammar to learn than almost any. Russian is unbelievably complicated. Inflected languages—German is like Latin in this respect—are really rather backward; it has been a great recommendation that English has been more progressive in this respect in simplifying itself" (p. 5). The chauvinism of this passage is stunning. Still later, Rowse recounts how he once talked with President Reagan about Reagan's having played Petruchio in his youth and then says (of Reagan): "In Britain last year we saw a fine performance of his on horseback in Windsor Park alongside of Queen Elizabeth II—very familiar ground to William Shakespeare and Queen Elizabeth I, as we know from *The Merry Wives of Windsor*" (p. 8). The national poet, Queen Elizabeth I, Queen Elizabeth II, the President of the United States—they are all implicity conjoined in the project of preserving the West and its "progressive" language and culture.

One of the many ironies of Rowse's undertaking, however, is that in using Shakespeare to build a bridge between England's past and present greatness, Rowse has to erase all signs of Shakespeare's historical difference, his otherness, partly as that is manifest in linguistic difference. While most editions gloss hard words in the margins or the footnotes, Rowse does it silently, through substitutions within the text. The Elizabethan and the modern become one, and the traces of the join are erased. What is muted, as well, is the sense of linguistic difference *within* the plays. The characters—thanks to Rowse's modernizations and his emphasis on "correctness" in grammar—sound more alike than they should, the rougher edges of class, gender, or regional differences shaved away. Instead, we get a donnish "correct" Shakespeare, useful for teaching English to "foreigners." The point is not that Rowse dares to tamper with the Shakespearean text. The more we learn about the way compositors, actors, editors, and even perhaps Shakespeare himself have continuously "tampered" with the Shakespearean text, the more we may have to acknowledge the inescapability of this activity. To read, to act, to edit Shakespeare is to rewrite him continuously. But that does not mean one should not resist those rewritings, like Rowse's, which suppress history and actively beat the drums for notions of national superiority and practices of cultural imperialism that the world can well do without.

By contrast, the New Cambridge Shakespeare editions proceed more cautiously. Philip Brockbank's general preface says of the undertaking: "while offering ample academic guidance, it reflects current critical interests and is more attentive than some earlier editions have been to the realisation of the plays on the stage, and to their social and cultural settings. . . . Although modernised, the edition conserves forms that appear to be expressive and characteristically Shakespearean, and it does not attempt to disguise the fact that the plays were written in a language other than that of our own time" (p. v).

The note of moderation stuck in these lines (scholarly but up to date, modernized but conservative) is fully exemplified in Elizabeth

Story Donno's edition of *Twelfth Night.* Her notes on the text are copious and helpful and the introductory essay thoroughly professional, though that introduction adds little to conventional views of the play. There is, for example, almost no discussion of the work's social and cultural setting, as promised by Brockbank, even though it may be the comedies which stand most in need of such an analysis; nor does the critical commentary go much beyond a discussion of the major characters: their popularity and function. What particularly distinguishes Donno's edition is the degree to which attention is paid to stage history and staging possibilities both in the introductory essay and in the textual commentary. A number of photos and illustrations accompany the introduction, showing scenes from notable productions of the play or instances of famous actors engaging one of its roles.

Russell Fraser's edition of *All's Well That Ends Well* resembles Donno's generally cautious mode of proceeding, except that the textual annotations are less extensive and less attention is paid to the performance potential and history of the play. In fact, Fraser argues in his introduction that there is much in the plays that is not able to be conveyed on the stage. To appreciate these things one must "follow Lamb's advice and read and ponder Shakespeare in your closet" (p. 13). The play is not historically contextualized, nor is there any mention of the new critical approaches to Shakespeare that reach beyond a concern for theme and character.

Obviously the volumes of this or any series vary considerably. Last year's *Richard II*, edited by Andrew Gurr, did strive to attend in a fresh way to the cultural matrix producing the text. But in the largest sense the *need* for this new edition of Shakespeare remains unclear. Each volume is handsomely produced (though I could do without the undistinguished illustrations by C. Walter Hodges), but expensive: $29.95 for each of the hardback editions sent for review. Though freshly edited, like most modern editions the New Cambridge seems to produce a conflation of quarto and folio readings where more than one text is available; like most modern editions it somewhat modernizes spelling and punctuation without "updating" Shakespeare in anything like Rowse's manner. In short, it is an edition that, while handsome and freighted with copious scholarship, takes few risks and does not represent a major alternative to existing editions such as the Arden Shakespeare. It is not an undertaking that—at least in the volumes I have seen—opens itself very widely to the current critical and editorial debates which supposedly are what called it forth and justified its predecessor's, *The New Shakespeare*'s, supersession.

By contrast, the new single-volume, modern-spelling Oxford Shakespeare has a surplus of innovation. Not being a textual scholar, I do not have the expertise to evaluate a number of the choices made in this edition, but let me describe some of its salient features and comment on a few of them. First, this edition expands the Shakespearean canon by including "various poems," of which the notorious "Shall I die" is one, the passages from *Sir Thomas More* attributed to Shakespeare, and *Two Noble Kinsmen,* which other editions have also included. It arranges the plays in the order of their supposed composition, rather than generically; and it lists them under their original titles. Thus, *3 Henry VI* is listed as *The True Tragedy of Richard Duke of York and the Good King Henry the Sixth* and is printed before *The First Part of Henry the Sixth; The Tragedy of Hamlet Prince of Denmark* precedes *Twelfth Night, or What You Will,* and *Henry VIII* appears as *All is True.*

More significantly, the editors have decided "when possible, to print the more theatrical version of each play. In some cases, this requires the omission from the body of the text of lines that Shakespeare certainly wrote; there is, of course, no suggestion that these lines are unworthy of their author; merely that, in some if not all performances, he and his company found that the play's overall structure and pace were better without them. All such lines are printed as Additional Passages at the end of the play" (p. xxxv). In practice, this means, for example, that the speech in which Horatio describes the eerie events in Rome before the death of Julius Caesar is printed among the "additional passages" at the end of the play since it appears only in Q2 and not in the Folio, which is deemed the most theatrical of the available texts. Furthermore, as one would expect, *King Lear,* which the editors believe was significantly revised by Shakespeare, appears in its entirety in two versions, one representing the folio and one the quarto text. The other four plays identified as having undergone revision after initial theatrical presentation—*Othello, Troilus and Cressida, 2 Henry IV,* and *Hamlet*—do not, however, appear in two separate versions. Rather than use a conflated text, though, the "more theatrical" copytext is followed.

Unfortunately, as of this writing, the supplemental volume, *William Shakespeare: A Textual Companion*, has not appeared. This volume will contain "a discussion of the text of each of Shakespeare's works accompanied by detailed notes on individual readings, lists of departures from the early editions, a reprint of the stage directions in the primary text of each play, an Appendix recording changes of lineation, and other relevant material" (quoted from page 1 of a publicity sheet distributed by Oxford Univ. Press). Also unavailable is the old-spelling single-volume edition of the plays which will parallel the volume under review, but will attempt as much as possible to duplicate the spelling, punctuation, stage directions, and scene divisions of the Renaissance scripts.

In principle I welcome a text prepared by "the new textual scholars" because it provides the occasion to raise basic questions about how we establish the "legitimacy" of a text, how an author's "canon" gets established and why we worry about the integrity of that canon, and why we would give priority to one authorial script over another or to an authorial script over one altered by other hands in the complicated process of theatrical production. In short, the Oxford volume provides the occasion to raise these important questions with students. I doubt, however, that it will ever appear in my undergraduate classroom because it doesn't meet *other* needs students have. It costs $45; it is extremely bulky; and it contains no explanatory notes of any kind and only the most cursory of one-page introductions to each play. While some editions freight the text with an overbearing apparatus that intimidates students, this is not always so. A text without notes, by contrast, implies that the passage of time doesn't matter and that words and their meanings are self-evident and unchanging. A text that puts all the notes in a companion volume, which I assume will also be expensive, asks students to move back and forth between two hefty books during the reading process. It won't happen. Presumably the old-spelling edition is meant for established scholars, and these objections don't pertain. The issuing of a modern-spelling edition with updated stage directions and punctuation and with modernized act divisions, however, implies that a student or general reader was imagined for the volume sent me for review. The present volume simply doesn't meet the needs of those readers. Undoubtedly it will make its way in the world because of its Oxford imprint and the amount of publicity that will be generated by the novelty of some of its editorial decisions. I wish it combined novelty with more attention to the general reader. And I wish some press would issue a paperback, well-annotated edition of the two texts of *Lear* and/or the three texts of *Hamlet*. It would be invaluable in the classroom and would let one address a number of important issues raised by the Oxford undertaking. It would also cost a lot less.

Also appearing this year is a useful edition of *A Yorkshire Tragedy*, edited by A. C. Cawley and Barry Gaines, for The Revels Plays, a series which has consistently made little-known plays of the Renaissance available in excellent modern editions. And Cambridge University Press has issued *The Selected Plays of John Ford*, edited by Colin Gibson, which includes *The Broken Heart, 'Tis pity She's A Whore,* and *Perkin Warbeck.*

VII

For reprints, this year saw the reissuing of Paul A. Jorgenson's 1962 monograph *Redeeming Shakespeare's Words* which looks—not at images—but at key words in selected plays such as *honesty* in *Othello* or *noble* in *Coriolanus.* Also reissued this year is an expanded version of R. S. White's *Shakespeare and the Romance Ending* (privately printed in 1981), now bearing the title *"Let Wonder Seem Familiar,"* and also White's *Innocent Victims: Poetic Injustice in Shakespearean Tragedy* (privately printed in 1982). The first examines the function of romance conventions in Shakespeare's comic conclusions; the second studies Shakespearean characters, especially women and children, who suffer unjustly and whose function is to "awaken our moral imaginations to the existence of injustice, and to train our own moral faculties" (p. 113).

Reference works published this year include, first, Michael Wentworth's *Thomas Heywood: A Reference Guide* which provides succinct annotations of material on Heywood published between 1808, when Lamb's *Specimens of English Dramatic Poets* appeared, and 1981-82. An introductory essay gives a brief history of Heywood criticism from the Elizabethan period to the present day; the body of the book arranges entries by year of publication, with the material for each arranged alphabetically by author's name. This lets one see how the issues of interest to Heywood scholars have changed over time, but it makes it difficult to locate all the material written about a particular play. An extremely comprehensive index, however, somewhat alleviates this problem since each play title is listed separately.

Mark Lidman's *Studies in Jacobean Drama, 1973-1984* is less successful. Presented as an update to Logan and Smith's *Recent Studies in Jacobean Drama,* the volume opens with a section on general studies of Jacobean theater between 1973 and 1984, and then provides separate sections on eleven dramatists of the Jacobean period (Chapman, Dekker, Thomas Heywood, Tourneur, Marston, Middleton, Webster, Massinger, Ford, Brome, and Shirley). Within each section, editions are listed first and then criticism, with entries arranged alphabetically by name of the critic. Consequently, one neither gets a sense of the year-by-year progression of the scholarship on a given author, nor a grouping of material on specific plays. No play or subject index is provided; the index simply lists the names of critics.

Reference works received dealing primarily with Shakespeare include, first, volume 3 of the series *Shakespearean Criticism* put out by the Gale Research Company. Intended for advanced high school and beginning college students, each volume offers a selection of criticism on four to six Shakespeare plays. Volume 3, edited by Laurie Harris and Mark Scott, treats *Macbeth, Midsummer Night's Dream, Troilus and Cressida,* and the three parts of *Henry VI.* Commentary on the plays is arranged historically; for *Macbeth,* for example, the first snippets are from Samuel Pepys, the last from Stephen Booth. At $82, the volume will be used in the library, presumably to show beginning students that the criticism of Shakespeare does, indeed, have a history, and that what texts mean has something to do with the historical conditions under which they are read. This may be the effect, as well, of the more ambitious Shakespeare Criticism series being published by Garland. This year three volumes are produced in this series: *"Twelfth Night": Critical Essays,* edited by Stanley Wells, *"Henry the Fourth Parts I and II": Critical Essays,* edited by David Bevington, and *"Hamlet": Critical Essays,* edited by Joseph Price. Each volume includes criticism by modern scholars, reviews of seminal performances, and essays of historical interest by figures such as Samuel Johnson, William Hazlitt, and Charles Lamb. The volumes are expensive ($54 and $62), but are well edited and well produced.

Another resource book suitable for actual use in the classroom is Graham Nicholls's brief paperback on *Measure for Measure* in Macmillan's Text and Performance series. Pitched, I feel, to students of high school age or to college freshmen, the book offers forty pages of basic commentary on the play and forty pages of discussion—with pictures—of four major stage or television productions of it. No substitute for going to a performance, the book nonetheless invites discussion of the difference between watching and reading a play and of performance as interpretation.

The year also brings two more volumes of the Garland Shakespeare Bibliographies. James Moore has done very well by *Richard III.* From opening essay to exhaustive index, the volume shows every sign of having been carefully put together. Along with criticism, editions, textual studies, and so forth, Moore also deals with such things as parodies of the play, and film, television, and recorded versions. D. Allen Carroll and Gary Jay Williams have produced a similar, if somewhat less strenuously inclusive, volume on *Midsummer Night's Dream*. The final bibliography for the year is Larry Champion's *The Essential Shakespeare: An Annotated Bibliography of Major Modern Studies*. Arranged primarily by plays, the book offers summaries of major criticism written between 1900 and 1984 and has a subject and author index.

And, finally, there has appeared a revised and enlarged edition of C. T. Onions's *A Shakespeare Glossary*. Prepared by Robert D. Eagleson, this edition has been able to take advantage of the computer-based concordances compiled since the second editon of 1919, as well as modern scholarship on Shakespeare's language. The result is an expanded and regularized reference tool of value to both beginning and seasoned scholars.

BOOKS RECEIVED

Anzai, Tetsuo, *Shakespeare and Montaigne Reconsidered*. Renaissance Monographs 12. Tokyo: Sophia Univ., 1986, Pp. 96. $25.00.

Bale, John. *The Complete Plays of John Bale*, vol. 1. Ed. Peter Happé. Woodbridge, Suffolk, and Dover, NH: Boydell and Brewer, 1985. Pp. 167. $41.25. ISBN 0-85991-174-8.

Barber, C. L., and Wheeler, Richard P. *The Whole Journey: Shakespeare's Power of Development*. Berkeley and London: Univ. of California Press, 1986. Pp. xxix + 354. $37.50. ISBN 0-520-05432-6.

Barroll, J. Leeds, ed. *Medieval & Renaissance Drama in England: An Annual Gathering of Research, Criticism, and Reviews*, vol. 2. New York: AMS Press, 1985. Pp. xiii + 364. $42.50. ISSN 0731-3403. ISBN 0-404-62300-X, set. ISBN 0-404-62302-6, vol. 2.

Bevington, David, ed. *"Henry the Fourth Parts I and II": Critical Essays*. New York and London: Garland, 1986. Pp. xxii + 457. $62.00. ISBN 0-8240-8706-2.

Braunmuller, A. R., and Bulman, J. C., eds. *Comedy from Shakespeare to Sheridan*. Newark: Univ. of Delaware Press, and London: Associated Univ. Presses, 1986. Pp. 290. $37.50. ISBN 0-87413-276-2.

Brennan, Anthony. *Shakespeare's Dramatic Structures*. London and Boston: Routledge & Kegan Paul, 1986. Pp. viii + 163. $49.95. ISBN 0-7102-0450-7.

Brockbank, Philip, ed. *Players of Shakespeare: Essays in Shakespearean Performance by Twelve Players with the Royal Shakespeare Company*. Cambridge and New York: Cambridge Univ. Press, 1985. Pp. xxi + 179. $22.95. ISBN 0-521-24428-5.

Bryant, J. A., Jr. *Shakespeare and the Uses of Comedy*. Lexington: Univ. Press of Kentucky, 1986. Pp. ix + 270. $26.00. ISBN 0-8131-1595-7.

Calderwood, James L. *If It Were Done: "Macbeth" and Tragic Action*. Amherst: Univ. of Massachusetts Press, 1986. Pp. xvii + 151. $17.50. ISBN 0-87023-534-6.

Carroll, D. Allen, and Williams, Gary Jay. *"A Midsummer Night's Dream": An Annotated Bibliography*. New York and London: Garland, 1986. Pp. xxxvii + 641. $75.00. ISBN 0-8240-9073-X.

Cawley, A.C., and Gaines, Barry, eds. *A Yorkshire Tragedy*. Manchester: Univ. Press, 1986. Pp. xii + 123. $25.00. ISBN 0-7190-1535-9.

Champion, Larry S. *The Essential Shakespeare: An Annotated Bibliography of Major Modern Studies*. Boston: G. K. Hall, 1986. Pp. xiv + 463. $55.00. ISBN 0-8161-8731-2.

Cornelius, R. M. *Christopher Marlowe's Use of the Bible*. American Univ. Studies. New York and Berne: Peter Lang, 1984. Pp. xiii + 321. $32.00. ISBN 0-8204-0193-5. SFR 73,60.

Coursen, H. R. *The Compensatory Psyche: A Jungian Approach to Shakespeare*. Lanham and London: Univ. Press of America, 1986. Pp. xxi + 217. $12.75. ISBN 0-8191-5278-1.

Crawford, John W. *Early Shakespearean Actresses*. American Univ. Studies. New York and Berne: Peter Lang, 1984. Pp. 199. $25.00. ISBN 0-8204-0099-8. SFR 57,50.

Currie, Hector. *Cinema Drama Schema: Eastern Metaphysic in Western Art*. New York: Philosophical Library, 1985. Pp. ix + 225. $14.95. ISBN 0-8022-2461-X.

Davidson, Clifford, Gianakaris, C. J., and Stroupe, John H., eds. *Drama in the Renaissance: Comparative and Critical Essays*. New York: AMS Press, 1986. Pp. xviii + 342. $34.50. ISBN 0-404-62282-8.

Dessen, Alan C. *Shakespeare and the Late Moral Plays*. Lincoln and London: Univ. of Nebraska, 1986. Pp. 196. $19.95. ISBN 0-8032-1671-8.

Dreher, Diane Elizabeth. *Domination and Defiance: Fathers and Daughters in Shakespeare*. Lexington: Univ. Press of Kentucky, 1986. Pp. x + 204. $21.00. ISBN 0-8131-1557-4.

Dymkowski, Christine. *Harley Granville Baker: A Preface to Modern Shakespeare*. Washington: Folger Shakespeare Library, and London: Associated Univ. Presses, 1986. Pp. 240. $32.50. ISBN 0-918016-82-7.

Eagleton, Terry. *William Shakespeare*. New York: Basil Blackwell, 1986. Pp. x + 114. $14.95. ISBN 0-631-14553-2.

Edwards, Philip. *Shakespeare: A Writer's Progress*. Oxford: Oxford Univ. Press, 1986. Pp. vi + 204. $22.50 cloth, ISBN 0-19-219184-5. $6.95 paper, ISBN 0-19-281966-9.

Empson, William. *Essays on Shakespeare*, ed. David B. Pirie. Cambridge and New York: Cambridge Univ. Press, 1986. Pp. ix + 246. $12.95 paper, ISBN 0-521-31150-0. $39.50 cloth, ISBN 0-521-25577-5.

Evans, Malcolm. *Signifying Nothing: Truth's True Contents in Shakespeare's Texts*. Athens: Univ. of Georgia Press, 1986. Pp. x + 291. $25.00. ISBN 0-8203-0837-4.

Faas, Ekbert. *Shakespeare's Poetics.* New York: Cambridge Univ. Press, 1986. Pp. xxiv + 263. $34.50. ISBN 0-521-30825-9.

Ford, John. *The Selected Plays.* Ed. Colin Gibson. Plays by Renaissance and Restoration Dramatists. Cambridge and New York: Cambridge Univ. Press, 1986. Pp. xviii + 356. $49.50 cloth, ISBN 0-521-22543-3. $18.95 paper, ISBN 0-521-29545-9.

Forker, Charles R. *Skull Beneath the Skin: The Achievement of John Webster.* Carbondale and Edwardsville: Southern Illinois Univ. Press, 1986. Pp. xiv + 612. $45.00 ISBN 0-8093-1279-4.

Foulkes, Richard, ed. *Shakespeare and the Victorian Stage.* Cambridge and New York: Cambridge Univ. Press, 1986. Pp. xviii + 311. Price not set. ISBN 0-521-30110-6.

Frye, Northrop. *On Shakespeare.* New Haven: Yale Univ. Press, 1986. 224 pp. $17.95. ISBN 0-300-03711-2.

Goy-Blanquet, Dominique. *Le Roi mis à Nu: l'Historie d'Henri VI de Hall à Shakespeare.* Études Anglaises, 92. Paris: Didier Érudition, 1986. Pp. 420. ISBN 2-86460-075-7.

Greer, Germaine. *Shakespeare.* Oxford and New York: Oxford Univ. Press, 1986. Pp. 136. $13.95. ISBN 0-19-287539-6.

Greetham, D.C., and Hill, W. Speed, eds. *TEXT: Transactions of the Society for Textual Scholarship,* vol. 2. New York: AMS Press, 1985. Pp. xii + 280. $37.50. ISBN 0-404-62552-5.

Gruber, William E. *Comic Theaters: Studies in Performance and Audience Response.* Athens and London: Univ. of Georgia Press, 1986. Pp. 198. $20.00. ISBN 0-8203-0829-3.

Harris, Laurie Lanzen, and Scott, Mark W., eds. *Shakespearean Criticism,* vol. 3. Detroit: Gale Research, 1986. Pp. 680. $82.00. ISSN 0883-9123. ISBN 0-8103-6127-2.

Hawkes, Terence. *That Shakespeherian Rag.* London and New York: Methuen, 1986. Pp. x + 131. $11.95. ISBN 0-416-38540-0.

Homan, Sidney. *Shakespeare's Theater of Presence: Language, Spectacle, and the Audience.* Lewisburg: Bucknell Univ. Press, and Cranbury, NJ: Associated Univ. Presses, 1986. Pp. 253. $32.50. ISBN 0-8387-5105-9.

Honigmann, E. A. J., ed. *Shakespeare and his Contemporaries: Essays in Comparison.* The Revels Plays Companion Library. Oxford and Dover, NH: Manchester Univ. Press, 1986. Pp. xii + 143. $35.00. ISBN 0-7190-1812-9.

Humphries, Jefferson. *Losing the Text: Readings in Literary Desire.* Athens and London: Univ. of Georgia Press, 1986. Pp. xiii + 218. $25.00. ISBN 0-8203-0857-9.

Jensen, Ejner J. *Jonson's Comedies on the Modern Stage.* Ann Arbor: UMI Research Press, 1985. Pp. viii + 158. $34.95. ISBN 0-8357-1632-5.

Jones, Robert C. *Engagement With Knavery: Point of View in Richard III, The Jew of Malta, Volpone, and The Revenger's Tragedy.* Durham: Duke Univ. Press, 1986. Pp. 179. $22.50. ISBN 0-8223-0520-8.

Jorgensen, Paul A. *Redeeming Shakespeare's Words.* Berkeley and London: Univ. of California Press, rpt. 1985. Pp. x + 131. $19.50. ISBN 0-520-05470-9.

Kogan, Stephen. *The Hieroglyphic King: Wisdom and Idolatry in the Seventeenth-Century Masque.* Rutherford: Fairleigh Dickinson Univ. Press, and London: Associated Univ. Presses, 1986. Pp. 311. $39.50. ISBN 0-8386-3229-7.

Leech, Clifford. *Christopher Marlowe: Poet for the Stage.* New York: AMS Press, 1986. Pp. viii + 250. $37.50. ISBN 0-404-62281-X.

Leinwand, Theodore B. *The City Staged: Jacobean Comedy, 1603-13.* Madison: Univ. of Wisconsin Press, 1986. Pp. viiii + 233. $25.00. ISBN 0-299-10670-5.

Levin, Richard A. *Love and Society in Shakespearean Comedy: A Study of Dramatic Form and Content.* Newark: Univ. of Delaware Press, and London: Associated Univ. Presses, 1985. Pp. 203. $26.50. ISBN 0-87413-266-5.

Lidman, Mark J. *Studies in Jacobean Drama, 1973-1984. An Annotated Bibliography.* New York and London: Garland, 1986. Pp. viii + 278. $37.00. ISBN 0-8240-8725-9.

Limon, Jerzy. *Dangerous Matter: English Drama and Politics in 1623/24.* Cambridge and New York: Cambridge Univ. Press, 1986. Pp. vii + 174. $34.50. ISBN 0-521-30664-7.

McGann, Jerome J., ed. *Textual Criticism and Literary Interpretation.* Chicago and London: Univ. of Chicago Press, 1985. Pp. xi + 239. $10.95. ISBN 0-226-55843-6.

Marcus, Leah S. *The Politics of Mirth: Jonson, Herrick, Milton, Marvell, and the Defense of Old Holiday Pastimes.* Chicago and London: Univ. of Chicago Press, 1986. Pp. ix + 319. $29.00. ISBN 0-226-50451-4.

Marienstras, Richard. *New Perspectives on the Shakespearean World.* Trans. Janet Lloyd. Cambridge and New York: Cambridge Univ. Press, 1986. Pp. viii + 273. $44.50. ISBN 0-521-25265-2.

Moore, James A. *"Richard III": An Annotated Bibliography.* New York and London: Garland Publishing, 1986. Pp. li + 867. $100.00. ISBN 0-8240-9112-4.

Morris, Harry. *Last Things in Shakespeare.* Tallahassee: Florida State Univ. Press, 1986. Pp. xii + 348. $30.00. ISBN 0-8130-0794-1.

Nicholls, Graham. *Measure for Measure: Text and Performance,* ed. Michael Scott. London: Macmillan Education, and Atlantic Highlands, NJ: Humanities Press, 1986. Pp. 94. $7.95. ISBN 0-333-34982-2.

Onions, C. T. *A Shakespeare Glossary,* rev. Robert D. Eagleson. Oxford: Clarendon Press, 1986. Pp. xviii + 326. $24.95. ISBN 0-19-811199-1.

Ornstein, Robert. *Shakespeare's Comedies: From Roman Farce to Romantic Mystery.* Newark: Univ. of Delaware Press; and London and Toronto: Associated Univ. Presses, 1986. Pp. 265. $34.50. ISBN 0-87413-298-3.

Parker, Patricia, and Hartman, Geoffrey, eds. *Shakespeare and the Question of Theory.* New York and London: Methuen, 1986. Pp. xiii + 333. $27.00. ISBN 0-416-36920-0.

Price, Joseph G. *"Hamlet": Critical Essays.* New York and London: Garland, 1986. Pp. xviii + 516. $54.00. ISBN 0-8240-9241-4.

Randall, Dale B. J. *"Theatres of Greatness": A Revisionary View of Ford's "Perkin Warbeck."* English Literary Studies 27. Victoria, B.C.: Univ. of Victoria, 1986. Pp. 80. ISBN 0-920604-27-7.

Salingar, Leo. *Dramatic Form in Shakespeare and the Jacobeans.* Cambridge and New York: Cambridge Univ. Press, 1986. Pp. x + 292. $39.50. ISBN 0-521-30856-9.

Sams, Eric. *Shakespeare's Lost Play: "Edmund Ironside."* New York: St. Martin's Press, 1985. Pp. 383. $37.50. ISBN 0-312-71432-7.

Sandler, Robert, ed. *Northrop Frye on Shakespeare.* New Haven and London: Yale Univ. Press, 1986. Pp. vi + 186. $17.95. ISBN 0-300-03711-2.

Schoenbaum, S. *Shakespeare and Others.* Washington: Folger Shakespeare Library, and London: Scolar Press, 1985. Pp. 285. $28.50. ISBN 0-918016-67-3.

Shakespeare, William. *All's Well that Ends Well,* ed. Russell Fraser. Cambridge and New York: Cambridge Univ. Press, 1986. Pp. xiii + 154. $29.95. ISBN 0-521-221501.

Shakespeare, William. *Antony and Cleopatra,* ed. A. L. Rowse. Lanham: Univ. Press of America, 1986. Pp. 152. $3.45. ISBN 0-8191-3931-9.

Shakespeare, William. *The Complete Works,* ed. Stanley Wells and Gary Taylor. Oxford and New York: Oxford Univ. Press, 1986. Pp. xlviii + 1432. $45.00. ISBN 0-19-812926-2.

Shakespeare, William. *King Henry the Fourth, Part 1,* ed. A. L. Rowse. Lanham: Univ. Press of America, 1986. Pp. 127. $3.45. ISBN 0-8191-3926-2.

Shakespeare, William. *King Henry the Fourth, Part 2,* ed. A. L. Rowse. Lanham: Univ. Press of America, 1986. Pp. 135. $3.45. ISBN 0-8191-3927-0.

Shakespeare, William. *Love's Labour's Lost,* ed. A. L. Rowse. Lanham: Univ. Press of America, 1986. Pp. 125. $3.45. ISBN 0-8191-3923-8.

Shakespeare, William. *Measure for Measure,* ed. A. L. Rowse. Lanham: Univ. Press of America, 1986. Pp. 122. $3.45. ISBN 0-8191-3930-0.

Shakespeare, William. *The Merry Wives of Windsor,* ed. A. L. Rowse. Lanham: Univ. Press of America, 1986. Pp. 113. $3.45. ISBN 0-8191-3929-7.

Shakespeare, William. *Othello,* ed. A. L. Rowse. Lanham: Univ. Press of America, 1986. Pp. 153. $3.45. ISBN 0-8191-3925-4.

Shakespeare, William. *Troilus and Cressida,* ed. A. L. Rowse. Lanham: Univ. Press of America, 1986. Pp. 146. $3.45. ISBN 0-8191-3932-7.

Shakespeare, William. *Twelfth Night, or What You Will,* ed. Elizabeth Story Donno. The New Cambridge Shakespeare. Cambridge and New York: Cambridge Univ. Press, 1985. Pp. xvi + 158. $29.95. ISBN 0-521-22752-6.

Shakespeare, William. *Two Gentlemen of Verona,* ed. A. L. Rowse. Lanham: Univ. Press of America, 1986. Pp. 105. $3.45. ISBN 0-8191-3933-5.

Shakespeare, William. *The Winter's Tale,* ed. A. L. Rowse. Lanham: Univ. Press of America, 1986. Pp. 133. $3.45. ISBN 0-8191-3924-6.

Shepherd, Simon. *Marlowe and the Politics of the Elizabethan Theatre.* New York: St. Martin's Press, 1986. Pp. xix + 231. $27.50. ISBN 0-312-51546-4.

Sherbo, Arthur. *The Birth of Shakespeare Studies: Commentators from Rowe (1709) to Boswell-Malone (1821).* East Lansing: Colleagues Press, 1986. Pp. xvi + 203. $21.95. ISBN 0-937191-00-0.

Shershow, Scott Cutler. *The Paradox of Comedy.* Amherst: Univ. of Massachusetts Press, 1986. Pp. xi + 151. $20.00. ISBN 0-87023-509-5.

Siegel, Paul N. *Shakespeare's English and Roman History Plays: A Marxist Approach.* Rutherford, NJ: Fairleigh Dickinson Univ. Press; and London and Toronto: Associated Univ. Presses, 1986. Pp. 168. $25.00. ISBN 0-8386-3251-3.

Streitberger, W. R. *Edmond Tyllney: Master of the Revels and Censor of Plays: A Descriptive Index to His Diplomatic Manual on Europe.* AMS Studies in the Renaissance. New York: AMS Press, 1986. Pp. xiv + 145. $37.50. ISBN 0-404-62285-2. ISSN 0195-657X.

Summers, Joseph H. *Dreams of Love and Power: On Shakespeare's Plays.* Oxford: Clarendon Press, 1984. viii + 161. $19.95. ISBN 0-19-812823-1.

Tydeman, William. *English Medieval Theatre 1400-1500.* London and Boston: Routledge & Kegan Paul, 1986. Pp. xiv + 221. $49.95. ISBN 0-7100-9850-2.

Velz, John W., and Teague, Frances N., eds. *"One Touch of Shakespeare": Letters of Joseph Crosby to Joseph Parker Norris, 1875-1878.* Washington: Folger Shakespeare Library, and London: Associated Univ. Presses, 1986. Pp. 359. $48.50. ISBN 0-918016-74-6.

Wells, Stanley, ed. *Shakespeare Survey 38.* Cambridge and New York: Cambridge Univ. Press, 1985. Pp. viii + 262. $39.50. ISBN 0-521-32026-7.

Wells, Stanley. *"Twelfth Night": Critical Essays.* Shakespearean Criticism, vol. 3. New York and London: Garland, 1986. Pp. xiv + 312. $54.00. ISBN 0-8240-9239-2.

Wells, Susan. *The Dialectics of Representation.* Baltimore and London: Johns Hopkins Univ. Press, 1985. Pp. x + 195. $19.50. ISBN 0-8018-2506-7.

Wentworth, Michael. *Thomas Heywood: A Reference Guide.* Boston: G. K. Hall, 1986. Pp. xxxii + 315. $55.00. ISBN 0-8161-8575-1.

White, Jerry D. *Early English Drama, "Everyman" to 1580: A Reference Guide.* Boston: G. K. Hall & Co., 1986. Pp. xx + 289. $50.00. ISBN 0-8161-8338-4.

White, R. S. *Innocent Victims: Poetic Injustice in Shakespearean Tragedy.* Atlantic Highlands: Humanities Press, 1986. Pp. 149. $39.95. ISBN 0-485-11295-7.

White, R. S. *"Let Wonder Seem Familiar": Endings in Shakespeare's Romance Vision.* Atlantic Highlands: Humanities Press, and London: Athlone Press, 1986. Pp. 203. $17.95. ISBN 0-391-03194-5.

Williamson, Marilyn L. *The Patriarchy of Shakespeare's Comedies.* Detroit: Wayne State Univ. Press, 1986. Pp. 207. $24.95. ISBN 0-8143-1807-X.

Wymer, Rowland. *Suicide and Despair in the Jacobean Drama.* New York: St. Martin's Press, 1986. Pp. xiii + 193. $25.00. ISBN 0-312-77526-1.

Ziegler, Georgianna, ed. *Shakespeare Study Today.* New York: AMS Press, 1986. Pp. x + 200. $29.50. ISBN 0-404-62283-6.

SEL

Studies in ENGLISH LITERATURE 1500-1900

Restoration and Eighteenth Century

VOLUME 27 SUMMER 1987 NUMBER 3

Studies in English Literature
1500 - 1900

VOLUME 27 SUMMER 1987 NUMBER 3

PUBLISHED BY RICE UNIVERSITY

CONTENTS

Dryden's Poetry and the Language of Magic — J. M. Armistead — 381

A Vindication of the Press and the Defoe Canon — Maximillian E. Novak — 399

"Heaven's Last Best Work": Pope's "Epistle to a Lady" — Taylor Corse — 413

The Mythical Implications in Pope's "Epistle to a Lady" — Molly Smith — 427

Pope and Antithesis: "Law and War With Words" — Vicki Sapp Bailey — 437

Mirror, Mirror: The Didactic Dilemma of *The Female Quixote* — Deborah Ross — 455

The Presence of "the Word" in Cowper's *The Task* — W. G. Marshall — 475

Blake Reads "The Bard": Contextual Displacement, and Conditions of Readability in *Jerusalem* — Molly Anne Rothenberg — 489

Recent Studies in the Restoration and Eighteenth Century — Robert Folkenflik — 503

Studies in English Literature 1500 - 1900

PUBLISHED BY RICE UNIVERSITY

Studies in English Literature is a quarterly journal of historical and critical studies. Each issue will be devoted to one of four fields:

WINTER: The English Renaissance
SPRING: Elizabethan and Jacobean Drama
SUMMER: Restoration and Eighteenth Century
AUTUMN: The Nineteenth Century

SEL: Studies in English Literature, 1500–1900 (ISSN: 0039-3657) is published quarterly (February, May, August, and November) at $15.00 per year for individuals, $20.00 per year for U.S. institutions, $25.00 per year for foreign institutions, and $6.00 per single issue, by Rice University, 6100 South Main Street, P.O. Box 1892, Houston, Texas 77251. Second-class postage paid at Houston, Texas. **Postmaster:** Send address changes to the Business Manager, *SEL,* Rice University, P.O. Box 1892, Houston, TX 77251.

Studies in English Literature invites historical and critical essays of moderate length (ten to twenty-five pages) that contribute significantly to the understanding of English Literature, 1500-1900. Typescripts should be double-spaced throughout and prepared in conformity with the Chicago Manual of Style. Clean photocopy on uncoated paper is acceptable in place of the ribbon copy. We will not consider articles being simultaneously submitted elsewhere, nor will we print essays to appear in a book published within a year of scheduled publication of *SEL*. Those wishing to omit their identities from manuscripts may do so, but should include a covering letter.

Manuscripts submitted for publication should be addressed to the Editor, *Studies in English Literature,* Rice University, P.O. Box 1892, Houston, TX 77251. They must be accompanied by a sufficient number of unattached stamps for return. Receipt of manuscripts will be acknowledged by postcard. Editorial decisions usually take a minimum of three months.

Annual subscription rates: $15.00 for individuals, $20.00 for U. S. institutions, $25.00 for foreign institutions, $6.00 per issue for partial subscriptions and single copies. Regular subscriptions may be obtained for any or all quarterly issues. Remittance should accompany subscription requests. Notice of non-receipt of an issue must be made within ninety (90) days following the publication of that issue. No refunds or cancellations. Business communications should be addressed to Business Manager, *Studies in English Literature,* Rice University, P. O. Box 1892, Houston, TX 77251.

Microfilms of previous volumes (Vols. 1-26) may be obtained from University Microfilms, Inc., 300 N. Zeeb Road, Ann Arbor, Michigan 48106; xerox copies of individual articles may be ordered by calling (800) 521-0600 (toll free). Copies of articles are also available from ISI's The Genuine Article service, 3501 Market Street, Philadelphia, PA 19104; phone (800) 523-1850; telex 84-5305; electronic mail through CLASS; or facsimile transmission via FAXPAX.

Volumes 1 through 3 and 5 through 10 of *Studies in English Literature* are available from Johnson Reprint Corporation, 111 Fifth Avenue, New York, N. Y. 10003, or Berkeley Square House, London W. 1, England.

SEL 27 (1987)
ISSN 0039-3657

Dryden's Poetry and the Language of Magic

JACK M. ARMISTEAD

To learn how John Dryden makes the occult an important part of his vision is to learn a great deal about the intellectual assumptions that shaped Restoration culture. It is well to remember that for Dryden, as for many of his contemporaries, some of them staunch members of the Royal Society, the occult and visible worlds were intertwined. The existence of spiritual intelligences, the efficacy of talismans, the ancient truths buried in alchemical documents, the validity of astrology—these and related issues were being probed earnestly by thinkers already deeply committed to the inductive, materialistic, experimental frame of mind. Elsewhere I have examined some of the ways in which this curious angle of vision seems to affect the dramatic works of Dryden and his contemporaries, especially Shadwell and Lee.[1] In this essay I shall examine Dryden's allusions to magic in the poetry, with special attention to his analyses of power.[2] Such an enterprise clearly reveals that he belonged to what Charles Webster calls "the intellectual elite" of the later seventeenth century, who continued to find in "the conceptual infrastructure of magic" an instructive fiction.[3]

From the outset Dryden's use of this fiction presumes that the reader can distinguish various types of magical art and their moral implications.[4] At one moral extreme was the daemonic black magician, the practitioner of goety, who used forbidden ceremonies to invoke the power of evil spirits. Somewhat less objectionable, but still condemned by most orthodox Christians, was the daemonic

Professor of English and Director of Undergraduate Studies at the University of Tennessee, Knoxville, Jack Armistead is the editor of *Restoration: Studies in English Literary Culture, 1660-1700* and of *The First English Novelists* (Tennessee, 1985); he is author of *Nathaniel Lee* (Twayne, 1979) and *Four Restoration Playwrights* (G. K. Hall, 1984). This article forms part of the introduction to a study of occult imagery and ideas in Dryden's plays.

white magician, the theurge, who ceremonially invoked and manipulated neoplatonic middle spirits, elemental beings, or angels. One variety of such "white" wizardry, cabbalistic magic, had gained some credence in the Church, because it purported to capture the influence of stars or angels by manipulating Hebrew letters and their numerical equivalents. Of all the practitioners of magic, however, the most widely accepted were the natural magicians, the alchemists and purveyors of sympathetic medicine, for they eschewed daemonic powers altogether. Instead, they worked to release and guide the hidden forces within and between all objects in the physical world.[5]

By the time of Dryden in the later part of the century, these distinctions had become blurred by the growing interest in inductive science. Francis Bacon had popularized the notion that the scientific method would make practicable a true natural magic, and Robert Boyle and his colleagues carried this concept into the fledgling scientific establishment after the Restoration.[6] At the same time, the influence of Paracelsus and his disciples encouraged many of the "new" philosophers to insist that much of the ancient natural magic was essentially scientific,[7] and Henry More led the Cambridge Platonists through an effort to find buried in cabbalistic and neoplatonic thought a set of truths that would reconcile demonology with atomism, heliocentrism, and a quantitatively structured world.[8] Only the rawest forms of daemonic magic were omitted from these respectable deliberations. The practicing conjurers either kept very quiet, as did Elias Ashmole, or found themselves consigned to the lunatic fringe, as did John Heydon and Samuel Pordage.[9]

Dryden himself employs occult phenomena in plays of the 1660s and 1670s, and during the same period writes prose conjectures about the world of daemons, specters, half-devils, witches, magicians, prodigies, and oracles.[10] But not until 1677 does he take a personal stand. In "The Author's Apology for Heroic Poetry and Poetic License," he speaks for the first time of "things above us" as existing in realms beyond the human mind, and he approves the use of biblically authorized imagery to represent them.[11] What is new about this train of thought is neither the interest in persistent folk beliefs about the supernatural nor the reference to demonology in classical literature. Several times in previous years Dryden had used these precedents to explain the employment of magic and prophecy in his plays. The novelty appears as he injects the scriptures into the equation. On the one hand, he seems to keep his philosophical distance, emphasizing that the Bible authorizes the "description" of "immaterial substances," rather than the belief in them, and that only the "vulgar" populace accepts such descriptions as genuine.

But on the other hand, he clearly affirms the existence of "things above us" that can only be conceived by analogy with "beings more within our knowledge." In the 1680s and 1690s he further approves the imagery of spirit life found in the writings of Christian platonists.[12]

This shift in orientation has an equivalent not only in the plays, but also in the poems about public life and the arts. In his public poetry we can see him moving from the imagery of old-style magic—with its proud, solitary operators producing effects by secret means—to that of the more communal, open experimentation with occult forces and sympathies that characterized the type of natural magic espoused by many of Dryden's contemporaries. In the 1680s, however, in keeping with his prose comments about Christian platonism, he begins to emphasize daemonic magic, theurgy, and goety, and the vocabulary of natural magic is employed to a lesser extent.

In the earliest public poems, the true magicians are the divinely ordained leaders and their chosen ministers. As the sun and other stars convey divine power to the rest of creation, so these great souls become conduits for God's energy in society. As rational beings, however, they must have techniques of communicating this power. In the case of Oliver Cromwell, as depicted in the "Heroique Stanzas" (1659),[13] the technique is that of the uniquely gifted military hero who selects his generals and plots his strategies with the almost mystical skill of the consummate alchemist:

> For from all tempers he could service draw;
> The worth of each with its alloy he knew;
> And as the *Confident* of *Nature* saw
> How she Complexions did divide and brew.
>
> . . . .
>
> When such *Heroique Vertue* Heav'n sets out,
> The Starrs like *Commons* sullenly obey;
> Because it draines them when it comes about.
>
> (97-107)

Like the old-fashioned alchemist, however, Cromwell operates in isolation, founding his strategy of reform and conquest upon "deep Secrets" (128) that are not shared with his retainers. His heroic potency is a unique gift of God, and in his absence only the blueprint of order, the "*faire Designment*" (96), remains.[14]

After the Restoration, power is returned to its natural agent, the monarch, and political magic loses its mystery. In *Astraea Redux*

(1660), Charles's return is heralded by General Monck's measured, systematic preparations (151-72), which are contrasted to the hasty and untimely efforts of "Chymists" (162) and enchanters (190). As Charles is crowned in *To His Sacred Majesty* (1661), the alchemy of conquest is displaced by the natural magic of "love," which is "destin'd to [his] Countries peace" (122):

> Now while the sacred Oyl annoints your head,
> And fragrant scents, begun from you, are spread
> Through the large Dome, the peoples joyful sound,
> Sent back, is still preserv'd in hallow'd ground:
> Which in one blessing mixt descends on you,
> As heightned spirits fall in richer dew.
>
> (59-64)

The public, communal nature of this process, sharply contrasting with Cromwell's personal mode, predicts the shape of things to come. Unlike his predecessor, Charles operates from the center of a natural structure, whose parts are informed and bound together by his love.[15] In "To My Lord Chancellor" (1662), the king's relation to subordinates is equated with that between God and the stars (83-86), sun and moon (47-48), sun and planets (149-54), mines and streams (66). The mechanics of this system are not founded on "deep Secrets"; their basis can be discovered: "we might unwind the clue / As men do Nature" (71-72), until we come, for instance, to the Earl of Clarendon, who is spoken of in Pythagorean terms as the "Soul" of public "harmony" (116).[16]

The peak of Dryden's interest in natural magic as a source of telling imagery comes in *Annus Mirabilis* (1667). There Charles is presented as a kind of supervising alchemist of the post-Baconian variety, and the events associated with the Dutch Wars and the Great Fire are treated as parts of a grand chemical reaction. He studies the ingredients of war "with careful eyes" and judges that they will behave "like vapours that from Limbecks rise," only to "descend again" in "richer showers" (49-52). Like the Dutch enemy, the fiendish fire is incited by an alchemical dream of material self-indulgence, "By pow'rful charms" of literal "gold and silver" (943-44). But again, Charles, the new-style Christian alchemist, loving, corporate-minded, and in touch with Providence, understands that the "Chymick flame" will produce a more enduring, utilitarian result, "a City of more precious mold" (1169-70). And while his enemies work feverishly to achieve their "proud designs" (137), he relies on what "all-maturing time" can "bring to light" as he, "like

Heav'n, does each day's labour bless" (559-60).[17]

In this providential laboratory, the monarch-magician and his assistants no longer need miracles or sorcery. Using a "scientific" knowledge of naval strategy, Albemarle saves his crippled fleet without the aid of those "flaming pillars, and . . . clouds" upon which the escaping Israelites depended (368).[18] And the fiends, specters, and witches that seem to promote their own wicked ends through the great fire (890-92, 989-92) are finally no match for the divine alchemy that Charles has witnessed and sponsored, an alchemy whose methods he enshrines in the Royal Society:

> O truly Royal! who behold the Law,
> And rule of beings in your Maker's mind,
> And thence, like Limbecks, rich Idea's draw,
> To fit the levell'd use of humane kind.
>
> (661-64)

The fiends (545, 991), ghosts (321, 739, 889), genii (1127), and angels (62, 893) that briefly appear in *Annus Mirabilis* belong among the "separated beings"[19] that Dryden tends to invoke, as in his heroic plays of this period, only when he needs a language to represent major changes in the natural order. In the poetry devoted to extraliterary subjects, to politics and private life, such beings do not begin to play an important role until the 1680s, when he begins to employ them in his analyses of the domestic troubles that threaten Charles's peaceable kingdom of love. Since the monarch and his deputized natural magicians have now established their providential function within the natural order, surely, says the narrator of *Absalom and Achitophel* (1681), the emerging treason must indicate diabolical intervention:

> when to Sin our byast Nature leans,
> The carefull Devil is still at hand with means;
> And providently Pimps for ill desires.
>
> (79-81)

Throughout *Absalom and Achitophel* and *The Medal* (1682), the radical Whigs, led by Shaftesbury, are spoken of as either fiends or magicians. Their arts threatened the "Form and Order" (*AA,* 531) fostered by Charles and maintained by those "Holy Bands" of nature (*AA*, 339) that constitute "our native Strength" (*M*, 72). In *The Medal* Shaftesbury seeks "Pow'r" (50) by "wicked means" which he, "like white Witches" (62), fools himself into considering pious. He intends to "clip" the king's "regal Rights within the Ring" (229), in effect to penetrate "the magic circle of kingship symbolized by the . . . national currency" and to substitute his own portrait for that of his monarch at the powerful center.[20] While he sits as model for this portrait, his worshipful artists, like hermetic priests, work to draw his own spiritual potency into the image. Ironically, they succeed; the "Idol seem'd . . . alive" with his true nature, the "*Lucifer*" (21) within him, "the Fiend confess'd, without a vaile" (81).[21] This link between Shaftesbury and the Egyptian form of diabolical magic is strengthened later in the poem where he is said to employ a false "*Mercury*" (263) in the chemistry of politics. "*Mercury*" alludes not only to Shaftesbury's slippery nature, to the Protestant newspapers (with *Mercury* in their titles) which spread the Whig propaganda, and to a dangerous remedy for syphilis,[22] but also to one of the key elements in the alchemy supposedly invented by Mercurius Trismegistus, the ancient Egyptian magus-king.[23] In hermetic alchemy, mercury was considered "a sharpe liquor, passable, and penetrable . . . most pure . . . quickning, and . . . the foode of life."[24] However, when applied for Shaftesbury's infernal purposes, it "pass'd through every Sect, or theirs through Thee" (264-66), without rarefying the treasonous concoction.[25]

Likewise, the Whigs of *Absalom and Achitophel* seek raw power through illegitimate means, as if there were no divine energy informing natural phenomena and hence no divinely sponsored method for tapping it. Zimri is a bumbling "Chymist" whose "peculiar Art" lies in "squandring Wealth" (550, 559). Shimei misapplies "Power" (612) gained from the London mob to "free the suffring Saint from Humane Laws" (609). Corah becomes the converse of Moses' magical brass serpent; instead of counteracting the venom of rebellion, he protects and incites the rebels (632-35).[26] Achitophel himself employs "Impious Arts" (498, and see 289 and 402) of rhetoric and bribery to orchestrate a revolution. To recruit Absalom, he interprets the conflict between himself and King David as a competition between rival forms of magic. Absalom, he insists, has been chosen by good fortune to revive the mosaical kingdom of theurgy and miracles, visions, dreams, and sacred prophecies (230-39);[27] David, on the other hand, is a fallen angel (273) who has been "Charm'd into Ease" (708) and now tries to "Enchant" (423) his son with "Love," which is "Nature's trick" (423-24).[28]

The narrator, of course, insures that we see through this diabolical propaganda. It is Absalom who is the victim of infernal designs, and it is the resurgent king, invoking the divine presence, who wields "Lawfull Pow'r" (1024).[29] The full potency of "Establish'd Pow'r"

993), we are told, is accessible only to the "faithful Band / Of Worthies" (914-15) who perform their rituals within nature's divinely ordained order. In describing Thomas, Earl of Ossory, as one of these, the narrator conflates the traditional image of perfection with the magician's conjuring circle, implying that Ossory's life had magical potency because it was centered on his faithful soul: "O Narrow Circle but of Pow'r Divine" (838).[30]

In writing Charles's funeral ode, *Threnodia Augustalis* (1685), Dryden seems to have sensed that England was passing into a new phase of its history. Charles had weeded out rebels and cultivated the arts and sciences, leaving behind a demi-paradise. If Cromwell had been the *Confident of Nature,*" absorbing stellar power (above, p. 383), Charles had become the more sociable confidant of scientific virtuosi, draining, filtering, and directing their best work (341-45).[31] Now that the "Promis'd Land [is] in view," however, the chosen flock needs no further "Miracles" (427-28). The dying king's physicians are "Sons of Art" (160), heirs of his own patronage of natural magic in its modern guise, but they cannot finally counteract fate. By acting as "second Causes" (110) with their "Charms of Art" (151), they can only briefly prevent "the Royal Soul" (150) from returning to "her Native Sphear" (150-52). As Anne Barbeau Gardiner has pointed out, these medical men are like the sorcerers in Pliny and Lucian, vainly "calling the distressed moon down from the sky to save it from [the] eclipse" that is part of God's primary magic.[32] Meanwhile, the country's martial spirit is released from Charles's own "Charms" (471) of loving husbandry as James assumes the throne. An era of "Arts," "Science," and "soft Humanity" (348-50) is displaced by one of expanding empire.

But James is not able to move his country in the new direction. Instead, he spends his brief, tumultuous reign confronting one domestic crisis after another. In *The Hind and the Panther* (1687), as in *Absalom and Achitophel,* Dryden once again senses that "the *Daemon*" is being permitted into the garden (pt. 3, 314). The radical Whigs, those "dire Magicians" (pt. 3, 721) of the Puritan persuasion, were exposed during Charles's reign before they could thoroughly infect the Protestant cause; now the Panther/Anglican Church has been charmed again (pt. 3, 725), and without the divinely sponsored power of James and his mother faith, it is impossible to undo the enchantment. On their own, the Anglicans are outside the true magic circle: "like *Aegyptian* Sorcerers," they "vainly lift" the "magick wand," only to discover that they could, "with like infernal force / Produce the plague" of sectarian enthusiasm, "but not arrest the course" (pt. 2, 538-42).

In his last great public poem, *Britannia Rediviva* (1688), Dryden hopes that the birth of an heir to James will point the way out of the current troubles. He envisions the prince as embodying potent holy power that can resist the diabolical magic, the "fascinating Eyes," "Spells, and Sorceries" (203, 200), of the Whig "Fiends" (122). In developing this idea, he compares the prince not only to Christ, "the Godhead cloath'd in Earth" (123), but also to "the Sacred *Tetragrammaton*" (197). In this his only overt reference to cabbalistic magic, he implies that the prince is like the four-lettered name of God (in Hebrew) upon which Christian cabbalists, following Pico della Mirandola's example, would meditate. As a potent symbol for the ineffable creative Word, the Tetragrammaton gave access to both stellar and angelical forces; it became the ultimate door to magical power.[33]

In the poem, then, this reference suggests that the prince will in some way complete the magical cycle of history begun with Charles's reign of love and continued in what this poem calls James's reign of "Justice" (355).[34] As we have seen, Dryden symbolized the former as Christlike cooperation with natural forces through post-Baconian natural magic; justice, however, raises the magic higher, to "Heav'ns self" (355), implying more direct access to divine power. The prince will in some way "fill the *Trine*" (327), become the third part of the "*Unit*" (326), not only in the biological, astrological, and trinitarian senses,[35] but in the sense of rounding out the age of love and justice with a monarchy of more transcendent virtue. Beyond such visions the poet cannot go, however, for he cannot expect to "read the Book which Angels cannot read" (227).

Events, of course, proved that these pious hopes could not be realized. Public life went its Whiggish way, and a dispossessed Dryden turned to safer, narrower, more private subjects. Even in the late poems, however, the imagery and vocabulary of magic contributes to the development of important themes. In "To . . . The Duchess of Ormond" (1700), God is seen as the ultimate alchemist, weighing and mixing the elements for the Duchess's body to fashion "so sweet a cage, / A soul might well be pleas'd to pass an age" (118-19).[36] Nevertheless, the elegant container is invaded by disease. When the attending physician, Christopher Morley, finds his natural magic as weak as that of the doctors who failed to save Charles II in *Threnodia Augustalis*, he is "inspir'd" by the lady's guardian "angel" to "find the remedy" (131-32), "As once the Macedon, by Jove's decree, / Was taught to dream an herb for Ptolomee" (133-34). In "On the Death of a Very Young Gentleman" (c. 1687-1693) the author offers the survivors an alchemical consolation. Try to think of the boy not as dead but rather as having been "rarify'd" (23); surely "His great Creator drew / His spirit, as the Sun the Morning Dew" (25-26). Although this is the true alchemy, Dryden implies, you the parents can apply the same process psychologically by treating your relationship with the other offspring as a kind of alembic:

> divide
> That Love in many which in one was ty'd.
> . . . .
> Love him by Parts, in all your num'rous Race,
> And from those Parts form one collected Grace;
> Then, when you have refin'd to that degree,
> Imagine all in one, and think that one is He.
> (46, 52-55)

This exhortation to "imagine" the process of alchemy leads us to another sphere of activity for the interpretation of which Dryden found the metaphor of magic particularly useful: art itself, especially literary art, music, and painting. Early in his career he speaks of artistic endeavours in the most exalted terms of Renaissance wizardry, but by the later 1660s, just as he begins to use the idiom of natural magic to describe the management of political power, he likewise begins to compare the artist's skill to the natural magician's virtuosity. Then, as his personal difficulties mount in the 1680s, his vision of the artist darkens; the times are unpropitious, and the bard becomes the inhibited craftsman.

At first, however, the enthusiastic patronage of Charles and his ministers must have given Dryden grounds for the highest expectations. In "To My Lord Chancellor" (1662) he rejoices that

> At length the Muses stand restor'd again
> To that great charge which Nature did ordain;
> And their lov'd Druids seem reviv'd by Fate,
> While you dispence the Laws and guide the State.
> (23-26)

Interest in the British druids, those ancient magician-priest-poets, had been revived earlier in the century when poets like Carew and Drayton traced the British monarchy and, by implication, their own lineage, back to an ancient world in which bards embodied political and priestly powers. The last druids, those in Wales, were considered heirs of Noah and of the magical theology of Hermes Trismegistus,

Orpheus, and Pythagoras; later, the druidical union of lawgiver and wizard split into the partnership of king and magician-bard typified by Arthur and Merlin.[37] Although less popular in the Restoration, this tradition obviously appealed to Dryden, since in his "Life of Plutarch" (1683) he discusses "our *Druydes*, who were nearest to the *Pythagoreans* of any Sect,"[38] and in *King Arthur* (1691) he gives a major role to Merlin.

During the 1660s, then, he seems to endow poets, including himself, with druidical powers. Appropriately, however, these modern druids see nature not as a living organism but rather as a mechanical structure shaped and moved by spiritual forces that realize God's law. The poems by Sir Robert Howard, writes Dryden in the epistle to his "Honored Friend" (1660), figure forth a "providence of wit" (34), a sub-creation whose "Atoms" (31) are so subtly controlled by Howard's "Genius" (35) that "dull souls, admire, but cannot see / What hidden springs within the Engine be" (21-22). Such artistry restores poetry's dominion over "Morall Knowledge" (45) just as "*Charls* ascends the Throne" (105) of political power.[39] The poet, then, becomes a natural magician whose manipulation of images and language through the spiritual potency of his "genius" corresponds to God's handling of corpuscular reality and the king's governance of society.

The same analogies are implicit in Dryden's response to the critics in his "Prologue" to *The Indian Emperour* (1665), with the addition that here poetic force is ascribed more directly to heaven. As God's surrogate and champion against the "pow'r" that critics derive from "the Devil" (2-3), the playwright offers a little world so complex that "each man" should "take but what he understands, / And leave the rest upon the Poets hands" (28-29). The dramatist has veiled his deepest impulses and structures from all but the most adept and pious interpreters, just as "Heav'n" in *Religio Laici* is said to hide "from humane Sense / . . . the secret paths of *Providence*" (186-87).[40]

By 1667 Dryden is assigning a somewhat lower status to the poetry of his own time, though he continues to use the metaphor of magic to describe it. Beginning with the "Prologue" to *The Tempest* (1667), he distinguishes between the poet-magus of the past, such as Shakespeare, who created virtually a second nature (8) and gave it laws (7) which his successors can only follow, and the modern poet-scientist who imitates and improves but cannot really create. Dryden reinforces this distinction with the vocabulary of daemonic magic: "*Shakespear's* Magick could not copy'd be, / Within that Circle none durst walk but he" (19-20); his "pow'r is sacred as a King's" (24) and presumably derives from the same divine source. As

Charles becomes the presiding alchemist in *Annus Mirabilis*, Shakespeare becomes the presiding theurge in this prologue, and the bards of the Restoration become, by implication, his proteges, his Clarendons and Albemarles; only through painstaking study of his artistic works and the natural creations of his divine master can they reach the highest level of achievement possible for them, the level of natural magic. For them, as for Charles's deputies and successors, the age of miracles is over.[41]

Thus, the best modern poetry is the product of careful study and imitation. Lesser poets are mere quacks, says the speaker of the "Prologue . . . to the University of Oxon." (1673); they

> build their Poems the *Lucretian* way,
> So many Huddled Atoms make a Play,
> And if they hit in Order by some Chance,
> They call that Nature, which is Ignorance.
>
> (32-35)[42]

More accomplished writers examine "with Care th' Anatomy of Man" and draw "Fame from Science, not from Fortune" (25-27). In the "Epilogue" to the "University of Oxon." (1673) this scientific art is distinguished from mere "Art Magique" (25), the mindless exploitation of vulgar tastes for spectacular effects on stage. Perhaps in order to remove the scenes of magic and demonology in his own plays from this category of "Art Magique," Dryden explains in some of his critical essays how daemons and sorcery can legitimately be represented both in the drama and in heroic poetry: the poet uses his well-informed fancy to combine images derived from experience, popular beliefs, philosophy, or, indeed, Shakespeare. With something like this principle in mind, Dryden can use the speaker of his prologue to *Tyrannick Love* (1669) to praise the "conjuring" dramatist who "Allow'd his Fancy the full scope and swing" (16-17).[43]

It is difficult not to hear notes of regret in Dryden's espousal of a "modern" role for the poets of his day. The language used in his famous renunciation of rhyme in the "Prologue" to *Aureng-Zebe* (1675) implies that he felt inhibited by more than a verse form: "Nature," says the speaker, "flies him like Enchanted Ground" (10). This is the same phrase he would use a few years later in *Religio Laici* (1682) to describe the failure of the great ancient philosophers to achieve a unified theory of happiness: "For *Happiness* was never to be found; / But vanish'd from 'em like Enchanted ground" (27-28). Their problem, and perhaps Dryden suspected it was his own as well, was that their "*anxious Thoughts* in *endless Circles* roul, / Without a *Centre* where to fix the *Soul*" (36-37). In theology, only "*Reveal'd Religion*" (68) could provide the center. In the circle of poetry, Dryden seems to feel, "sacred" potency has been inaccessible since Shakespeare, so that now, as he puts it in the "Epilogue" to *Aureng-Zebe*, "a Poet must confess, / His Art's like Physick, but a happy ghess" (11-12).[44]

When he returned to the theme of artistic magic in the 1680s, Dryden's estimation of the prospects for great achievement had dropped still further. Aware that none of the early Christian geniuses, the Shakespeares and Raphaels, had borne offspring in Restoration England, he felt that somehow the progress of art had been stymied. In "A Song for St. Cecilia's Day, 1687," God's creative magic is represented in musical terms; it is a composition that unites the physical and supernal dimensions of reality in a harmony "closing full in Man" (15). Its lower range is first recreated by the pagan musician Orpheus, whose tuneful wizardry could command plants, animals, and human passions. Then, with her faith-inspired organ, St. Cecilia "rais'd the wonder high'r" (51), unwittingly conjuring "An angel" (53) from the supernal realm.[45] A similar contrast is drawn in "Alexander's Feast" (1697). There Timotheus is the Orpheus figure,[46] egotistically manipulating emotions through masterful fiction-making that is in one instance compared to necromancy (138-46). Again, St. Cecilia, adding the sacred "arts" of the organ to "nature's mother wit," enlarges the "narrow bounds" of pagan music and is able to invoke "an angel" (161-70).[47] Of the composers in Dryden's time only Purcell could approach such musical magic. In "An Ode, on the Death of Mr. Henry Purcell" (1696) he is both "our *Orpheus*" (16), with power to tune the discord of hell (21-22), and the teacher of angel singers (23). Thus he might have linked nature and heaven in the full "Scale of Musick" (24); unfortunately, "the God-like Man, / . . . too soon retir'd, / As He too late began" (13-15).[48]

On the other hand, had Purcell lived he might well have met the fate of other Restoration artists. "'Tis hard, my friend," Dryden lamented in his epistle to Motteux (1698),

> to write in such an age,
> As damns not only poets, but the stage.
> That sacred art, by heav'n itself infus'd,
> Which Moses, David, Solomon have us'd,
> Is now to be no more: the Muses' foes
> Would sink their Maker's praises into prose.
>
> (1-6)

And so with the finest Restoration painter. In the epistle "To Sir Godfrey Kneller" (1694) Dryden compares his own poetic subordination to Shakespeare with Kneller's relation to Raphael and Titian. They were truly creative spirits, true magicians of painting as Shakespeare was a true magician of poetry. Kneller, like Dryden himself, should be "Proud to be less; but of [their] Godlike Race" (76). "Bounded by the Times" (147), he must be content with "imitating Life" (18) rather than contending "with Heroes Memory" (119). Kneller has taken his craft as far as anyone can in "these inferior times" (118); it remains earthbound and lacks the Promethean "Fire" (25) that Dryden once expected the greatest Restoration artists to possess. But in the final analysis, it imitates life so well, exists in such complete harmony with "Nature" (8), that "Time" will "Add every Grace" that the painter could not provide (176-81).[49]

Through the efforts of scholars like Steven Zwicker and James Garrison, we have seen that Dryden's religious conversion in the 1680s was accompanied by a gradual abandonment of his political dream, the dream of a redeemed, civilized community centering on a providentially sponsored patriarch-king.[50] In this study I have tried to show that this dream and its loss were bound up with Dryden's understanding of power, and that the "infrastructure" of magic provided him with a language to interpret important aspects of the appropriation of power. To examine the genius of a Cromwell or a Shakespeare he found the lenses of Renaissance alchemy or theurgy most revealing, but as he moved into the early Restoration for his subjects, he turned to the kind of natural magic promoted by Bacon and the Royal Society. The poets and kings of the new age, working from the center of society, would be disciplined, sociable observers and promoters of providence at work through secondary causes. When the political scene darkened in the 1680s, Dryden found richer interpretive possibilities in the imagery of daemonic and cabbalistic magic. He began to see both artists and monarchs as victims of an evil wizardry that had been permitted to frustrate the unfolding of a higher art and a higher politics. Divinely ordained power had been withdrawn to the private soul and to time itself, the last magician of the age,

for former things
Are set aside, like abdicated kings;
And every moment alters what is done,
And innovates some act till then unknown.

(274-77)[51]

NOTES

[1]See "Occultism in Restoration Drama: Motives for Revaluation," *MLS* 9 (1979):60-67; "Dryden and the Popular Tradition: Backgrounds for *King Arthur* and *The Indian Emperour*," *N&Q* 229 (1984):342-44; "Dryden's Prospero and his Predecessors," *SAR* 50 (1985):23-33; "Calista and the 'equal empire' of her 'sacred sex'," *Studies in Eighteenth-Century Culture* 15 (1985):173-85; "Egypt in the Restoration: A Perspective on *All for Love*," *PLL* 22 (1986):139-53; "The Occultism of Dryden's 'American' Plays in Context," *The Seventeenth Century* 1 (1986):127-52.

[2]Jackson I. Cope relates Dryden's interest in magicians and spirits to More and Glanvill; see "Dryden vs Hobbes: An Adaptation from the Platonists," *JEGP* 57 (1958):444-48. Maximillian E. Novak documents the spirit lore in early plays: "The Demonology of Dryden's *Tyrannick Love* and 'Anti-Scot'," *ELN* 4 (1966):95-98. Michael McKeon notices the astrology and alchemy in *Annus Mirabilis,* in *Politics and Poetry in Restoration England* (Cambridge, Mass., and London: Harvard Univ. Press, 1975). And Cedric D. Reverand mentions the magician's circle in "Patterns of Imagery and Metaphor in Dryden's *The Medall,*" *YES* 2 (1972):103-14.

[3]Charles Webster, *From Paracelsus to Newton* (Cambridge: Cambridge Univ. Press, 1982), p. 11.

[4]The ensuing survey of categories draws heavily not only from my reading in primary sources but also from Robert Hunter West's two books, *The Invisible World: A Study in Pneumotology in Elizabethan Drama* (1939; rpt. New York: Octagon, 1969), esp. ch. 3, and *Milton and the Angels* (Athens: Univ. of Georgia Press, 1955), esp. chs. 4-5; Frances A. Yates, *The Occult Philosophy in the Elizabethan Age* (London: Routledge & Kegan Paul, 1979), esp. pp. 1-74; Allen G. Debus, *The English Paracelsians* (London: Oldbourne, 1965), esp. pp. 13-136; Keith Thomas, *Religion and the Decline of Magic* (1971; rpt. Harmondsworth: Penguin, 1973), esp. chs. 7-9; and Brian Easlea, *Witch-hunting, Magic & the New Philosophy* (Brighton: Harvester, 1980).

[5]Although astrological knowledge formed an important part of the wizard's lore, it was not regarded as a kind of magic but rather as a method of choosing opportune conditions for magical enterprises, since it enabled one to estimate future configurations of stellar influence.

[6]On Bacon's ideas about magic, see Paolo Rossi, *Francis Bacon: From Magic to Science* (1957; trans. Sacha Rabinovitch; rpt. Chicago: Univ. of Chicago Press; London: Routledge & Kegan Paul, 1968), pp. 16-56. Boyle and the magical tradition is discussed by J. R. Jacob in *Robert Boyle and the English Revolution* (New York: Burt Franklin, 1977), pp. 65-163.

[7]The extent to which various kinds of magic, including Paracelsian natural magic, made its way into the Restoration science is discussed by P. M. Rattansi, "Paracelsus and the Puritan Revolution," *Ambix* 11 (1963):24-32; K. Theodore Hoppen, "The Nature of the Early Royal Society," pts. 1 and 2, *The British Journal for the History of Science* 9 (1976):1-24, 243-73; and Charles Webster, *From Paracelsus to Newton.*

[8]See Arlene Miller Guinsburg, "Henry More, Thomas Vaughan and the Late Renaissance Magical Tradition," *Ambix* 27 (1980):36-58.

[9]On Ashmole, see C. H. Josten, "Introduction," *Elias Ashmole (1617-1692)*... *Sources Relating to his Life and Work,* 5 vols. (Oxford: Clarendon Press, 1966),

1:1-308. On Heydon, see Thomas, pp. 408, 445, and Bernard Capp, *English Almanacs 1500-1800: Astrology and the Popular Press* (London: Faber and Faber, 1979), pp. 86, 89, 161, 184, 190, 406. Pordage was "lame *Mephibosheth* the Wisard's Son" in "The Second Part of Absalom and Achitophel" (1682), *The Works of John Dryden*, gen. eds. Edward Niles Hooker and H. T. Swedenberg, Jr., 19 vols. (Berkeley and London: Univ. of California Press, 1956-). Vol. 2, *Poems 1681-1684*, ed. H. T. Swedenberg and Vinton A. Dearing, line 405, p. 74, and see note on p. 332. Hereafter, the California edition will be cited as *Works*.

[10]"Of Heroic Plays: An Essay," "Preface" to *Tyrannic Love,* and "The Grounds of Criticism in Tragedy," in *Of Dramatic Poesy and Other Critical Essays*, ed. George Watson, 2 vols. (London: Dent; New York: Dutton, 1962), 1:161, 142, and 253. Hereafter, this edition will be cited as *Critical Essays*.

[11]In *Critical Essays*, 1:204. These remarks were appended to *The State of Innocence*, Dryden's operatic adaptation of Milton's *Paradise Lost*, and it may well be that such intimacy with Milton's biblical demonology contributed to what grew into a new direction in Dryden's orientation toward the occult.

[12]See "The Life of Plutarch," in *Works*, vol. 17, ed. Samuel Holt Monk, et al., pp. 256-57. Watson omits this section from his edition. For later remarks, see "A Discourse Concerning . . . Satire" (1693) and a letter to John Dennis (c. March 1694), in *Critical Essays*, 2:89-93, 178. See also the "Preface" to *Fables* (1700), in *Critical Essays*, 2:292-93.

[13]All quotations from the poetry of 1649-1696 are taken from *Works*, vols. 1-4. Parenthetical references will be given by line only.

[14]Jackson I. Cope comments on the synthesis of mechanistic and providential ideas in this poem but does not develop the implications; see "Science, Christ, and Cromwell in Dryden's *Heroic Stanzas*," *MLN* 71 (1956):483-85. In *Works*, 1:204, Hooker and Swedenberg think it unlikely that Dryden had in mind "the wonder-working alchemist," and in *Dryden's Poetic Kingdoms* (London: Routledge & Kegan Paul, 1965), pp. 59-60, Alan Roper sees Cromwell as "a sort of superior machine-minder" who is himself a surrogate god. To me, however, the alchemical reference is unavoidable, and it reinforces Steven N. Zwicker's sense that Cromwell exhibits "uncanny understanding" and "seems to exercise a power beyond human politics": see *Politics and Language in Dryden's Poetry* (Princeton: Princeton Univ. Press, 1984), pp. 80-81.

[15]For Dryden, Charles's other virtues seem to have been subsumed in this one, which was, as Roper indicates (pp. 22-23), traditionally equated with harmony in the state. One wonders if Dryden was acquainted with the neoplatonist formulation that "all the power of magic consists in love" (Ficino's *Commentaire sur le Banquet de Platon*, trans. R. Marcel, 1956, cited in Easlea, p. 94). For discussions of Dryden's Charles, see Dustin Griffin, "Dryden's Charles: The Ending of *Absalom and Achitophel*," *PQ* 57 (1978):359-82; Bernard N. Schilling, *Dryden and the Conservative Myth* (New Haven and London: Yale Univ. Press, 1961), pp. 270-74; and Richard Wendorf, "Dryden, Charles II, and the Interpretation of Historical Character," *PQ* 56 (1977):82-103.

[16]On the Pythagorean analogies, see S. K. Heninger, Jr., *Touches of Sweet Harmony* (San Marino: Huntington Library, 1974), esp. pp. 103-104, 178-89.

[17]Because I am placing my reading of Dryden's alchemical imagery in the larger context of his other poems and of the history of science, I note implications beyond those discussed by Bruce A. Rosenberg in "*Annus Mirabilis*

Distilled," *PMLA* 79 (1964):254-58. The best reading of this imagery in its political context is by McKeon, esp. pp. 72-73, 165, 170, 181.

[18]Steven Zwicker in *Dryden's Political Poetry* (Providence: Brown Univ. Press, 1972), p. 80, reads the flaming pillars as "symbols of God's presence among the Israelites" (and see pp. 91-92).

[19]"Of Heroic Plays: An Essay," in *Critical Essays*, 1:161.

[20]I quote Sanford Budick, *Poetry of Civilization* (New Haven and London: Yale Univ. Press, 1974), p. 108, whose observation was anticipated by Cedric D. Reverand, "Patterns of Imagery and Metaphor in Dryden's *The Medal*," *YES* 2 (1972):108-109; Reverand compares the clipping of a coin to invading "the circle . . . in necromancy."

[21]See Roper's discussion of Shaftesbury as Satan in this poem (*Dryden's Poetic Kingdoms*, pp. 87-103).

[22]These allusions were identified by H. T. Swedenberg, Jr., in *Works*, 2:298, and Anne Barbeau Gardiner, "Dryden's *The Medall* and the Principle of Continuous Transmission of Laws," *CLIO* 14 (1984):65.

[23]For a survey of the various connotations of "mercury," see Douglas Brooks-Davies, *The Mercurian Monarch* (Manchester: Manchester Univ. Press, 1983), pp. 1-10.

[24]Joseph Quercetanus Duchesne, *The Practise of Chymicall, and Hermeticall Physicke*, trans. Th. Thymme (London, 1605), sig. DI (v), cited by Debus, *The English Paracelsians*, p. 93.

[25]Anne Barbeau Gardiner, "Dryden's *The Medall*," also notes that these lines refer to "the interpenetration of Jesus, the Father, and his disciples" (p. 65), which reinforces my sense that through his diabolical arts Shaftesbury ineffectually apes the divine alchemy.

[26]See Numbers 21:6-9; in *Dryden's Political Poetry*, pp. 97-98, Zwicker fully analyzes this image.

[27]The Renaissance demonologists were fond of citing the contest of Moses (and Aaron) against the Pharoah's magicians as an example of heavenly versus diabolical magic. See West's account of Deacon, Walker, and Bodin on this matter in *The Invisible World*, pp. 33, 44.

[28]Of course, Shaftesbury was identified with necromancy and Satanism in contemporary pamphlet literature, as noted by Rachel A. Miller, "Political Satire in the Malicorne-Melanax Scenes of *The Duke of Guise*," *ELN* 16 (1979):212-18. But even though Achitophel's diabolical rhetoric has been analyzed many times, it has never, as far as I know, been examined in terms of allusions to magic. For examples, see Schilling, pp. 175-99, and Arthur W. Hoffman, *John Dryden's Imagery* (Gainesville: Univ. of Florida Press, 1962), pp. 76-88.

[29]In *Poetry of Civilization*, pp. 102-105, Sanford Budick instructively analyzes the relationship between power and design in this poem. Schilling reviews seventeenth-century ideas of "law" (pp. 147-53). David/Charles is a godlike creative force in Thomas E. Maresca's reading, "The Context of Dryden's *Absalom and Achitophel*," *ELH* 41 (1974):340-58.

[30]In the dedication of *Don Sebastian*, Dryden writes admiringly of the individual "who centring on himself, remains immovable, and smiles at the madness of the dance about him": *Works*, 15:60. J. Douglas Canfield cites this passage in "The Image of the Circle in Dryden's 'To My Honour'd Kinsman',"

PLL 11 (1975):168-76, where he reviews the various connotations of circles but does not include the magician's circle; in the section on Barzillai's son, as in the letter to "My . . . Kinsman," says Canfield, the "circle implies the perfection of the soul" (p. 173).

[31]For this observation I am indebted to Anne Barbeau Gardiner's unpublished manuscript, "Dryden and the Royal Brothers: *Threnodia Augustalis* in its Historical Context," pp. 34-36.

[32]"Dryden and the Royal Brothers," p. 19.

[33]Anne Barbeau Gardiner overlooks this allusion in her otherwise revealing study, "Dryden's *Britannia Rediviva*: Interpreting the Signs of the Times in June 1688," *HLQ* 48 (1985):257-84.

[34]See James D. Garrison, *Dryden and the Tradition of Panegyric* (Berkeley and London: Univ. of California Press, 1975), p. 186. "The merciful king of *Astraea Redux*, challenged in *Absalom and Achitophel*, gives way to the just king of *Britannia Rediviva*." In *The Secular Masque*, of course, Charles's reign is symbolized by Venus.

[35]See Earl Miner's note to line 327 in *Works*, 3:482.

[36]Citations of poems from 1697-1700 refer to the versions in *The Poetical Works of Dryden*, 2nd edn., ed. George R. Noyes (Boston: Houghton Mifflin, 1950).

[37]The tradition is documented by Brooks-Davies in an interesting chapter, "Druids, Egyptians, and the Norman Yoke," in *The Mercurian Monarch*, pp. 150-79.

[38]*Works*, 17:256.

[39]Roper's instructive reading of this imagery, p. 157, does not pick up the magical implications.

[40]As the Inca puts it in *The Indian Queen*, "humane actions hang on springs that be / Too small, or too remote for us to see" (II.i.75-76).

[41]The best interpretation of the prologue is by Maximillian E. Novak, "Commentary" on *The Tempest*, in *Works*, 10, esp. pp. 328, 346-49.

[42]Hoffman's commentary on this imagery does not deal with magic (see pp. 42-43).

[43]A point not made by Novak in his "Commentary" on the play in *Works*, 10:406-408.

[44]Sanford Budick discusses the passage from *Religio Laici* in *Dryden and the Abyss of Light* (New Haven and London: Yale Univ. Press, 1970), p. 106, but overlooks the magical implications.

[45]The best analyses of this poem are those of John Hollander, *The Untuning of the Sky* (1961; rpt. New York: Norton, 1970), pp. 404-10, and of Jay Arnold Levine, "Dryden's *Song for St. Cecilia's Day, 1687*," *PQ* 44 (1965):38-50. Levine reminds us that in Clement of Alexandria, Orpheus is spoken of as "influenced by daemons" (p. 47); clearly, says Levine, Dryden considers the harps of Orpheus and Jubal inferior to Cecilia's organ, which more closely approximates the celestial harmony.

[46]See Hollander, pp. 412-21.

[47]See John Dawson Carl Buck, "The Ascetic's Banquet: The Morality of *Alexander's Feast*," *TSLL* 17 (1975):573-89, and W. B. Carnochan, "Dryden's Alexander," in *The English Hero, 1660-1800*, ed. Robert Folkenflik (Newark: Univ. of Delaware Press; London and Toronto: Associated Univ. Presses, 1982), pp. 46-60.

[48]On this poem, see Hollander, p. 404, and Earl Miner, *Dryden's Poetry* (Bloomington and London: Indiana Univ. Press, 1967), pp. 252-54.

[49]Though he does not take up the topic of magic, Cedric D. Reverand II provides an instructive close reading of the imagery of this poem in "Dryden on Dryden in 'To Sir Godfrey Kneller'," *PLL* 17 (1981):164-80. For a recent discussion of Dryden's notion of imitation, see John L. Mahoney, *The Whole Internal Universe: Imitation and the New Defense of Poetry in British Criticism, 1660-1830* (New York: Fordham Univ. Press, 1985), pp. 22-32.

[50]Roper notes a "shift in emphasis from Saturnian times to the Garden of Eden," from "the familial analogy" to the analogy of God's relation to mankind (p. 106). Zwicker believes that Dryden loses "the ability . . . to see the nation and king in terms of sacred metaphor" (*Dryden's Political Poetry*, p. 109) and endows individuals with "the correlative relationship with the Old Testament elect that had earlier illuminated the trials of the whole nation" (p. 103). In general the later Dryden was losing his "belief in the possibility of political redemption" (p. 120). Unlike Pope, says Garrison, Dryden does not take up antigovernment satire; instead, he turns away from what Maynard Mack calls "the throne as center of the dream of the civilized community" (*Dryden and . . . Panegyric*, p. 196).

[51]"Of the Pythagorean Philosophy," in Noyes, *Poetical Works*, p. 882. In *Politics and Language* Zwicker argues that in this passage Dryden becomes reconciled "with a universe that is disturbing, at points incomprehensible" (p. 173). I am more inclined to think that it signals not reconciliation but resignation, as in *The Secular Masque*: "All, all, of a piece, throughout" (87).

SEL 27 (1987)
ISSN 0039-3657

A Vindication of the Press and the Defoe Canon

MAXIMILLIAN E. NOVAK

When George Watson asked me if I would do the Defoe entry in the *New Cambridge Bibliography of English Literature* I agreed reluctantly. I felt a little like Martin in Jonathan Swift's *A Tale of a Tub*, who, knowing the coat (*i.e.* the holy text) he and his brothers had inherited from their father had become covered with decorations by his brother, Peter, to an extent that attempting to restore it to its original plainness might result in a completely tattered garment (such as his brother, Jack, had managed to produce upon his discovery of Peter's errors) decided to proceed slowly and carefully for fear of destroying the basic properties of the garment. My situation differed somewhat in that there had never been any simple and true ur-bibliography for Defoe. When John Robert Moore published his *Checklist* in 1961, he believed that every item was certainly by Defoe, even though a number of his ascriptions had been challenged. The very number of entries, 547, created some skeptics. The number that he had added to the canon was not proportionally great, but he continued to add entries to various revised editions. The reputation of the *Checklist* depended on his ability to defend his selection. After he died on 18 July 1973, the challenges to his ascriptions increased.[1] When Frank Bastian published a list of twenty-four new ascriptions with his biography of Defoe, in 1981, it was clear that the authority of Moore's *Checklist* had crumbled and that the notion of a firmly established canon for Defoe had vanished. Bastian presented little detail on why he considered these pieces by Defoe, feeling, apparently, that his guess was as good as Moore's or anyone else.[2] My effort at averting anarchy had not succeeded.

My intention in this essay is double: I want to examine the grounds

Maximillian Novak is professor of English at the University of California, Los Angeles. He is the author of several books on Defoe, and is currently engaged in writing his biography.

put forward by P. N. Furbank and W. R. Owens for removing item number 399, *A Vindication of the Press* (1718),[3] from the Defoe canon; and I want to add two new works to the Defoe canon, explaining why I feel there is a high probability that these works are by Defoe. I should say, at the outset, that a thorough discussion of the grounds for inclusion of works in the canon or exclusion therefrom is so rare in the bibliographical literature on Defoe that the effort of Furbank and Owens must be considered a welcome addition to any attempt at establishing the canon. I regard it, however, as part of a dialogue. My response is not a dismissal of their questions but rather an attempt to answer some of the issues they raise.

Since Defoe signed so few works, the presence of *A Vindication of the Press* in any list of Defoe's works depends on probability and the authority of previous scholars. Probability and authority are not the best bases for a definitive list of Defoe's writings, but were that list to include only such works as he openly acknowledged, he could not be assigned *Robinson Crusoe, Captain Singleton, Moll Flanders, Colonel Jack, A Journal of the Plague Year,* and *Roxana*—all of his important works of fiction upon which his modern reputation is based. Surely no one is so attached to certainty as to trade the great Defoe of modern literary history for the somewhat lively but clearly minor poet and journalist who identified himself as the author of *The True-Born Englishman.*

Although Defoe's enemies often accused him of writing various pamphlets, the first list compiled by a friendly biographer appeared toward the end of Robert Shiel's sympathetic sketch of Defoe's career. He named Defoe's "principal performances" as: "*A Plan of Commerce, Memoirs of the Plague, Religious Courtship, Family Instructor, History of Apparitions, Robinson Crusoe, Political History of the Devil, History of Magic, Caledonia, De Jure Devino, English Tradesman, History of Colonel Jack.*"[4] The preponderance of works from the 1720s suggests that Defoe's authorship of works during this period was an open secret, whether written anonymously or pseudonymously. The omissions are notable, but any Defoe bibliographer would like to know whence he had his information. His only mistake appeared in a footnote that supplied the information, "Cleveland's Memoirs etc. are also said to be his."[5] Footnote or not, error haunted lists of Defoe's writings from the start.

The list has grown since Shiel's early effort. When Abel Boyer accused Defoe of producing some sixteen pamphlets from his "Forge" in 1716, he turned out to be right on almost all of them.[6] He claimed to have recognized Defoe's style; more likely he had very good inside information through the printing trade. In his own day,

Defoe complained that every incendiary pamphlet was assigned to him and he "abused for being the Author of it."[7] In the nineteenth century the practice continued, for booksellers knew that a work by Defoe would fetch higher prices than one by an unidentified author. Hence he was assigned works such as *Some Memoirs and Amours of a Certain Irish Dean* (1728), a piece in a manner wholly unlike anything Defoe ever produced.[8] John Robert Moore made mistakes. He once announced that he knew Defoe's writings as a father knows his own son, forgetting another proverb that suggested how uncommon such recognition might be. To study his correspondence is to know how often he changed his mind. Contrary to the belief of some of his critics, he omitted works about which he felt any doubt.[9] His authority has to be given some weight.

This is why the dismissal of Moore's authority in the matter of *A Vindication of the Press* strikes me as hasty. Along with Moore's opinion, also dismissed are the opinions of William Trent, Otho Clinton Williams (who edited it for the Augustan Reprint Society), Henry Hutchinson, and myself.[10] Paul Dottin put an asterisk next to it in his list, signaling some doubt, but he included it nevertheless.[11] All of these scholars had various tests by which they tried to determine if the work was by Defoe and concluded that he wrote it. William Trent was the first to place the work in the canon. He examined the pamphlet at the request of Joel Spingarn of the New York Public Library, which had obtained a copy of the pamphlet with two ascriptions to Defoe on the title page. One of these is in a nineteenth-century hand and bears little weight, but the second, with the explicit identification "by D. De Foe," appears to be written in a hand that could have belonged to a contemporary of Defoe. Trent replied to Spingarn on 21 February 1909:

> I am very sure that was my Defoe, and I'm glad to get the reference; not that it is specially important in itself but because it is a tiny fact—belonging to a year almost entirely barren of them.
>
> I have made a careful analysis of it and think that it is certainly Defoe's. Curiously enough I forgot when I first saw it that it was one which an advertisement had led me to suspect to be Defoe's. I had looked it up in the B.M. and failed to run it down.[12]

Trent's reasons for ascribing the pamphlet to Defoe, then, included what may be a contemporary ascription, an advertisement (perhaps one that listed *A Vindication of the Press*) with some other works known to be by Defoe, and "careful" study of the style, all of them good reasons for a probable ascription. Under these circumstances, the arguments of Furbank and Owens must be examined with great care. What is their evidence and how strong must such evidence be to overturn the opinions of these scholars?

The argument that inspires least confidence comes at the end when they maintain that the ideas are banal and that the work is unworthy of a great writer. Defoe described himself as the master of a kind of writing factory in *The Manufacturer* (1719-1720),[13] and in his reply to Boyer's attack upon him, he spoke of having only a part in some of the pamphlets ascribed to him.[14] During the three years that preceded the publication of *Robinson Crusoe* in 1719, Defoe was as much an editor as a writer, and there is little question that the quality of his productions suffered. Despite this adulteration, many Defoe scholars believed they could detect his hand in many pamphlets written during these years. Certainly the quality of the work should not be a major criterion for making a judgment about authorship.

Another weak argument presented by Furbank and Owens is their claim that there seems to be no reason for Defoe to have written the piece. I have not found any parliamentary debates about press censorship at this time, but the question was very much in the air. The government had decided to censor a speech made at the gallows by James Shepeard, a young Jacobite who had attempted to assassinate George I. Moore's *Checklist* attributes at least one pamphlet to Defoe on this controversy.[15] A related matter concerned the swirl of controversy around Benjamin Hoadly, Bishop of Bangor. In the introduction to his reprint, Clement Williams mentioned the Bangorian Controversy as a possible cause but tended to dismiss it—all too lightly I think.[16] After Benjamin Hoadly had been accused of having changed his sermon when he had it printed, charges of lying and insincerity were hurled by all parties to the dispute. James Shepeard's speech had mentioned "Bangorian Sincerity" as a code word for its opposite.[17] And what was most startling was the way in which the battle between bishops of the Church of England was carried forth in the daily press. There may have been a precedent for the use of newspapers for this purpose but none comes easily to mind. The attacks and replies were so extensive that several guides to the battles were published including one, *A Muster-Roll of the B. of B-ng-rs Seconds,* that appeared as late as 1720.[18] The controversy certainly makes its appearance in *A Vindication of the Press.*[19] Furbank and Owens seem to have underestimated its importance.

But why would Defoe defend liberty of the press at this time? Was he not operating mainly as a spokesman for the government? Would self-interest be too base a motive to suggest? Defoe was making his living by writing and editing newspapers, and he was being paid handsomely to remove the "sting" from the opposition press. In the very month in which this pamphlet appeared, on 26 April 1718, Defoe wrote one of his most revealing letters on his activities to Charles de la Faye. He explained how difficult it was to have complete control and explained that whatever seditious material was published had to be regarded as having evaded his watchful eye.[20] As a letter written a month later, on 23 May, reveals, Defoe had been trying for years to preserve Morphew, one of his publishers, from persecution by the government.[21] Censorship had to be in his mind, and he probably felt that a defense of the press would serve a useful purpose at this time.

Two other pieces of evidence that are educed to demonstrate that Defoe did not write this work are "contemptuous remarks about the Quakers" and a praise of Congreve. Now it should be pointed out that despite Defoe's general respect for Quakers, he was not above finding some amusement in their mannerisms. His imitation of Quaker style actually drew an angry response from the Quaker community, causing him to issue an apology.[22] And as for Congreve, Defoe not only has occasional echoes of Congreve in his work but also assigns to him the realm of comedy in *The Pacificator*, his version of the battle between the ancients and moderns.[23] He clearly disliked what he considered to be the immorality of Congreve's comedies, but as with his appreciation of Rochester, it would not have prevented his admiring Congreve's wit.

What then is left? The final footnote speaks of some "statistical tests" that appear to rule out Defoe's authorship, but no details are provided about them. I too have used a computer concordance and various stylistic tests of a statistical nature on Defoe's style and vocabulary. Such tests work well enough when there is a control. I could demonstrate that Addison employed a different sentence structure and a distinctly different paragraph structure from Defoe. But I could not prove that some anonymous journalist might not reveal a style similar to that of Defoe. Frank Bastian was certain that Defoe must have written some of the works ascribed to Guy Miege, but some of the characteristic aspects of Defoe's prose style appear in a work by Miege written when Defoe was an infant. Unless we are ready to posit an extraordinarily precocious Defoe, we will have to conclude that simple resemblances cannot be the basis for an ascription.[24]

Unfortunately for the case made by Furbank and Owens, the case for stylistic resemblances between *A Vindication of the Press* and

Defoe's writings extend beyond a few simple phrases. Paragraph beginnings are fairly typical of Defoe's mannerisms, including "'Tis owing," "As for," "This was," "This is," and the very typical, "'Tis true." The author numbers his points; he uses "viz." a number of times; and his use of irony is similar to Defoe's.[25] The variation in the lengths of paragraphs would be typical of Defoe, with some as short as eight lines and others extending to forty-four.[26] Punctuation within paragraphs is also much in the manner of Defoe. Phrases such as the "meer scholar" and "the Eyes of the People would bee open" are very much in the manner of Defoe. And the ideas and references are much like those of Defoe. The author seems to know something about the Turks and Scots;[27] he is an admirer of Milton and Jeremy Taylor;[28] he speaks in open praise of knowing about geography and commerce. Finally, the publisher, Thomas Warner, had published many works by Defoe before this piece and was to publish many more.[29]

One of the key passages in *A Vindication of the Press* is a praise of Defoe as a "Person of little Learning, but of prodigious Natural Parts," and a praise of the popular success of *The True-Born Englishman*.[30] At this point the author compares Defoe to Shakespeare, who was emerging at this time as England's greatest writer—a writer who appealed to a wide audience and who was a natural genius as opposed to a writer who drew upon traditional learning. Furbank and Owens suggest that Defoe would have been unlikely to have disparaged his own learning in this manner.[31] Unfortunately for this argument, the notion of "learning" at the time almost always referred to knowledge of the Greek and Latin classics, and Defoe, who was not the "meer scholar" disparaged by *A Vindication of the Press*, might have appreciated the compliment more in 1718 than in his earlier years when he regarded plays as morally suspect.

I think that Defoe had enough of a following by 1718 to have received such a compliment from a complete stranger, but I doubt very much that praise of this kind would have been forthcoming from the supposed writer—a young man who had studied to become a clergyman in the Church of England. Just a year later Charles Gildon was to attack *Robinson Crusoe* for its appeal to a general rather than a learned audience.[32] From a writer who purports to belong to the established church and who offers what Otho Clinton Williams calls "the critical commonplaces of the time," praise of a political poem such as *The True-Born Englishman* must appear somewhat odd.[33] One would expect more quotations from Latin and Greek as well as a somewhat more "elegant" style. Once the autobiographical claims of the ostensible writer are opened to question the notion of the author being exactly who he claims to be appears extremely doubtful. That allows the possibility that such a compliment may have come from someone working under Defoe's general direction or from Defoe himself. He was certainly proud enough of his popularity—proud enough to have reminded his readers of it or to have allowed it to stand if one of his assistants composed it. If, then, this passage cannot be used as a sure indication of a connection with Defoe, it cannot be used to dismiss Defoe's role in the work.

II

Having made my point about the caution that ought to be used in removing works from the Defoe canon, I should warn of the equal care necessary in suggesting additions to the canon. In putting forward two new works for possible inclusion in the canon, I acknowledge that I am proceeding on probability rather than certainty. There is no signature appended to either of these pamphlets. My evidence involves a combination of factors including style, the nature of the ideas, the attitudes, and, with one of them, the publisher.

The first is titled, *The Case of a Standing Army Freely and Impartially Stated.* The title page provides no publisher; only the date and place, London, 1698. It has all the appearance of being one of many pamphlets that Defoe wrote on the subject of a standing army. He supported William III's request for such forces after the Treaty of Ryswick had seemingly ended the war between England and France. His opponents were the members of the country party, always suspicious of the power of the court, "classical republicans," who believed that a militia was the best protection against tyranny and Tories. So far as we know this was the first controversy in which Defoe used the method of overwhelming his enemies by the sheer volume of pamphlets.[34] Moore added several in revised editions of his *Checklist,* and others may yet be added, since Defoe regarded an armed England as crucial to keeping the ambitions of Louis XIV in check.[35]

One of the advantages of having so many pamphlets written on the same subject is that some repetition must become inevitable. *The Case of a Standing Army* has so many of these repetitions that it sometimes assumes the quality of a pastiche. As in his *An Argument Shewing That a Standing Army Without Consent of Parliament Is Not Inconsistent with a Free Government* (1698), he maintains that the entire nation has changed to a modern, money economy and that under such conditions, the House of Commons must always have control of the purse. J. G. A. Pocock sees this as Defoe's most original contribution to the debate and a direct response to the ideas of Fletcher of Saltoun:

> Defoe asserted that a society built on military service and tenure was not only feudal but baronial, uncultivated, violent, and repressive; true freedom was modern and could only be found in commercial society, where the individual might profit by wealth and enlightenment and did not risk his liberty in paying others to defend and govern him, so long as he retained parliamentary control of the purse strings. . . . The confrontation of Fletcher with Defoe supplies an antithesis between virtue and commerce, republicanism and liberalism, classicism and progressivism. The Old Whigs identified freedom with virtue and located it in a past; the Modern Whigs identified it with wealth, enlightenment, and progress toward a future.[36]

As in the pamphlets ascribed to Defoe, the author of *The Case of a Standing Army* insists on the distinction between England under William III and the past. "England" the author urges, "now is in sundry Circumstances, different from England formerly, with respect to the manner of Fighting, the Circumstances of our Neighbours, and of ourselves."[37]

In *A Brief Reply to the History of Standing Armies* (1698), he complained of "Grumbletonians" or "Murmerers" against the army.[38] He repeated similar phrases in *Some Reflections on a Pamphlet Lately Published, Entitled An Argument Shewing that A Standing Army is Inconsistent with a Free Government* (1697), a work to which he appended his initials.[39] In *The Case of a Standing Army*, he refers to "Grumbletonians" and "Malcontents."[40] As in a work with a similar title, *The Case of Disbanding the Army* (1698), he warns against cries about "Liberty" as a snare for the "unthinking."[41] And as in *Some Reflections*, he notes that Poland, which has no standing army, has been ravaged by "Swedes, Muscovites, and Tartars."[42] That two of the works he quotes for evidence appear in the catalogue of his library[43] may also be offered as evidence along with his use of ideas he was to offer many times during his career—an attack on Charles II for introducing luxury into England and his defense of the ordinary English soldier.

The work has wide paragraph length variations, an important indication of Defoe's style. Some paragraphs have only eight lines with others extending to forty. Punctuation within paragraphs is typical of Defoe, who apparently gave general instructions to favor commas, semi-colons, and colons rather than periods within paragraphs.[44] Certain signs of Defoe's mannerisms are everywhere present: "Viz," "I think," "as he calls it." Paragraph beginnings with generalized phrases such as "'Tis" are common. I think that anyone reading through his other tracts in defense of a standing army would recognize this pamphlet as Defoe's.

My second ascription, *Some Remarks upon the Late Differences among the Dissenting Ministers and Preachers. With a Brief Answer to Mr. Pierce of Exeter* was published by William Boreham in 1719. I have claimed two other tracts published by Boreham during 1718 for Defoe, and I feel that every tract published by him has to be examined carefully for signs of Defoe's hand.[45] He was clearly Defoe's most important publisher during these years both for tracts and newspapers.

The stylistic evidence for Defoe's hand in this work is overwhelming. Defoeisms include: "In a word," "viz." (used five times), "Upon this Foot," "I say." Paragraph length variation is from those with three lines to others with more than forty. Paragraph beginnings are again typical, if somewhat more complex. They include: "It is said," "I say," "It is," "I know," "As to the." And the ideas are those of the man who was to defend the Christian concept of the Trinity in a lengthy blank verse poem contained in *A New Family Instructor* published nine years later—the "orthodox" Christian view as Defoe saw it.

The occasion for the pamphlet was the meeting at Salter's Hall to consider what was clearly an outbreak of arianism among a number of Nonconformist congregations. Although the best known among the group was an old acquaintance of Defoe, James Peirce, the congregation of Defoe's village, Stoke Newington, was also involved.[46] The controversy threatened to destroy any unity among the Dissenters, particularly when one group decided that an oath affirming belief in the Trinity would clear the air. Many refused to sign, some, at least, on the grounds that it was an infringement of their civil liberties. Without condemning those who openly stated their sincere doubts about the concept of the Trinity, Defoe lined up with the subscribers. He always insisted that his own inability to conform was based on fairly narrow differences. But those differences were based on sincerely held beliefs. He regarded arianism, on the other hand, as a fundamental error and was to give over a large portion of *The Political History of the Devil* (1726) to an attack on those attracted to it.[47] Like many of the works Defoe was to write from this time forward, the author of *Some Remarks upon the Late Differences among the Dissenting Ministers* writes in a manner that seems to announce to its readers that they will know (or ought to know) the identity of the author. Defoe was the foremost propagandist for the Dissenters from the beginning of the century, and he might well have assumed that his readers would recognize his mannerisms. The reference to "Mr. T—— a Dissenting Minister near *London*" as a person who had changed his mind about the Trinity, is clearly to Martin Tompkins of Stoke Newington. Defoe is even harsher on Peirce, whom he accuses of using the language of equivocation: "*Mr. Peirce* is too much a Master of Language to want Words more fully to have expressed himself, tho' he had not joyn'd any Epithets of abhorrence to Distinguish himself."[48] The author does not accuse Peirce of being a doctrinaire arian but rather of having doubts about the Trinity which he has not resolved. What Defoe asks for is a confession of those doubts, though he believes that the controversy may have had a devastating and permanent effect upon Christianity in Britain. I feel confident about Defoe's authorship of this tract, but I have to admit that my certainty about the evidence can only be translated into a probability for Defoe's authorship.

Certain remarks that Professor Furbank has made in a review of some books on Defoe suggest that his sense of what Defoe wrote and did not write is more assured than the position that I have been putting forward in this article.[49] He and Owens are about to embark on a book concerned with the Defoe canon. It is a project which Rodney Baine began several years ago before abandoning it and one which needs desperately to be done.[50] I would hope that they would offer some of their conclusions as they proceed in their task. In matters of probability, the entire case for and against a conclusion should be laid out. And I would urge a procedure somewhat different from that followed in treating *A Vindication of the Press,* a work which, on balance, seems very likely to have been written by Defoe.[51]

NOTES

[1]Perhaps no attack on Moore's ascriptions and on the entire tradition of ascribing works to Defoe was more devastating than Rodney Baine's demonstration that William Bond was a more likely author of works surrounding the deaf claimant to second sight, Duncan Campbell, than Defoe. See *Defoe and the Supernatural* (Athens: Georgia Univ. Press, 1968), pp. 137-98; and John Robert Moore, *A Checklist of the Writings of Daniel Defoe* (Bloomington: Indiana Univ. Press, 1960), p. 173, item 432. For a recent update of Moore's *Checklist*, see Pat Rogers, "Addenda and Corrigenda: Moore's *Checklist*," *PBSA* 75 (1981): 60-64.

[2]F. Bastian, *Defoe's Early Life* (London: Macmillan, 1981), pp. 307-18. Perhaps the strangest ascription is that of *The History of the Press Yard* (1717). Although it has often been ascribed to Defoe by libraries, no important writer on Defoe has accepted it as an authentic work by Defoe. Bastian's inclusion of this work among his "New Attributions" was as good as an announcement that all previous judgments on the canon might be ignored.

[3]P. N. Furbank and W. R. Owens, "*A Vindication of the Press* (1718): Not by Defoe?" *PBSA* 78 (1984): 355-68.

[4]Theophilus Cibber, et al., *The Lives of the Poets of Great Britain and Ireland*, 5 vols. (London: R. Griffiths, 1753), 4:323.

[5]Ibid., 4:323. The association between this work by Abbé Prevost d'Exiles and Defoe is of literary interest even though the first translation did not appear until 1732, a year after Defoe's death.

[6]Abel Boyer, *The Political State* (February 1717), p. 123; and (June 1717), pp. 632-33. See also Defoe, *Mercurius Politicus* (July 1717), pp. 472-73.

[7]Daniel Defoe, *An Appeal to Honour and Justice*, in *The Novels & Selected Writings of Daniel Defoe*, 14 vols. (Stratford-Upon-Avon: Shakespeare Head Press, 1927-1928), 13:211.

[8]It appeared as late as 1941 in the list compiled for the first *CBEL* by Henry Hutchinson.

[9]See, for example, the correspondence at the William Andrews Clark Memorial Library between John Robert Moore and Edna Davis.

[10]See Williams's introduction to *A Vindication of the Press*, Augustan Reprint Society no. 29 (Los Angeles: William Andrews Clark Memorial Library, 1951), pp. i-v.

[11]Paul Dottin, *Daniel Defoe et ses romans*, 3 vols. (Paris: Les Presses Universitairies de France, 1924), 3:830.

[12]Spingarn papers, New York Public Library.

[13]Defoe, *The Manufacturer*, ed. Robert Gosselink (Delmar, New York: Scholars' Facsimilies & Reprints, 1978), pp. xiv-xvii, and no. 44, 18 May 1720.

[14]*Mercurius Politicus* (July 1717):472-73.

[15]John Robert Moore, *Checklist*, p. 156, item 395. See also James Shepeard, *Last Speech* (n.p., n.d.), folio half sheet in the Bodleian Library (Ms. Rawl. D. 383).

[16]*Vindication of the Press*, p. ii.

[17]See my discussion of the ways in which the entire nature of "sincerity" became a crucial part of these debates in "Sincerity, Delusion, and Character in the Fiction of Daniel Defoe and the Sincerity Crisis of his Times," *Augustan Studies: Essays in Honor of Irvin Ehrenpreis*, ed. Douglas Lane Patey and Timothy Keegan (Newark: Univ. of Delware Press, 1985), pp. 109-26.

[18]See also *A Collection of Papers Scatter'd Lately about the Town in The Daily Courant, St. James's Post, etc.*, 2nd edn. (London, 1717), especially pp. 2-4.

[19]Pp. 10-11.

[20]*The Letters of Daniel Defoe,* ed. George Harris Healey (Oxford: Clarendon Press, 1955), pp. 450-54.

[21]*Letters,* p. 456, n. 1.

[22] Defoe's parody of Quaker style is not exactly malicious, but its exaggeration of Quaker mannerisms was certainly intended to be amusing. Any comparison between pamphlets such as *A Declaration of Truth to Parson Benjamin* and the writings of one of Defoe's Quaker correspondents, Benjamin Coole, reveals how comic the supposed author must have seemed to Defoe and his readers. For Defoe's unpleasant encounter with Quaker resentment over his parodies, see Thomas Wright, *The Life of Daniel Defoe* (London: C. J. Farncombe and Sons, 1931), p. 206.

[23]See *A True Collection of the Writings of the True-Born Englishman,* 2 vols. (London, 1703-1705), 2:167.

[24]See Guy Miege, *A Relation of Three Embassies from His Sacred Majestie Charles II to the Great Duke of Muscovie* (London: J. Starkey, 1669), pp. 18, 47, passim.

[25]The most convenient summary of some of Defoe's favorite expressions may be found in William Lee, *Daniel Defoe: His Life and Recently Discovered Writings,* 3 vols. (London: J. C. Hotten 1869), 1:vi.

[26]A broad sampling of paragraphs from Defoe's writings shows that he tends to vary their lengths from fewer than 20 words to the occasional very long one of five hundred words. Average paragraphs seldom extend beyond a hundred words or so. But there is what would appear to be a deliberate attempt to achieve a change of rhythm through altering the size of paragraphs. Of course his methods changed somewhat over his entire career. His earliest writings were composed of many very brief paragraphs, and he tended to use longer ones as he grew older; but the strong pattern of variation remained. In contrast, Swift's paragraphs in *The Examiner*, to take a random example, will run as long as seven or even eight hundred words without any noticeable pattern of variation. Addison's paragraphs are somewhat shorter but they tend toward a uniform length.

[27]Defoe lived in Scotland for several years during the reign of Queen Anne. He often boasted of his knowledge of Turkish history and even produced a continuation of Marana's *Letters of a Turkish Spy* in 1718.

[28]Defoe was thoroughly familiar with both writers. *The Political History of the Devil* (1726) has several chapters devoted to a discussion of Milton's concept of Satan and Christ, while *Conjugal Lewdness* (1728) drew heavily on Taylor from the standpoint of both his ideas and style. I choose these works to illustrate my point because they show the fullest uses of these writers, but Defoe has ample references to both writers before 1718.

[29]Moore, *Checklist,* p. 239.

[30]Pp. 29-30.

[31]Furbank and Owens, p. 357.

[32]See *Robinson Crusoe Examin'd and Criticis'd,* ed. Paul Dottin (London: J. M. Dent, 1923), pp. 71-72, 112.

[33]I am suggesting, in short, that although many of the critical statements represent contemporary commonplaces, there are some that do not fit together very well. What seems like pure criticism should be viewed as a screen for political statements.

[34]He did this most notably after the death of Queen Anne when he was trying to defend his patron, Robert Harley, and himself, but the effect of such an effusion of print upon any debate was not lost on some of his earliest critics. One of them described him as a writer whose prolific output might make the regulation of the press necessary:

Whose Pen show'rs Ink like the descending Rain,
And speaks the diabetes *of his brain.*

The True-born-Hugonot: or, Daniel deFoe. A Satyr (London, 1703), p. 3.

[35]Items 17a, *Some Queries concerning the Disbanding of the Army* (1698), and 19a, *The Case of Disbanding the Army* (1698), were added to the *Checklist* after its appearance in 1960.

[36]J. G. A. Pocock, *Virtue, Commerce, and History: Essays on Political Thought and History* (Cambridge and New York: Cambridge Univ. Press, 1985), p. 231.

[37]Sig. A2.

[38]Sig. A2.

[39]See p. 2.

[40]P. 2.

[41](London, 1698), p. 10. Compare *Case of a Standing Army*, p. 3.

[42]*Case of a Standing Army*, p. 26. Compare *Some Reflections*, p. 22.

[43]Helmut Heidenreich, ed., *The Libraries of Daniel Defoe and Phillips Farewell* (Berlin: H. Heidenreich, 1970), items 124 and 230. These are works on the wars in Flanders by Guido Bentivoglio and Famiano Strada.

[44]Defoe must have given general instructions to the printer, since in the manuscripts of "The Complete English Gentleman" and "Of Royall Educacion," Defoe uses a dash for most punctuation within paragraphs. The paragraph is made the unit of thought with periods coming mainly at its conclusion.

[45]See my attribution of *Two Arguments Never Brought Yet* in *N&Q* 22 (1975):345-47.

[46]Peirce is listed as Defoe's man in Exeter in the list of his correspondents. See *Letters*, p. 116.

[47]Especially pp. 74-75.

[48]*Some Remarks upon the Late Differences*, p. 29.

[49]*The London Review of Books* (19 September 1985): 14.

[50]See Rodney M. Baine, "Chalmers' First Bibliography of Daniel Defoe," *TSLL* 10 (1969):547-68.

[51]Although he had the same methods as most Defoe scholars for detecting the presence of Defoe, William Trent established what seems to me to be the best *tone* for trying to establish the Defoe canon. He confessed his prejudices, his lack of evidence, his occasional failure to convince himself that there was sufficient reason for ascribing a work to Defoe even though he might have wished that Defoe had written it. Like Furbank and Owens, he was willing to allow doubtful works to drop from the canon if he thought them inferior productions, but he was interested in eliminating them by open and balanced discussion. See his articles in *The Nation* 85 (1907):516-8, 180-82, 19-32.

SEL 27 (1987)
ISSN 0039-3657

Heaven's "Last Best Work": Pope's "Epistle to a Lady"

TAYLOR CORSE

Toward the end of his second Moral Essay, "Of the Characters of Women," Alexander Pope writes about the genesis of one particular woman, his lifelong friend Martha Blount:

> Heav'n, when it strives to polish all it can
> Its last best work, but forms a softer Man.[1]
>
> (271-72)

It has recently been argued that Pope's "misogyny" extends even to the woman "whom he means to dissociate from the general failings of her sex."[2] I shall argue in this essay that Pope is not a male supremacist, and that his ideas about women derive from several sources, a consideration of which may affect our understanding of the Lady in Pope's "Epistle." His portrait of Martha Blount is drawn from life, but it also draws on literary precedence (Milton in particular), on contemporary feminism, on theology and scripture, and on ethical concerns which were formulated, long ago, in classical antiquity. The supreme ease with which Pope achieves this remarkable synthesis makes it difficult to reconstruct, however sketchily, the "background" of his poem. My own attempt to provide such a scaffolding will begin with the well-known couplet (271-72), lines which have been the focus of much discussion over the years.

Several critics have noted the androgynous nature of this "softer Man": according to Martin Price, Martha Blount "becomes a fusion

---

Taylor Corse, Assistant Professor of English at the University of Tennessee at Martin, is the author of a forthcoming essay on Pope, "Force and Fraud in *The Rape of the Lock*" (*Philological Quarterly*). He is presently at work on a book-length study of Dryden's *Aeneid*.

of the charm, variety, and energy of feminine passion, and the stability, directness, and strength of masculine reason";[3] she "benefits," says Wallace Jackson, "from the paradoxical coalescence of male and female qualities within herself";[4] she "avoids," says David B. Morris, "the defects of traditional masculine and feminine conduct while she simultaneously unites the traditionally divided virtues of womanly softness and manly strength."[5] The unanimous consensus of these critics, including Howard D. Weinbrot, is that Pope's Lady is "an amalgam of the best of both sexes."[6] Astute as these assessments are, they overlook, it seems to me, the influence of Milton, and the variety of Miltonic contexts on which Pope is drawing.

Pope's language recalls in various ways the language of Milton. The process whereby Heaven "forms" Miss Blount is like the "forming" process whereby God created Eve:

> Under his forming hands a Creature grew,
> Manlike, but different sex.
>
> (*Paradise Lost* VIII.470-71)[7]

Miss Blount, moreover, is called a "softer Man" for the same reason that Eve is said to have a "Heav'nly form / Angelic, but more soft, and Feminine" (*PL* IX.457-58). Softness is a relative, not an absolute, quality. In comparison to the rest of her sex ("Too soft a lasting mark to bear," 3), Miss Blount is made of fairly firm stuff; she has been "tempered," as it were, or brought to a certain degree of resiliency and strength. It is well to remember that Eve is formed for "softness" and "sweet attractive Grace" (*PL* IV.298). It is Eve's "softness," her ability to yield, which softens Adam's heart and which sets in motion the process of redemption and reconciliation described in Book X. When Pope addresses Martha Blount as a "softer Man," he identifies her as a daughter of Eve; Eve, of course, had other daughters, one of whom was Blount's contemporary, Esther Johnson. Expressing the same sense of wonderment as Pope, thus Jonathan Swift, in his poem "To Stella, Written on the Day of Her Birth, But Not on the Subject, When I was Sick in Bed," marvels at the paradox of his own lady friend:

> When, among scholars, can we find
> So *soft*, and yet so *firm* a mind?[8]

Although Swift is writing in a lighter vein than Pope, both poets find in their respective ladies a combination of certain traits (Stella, says Swift, "seems to feel my pains alone, / And is a Stoic in her own") which make each woman a model of Christian softness, someone who can pity the infirmities of others, and Stoic firmness, someone who can endure her own afflictions. Pope goes much further than Swift in pursuing the implications of this theme. The heterogeneous character of Martha Blount unites not only "Courage with Softness," but "Modesty with Pride" (278); this combination of contradictory qualities, of masculine and feminine traits, was present, moreover, from the very beginning in Eve's composite character. Consider, for instance, that oxymoronic union—"Modesty with Pride." The same locution appears in the fourth book of *Paradise Lost*, when Adam praises Eve for her many attractive graces, not the least of which, according to Milton, is her "modest pride" (310). In Pope as in Milton, opposites come together to create a kind of *concordia discors*. It would therefore seem that the virtues ascribed to Martha Blount are not "traditionally divided," as Morris and other critics assume; on the contrary, they are traditionally *united* virtues.

The making of Miss Blount has its comic side of course. Like some master chef, Pope's creator "Picks" (273) and "Blends" (275) the best ingredients, "Shakes [them] all together, and produces—You" (280). This final gesture is the rhetorical flourish of an artist showing off his masterpiece, his *pièce de résistance*. Pope seems to have borrowed this comic recipe for a human being from his friend Jonathan Swift, whose poem "On Mrs. Biddy Floyd" was widely admired and often imitated. Swift's recipe contains many of the same ingredients as Pope's ("Truth," "good nature," "look serene," "decent pride"), and the two eulogies are remarkably similar in tone as well as substance:

> Jove mixed all up, and his best clay employed;
> Then called the happy composition Floyd.[9]

Irvin Ehrenpreis has said that "all Mrs. Floyd's attractions are moral or intellectual";[10] the same thing may be said of Martha Blount. Although both women are praised for their beauty, there is little attention given to physical appearance in either poem. Martha's "blue eyes" (284) are the one physical trait that Pope puts into his inventory of personal attributes, and this particular detail seems all the more striking since everything else lays stress upon her manners and morals.

Pope strengthens the association between the Lady of his "Epistle" and the Lady of *Paradise Lost* by calling her heaven's "last best work." On more than one occasion, Adam also piles superlative upon superlative in his praise of Eve:

> Awake
> My fairest, my espous'd, my latest found,
> Heav'n's last best gift.
>
> (*PL* V.17-19)

In Book VIII, Adam issues a torrent of hyperboles—"wisest, virtuousest, discreetest, best" (550). Difficult to pronounce, the line calls such attention to itself that its own validity is called into question; Raphael, in fact, finds it necessary to rebuke Adam for being overly adulatory. In Book IX (896-97), Adam himself discovers what it means to be uxorious:

> O fairest of Creation, last and best
> Of all God's Works.

This final tribute, in which Adam reproaches Eve for tasting the forbidden fruit, echoes the earlier tribute in Book V, thereby reminding us of Eve's happy state before the fall. Pope brings together all these passages, and the movement of his verse makes it one of the most "arresting" moments in the poem: "Heav'n, when it strives to polish all it can / Its last best work, but forms a softer Man." No two readers will probably agree upon the precise significance of this allusion; there is little doubt, however, that Pope is paying a gallant compliment when he concurs with Milton that woman, who came "last" in the order of created beings, is therefore "best." John Dryden makes the same point in his "Prologue to *Amphitryon*," where the actress Mrs. Bracegirdle, speaking on behalf of her sex, voices a similar view of woman—to the chagrin, moreover, of the male audience:

> Our Sex, you know, was after yours design'd;
> The last perfection of the Maker's mind.[11]

Here the preposition "after" does double duty: it means both "later in time" and "in closer imitation of." Pope and Dryden clearly invoke the authority of Milton, and both exemplify a common poetic attitude.

Eve is a woman of many virtues, and Adam singles out, for special mention, her "Innocence and Virgin Modesty" (*PL* VIII.501). "Virgin Modesty" also finds its way into Pope's panegyric, when

Miss Blount is praised for the way in which

> Serene in Virgin Modesty she shines,
> And unobserv'd the glaring Orb declines.
>
> (255-56)

Nowadays we tend to think of a modest person as someone who is shy and unassuming; in Pope's day, however, as in Milton's, "modesty" had much stronger connotations. *Modestia*, from which our modern word derives, means "self-control." Being modest, Miss Blount is "Mistress of herself" (268); being immodest, other women are changeable creatures, "Chameleons" (156) or "Cynthia[s] of this minute" (20). It may be useful in this context to recall the Virgin Queens, Elizabeth and Anne, both of whom are associated in Pope's early poem, *Windsor Forest*, with the goddess Diana, the chaste huntress of classical mythology.[12] In Pope's "Epistle," where "Ev'ry Lady," including, one supposes, Caroline herself, "would be Queen for life" (218), Martha Blount is the notable and noteworthy exception. Only she, moreover, is associated with the moon, whose tutelary deity is of course Diana (Cynthia, also a version of Diana, represents, however, mutability).

In the eighth book of *Paradise Lost*, Milton speaks of the sun and moon as "communicating," respectively, "Male and Female light, / which two great Sexes animate the World" (150-51). Pliny the Elder, from whom Milton takes much of his cosmology, ascribes different attributes to these two stars. The sun, according to Pliny, is "a masculine star, burning up and absorbing everything," whereas the moon, by contrast, is "a feminine and delicate planet."[13] These traditional associations seem to have some bearing on the solar/lunar imagery of Pope's "Epistle." In juxtaposing the "glaring Orb" of the sun with the "more sober light" of the moon (254), Pope calls attention not only to a sexual dichotomy, but to a confusion and perversion of sexual roles. In usurping the male light of the sun, vain and presumptuous women arrogate to themselves "the full light" in which men's "bolder Talents" are properly "display'd" (201). Such women who expose themselves to the burning glare of public scrutiny suffer the consequence: "Worn out in public, [they] weary ev'ry eye" (229). Yet even men, Pope suggests, should limit their engagement in, and exposure to, public life:

> But grant, in Public Men sometimes are shown,
> A Woman's seen in Private life alone.
>
> (199-200)

The subdued pun on "shown" ("shone") and the radical pun on "Private" (from the Latin *privatus,* "taken away from public affairs") indicate that sensible people, regardless of sex, appreciate the value of a "well-timed Retreat" (225), whether from politics, business, or that most exhausting activity—pursuit of pleasure.

Another quality which distinguishes Miss Blount from the vicious female characters who populate Pope's "Epistle" is her capacity for love, and "Love," as Milton defines it, is that which "refines / The thoughts and heart enlarges" (*PL* VIII.589-90). Pope seems to have this all-embracing definition of love in mind when he exhorts his friend, "To raise the Thought and touch the Heart, be thine!" (250). In striking contrast to a woman like Cloe, who can think but cannot feel ("'Say what can Cloe want?'—she wants a heart," 160), or to a woman like Atossa, who can feel but cannot think ("No Passion gratify'd except her Rage," 126), Martha Blount possesses sense and sensibility.

There can be no doubt that this *mulier bona* is the epitome of womankind. What is strange, however, is that Pope seems to have given her a double identity. The woman he describes in lines 257-68, who has a "Husband" and a "Daughter," is markedly different from the woman addressed at the end of the poem, whom Phoebus gave "Beauty, but deny'd the Pelf / Which buys your sex a Tyrant o'er itself" (287-88). Many critics, such as Irvin Ehrenpreis, assume that this is one and the same woman and that Pope has introduced these fictive details to protect the identity of his maiden lady.[14] It seems to me, however, that Pope is presenting two different women—one married, the other unmarried—and that he does this so that his portrait will be fully representative. The sort of marriage which Martha Blount might have had, if her parents had been able to buy her a husband (i.e., a "Tyrant"), is set against her actual lot in life: a spinster whom providence has compensated by giving her "Sense, Good-humour, and a Poet" (i.e., Alexander Pope). This dual portrait complements the many dualities in Pope's "Epistle": the duality of reason and passion, of public and private life, of sun and moon, of male and female light, of Apollo and Diana, and of art and life. Pope does not insist on a necessary dichotomy between these various forces, any more than he insists on a necessary dichotomy between men and women. On the contrary, his vision of woman as a "softer Man" reflects his deep concern with reconciliation in general, and with the complex whole created by the harmonization of opposites.

Pope's equation of husband and tyrant is of a piece with his opinion that women, in general, are "by Man's oppression curst"

(213). In her eloquent treatise, *Some Reflections upon Marriage* (1730), Mary Astell comments at bitter length on the oppression of women: "Whatever may be said against Passive Obedience in another Case, I suppose there's no Man but likes it very well in this; how much soever Arbitrary Power may be dislik'd on a Throne, not Milton . . . nor any of the advocates of Resistance, would cry up Liberty to poor *Female Slaves,* or plead for the lawfulness of Resisting a private Tyranny."[15] The counsel which Astell offers to "poor *Female Slaves*" who groan under the yoke of a "private Tyranny" is patience (the martyrlike ability to suffer or endure) and submission: "A Woman that is not Mistress of her Passions, that cannot patiently submit, . . . will never be acceptable to such an absolute Sovereign as a Husband."[16] Astell plainly wishes that subjection were not a necessary condition of marriage; she also wishes that women would not "marry off in haste, for perhaps if they took Time to consider and reflect upon it, they seldom would marry."[17]

A wife can make the best of a bad situation, provided she is "Mistress of her Passions," or, as Pope puts it, "Mistress of herself" (268). Such a woman

> Charms by accepting, by submitting sways,
> And has her humour most, when she obeys.
>
> (263-64)

Here, once again, Pope's language recalls the language of Milton. We find Adam, in Book IV, enamoured of Eve's "Beauty and submissive Charms" (498), yet her subjection, Milton tells us, is not something forced, "but requir'd with gentle sway" (308) and "Yielded with coy submission, modest pride" (310). In this ideal state of affairs before the fall, Milton softens such harsh injunctions as that of Paul in Hebrews 13:17 ("Obey them that have the rule over you, and submit yourselves") and in Colossians 3:18 ("Wives, submit yourselves unto your husbands"). In a fallen world, however, where a husband is often a "Tyrant," the only way many a woman can preserve her independence and identity is by dissembling. "He that knows not how to Dissemble," so goes an ancient proverb, "knows not how to Live."[18] The ideal married woman in Pope's *Epistle* is one who

> ne'er answers till a Husband cools,
> Or, if she rules him, never shows she rules.
>
> (261-62)

She is someone, in other words, who knows how to dissemble. Only thus can she subvert "them that have the rule over" her.

Married or unmarried, men and women alike would do well to emulate the "serene" disposition of Martha Blount:.

> Oh! blest with Temper, whose unclouded ray
> Can make to morrow chearful as to day.
>
> (257-58)

In a letter to Jonathan Swift, dated 16 February 1733-1734, Pope indicates what he may mean by the word "Temper": "Your Lady friend is *Semper Eadem,* and I have written an Epistle to her on that qualification in a female character."[19] *Semper Eadem* ("always the same") was the motto of Queen Elizabeth and Queen Anne.[20] There is good reason to believe that Pope is being serious when he applies this motto to his own "Lady friend." In a universe where everything is subject to change, an even "Temper" assures some measure of stability and continuity. A blessing in itself and a blessing to others, it "Can make to morrow chearful as to day." Such a "qualification" is no less desirable in a private person like Martha Blount than it is in a public figure like Elizabeth or Anne.[21] Within the intimate circle (or microcosm) of Pope's personal friends, Miss Blount holds a position analogous to that of a royal sovereign in the larger world (or macrocosm) of English society. Although Pope nowhere mentions the Christian term "soul," the idea seems essential to his conception of self and personality. Mary Astell, a contemporary of Martha Blount, says, "I know not whether or no Women are allow'd to have Souls."[22] Astell does not claim to be a theologian, and she sees the imputation that women have no souls as an egregious symptom of masculine tyranny. The casual remark "let fall" by Martha Blount ("'Most Women have no Characters at all'") suggests another, more serious, deficiency: lack of character implies a lack of soul.

George Sherburn suggested, some thirty years ago, yet another reason why the Latin tag, *Semper Eadem,* is crucial to Pope's "Epistle": "This quality—constancy of temper as contrasted with variability—is the compliment paid to Martha Blount at the expense of the rest of her sex."[23] The person in the poem who best represents variability is Atossa: "Scarce once herself, by turns all Womankind!" (116). Perhaps the most famous portrait in Western literature of variability is Virgil's Dido: *"varium & mutabile semper femina,"* says Dryden in the Dedication of the *Aeneis,* "is the sharpest Satire in the fewest words that was ever made on Womankind."[24] *Semper Eadem* pays just as sharp a compliment, in even fewer words. This quality, of course, is a common topic in the genre of panegyric. Thus Jonathan Swift, in his Dedication of *A Tale of the Tub*, commends Lord Somers for "Evenness of Temper in all the Scenes of Life."[25] The ethical import of Pope's encomium (as well as Swift's) should not be underestimated. Constancy of temper is one of the cardinal Stoic virtues, and behind it lies a tradition of moral philosophy stretching back to the time of Cicero.

While I do not wish to claim here specific indebtedness, I do want to stress the fact that Cicero (arguably the most influential ancient author throughout the eighteenth century) was a forceful and eloquent spokesman for the Stoic ideal embodied in the catch phrase *Semper Eadem*. In his third *Tusculan Disputation*, Cicero maintains that no one better exemplified this particular virtue than Socrates: "iure autem erat *semper idem* vultus, cum mentis a qua is fingitur nulla fieret mutatio" (my italics).[26] As translated by Christopher Wase (1683): "And well might it be always the same countenance, when there was no alteration in the mind, by which the looks are fashion'd."[27] Cicero, an apparent believer in physiognomy, regarded the human countenance as a kind of index or mirror of the soul. Since Socrates never changed his mind, it follows that his face was always the same (*semper idem*). Such firmness, however, is not to be confused with rigidity; Cicero, in fact, makes a point of distinguishing the demeanor of Socrates (*tranquilla et serena*) from that of someone like Crassus, a person who was said to have "laugh'd but once in all his life-time."[28] Pope himself, on another occasion, upbraids his noble friend Bolingbroke for his apparent insensibility and insensitivity: "You never change one muscle of your face."[29] The serene (literally "clear" and "unclouded") composure of Martha Blount is a different matter altogether. A woman of "fixed Principles" (279), she is

> blest with Temper, whose unclouded ray
> Can make to morrow chearful as to day.

Equanimity is also an important topic in that famous courtesy book, *De Officiis*. "Next to the Bible," says Ben R. Schneider, "perhaps no other guide to conduct had such an influence on Western manners during and since the Renaissance as 'Tully's Offices.' "[30] Alongside Pope's verses in praise of Martha Blount, we may place the following passage in praise of Socrates: "praeclaraque est aequabilitas in omni vita et idem *semper* vultus *eademque* frons, ut de Socrate . . . accepimus" (my italics).[31] As Roger L'Estrange (1681) translates: "And it is an Excellent Thing to observe an Equal

Tenor of Life, and to have still the same humour, and the same countenance; as we find it recorded of *Socrates*."[32] Of all the women in Pope's "Epistle," only Miss Blount achieves the Ciceronian ideal: "to have still the same humour [temperament] and the same countenance." Only she, moreover, has genuine "character"—in the original sense of a "mark engraved or impressed" (from the Greek *χαρακτήρ*). Her complexion, furthermore, had been marred by smallpox, the lasting marks of which she not only learned to bear, but to rise above:

> Spleen, Vapours, or Small-pox, above them all,
> And Mistress of herself, tho' China fall.
>
> (267-68)

That such a countenance and such a stigma should fail to dismay shows, at the very least, considerable strength of character.

In his portrait of Martha Blount, Pope suggests a subtle correspondence between external and internal traits; he dwells, however, at the end of the poem on the intrinsic worth of the inner self.[33] Here, strangely enough, the goddess Diana gives way to Apollo,

> The gen'rous God, who Wit and Gold refines,
> And ripens Spirits as he ripens Mines.
>
> (289-90)

What was once a "glaring Orb" has now become a nourishing, enriching power. The reader may ask how the sun can exert an influence that is maleficent and sterile on the one hand, and beneficent and fertile on the other. This paradox, like so many others in the poem, is a paradox in Milton. Raphael, in the eighth book of *Paradise Lost*, discourses on the mysteries of creation, one of which is the sun

> that barren shines,
> Whose virtue in itself works no effect,
> But in the fruitful Earth; there first receiv'd,
> His beams, unactive else, thir vigor find.
>
> (94-97)

The alchemical operation of the sun, which transmutes base metal into gold, can only work its magic in hidden places: the bowels of the "fruitful Earth" and the recesses of the human psyche.[34] Phoebus Apollo is a "gen'rous God"—generous in being munificent (*generosus*) and procreative (*generare*); thus he "ripens Spirits as he ripens Mines." As a "glaring Orb," he burns up everything, including the men and women who expose themselves to his consuming rays; but as a hidden god, what the theologians would call a *deus absconditus*, he "refines" both "Wit" and "Gold" (the zeugma indicates that each substance is equally precious).

Mere "Pelf," base and barren metal, can purchase goods (even a husband), but it lacks the "virtue" or inherent power to produce what Pope regards as being of greatest value: "Sense, Good-humour, and a Poet." A modern reader may wonder why Pope should assign the same importance to "Sense" and "Good-humour" as he does to poetry ("Poet," the last item in the list, is probably *primus inter pares*).[35] These terms, which meant more in Pope's day than they do in ours, could not be equated with each other unless they were also, in some way, closely related. Dryden understood, as well as anyone, the larger significance of these interrelated terms. "Good Sence and good Nature," says Dryden in his "Discourse concerning Satire," "are never separated, tho' the Ignorant World has thought otherwise."[36] Dryden sees "good Nature" as the "Product of right Reason";[37] he also sees it as "the most God-like Commendation of a Man."[38] Justice and Mercy are the two essential attributes of the Christian god, and "good Nature," according to Dryden, means "Candor" (the ability to judge and discriminate) and "Beneficence" (giving "Allowance to the Failings of others").[39] The context of the entire discussion, needless to say, is that of poetry and criticism. As Charles, Earl of Dorset, was the publicly acknowledged patron of Dryden, so Martha Blount in effect becomes, at the end of this *Epistle*, the private, personal patron of Pope. Pope never divulges her true identity, and even to the end conceals what he reveals.

The ambiguous gender of this "softer Man" confirms her status as a daughter of Eve ("Manlike, but different sex"). Her character, as Pope conceives it, is grounded in classical and Christian tradition. For a different, and far less humane, view of womankind, we have only to turn to Richardson's *Pamela* (1737), a novel which embodies, according to Ian Watt, "a more complete and comprehensive separation between the male and female roles than had previously existed."[40] No such separation can be said to exist in Pope's Miltonic Lady.

NOTES

[1]*Epistles to Several Persons*, ed. F. W. Bateson, The Twickenham Edition of the Poems of Alexander Pope, 11 vols. (London: Metheun, 1961), 3,2:70. References to Pope's poems will be given in line numbers in the text.

[2]Ellen M. Pollak, "Pope and Sexual Difference: Woman as Part and Counterpart in the 'Epistle to a Lady,'" *SEL* 24,3 (1984):461-62.

[3]Martin Price, *To the Palace of Wisdom: Studies in Order and Energy from Dryden to Pope* (Garden City: Doubleday, 1964), p. 163.

[4]Wallace Jackson, *Vision and Revision in Alexander Pope* (Detroit: Wayne State Univ. Press, 1984), p. 92.

[5]David B. Morris, *Alexander Pope: The Genius of Sense* (Cambridge, Mass.: Harvard Univ. Press, 1984), p. 44.

[6]Howard D. Weinbrot, *Alexander Pope and the Traditions of Formal Verse Satire* (Princeton: Princeton Univ. Press, 1982), p. 196.

[7]*PL* VIII.470-71, in *John Milton: Complete Poems and Major Prose*, ed. Merritt Y. Hughes (Indianapolis: Bobbs-Merrill, 1957). All further references to *PL* are cited from this edition and are given in the text by line.

[8]Lines 19-20, my italics. *Jonathan Swift: The Complete Poems*, ed. Pat Rogers (New Haven: Yale Univ. Press, 1983), p. 268.

[9]Lines 11-12, p. 100.

[10]Irvin Ehrenpreis, *Swift, the Man, His Works, and the Age*, 2 vols. (Cambridge, Mass.: Harvard Univ. Press, 1967), 2:309.

[11]Lines 32-33. *The Poems of John Dryden*, ed. James Kinsley, 4 vols. (Oxford: Clarendon Press, 1958), 2:559.

[12]See lines 159-64.

[13]Quoted by George Wesley Whiting, *Milton's Literary Milieu* (Chapel Hill: Univ. of North Carolina Press, 1939), p. 78.

[14]Irvin Ehrenpreis, "The Cistern and the Fountain: Art and Reality in Pope and Gray," *Studies in Criticism and Aesthetics, 1600-1800: Essays in Honor of Samuel Holt Monk* (Minneapolis: Univ. of Minnesota Press, 1969), pp. 165-66.

[15]Mary Astell, *Some Reflections upon Marriage*, 4th edn. (London, 1730; rpt. New York: Source Book Press, 1970), pp. 34-35.

[16]Ibid., p. 59.

[17]Ibid., p. 88.

[18]See Aubrey L. Williams, *An Approach to Congreve* (New Haven: Yale Univ. Press, 1979), p. 110.

[19]*The Correspondence of Alexander Pope*, ed. George Sherburn, 5 vols. (Oxford: Clarendon Press, 1956), 3:349.

[20]For an extensive treatment of *Semper Eadem*, see Larry Vonalt, "Pope's *Epistles to Several Persons*," Ph.D. Diss. Univ. of Florida, 1968, pp. 45-101.

[21]There is scriptural authority for Pope's "qualification" which makes it an appropriate motto for Martha Blount as well. In Heb. 1:12, Paul says of Jesus Christ, "Thou art the same, and thy years shalt not fail." A related verse, in Heb. 13:8, speaks of Christ as "the same, yesterday, and to day, and for ever." To be *Semper Eadem* is thus to imitate, in some imperfect way, the character of Christ.

[22]Astell, *Some Reflections upon Marriage*, p. 55.

[23]See Sherburn's note, *Correspondence*, 3:349.

[24]*The Poems of John Dryden*, 3:1029.

[25]*The Prose Works of Jonathan Swift*, ed. Herbert Davis, 14 vols. (Oxford: Basil Blackwell, 1939—), 1:15.

[26]*Tusculan Disputations*, ed. and trans. J. E. King, The Loeb Classical Library (1927; rpt. Cambridge, Mass.: Harvard Univ. Press, 1960), p. 264.

[27]*The Five Days DEBATE at Cicero's House in Tusculum* (London, 1683), p. 172. A famous variation on this theme appears in Shakespeare's Sonnet 116: "Love is not love / Which alters when it alteration finds."

[28]Ibid.

[29]*The First Epistle of the First Book of Horace Imitated*, 6:459, line 171.

[30]Ben R. Schneider, *The Ethos of Restoration Comedy* (Urbana: Univ. of Illinois Press, 1971), p. 23. The works of Cicero are included in Maynard Mack's "Finding List of Books Surviving from Pope's Library." See *Collected in Himself* (Newark: Univ. of Delaware Press, 1982), pp. 401-402.

[31]*De Officiis*, ed. and trans. Walter Miller, The Loeb Classical Library (1913; rpt. Cambridge, Mass.: Harvard Univ. Press, 1961), p. 92.

[32]*Tully's Offices, in Three Books, Turn'd out of Latin into English. By Sr. Ro. L'Estrange*, 4th edn. (London, 1688), p. 44.

[33]According to Pollak, Martha "is no more an id/entity, no more intrinsic to herself, no more unmixed or less impure than Pope's adulterous and vicious scattered women" (p. 479).

[34]The alchemical operation of the sun can also be seen in *PL* III.583-87.

[35]Patricia Meyer Spacks, *An Argument of Images: The Poetry of Alexander Pope* (Cambridge, Mass.: Harvard Univ. Press, 1971), discusses why the poet has "the climactic position in this list of blessings" (p. 167).

[36]*The Poems of John Dryden*, 2:602.

[37]"*RIGHT REASON*," says Justus Lipsius, author of the popular Christian Stoic tract *De Constantia*, is nothing less than "A True sense and judgement of thinges humane and divine." *Two Bookes of Constancie, Written in Latine by Justus Lipsius, Englished by Sir John Stradling* (London, 1594), ed. Rudolf Kirk (New Brunswick: Rutgers Univ. Press, 1939), p. 79.

[38]Dryden, 2:603.

[39]Ibid., 602.

[40]Ian Watt, *The Rise of the Novel: Studies in Defoe, Richardson, and Fielding* (Berkeley: Univ. of California Press, 1957), p. 162.

SEL 27 (1987)
ISSN 0039-3657

The Mythical Implications in Pope's "Epistle to a Lady"

MOLLY SMITH

Until recently criticism has viewed Pope's "Epistle to a Lady" as posing no problems, as being straightforward in its eulogy of Martha Blount and in its somewhat harsh but nevertheless tolerant criticism of her sex. Recently, in an illuminating but by no means conclusive article, Ellen Pollak has indicated that there are problems in viewing the poem as simply following the pattern of blame and praise through the use of contrasting models. She argues that the portrait of Martha may be read "more fundamentally as the vehicle for the conception of the female as a lack"; Martha, according to Pollak, is the focus of "a discourse that can render woman only as negation," and "the margins Miss Blount inhabits occupy the same conceptual space on which the 'characters' of Narcissa and Atossa have been drawn."[1] Though Pollak is the first to make this point about the collapsed distinction between the earlier portraits and that of Martha Blount, she is by no means the first to see the nature of Pope's culminating eulogy in the poem as, to say the least, problematic. Felicity Nussbaum, in what seems to point to a rather ambivalent stand, insists that "Miss Blount's identity poses no puzzle" and then goes on to point out that underlying Pope's eulogy is the "suggestion that only one thin layer beneath, the ideal woman may resemble the rest of her sex."[2] Rebecca Parkin notes likewise that "his eulogy on Martha . . . is amusingly undercut."[3] Indeed the poem seems to suggest that Pope intends to portray Martha as an ideal, but that she is an ideal whose value as a model is nevertheless tenuous; the ambivalence in her portraiture is intentional and one might better

Molly Smith is a candidate for the doctoral degree at Auburn University.

come to terms with it by understanding the nature of the relationship between Pope and Martha, which in turn emerges as ambivalent and complex.

"Thwarted in his early attempts to gain a wife" and "constrained throughout his life to relations with women in which ridicule was a constant possibility,"[4] Pope emerges in his letters to Martha as a figure highly conscious of his physical deficiencies and well aware of the unlikelihood of having a conventional relationship with her. Thus, Martha's chastity, which is an ideal to be complimented in the poem, as the comparison with the moon suggests, is also implicitly a shortcoming, for it was in reality the factor that rendered impossible on Pope's part any attitude more intense than that of an admirer and friend. The praise is, therefore, necessarily muted, and the poem evolves an understandable but extremely complex paradox—to be admired Martha has to be an ideal, but as an ideal she demands admiration and rejects any stronger emotional commitments. Pope's depiction is a painfully poignant but analytically superior projection of this complex emotional state.

Pope's early letters, which show an equal esteem for both the Blount sisters, are illuminating for the awareness he shows of his own limitations and for the resulting tentativeness apparent in his emotional confessions. In August 1716 Pope writes to Teresa: "Madam,—I have so much Esteem for you, and so much of the other thing, that were I a handsome fellow I should do you a vast deal of good: but as it is, all I am good for is to write a civil letter or to make a fine speech."[5] There is a conscious ambivalence in these letters not unlike that in "Epistle to a Lady," and as James A. Winn points out, "what amount to confessions of love are disguised" by wit or by comical strategies.[6] The possibility of mockery seems to have been a constant concern to Pope, a concern he sometimes tries to ward off by openly admitting its existence: "May you have all possible success both at your Devotions this week, & your Masquerade the next: Whether you repent or Sin, may you do all you wish; and when you think of me, either laugh at me or pray for me, which you please" (1:339). In 1717, in one of his more serious letters, Pope writes again to both sisters:

> If you had any Love for me, I should be always glad to gratify you with an Object that you thought agreable. But as your regard is Friendship & Esteem; those are things that are as well, perhaps better, preservd Absent than Present. . . .
>
> Let me open my whole heart to you: I have some times found myself inclined to be in love with you: and as I have

> reason to know from your Temper & Conduct how miserably I should be used in that circumstance, it is worth my while to avoid it; It is enough to be Disagreable without adding Fool to it, by constant Slavery.
>
> (1:455-56)

In 1734 Pope's attitude in "Epistle to a Lady" is not significantly different. If anything, it is more markedly ambivalent, and paradoxically, the poem is both complimentary and critical. Martha may be a contrast to the other women in the poem, but she is also limited like them to an inherent duality, which in Pope's vision seems to lie at the base of womanhood itself.

In its ambivalence, the poem, like the correspondence between Pope and Martha, is testimony to the complexity of their relationship. Ehrenpreis's statement that "the poem overflows, reaching beyond literature into reality"[7] is true in more ways than he acknowledges. While the poem shows Pope's usual concern with images of light and darkness and nakedness, it seems to revolve primarily around the image of Cynthia or the moon. This highly compressed and pervasive image provides Pope with what Patricia M. Spacks terms "a mythology of control."[8] It is an emblematic control possible only within the artificial precincts of the poem and intended as a reversal of the situation in reality, a situation over which Pope, inhibited by his physical and psychological shortcomings, could never hope to gain control. The poem is evidence also of the poet's ability to put to original use this traditional and even hackneyed image.

Pope indicates early in the poem the use he intends to make of this image:

> Come then, the Colours and the ground prepare!
> Dip in the Rainbow, trick her off in Air,
> Chuse a firm Cloud, before it fall, and in it
> Catch, ere she change, the Cynthia of this minute.[9]

The lines draw the analogy with painting, which is insistently echoed at various points in the poem, even as they touch on the major theme of the poem—the changeability and temporality of female nature. That Pope refers to his portraits as Cynthias "of this minute," and then concludes the poem by drawing an analogy between the Lady and the Moon, is the most important indication we have that the final portrait is not entirely eulogistic. The earlier portraits then become false Cynthias linked by their overt sexuality with Apollo and a contrast to the true Cynthia, Diana:

So when the Sun's broad beam has tir'd the sight,
All mild ascends the Moon's more sober light,
Serene in Virgin Modesty she shines
And unobserv'd the glaring orb declines.

(253-56)

Diana is obviously an important figure in the poem; as Ehrenpreis points out, "Since the lady happens to be a spinster, the lunar tones appropriately suggest Diana and chastity."[10] The last lines of the poem devoted to Phoebus's approval of Martha also amplify the analogy between Martha and Diana, for Phoebus is, after all, Diana's twin brother.

It may be significant that, including the final portrait of Martha, there are twenty-eight Cynthias referred to in the poem, representing possibly the twenty-eight days of the lunar cycle. The first thirteen portraits, which are not fully developed, are treated with a certain amount of gaiety. Then follow three more impressive portraits of the seeming wits—Narcissa, Flavia, and Philomede. Lucretia and Rosamonda are passingly referred to in the description of Philomede. Then follows, starting with Simo's mate, a description of the five non-wits who also remain nameless because they are not important socially. The four figures who follow—Atossa, Cloe, the Queen, and Queensbury—complement and contrast with the previous group by being important social figures. The description of the Lady (the true Cynthia?) completes the portrait-gallery tour. She is, of course, significantly different from the false Cynthias of the preceding lines and is therefore set apart from them by an intervening analysis of the differences between men and women.

The applicability of the analogy between Diana and Martha is manifold. As a spinster, Martha naturally suggests the goddess of chastity. Also, being comprised of the best of man and woman, she becomes a natural counterpart to the androgynous goddess of chastity, childbirth, and the hunt. The metaphor is a compressed but succinct commentary on the relationship between the poet and the lady. By implication, the analogy calls to mind the popular myths associated with Diana/Artemis. These myths in all their variations suggest the duality inherent in this highly androgynous goddess—her chastity and her power, a power often ruthless which almost always manifests itself as a result of her desire to preserve her virtue. If Martha is by implication allied to Diana/Artemis, Pope naturally allies himself with Actaeon, Orion, and Hippolytus, the important cofigures in the myths. Actaeon's vision of Diana naked at the fountain results in his transformation into a deer and his subsequent destruction by his hounds. Pope as a serious artist is painting women, including Martha, in their nakedness in the poem. He makes the analogy himself:

> Poets heap Virtues, Painters Gems at will,
> And show their zeal, and hide their want of skill.
> 'Tis well—but, Artists! who can paint or write,
> To draw the Naked is your true delight.
>
> (185-88)

The metaphor is also used repeatedly in his letters: "I must be content to show my taste in Life as I do my taste in Painting, by loving to have as little Drapery as possible. Not that I think every body naked, altogether so fine a sight as yourself and a few more would be: but because 'tis good to use people to what they must be acquainted with" (1:353). By extension, therefore, Pope's vision of Martha as an ideal, like Actaeon's vision of Diana naked, is self-destructive. The burden of guilt for Actaeon's death in the myth lies wholly on the ruthlessly chaste goddess. Pope must certainly have used the analogy between Martha and the moon with some awareness of its ultimately critical implications.

Ellen Pollak raises the interesting point about Martha's relative silence in the poem as further evidence of her negation.[11] Her silence seems to me a necessary prerequisite to Pope's establishing a principle of control in the poem. Nancy J. Vickers, in an interesting article on the use of the Diana-Actaeon myth in Petrarch's poetry, points out that in using the myth, poets establish their artificial control by reversing the order of the mythological story. Actaeon had in the story lost his voice, and, unable to call to his hounds or his hunters, had lost his life as well. As Vickers points out, "a modern Actaeon affirming himself as a poet cannot permit Ovid's goddess to speak her displeasure and deny his voice; his speech requires her silence"; the poet similarly revenges his psychological and emotional dismemberment at the hands of the goddess and "repeatedly, although reverently, scatters her through his rhymes."[12] Thus, Cynthia is scattered in twenty-eight figures in the poem. Martha's relative silence in the poem and the scattering of Cynthias, like the use of the myth itself which is ultimately critical in its implications, are thus emblematic of the "mythology of control" that Pope achieves by an artificial reversal of the situation in reality.

Orion's encounter with the goddess in the myth, unlike Actaeon's, is more than an accident, though not any the less to be pitied. While in a drunken state he desires the goddess and actually tries to rape her, a foolhardy forwardness that results in his death. Like Actaeon, he is partly responsible for his own destruction through desiring the virgin goddess, and Diana's revenge, as in the Actaeon myth, is the result of her desire to preserve her purity and chastity. The analogy between Martha and the moon goddess, therefore, necessarily implies a criticism of her chastity as a result of which Pope, like Actaeon and Orion, is psychologically trapped by a self-destructive admiration of beauty. The eulogistic nature of the concluding vision of Martha is depressed thus, not only with reference to Martha, as Ellen Pollak seems to suggest,[13] but also with reference to Pope, the recipient of this vision, who is necessarily trapped by the seemingly illogical juxtaposition of true beauty and unapproachability.

There are two classical sources for the Diana-Hippolytus myth—Ovid's account in *Metamorphoses* XV, 492-546, and Euripides' play. While Ovid is certainly the immediate source, Pope seems to owe as much to Euripides. It would, of course, be difficult to determine if Pope actually knew the play, but the last section of "Epistle to a Lady" seems to owe something to the opening of Euripides' play. In the play, Hippolytus, an ardent admirer of Diana, presents the goddess with a garland and the following praise:

> Loved mistress, here I offer you this coronal;
> it is a true worshipper's hand that gives it you
> to crown the golden glory of your hair.
> With no man else I share this privilege.[14]

Pope is making a similar gesture when he concludes his poem with a "garland" of praise. He closes with a reference to the fact that Martha can claim a poet to sing her praise, a line sharply reminiscent of Hippolytus's statement that Diana can likewise claim him alone among mortal men. Irrespective of whether this alliance exists between the play and the poem, Pope's references to the moon while speaking of Martha call into play a reference to the Diana-Hippolytus myth. The choice of image seems to indicate Pope's awareness of the fact that his admiration for Martha is necessarily self-destructive even as Hippolytus's worship of Diana had been. Pope's choice of this rather ambiguous analogy between Martha and Diana raises some rather interesting possibilities. Has Pope, like Hippolytus, destroyed himself by a foolish attachment to an impractical ideal? Does Martha's rejection of the physical make her a saint or a ruthlessly irrational figure not to be emulated? In raising her to the status of a goddess, is Pope implicitly drawing attention to her failure as a woman? Pope writes within the tradition in which poets confer immortality on their beloved through verse, but in this conferment of immortality there is an implied irony, a recognition of the power of the poet himself who, while acknowledging the ideal nature of his beloved, necessarily conveys to the world his impression of her very shortcomings as an ideal. The concluding statement—"The gen'rous God . . . To you gave Sense, Good Humour and a Poet"—is a charged acknowledgement of his own poetic power over the Lady, and functions dramatically in a fashion similar to that effected by the reversal of the mythological stories of Actaeon and Orion. The poem, in other words, functions as a Freudian dream fulfillment seeking to rectify an unsatisfactory reality. The control of psychological and emotional power imposed by Martha in reality becomes the foundation for the poet's control by artistic power and ironic suggestion in the poem. According to Freud, who conceives of the writer as dreamer and the work of art as a personal fantasy, "unsatisfied wishes are the driving power behind phantasies; every phantasy contains the fulfillment of a wish, and improves an unsatisfactory reality."[15] Pope, dissatisfied with an actual situation, makes it the basis for a faithful but ironic depiction, which transfers, by his awareness of the permanence of art over reality, the ultimate power into his own hands.

Another myth which seems to be relevant to the poem is that of Niobe and her children. Diana destroys Niobe's female children when Niobe insults Leta, Diana's mother. The act points again to the goddess's power and ruthlessness. But the myth has also led to the association of Diana with the death of females. It may be significant that Pope begins the poem with what amounts to a verbal slaughter of women by Martha: "Nothing so true as what you once let fall, / 'Most women have no Characters at all'" (1-2). By this statement, Martha sets herself apart from women, even as she sets herself apart from men by her chastity. Her association with the androgynous moon goddess is thus particularly apt. Pope must also have found the figures of Actaeon, Orion, and Hippolytus psychologically satisfying as counterparts to himself. Each of these figures was, of course, deformed in his interaction with Diana; Actaeon was transformed into a deer, Hippolytus (in Ovid's account) into an old man, and Orion into a constellation. Each, in other words, was either dehumanized or made impotent. There seems to be at least a small suggestion that Pope is laying the blame for his psychological deformity at Martha's door, that he attributes his subsequent failure with the opposite sex to the precipitous nature of his relationship with Martha.

Something needs to be said also about Pope's reference to Phoebus, Diana's twin brother, towards the end of the poem. Pope seems here to be drawing an analogy between himself and the god of poetry. The analogy may be relevant for several reasons: Pope and Martha were of about the same age; Pope was not above seeing himself as equal in rank to the poetic muse; and in the concluding line of the poem, Pope is, by his reference to the poet, nodding his approval of Martha as Phoebus had in the earlier passage. The reference implies an interesting possibility. Phoebus, like Diana, is a composite of opposites, but unlike her, a lover of both men and women. He thus resembles her most and differs from her most in his bisexuality. In a letter to the Earl of Peterborough, Pope refers to himself as "abominably Epicoene."[16] The expression is, of course, metaphoric,[17] even as the lunar tones in the description of Martha are. But the choice of Phoebus may be an unconscious revelation by the poet, pointing to an essential physical inadequacy that made impossible any satisfactory relationships with women. But whether the analogy is psychologically revealing or not, the image is yet another indication of the tragic dilemma underlying the relationship between Pope and Martha. Like Apollo and Diana, Pope and Martha are necessarily bonded; but, as the metaphor suggests, they are also necessarily separate because anything more would be tantamount to intellectual and spiritual incest. Thus Pope's characterization—"Woman's at best a Contradiction still" (270)—is more than just a simple paradox.

Pope's attitude towards Martha in the poem is not unlike his attitude towards Belinda, whom he both loves and satirizes. The difference lies, however, in the tone of the later work which is considerably less gay than *The Rape of the Lock*. I suspect that there is more truth than is generally acknowledged to Benjamin Boyce's statement that Pope seems to owe as much to Juvenal as to Horace.[18] In his later poetry, Pope seems to be moving towards Juvenalian satire. In the context of the poem, which is reminiscent of Juvenal's satire on women, there seems to be no way out for a woman. She can either be charmingly false like the twenty-seven false Cynthias, or cold and perfect like the Lady. Pope may show an awareness that a woman's role was limited by the imposition of eighteenth-century society,[19] but his poem is most certainly anti-feminist in its implications. As Dustin H. Griffin points out, "the poem has made it abundantly clear that in such a world a woman has no life except in marriage," restraining though such a situation might be.[20] Martha may be exemplary in her nature, but she falls short in her role as a woman by not combining her "Good-humours" with the role that society has mapped out for her. The perfect golden mean between the extremes of overt sexuality and cold chastity is the woman whose portrait is missing in the gallery (and by implication, in life):

> She who can love a Sister's charms, or hear
> Sighs for a Daughter with unwounded ear;
> She who n'er answers till a Husband cools,
> Or, if she rules him, never shows she rules;
> Charms by accepting, by submitting sways,
> Yet has her humour most, when she obeys.
>
> (259-64)

That such an outlook is probably the result of Pope's physical shortcomings and the resulting frustrations in his relationships with women, and that it is certainly not atypical of the general social temper of the period are facts that do not require much corroboration. Neither does our awareness of the presence of this dark and tragic outlook in the poem reduce its worth as a complex and highly structured work of ethical seriousness. As Pope himself intended it, it shows him "most to advantage."[21]

The poem in its undercutting of the eulogy to Martha follows a structural pattern similar to that of "Epistle I," where the lines on Cobham are "in some degree undercut by satire."[22] What Winn calls a "relative lack of surface emotion and sexuality"[23] is only an intellectual guise, and the central image of the moon is the key to its unmasking. By using the image of the moon to characterize simultaneously the introductory negative portraits and Martha Blount, the poet necessarily undercuts his eulogy. By his choice of myth, by comparing Martha to the chaste but ruthless and unapproachable goddess, he likewise implies a criticism of the very virtues he appears to be praising. Most significantly, by allying himself with Actaeon, Orion, and Hippolytus, pathetic victims of the goddess's injustice, he draws attention to Martha's destructive power over himself, and with conscious irony he reverses the situation through poetry to claim for himself the ultimate power.

NOTES

[1]Ellen Pollak, "Woman as Part and Counterpart in the 'Epistle to a Lady,'" in *The Poetics of Sexual Myth* (Chicago: Univ. of Chicago Press, 1985), pp. 109-11, 117. (Originally published in *SEL* 24, 3 [1984]: 461-81.)

[2]Felicity Nussbaum, "Pope's 'To a Lady' and Eighteenth Century Woman," *PQ* 54 (1975):444, 451.

[3]Rebecca Parkin, *The Poetic Workmanship of Alexander Pope* (Minneapolis: Univ. of Minnesota Press, 1955), p. 217.

[4]James A. Winn, "Pope Plays the Rake: His Letters to Ladies and the Making of Eloisa," in *The Art of Alexander Pope*, ed. Howard Erskine-Hill and Anne Smith (London: Vision Press, 1979), pp. 114-15.

[5]*The Correspondence of Alexander Pope*, ed. George Sherburn, 5 vols. (Oxford: Clarendon Press, 1956), 1:349-50. All further citations from Pope's letters will be from this edition; volume and page numbers will appear in the body of the paper.

[6]Winn, p. 96.

[7]Irvin Ehrenpreis, "The Cistern and the Fountain: Art and Reality in Pope and Gray," in *Studies in Criticism and Aesthetics 1600-1800: Essays in Honor of Samuel Holt Monk*, ed. Howard D. Anderson and John S. Shea (Minneapolis: Univ. of Minnesota Press, 1967), p. 165.

[8]Patricia Meyer Spacks, *An Argument of Images: The Poetry of Alexander Pope* (Cambridge, Mass.: Harvard Univ. Press, 1971), p. 6.

[9]"Epistle to a Lady," in Alexander Pope, *Epistles to Several Persons (Moral Essays)*, ed. F. W. Bateson, in The Twickenham Edition of the Poems of Alexander Pope, gen. ed. John Butt, 6 vols. (London: Methuen, 1951), 3,2:48-49, lines 17-20. All further citations from "Epistle to a Lady" will be from this edition; line numbers will appear in the body of the paper.

[10]Ehrenpreis, p. 165.

[11]Pollak, p. 111.

[12]Nancy J. Vickers, "Diana Described: Scattered Woman and Scattered Rhyme," *CritI* 8(Winter 1981):265-79, 279.

[13]Pollak, pp. 109-17.

[14]Euripides, *Hippolytus*, trans. David Greene, in *Euripides I*, ed. David Greene and Richmond Lattimore (Chicago: Univ. of Chicago Press, 1955), lines 81-84.

[15]Sigmund Freud, *On Creativity and the Unconscious: Papers on the Psychology of Art, Literature, Love, Religion* (New York: Harper and Row, 1958), p. 47.

[16]*Correspondence*, 2: 189.

[17]Jean H. Hagstrum, *Sex and Sensibility: Ideal and Erotic Love from Milton to Mozart* (Chicago: Univ. of Chicago Press, 1980), p. 137.

[18]Benjamin Boyce, *The Character Sketches in Pope's Poems* (Durham: Duke Univ. Press, 1962), p. 4.

[19]Felicity Nussbaum, *The Brink of All We Hate: English Satires on Women 1660-1750* (Lexington: Univ. Press of Kentucky, 1984), p. 139.

[20]Dustin H. Griffin, *Alexander Pope, the Poet in the Poems* (Princeton: Princeton Univ. Press, 1978), p. 125.

[21]*Correspondence*, 4: 448.

[22]Parkin, p. 217.

[23]Winn, p. 115.

SEL 27 (1987)
ISSN 0039-3657

Pope and Antithesis: "Law and War With Words"

VICKI SAPP BAILEY

In *The Arte of English Poesie* George Puttenham colorfully personifies the rhetorical figure of antithesis:

> Ye haue another figure very pleasant and fit for amplification, which to answer the Greeke terme, we may call the encounter, but following the Latine name by reason of his contentious nature, we may call him the Quarreller, for so be al such persons as delight in taking the contrary part of whatsoeuer shalbe spoken.[1]

For the eighteenth-century writer, antithesis proved a natural extension of the empirical epistemology; the requisite shared experience of "self" and "social" must certainly include dissention as well as agreement. Antithesis illustrates the power of the human mind to freeze, or reorder the process of experience into manageable models; to find similarity in difference and order in chaos; and to use language most flexibly, but to the ends of reason. The formal bond of this figure shows us that however discrete, different, or "contentious" two elements might be, they can (and must) share in the great whole which is creation—or society—and co-exist in a meaningful way. The writer employing antithesis skillfully searches out these connections and asserts or discloses them. Puttenham, speaking of the manipulative potential of the "sententious" figures (including, and especially, antithesis) concludes: "For to say truely, what els is man

---

Vicki Sapp Bailey has an M.A. in Comparative Literature from the University of North Carolina at Chapel Hill. She is currently a graduate student in English at Rice University and is working in critical theory and eighteenth-century studies while teaching full time in the Rice Intensive English Program (ESL) and in the University Writing Center.

but his minde? which, whosoeuer haue skil to compasse, and make yeelding and flexible, what may not he commaund the body to perfourme?"[2] The eighteenth-century mind framing the world antithetically followed the Newtonian paradigm in working within the great cosmic paradox, that "it was the tension of opposing forces that made the structure one."[3] The rhetorical manifestation of this paradigm thus constituted a very powerful figure.

Alexander Pope used antithesis to dramatize the paradox of individual life sharing in an infinite and infinitely complex universe. Paul Fussell expresses this paradox as Pope himself may have considered it:

> Man is thus a mighty curious creature. A flesh-machine of self-destructive depravity fraught with ignorance and vanity, and at the same time inspired somehow with an anima which has it in its power to redeem all defects except . . . mortality, he is a wandering paradox perpetually looking for a place now to hide and now to exhibit himself.[4]

Pope's concern lay with particularity in an ideal context of universal wholeness and truth, and his couplets illuminate the paradoxical and often contentious aspects of this fundamental part-whole relationship. Antithesis works ideally for the heroic couplet in several ways: (1) it posits two poles, or an encounter of two unlike or contrary positions; (2) its difference-in-contiguity implies a common aim or base of comparison, and therefore the opportunity for judgment; and (3) it brings the two values—whether ideas, entities, qualities, names, etc.—close together as particulars in order that the poet might closely scrutinize, compare, and resolve them into a larger field. The tight closure of the couplet itself and the gathering device of antithesis bring temporarily together within the control of language conflicting or chaotic elements, for rational experimentation by the poet. Such poetic discourse provides a "holding-place" for the process of empirical experience, and therefore, an experimental field for the poet. Life may seem to be confused, unjust, or disconnected; yet the poet can rhetorically frame it against the backdrop or in the plan of a universal ideal:

> HERE then we rest: the Universal Cause
> Acts to one end, but acts by various laws.[5]

The "one" and "various" both point, antithetically, to "Universal Cause"; within the couplet and with antithesis, Pope "presents us with one great style and one great vision . . . that of unity in diversity, of order in variety, of actual pattern in apparent chaos," and attempts to bring "into the focus of common sense the certainty that creation entire, despite the many observable imperfections of the human condition, is perfect and good."[6]

The perfection of nature as model included for Pope human nature. Nature essentially embraced "the nature of the human being and the milieu created by him, cities and estates, politics, society, and business, poetry and conversation."[7] Pope certainly accepted Quintilian's prescription: "Fix your eyes on nature and follow her. All eloquence is concerned with the activities of life . . . and the mind is always readiest to accept what it recognizes to be true to nature."[8] Confronted also with the ignorance, dullness, and conflict he observed around him, Pope necessarily assumed an antithetical attitude toward life. In "Epistle to Dr. Arbuthnot," Pope uses antithesis self-consciously in an ironic and humorous gesture, in his assault on "Sporus," Lord Hervey, "one vile Antithesis" who "Now trips a Lady, / and now struts a Lord" (325, 329). Sporus's "vile Antithesis" describes both a social and a natural monstrosity, and a destructive, not constructive force in society and creation. Pope slips briefly out of the couplet form for Sporus's sake:

> His wit all seesaw, between *that* and *this*,
> Now high, now low, now master up, now miss,
> And he himself one vile Antithesis.
>
> (323-25)

The effeminate Sporus of the nonsignifying "wit" does not fit within the balanced discourse of the heroic couplet and constructive binary tension of antithesis. Pope places him in a triplet with his mind meaninglessly oscillating between the empty deictics of "that" and "this," a pseudo-antithesis. Pope thus informs the reader (rhetorically as well) that Sporus/Hervey is finally "antithetical" to what good antithesis should be: a productive tension of opposing forces. The use of "one" instead of "a" in line 325 further reinforces Pope's rhetorical play: an "antithesis" should never be a simple "one" but should guard the individualism of its parts as they share in the proposed relationship. Pope intricately plays with the fact that, although Sporus's nature is, unfortunately, "true" (that is, to be observed in mankind)—it is also "antithetical" to the true nature that consists of the productively antithetical One-Many paradox that should define a healthy society. Sporus/Hervey as "one vile Antithesis" previews the triumph of duncery in *The Dunciad: Book the Fourth.* Just as Pope can recognize and prove to the reader Sporus's offensive and destructive nature, he can report the universal domination of this nature in the *Dunciad*'s world. In both cases, perverse antithesis betrays a "Quarrel" in the mind of the poet straining rhetorically to reflect something like a universal ideal. And, in both cases, Pope's humor finally reveals itself as an antithesis of control and capitulation. For Pope, reason decreed that "it is necessary for limits to be put on human intellectual ambitions and, contrariwise, that the human mind, working within its proper limits, has tremendous powers."[9] Pope's couplets, and especially his antitheses, stand as "efforts of recovery and resistance,"[10] where the poet's mind can test its powers against its limitations. However, although the recovery and resistance effort might become quite demanding and frustrating, the poet always controls his experimental field.

As Fussell recognizes in Pope's poetry, "antitheses swarm everywhere," in "*this* and *that*, wit and judgment, reason and passion, art and nature, city and country, ancient and modern, uniformity and variety, sublime and beautiful."[11] Pope used all the modes of antithesis described by Quintilian, including single words with single words, pairs of words (or phrases) with pairs, sentences with sentences. Words repeated in antithesis show different cases, moods, tenses. Often, words of similar appearance but different meaning are paired. At times, "special elegance . . . may be secured by placing names in antithesis."[12] Pope used antithesis in its diverse potentialities as a barometer of his attitude toward the capacity for harmony between man and the universe, the individual and society—and of the poet's power to frame opposites or seemingly unrelated particulars in fruitful tension. The remainder of this essay addresses Pope's use of antithesis in three texts: *Windsor Forest* (1713), *An Essay on Man* (Epistle I) (1733-34) and *The Dunciad* (Book the Fourth) (1743). These poems not only exhibit Pope's great antithetical range, but also rhetorically trace his changing world view throughout his career. Antithesis is the dominant figure in the *Essay*; in the other two texts, its relative scarcity is revelatory of change.

Windsor Forest, the product of Pope's enthusiastic youth, shows the poetic reach aimed at absolute control over a responsive world. Time and space in the abstract call through specific time and place, to be harnessed and manipulated by the poet:

Thy forests, Windsor! and thy green retreats,
At once the Monarch's and the Muse's seats,
Invite my lays.
. . . .
GRANVILLE commands; your aid, O Muses, bring!
What Muse for GRANVILLE can refuse to sing?
        The Groves of Eden vanished now so long,
Live in description, and look green in song:
These, were my breast inspired with equal flame,
Like them in beauty, should be like in fame.

(1-10)

Opening the poem with chiasmus and antithesis, Pope brings together the physical/human (Monarch, green retreats, Granville) and the metaphysical/divine (Muses, the timeless forest linked with Eden). His poem will both respond to, and reflect, the human and eternal orders. Lines 7-10 announce the poet's intention to immortalize the forest in his verse, thus bringing space and time under his control.

Lines 11-20 form a node of antithesis that should further reinforce our conception of the poet's power, of his command-post over specific subject and world, general space and time:

Here hills and vales, the woodland and the plain,
Here earth and water seem to strive again;
Not Chaos-like together crushed and bruised,
But, as the world, harmoniously confused:
Where order in variety we see,
And where, though all things differ, all agree.
Here waving groves a chequered scene display,
And part admit, and part exclude the day;
As some coy nymph her lover's warm address
Nor quite indulges, nor can quite repress.

(11-20)

Three substantive antitheses introduce this overview: hills/vales, woodland/plain, and earth/water comprise not so much opposites as complementary disparate elements that form our world. This difference-in-harmony is a continuous process, as all "seem to strive again": these particulars work within each phrase, and each phrase works within the other two phrases in the couplet in an effort to describe a timeless, transcendent harmony. The "Chaos" and "together" of lines 13-14 are terms linking here respectively disorder and dissipation (moving apart), and harmony and union; these two terms do not ordinarily modify each other, but are crushed together in harmony in these lines, as in the world as aspects of the creation. "Harmoniously confused" follows chiasmically in line 14. The poet places "the world," poised as it is between chaos and harmony, between these two antitheses in lines 13-14 which are themselves syntactically emblematic of this balance. The "as," a correlative conjunction, links the world with the hills and vales, woodland and plain, earth and water of the previous lines. The poet has swept the reader up from the world's particulars to an empyreal view of the world in one great leap; this reader, who looks and sees that indeed all is not "chaos," must agree with the poet that the world may be multifarious and even confusing, but the orderly appearance of these natural phenomena from this new perspective assures that the world must be, at worst, "harmoniously confused." Lines 15-16 continue the panoramic view of this section of earth, where "order in variety we see"—this natural order preexisting (again, syntactically) both the variety and our perception of it—and then equate our perception with the natural order by the repetition of "where," the agent of line 16 being "all things" which both "differ" and "agree." Thus, a subtle antithesis exists between the individual and nature in lines 15-16, and finds resolution in the mirroring of our perception and the way things naturally are: the end-rhyme here implies that we cannot "see" and fail to "agree."

The antithesis in line 17 combines motion and stasis; from his lofty vantage-point, the poet can view the "waving groves" (the participle evoking continuous motion) as a "chequered scene," and can fix the changing real into an abstract grid. The antithetical phrases "and part admit, and part exclude the day" recapitulate order and chaos, vision and blindness, in the allusion to light and dark; the world naturally admits both, as in the perfect checkerboard balance of night and day. The reader finds himself back down in the forest, moving through light and shadow. Finally, a second "as" draws in the human context. The "coy nymph" whose human will should stand antithetical to the deterministic natural world, is brought by parallel antithesis into the poet's scheme. "Nor quite indulges, nor can quite repress" (see line 18, "and part admit, and part exclude the day") fulfills for the human context the "harmonious confusion" of the world. This human particular is also of the most general, abstract quality, a literary allusion to the eternal antithesis of desire and reticence that defines human passion.

Windsor Forest reveals the youthful Pope's exuberant desire to bring paradox within the scope of reason, to prove it a matter of perspective. Pope seeks to establish rhetorical control at the very beginning of the poem. He strikes out from the start to bring fundamental abstractions—space and time, man and nature, chaos and harmony—under his intellectual and artistic command. Although other antitheses do occur scattered throughout the poem, such as the striking couplet: "Make sacred Charles' tomb for ever known/(Obscure the place, and uninscribed the stone)" (319-20), Pope concentrates the figure in the poem's opening lines to establish bardic scope and power. W. B. Piper questions Pope's power to convince us truly in these lines of nature's "harmonious confusion," and of his verses' ultimate efficacy in proving the predominance of harmony: "We know, at any rate, that the range of nature is much greater than the range of the poet's descriptive medium; that its variety, its apparent confusion, is much greater than such a form of description can indicate."[13] However, it seems that the young poet, convinced of his success in capturing and patterning disparate elements (including the greatest abstraction and paradox) in the tightly woven antitheses of the poem's first twenty lines, felt that he had won the audience from the start and could proceed without too much further antithetical dramatization to assert the poet's rhetorical control over creation.

An Essay on Man crowns the ripeness of Pope's career, and displays the poet's fulfillment of his potential for rhetorical control through antithesis tested in the opening lines of *Windsor Forest*. In the *Essay*, Pope not only increases and intensifies the use of antithesis, he moves through an extensive range of particulars to build his figures; the *Essay* emerges finally as a great fabric—or chain—of particulars in antithesis. Here, the mature poet realizes the unlimited scope and diversity of his subject: man, his place in and multiple perspectives on creation entire. He simultaneously reinforces rhetorically his assertion of the ultimate harmonious unity and purpose of creation; thus, the *Essay* constitutes a macrocosmic content-form paradox. Antithesis is the ideal form for the display of the greatest paradox: that although "the objects of the universe are particular and disjunct, yet . . . it is still a universe: there is something that is 'changed through all, and yet in all the same'."[14]

Antithesis, in the gathering of contraries or seemingly incompatible elements within a common point of view, allows for a continuous experimentation with particular experience within the premise of general unity. In the *Essay*, Pope attempts to move across all creation in this task, all along "The Great Chain of Being." With him is his St. John, another individual man, whom he calls into conversation, social activity, sharing of the experience. The reader is, naturally, also included in this experience and conversation; we now have an expansive society. The community of poet-St. John-reader, as individual men and mankind, can now embrace experience, self-knowledge, and social relation as a necessary triad of truth. This "triad" actually reflects the antithetical tension of the one-many paradox, of the individual working in the cooperative resolution that is society. Pope will put the triad through drastic reinterpretation in the *Dunciad,* where it loses its antithetical core and comes to represent instead an unresolvable string of monads.

The *Essay* is so replete in antitheses that to touch upon even a portion of them as they appear throughout the poem would far exceed the scope of this paper. Pope weaves the rich antithetical texture of the poem by placing in antithesis words, phrases, lines and couplets, nouns, verbs, and modifiers, the greatest abstractions and the most minute particulars. The profusion, variety, rhetorical strength, and complexity of this antithetical system cannot help but argue for the poet's powers of reason and grasp of a perfect order in creation. This power and reach shine from such larger antithetical constructs as:

> Presumptuous Man! the reason wouldst thou find,
> Why formed so weak, so little, and so blind!
> First, if thou canst, the harder reason guess,
> Why formed no weaker, blinder, and no less!
>
> (I, 35-38)

Pope illumines, with the simplest diction and repetition of terms, the classic epistemological problem: how can we know for certain what is outside of our own experience? He rhetorically "neutralizes" the question, with "so" and then "no," indicating simultaneously the great folly—and wonderful wisdom—of the question. Out of this epistemological paradox Pope will proceed, eventually, to consider a vast, comprehensive range of particulars. He will not only "vindicate the ways of God to man" (I, 16), but will also, in a mirror-image, "vindicate the ways of man to God" rhetorically as he takes on the "Vast chain of Being" as the object of his investigation.

At the time he wrote the *Essay*, Pope's great faith in himself, in society, and in a perfect universal order (which he as poet must necessarily reflect in his own creation) allowed him the presumptuous liberty of taking on nothing less than "the vast chain of Being" as experimental field. As a poet who grasps and expresses this system's logic, Pope acts as both man and God, his human rhetoric a model of the "creating Word."

Vast chain of Being! which from God began,
Natures ethereal, human, angel, man,
Beast, bird, fish, insect, what no eye can see,
No glass can reach; from Infinite to thee,
From thee to Nothing.—On superior powers
Were we to press, inferior might on ours;
Or in the full creation leave a void,
Where, one step broken, the great scale's destroyed:
From Nature's chain whatever link you strike,
Tenth or ten thousandth, breaks the chain alike.
(I, 237-46)

This passage is a chain of antitheses moving from the most general to the most particular, and back again to the most general. "Vast chain of Being" includes everything in creation, beginning with God who is infinite and thereby simultaneously part of and transcendent of all category. "Natures ethereal, human" are antithetical concepts; "angel, man" describe particular manifestations of the former conceptual antithesis. Lines 238-39 ("Beast, bird," etc.) provide the particular, perceptual analysis of the chain; lines 239-40 (postmedial caesura, "what no eye can see, / No glass can reach") refine the perceptual by the conceptual comprehension. Thus, this division at the semicolon in line 240 creates a parallel construction that is formally antithetical; both particular and conceptual demonstrate the "vast chain of Being." However, the particular breakdown forms a chain with "man" (a general concept) in the center—while the conceptual comprehension places the rhetorically specific "thee" (a particular) at the center, or between "Infinite" and "Nothing." Man's position is paradoxical in that he is, on the one hand, the general in the particular, and on the other, the particular in the general. He seems to stand at the midpoint of creation; he makes possible the antithesis of lines 241-42, of "superior" and "inferior" powers. Man can both act, and be acted upon. Pope quickly informs us, however, that in spite of man's "central" position, he enjoys the simultaneous status as merely one link in the great chain, equal to all other links: with the unreachable infinite at one end, and nothing at the other, man cannot possibly exist as a true, fixed "center." In the following couplet, "The least confusion but in one, not all / That system only, but the Whole must fall" (249-50), the enjambment in line 250 breaks the premature antithesis of "but in one, not all," by proving the "all" part of another "one"—"that system only"—which proves, in turn, to be part of another "all"—"the Whole." Other antitheses in this couplet are: confusion/system, and "but in one / but the Whole." Pope forges a chain of antitheses to refine the propositions of lines 237-48, and to prove how the least and the most, the one and the all, and everything in between, coexist as separate particulars sharing the relationship of being parts integral to the great whole. Pope's rhetorical chain reveals the dynamics of the "vast chain of Being," and suggests a "proof" of creation as an ultimate antithesis of particular/general, part/whole.

Man lives the truth of such paradox as an individual member of a society, and as participant in the certainty/uncertainty of mortal and eternal life. In the *Essay*, Pope presupposes a society composed of individual members capable of reason, productive exchange, and good judgment. These individual members can work together to relieve uncertainty, reduce conflict, and reach agreement to meet the individual's and society's needs. Antithesis presupposes the possibility of resolution, or of a unifying point of view capable of seeing similarity in difference, and of achieving and expressing a harmonious relationship between and among conflicting particulars—of conceptualizing a comprehensible great "chain of Being." The poet of the *Essay* functions as this unifying point of view and expresses this model possibility to his fellow man. The poet who unifies, comprehends, and reveals the system offers a rhetorical model of the "creating Word." He is both a part of the system and the whole; as creator who observes his work, he both pervades and transcends the system.

The Dunciad (I focus here exclusively on Book the Fourth) presents a radically different scenario: the poet divided from the society of men. This poet proposes the final triumph of "Dulness" over society and creation entire. Presumption, pride, ignorance, hypocrisy, and folly—in law and letter—preclude the possibility of productive exchange and the resolution of doubt and conflict in society. The failure of the microcosm—the individual member—entails the collapse of the universal; the part no longer participates constructively in the whole. Maynard Mack describes a malignant destruction from the part through the whole in Books 1-3 of *The Dunciad*, a "systolic" movement where "persons and things tend to move outward from centers of idiocy to touch, taint, deafen, overwhelm, possess." In Book the Fourth, this dissemination turns back into a centering process.[15] I see this "centering" as a collapse from the scattered many, to a nonsignifying unit of one. The whole, represented by the triumphant goddess Dulness, swallows and subverts the parts. This "deity" appears to resist the part-whole antithesis by denying the parts' separate-and-equal status; her creation is no "chain," but an undifferentiated, inert mass of dullness.

When community is no longer possible, each man finds himself alone in his helpless particularity. From his isolation, he can learn nothing about himself, others, or the world; he can be no link in any "vast chain of Being." Sharing, comparing, and reasoning necessitate community. What happens when "dulness" deflects the reach of self to society, and vice versa? Paul Fussell offers an explanation:

> The aim of Dulness is sameness, the utter absence of the differentiation that makes order possible. . . . In such a state intelligence has no place, for there are no qualitative differences to be discriminated. Dulness melts down and levels off the structural order of "degree" that had been the imagination's dream since the beginning of thought.[16]

In the absence of the various "many," of differentiation, degree, and the possibility of comparison—the figure of antithesis finds no work. Pope's world view had changed by the end of his career; he still uses antithesis in *Dunciad* IV, but here this key constructive figure appears much changed in force and function. In general, we no longer find the self-sufficient, well-balanced, clear, and comprehensive antitheses of the *Essay*. The relatively scant, fragmentary, and strained antitheses of *Dunciad* IV imply Pope's relaxation or even renunciation of the effort to describe (or "reflect") rhetorically the productive tension of that awesome paradoxical whole, the creation. Or, we can see the strained rhetoric as the conflict between the poet's constructive power and his compulsion to reflect accurately the dissolute world he observes. In any case, Pope now turns his rhetoric to an attack on the society of learning, and especially letters, whose "dulness" renders poetry impotent and even absurd.

The changes in antithesis in *Dunciad* IV serve as an index to the changed universe Pope presents at the end of his career. From the *Essay* to *Dunciad* IV, three main alterations occur in this figure: (a) antitheses become strained, "neutralized," or otherwise weak; (b) they become "perverse," and (c) they give way to three-term constructs where the possibility of comparison and judgment is weakened, thwarted, or absurd. This last category also, significantly, enacts rhetorically the central drama of *Dunciad* IV.

The first four couplets of *Dunciad* IV contain category (a) antitheses:

Yet, yet a moment, one dim ray of light
Indulge, dread Chaos, and eternal Night!
Of darkness visible so much be lent,
As half to show, half veil the deep Intent.
Ye Powers! whose Mysteries restored I sing,
To whom Time bears me on his rapid wing,
Suspend a while your Force inertly strong,
Then take at once the poet and the Song.

(1-8)

The "moment" of "one dim ray of light" strains impotently against "dread Chaos, and eternal night," a strain of diction and logic. Line three's "darkness visible" poses a neutralized, because impossible, antithesis. Line seven's "inertly strong" offers another example of the nullifying effect of logical impossibility; this finds its apotheosis shortly thereafter:

Mad *Mathesis* alone was unconfined,
Too mad for mere material chains to bind,
Now to pure Space lifts her ecstatic stare,
Now running round the Circle finds it square.

(31-34)

Although the goddess Dulness has imprisoned all of mankind's constructive sciences and arts, she need not bind "mathésis," pure mathematics, as the latter already occupies a logically impossible realm, the ultimate unresolvable antithesis (worse than Sporus, "one vile Antithesis") of the square circle. It is also possible that Pope considered the Greek root meaning of *mathesis*, as learning, mental discipline itself; under the goddess's sway, all of mankind's intellectual enterprise falls to nonsignifying "ecstacy," having lost its force to bind the world's phenomena into coherent patterns.

The following couplet "mocks" antithesis by repeating the derogatory nouns, as well as by proffering weak end-rhymes, to produce a silly and weak "antithesis":

Dunce scorning Dunce beholds the next advance
But Fop shows Fop superior complaisance.

(137-38)

In each line, two identical terms are "opposed"; one line nonsensically opposes the other. A strain appears in the scorn of "Dunce" for "Dunce," and the "superior complaisance" exhibited by "Fop" for "Fop": such is tantamount to nonsense, as the ordering or degree rhetorically implied here is absurd.

In other cases of category (a), the antitheses seem incapable of effecting any new and improved viewpoint or judgment:

> A poet the first day, he dips his quill
> And what the last? a very Poet still.
>
> (164-65)

> It fled, I followed; now in hope, now pain;
> It stopped, I stopped; it moved, I moved again.
>
> (427-28)

These "antitheses" employ useless repetition and nonsignifying juxtaposition. Often Pope places in contiguity terms that resemble antithesis by virtue of their situation in the rhetoric of comparison. Sometimes, he uses "or" to link terms that constitute a *trompe l'oeil* antithesis because of the presence of this conjunction:

> To the same notes thy sons shall hum, or snore.
>
> (59)

> Sneers at another, in toupee or gown.
>
> (88)

> By the French horn, or by the opening hound.
>
> (278)

Such constructions generate no productive tension, and also seem to "mock" the figure's former full-power proliferation, as in the *Essay* where we encountered such key usages as, "A hero perish, or a sparrow fall," and "Atoms or systems into ruin hurled" (I, 85-90).

I call category (b) antitheses "perverse" because they draw together bizarre, grotesque, or quasi-meaningless elements: "Impale a Glow-worm, or Vertu profess" (569). In a grotesque twist, Pope reverses the previous assertion that unity and harmony "reign" over division and confusion: "Joy to great Chaos! let division reign" (54). Some antitheses are gruesome, violent, uselessly destructive:

> When Dulness, smiling—Thus revive the Wits!
> But murder first, and mince them all to bits.
>
> (119-20)

> Appear more glorious as more hacked and torn.
>
> (124)

A morbid and destructive association of writing (creation) with death occurs in the following:

> Leave not a foot of verse, a foot of stone,
> A Page, a Grave, that they can call their own.
>
> (127-28)

> Now to thy gentle shadow all are shrunk,
> All melted down, in pension, or in Punk!
> So K __ so B __ sneaked into the grave,
> A Monarch's half, and half a harlot's slave.
>
> (509-12)

Category (b) antitheses may be "antithetical" merely by virtue of sound, as different signifiers emptied of meaning, or as simple enumerations of seemingly unrelated terms:

> A Nest, a Toad, a Fungus, or a Flower.
>
> (400)

> Cibberian forehead, or Cimmerian gloom.
>
> (532)

> one
> Rose a Gregorian, one a Gormogon.
>
> (575-76)

Pope rhetorically illustrates the poem's central message—that the concepts of societal and universal order are now emptied of meaning, reduced to mere scribbling or noise—in lines such as the following with their "empty" antitheses:

> 'Tis true, on Words is still our whole debate,
> Disputes of Me or Te, of *aut* or *at*,
> To sound or sink in *cano*, O or A,
> Or to give up Cicero to C or K.
>
> (219-22)

Even when not precisely "antithetical," these category (b) examples reveal the bringing together of different elements into a relationship or contiguity, where the only or strongest possibility of communion may be graphic, superficial resemblance, or even simple physical existence. This rhetorical strategy suggests the vain struggle to make meaning and establish unity in an incoherent and illogical context: the society of men, of minds, the world. Also, perhaps, the very opaque allusions in these antitheses, when compared to the very clear antitheses in the *Essay*, betray the poet's retreat into self, his diminished interest in communicating his thought to others—the very foundation of eighteenth-century society—and a purposeful turning of the mirror inward toward the discontents and deformations of the poet's own world view.

Category (c) explores three-term relationships. Where two poles readily admit challenge, dialogue, and comparison, three tend to dilute, extend, and otherwise retard the process of comparison and resolution. *Dunciad* IV contains these significant triads:

> One Trill shall harmonize joy, grief and rage.
> (57)

> But wherefore waste I words, I see advance
> Whore, pupil, and laced Governor from France.
> (271-72)

> As much Estate, and Principle, and Wit
> As Jansen, Fleetwood, Cibber shall think fit.
> (325-26)

> Unseen at Church, at Senate, or at Court.
> (338)

The goddess Dulness hands down her *modus vivendi* to society:

> All my commands are easy, short and full:
> My Sons! Be proud, be selfish, and be dull.
> (582)

The goddess fantasizes her final takeover of society, at the scepter of some "daring son," who

> Tyrant supreme! shall three estates command,
> And MAKE ONE MIGHTY DUNCIAD OF THE LAND!
> (603-604)

Here, the number three entails the collapse into one, the universe of sameness predicted by Fussell, not the "One" which represents creation as a perfectly resolved antithesis of the individual and the universal, as explicated in the *Essay*. We now see a three-term relationship dominant over the two-term: the poet, the society of men, and the "universal" (as ruled by the goddess Dulness) separate into the fragments of a fallen unity. As long as the poet could ally himself with his society (relating the two terms into one), he could create sound, productive, binary antitheses from the model of that absolute antithesis, particularity-generality. Now the poet turns from that society, causing the whole system to topple ("from Nature's chain whatever link you strike, / Tenth or ten thousandth, breaks the chain alike," *Essay*, I, 245-46). He retains his own powers, but establishes no experimental field. How will he redefine his relationship with the "universal"? He reframes the universal as the domain-by-usurpation of the goddess Dulness—that very principle which undercuts the possibility of a "universal," a coherent totality of various particulars. "She" destroys the unifying power by rendering comparison and judgment irrelevant in her universe of sameness.

In the final lines of *Dunciad* IV, however, antithesis once again signals a critical maneuver by the poet. He actually *revives* antithesis, wielding it in its former full power and clarity, to perform a last, vital task. The final fanfare of this powerful rhetorical device of conflict and resolution, order-in-chaos, unity-in-division, will conclude the poem that appears to cede the triumph to the goddess Dulness with her division, chaos, and nullity:

> No public Flame, nor private, dares to shine;
> No human Spark is left, nor Glimpse divine!
> Lo! thy dread Empire, CHAOS! is restored;
> Light dies before thy uncreating word;
> Thy hand, great Anarch! lets the curtain fall;
> And universal Darkness buries All.

In a final, ironic flourish, Pope nullifies the universe in a vision of absolute separation of the social and individual, man and God. In what are perhaps his most powerful—and certainly most startling—antitheses, Pope brings all process, including and especially his poem, to a halt. As he is "there" to witness this process, he must be somehow "outside" of this decreation. As a man of letters, however, he is also necessarily a part of his society and of such a dissolute universe, however unfortunately (having been there to "make a new *Invocation*; as the greater Poets are wont, where some high and worthy matter is to be sung"—"Book the Fourth: Argument"). In *Dunciad* IV, the poet remains the unifying point of view, simultaneously part, whole, and "outside" of the system.[17] But unlike the poet-creator of the *Essay*, this poet will *uncreate* the system. To this end, he needs a figure like the goddess Dulness as a sort of antiforce to the coherent universe once depicted or made possible by "the greater poets." This poet arms her with the "uncreating word" so that she might destroy the poet-creator's workshop—the rhetoric of reason, judgment, and wit. The strain in Pope's rhetoric in *Dunciad* IV enacts the drama of the particular individual struggling against the divisive force that he himself has created by willful capitulation to the enemy.

We do see, in the poem's final couplets, how the poet's powers have actually remained fully intact, to the last curtain-fall. Like a vengeful God, he has created and loosed the anti-force upon the creation as an ironically masterful gesture of capitulation. He then leaves the scene where nothing remains with which to work. He endures, the One without the many, a nullity—or unresolvable antithesis of silent voice.

The *Essay* and *Dunciad* IV, with reliance on antithesis, demonstrate the poet's rhetorical power to create, and uncreate, the "universe." Pope's universe consisted of his belief in an absolute order whose perfection was verified by the poet's ability to model (or mirror) that perfection in his work. In the end, he felt compelled to cancel the very possibility of a unified and harmonious creation with the very instrument he had once used so potently and precisely to model it. Pope's deteriorated antitheses poignantly illustrate the dissolution of the poet's universe as his own vengeful and deliberate decreation. The concluding couplets of *Dunciad* IV prove as a locus of extreme rhetorical control that the poet has lost his faith, but not his power. He remains the absolute center of experience who, following his will, might "give law to words, or war with words alone," to borrow his own bitter and ultimately self-referential antithesis.

NOTES

[1]George Puttenham, *The Arte of English Poesie*, ed. Gladys Doidge Willcock and Alice Walker (Cambridge: Cambridge Univ. Press, 1936), pp. 210-11.

[2]Ibid., p. 197.

[3]Maynard Mack, *Alexander Pope: A Life* (New Haven: Yale Univ. Press, 1985), p. 542.

[4]Paul Fussell, *The Rhetorical World of Augustan Humanism* (Oxford: Clarendon Press, 1965), p. 110.

[5]*Alexander Pope: Selected Poetry and Prose*, ed. William K. Wimsatt (New York: Holt, Rinehart and Winston, 1972), p. 211. This excerpt is from *An Essay on Man,* Epistle III, lines 1-2. All subsequent quotations from Pope's poetry are taken from this text and will be cited in the text by line, and by Epistle in the case of the *Essay* (all selections from the *Dunciad* are from Book the Fourth).

[6]William Bowman Piper, *The Heroic Couplet* (Cleveland: Case Western Reserve, 1969), pp. 145, 147-48.

[7]Wimsatt, p. xxix.

[8]Quintilian, *Institutio Oratoria*, trans. H. E. Butler, Loeb Classical Library (London: William Heinemann, 1921), Book VIII, p. 251.

[9]Piper, p. 137.

[10]Fredric V. Bogel, *Acts of Knowledge: Pope's Later Poems* (Lewisburg: Bucknell Univ. Press, 1981), p. 36.

[11]Fussell, p. 115.

[12]Quintilian, Book IX, pp. 495-97.

[13]Piper, p. 147.

[14]Alexander Pope, *An Essay on Man*, ed. Maynard Mack. Twickenham edition of the poems of Alexander Pope (London: Methuen, 1950), p. lvi.

[15]Mack, *Alexander Pope: A Life*, p. 542.

[16]Fussell, p. 120.

[17]It might be said that the poet of the *Dunciad*, because he is able to posit something like a "dunciad" and therefore to step out of the system to observe it, still commands the powers of comparison, judgment, and ordering. He can witness "the Universal Darkness" only because he yet retains some "light": "At precisely the point where Pope dramatizes the pathos of his own expendable art . . . that art is at its most assured. If 'Universal Darkness' has not yet buried all it is because the dead wits at least are still alive, reaching us from outside our own vortex. Creativity is a condition of life; without it . . . we are composed . . . to everlasting rest" (Mack, *A Life*, p. 796).

SEL 27 (1987)
ISSN 0039-3657

Mirror, Mirror: The Didactic Dilemma of *The Female Quixote*

DEBORAH ROSS

The world's male chivalry has perished out,
But women are knights-errant to the last;
And, if Cervantes had been greater still,
He had made his Don a Donna.

E. B. Browning, *Aurora Leigh*

We are handsome, my dear Charlotte, very handsome and the greatest of our Perfections is, that, we are entirely insensible of them ourselves.

Jane Austen, "Lesley Castle"

In writing *Don Quixote* Cervantes can be said to have begun the perpetual struggle of each new generation of novelists to make their works more realistic than those that came before.[1] Cervantes established his hero's verisimilitude through contrast with the older romance hero, Amadis, much as Jane Austen would later use Radcliffe's romantic Emily St. Aubert to help define the ordinariness of her own Catherine Morland. But reality is always running a step ahead of the novelist. Even Catherine would seem unrealistic—far too even-tempered—in the age of the Brontës. In Austen's novel, written in 1803, *Sir Charles Grandison* appears as an amusingly placid antithesis to the absurdly unrealistic gothic romance. But in America in 1808, Tabitha Tenney used *Grandison* as an absurd romance that, as her title *Female Quixotism* implies, could itself induce outrageous, quixotic behavior.[2]

Deborah L. Ross received her doctorate from the University of Rochester and was an assistant professor of English at the University of Hawaii before accepting her current position at Hawaii Pacific College. The following essay is part of a longer work in progress on romance, realism, and didacticism in novels by women from Aphra Behn through Jane Austen.

Tenney's source for *Female Quixotism* was Charlotte Lennox's widely popular *The Female Quixote.* Never did a novel so loudly proclaim its own realism in direct opposition to the romance, which Lennox's narrator seems unequivocally to condemn.[3] Yet it is a highly equivocal novel, despite its ostensible thesis, because the traditional theory of the novel to which Lennox subscribed exaggerated the difference between novel and romance.

Naturally, in the early days of the novel theorists felt a need to distinguish it from its fanciful, much-aspersed ancestor. As Laurie Langbauer remarks, precise definition was much less important than the general notion that "romance was what the novel was *not.*"[4] There were attempts to draw the lines, however. In 1691, Congreve described romance as

> generally composed of the Constant Loves and invincible Courages of Hero's, Heroins, Kings and Queens, Mortals of the first Rank, and so forth; where lofty Language, miraculous Contingencies and impossible Performances, elevate and surprize the Reader into a giddy Delight, which leaves him flat upon the Ground whenever he gives of [sic], and vexes him to think how he has suffer'd himself to be pleased and transported, concern'd and afflicted at the several Passages which he has Read . . . when he is forced to be very well convinced that 'tis all a lye.

Novels, however, "Come near us, and represent to us Intrigues in practice, delight us with Accidents and odd Events, but not such as are wholly unusual or unpresidented, such which not being so distant from our Belief bring also the pleasure nearer us." The passage concludes with a neat antithesis: "Romances give more of Wonder, Novels more Delight."[5]

Like many neoclassical formulae, this one is deceptively neat. Congreve made so much of the difference between novel and romance because the "wonder" of the seventeenth-century French romances was lost on the middle-class reading public of his time. The biggest wonder of romance, one feels by the end of Congreve's definition, is that the reader has been drawn in at all. Realism was meant to restore at least a degree of wonder to a genre that had ceased to inspire it: that is, to appeal to a new audience that could find wonder or excitement only in adventures that might really happen to them. Aphra Behn's *Oroonoko,* for instance, purports to be (and probably was, to an extent) factual, but the events it describes are far from ordinary. Because in the real world the reader "finds Diversions for every Minute, new and strange," the author has omitted all but the most exciting part of her hero's life.[6] Congreve emphasized the difference he saw as important and obscured the fact that the novel was really a new kind of romance that owed a part of its "delight" to the rich plotting of its ancestor.

In fact, both Horatian goals of *dulce* and *utile* kept the novel tied to its romantic mother. Charlotte Lennox's friend and patron, Samuel Johnson—also a definer (and confuser) of the novel—followed Congreve in preferring the new form to the "heroic romance" adored by the heroine of *The Female Quixote* because of the new works' "natural" plot development, their reliance on human probability rather than "machines and expedients." He believed in Congreve's "wonder vs. delight" dichotomy. But Johnson more openly acknowledged the relation of novel to romance by labeling the work of his contemporaries "comedy of romance." And because of his insistence on its instructive mission, other romance elements crept into his definition of the novel. Johnson believed that characters should not be "mixed," and that virtue should be rewarded and vice punished. (Like Wilde's Miss Prism, he felt "that is what Fiction means.") While endorsing the new fiction, then, he also directed the novelist to polarize values and preserve perfect justice—in a sense to present a romantic rather than a realistic world.[7]

For many of Johnson's female protégées, writing as if the novel were completely separate from the romance was like following a clearly marked path into a bog. Novel-writing for them meant trying to satisfy several contradictory demands. They wanted their works to be modern and realistic, concerned with the daily lives of characters much like their readers. They also wanted to provide models of virtue, which meant borrowing romantic plot manipulations and "unmixed" characters to bring about justice. And a third goal made the task even more difficult: they wanted, as all writers do whether they admit it or not, to express something of their inner lives, their dreams and desires. For this goal, factual realism would not do; for as Madame de Genlis once remarked, "The life of every Woman is a Romance!"[8] The earliest women novelists particularly liked the romance's glorification of love, and hence its elevation of women far above the status they enjoyed in their daily lives.[9] This love of love persisted into mid-century and underlies—or undercuts—the novels of the most moral of the female moralists. In the best of these novels the contradictions generate irony and richness. But even in the best, the tension between romantic and realistic elements creates a foggy moral universe. Hence it was not actually possible to learn good conduct from many novels that seemed to promise such instruction.

Charlotte Lennox's *The Female Quixote,* published in 1752, is wonderfully suited to the study of these conflicting elements because, like *Don Quixote,* it is both a romance and a satire of romance. The paradox is appropriate to *Don Quixote*'s complex message. Though the hero clearly reads romances the wrong way, all the sympathetic, educated characters do read them, and only the unsympathetic characters try to destroy them. Cervantes allows the romance form subtly to support the hero even as each new adventure makes him more ridiculous. By Part II, Don Quixote is the renowned hero he planned to be in Part I, though we've been laughing at him all the time. *The Female Quixote* makes use of the same romance/anti-romance paradox. But in Lennox's hands the contradiction is sometimes confusing, because neither she nor her readers would have accepted Cervantes's complex vision. After all, she was writing in a tradition that elevated the novel and deprecated the romance.[10] When Don Quixote loses his delusion, the spell is broken, he dies, the book ends, the reader is sad. When Arabella loses hers, she is cured and can get married and live happily ever after. But Lennox was more like Cervantes than she admitted. Undercurrents of sympathy with the romance in *The Female Quixote*—though much less obvious than those in *Don Quixote*—prevent the reader from rejoicing at this fairy-tale dénouement.

On the surface, Lennox uses romantic elements in *The Female Quixote* only to satirize them. The novel opens with a common romantic situation which, given her work on Shakespeare, the author may have borrowed from *The Tempest.* Arabella's father has been tricked out of favor at court and has retired to a remote castle where, his wife dying, he must bring up his daughter alone.[11] The seclusion of the heroine's life thus makes any extraordinary behavior more or less plausible, like the magic we allow on Prospero's island. This romantic background established, Lennox begins to play with its satiric possibilities. The hero, Arabella's cousin Glanville, is "violent and hasty" enough to be the romantic lover he pretends to be to humor Arabella in volume two; he recalls Dorothea in *Don Quixote,* who is little less romantic than the Princess Micomicona she counterfeits (*FQ* 1:45). Like Cervantes, Lennox has great fun piling up levels of fiction; at one point she has an actress disguised as a princess recite the romance of her life, in which she meets a prince, who recites the romance of his life.

Lennox also satirizes many obstacles to the movement of the romance plot. So modest are the typical hero and heroine that their coming together can be difficult to arrange. First the hero must

> struggle with the Violence of his Passion, till it has cast him into a Fever. . . . Thus he must suffer, rejoicing at the Approach of Death, which will free him from all his Torments, without violating the Respect he owes to the Divine Object of his Flame. At length, when he has but a few Hours to live, his Mistress . . . conjures him to tell her the Cause of his Despair. . . . [H]e acknowledges his Passion with the utmost Contrition for having offended her. . . . The Lady is touch'd at his Condition, commands him to live, and if necessary, permits him to hope.
>
> (*FQ* 2:169)

Lennox's own hero wins Arabella in much the same way—and Arabella herself must become conveniently ill before she can reform.[12]

Lennox's criticism of romance is to be taken much more seriously than Cervantes's. To the narrator of *The Female Quixote,* the romances Arabella reads lack even the aesthetic merit that in Cervantes saves Amadis of Gaul from the flames. In fact, one of the heroic labors the heroine exacts from Glanville is to read her favorite books. The clergyman who ultimately converts Arabella (in a speech that may have been written by Johnson) argues that "the only Excellence of Falsehood . . . is its Resemblance to Truth" (*FQ* 2:313).[13] By this standard, Arabella's books aren't even good lies.

But more importantly, *romances are lies,* hence morally dangerous as well as aesthetically flawed. Everyone, including Arabella, believes that books should help one through life. But whereas she considers romances "Books from which all useful Knowledge may be drawn," Lennox informs the reader rather that this "Study" has prevented the heroine from acquiring "a great Proficiency in all useful Knowledge" (*FQ* 1:69, 4). "Books ought to supply an Antidote to Example," aphorizes the Johnsonian clergyman; for this reason only may they depart from reality. But romances swerve from truth merely for excitement, and thus "they teach young Minds to expect strange Adventures and sudden Vicissitudes, and therefore encourage them often to trust to Chance" (*FQ* 2:317, 314). Worse, they give "new Fire to the Passions of Revenge and Love" instead of helping "Reason and Piety to suppress" those passions; and we must suppress them, "if we hope to be approved in the Sight of the only Being whose Approbation can make us happy" (*FQ* 2:317). An eighteenth-century Englishman would be hanged for many deeds romances present as heroic, as Cousin Charlotte fears.[14] Thus, the biggest cause of Arabella's remorse at the end of the novel is her having incited Glanville (as she believes) to kill a rival in her behalf.

By contrast, *The Female Quixote* does its Christian duty by presenting as absurd the quixotic temptation to seek personal fulfillment outside the social order. Its plot—or one might say its lack of plot—shows how effectively civilization has eliminated the "Vicissitudes" that so fill the lives of heroes and heroines of romance. Arabella's fearfulness appears paranoiac; she won't grant her own cousin a "private Conversation" for fear he will molest her. Her unnecessary dread of rape even leads her to a criminal act when she orders her servants to assault the innocent Hervey (*FQ* 1:24).

The only real dangers Arabella encounters result from her own willfulness and perversity: she does not know how to value the safety of the real world. Fearing attack from Edward, a gardener who she believes is a disguised nobleman, she runs out of her house in the middle of the night and throws herself upon the first man who passes, asking this "Generous Stranger" for assistance. Here she really is threatened with rape: the gentleman is "extremely glad at having so beautiful a Creature in his Power" and eager "to have her at his own House" (*FQ* 1:151). Charlotte Glanville points out the foolishness of Arabella's flight: "Sure nobody would be so mad to attempt such an Action" as rape in a woman's own well-guarded house (*FQ* 1:148). But even a gentleman might feel justified in molesting a woman who would run around the streets at night alone. Thus the heroine demonstrates Lennox's thesis that only a woman who wants adventures will have them; and also the corollary, that she will be thought to deserve them.

Such a woman is as ignorant of the benefits of a stable class structure as she is reckless of her own safety. The stairs a rapist/gardener would have to climb symbolize the social distance between him and his mistress; Arabella abandons this eminence when she leaves her house. Her carelessness shows the extent to which romances have confused her, since they contain only royalty dressed as royalty and royalty disguised as peasantry. As Don Quixote explains to Sancho, romance seeks to reestablish the original God-given social hierarchy that has crumbled to chaos in a fallen world. That is why a large part of romance is finding out who one really is, and why every peasant with an aristocratic air turns out to be a duke. But in Lennox's view, the social hierarchy found in the real world needs no correction. Edward may seem genteel for a gardener, but there is a perfectly reasonable explanation for his good manners: "he had contracted . . . a great deal of second-hand Politeness" as a servant in London (*FQ* 1:27-28). Anyone less deluded than Arabella would know Edward is only a servant when he is caught trying to steal carp from her fish-pond. The heroine reasons thus: no gentleman would steal, Edward is a gentleman, therefore Edward would not steal. The reader accepts the first premise, but knows the second premise is false: Edward has been caught red-handed. Thus the novel forces the reader to conclude that Edward is no gentleman; he is perfectly suited to his rank in life.

Arabella is similarly perverse in her treatment of her father. From the first moment, Lennox endorses the man the Marquis benignly proposes as a husband.[15] Arabella herself is impressed by his handsome face and figure, intelligence, good nature, and charm (*FQ* 1:37, 40). But according to her inverted values, cooperation with her father would be "Impropriety," as the narrator ironically notes: "What Lady in Romance ever married the Man that was chose for her? In those Cases the Remonstrances of a Parent are called Persecutions; obstinate Resistance, Constancy and Courage; and an Aptitude to dislike the Person proposed to them, a noble Freedom of Mind which disdains to love or hate by the Caprice of others" (*FQ* 1:36). Her "Repugnance" arises merely from having to see Glanville as an approved suitor.[16] Her "heroic Disobedience" is especially foolish because her father is not Clarissa Harlowe's (*FQ* 1:41). He simply expresses the wish that his daughter marry the man of his choice, and hopes that her filial piety will rather incline her to accept than otherwise. When Arabella miscasts her father as the tyrant of romance (descendant of the *senex iratus* of Greek New Comedy), she nearly loses her Prince Charming.[17] According to the novel, the clearest path to personal happiness is obedience to just authority.

Lennox's didactic message shows how far she was from accepting the values inherent in romance. Yet if she really meant to condemn romance whole-heartedly, she grossly underestimated its power. Once one rubs the magic lamp, it's not so easy to get rid of the genie. Any romance heroine has power simply by virtue of her role, supported by the weight of centuries-long tradition. Thus the reader cannot avoid feeling that Arabella, who is supposed to be wrong, is actually right, because this is her story. Furthermore, as we read on, we begin to sense Lennox's real sympathy for Arabella; she is drawn with a conviction that seems to have come from the author's own experience.[18] By adding realistic details about growing up female in the eighteenth century, Lennox further enlists the reader's sympathies on what the novel formally designates as the wrong side.

Arabella is designed in part to teach young girls what not to be. Thus, she is given traits—including an interest in sex—from which model heroines like Clarissa are supposedly free. To an extent, Lennox acknowledges her heroine's sexuality, linking it with the part of her character that needs satiric correction. The narrator tells us Arabella's romantic chastity is affected. After sternly forbidding her maid to accept any love-letters from her first suitor, Hervey, Arabella dismisses her, "not without an Apprehension of being too well obeyed"; and when Lucy does deliver a letter, "in Reality, she was not displeased, yet, being a strict Observer of romantic Forms, she chid her Woman severely for taking it" (*FQ* 1:11, 14). Her obsessive chastity is comic because it reveals a most unmaidenly forwardness. Hervey interprets Lucy's warning not to give her a letter—"I beg you will not offer to bribe me"—as what it is in fact: an invitation (*FQ* 1:12). Paradoxically, reading romances has made Arabella far too ready for love.[19]

This wantonness is clearly meant to be more apparent than real. In the second half of the novel, Arabella appears as an angel of delicacy compared to the London ladies. Yet post-Freudian readers will see a sexuality in Arabella beyond what Lennox openly acknowledges, expressed in symbols of considerable subliminal power. The Marquis's house literally and symbolically preserves virginity, as Arabella knows; her own euphemism for rape is "[to] be carried away by Force from my own House" (*FQ* 1:138-39). Therefore, when she "escapes" the house the night of Edward's imaginary attack, she seeks sex as much as she avoids it.

The rooms in which the "rape" takes place—Arabella's antechamber, bedchamber, and closet—also help to reveal the heroine's hidden sexuality. The scene opens with Lucy and Arabella conferring in the closet, symbolic of the heroine's most private self. There is a knock at the door of the antechamber (the most public room), and Arabella commands Lucy to go talk to the supposed attackers. As the terrified maid shouts through the locked antechamber door, Arabella "advanced as far as the Bedchamber, longing to know what sort of Conference Lucy was holding with her intended Ravisher" (*FQ* 1:142). Arabella's sexual curiosity thus leads her to the bedchamber, which lies appropriately between her private self and the outside world.[20]

Arabella's sexuality, both overt and implicit, helps give her a complexity with which the reader can identify, so that we cannot enjoy seeing her crushed, or cured, at the end of the novel. In other ways as well, the novel makes us sympathize with the heroine by showing that suppression, while virtuous, requires considerable struggle. Despite Lennox's stated intention, she does make us see the old Marquis as the archetypical male tyrant when he orders his daughter to write an apologetic letter to Glanville, whom she has indignantly dismissed from the house. Because Arabella has no good reason to be angry with Glanville, her resistance to her father's command is clearly wrong. Nevertheless, it hurts to watch her father "leading her to *his* Writing-Desk [my emphasis]," commanding her to write, and finally telling the "sobbing" heroine what she must say. One is glad to see from the letter that the Marquis finally cannot rob her of her voice (or in current terminology, her "mode of discourse"), deranged though it may be:[21] "It is not by the Power I have over you, that I command you to return, for I disclaim any Empire over so unworthy a Subject; but since it is my Father's Pleasure I should invite you back, I must let you know, that I repeal your Banishment" (*FQ* 1:55, 56).

The Marquis's anger arises from the "Rudeness" of his daughter's commanding his guest to leave his house. Arabella often gives the appearance of bad manners because her reading has failed to teach her to suppress her feelings. Conversely, Arabella's only complaint against Glanville is his self-command. He is reasonably distraught when Arabella has fled and cannot be found; but she expects him to "strike his Bosom with the Vehemence of his Grief; and cast his accusing and despairing Eyes to Heaven, which had permitted such a Misfortune to befall" (*FQ* 1:165). She likes Glanville best when, "a little elevated with the Wine," he ignores what Fielding might have called her "violent modesty" and throws himself at her feet, venting his feelings in romantic but sincere hyperbole (*FQ* 1:189-90). The surface message is thus that real feeling is all around Arabella, if only she could recognize it through the calm expressions of real life.

Yet the novel also conveys the sad fact that, though Glanville may express real love, Arabella can never have that freedom. Emotional expressiveness for her is, at best, rudeness—at worst, vice. No wonder, the reader feels, the heroine wants more excitement in her life. And the more one enjoys reading Arabella's story, the more one is forced to side with her. Without her delusions there would be no plot—hence chapter headings such as "Contains a Turn at Court, neither new nor surprizing," "A Mistake which produces no great Consequences," "An extraordinary Comment upon a Behaviour natural enough." Once Arabella comes to her senses and marries Glanville, she will cease to be interesting: "all her Adventures are at an end for the future" (*FQ* 1:209).

In fact, the novel demonstrates, as Gilbert and Gubar might put it, that a good girl should have no story.[22] When Arabella asks that model of virtue, the "celebrated Countess of — ," to tell of her Adventures, the Countess is embarrassed and explains that "the

Word Adventures carries in it so free and licentious a Sound in the Apprehensions of People at this Period of Time" that to ask such a question is insulting. Her own life has been adventureless: "I was born and christen'd, had a useful and proper Education, receiv'd the Addresses of my Lord — through the recommendation of my Parents, and marry'd him with their Consents and my own Inclination, and . . . since we have liv'd in great Harmony together" (*FQ* 2:237). The Countess has no rebellious spirit to be suppressed into obedience; she naturally feels what she ought to feel—and so, she claims, do most "other Women of the same Rank, who have a moderate Share of Sense, Prudence and Virtue" (*FQ* 2:237). The Countess shows that good girls should appreciate how lucky they are to be able to live without Adventure—that is, without conflict.

But Arabella is slow to get this message, perhaps because the life the Countess describes, unlike that of romance heroines, fails to satisfy her will to power—that drive so dangerous to the eighteenth-century social structure, so appealing to the "raised consciousness" of today.[23] She feels she deserves to be the center of attention, cannot "comprehend, how any Solitude could be obscure enough to conceal a Beauty like hers from Notice," and expects "the Reputation of her Charms sufficient to bring a Croud of Adorers to demand her of her Father" (*FQ* 1:5-6). She speaks like a goddess to whom her lovers must give "Signs of Contrition" and "true Repentance" (*FQ* 1:67). Like the pope, she "grants Audience" to her worshippers—in whose number she includes her bewildered uncle (*FQ* 1:170). The baronet complains, "Why, Madam, . . . you want to carry your Power farther than ever any Beauty did before you; since you pretend to make People sick and well, whenever you please" (*FQ* 1:222). But Arabella believes her magical powers do have precedence, because she believes romance is history—told from a perspective that makes women central figures. Thus she claims that Pisistratus took over Athens, not out of ambition, but out of love for Cleorante, supposed mistress of Lycurgus (*FQ* 2:140-41). And beauty is not these women's only power. The heroines she admires lead armies and swim the Tiber (*FQ* 1:191-92; 2:289-90).

Unfortunately, Arabella's pathetic attempt to emulate Clelia and swim the Thames nearly results in her death. Despite the apparent joy with which Lennox created her heroine, she refuses to spare the rod. Yet her strictness need not conflict with her sympathy.[24] The novel contains many signs that if Arabella must "dwindle into a wife," it is by worldly rather than divine injunction. We see here a dominant trait of the women's novel of the mid-eighteenth century: a pragmatic didacticism, almost an amoral morality, in which what *is* clearly but inevitably differs from what *should be*, and in which the author gives advice that would not be necessary in a fairer world.

This double perspective appears even more sharply in Lennox's less complex novel of the previous year, *Harriot Stuart*.[25] Like Arabella, Harriot is preoccupied with men and thus reveals her sexuality to the modern reader. Unlike Arabella, Harriot is an avowed coquette. But to readers of Lennox's time this sin, though real, is venial, for she is driven not by lasciviousness but by a lust for conquest. She deserves correction, but the author clearly shows that her punishment is out of all proportion to her crime. On one occasion, Harriot is thrilled to find herself the only young woman on a ship on the Atlantic, and she flirts shamelessly with several of the crew. The captain, one of a majority of men in the novel for whom love is merely the desire to possess, tries to rape Harriot, but she manages to stab him. For a time the captain appears to be dead, and the crew seeks revenge, crying, "What, our captain murdered by a girl, for such a paultry trifle as a rape, and not committed neither! Hang law, and a court of justice, as she talks of; deliver her up to us, noble lieutenant; let us punish her our own way."[26] If Harriot learns from this experience to be more circumspect, it is only because men are so uncivilized. We can tell who is right and who is wrong, but that issue is less important than who is weak and who is strong.[27]

The Female Quixote similarly stresses the unfairness of the punishments visited on women who lack self-restraint. Part of Arabella's education in the way of the world comes from the history of the fallen Miss Groves, whose brazenness has been her undoing. Unlike her "serious, reserved, and pious" foster-sisters, Miss Groves spent her childhood as "a great Romp" who enjoyed "masculine Exercises" (*FQ* 1:105). Because she had no self-discipline, she was easily seduced and became pregnant (or as her maid says, "ill"). The child died. When she became pregnant a second time, she was betrayed by her servants and abandoned by her lover, who took the child and spread the word that she was "too easy a Conquest" (*FQ* 1:111-13). When Arabella and the reader meet Miss Groves, she seems to have no choice but to go her highspirited way along the road to ruin. Unfortunately, Arabella cannot learn much from this harrowing story, because her romantic delusions make her believe Miss Groves is chaste but misunderstood, like Scudéry's "unfortunate Cleopatra." But the female reader learns to fear the consequences of free behavior without forfeiting her awareness that if Miss Groves is bad, her cruel, hypocritical lover is much worse.

One can easily imagine Charlotte Lennox's own adolescence from these two novels. And though such speculation is dangerous, there is evidence in her early writings to suggest, as Philippe Séjourné has done, that the author did find oppressive the very proprieties *The Female Quixote* preaches. Séjourné believes growing up outside London (perhaps in America) made Lennox a bit too wild for bluestocking tastes, and thus her works before *The Female Quixote* were not well received.[28] In her poem "The Art of Coquetry," for example, the narrator runs down a list of various types of men, giving clues on how to conquer their hearts.[29] Like Arabella, the persona uses chivalric conventions to satisfy the feminine will to power, thus facetiously contradicting the anti-romantic principles the author would later espouse in *The Female Quixote*. The bluestockings were shocked.[30] So in her first popular novel, Lennox would show—with some sadness, as we have seen—that this lust for power is an adolescent phase that must be painfully outgrown.

One might say the woman novelist assumed an attitude of enlightened resignation—a stance that enriches Lennox's satire by giving it a double edge. During most of volume one Arabella appears ludicrous; during most of volume two, she is seen as unique, a Juvenalian norm used to measure the vices and follies of the world (often represented by Glanville's sister, Charlotte).[31] One way the world is especially deficient is in its opinion of feminine intelligence. Though Arabella may read the wrong books, she does read—unlike most of the Londoners she meets. All of London admires the Countess, who, like a Richardsonian heroine, receives their good opinion because she is above caring for it. Yet she is also sneered at for knowing "too much for a Lady" (*FQ* 2: 245); and so we are invited to sneer at London. The novel supports Arabella for possessing such uncommon learning and intelligence: "if she had been a Man," brags her uncle, "she would have made a great Figure in Parliament" (*FQ* 2:211). Interestingly, the greatest ignoramuses of London are male. Lennox takes the old fop and pedant, familiar since the days of Jacobean drama, and adapts them to her feminist purpose by enlisting them on the losing side of the battle of the sexes. Arabella innocently exposes their folly, and they bitterly resent being "posed by a Girl" (*FQ* 2: 139).[32] The heroine's absurdity is nothing to theirs.

Enlightened resignation may make the irony rich, but it makes the morality foggy. A reader seeking wisdom from *The Female Quixote* would often be unsure whether to view Arabella as a model or as a warning. And even when a virtue can be clearly identified, it cannot be imitated. For, like most eighteenth-century heroines, Arabella is most virtuous when she is least imitable. Compared to Charlotte, Arabella is natural and artless. And who can learn to be natural?

This paradox is full of comic possibilities, as Cervantes shows when Sancho boasts of his charming simplicity. Lennox similarly exploits the humor of Arabella's studied carelessness. Only her hairdresser knows for sure how she gets her romantic coiffure: "Her fine black Hair hung upon her Neck in Curls, which had so much the Appearance of being artless, that all but her Maid, whose Employment it was to give them that Form, imagined they were so" (*FQ* 1:7). Further, Lennox uses the paradox to make a satiric point: that romance heroines are useless as moral models. Just as Don Quixote cannot will himself to go mad like his hero Amadis, no amount of conscious effort will make Arabella as modest as her favorite heroines. On one occasion, Arabella orders her poor maid, Lucy, to play romance confidante and narrate the story of her mistress's life. But Lucy spoils the game by asking "what she must say"; now Arabella cannot ask her "to soften those Parts of my History where you have greatest Room to flatter; and to conceal, if possible, some of those Disorders my Beauty has occasioned" (*FQ* 1:185). Though she tries, Arabella simply cannot conceal the egoism that makes her expect Lucy to "be able, not only to recount all my Words and Actions . . . , but also all my Thoughts, however instantaneous" (*FQ* 1:185). Because Arabella reads romances, she is automatically barred from becoming a spontaneous romance heroine. Thus her whole value system is built on sand.

But this satire backfires on Lennox and her heroine; Arabella is also ineffective as a model, and for the same reason. One day Charlotte spends four hours getting dressed, "in order, if possible, to eclipse her lovely Cousin." When she goes to Arabella's chamber shortly before they are to go out, she finds the heroine still undressed. She prepares with "Haste and Negligence," but "notwithstanding her Indifference, nothing could appear more lovely and genteel" (*FQ* 1:124-25). Charlotte is understandably frustrated. What can she do? She might imitate Arabella by becoming careless of her appearance and by forgetting the protocol and decorum of fashionable life. But would she then be as adorable as Arabella? Since she can only admire perfection without hope of acquiring it, she is jealous. And since the young female reader is in exactly the same position, she will most likely share Charlotte's bitterness.

Of course, Arabella's careless beauty is simply the visible manifestation of her artless goodness. In important matters, the self-conscious heroine completely lacks self-awareness. Her preoccupation with love does not make her unchaste because, like Pamela and all her innocent daughters, she knows much less of the state of her heart than the reader does. Lennox confides only to us that

Glanville's faithfulness is "of more Consequence to her Happiness, than she was yet aware of" (*FQ* 1:197). During one comic misunderstanding we even catch her in the act of self-deception. Thinking she has discovered that Glanville is indifferent, "As she was unwilling to acknowledge, even to herself, that the Grief she felt at this Discovery, proceeded from any Affection for her Cousin, she imputed it to the Shame of seeing herself so basely forsaken and neglected" (*FQ* 1:261). Like Jane Austen's Emma, she does not discover "the true State of her Heart" until a rival appears to stir up "all the Passions which attend disappointed Love" (*FQ* 2:271). But by ridiculing Arabella, Lennox invites the reader to examine the state of her own heart, and to acquire self-knowledge superior to the heroine's. And once she has done so, her innocence is lost.

Arabella's artlessness would pose no didactic problem in an avowed romance, like the fairy tale Snow White. The two stories are very similar in theme. Like Charlotte, the wicked queen in the fairy tale is a slave to her mirror; yet she fails to be as beautiful as Snow White, the *unreflecting* heroine. Whereas Charlotte and the queen are punished for their vanity, Arabella and Snow White marry the handsome prince. The fairy tale might teach a child not to be vain. But she would not learn simply by taking Snow White as a model and the queen as a warning. Rather she would identify with both the heroine and the villainess, working out her inner struggles through the conflict in the story. Thus the fairy tale helps the child acknowledge and accept inner feelings it may be "wrong" to express: what Bruno Bettelheim calls "the dark side of man." Johnsonian didactic fiction, on the other hand, encourages the suppression of all qualities not found in the character designated as ideal. And since in *The Female Quixote* the ideal female is unselfconscious, the novel cannot point out a safe path from the world of innocence into the world of experience. Here, to lose innocence is to fall irredeemably. The reader, self-conscious by definition, is already lost. Comparing herself with the heroine can only make her, in Bettelheim's phrase, "a monster in [her] own eyes."[33]

Clearly, and despite all Lennox's satire, Arabella is Snow White's daughter: a heroine in the old romance tradition. Her "natural" curls may be an illusion, but in the assembly room at Bath she gets the attention Austen's Catherine Morland could only dream about. Charlotte hopes everyone will laugh at her cousin, dressed outlandishly as Princess Julia. But "her noble Air, the native Dignity in her Looks, the inexpressible Grace which accompany'd all her Motions, and the consummate Loveliness of her Form" win the day (*FQ* 2:150). Langbauer sees this romantic turn as a sign of Lennox's lack of control; Warren sees it as subtle and deliberate irony.[34] The novelist must at least have seen what her heroine had become. Yet she could not have expected her readers to switch their orientation suddenly and begin reading *The Female Quixote* as if it belonged to a completely distinct (and inferior) genre. Lennox presents the romantic Arabella as if she were real, thus demonstrating the practical results of an oversimplified theory of the novel. When writers of Lennox's time denied the romantic roots of fiction, they presented a whole century of young women with heroines whose artlessness made them useless as moral models.

One might understand how male novelists would fail to see the problem with such heroines: a man might believe the allure of an unreflecting Beatrice or Laura could inspire a love of virtue in the reader. So Richardson expected his readers to fall in love with Pamela and hence gradually, like Mr. B, with the innocence she represents. But Henry Fielding was perceptive enough to point out that giving the artless angel a point of view of her own automatically makes her inconsistent and hypocritical. His Shamela, in consciously pretending to be unconscious—literally, when she pretends to faint—is any woman trying to imitate the childlike heroine of eighteenth-century fiction.

If Fielding could see the problem, how then could women themselves cooperate in the attempt to make this mythical character seem real? One possible answer is that (as *The Madwoman in the Attic* points out) writing in itself was felt to be a male generative act. And since form and content cannot really be separated, the genres in which a writer might publish reflected the values and fantasies of men. For example, Lennox's "The Art of Coquetry," discussed above, is a verse essay that seems to attempt a mildly ironic view of women much like Pope's. But because of Lennox's gender, the satiric detachment is confusing, rather like Mary Wollstonecraft's referring to women as "they." Thus contemporary readers like Elizabeth Carter could not catch the tone of the poem and took it as serious advice to power-seeking flirts.

The bluestockings' reaction to the poem also suggests that women really believed artlessness was the highest form of female beauty. No wonder these writers were so insecure and inconsistent in their attitudes about their own writing—some, like Madame de Genlis, even publishing the sentiment that women should not write, and especially should not publish.[35] Satire, hitherto the province of sage male authority, was considered particularly unmannerly and unfeminine. Even Lennox, whose poem is so full of conscious satiric purpose, has Arabella "decry" raillery for a whole chapter, just before which the heroine has unconsciously exposed the folly of a pedant.[36] Thus the author—with some wistfulness, perhaps—gives her fictional woman a quality of innocence no longer available to herself.

Women writers did accept the beauty of artlessness; but they also gave their heroines the flaws born of self-consciousness. At first those flaws existed side by side, rather inconsistently, with the romance heroine's perfect simplicity. Thus Arabella (and most of Fanny Burney's heroines as well) inhabit a confusing universe. Their failure to conform appears sometimes like a vice, sometimes like a rare virtue. Unable to move either forward into experience or backward into innocence, they (and their readers) are condemned to an eternal adolescence.[37]

However frustrating this inconsistency might have been to contemporary readers, novel-lovers of our own time must be grateful for it: for it was this inconsistency that led the novel in its modern direction. Johnson wanted novels to present a model moral universe. The women novelists of his time persisted in presenting the real universe, showing its unfairness without advocating rebellion. Thus novels began to focus on the moral problems resulting from trying to live in an imperfect world.[38]

Not content with depicting the facts of their outer lives, eighteenth-century women novelists also gave us detailed accounts of their fantasies of love and power. For these accounts they made use of old romantic archetypes, and in doing so provided an underground service for an age that, after all, could only pretend not to like "wonder." Dr. Johnson himself loved romances, while blaming them for "that unsettled turn of mind which prevented his ever fixing in any profession."[39] Lennox's novel embodies this same repressive self-criticism, satirizing and exploiting the romance at the same time. And so, despite the author's stated intention, the cure of Arabella is as much to be mourned as the death of Don Quixote.

NOTES

[1]Susan Staves, "Don Quioxte in Eighteenth-Century England," *CompL* 24, 3 (1972):193.

[2]Miriam Small, *Charlotte Ramsay Lennox* (New Haven: Yale Univ. Press, 1935), p. 112.

[3]Laurie Langbauer writes, "By deriding romance, construing it as the realm of excess and nonsense, *The Female Quixote* veils its own excesses, tries to appear stable and controlled." See "Romance Revised: Charlotte Lennox's *The Female Quixote*," *Novel* 18(Fall 1984):29.

[4]Langbauer, p. 29.

[5]William Congreve, Preface to *Incognita, The Complete Works of William Congreve*, 4 vols. (London: Nonesuch, 1923), 1:111. Bridget MacCarthy notes that Congreve, like Lennox, "adhered" to the romance tradition while criticizing it. See B. G. MacCarthy, *The Female Pen: Women Writers, Their Contribution to the English Novel 1621-1744*, 2 vols. (Cork: Cork Univ. Press, 1947), 1:226.

[6]Aphra Behn, *Oroonoko* (New York: Norton, 1973), p. 1.

[7]Samuel Johnson, *Rambler* no. 4, *Essays from the Rambler, Adventurer, and Idler* (New Haven: Yale Univ. Press, 1968), pp. 9-15.

[8]Patricia Meyer Spacks, *Imagining a Self* (Cambridge, Mass.: Harvard Univ. Press, 1970), p. 191.

[9]By inventing a narrator who rates women on an amatory rather than a moral scale, Delariviere Manley vindicates her own "fallen" life in her *Adventures of Rivella*.

[10]Susan Staves notes that few writers of the eighteenth century saw Don Quixote's quest as anything but ridiculous. She excepts Addison and Steele (pp. 194, 205, 209-210). Ronald Paulson notes that Whig writers in general showed more sympathy for such eccentric characters. See *Satire and the Novel in Eighteenth-Century England* (New Haven: Yale Univ. Press, 1967), pp. 62, 63, 69. Marilyn Butler mentions Charles Lucas's *The Infernal Quixote* as part of the anti-Jacobin movement of the end of the eighteenth century. See *Jane Austen and the War of Ideas* (Oxford: Clarendon Press, 1975), pp. 107-18.

[11]Charlotte Lennox, *The Female Quixote*, 2 vols. in 1 (Upper Saddle River, N.J.: Gregg Press, 1970), 1:1-3. Subsequent references to this novel are incorporated in the text, using the abbreviation *FQ*, cited by volume and page.

[12]Langbauer points out Lennox's debt to the romance for her own plot structure, but seems to see the borrowing as unintentional. She does show that Lennox did not want her novel to be too long, like the romances she satirized (p. 35).

[13]Miriam Small says Johnson wrote the chapter (pp. 2-7); Staves says Johnson may have written it (p. 197). Duncan Isles says there is no evidence he did. See "Johnson and Charlotte Lennox," *New Rambler*, serial C, no. 3 (June 1967):43. John Fyvie feels the chapter is unworthy of Johnson. See *Some Famous Women of Wit and Beauty* (London: Constable, 1905), p. 186. To Langbauer, the only "material" point is that the chapter is in Johnson's style (pp. 42-43).

[14]Langbauer, p. 39.

[15]Thus it is Arabella's own fault that she faces the normal heroine's choice between lover and father described by Nancy K. Miller in *The Heroine's Text* (New York: Columbia Univ. Press, 1980), p. 149.

[16]See Spacks, *The Adolescent Idea* (New York: Basic Books, 1978), p. 133.

[17]Northrop Frye, *Anatomy of Criticism: Four Essays* (Princeton: Princeton Univ. Press, 1957), p. 172.

[18]Langbauer points out that by 1752, the magical power of romances was more of a "danger" to novelists than to the public, which had largely ceased to read them. Thus Arabella's struggle is really the author's (p. 30). Spacks notes that the typical woman novelist of the period sympathized with even her erring heroines (*Imagining a Self*, p. 129).

[19]Langbauer, p. 40.

[20]For further discussion of space and enclosure, see Sandra Gilbert and Susan Gubar, *The Madwoman in the Attic* (New Haven: Yale Univ. Press, 1979), p. 84.

[21]Both Langbauer and Leland Warren note the importance of the language of romance to Arabella's self-definition. See Langbauer, p. 33, and Warren, "Of the Conversation of Women: *The Female Quixote* and the Dream of Perfection," *SECC* 11 (1982):368. Langbauer also argues that Gilbert and Gubar would attribute this voice to a male author rather than to Arabella (p. 41). Of course, the Johnsonian language Arabella eventually adopts is not really hers either (Warren, p. 374).

[22]See Gilbert and Gubar, pp. 22-23, 39. In his review of *The Female Quixote*, Henry Fielding notes that feminine passivity makes the plot necessarily inferior to that of *Don Quixote*. See *The Covent-Garden Journal*, 2 vols. (New York: Russell and Russell, 1964), 1:280. Sandra Shulman agrees with this assessment. See *The Female Quixote* (New York: Pandora Press, 1986), p. xiii. Paulson comments, however, that even sentimental heroes are comparatively passive (p. 244).

[23]Langbauer, p. 45.

[24]Warren notes that the men in Lennox's novel—like those in her society—were also ambivalent about romance and its language (p. 368).

[25]This novel is remarkably similar to Eliza Haywood's *Betsy Thoughtless*, published the same year (1751), according to Small (p. 248). Dale Spender notes the similarity but dates Haywood's novel a year earlier. See *Mothers of the Novel* (London: Pandora Press, 1986), p. 200. Margaret Dalziel gives the date as December 1750. See *The Female Quixote* (London: Oxford Univ. Press, 1970), p. xxi. The title page reads 1751 (see note 26).

[26]Charlotte Lennox, *Harriot Stuart*, 2 vols. (London: Payne, 1751), 1:204.

[27]Dale Spender discusses Eliza Haywood's advice to women in the *Female Spectator* in similar terms (pp. 103-104).

[28]Philippe Séjourné, *The Mystery of Charlotte Lennox* (Aix-en-Provence: Publications des annales de la faculté des lettres, 1967), p. 23. Marilyn Butler notes that many writers' first novels were anti-romances. See *Maria Edgeworth: A Literary Biography* (Oxford: Clarendon Press, 1972), p. 307. That Lennox didn't write anti-romance till her second novel may confirm Séjourné's view. Langbauer emphasizes another significant biographical fact: that Lennox and her writing were much more popular with men than with women (p. 42). Dale Spender, however, attributes this "fact" to prejudice against women (pp. 198-99).

[29]Small, pp. 233-35.

[30]Elizabeth Carter and her friends, in particular. Lady Mary Wortley Montagu called it "The Art of Tormenting" (Small, pp. 9 and 86).

[31]Shulman comments that the novel demonstrates how dangerous it is to isolate women from the world, and how reasonable it is for such women to prefer the world of fiction (p. xiii).

[32]Langbauer, p. 47.

[33]Bruno Bettelheim, *The Uses of Enchantment* (New York: Random House, 1977), p. 7. On Snow White, see Gilbert and Gubar, pp. 37-38. Also of interest is Donald Barthelme's version of Snow White, in which the heroine goes to college and becomes self-aware, discontented, and impossible to live with. See *Snow White* (New York: Atheneum, 1982).

[34]Langbauer, p. 32; Warren, pp. 368-69.

[35]Gilbert and Gubar, p. 116.

[36]Langbauer, pp. 33-34.

[37]Jane Austen found one solution to this problem. Her Emma has the perfect beauty and high rank of a romance heroine, but in her realistic setting those attributes produce conceit—a vice to which only reflecting people are liable. However, Bridget MacCarthy points out that even the unromantic Austen could not escape the archetype of the lovely heroine. Though Anne Elliot is in many ways far from typical, even she must have a second bloom. See *The Female Pen: The Later Women Novelists 1744-1818*, 2 vols. (Cork: Cork Univ. Press, 1947), 2:279.

[38]Critics often assume that as the novel moved toward realism it moved away from didacticism. Thus Lennox and Burney are typically described as declining as their works became more instructive. But the real development was away from theoretical and towards practical didacticism, a development that took place largely in the works of women. Dale Spender is rare in recognizing that didacticism was an indication that women took their reading and writing seriously (pp. 92-93).

[39]James Boswell, *The Life of Johnson* (London: Oxford Univ. Press, 1970), p. 36.

SEL 27 (1987)
ISSN 0039-3657

The Presence of "the Word" in Cowper's *The Task*

W. GERALD MARSHALL

Throughout his poetic career, William Cowper maintained a strong Christian faith, one rooted in the Evangelicalism of eighteenth-century England.[1] A major aspect of that faith involves Cowper's understanding of the *Logos,* a concept which influences a number of his works. In his commentary on the Gospel of St. John, a fragmentary composition which, to my knowledge, has been totally ignored in Cowper studies, the poet asserts his belief in Christ as the Word of God, and he stresses the creative function of the *Logos*: "By the Word is to be understood the Son of God; Christ was that Word . . . the Word of God . . . the same Word created all things . . . Christ, therefore, is God the Creator . . . in Him dwelleth the fulness of the Godhead bodily."[2] Christ, then, is "the efficacious Word, the fiat," as Walter Ong expresses it,[3] who creates light out of darkness, order and harmony from the original chaos. Cowper also suggests that the Word is the sustaining force of the natural creation. He writes in his brief commentary that "the Word" is actively present "in all things created."[4]

Cowper places greatest emphasis, however, upon the written Word of God. The poet suggests in his remarks on St. John's Gospel that man should continually "feed" upon the "Word" in Scripture.[5] Indeed, it is the written Word to which a troubled poet could turn for peace: "O How I love thy holy word," Cowper writes in his hymn, "Afflictions Sanctified by the Word," for "It guides me in the

W. Gerald Marshall is Associate Professor of English at the University of Hawaii-Manoa. He has published on Wycherley, Dryden, Richardson, and Pope; and he presently is engaged in a book-length study of Restoration biography.

peaceful way / I think upon it all the day."[6] And in his hymn, "The Light and Glory of the Word," Cowper uses images of brillant light to convey his belief in the inspired word of scripture:

> The Spirit breathes upon the Word,
> And brings the truth to sight
> . . . .
> A glory gilds the sacred page
> Majestic like the sun;
> It gives a light to ev'ry age.[7]

These brief, representative statements bring us to the Cowper of *The Task*, who develops with depth and complexity these fundamental concepts of the *Logos*. *The Task*, of course, is often seen as a rambling, disunified piece,[8] but the theme of the Word, as we shall see, unites at least the poem's main topics: Nature, horticulture, the value of meditative reading in the rural environment, city life and the concomitant discussion of public education, the press, and sermons. This approach to the poem is in keeping with Cowper's own statement regarding the overall intent of *The Task*: "to discountenance the modern enthusiasm after a London life, and to recommend rural ease and leisure as friendly to the cause of piety and virtue."[9] For the poem ultimately asserts that country life is to be preferred to city life because of its closeness to the Word as revealed in the "book" of Nature and in quiet reflection upon Scripture. The city, on the other hand, is depicted as a modern Babylon which has so neglected and abused the Word that it has lost touch with the efficacious source of all life and meaning. Or, as Cowper writes in *The Task*:

> Their only point of rest, eternal Word!
> From thee departing, they are lost, and rove
> . . . .
> From thee is all that sooths the life of man.[10]

The important nature scenes in the poem certainly emphasize the essential and primary link between the "eternal Word" just referred to and the natural creation, for all of Nature is presented as the wondrous fruit of the engendering Word, the fiat. The English countryside "leaps forth at once" to the command of God's Word which "calls for things that are not, and they come" (V, 686-87). Beautiful, harmonious nature is "worthy of the word / That, finding an interminable space / Unoccupied, has fill"d the void so well" (IV, 551, 57). The poem also speaks of that "voice, / Which winds and waves obey" (II, 113-14).

Not only is nature created by the Word, but also it is sustained by the *Logos* which speaks to man in and through the creation. The poem opens with a variety of sounds such as "Wintry torrents roaring loud," and "rural sounds" which speak to "the spirit" and restore "the Tone of languid Nature" (I, 181-53). Cowper asserts that all such sounds merge to create a "voice . . . to sooth" (I, 191 and 199). This voice becomes the natural "word." Indeed, nature becomes, metaphorically, God's great *book,*[11] for in his works God "Commands us [as] in his word / To seek *him,*" and in nature man may "read his wonders" (III, 228; V, 798). Through contemplating nature, man may have a deeply spiritual epiphany, an existential experience of the living Word just behind the surface: "Nature [throws] wide / Her veil opaque, discloses with a smile, the author of her beauties . . . eternal Word" (V, 892-97). And the poem concludes, "So *reads* he nature whom the laws of truth / Illuminate. Thy laws, mysterious Word!" (V, 845-46, my emphasis). The poem thus adopts a sacramental view of Nature as providing tangible phenomena which contain the Word as the mysterious, spiritual force which speaks to man of its own order, harmony, and beauty.

We can now see how Cowper begins to develop more deeply the poem's sense of the Word in relationship to the country environment. The poem suggests that one way man may imitate and even participate in the creative expression of the fiat is through the art of gardening. Martin Battestin, summarizing a commonplace aesthetic position of Neoclassical England, suggests that for the poet of the eighteenth century the paradigmatic act of history, to be emulated both in works of art and in the moral life, is the "Logos, whose fiat first brought order out of chaos."[12] The essential creative principle inherent in the Word is, of course, that of *concordia discors*: "harmony and proportion, symmetry and balance" which arise from variety or apparent discord. Such aesthetic principles, Battestin demonstrates, often were applied to the "art" of gardening in the eighteenth century. Samuel Clark, for example, writes that the "true" gardener creates "a work infinitely various, but formally ordered."[13]

Similarly, in Cowper's poem, the true gardener creates not only a literal garden, but a microcosm of the universal order; once again, the fiat becomes the paradigmatic act of history to be imitated, even in the art of gardening. Note the planetary imagery, the imagery of universal wholeness and harmony reflected in the simple, rural garden. The gardener

> Has made a heav'n on earth; with suns and moons
> Of close-ramm'd stones has charg'd th' encumber'd soil,
> And fairly laid the zodiac in the dust.
> He, therefore, who would see his flow'rs dispos'd
> Sightly and in just order, ere he gives
> The beds the trusted treasure of their seeds,
> Forecasts the future whole; that, when the scene
> Shall break into its preconceiv'd display,
> Each for itself, and all as with *one voice*
> Conspiring, may attest his bright design.
> (III, 645-54, my emphasis)

Like the fiat, the gardener creates upon the principle of *concordia discors*. The separate and various elements of the landscape garden ("each for itself") harmonize, as with "one voice," to create a sense of unity in the "future whole." Therein they echo that single "voice" heard at creation which brought forth God's "preconceived" design.

Such is the natural, moral use of the art of gardening. Indeed, Cowper reminisces about a time when rural land was passed down from father to son, when "landscapes" were not simply "gazed upon awhile / then advertised, and auctioneer'd away" (III, 750-56). But now, Cowper suggests, rich landowners from the city destroy the "venerable" homes and land of "our forefathers" in order to make highly expensive, gaudy gardens. Though the older landscape gardens were not as elegant as those created by the wealthy, they were, at least, adhering to the natural countours of the land. The landscape gardener, "Brown" (Lancelot Brown), is hired by the wealthy to create new and elegant gardens in the country, but his creations come at the expense of the poor who must lose their land so that his lavish and, indeed, unnatural gardens can appear. In order to satirize such uses of gardening, Cowper presents Brown as engaging in a devastating parody of the original creation rendered by fiat. In doing so, Cowper establishes a crucially important pattern for the entire poem, in which there are satires on "uncreating words" which stand in contradistinction to the "creating" Word of God. Indeed, Brown *calls* a garden into existence:

> He speaks. The lake in front becomes a lawn;
> Woods vanish, hills subside, and vallies rise:
> And streams, as if created for his use,
> Pursue the track of his directing wand,
> . . . .
> Ev'n as he bids! Th' enraptur'd owner smiles.
> (III, 774-82)

Like the fiat which calls nature into being, Brown's word generates a garden, but unlike creation, Brown's garden violates natural order and perspective: what should be land is water, what should rise falls, what should be deep is elevated. Certainly, Brown's garden lacks "a grace" (III, 82), for there is no harmonious blending of various elements, only increasing disorder, as Brown assumes that nature can be perverted "for his use." Brown's garden is thus presented as the unnatural trickery of a "magician" who parodies the "omnipotent" God (III, 756). Indeed, Brown is presented in much the same manner that Pope presents the goddess, "Dulness," in *The Dunciad.* Pope suggests that Dulness is the "uncreating word" whose voice *uncreates* the natural order of things; what Aubrey Williams says of Pope's poem applies here, for Brown would return the rural harmony to its original "chaos," thus becoming a parody of the Word which generates order from chaos.[14] The Word and its creation thus serve as the standard, the paradigm of gardening, a model clearly imitated by the true gardener. Brown and others who would pervert nature, however, are not welcome in Cowper's rural paradise, and they must return to "London" where "Ambition . . . and vice [and] vanity . . . engulf them all!" (III, 817).

Cowper now suggests yet another way of experiencing the Word which is fostered by the rural environment: quiet meditation upon the written Word. We have presented to us, in various sections of the poem, the poet/narrator alone in his rural retreat, reading works of history (III,140), or poetry (III, 255)—but especially, "His word" that teaches man "To seek him" (III, 224); "his word sagacious" (III, 254); "His most holy book" (VI, 650). It is, perhaps, scriptural prophecy which offers the greatest hope for the narrator and modern man, for "Sweet is the harp of prophecy" which gives assurance that "all Must be at length" reunited to God (VI, 747 and 819).

In the country, then, the Word may be experienced as: 1) the fundamental reality, the ground of being for the natural creation; 2) the primary aesthetic principle, as symbolized in the art of gardening; 3) intellectual and spiritual nourishment that is discovered in quiet, meditative reading of the Word of Scripture.

We can now shift emphasis and begin to see how the poem depicts city life—a major topic of *The Task.* A central element of London life is the press. The daily paper which is received by the poet/narrator is depicted as the mirror of London, the modern Babylon: through the reading of the paper, the poet is permitted a "peep" at "the great Babel" (IV, 90-91). At the outset of *The Task*, we were presented with an array of delightful, natural sounds. In contradistinction, the newspaper, which provides an overview of the city and its values, is "the herald of a noisy world," and the delivery boy comes "with twanging horn o'er yonder ridge" (IV, 5 and 1). Already, the paper is associated with abuses of "sound."

Moreover, it is of crucial importance to see that the "word" of the press ultimately is depicted as a parody of the Divine Word, the fiat. Once again, then, we have uncreating words, but now the poem has shifted its vision from the garden to the city. The writer of the news has a potent pen, a "fluent quill" which senselessly lumps together "words" about "Houses in ashes, and the fall of stocks, / Births, deaths, and marriages, epistles" (IV, 16-19). And the press, with one "voice" (IV, 35), reports political debate concerning Britain's treatment of India: "The grand debate, / The popular harangue" (IV, 30-31). Since it seems painfully obvious to the poet that the people of India, like all people, should be free, he finds such debate to be a "loud laugh" (IV, 33). He goes on to show that the actual words of the press—prideful political speeches, gossip, and trivial reports—are presented as a microcosm (as a *world* which springs from *words*) which parodies the fiat and its creation. The words of the London press are a "map of busy life," which often reports the ambition of city politicians (IV, 55). Indeed, the words metaphorically create an inky world:

> Here runs the mountainous and craggy ridge
> That tempts ambition. On the summit see
> The seals of office glitter in his [the politician's] eyes;
> He climbs, he pants, he grasps at them! At his heels,
> Close at his heels, a demagogue ascends,
> . . . .
> Here rills of oily eloquence in soft
> Meanders lubricate the course they take.
>
> (IV, 57-65)

These politicians thus manage to get their speeches and activity recorded in the press. But this is all "trivial" and represents a "dearth of information and good sense" (IV, 56-71). Thus, the London press contains meaningless "Cat'racts of declamation [which] thunder here" and "forests of meaning [which] spread the page, / In which all comprehension wanders, lost" (IV, 73-75). The rest of the paper "appears a wilderness of strange / But gay confusion . . . Heav'n, earth, and ocean, plunder'd of their seats" (IV, 78-82). Lumped together in this chaos are "Sermons, and city feasts, and fav'rite airs, / Aethereal journies, submarine exploits, / And Katterfelto, with his hair on end" (IV, 84-86). The writer's quill, which generates the news, is a parody of the divine, generative principle, as it gives "voice and utt'rance" to a "noisy" world. For the *world* created in the press, with its *ridges* of prideful statements, *summits* of power, *rills* of false eloquence, and *cataracts* of meaningless words represents an uncreation of order. It is a bathetic world of thunderous declamation with no content, of mountains of words built on illusions of grandeur, of words separated from meaning. The press, finally, is a sterile world, a "wilderness"—the ultimate travesty of a world teeming with life which is engendered by the *Logos*. The words of the press thus create a world of language which is a parody of *the Word* itself and the world it has generated, a world of harmony, order, and substantial meaning. The London press thus stands condemned in its own triviality by the Divine Word to which it is compared through the technique of allusion. An abuse of words is an abuse of *the Word*.

Similar abuses appear in the city's educational system. Cowper asserts that "in ancient days" (II, 699) English public education upheld high principles. Education was, metaphorically, presided over by a "sage call'd Discipline" whose *word* was sacred and "*Bespoke* him past the bounds of freakish youth" (II, 704, my emphasis). Just as the *Logos*, itself, speaks with wisdom, righteousness, love, and truth, so Discipline speaks forth his word: "in his speech was heard / Paternal sweetness, dignity, and love," along with "learning, virtue, piety, and truth" (II, 706-707; 700). His "voice" (II, 721), like the fiat itself, creates order from the potential chaos of classrooms, for he "held" the "passions," and his words "shook the delinquent with . . . fits of awe." Under the *efficacious* power of his word, there grew a little "garden" of learning: "Learning grew, / Beneath his care, a thriv'ng, vig'rous plant" (II, 715, 722, 713-14).

But modern London has lost such educational values, Cowper suggests, and abuses the word of education. Discipline has now lost his *voice* in the public schools: "his voice, unstrung, / Grew tremulous, and mov'd derision more / Than rev'rence in perverse rebellious youth" (II, 728-29). In the cities, Discipline has been replaced by "Ignorance," who is also directly associated with words and voices: "With parrot tongue," Ignorance "perform'd the scholars' part, / Proceeding soon a graduated dunce" (II, 738-39). The parrot metaphor suggests that the word of Ignorance is highly uncreative, that it merely repeats and reflects the thoughts expressed by other dunces, and it can hardly be said to be inherently generative as is the *Logos*. Indeed, this parrot tongue becomes an uncreating word that would transform the once orderly world of public education into chaos:

> A dissolution of all bonds ensued;
> The curbs, invented for the mulish mouth
> Of head-strong youth, were broken . . .
> . . . .
> A mock'ry of the world!
>
> (II, 743-50)

The uncreating word of Ignorance and its resultant chaos are a parody of the orderly creation of God.

A central hope in the poem for some sort of reform lies in the *preaching* of the Word of God to the people of "Babylon." To Cowper's thinking, sermons are inspired by "His most holy book" of scripture (VI, 650) and are a most important means of communicating God's Word to man. Hence, the true preacher should hold his office as "sacred," for his sermon is the earthly expression of the eternal Word: he is the "legate of the skies" (II, 337-38). The minister's sermon, like the sacred text, itself, should be filled with power when the homilist "*speaks out* [my emphasis]" against violations of divine law and "thunders" forth his sermons (II, 340-41). At the same time, the effective sermon must bring the soothing, peaceful message of the Gospel—the expression of the incarnate Word, Himself; the minister must remember that "the gospel *whispers* peace [my emphasis]" and that, like the redeeming Word of Christ, his word "restores the weak" (II, 342-43). The minister should display an eloquence and skill which carry with them the very heart of the Word of scripture: "[the preacher] in strains . . . sweet . . . Reclaims the wand'rer, binds the broken heart" (II, 341-43).

Unfortunately, the poem suggests, such ministers have all but vanished in the modern city and have been replaced by abusers of words. Such preachers use language which contains no inherent meaning and they preach sermons void of the efficacious power of the Word upon which they base their text. These false preachers, these "things that mount the rostrum with a skip," simply

> pronounce a text;
> Cry-hem: and, reading what they never wrote
> Just fifteen minutes, huddle up their work,
> And with a well-bred whisper close the scene!
>
> (III, 409-13)

Such an abuse of words parodies the creation by fiat, for these ministers symbolically have descended the chain of being to the level of a "thing," thus speaking themselves out of their own humanity. Moreover, such a minister makes a mere show of words: "He seek[s] to dazzle me with his tropes . . . and play his brilliant parts before my eyes" (II, 423-25). His word, unlike the *reality* of *the Word,* is a mere show or illusion. Not allowing his listeners to "feed" upon the Word of scripture, he "starves his flock!" (II, 429). To misuse words in sermons is, in the world of *The Task,* to parody God himself; and, again, to abuse words is to abuse the Word: "He [the preacher] mocks his Maker, prostitutes and shames / His noble office" (II, 427-28). Little wonder these abuses in speech exist, since the fake minister has been taught by a false Doctor or teacher of ministers, whose "voice" (II, 351) is one which

> sells accent, tone,
> And emphasis in score, and gives to pray'r
> Th' *adagio* and *andante* it demands.
> He grinds divinity of other days
> Down into modern use; transforms old print
> To zig-zag manuscript, and cheats the eyes.
>
> (II, 359-64)

These are clearly abuses of words: selling homiletical skills for profit, using form and eloquence with no spiritual content, depriving words of those qualities which Cowper, Pope, and other Augustan writers would see as essential. For here, words have lost their efficacious, redeeming and enlightening aspects. The "word" of the "Doctor," unlike the Word of scripture, uses form with no substantial content, words severed from truth and meaning.

It is within the general context of scripture and preaching that we now find a final rendering of the Word. Cowper certainly implies that pulpits have failed to transform modern London. As an alternative, he suggests that literature—indeed, his own poem—can be an important means of providing scriptural teaching and the homiletic force that seem to be lacking elsewhere. Occasionally, *The Task* closely mirrors—in tone, imagery, and theme—scriptural passages.[15] Let us first note such activity in the poetic text and then examine further implications as regards the central theme of the Word.

Cowper closely follows well-known scriptural passages when he asserts that "all below" is vanity, that "Nothing is proof against the gen'ral curse / Of vanity, that seizes all below" (III, 266-67). The source for the passage is, of course, the Book of Ecclesiastes: "All is vanity . . . I have seen all the works that are done under the sun; and, behold, all *is* vanity" (Eccles. 1:3 and 14, KJV). Emphasizing the transitoriness of life, the poet writes in the same passage: "All flesh is grass, and all its glory fades" (III, 261). Here are precisely the same words in the Book of Isaiah: "All flesh is grass . . . the grass withereth, the flower fadeth" (Isa. 40:6-7).

But the poem also offers a vision of hope and, again, Cowper turns to the prophet Isaiah and his vision of the millennium:

> Rivers of gladness water all the earth,
> The various seasons woven into one,
> And that one season an eternal spring,
>
> . . . .
>
> The lion, and the libbard, and the bear
> Graze with fearless flocks; all bask at noon
>
> . . . .
>
> Antipathies are none. No foe to man
> Lurks in the serpent now: the mother sees,
> And smiles to see, her infant's playful hand
> Stretch'd forth to dally with the crested worm,
>
> . . . .
>
> All creatures worship man, and all mankind
> One Lord, one Father.
>
> (VI, 763-84)

Here is Isaiah's scriptural account of the millennium: "the wolf also shall dwell with the lamb . . . and a little child shall lead them. . . . And the sucking child shall play on the hole of the asp . . . for the earth shall be full of the knowledge of the lord, as the waters cover the sea. . . . And in that day [all] shall say, praise the Lord" (Isa. 11:5-9; 12:4).

This is immediately followed by further direct parallels with biblical prophecy, this time elements of the vision of St. John in the Book of Revelation. A prophetic voice describes the end-time, when

> One song employs all nations; and all cry,
> "Worthy the Lamb, for he was slain for us!"
>
> . . . .
>
> Till, nation after nation taught the strain,
>
> . . . .
>
> All kingdoms and all princes of the earth
> Flock to that light.
>
> (VI, 791-802)

Paralleling the poem are these lines in Revelation: "And I beheld, and I heard the voice of many angels . . . Saying with a loud voice, Worthy is the Lamb that was slain . . . And every creature which is in heaven, and on the earth . . . [said] Blessing . . . to Him who sitteth on the throne, and unto the Lamb"(Rev., 5:11-13). Immediately after these passages, the poem offers a brief *commentary* on the scriptural "text" which has just ended: "Thus heav'n-ward all things tend. For all were once / Perfect, and all must be at length restor'd" (VI, 818-19). This brief commentary certainly heightens the scriptural nature of the prophetic passages, since, of course, biblical passages would receive such analysis in popular commentaries of the period.

The chief way in which the passages we have examined relate to the theme of the Word is that they emphasize the value of Scripture, the written Word of God; these sections of the poem are, then, meant to stand in direct contrast to the abuses of the Word revealed by the false preachers and teachers of London who were discussed earlier. The sections which so closely mirror biblical writings are certainly among the most eloquent and memorable in *The Task*, and it is through them that Cowper has chosen to provide the reader with the most all-encompassing vision, both of human weakness and of man's possibility for renewal. With the power of the Word itself, the passages suggest that city life, with its neglect and abuse of the Word, is a world of vanity and empty dreams much like the world described by "the preacher" in Ecclesiastes; but modern man, after realizing his situation, can participate in the vision of a future which is immersed in the presence of the living Word in the heavenly Jerusalem, a vision found in Scripture. When Cowper wishes to make his point this far-reaching, even visionary, he turns to the Word of Scripture to provide depth and persuasive expression. The poet/narrator thus becomes much like the true preacher who uses the Word in proper ways.

Moreover, there is a somewhat deeper element here. In the sections of the poem which are modeled after biblical passages, the reader has a poetic text which he is invited to read as though it were a Scriptural text, and he has a narrative voice that he is now asked to "hear" as though it were a biblical voice. Ultimately, this technique becomes an important *symbolic* element of the poem: it suggests that the poetic text gives priority to the scriptural text which it has, essentially, become; that the poem speaks with greater force and dignity when it permits *the Word* to consume the mere poet's words with its own holy presence. The poem, like the book of nature, thus becomes *sacramental*: the visible phenomenon of the poetic text occasionally parts or symbolically vanishes to reveal *the Word* as fundamental ground of its own "being," just as it is for Nature itself.

We can, then, perceive that *The Task* has a central, unifying statement: the modern city has abused and lost contact with the Word, the source and meaning of life and the source and meaning of all significant uses of words themselves. This Word may best be experienced in a peaceful, rural environment through contemplation of the "book" of Nature, and through reflection upon Scripture and literary works, such as *The Task*, which speak to "noisy" (IV, 5) Babylon of a Word beyond sound.

NOTES

[1]For an excellent discussion of Cowper's religion, see Norman Nicholson, *William Cowper* (London: John Lehmann, 1951), pp. 26-45.

[2]I am deeply indebted to Mr. Joseph Bourneau of Widener Library, Harvard University, for invaluable assistance in locating this work. Cowper's "Notes on St. John's Gospel" is printed in the Reverend Josiah Bull's *John Newton: An Autobiograghy and Narrative* (London: The Religious Tract Society, 1868), pp. 373-77. This passage covers pp. 373-75.

[3]Walter J. Ong, S.J., *The Presence of the Word* (New Haven: Yale Univ. Press, 1967), p. 288. Obviously, I am indebted to Father Ong for the title of my own essay.

[4]"Notes on St. John's Gospel," p. 374.

[5]"Notes on St. John's Gospel," p. 377.

[6]*The Poetical Works of William Cowper*, ed. H. S. Milford (London: Oxford Univ. Press, 1934), pp. 456-57, hereafter referred to as *Poetical Works.*

[7]*Poetical Works*, p. 452.

[8]For studies of the poem see Gilbert Thomas, *William Cowper and the Eighteenth Century* (London: George, Allen and Unwin, 1948), pp. 256-97; Roderick Huang, *William Cowper, Nature Poet* (Oxford: Oxford Univ. Press, 1957), pp. 67-92; Hoosag K. Gregory, "Cowper's Love of Subhuman Nature: A Psychoanalytic Approach," *PQ* 46, 1 (January 1967):42-57; William N. Free, *William Cowper* (New York: Twayne, 1970); Vincent Newey, "Cowper and the Description of Nature," *EIC* 23, 1 (January 1973):102-108, and *Cowper's Poetry* (Totowa, N.J.:Barnes and Noble, 1982), pp. 16-42, 93-207; David Boyd, "Satire and Pastoral in The Task," *PLL* 10, 4 (Fall 1974): 363-77; Dustin Griffin, "Cowper, Milton, and the Recovery of Paradise," *EIC* 31, 1 (January 1981):15-26; P. M. S. Dawson, "Cowper's Equivocations," *EIC* 33, 1 (January 1983):19-35; and Martin Priestman, *Cowper's 'Task': Structure and Influence* (London and New York: Cambridge Univ. Press, 1983). Priestman deals with the idea of Cowper's "self-recreation in the shape of the truly exemplary figure" in the poem (p. 5). The study thus sees the poem as an attempt by the poet to define himself.

The most serious attempt to establish unity in the poem, other than my own, is that of Thomas E. Blom, "The Structure and Meaning of *The Task*," *PCP* 5 (1970):12-18. This essay emphasizes the theme of the "fall" and redemption as being central to the poem. But this theme is much too commonplace, even inherent, in retirement literature to bear the weight Blom assigns it. Rather, the inherent concern with fall and redemption, as we shall see, becomes only a part of the poem's much larger discussion of the Word. Blom also points out some passages in the poem which echo Biblical prophecy. My own work offers more extensive uses of scriptural allusions in the poem and relates such elements to the theme of the Word, which Blom does not mention.

[9]The passage is found in Cowper's letter of 10 October 1784 to the Rev. William Unwin. Cited in Nicholson's *William Cowper,* pp. 89-90. See note 1.

[10]*Poetical Works*, V, 897-98, p. 219. Hereafter, references to the poem are to this edition and are cited by book and line.

[11]The idea that Nature is God's "book" is commonplace in seventeenth and eighteenth-century English theology. For example, Bishop Peter Browne (whose works appear in Cowper's personal library), asserts that the world is a "book to be read," a book which contains the "living Word." See *Things Divine and Supernatural* (London, 1733), p. 9. Cowper's library holdings appear in Thomas Wright, *The Life of William Cowper* (London: T. Fisher Unwin, 1892), pp. 659-65.

[12]Martin C. Battestin, *The Providence of Wit* (Oxford: Clarendon Press, 1974), p. 56.

[13]Cited in Battestin, pp. 79-80, 46-57.

[14]*Pope's Dunciad: A Study of its Meaning* (New Haven: Yale Univ. Press, 1967), pp. 143 and 139. Williams refers to the goddess, Dulness, as an "anti-*Logos*" (p. 154). Williams also points out that in Pope's poem abuses of *words* in literary art, in the press, and in public speaking represent abuses of *the Word* itself, the *Logos*. Similar ideas are expressed by other writers of the Neoclassical period. For example, in Dryden's "MacFlecknoe," Shadwell, through his abuses of writing, is presented as a parody of Christ, the Word. See Michael Wilding, "*MacFlecknoe*," *EIC* 19, 4 (1969):355-70.

[15]Blom has noted some of the poem's prophetic allusions, but his use of this material differs greatly from my own. See note 8.

SEL 27 (1987)
ISSN 0039-3657

Blake Reads "The Bard": Contextual Displacement and Conditions of Readability in *Jerusalem*

MOLLY ANNE ROTHENBERG

The reader who seeks to unlock *Jerusalem* must devise a reading strategy to handle the poem's apparent incoherencies. At the outset of the poem, the reader's situation is complicated by assurances that the "origin" of the work guarantees its coherence; the much-quoted address to the public provides for two possible, and mutually exclusive, sources of the poem. Blake explains first that the origin is some external power which "dictated" the poem to him, but he immediately contradicts himself by claiming responsibility for the choice of a novel type of verse that encompasses a variety of meters and styles:

> When this Verse was first dictated to me I consider'd a Monotonous Cadence like that used by Milton & Shakespeare & all writers of English Blank Verse, derived from the modern bondage of Rhyming, to be a necessary and indispensable part of Verse. But I soon found that in the mouth of a true Orator such monotony was not only awkward, but as much a bondage as rhyme itself. I therefore have produced a variety in every line, both of the cadences & number of syllables. Every word and every letter is studied and put into its fit place.[1]

The "dictated" poem and the poem constructed syllable by syllable do not arise from reconcilable sources.[2]

However, Blake offers yet another possibility for the "origin" of the poem at its conclusion:

Molly Ann Rothenberg is Assistant Professor of English at Beloit College and Chair of Comparative Literature. She has completed a book on Blake's *Jerusalem*.

All Human Forms identified even Tree Metal Earth & Stone. all
Human Forms identified, living going forth & returning wearied
Into the Planetary lives of Years Months Days & Hours reposing
And then Awaking into his Bosom in the life of immortality.
And I heard the Name of their Emanations they are named Jerusalem

The End of The Song
of Jerusalem

(Plate 99, E258-59)

This conclusion suggests that Jerusalem may be the composer of the "song" that we know as the poem entitled *Jerusalem*. And since "Jerusalem" is not simply a character in the poem, but also the name of the emanations of all human forms, this poem can be understood as being produced by itself, as a form of *auto-citation*. This poem announces itself as coextensive with its source, its location, its readership: above all, this text takes itself as its own context, or (what may be the same thing) treats all possible contexts as determining its meaning. This property of self-citation and recursive contextualization creates the conditions of "readability" that Blake presents as Vision in this poem.

Contextual Rupture and Readability

Blake's rhetorical problem was to write a poem that did not recreate in its relations to its readers the social and intellectual tyranny he was seeking to subvert. Blake believed that tyranny arises from a misconceived relationship between self and world, what he called the "possessive Self-hood"; his primary task was to help his readers confront the ways in which they established that tyrannical relationship to the world. Since all perception involves an act of interpretation, a poem that calls a reader's interpretive strategies into question could help re-educate that reader into a visionary relationship with the world. By undermining the position of the author as the origin of the text, by making the source of the text both internal and external to the work, by refusing to provide a stable contextual determinant, by positively disallowing any recourse to such a context, Blake forces the reader to confront the ways in which he uses such contexts (such as the concept of author-as-origin) to create his interpretations. In fact, Blake compels the reader to recognize both the necessity for and the artificial and unstable existence of these contexts in the production of any meaning.

Language can mean only if it can be separated from an original, determinate context: we produce the meaning of words not by finding their source but by appropriating them to new contexts—our own. The "readability" of a text depends upon its dissociation from a definitive context or consciousness. It requires the disruption of context—from a particular reader, a particular point of view, a particular author—so that other contexts, other readers, other "writers," may come into play. The possibility that language will escape the intention of its author, that the text will free itself from its supposed referent, that the poem will sever itself from any determinate context, is the way language is able to mean at all. This must be true since language is composed of signifying forms, recognizable as such, without the imposition of conditions of intention. This is what makes it possible for us to appropriate the signifying forms of language for our own uses, although those language events necessarily carry with them the potential for their being used or understood in ways not under our control. Given that every signifying form can be put in quotation marks (cited), it can break with every given context, "engendering an infinity of new contexts in a manner which is absolutely illimitable. . . . This does not imply that the mark is valid outside of a context, but on the contrary, that there are only contexts without any center or absolute anchoring."[3] The text that cites itself, that disrupts its own original or teleological context, brings to the surface the inherent freedom to make language meaningful. In presenting itself as a citation, *Jerusalem* makes itself available for use in the unlimited production of meaning: "JERUSALEM IS NAMED LIBERTY AMONG THE SONS OF ALBION" (Plate 26, E171).

The poem anticipates the formalist objection that such an approach requires us to lose the hope of uncovering the significance of the poem, relegating the text to a chaotic jumble of senseless signs. As Derrida's quotation explains, all signifying forms achieve their validity within a context, and in the commentary on Chaos in the eternity of "readability" that appears in the closing plates of the poem, chaos is rescued from meaninglessness by the renewed and continuous production of meanings by the creation of different contexts. Thus Chaos "Brighten'd beneath, above, around! Eyed as the Peacock / According to the Human Nerves of Sensation" (Plate 98, E257). Here we see the power of multiple viewpoints, derived from the "expansion and contraction of the organs of perception."

These contextual shifts bring shifts in consciousness and transform perception, but they are not dominated by a single aim or origin. The unifying factor in Blake's Eternity as presented in the conclusion of the poem is the continually transforming and transformative text/context of *Jerusalem*, not some essence that pervades all things or a determinate origin. Without a multiplicity of viewpoints and contexts, there is no possibility of creation, no possibility of significance.

Without contextual rupture, writing becomes a kind of bondage, a "spectrous oath," linking word and object in an absolute symmetry. The interpretive strategy that insists on equating the origin and the meaning of the text is the same strategy that believes in the denotative nature of language, using nature as referent. But Derrida has shown that this founding origin, whether in nature or in consciousness, can never appear anywhere as absolutely present. It can only be figured in a series of substitutions:

> There has never been anything but writing; there have never been anything but supplements, substitutive significations which could only come forth in a chain of differential references, the "real" supervening, and being added only while taking on meaning from a trace and from an invocation of the supplement, etc. And thus to infinity, for we have read, *in the text*, that the absolute present [and] Nature . . . have always escaped, have never existed; that what opens meaning and language is writing as the disappearance of natural presence.[4]

In the final plates of *Jerusalem*, the contextual rupturing that founds the signifying process presents itself as a rhetorical function—the metonymic displacement of contexts. Plate 94, which begins the process of Albion's awakening, and thus serves as the climax of the poem, institutes a dramatic figuration of metonymic displacement. Each displacement results in an "awakening" and the appearance of a new subjectivity. At the same time, these individual metonymic displacements are successively gathered together into ever larger contexts: "England who is Brittannia enterd Albions bosom rejoicing . . . So spake the Vision of Albion & in him so spake in my hearing / The Universal Father" (Plates 96-97, E255-56). This process culminates in the ultimate identification of every thing by means of mutually transforming contexts: "All Human Forms identified even Tree Metal Earth & Stone . . . And I heard the Name of their Emanations they are named Jerusalem."

Each "awakening" makes language possible—this is the moment of "readability," the rupturing from a determinate context that permits signification: "And England who is Brittannia awoke from Death on Albions bosom . . . her voice pierc'd Albions clay cold ear. he moved upon the Rock / The Breath Divine went forth" (Plates 94-95, E254). The rupture is followed by the conferring of a name, a designation of a new context, which functions as a substitution or metaphor for the subject until the next rupture occurs. England becomes Brittannia and in so doing awakens Albion; at this point Albion becomes the sun which in turn reveals Jesus, who then appears in a simile as Los.

The conferring of the name, then, involves two modes of language. First, it functions as a mark of identity, of what is proper to the subject. This is the first step in the regeneration of a "determinate" meaning after the contextual rupture. (It is necessary for purposes of explication to describe this as a chronological process, although logically neither step is prior.) This first mode corresponds to the one-to-one designation of absolute reference so often marked in Blake's text by the activity of the Spectre of Reason, the "oath" or "law." This referential moment, however, is absolutely necessary for signification to appear, because it provides the element of sameness, of presence, on which signification depends. We can recognize that this is language seen in what Paul Ricoeur calls its *hermeneutic* function, its denotative or referential function, which requires a phenomenal here and now, a fixed point of view, a definite origin that governs the relationship between sign and referent.[5]

The second mode of language concerns its *rhetorical* function: Blake re-figures this referential moment as a rhetorical trope, a substitution by metaphor or simile. A name is already a metaphor, a turning away from identity as inherent; it consequently inscribes the possibility/necessity of difference or contextual definition. The rhetorical figure, then, functions as the sign of difference or context. Ricoeur says that we have recourse to the rhetorical function when the "original" authority appears as textually or rhetorically constituted. This rhetorical moment in the text, the stabilizing by a troping that is itself unstable, calls attention to the renewed possibility for contextual rupture, and the process begins again. By the end of the poem, Blake writes this continual movement of the figures, this continual troping, as producing *Jerusalem* itself.

Re-Citing "The Bard"/Re-Visioning the World

Plate 94 marks a turning point in the narrative and an interpretive crux. This plate instigates the series of metonymic substitutions that move us from Albion's death-like trance to his four-fold, Eternal form, but the *cause* of the transition is elided in the narrative:

> Albion cold lays on his Rock . . .
> . . . .
> The weeds of Death inwrap his hands & feet blown incessant
> . . . .
> And the Body of Albion was closed apart from all Nations.
> Over them the famishd Eagle screams on boney Wings and around
> Them howls the Wolf of famine deep heaves the Ocean black and thundering
> Around the wormy Garments of Albion: then pausing in deathlike silence
> Time was Finished! The Breath Divine Breathed over Albion
> . . . .
> And England who is Brittannia awoke.

This account represents its own lack of narrative causality by inserting the screaming eagle, howling wolf, and thundering ocean, whose meaningless sounds effect the ultimate rupture of "deathlike silence." More importantly, the text re-marks this rupture by means of an intertextual suturing, an allusion to Gray's "The Bard" which *also* comments upon the interplay of the referential and contextual signification.

According to Gray, "The Bard" reproduces the curse laid upon Edward the First by the last Welsh bard in reaction to Edward's execution of the Welsh poets; that is, the poem itself is a kind of citational rupture concerned with the disruption of the process of meaningful language. The Bard bemoans the loss of nature's voice that followed the murders:

> 'Hark, how each giant-oak, and desert cave,
> 'Sighs to the torrent's awful voice beneath!
> . . . .
> 'Vocal no more, since Cambria's fatal day,
> 'To high-born Joel's harp, or soft Llewellyn's lay.[6]

The death of the poets renders nature's voice unintelligible, but the last bard is unable to change this until the dead poets reappear. The conditions preceding their return are these:

'Far, far aloof th'affrighted ravens sail;
'The famished eagle screams, and passes by.
'Dear lost companions of my tuneful art,
'Dear, as the light that visits these sad eyes,
'Dear, as the ruddy drops that warm my heart,
'Ye died amidst your dying country's cries—
'No more I weep. They do not sleep.
'On yonder cliffs, a grisly band,
'I see them sit.

(lines 37-45)

Upon their re-appearance, they join the Bard "in dreadful harmony . . . And weave with bloody hands the tissue of [Edward's] line" (lines 47-48). The effectiveness of the curse as a prophecy of Edward's demise depends upon the multiplicity of voices, the conjoining of prior texts. Here, as in the climax of *Jerusalem*, "the famished eagle" announces a transfiguration and a renewed access to signifying power.

However, in Gray's poem the loss of "natural" language marks the crisis. The Bard needs "natural" language to prophesy the actual destruction of Edward and his (un)natural descendants of his union with the "she-wolf of France." Consequently, the Bard privileges the referential power of language, its presentation of itself as a natural sign, a sign that "erases" its own representing, tropological function. In Gray's poem and in Blake's, the screaming of the eagle signifies the breaking of the link between sign and (natural) referent, subverting nature as a determinate context. In "The Bard," however, the break occasions despair; in Blake's poem, the rupture is liberating.

We know that Albion's stony sleep is a figure for the domination of just that referential aspect of language, the priority of the designated object as origin, as "property," as fixed identity. We only need to refer to Albion's opening speech in the poem for a description of this mode of language. His reply to Jesus' request for mutuality and metonymic displacement ("I am in you and you in me") establishes Albion as a centralized, possessive selfhood, totally unaware of the rhetorical function of his own self-proclaimed denotative discourse:

But the perturbed Man away turns down the valleys dark;
Saying. We are not One! we are Many, thou most simulative
[deleted in most printings]
Phantom of the over heated brain! shadow of immortality!
Seeking to keep my soul a victim to thy Love! which binds

Man the enemy of man into deceitful friendships:.
Jerusalem is not! her daughters are indefinite:
By demonstration, man alone can live, and not by faith.
My mountains are my own, and I will keep them to myself!
The Malvern and the Cheviot, the Wolds Plinlimmon &
    Snowdon
Are mine. here will I build my Laws of Moral Virtue!
Humanity shall be no more: but war & princedom & victory!
So spoke Albion in jealous fears, hiding his Emanation
Upon the Thames and Medway, rivers of Beulah:
    dissembling.

(Plate 4, E146-7)

These lines are usually cited as instancing the error that leads to Albion's fall: his empiricist blindness to the limitations of the rationalist method leads him to privilege demonstration over faith. Yet Albion errs only in not recognizing the rhetorical mode of his own language, the truth he speaks despite himself. He appears to assert that man must rely solely upon demonstration rather than faith, but the line may also be read "By relying upon demonstration alone, without faith, man will only be able to live in solitude." In his denial of the figurative properties of language, its rhetorical mode, in his condemnation of Jesus' "simulative" or simulating powers, Albion establishes himself, his intention, and his property as the total context within which language is to function. Consequently he loses access to the truth of his own discourse, a truth that appears only when his words receive another context. Blake signals Albion's refusal of figuration with a trope: Albion "away turns"; he is without trope, a-verse. The attempted elision of the rhetorical results in a "stonified," denotative, referential language with pretensions to univocity (one law) that its very forms belie. For the key to this speech lies in its figuration: in the polysemy of "alone," for example.

Albion's own language escapes his authority, since he must have recourse to the very "simulative" language he deplores in Jesus. Although Albion correctly sees that the mode of existence Jesus embodies subverts the central, possessive selfhood (Albion has "jealous fears," fears of being displaced), he must himself rely upon tropes, metonymically re-figuring Jesus as a "phantom of the over-heated brain! shadow of immortality!" Here he confirms Jesus' claim that Jesus resides in Albion as a representation of his own eternal state. Thus Albion reproduces the "simulative" characteristics of Jesus, a rhetoric of similitude that permits metonymic displacement, at the very moment that he seeks to deny them. Blake reminds the reader of this recourse to rhetoricity by the word "dissembling," an operation that denies similarity—dissemblance—*and* affirms it, by substituting a lie for the truth. Once the reader sees the interdependence of referentiality and rhetoricity in the production of meaning, Albion's speech no longer stands in opposition to Jesus' as a negation, but rather as a kind of reflection or incorporation. Each implies the other.

In Gray's poem we also find that troping makes referentiality possible and gives it a provisional stability. At the moment that language achieves its fullest power in the poem, the power of the prophetic curse, the poetic voices create a metonymy in the metaphorical "weaving" of the "line." Here too Gray provides Blake with the figure for the metonymic substitution that makes Albion appear in his fourfold guise in Plates 96 and following. The Bard taunts Edward and then throws himself from the cliff into "endless night," dying in order to "triumph":

> 'Fond impious man, think'st thou yon sanguine cloud,
> 'Raised by thy breath, has quenched the orb of day?
> 'To-morrow he repairs the golden flood,
> 'And warms the nations with redoubled ray.
> 'Enough for me: with joy I see
> 'The different dooms our fates assign.
> 'Be thine despair, and sceptered care,
> 'To triumph and to die are mine.'
> He spoke and headlong from the mountain's height
> Deep in the roaring tide he plunged to endless night.
> (lines 135-44)

The Bard proposes as his substitute the figure of the sun who "repairs the golden flood, / And warms the nations with redoubled ray." In Plate 96 Albion also sacrifices himself, throwing himself into the "Furnaces of Affliction," but he has already appeared in Plate 95 as the fulfillment of the Bard's sacrifice, as the figure of the sun who arises from the "endless night" of his "stony sleep." Albion's reawakening as the sun parallels the Bard's vision. Blake even puns on Gray's "redoubled ray" for Albion and his Bow are four-fold, re-doubled. The cloud, the gold flood, the nations of the earth, the mountain all appear in the climax of *Jerusalem* through the regeneration of Edward's "sanguine breath"—the Breath Divine, an analogue for the rhetorical power of language:

> Albion rose in anger: the wrath of god breaking bright
> flaming on all sides around

. . . .

Thou seest the Sun in heavy clouds
Struggling to rise above the Mountains. in his burning hand
He takes his Bow, then chooses out his arrows of flaming gold
Murmuring the Bowstring breathes with ardor! clouds roll around the
Horns of the wide Bow, loud sounding winds sport on the mountain brows

. . . .

the Cloud overshadowing divided them asunder

. . . .

So Albion spoke & threw himself into the Furnaces of affliction
All was a Vision, all a Dream: the Furnaces became
Fountains of Living Waters flowing from the Humanity Divine
And all the Cities of Albion rose from their Slumber

. . . .

Then Albion stood before Jesus in the Clouds
Of Heaven Fourfold among the Visions of God in Eternity
(Plates 95-96)

Here the movement of the allusion, begun by the scream of the eagle which both linked and divided Blake's and Gray's texts, has transfigured the rhetorical figures of "The Bard," figures which project the necessity of their transfiguration in order to achieve efficacy or significance. Blake has managed to use the oppositional categories established by Gray's poem without replicating their mutual negation: they are regenerated to a redemptive purpose.

Blake's presentation of Albion's mistaken reliance upon denotation and demonstration, as presented at the outset of the poem, effects another contextual rupture/suture, for his "demonstrative" credo echoes and transforms the text of Jesus' temptation in the wilderness. We can see the relevance of this allusion easily by focusing upon the function of citation (as a contextual rupture which calls for a determinacy that can only be given tropologically) itself in the New Testament text.[7]

When Jesus is offered the option of satisfying his hunger by turning stones into bread, he answers Satan: "It is written, Man shall not live by bread alone, but by every word that proceedeth out of the mouth of God" (Matt. 4.4). Unlike Albion, who organizes the world around himself, motivated by "jealous fears" that limit his perception of available contexts for producing meaning, Jesus refuses to assert the priority of his self (his hunger) as motivation or origin. Jesus will not produce a univocal, tyrannical relationship between word and thing, between self and world. The life of the self that asserts referentiality as the only principle of language is no life at all. Instead, Jesus performs the transformation of stone into bread through a trope, referring to "bread" that does not exist in the world before him *except in potentia*, in his power to transfigure the stones. Bread and stones are equivalent in their inability to satisfy and in their availability for rhetorical transfiguration, metaphorically identical in Jesus' discourse that posits another principle by which meaning emerges—"every word that proceedeth out of the mouth of God."

Jesus' reference to the Mosaic text seems to suggest God as the definitive context for meaningful language/existence. Satan's second temptation makes it clear that he, at least, interprets Jesus' allusion as privileging a hermeneutic view of language, as an attempt to provide a unique origin that governs meaning: the Word of God as "it is written" in Scripture, Satan reasons, must have the same meaning and power, no matter what the scriptural context. Scripture, therefore, is to be read univocally rather than figuratively. This encourages Satan to quote another text from Scripture as his authority for tempting Jesus to throw himself from the pinnacle of the temple. In so doing, Satan displaces Jesus, moving him from wilderness to city, providing a new context for his actions. Jesus, however, follows this rhetorical strategy and performs the same contextual displacement in the scriptural text itself, citing a counter text and thereby undermining the univocity of Scripture and opening up a gap between God's word as origin and God's word as intention, emphasizing the rhetorical rather than the hermeneutical foundation of interpretation.

For Jesus, Scripture is not a univocal text that can be applied, or referred to, with the same result in every situation or context. Instead, he sees it as a collection of tropological maneuvers which allow referentiality to appear as an *effect*. Jesus' troping does not privilege referentiality, but it does produce a designation of the tempter as "Satan." The name—which we are accustomed to think of as denotative—appears out of a tropological moment in the text (which has its representation in the action Jesus proposes, the "turn": "Get thee behind me"—Luke 4.8). Furthermore, the entire process by which names emerge from tropological gestures that efface themselves in a simulation of grounded referentiality appears in this text as a re-contextualization of its predecessor text, Deuteronomy 8.3.

In the predecessor text, Moses chastises the Israelites for complaining of hunger when they are receiving the Law. Moses explains that God sent manna in place of bread—an entirely new creation, a substitution they had never conceived before—in order to make them familiar with the tropes by which meaning emerges: "And he humbled thee, and suffered thee to hunger, and fed thee with manna, which thou knewest not, neither did thy fathers know; that he might make thee know that man doth not live by bread only, but by every word that proceedeth out of the mouth of the Lord doth man live." The literal manna, therefore, stands in for bread, but it also figures what it literally is not, the Word of God. Moses' text sets up a dominating referential principle—the Word of God—that governs the meaning of every thing in the world. Yet that principle appears in a figurative moment in the text. Thus, when Moses produces the commandments, the "Moral Law" that Albion holds so dear and Blake despises, he is binding language into its referential function by means of figuration.

Here we are faced with a complex intertextual relationship that speaks to the issue of authorizing interpretation by reference to a "stable" referential system or an intentional act. We can say that Albion, unlike Moses and Jesus, displaces the Word of God with his own intentionality, but that in order to achieve this position of centrality he must at the same time rely upon the primacy of those predecessor texts and their rhetorical strategies. I believe that Blake does not criticize Albion on the grounds of impiety but rather provides the reader with an opportunity to see that the illusion of referentiality is *created* rhetorically. Blake uses these allusions to criticize our reliance upon *any* determinate grounding for meaning, whether divine or natural, while demonstrating the function of context in the creation of meaning. For example, in his effort to make himself the origin of all texts, the guarantor of language, Albion must resort to the secondary nature of his self-naming—its figurative constitution—which always returns to haunt him as a "simulative phantom." In a precise contrary to Albion's gesture, the "naming" of the emanations of "All Human Forms" as Jerusalem is a kind of liberating *un-naming*, since it undermines the denotative function of proper names that isolate individuals.

In any event, the act of reading the text itself requires that we become authors who do not stand in an "originary" position vis-a-vis their own texts because the texts are always constructed out of the rupturing/suturing of other texts/contexts. Ricoeur comments that "by any supposition reading is a linking together of a new discourse to the discourse of the text" (p. 144), and my point is that, for Blake, the meaningfulness of this linking/writing does not emerge solely by recourse to the intention of the author nor to the "natural" sign but rather by the rhetorical construction of authority and the tropological play that shifts us from set to set of constricting categorical oppositions.

Blake struggles against our need for determinacy, but he does not deny the need. The figurative and the denotative are interdependent; where one creates a sense of giddiness at the infinite plenum of meaning available, the other halts the glissade into *meaninglessness* that lingers on the dark side of linguistic polyvalence. Yet Blake finally seems more concerned that our fears of indeterminacy will goad us to produce increasingly constricted visions of reality. In particular, he forces us to confront our tendency to mistake our time- and culture-bound interpretive groundings, the limits on language we impose by positing the equivalence of origin and aim, for eternal truth. The institutionalization of interpretation is a striking case among many to be found in our everyday perception of the world, of our willingness to sacrifice creativity and liberty for security, since any interpretation will only seem inevitable within a given context. Blake shows us that the tropological strategies of contextual displacement are necessary to undermine the tyranny of that seeming inexorability. In so doing, he displaces himself as the determinant of the text. Readers who follow his example will find in *Jerusalem* the tools for breaking their own "mind-forg'd manacles."

NOTES

[1]*The Complete Poetry and Prose of William Blake*, ed. David V. Erdman (Berkeley: Univ. of California Press, 1982), pp. 145-46. All subsequent Blake quotations are taken from this edition and will be cited in the standard way, by plate number and by page number preceded by the letter "E".

[2]A third possible "origin" emerges in the address, when Blake exhorts his reader to "[forgive] what you do not approve, & [love] me for this energetic exertion of my talent" (Plate 3, E145). Although the bracketed words are conjectural readings, they accord with a prior statement that the author hopes the "Reader will be with me, wholly One in Jesus our Lord, [whose] Spirit is . . . continual forgiveness of Sin." In identifying the reader with Jesus, the origin of the coherence of the poem may be found in the reader's unifying (because forgiving and loving) conception of the work. This possibility only strengthens the argument I make subsequently.

[3]Jacques Derrida, "Signature Event Context" in *Margins of Philosophy*, trans. Alan Bass (Chicago: Univ. of Chicago Press, 1982), p. 186.

[4]Jacques Derrida, *Of Grammatology*, trans. Gayatri Chakravorty Spivak (Baltimore: Johns Hopkins Univ. Press, 1974), p. 159.

[5]David M. Rasmussen, *Mythic-symbolic Language and Philosophical Anthropology, A Constructive Interpretation of the Thought of Paul Ricoeur* (The Hague: Martinus Nijhoff, 1971), pp. 148-49, "What is a Text?"

[6]Thomas Gray, "The Bard," in *The Complete English Poems of Thomas Gray,* ed. James Reeves (New York: Harper & Row, 1973), pp. 77-82, lines 23-28. All subsequent references to "The Bard" are from this edition.

[7]All biblical references are from the King James version. My readers no doubt see that the tracing of citations and allusions can have no end. All writing is already a "citation." At this juncture, I am concerned with the way in which the citation in the text functions as a sign of intertextuality, rather than simply meaning the content *(énoncé)* of the quotation itself. Antoine Compagnon, in *La seconde main ou le travail de la citation* (Paris: Editions du Seuil, 1979), has described the citation as "un operateur trivial d'intertextualité" (p. 44). We are not so much interested in the material contained in the citation, since "elle n'a pas de sens hors de la force qui l'agit, qui la saisit, l'exploite et l'incorpore" (p. 38). This force, seizure, incorporation are all part of the contextual rupturing/suturing that produces meaning. The citation, then, is the paradigmatic case—or the most trivial case, the most obvious case—of reading as contextual displacement. It is clear that in the act of citing, the subject of the enunciation becomes displaced, with the result that writing viewed as citational appears without recourse to one single, originating intention. Compagnon says "en un sens, il n'y a de sujet de la citation qu'en regime democratique de l'écriture" (p. 39). This democratizing effect accords well with the liberating aims of the Blakean text.

SEL 27 (1987)
ISSN 0039-3657

Recent Studies in the Restoration and Eighteenth Century

ROBERT FOLKENFLIK

First, the ground rules. I have not commented on books that are reprints of earlier productions. I also have little to say of anthologies, or of miscellaneous collections, as opposed to those with a unifying idea behind them. The treatment of books that devote only a chapter or two to our period is necessarily selective. Bowing to the canons of *SEL*, I have grudgingly left Austen, Blake, and some others to the Autumn issue reviewer.

In 1981 and 1982 Richard Schwartz and Maximillian Novak respectively found fifty books to review for *SEL*. In 1984 and 1985 Morris Brownell and Howard Weinbrot reviewed over eighty each. This year's list exceeds one hundred. It includes all books received by me with April 1987 or earlier publication dates and a handful of stragglers.

I will start with the novel and with feminist and gender studies, which usually pay central attention to the novel, because these seem to me of most interest this year as a group. Otherwise general books will normally be found in that section of the standard triad, Restoration, early, and late eighteenth century, in which their subjects are weighted most heavily.

Since 1957 Ian Watt's *The Rise of the Novel* has held the field as the single most important and influential interpretation of the early eighteenth-century novel. During that period numerous attempts have been made to modify or overturn the Watt paradigm, among

---

Robert Folkenflik, Professor of English at the University of California, Irvine, is the author of *Samuel Johnson, Biographer* and is currently working on The Artist as Hero, 1660-1820, for which he held a Guggenheim Fellowship. He is General Editor of Irvine Studies in the Humanities.

them G. A. Starr's and J. Paul Hunter's religious readings, John Richetti's emphasis on popular fiction, Wayne Booth's passing attack on the normative criterion of "realism," Robert Alter's countertradition of the self-conscious novel, Lennard Davis's positing the novel as part of a Foucauldian news/novel discourse, and the feminist insistence on the importance of women novelists (see below). Now Michael McKeon's ambitious and impressive *The Origins of the English Novel 1600-1740* bids to replace Watt as the farthest reaching synthesis and the most original account of a new understanding of the novel.

This book, like Watt's (whose title seems to allude to the rise of the middle class and Tawney's *Religion and the Rise of Capitalism* among other things) is based on social theory. It represents another stage of Marxist understanding which goes directly to Marx for the key notion of the "simple abstraction." In effect McKeon works out the prehistory of the novel—the *longue durée* from Greek and Roman narrative. He stresses the analogy between social instability and the instability of the novel as genre. The stabilization of the novel as concept in the middle of the eighteenth century provides the point of departure for his look backward at the "pregivenness" of the form. And he finds the key to reading the novel in the dialectics of genre, though one could come to this last convincing conclusion through a range of different theories. His account of the "dialectical constitution of the novel" finds room for Swift (the category of the novel was unstable enough that it may be included, despite the discontinuities of character) as well as Bunyan, along with the familiar trio of Watt's and most canons—Defoe, Richardson, and Fielding, but he deals with a vast range of other narratives ("saint's lives to spiritual biography," "picaresque to criminal biography," "Christian pilgrimage to scientific travel," and many romances). He pursues his inquiry through "questions of truth," which deal with problems set up by an "epistemological crisis," and "questions of virtue," which deal with the problems of "social and ethical crisis." He charts the dialectical movement of epistemological premises from "aristocratic idealism" to "naive empiricism" to "extreme skepticism," dependent on aristocratic, progressive, and conservative ideologies which produce as narrative equivalents romance, anti-romance, and "true history."

He does not place new passages at the center of his readings of the canonical novelists nor does he reinterpret the familiar ones so much as place the significance of novelistic discourse differently and suggest a different meaning for what we find. This book is most impressive not for its individual readings (a chapter on Defoe comes after three hundred pages, three-quarters of the way through the text), but for the intellectual and social context he has set up for his discussions of the English novelists he considers (many of the passages he finds in doing this are strikingly new), and his credentials as a student of the Restoration put him in an excellent position to understand the historical and literary situation in the period immediately before the tradition of the novel as we know it begins. Perhaps the best of his individual chapters on novelists (they are all of very high quality) is "The Institutionalization of Conflict (I): Richardson and the Domestication of Service" where the long view pays off in the delineation of the meaning of the shifting relations of master and servant.

When he finally finds generic stability around 1750 with the relations set up between the work of Fielding and Richardson (*Pamela, Shamela, Joseph Andrews*), his book comes to an end with the same figures whom Watt takes as his effective conclusion, though Watt comments on Sterne and Austen. I would say, however, that here the generic stability he finds does not correspond to the actual continuance of flux in title pages, prefaces, and critical remarks about novel and romance. And the historical instability he finds lasts a very long time, perhaps too neatly from feudalism to capitalism. But apart from these reservations and a minor quibble about his theoretical attempt to get Levi-Strauss and Northrop Frye into the same tent as "archetypalists," I find his synthesis a remarkable achievement.

One may miss Watt's urbanity and wit, but McKeon has his own distinctive lucidity and eloquence. The poise with which he writes may mask to some extent the enormous difficulty of the task he has set himself. The whole is remarkably assured, learned, and mature. Whether McKeon's "questions of truth" and "questions of virtue" will replace Watt's "realism of presentation" and "realism of assessment" remains to be seen, but I think it at the very least the book of the year.

Dale Spender's *Mothers of the Novel: 100 Good Women Writers Before Jane Austen* functions as the manifesto volume for the useful reprint series of that name. It is like reading a 350-page jacket blurb. The topic is valid and important, but Spender seems to have discovered the Restoration and eighteenth century the day before she started writing the book. Chatty and long-winded, it is easily the worst I have read this year. Spender's canon-making sounds like nothing so much as a late seventeenth-century collective biographer like William Winstanley, who is willing to say a good word about every poet in his book, however slight. Midway through the book she springs a list of 106 women novelists and their 568 novels. Her claim that there are fewer underrated male novelists than female is a useful shock tactic (and possibly defensible), but her list of the underrated males displays a woefully inadequate idea of what the canon she is attempting to displace consists. Ian Watt is the major villain because his authoritative account scants early women novelists. The status of some women novelists has been growing. Both Terry Castle and Gary Kelly have argued for the importance of Elizabeth Inchbald's *A Simple Story*.

The series itself can only be welcome, though with some caveats. The introductions tend to be very short (Sandra Shulman's to Charlotte Lennox's *The Female Quixote*—the only one to come my way this year—is also weak) and the newly edited texts have no indication of editor or copy-text. A few volumes in the Virago series have appeared this year. Sarah Scott's *Millenium Hall* is prefaced by Jane Spencer's even-handed short account. Aphra Behn's *Love Letters Between a Nobleman and his Sister* has a preface by Maureen Duffy, and Fanny Burney's *Cecilia*, by Judy Simons. The first two have texts such as those found in the Pandora series. The last simply reprints an unattractive 1904 edition. Where possible, World's Classics are preferable, for example, Edward and Lillian Bloom's *Camilla*. But a number of these books from the Oxford Novels series are out of print or prohibitive for classes.

Fortunately Jane Spencer's *The Rise of the Woman Novelist: From Aphra Behn to Jane Austen*, which covers much of the same territory as Spender, if not so broadly, is another thing altogether. Her title echoes Watt's and challenges his canon, but she conducts her neatly formulated inquiry with high competence. From the first chapter on "wit's mild empire," she is attuned to the ironies of her topic. One of her strongest points is that Richardson's seeming preeminence as a model for female novelists masks a tradition that goes back to women who wrote before him in the same vein. She also notices the paradox in the later eighteenth century that women novelists were creating public careers "by recommending a private, domestic life for their heroines." Her title can be paraphrased as the establishment of female literary authority.

In a chapter on three autobiographical novelists, she separates the often linked Aphra Behn and Delariviere Manley (who appears in the books I discuss with and without "Mary," with and without the accent) by claiming that "where Behn widened the woman writer's scope, Manley declared that love was the only subject for a woman." This is a move from "a declaration of independence" to "an attempt to found the woman writer's authority" on erotic femininity. Yet though Spencer tends to see Behn as *sui generis*, she and Manley do provide models of the erotic woman for later writers, as her third figure, the virginal Jane Barker, is in the chaste tradition that derives from Katherine Phillips. Spencer takes note frequently of the female models and mentors for the novelists she discusses. (Or, in the case of Behn, the conscious acceptance of male models.) She considers women's novels as leading to three sorts of heroines, seduced, reformed, and romance—which represent three relations to reality: protest, acceptance (which permits a role as teacher, the "didactic" tradition), and escape.

In this book Spencer focuses on two dozen novelists though others receive passing mention. Her distinction between the two models of female writers has been anticipated by Nancy Cotton, who identified them as the "Orinda" and "Astrea" modes, after Phillips and Behn. Although I believe there are difficulties (as well as gains) in emphasizing the "self-portrait" aspect of the early novels, not least with the problematic *Oroonoko*, she is successful in opening up lines of thought and dealing with feminine traditions in the novel. She opposes the notion that all women's writing has, however hidden, "a feminist meaning." Spencer argues that the woman writer was not "totally suppressed" by patriarchal society but was often encouraged, especially in directions that could be put to use as male ideology. (Nancy Armstrong's *Desire and Domestic Fiction*, which appeared too late for this review, speaks to such issues.) Feminist criticism can build from such a position.

Constance Clark's *Three Augustan Women Playwrights* should be a companion piece to Spencer's, but it is slighter in every way. This study of Catherine Trotter, Delariviere Manley, and Mary Griffith Pix reads like an unrevised dissertation, and not a good one at that. Authorities are dutifully quoted, short biographies deployed.

Ruth Perry's *The Celebrated Mary Astell: An Early English Feminist* is a biography of a woman who left relatively few traces besides her work. The title suggests the sort of measured judgment, though fully sympathetic, found in the text. The claim for her as "England's first feminist" comes in the chapter on *A Serious Proposal to the Ladies*. It is a position echoed in the title of Bridget Hill's useful anthology of Astell's writings, which forms the necessary complement to this one: *The First English Feminist*. As Perry recognizes, the Tory and conservative Astell is not an ideal feminist heroine, but she deserves this substantial account. The tone is successful, and the narrative convinces, as in the excruciating description of the mastectomy which Astell underwent, in which Perry makes a knowledge of early eighteenth-century medicine fill in the details of an account based on George Ballard's slight biography. (Though how she can dismiss out of hand Ballard's claim that Astell's feminism came from an unhappy love affair is not clear. It does sound suspicious, but he had her friend Elizabeth Elstob as a possible source.) Happily, Perry has found forty unknown letters by Astell, which appear in an appendix. Poems from the Rawlinson manuscript appear in another. This recovery is one of the fruits of the new feminist scholarship.

Fetter'd or Free? British Women Novelists, 1670-1815, edited by Mary Anne Schofield and Cecilia Macheski, brings together nearly two dozen essays on such writers as Austen, Burney, Behn, Mary Brunton, Edgeworth, Ann Masterman, Heywood, More, Radcliffe, Frances Sheridan, and Charlotte Smith, all of whom receive separate treatment, and a range of feminist topics. Patricia Meyer Spacks compares Austen with Charlotte Lennox and Jane West on the use of sisters in fiction. Susan Staves continues her work on law and fiction, and Mitzi Myers hers on "female ideology." Landscape receives attention in the work of Manley, Haywood, Aubin (April London), and Radcliffe (Rhoda L. Flaxman). Cecilia Macheski writes a resourceful account of "images of needlework in eighteenth-century literature." Her "Penelope's Daughters" takes as its point of departure Richardson's comment that "the pen is almost as pretty an implement in a woman's fingers as a needle." Gary Kelly summarizes the relation of Jane Austen to Jacobin and anti-Jacobin novels. The collection, which also includes essays by Margaret Anne Doody, Paula R. Backscheider, Jerry C. Beasley, and Robert A. Day, is intelligently conceived and useful. It concludes with Roger Lund's bibliographical essay.

A few books attempt to bridge the gender gap in their different ways. Roy Roussel's *The Conversation of the Sexes: Seduction and Equality in Selected Seventeenth- and Eighteenth-Century Texts* is an attempt to read androgynously, most explicitly so in the case of *Fanny Hill,* where the appeal would seem to be very strongly to the male reader. After an initial chapter on Donne's "The Flea" he also discusses *Pamela, Les Liaisons Dangereuses,* and Congreve's comedies (in that order). These are feminocentric works by male authors. He finds that such literature puts in question traditional notions of male and female experience. Drawing on feminist criticism, he focuses on the responses to desire in characters and readers. He recognizes that what he is talking about is "men's imagination of women's experience."

While I do not think his account of *Fanny Hill* will win over many feminists, it is the most searching and serious account of that fiction.

The problem is in part that the intelligence of the close reading leads to the position that "Fanny Hill . . . establishes an ambivalence within its readers by encouraging their masculine selves to confront their feminine selves," a formula which seems highly dubious.

The essay on *Pamela* emphasizes the feminization of Mr. B as a result of reading Pamela's letters (therefore a model for the reader). Throughout the book Roussel links reader and observer (analogous to the voyeurs within several of the novels). In his discussion of the importance of distance in *Pamela,* he seems unaware of significant work, which leads him at times to repeat unknowingly what others have already said.

This book is a sophisticated treatment of the topic, yet I wonder if the implications of the central ambiguity of the title (which operates for us as a pun) will be much admired by feminists. Can a conversation take place only through sexual means? And are the male authors and readers in this book in the end only talking to themselves? That Roussel is aware of these dangers is one indication of the value of his seductive enterprise.

Although not the sort of book I have in mind, perhaps here is the most appropriate place to mention that Peter Wagner has a short chapter on England in his bilingual *Lust and Love in the Rococo Period* which deals with erotic book illustrations and engravings. This volume seems to exist for the copious illustrations. England makes, not surprisingly, a less salacious showing than France. Perhaps his book in progress will treat the subject more successfully. It will be easy to treat it in more depth.

Ann Messenger's *His and Hers* attempts to canonize a range of women writers through a series of chapters which generally pair a canonical male with a marginal female (she sometimes refers to them as "brother" writers, which with its suggestions of equality is a nice touch). Her intention is also to discover the specifically feminine nature of women's writing, if possible, and she knows the implications of her method in the context of women's studies. The number of novels considered is surprisingly small (just Behn's *Oroonoko* and Frances Brooke's *The History of Emily Montague* receive central attention). Given her interest in "brother writers," she might have tried Sarah and Henry Fielding. The links are different in the various cases: Dryden praises Killigrew, Southerne adapts Behn, Knight writes a sequel to Johnson's *Rasselas,* Brooke has a character named Arabella Fermor after the original of Pope's Belinda, Lady Mary claims a poem often attributed to John Gay. What we have then is writers compared who work in the same genre or in some cases rework the same material. And though the women usually derive from the men in some way (the last chapter asks "Women's Writing: Derivative or Mainstream?"—a question easily recognized as a false dichotomy), Behn, who may certainly be thought more important than Southerne, is the source of his play. Killigrew is usually mentioned in the classroom only as a textbook example that panegyrics are not to be taken as literal praise. This point should be made less smugly, and Messenger would attempt to rouse a cheer or two for her work. She recognizes that Lady Mary is "best known" for her letters, but does not bother to valorize the genre nor to place her in relationship to a male letter writer as Bruce Redford, who chooses Cowper, does in *The Converse of the Pen*. Pope would have made a fine contrast. The genres are varied. Her longest chapter discusses Addison, Steele, and Eliza Haywood as essayists. (Simon Varey has edited *Bath Intrigues* for the Augustan Reprint series this year; and Kathryn Shevelow considers *The Tatler* from the perspective of women readers in *Gender and Reading*.) I would like Messenger's book better if she were a better critic. She identifies her own stance as "new critical," which it is not. She has in mind close reading or direct inspection, though she confesses that "perhaps what I do can best be described as 'appreciation.' " Her designation of a work as "a good read" (Behn's *The Lucky Mistake*) or "a jolly good read" (Knight's *Dinarbus*) points to the distinct limits of her method. Rose Zimbardo's incisive comparison of Behn and Southerne makes more of the necessary critical and feminist distinctions in a few pages than Messenger does in her chapter on the pair.

Robert Erickson's *Mother Midnight* is a provocative account of fate and the Fates in four major eighteenth-century novels from the perspective of what I would call ambiguous femininity. It focuses on the role of the midwife and her relation to the whore and the witch (both good and evil). By relating this central figure to the fates, it deals with the mythic as well as the historical. Erickson combines a well-grounded historical knowledge of the literature concerning these figures with the ability to read the novels closely and intelligently in terms of what he finds.

In all of his chapters he takes as his point of departure the intricacies of character relationships: Moll and her "governess"; Pamela and Mrs. Jewkes; Clarissa, Lovelace, and Mrs. Sinclair; Tristam and the male and female midwives. Yet the work as a whole is hardly a character study, but rather full readings of the novels in terms of their implications. If the women are associated with the Fates, he is highly concerned with the fate of the novel. And he is also strongly aware of the importance of genre. He initially owes this orientation to Northrop Frye, but he has developed it to good effect on his own, and one can best see it in operation in the chapter on *Tristram Shandy.*

He has a very good eye for detail and motifs. For example, he notices the importance of the references to Mrs. Jewkes's hand in *Pamela,* and the emphasis is significant whether we wish to consider its source as the emphasis on what Pope would call the "obstetric hand" of the midwife or not. He is also full of fresh observations, such as his awareness that B's "petticoat ruse" is in some ways a parallel to Pamela's when she fakes suicide. To put this another way, though I expect everyone to learn a good deal from this book, even those who are resistant to the thesis and find the midwife and related lore not central to their understanding of the novels will still profit from the attentiveness of his readings, his frequent insights, and his apt formulations. I do not expect any reader to be nodding his head in agreement at every point, but this is because Erickson willingly takes risks that a safer, duller writer would not take. At times I do not agree that the relation to the text of midwife or witch is significant, and I find his historical labors more convincing than his myth criticism, but for the most part he has brought such figures suggestively to bear upon the texts.

The writing is consistently brisk and lively, often witty or elegant. His insights are frequently conveyed in formulations that convince. Clarissa, he says is "more in love with the symbolic than the actual." One can also see his expansiveness, his urge to convey those things he knows that he wants to share with us, from the first page, with its dozen epigraphs. The rich and full footnotes are themselves highly valuable. In all this is a vital book, a welcome study of sexuality from an unexpected angle.

The most interesting of the books that discuss gender this year is Terry Castle's *Masquerade and Civilization: The Carnivalesque in Eighteenth-Century English Culture and Fiction,* a highly original Bakhtinian account of the masquerade and its function in a series of novels at the margins of the canon (*Pamela,* part 2, *Amelia, Cecilia* and *A Simple Story*). Following a brief history and phenomenology of the masquerade in England, Castle gives readings of the novels centered on the masquerade episodes (which she takes as synecdoches of the novel itself). She wishes to account for the bad press of the masquerade from the eighteenth century to ours and claims that the attacks of Addison, Pope, Hogarth, Johnson, Fielding, Richardson, and Burney "all paradoxically deny intellectual significance to the masquerade at the same time that they commemorate its excesses and suffuse its representation with an aura of excitement and moral danger."

Basically, she sees the maquerade in the novels she selects as "plot-engendering" and causally related to the happy events that occur. In some ways this is the *felix culpa* theory of evil. All things happen for the best (especially, I would add, in comic novels). Sir Hargrave Pollexfen attempts to rape Harriet Byron after abducting her from a masquerade, but she is saved by Sir Charles Grandison, and this "happy accidental meeting" on which the plot depends leads to her eventual marriage to Sir Charles. Later Castle finds in *Amelia* that the masquerade "cannot be glossed merely as the quintessential scene of vice, for though it has led Mrs. Bennet into an involuntary union with vice in the person of the Noble Peer, it has also led her into a union with virtue, in the person of Sergeant Atkinson." This sort of equivalence is very misleading. The novel's emphasis on experience includes the necessity of evil experience, but the happy ending here glosses over the way that her rape following the masquerade is a direct outcome of it and leads to venereal disease and her first husband's death. This cannot be equated with her happy second marriage. Do we think of Job's happy end as a divine comedy? A slippery notion of causality is also at work. While the repulsion/attraction of evil is certainly part of the effect (and one long-standing criticism of Richardson's fiction is based on his having things both ways), I'll accept Castle's argument fully when it is made convincingly for the role of Vanity Fair in *Pilgrim's Progress.*

She is alert and has frequent memorable formulations, but they are not always exactly applied. For example, she notices that if "the possibility of attending a masquerade is raised in an eighteenth-century novel, someone—and usually the heroine—will go." She observes that this runs against the grain of "didactic economy," for the dangers of the masquerade are usually inculcated. But the novel can be taken as precisely the genre that runs counter to didactic economy: the hero or heroine's reality is experiential.

Although Castle recognizes that the middle-class moralists indicted (perhaps literally in Fielding's case) the masquerade as "a foolish, irrational, and corrupt activity perpetrated by irresponsible people of fashion," she rarely considers its financial basis. She has very little on the cost of masquerades (five shillings seems to be the price of some tickets), and nothing at all to say about her illustration of a masquerade ticket of 1770 which "admits one Gentleman or two Ladies." Unaccompanied ladies might hesitate to come, but the sexual economy set up here should not be ignored. Nor does she comment on the fact that subscription tickets require the name of the person to whom the ticket is transferred. This suggests that the masquerade provided anonymity for some, though the novels would add that potential victims of seduction were generally known to their predators. (The sources of the very interesting illustrations spread throughout the book are given, but there is no table of them.)

The book explores the masquerade as the field of release from social inhibitions, a deinstitutionalizing institution devoted to gender-bending, freedom, democracy. Yet the examples she gives of "collective outbursts of popular insurgency" developing from "festive license" seem to have little in common with the masquerade. To my mind, *Humphry Clinker* is a better example of the carnivalesque—its very epigraph comes from a Horatian satire in which the servant cheeks his master during Saturnalia—than these novels. Castle's celebration of masquerade seems finally her own version of pastoral: "Its promiscuity was at heart joyful rather than degrading; its sensual delights revelatory and life-enhancing rather than cynical or satiating." Perhaps so; but I do not find any proof for this position in the phenomenological history that proceeds it.

Ultimately, the masquerade in this reading means most for women since it functions as a challenge to "patriarchal society." But it seems to me that the masquerade may only be patriarchal society with its mask on. For all Castle's awareness of the problematics, the book functions as ideology and fails to see the implications of the institution's economic basis and the upper-class control exerted in the novels, and possibly in the historical setting as well. It is as though someone today were to swallow the Playboy Philosophy whole as a means of liberation. Another way of putting this is that she simply takes Bakhtinian carnivalesque straight, and only asks in passing if carnival itself may have functioned as a mode of social control, nor does she mention that in its heyday carnival was usually against marginal figures—women, foreigners, Jews, etc.

But this is not where I want to conclude. Reading *Masquerade and Civilization* is a stimulating experience. The awareness Terry Castle brings to both the institution of the masquerade and the appearance of the masquerade in the novel is a challenge to conventional notions at a very high level. This is one of those rare books that forces the reader to rethink most of the assumptions on which he or she proceeds. Castle's inquiry is carried out with great deftness and a fittingly carnivalesque openness to variety, and the book can be enjoyed for its verve as well as its range. The topic brings her own dazzling kaleidoscope of insights into play. Is the novel a vehicle of social control or social subversion? Both, I would say, but Castle, for all her awareness of ambiguity, rejects the "safety valve" theory of "symbolic rituals of disorder."

It is worth noting in connection with Castle's book that Peter Stallybrass and Allon White have written a wide-ranging and engaging Bakhtinian series of essays in *The Politics and Poetics of Transgression*. Of primary interest is the chapter "Authorship in the Eighteenth Century," though the prior one, provocatively titled "The Fair, the Pig, Authorship," races through some eighteenth-century instances as well. An introductory chapter is a kind of advanced introduction to Bakhtinian ideas in the context of anthropology (Mary Douglas, Norbert Elias, and Victor Turner also figure in here). They are happily aware that the "uncritical populism" of carnival was frequently turned against minorities.

David Marshall's *The Figure of Theater* might not get the audience it deserves because its two philosophers and two novelists seem so disparate: Shaftesbury, Defoe, Adam Smith, and George Eliot. I consider it here because Marshall wants to treat all of his texts as "philosophical novels" and devotes the longest section to the novels of Defoe. This book, which derives, though hardly in an exclusive way, from Michael Fried's work on theatricality, investigates the way the self exists for an other and the possibilities of interiority. After a glance at the implications of Addison's Spectator, he looks closely at Shaftesbury's need for and fear of a public audience. The chapters on Shaftesbury lead him to a discussion of similar issues (despite the strong class differences) in Defoe. One might think first of Richardson or Fielding in discussing the relationship of eighteenth-century novelists to the theatrical, but Marshall develops the ambiguities of Defoe's position on theater, which parallel his position on fiction. The central insight here is that "the impersonations and fictions [used by Defoe's characters] are specifically theatrical in character; and implicit in this assertion (and my readings) is the assumption that as these characters metamorphose themselves into different parts and persons and stage realistic illusions that are taken for reality, they can be seen as figures for Daniel Defoe." His method is close reading, which takes the model but not the doctrine of psychoanalysis. He is also aware of a range of contemporary theoretical positions, some of which he assimilates.

For the rest, Smith's theory of sympathy leads to the theatricalization of society, as we all attempt to see our actions as they will be seen by others and as the "impartial spectator" views the theater of our actions. But most important here is the split of the self into actor and spectator at once, a *dédoublement* that runs all through Marshall's inquiry. George Eliot is seen as developing the eighteenth-century investigations of the theatrical in *Daniel Deronda*. Those skipping the George Eliot chapter will miss Marshall's thumbnail account of the eighteenth-century novel through the lining up of Defoe, Richardson, Fielding, and Sterne on the desirability of privileged views of the other. Marshall would by implication make larger claims for the figure of theater in eighteenth-century culture. The readings of his major writers are stimulating, fresh, and well-written.

This brings me to studies of specific novelists. Paula R. Backscheider's *Daniel Defoe: Ambition and Innovation*, like James Sutherland's shorter study, attempts to give a sense of the total career, a daunting prospect when one simply considers the known canon. She is at her best on historical ground. Her intention is to "trace Defoe's development as a teller of tales, argue the intensity and integrity of his artistic ambitions, and demonstrate that everything that Defoe wrote rests solidly upon his extensive reading of books published in England." She buries Defoe's claim, which supports her emphasis, that "good literature 'has always been my ambition and delight' " in the chapter on poetry.

Her account of the poetry combines a checklist of forms with some unsubstantiated comments on the value of the poetry: "Most of the longer lines of his odes are composed of heroic couplets with iambic hexameter indented lines, but he uses Alexandrines, dactylic feet, and alliteration to emphasize meter often enough to give the odes force and unusual beauty." Speaking of Defoe's "Pindaric odes," she does not notice that the poem which she rightly praises, beginning "Happy the Man, and happy he alone," is a translation of Horace's second epode, nor that Cowley, whom she had just been discussing, also translated it. On the other hand, she does not overvalue the poetry generally, and her introduction usefully reminds us that "although no one today thinks of Defoe as a poet, he wrote more verse than Milton or Dryden, and the signature he used most frequently on his published works identified him as the author of a poem."

The chapter on *Robinson Crusoe* is placed last, undoubtedly because she thinks it, as I do, the best of Defoe's fictions, but the reading lacks a center. Beginning with "our" fantasies of being on a desert island, it is almost all prolegomenon and influence. Perhaps despite its climactic position this is not the best place to see what she has to say of Defoe's fictions, for she has published several essays on *Crusoe* already. She might have pursued the suggestive comparison of Eliza Haywood's *Love in Excess*, also of 1719, which has more in common with *Crusoe* than one might think, and leads to *Moll*. This is the kind of observation that helps to show that the rise of the woman novelist should not be hermetically sealed but finds its full meaning in the context of male practice as well.

The idea of looking at Defoe in the "context of English literary history" is good, but she might say more about how it connects to the underrating of Defoe, despite his learning, because of his unwillingness to let "classicism dominate his conception of literature," another of her themes. Her account of him as "the indisputable father of the English novel" ("disputable" might be more accurate) points to his acquaintance with genres and his sense of himself as working in literary traditions.

With her frequent lists (of verse forms, authors alluded to in a single essay, pre-Crusoe fictions) and her penchant for honorifics, it sometimes seems that she is writing the epic of Daniel Defoe. Too often she will quote testimonials from later novelists or attempt to aggrandize Defoe's achievement by a sweeping comparison. Defoe's Cavalier is brought to the state "of the powerless, frustrated soldiers of books like *A Farewell to Arms, Catch 22,* and *If I Die in the Combat Zone.*" She also considers him "the dramatization of the powerful anti-war sentiment that would . . . find expression in the works of the greatest thinkers of the age: Hume, Gibbon, Adam Smith, Voltaire, and Rousseau." (For that matter, why not More, Erasmus, Colet, Milton?) I do not mean this characterization in a merely negative way, however: her strength lies in the hard labor of ferreting out all the facts she provides, and we may expect to see this ability put to good use in the biography of Defoe on which she is now at work.

Daniel Defoe and Diplomacy is appropriately the subject of a diplomatic historian, William Roosen, and he has an interesting case to make. Although there is no hint in the preface and the opening chapters suggest only that this brief book will acquaint us with Defoe's thoughts on foreign affairs, Roosen's real subject is that Defoe, rather than being simply a political propagandist, even in the Harley years, had a fairly consistent position, one identifiable in political terms as "realist," a set of ideas ultimately deriving from Machiavelli (though Defoe's ideas are not traced back to his sources) and obtaining strong support today.

The realist is concerned with effectiveness rather than morality. In canvassing Defoe's ideas, Roosen is aware of his nationalism as a limit to his realism, but he also quotes some clear-eyed passages by Defoe on the way in which such parochialism blinkers believers. Roosen's Defoe, whose province despite his interest in exotic places and the world at large is western Europe, eclectically supports such familiar ideas as the balance of power, which implies the necessity of some wars and a distrust of "exorbitant power." Nevertheless, Defoe's commitment to trade leads him to insist on the importance of peace. The balance of power suggests that allies may become enemies and vice versa. Roosen sometimes squares Defoe's public ideas with private by way of a letter to Harley, but how accurate such documents are as indices of Defoe's mind is open to question. The War of the Spanish Succession is given close attention as a test case.

This is a modest book, but its challenge to the dominant treatment of Defoe's politics, with its frequent implication that Defoe was a liar, is refreshing. Backscheider emphasizes Defoe's attributes as propagandist in her chapter on "Politics and Pamphlets" and attends to Defoe's rhetoric, so it forms a useful complement to Roosen, who prefers the term "publicist." Michael Seidel has a good chapter on *Robinson Crusoe* (along with another good one on *A Sentimental Journey*) in *Exile and the Narrative Imagination.*

Sylvia Kasey Marks is not aware of the improved standing of her subject in *Sir Charles Grandison: The Compleat Conduct Book.* She seems to think that only Margaret Doody has a good word for Richardson's last novel. She recognizes that others have worked on the relationship between Richardson and conduct literature, but her distinction in this short book is to treat Richardson's novel as conduct book rather than as drawing on conduct books. Hence, Richardson enlarges the conduct book, going beyond it by extensive dramatization of issues, and so forth. Although she considers the parallels between Richardson's own correspondence and his practice in the novel (recommendation of discretion, drawing up of balance sheets), for the most part she details a series of conduct topoi and shows how Richardson applies them (qualities of a true gentleman and lady, the professions, proper behavior of spouses). In speaking of "relative duties," she does not notice, though she has a number of things to say about the earlier novels, that both *Pamela* and *Clarissa* can be said to originate in the breakdown of relationships that would come under the rubric of relative duties (master-servant, parent-child). Despite her use of extensive manuscript sources, this is a slight, dutiful performance. Some of her findings will be useful, but none is surprising. Conduct books are being put to more sophisticated use recently, but she does not cite or employ such work.

Valerie Grosvenor Myer's collection, *Samuel Richardson: Passion and Prudence,* contains one essay on *Pamela* by J. W. Fisher (on "closet work"—it has already been done), six on *Clarissa,* one on *Grandison* and two essays on special topics—Pat Rogers's informative account of the bluestockings and Park Honan on the influence on Jane Austen. In the best of the rest Margaret Anne Doody intelligently considers the man-made world (with its attendant ironies) and Clarissa's work. The Angus Wilson piece is reprinted.

The editor tackles the relationship to Shakespeare. The collection as a whole is very uneven in quality. Richardson has also become a favorite for an eighteenth-century chapter in general books on the novel, as in those by Cohan, Kauffman, and Leites this year.

James J. Lynch's slim book, *Henry Fielding and the Heliodoran Novel: Romance, Epic, and Fielding's New Province of Writing*, is in the Baker-Miller-Goldberg line of comic romance. The Lynch variation allows for the epic (transformed into history) as well as romance, an improvement in dealing with so inclusive a writer as Fielding. The method consists largely of a phase by phase comparison of each Fielding novel with the "Heliodoran stucture." He considers the *Aetheopica*, Cervantes's *Persilles*, Scarron's *Roman Comique*, and Fielding's three novels. He sees Fielding's novels as a combination of romance conventions and the conventions of formal realism (his concession to Watt). He would not claim the direct influence of Heliodorus, and finds the burlesque version of Scarron the nearest progenitor. An early chapter considers critical response to Heliodorus by Amyot, Huet, and Scudery. For some notion of what can be done with the same sort of material, Michael McKeon's book on the novel, discussed above, should be consulted.

Simon Varey's *Henry Fielding* is frankly intended as a short introduction. The voice we hear is that of a knowledgeable and no-nonsense teacher ("for Fielding 'epic' would mean little more than 'long narrative' "—a point with which I would strongly disagree) who is suspicious of modern theory. While he claims that he is "not a synthesizer of modern scholarship," it would not be hard to pick up the main lines from his book. Battestin is the major influence. Sometimes the chore of engaging the sympathies of the young seems to take over from other priorities. In speaking of *The Tragedy of Tragedies,* he quotes some funny bits but has nothing to say of the satire on meaningless drama and criticism nor its connection to the Pope of *Peri Bathous* and *The Dunciad.* He does better in this respect with *Shamela.* The account of *Joseph Andrews* suggests that Varey knows many of the things that "epic" means to Fielding, yet both here and in the chapter on *Tom Jones* he stresses the romance elements. This is an informative book which raises a number of points that students need to know. He concludes with a judicious bibliography.

K. G. Simpson's collection *Henry Fielding: Justice Observed* centers, though not exclusively, on Fielding as magistrate. It includes Lance St. John Butler's cogent claim that the relationship of Fielding and Shaftesbury needs reexamination, Mark Kinkead-Weekes's lively argument for the role of love in *Tom Jones*, and a slight introduction and essay on "Technique as Judgement in *Tom Jones*" by the editor.

There are several Fielding editions this year. Hugh Amory has edited a diplomatic transcript of fragments of a Fielding legal manuscript, *An Institute of the Pleas of the Crown*. He has also edited *New Books by Fielding*, which in addition to being a catalogue of an exhibition drawn from the Hyde collection is worth reading for Amory's tidbits about the history of the book. Thomas Lockwood's facsimile of *The History of Our Own Times* contains his introduction and notes.

Arthur H. Cash's *Laurence Sterne: The Later Years* is the second and concluding volume in what now is the standard biography of Sterne. He claims that his narrative may be like those of Fitzgerald and Cross in outline, but "it differs in almost every detail." Nine chapters cover only eight years of Sterne's life, but they are the years of celebrity. Cash's focus is on the life, not the fiction, though he does make a number of necessary connections between the two. Cash gives us a far richer account of Sterne the churchman and believing Christian, and he writes a very urbane version of standard-life prose. His *Sterne* is an informed, lucid account and a solid achievement. The book has its limits, however. It may be a delight to find that Sterne was commissary of the Peculiar Court of Pickering and Pocklington, but there are times when a more enlightening set of relations between Sterne's life and art would be welcome. Nevertheless, biographies as good as this one do not come along every year.

Few bibliographies came my way this year. The familiar, indispensible, and tardy *ECCB*, edited by Jim Springer Borck, remains four years behind its imprint. George Wasserman's odd coupling *Samuel Butler and the Earl of Rochester: A Reference Guide* appears accurate and useful. He manages to catch some of the unobvious scholarship, such as Ronald Paulson's accounts of Hogarth's *Hudibras* engravings in several of his books. I discuss a bibliography of Junius with late eighteenth-century work.

Dustin Griffin displays a defensive traditionalism in the most ambitious book on poetry this year, *Regaining Paradise: Milton and the Eighteenth Century*. Basically, he wants to counter the ideas of Harold Bloom and W. J. Bate that Milton's greatness caused a widespread poetic anxiety and a more general notion that Milton's influence was "bad." Griffin suggests that the modern theoretically-oriented critics are of the devil's party. He faults older criticism for its "naive empiricism," a fair enough indictment of Good, Havens, and some others.

His argument in part is that the recent revaluation of eighteenth-century poetry helps us to see the real contribution of Milton, and he believes that Milton "set the agenda for the century." (It should be noted that Bloom has usually been unwilling to consider the relationships of Dryden and Pope to Milton because they do not make his canon of great poets, though his Chelsea series may change that.) Griffin ignores the brilliant article by Christopher Ricks "Allusion: The Poet as Heir," in *Studies in the Eighteenth Century III,* which considers the relationships of Dryden and Pope to their predecessors through close attention to their imagery. On the whole, Griffin's book provides a careful and conscientious examination of the topic with individual chapters devoted to Dryden, Pope, Thomson, Johnson, and Cowper. Given recent claims, however, there is surprisingly little attention to Collins.

Griffin traces a double tradition of John Milton, the influence of the man, and of his work (centering in the image of Satan), though I think he misses the pre-Blakean identification of the two. The chapter on Johnson does find "anxiety," but in Johnson's response to Milton's life, "his self-discipline, devotion and religious conviction"—a position which strikes me as quite wrong. In trying to make his point, he even cites as an example of Johnson's "respect for a man of opposing principles" (as opposed to his treatment of Milton), the "Life of Cheynel," the most vitriolic biography Johnson ever wrote. I find Lawrence Lipking, among others, more convincing on the relationship of Johnson and Milton.

Griffin's chapter on Pope appropriately devotes the most space to *An Essay on Man* and *The Dunciad.* Taking issue with Maynard Mack on the former, he finds that Pope uses Miltonic allusions "to advertise the differences" between the two poets and that Pope's departure from Milton is more "radical" than Mack allows. Griffin claims rightly that "whereas Milton's poem is obtrusively Christian, Pope's is only implicitly so," but I would add that Pope's specifically Christian resonance comes mainly from the allusions to Milton and the Bible. Griffin's pinpointing of Pope's differences from Milton (with the help of Barbara Lewalski and Douglas Canfield) is useful and lucidly presented. He accomplishes a good deal in brief compass. In considering *The Dunciad,* he takes Aubrey Williams's darkly religious view, still dominant, as the target and stresses instead the comedy. He finds the allusions to Milton are used to "belittle the dunces" and emphasize "the differences between Cibber and Satan, dunces and devils." Here I find him less successful than in dealing with doctrines. Although he is aware of the ambiguities of mock-epic (at least as a critical notion) he insists on the attempts of Pope (and eighteenth-century poets generally) to control the context, and he wishes to stress the comic (his own partial control), though he declares himself aware of the seriousness of the topic. Like Irvin Ehrenpreis, he wants to rein in the implications of allusiveness. This reading is intended as a "corrective," a point that could be made about the book as a whole.

While I find myself in frequent disagreement, his readings are succinct and often forceful. He has mastered a substantial body of material to present this overview, and he solidly canvasses a number of necessary issues, including "new" and traditional Miltonic genres, adaptations of Milton, the prevalence of Miltonic tags, and the status of Milton during the period. In connection with his topic, it is worth noting that Max Schulz's *Paradise Preserved: Recreations of Eden in Eighteenth- and Nineteenth-Century England* contains a preliminary chapter on the eighteenth century and another on Blake.

David Hopkins does well in his introductory *John Dryden* to overcome the annoying opening gambit of stringing together a paragraph of quoted praise from Johnson, Coleridge, Tennyson, G. M. Hopkins, and others. This is a balanced account that attempts to set Dryden within the context of a historiography out from under the whig interpretation. He intends the book for the novice, one who needs to be shown how to read a couplet. He wants the student to hear the music of Dryden's verse. In the portrait of Charles-David at the beginning of *Absalom and Achitophel* he sorts out the various meanings of the lines in order to suggest that the "wit . . . holds them in superfine equipoise" and that such meanings are "teasing hints" rather than "bald propositions." The treatment of Dryden's criticism lacks substance. It consists of a quick listing of themes, though he does effectively contrast Johnson's reasoned defense of tragicomedy with Dryden's account of tacking two plots together in *The Spanish Fryar*. He follows Robert Hume on Dryden's dramatic career, but he seems to take L. C. Knights's high moral line on the plays themselves: it would be hard to tell from his complaints about the triviality of the treatment of the themes that *Marriage à la Mode* is comic.

Instead of worrying whether Wordsworth really liked Dryden's poetry or not, he might have shown that it existed as a viable tradition in the work of Byron, who had Pope and Churchill before him. He uses the conclusion of his inadequate bibliography (nothing is suggested on the plays or criticism; apart from praise of Johnson—whom he often quotes to good effect—and Scott, he devotes his space to the premodern critical reception) to puff the work of a few friends when he might instead suggest a few stimulating articles, such as those of Brower and Ricks. Nevertheless, his writing is fresh, and the students for whom it is intended will find it readable and responsive to many of their needs.

Robert W. McHenry, Jr.'s volume in the Archon Contexts series, *Absalom and Achitophel*, reprints materials concerning the Popish Plot and the exclusion crisis, such as selections from Titus Oates's *True Narrative*, Andrew Marvell's *Growth of Popery, A True and Perfect Narrative of the . . . Murther of Sir Edmundberry Godfrey*, Burnet's *History of My Own Time*, and other sources as well as literary antecedents, and a few characters (Buckingham, Monmouth, York, and Bethel). McHenry contributes a short introduction, headnotes and footnotes. The texts, reproduced from originals, are sometimes difficult to read, and there's no reason for reproducing Burnet's *History* from a nineteenth-century version. Even a reduced reproduction of the first edition of 1734 would be better. On the whole, though, this is a useful collection.

In *The Restoration Newspaper and its Development* James Sutherland focuses on the brief span 1679-82 when the proroguing of parliament led to the lapse of the Licensing Act and a short respite from Stuart suppression of all but the official *London Gazette*. Successive chapters deal with London, country, and foreign news, followed by a chapter on politics and one on newspaper men and women, a chapter that would surely have been called "newspapermen" some years ago. There is also a proleptic look at the eighteenth-century newspaper. Much of the book is anecdotal. The account is enlivened by Sutherland's characteristic wit; it is good to see him still publishing at 86.

Graham Midgley's well-edited volume in *The Miscellaneous Works of John Bunyan* includes *The Barren Fig-Tree, The Strait Gate, and The Heavenly Foot-Man*. The solid introduction attempts to establish Bunyan's sermon methods and show their relationship to his published works. The annotations are informative, and the establishment of copy-texts is thoughtful.

In *Restoration Comedy in Performance* J. L. Styan has written a book on the elements of Restoration comedy. It might well have been titled, as he suggests, *A Celebration of Restoration Comedy*. His account of playhouse, actors and actresses, and the nature of performance is largely familiar (most topics, like the proviso scene, are given brief, pertinent consideration), but it provides a brisk refresher, and should be very useful for beginning students. His frequent reference to the early twentieth-century revival of Restoration comedy seems to be intended to show how reviewers frequently let their moral presuppositions mislead them, and how some modern actors and especially actresses played the roles effectively. He might, however, have discussed more recent productions that he had seen. The emphasis on performance, while hardly unprecedented—he is aware of the work of Holland, Oxenford, Powell, Milhous, Hume, and others, whom he draws upon sparingly—is welcome. The book is illustrated with a large number of photographs of modern productions and a few drawings of the early stage.

Harold Weber's *The Restoration Rake-Hero: Transformations in Sexual Understanding in Seventeenth-Century England* looks, as one might guess, primarily at comedy from 1660-1700. He does well to ground his themes on Jacobean and other pre-Restoration drama to show the changes that come about. He does not show the shift away from the rake in the eighteenth century; that theme was taken up early in this century by Krutch. By quoting Chesterfield's distinction in a letter to his son between a "rake" and a "man of pleasure," he shows the shifting conception of the term (which he here takes to be aimed at the Hobbesian libertine, while the man of pleasure has something in common with the philosophical libertine). He might also have quoted that sharper attack at mid-century by Samuel Johnson, who defines a "rake" as "a loose, disorderly, vicious, wild, gay, thoughtless fellow; a man addicted to pleasure"—such moral disapprobation extends to the OED definition. While he takes the rake's sexuality fairly enough as his defining feature, he does not examine any use of the term in the Restoration, an investigation that would have turned up a range of very different characteristics from the ones he notices (especially under "rakehell"). Using demonic notions of sexuality as a backdrop, he devotes successive chapters to the Hobbesian Libertine-Rake, the Philosophical Libertine, and the Female Libertine. The argument here is that the Restoration rake gives us a secularized version of sexuality for the earlier religious discourse. The last chapter carries the theme into the eighteenth-century novel as well, though I think that the libertine is more persistent than Weber suggests both in life and art.

A more widely-ranging book employing the notion of transformations prominently is Rose Zimbardo's *A Mirror to Nature: Transformations in Drama and Aesthetics, 1660-1732*. Her book is ambitious in scope, schematic in method, and breezy in style. She investigates the shifting conceptions of imitation embodied in comedy and tragedy between those years, which she lays out neatly in her second chapter. These comprise four stages which move from the actual to the ideal. In the sixties "drama imitates nature as the ideal." This turns out to be a microcosmic whole perceived as Carolinian Neoplatonism or as "the old three-tiered medieval universe secularized and modified by Hobbesian thought." This takes place through "mounting progression toward trandescent truth that is effected by dialectical juxtaposition and refinement." She may be said to reverse Eugene Waith's emphasis from "ideas of *greatness*" to "*ideas* of greatness," at least in the first part of her study. (Incidentally, this is exactly Davenant's emphasis.)

It should be noted throughout that the ideal and the actual are spatialized as up and down, so one would expect an approach to the actual as we move from heroic drama to comedy and satire (and indeed satiric drama plays an important role in her book), but she is not oblivious to this possibility and insists that in the sixties "comedy is not more 'realistic' or more closely approximate to life than tragedy."

In the next decade "drama imitates the interplay between the ideal and the actual." Dramatic satire becomes the exemplary form for this development. The last two decades of the century give us, to use the title of her fifth chapter, "Nature as the Experiential Actual." In stage three there is a movement "away altogether from the realm of idea towards the realm of actuality," which proceeds from the typical to particular humans and finally focuses on the "inner reality" of these individuals . In the last stage (1700-23) the dramatist was not trying "to imitate nature but to draw nature to imitate art." In a sense there is a fifth stage suggested by *The Conscious Lovers*, for in this comedy, as she notes, we find a return to the ideal.

I think she is right that this period witnessed a shift (which in addition to the title's "Transformations" is characterized as an "evolution" or even "revolution") from the ideal to the actual—with its own movement from type to individual to individual psychology—but the neatness of the early decades and the completeness of the shift raises some skepticism. To concentrate on comedy, she finds indicators about the status of comedy in the sixties in the persistence of type figures in the seemingly actual characterization of *The Man of Mode* ("Old Bellair is a *Senex Amans*; Nan, the Orangewoman is a figure of La Veille"), but surely types persist throughout the period in comic drama, which tends to be highly conservative in that respect. Some of the readings, like that of *The Man of Mode*, are skewed, but she is also capable of brisk, insightful interpretations, and she considers a good range of plays, and not just the familiar ones, if only in short scope.

This study bears some relation (though over a more sharply confined period and by strictly formalist means despite some reference to controlling philosophical ideas) to the kind of changes that Michael McKeon attempts to demonstrate for the novel. It might be useful to see how what she has done changes the perception of historical development as seen by other categorists of the period, such as Robert Hume or Laura Brown, though it is well to remember that she has been publishing on this topic for some time, and others have been learning from her.

Peter Dixon has edited Farquhar's *The Recruiting Officer* in the valuable Revels series with a substantial introduction (a brief account of Farquhar followed by the nature of the play with its links to Restoration types, stage and textual histories) and modernized text.

Augustan Studies: Essays in Honor of Irvin Ehrenpreis, edited by Douglas Lane Patey and Timothy Keegan, is a Festschrift turned memorial volume. The miscellaneous essays include Ralph Cohen's study of a seventeenth-century ballad, part of his ambitious generic literary history; Mary Lascelles on epitaph and elegy; Christopher Ricks on Clarendon; Susan Staves on "Restoration Plays Embedded in Eighteenth-Century Novels"; Maximillian E. Novak on Defoe and the "Sincerity Crisis"; Margaret Anne Doody on *Gulliver's Travels* and Virgil's *Georgics*; Leopold Damrosch, Jr. on *Rasselas*; Rachel Tricket on visual description; and G. A. Starr's "Sentimental De-education," part of his continuing study of sentimentalism. A list of Ehrenpreis's publications is appended.

Hermann J. Real and Heinz J. Vienken have rounded up twenty-five essays for *The Proceedings of The First Münster Symposium on Jonathan Swift.* Marie-Luise Spieckermann writes appropriately on Swift in Germany. The poetry is discussed by W. B. Carnochan, Andrew Carpenter and Alan Harrison, Arno Löffler, Charles Peake, and Peter Schakel, an indication of its current high status, the explicit subject of Schakel's essay. *Gulliver's Travels* still receives the lion's share of attention with essays by the editors, Heinz Kosok, Eric Rothstein, and Michael Treadwell, among others. J. A. Downey's essay on Swift's politics claims that "the ideal political system" in *Gulliver's Travels* "turns out to be not Tory in inspiration, but Whig." The pamphlets and periodicals receive attention from Frank H. Ellis (*Examiner*), Johann N. Schmidt (*Drapier's Letters*), James Woolley (*Intelligencer*). Maximillian Novak makes some intelligent iscriminations din discussing the slippery question of Swift and Defoe. Irvin Ehrenpreis, who died in a fall at the symposium, contributes a characteristic essay on "The Doctrine of A Tale of a Tub," which denies that Swift attacks atheism in his satire. Phillip Harth considers "Swift's Self-Image as a Satirist" in his letters to Pope. Clive Probyn's account of the *Abstract upon Mr C——n's Discourse of Free-Thinking* focuses upon concern for textual authority in his parody. W. A. Speck weighs Swift as a source for historians in *The History of the Four Last Years of the Queen.*

Following a thumbnail account of twentieth-century theoretical methods, Nigel Wood's introductory *Swift* divides into chapters on Dean, Bickerstaff, Gulliver, and Drapier, headings chosen mainly to echo, though not in order, Pope's famous apostrophe. A postmodernist emphasis surfaces from time to time, but it seems fairly tepid. He is capable of engaging readings, but he is under the impression that *Gulliver's Travels* is a novel (an unargued position for which McKeon's *Origins* provides a defense). It is not the sort of thing that should happen in an introductory book. Wood includes a highly selective bibliography.

Taking as his point of departure a squabble between Swift and Steele, Allan Ingram considers the fallen or post-commonwealth laugh in *Intricate Laughter in the Satire of Swift and Pope.* His first chapter, on the late seventeenth- and early eighteenth- century theories of laughter, sets up Hobbes's familiar notion of "sudden glory" as the paradigm to which such writers as Shaftesbury, Dryden, Addison, Steele, and Hughes responded. The second chapter uses Swift's "A Beautiful Young Nymph Going to Bed" as the basis for a discussion of modern psychological ideas (Bergson, Freud, Laing) on or related to laughter. He is of the school that finds compassion in Swift's poem, and he would even see "the satirist . . . within the process of laughter-making as [Laing's] ontologically secure person." I think this quite wrong, and since he concludes the chapter with a brief workout of Robert Elliott's point (a valid one) that satire kills (in the Partridge essays and a few poems), I am left wondering how he squares this with the ontologically secure person's recognition of the "reality and identity of others." From here we move to the physiological and anthropological status of the laugh by way of Darwin and modern investigators. A chapter on play draws on Huizinga (though not Caillois). The showpiece here is appropriately *The Dunciad,* and though I would dissent from some of his analysis, he finds a successful formulation that brings together play and judgment: "While we disapprove of the dunces' play, we have no choice but to endorse and enjoy the play of Pope which has framed it, for our childhood delight in play has been aroused in the same spectacle that calls upon our learned capacity for increasingly confident approval or disapproval."

This book is an agreeable, undemanding consideration of the topic that rehearses a good deal one would want to know in connection with the topic of laughter, though while we have much on the "silent bared teeth display" of monkeys, Chesterfield's famous comment that a gentleman should never laugh, with its strong implications for the social laugh, does not appear. And, of course, Swift himself is said never to have laughed.

In *The Unbalanced Mind: Pope and the Rule of Passion* Rebecca Ferguson traces the role of passion in Pope's poetry. She follows the arguments closely from poem to poem and finds a productive pairing in *The Rape of the Lock* and Pope's *Iliad*. We have to wait until the third chapter to discover the influences on Pope's theory of the passions and the various meanings the word has for them (a chapter not surprisingly on *An Essay on Man*), but she initially defines "passion"as "impulse, and especially motivational impulse, encompassing also its more modern meaning of 'intense emotion'; it might be defined as denoting the affective or emotional capacity of the soul." She is aware, however, of the frequent distinction between the "passions" and the "affections." She notes the importance of the passions for seventeenth- and eighteenth-century psychology, ethics, and literary criticism (especially affective aesthetics), though she might add art theory with its central concern for the passions to her list. Pope's account of the passions as "'modes of self-love,' individualistic desires and aversions," she later accurately traces to Hobbes, as Douglas H. White had before her. Although she does not put it this way, much of what Pope is doing in the *Essay on Man* can be described as an attempt to overcome the conclusions of Hobbes while accepting his terms. She does not deal with the similarity of Pope and Locke's *Essay on Human Understanding*, discussed by Kenneth McLean and minimized by White, though in her chapter on *The Dunciad* she uses Locke on education. She could also draw on dictionaries and encyclopedic sources. Chambers's *Cyclopedia* (1720), for example, gives a highly eclectic account of the passions that would help to establish the popular understanding.

She sees the ideas of the ruling passion in women put forward in "To a Lady" adumbrated in the 1712 "Epistle to Miss Blount," which is often linked to the later poem. Pope argues for "not the suppression of impulses but their restraint within a harmonious balance." (A quick glance back at *The Rape of the Lock* would be in order here.) And the poem is viewed as the most "complex and deeply considered" embodiment of the theory that he had undertaken. Despite her frequent quotations and glosses, some gaps exist. A couplet like "On life's vast ocean diversely we sail, / Reason the card, but Passion is the gale" needs closer attention than she gives it. It is striking that Jean-Francois Senault, whom she had just mentioned, uses the same metaphor in arguing for reason's ultimate control over the passions, as does *Spectator* no. 408. She is not as concerned with ideas and sources as White, yet she sometimes moves too quickly to abstraction. She uses some manuscript material, especially from the Morgan Library, to good effect and is aware of the implications of Pope's reordering of some of his portraits within the poems. This is a literate reading of Pope's major poems in the context of a crucial idea. It is surprising it had not been done sooner.

The other shoe has dropped on *The Prose Works of Alexander Pope*. Volume Two now appears some forty years after Norman Ault's first. The editor, Rosemary Cowler, has been assiduous in footnoting, but lacks the sure touch for what is needed. The volume is very welcome, but not up to the standards of Mack and Tillotson in introductions and annotation. The brief introduction to the "Preface to *Shakespear*" shows her awareness of the immediate critical influence, but the essay is neither placed in the theoretical tradition nor compared in any way to *An Essay on Criticism*. She does discuss Pope's editorial principles and some of the leading issues of the critical reception. Her editing itself appears to be highly accurate. If I find quite often that she is annotating the topic rather than the reference, there are those who will be grateful for the learning deployed.

John Sena's *The Best-Natured Man: Sir Samuel Garth, Physician and Poet* is in large part archival in intention. Sena would bring together the little that is known of the admirable Dr. Garth in a short book with Garth's thirty-one extant letters as an appendix. (As Sena points out, the primary correspondents, Sloane, Newcastle, and the Duchess of Marlborough, neatly represent his main interests, medicine, politics, and poetry.) This is a dependable if limited account, a state of affairs that may not be entirely Sena's fault. While some of his passing comments on the cultural implications of Garth's life are perceptive, and he leads us carefully through the thickets of the background of *The Dispensary*, his literary comments, such as those on allusion in this, Garth's best-known poem, do not go far. His treatment of Garth's deathbed humor suggests that there is a side to Garth that he may not catch: "Although he was noted throughout his life for his ingratiating humor, it is likely that much of the levity and nonchalance with which he faced death was a pose. It is hard to believe that even the most dedicated stoic could confront death with jollity, for even to him death is serious—if only because he can no longer practice his stoicism." Sena is a student of the history of medicine and is aware of the range of topics that Garth's life embodies, but I think something more interesting can be made of the combination of science, medicine, charity, and atheism in a biography of this man who interests us as a minor poet. This is, nevertheless, the best biography of Garth.

Stephen K. Land argues with clarity and rigor in *The Philosophy of Language in Britain: Major Theories from Hobbes to Thomas Reid.* His intention is to represent the major types of theories in the period with individual chapters on Hobbes (Formalism), Locke (Idealism), and Berkeley (Structuralism), and two pairing Smith and Monboddo (the search for origins), Harris and Reid (Rationalism and Common Sense). He tells us that the book was complete in 1978, and perhaps his subtext, a critique of the Chomskyian history of language theory, seemed more pressing at that time. He is fully aware that language theory often plays a secondary role in the philosophies he discusses. Relying on W. S. Howell and the Kneales, he fills in some of the history in passing. Ramus and Port-Royal, Wilkins and the Royal Society (though not Sprat), Condillac and Rousseau receive brief mention. Land's method is frankly expository. He looks for symmetry and completeness and discusses the difficulties attendant on the various theories. This would lead him toward parallel subsections of his chapters, but what it often shows instead is where the differences lie: Berkeley, for example, unlike Locke, has no theory of words. Frequent diagrams lay out his findings.

His short chapter on Hobbes emphasizes the difficulties in drawing a theory from his "cursory, repetitious, and inconsistent . . . treatment of the subject." He neatly differentiates Hobbes, who is concerned with interpretation, from Locke, who is concerned with utterance, in the understanding of words. Book III of Locke's *Essay* contains a "theory of *words*—not strictly of *language*." He does not think that any philosopher noticed in the eighteenth century that Locke's words exist as ideas in the individual mind, but he might have mentioned Sterne, who clearly did. He follows Norman Kretzmann in getting Locke off the hook for some of the difficulties raised by the solipsism of words as ideas in the speaker's mind. He would also insist that Locke (like Berkeley after him) is concerned not with natural language but "only with language used to communicate, in the form of propositions, information about the agreement and disagreement of ideas." Indeed, in a sharper version of this formulation, he argues that Locke, "like most philosophers before World War II," was interested in logic, not language.

Those a bit puzzled by the ascription of "stucturalism" to Berkeley will find at the end of the chapter that Land claims that if he was largely uninfluential in his own time as a theorist of language, he is uniquely a forerunner of Saussure (an idea he pursues in more recent work), promulgating "a theory in which words signify ideas and the meaning of an idea is determined by its place in an ordered structure or 'language' of ideas." In dealing with Smith and Monboddo he recognizes that the search for the origins of language is often really a search for "the principles of human nature," though he might also have noticed that it is a search for the origins of society. His account of Smith is devoted to what could be called the conjectural history of grammar.

The conclusion insists that none of these theories will "fit comfortably" into the terms of twentieth-century linguistics and philosophy. He finds them linked (with the exception of Hobbes) by the belief that a "systematic connection" exists "between the patterns of language and the universal (logical) operations of rational thought." Though the theories differ at many points, one can see the crucial importance of Locke in opening up the subject for investigation.

Carey McIntosh's *Common and Courtly Language: The Stylistics of Social Class in 18th-Century British Literature* is a preliminary study of the relationship between class and usage. Taking Shakespeare as a base for accepted usage in the Renaissance (for reasons not spelled out), he describes lower-class and "courtly-genteel" English from 1660-1800. Part of his achievement is to detail the insistence on "correctness" in eighteenth-century prescriptive grammarians and the rejection of usage that had been seemingly standard for earlier periods. Courtly-genteel prose consists of a diction drawn from court usage and expressed through a series of key abstractions ("honor," "favor," "obligation," "duty") found initially in such contexts as the language of diplomacy and love (courtship), letters of "high friendship," model letters, chivalric romance, and prayer. He claims convincingly that this prose became "such a familiar phenomenon" in a domesticated middle-class version "that its frequent use in such novels as *Tom Jones* and *Clarissa* has never been noticed," and associates it with "middle-class aspirations to gentility." His account of Defoe is very different from G. A. Starr's "Defoe's Style." His account of Richardson might profit from some use of the distinctly lower-class usage of *Pamela* along with that of *Clarissa*, but since his demonstration of the persistence of courtly-genteel prose is probably his finest achievement, one cannot regret its omission very much.

His last chapter applies the findings to Hawkesworth's revisions of Captain Cook, *Evelina, Tom Jones, Clarissa, Humphry Clinker*, and a number of "courtly letters." A nice final touch shows how Johnson's letter of supreme insult to Chesterfield remains thoroughly polite—it is McIntosh's own very graceful complimentary close. Some will find the lack of a theoretical framework disturbing, but the book as a whole is modest in the best sense. It may be taken as an early step in a field that has not been much investigated.

While I am somewhat resistant to the notion of the Age of

Johnson, this was certainly the year of Johnson, perhaps spurred by the bicentennial of Johnson's death in 1984. Paul Korshin's *Johnson After Two Hundred Years* consists of fourteen essays selected from the commemorative conference at Pembroke College, Oxford. They cover a good range of topics. Some deal with Johnson's biography: Bertram Davis on the 1764 visit to Percy, Elizabeth R. Lambert on the friendship with Burke, Thomas M. Curley on Johnson and Sir Robert Chambers. (Curley has now also edited the two-volume *Course of Lectures on the English Law* by Chambers, a work of importance quite apart from its Johnsonian connections.) James Gray considers Johnson's knowledge of French. Paul Korshin subjects his last days to close scrutiny. The late Frank Brady explores a topic which deserves more attention in the biographies, Johnson as public figure. (Brady's last completed publication, *Mickle, Boswell, Garrick and "The Siege of Marseilles,"* details from manuscript sources the cantankerous Mickle's unsuccessful attempts, with Boswell as intercessor, to get Garrick to take his play.) My own essay discusses the twentieth-century biographies of Johnson.

Most of the essays deal with the writings. John L. Abbott's "The Making of the Johnson Canon" surveys the difficulties. Curley's decision that Chambers could well have written his law lectures himself with minor help from Johnson is a demonstration of the problems of the canon, for E. L. McAdam, Jr. had long ago ascribed much of the writing to Johnson. Curley on occasion disproves him specifically, but the larger question remains open. J. D. Fleeman's "Johnsonian Prospectuses and Proposals" in *Augustan Studies* is of interest for the canon. Other essays discuss Johnson and the writing of history (Martine Watson Brownley), his relation to the early editors of Shakespeare (Peter Seary), his biographies (William Epstein and Brian Corman), his letters (Isobel Grundy) and the *Dictionary* (Robert DeMaria, Jr.). Of all the essays William Epstein's "Patronizing the Biographical Subject: Johnson's *Savage* and Pastoral Power" is the only one employing contemporary critical theory (largely from Foucault).

Two other papers from that conference have been collected by Magdi Wahba as *Samuel Johnson: Commemorative Lectures.* Howard Weinbrot's "Johnson and the Arts of Narration" is a typically learned cross-generic study of rhetorical and narrative devices in *The Life of Savage, The Vanity of Human Wishes,* and *Rasselas.* Donald Greene's "The Future of Johnsonian Biography" consists of some vigorous bashing of Greene's *bêtes noires*, Macaulay and Boswell, in the context of praise of modern biography. At the conference one participant wickedly complained that Greene was doing the most to keep Macaulay alive, and another said that Greene was himself highly Macaulayan. I think this last was meant as a compliment, however backhanded; I look forward to a trenchant, opinionated, thoroughly-researched biography of Johnson by Greene. The short farewell by J. D. Fleeman lays out a few problems and desiderata (including a wish for an edition of letters to Johnson). One Johnsonian desideratum has been taken care of this year: the late Bertrand Bronson's *Selections from "Johnson on Shakespeare"* makes a one-volume version of the Yale edition available in paperback.

As the title of Isobel Grundy's *Samuel Johnson and the Scale of Greatness* suggests, the book is at once concerned with theme (the most important, she would argue) and method. The topic deserves such sustained attention, and this fresh, well-written account is very welcome. It deals with some of those large questions of human achievement that were the topic of W. J. Bate's memorable book. She is familiar with an impressive range of Johnson's writing and does not duck the little-known pieces, and she also seems to be aware of almost all of the relevant scholarship. As in the Virgilian tag, this commits her to compare ("Comparison" is her first chapter) great things with small. Some of her topics are "vindication of littleness," "criticism of pettiness," competition, community, "Greatness and Heroism," "Greatness and Ourselves." One may notice here a series of antithetical pairs which at once structure her book and fairly represent the movement of Johnson's thought, whether in sentences, paragraphs, or books. While I would say that Johnson's comparisons do not lead to relativism but discrimination, her emphasis on the different perspectives in which he sees things is salutary. She puts Johnson's *Dictionary* to extensive use in defining a broad range of terms, and notices such important eighteenth-century oppositions as that between goodness and greatness. If the focus is strongly on Johnson, she also finds the influence of Swift on the parliamentary debates, putatively in Magna Lilliputa, the occasion for a comparative chapter. One could ask for other things, but by turning her microscope and telescope on Johnson, she gives us the feeling that she has presented a plenum while moving up and down her Johnsonian scale.

Robert DeMaria's *Johnson's "Dictionary" and the Language of Learning* began as part of an investigation into the history of reading. For him Johnson's book is a "teaching dictionary," an anatomy, a common-place book, a history of the known. The result is at once interesting and miscellaneous, a virtual epitome of the sort of encyclopedic knowledge which is the topic of his study. What he has done is to organize the topics illustrated by the *Dictionary*. Under "Arts and Sciences," for example, we find Critics and Criticism, Poetry and Poets, The Fine Arts,—Music, Painting and Architecture—The Professions of the Gown—Medicine, Divinity, Law. The point is that one can draw Johnson's, or at least the *Dictionary*'s attitude, towards these things: "The *Dictionary* hates servile traitors to the writing profession who flatter the rich, and it delights in mocking the attempts of the rich to achieve high status in the republic of letters by dint of momentary force." The introduction and the chapter on knowledge are particularly valuable. For the most part, however, one may want to use this book the way one uses a dictionary or encyclopedia. Testing what I know best I find that he is commonly right in his claims and judicious about the significance of the topics under discussion for Johnson, though frequently these are not surprising. (He has also written an incisive account of Johnson on language theory which appears in Korshin's collection.) The point in part is not that Johnson has simply registered usage through his illustrations, but that he has chosen them (and one may add shaped them, though this aspect is scanted) with didactic intent.

Richard Harp's *Dr. Johnson's Critical Vocabulary: A Selection from His Dictionary* is a fine idea put into execution. The selection, which includes illustrations as well as definitions, is specifically of great aid for the student of Johnson (and goes beyond J. E. Brown's well-known *The Critical Opinions of Samuel Johnson* in this respect), but it also provides a very good guide to eighteenth-century and earlier critical usage. (One could argue that this is the true subject.) When Johnson, for example, defines an elegy as "a simple poem without points or turns," the relation of the genre to other sorts of poetry and eighteenth-century norms looms into view. The introduction relies a bit too heavily on authoritative testimonials to Johnson's excellence and importance. The book is printed in a clear, ugly typescript and is inexpensive enough as a paperback to be recommended for students. It is altogether a much more valuable book than the selection chosen by Milne and McAdam. Though since they would delight and Harp would teach, a Horatian compromise is present.

Thomas Kaminski's *The Early Career of Samuel Johnson* is what its title suggests, not a biography but an account of Johnson's career as a professional writer from his arrival in London in 1737 to 1746. Hence it covers a smaller and more selective span than Clifford's *Dictionary Johnson*. His intention is to work on some of Johnson's least-known works rather than the major ones, though he happily does not overestimate them. This close scrutiny is marked by some judicious interpretation rather than striking new finds. Though given as narrative, this book has much in common with the "facts and problems" approach of such earlier scholars as R. W. Chapman, J. M. Osborn and, to some extent, Clifford himself. Perhaps he is at his characteristic best in the fourth chapter, in which he takes as his point of departure Johnson's reported comment in a letter of Lord Gower's that he would "rather die upon the road, than be starved to death in translating for booksellers" and manages to tease from skimpy evidence the persuasive finding that Johnson must have translated between four hundred and eight hundred pages of Sarpi's *History of the Council of Trent* now lost. He also establishes Johnson's likely pay for this venture (between ten shillings and one guinea per sheet) in showing why on the basis of other Cave projects Johnson would be paid to go on translating an abortive book. He concludes from this examination that Johnson was more translator than editor under Cave in the late thirties. This is a bit of virtuoso detective work. In the last chapter he discusses Johnson's intention to write a tragedy about Charles XII without commenting on the relation of this ineffectual plan to Johnson's most praised portrait in *The Vanity of Human Wishes*, and he might be more ready to believe Johnson admired Voltaire's biography of Charles had he noted the distinctly mock-heroic treatment of its subject.

It would be useful to have his findings in the book summarized, for a good deal of what he has to say is necessarily well known. When he claims at the end of chapter three that "our investigation has uncovered two obvious changes," the first, "the introduction of biographies," has been noted before without fanfare. Nevertheless, the *Early Career* is the work of a careful scholar and future biographers as well as students of Johnson will certainly be in his debt.

Alvin Kernan's gracefully written *Printing Technology, Letters and Samuel Johnson* disappoints. It would be good to have a book on Johnson which extended the work of Marshall McLuhan and Elizabeth Eisenstein, but what Kernan has to say is all too familiar. This is something of a puzzle because he has mastered most of the requisite scholarship. It seems there is a drive to tell Johnson's story; the chapter "Boswell's Johnson" really is Kernan's own thumbnail life with little focus on Boswell's shaping, though in dealing with Johnson's meeting with the king he emphasizes the way Boswell plays up Johnson's importance as a monarch of literature, a richer topic in the *Life* than he makes it. Since he takes Boswell's making of Johnson into a symbol as part of Johnson's meaning for us, anti-Boswellians will like the book less than I do. Perhaps the best result of his method is the account of the *Dictionary* as a product of print-logic:

> The *Dictionary* was in the first place a practical handbook needed by the printing business to establish the authoritative spellings and, to only a slightly lesser degree, the fixed meanings which print, with its inbuilt tendency toward systematic regularity, required for its day-to-day operations of editing manuscripts and setting type with some consistency. It was also a book whose conception owed much to print and its characteristic *esprit de système* which made it possible to think of and then produce a systematic arrangement of all the words in the English language.

This is part of a longer consideration. Although one misses that primary audience of students, foreigners, and others, his point is well-taken. Yet I was more impressed by the revelations that Hugh Kenner produced from his meditation on print culture, *The Counterfeiters*, nearly twenty years ago.

Another book that considers print technology is Jerome Christensen's *Practising Enlightenment: Hume and the Formation of a Literary Career*, an intellectual biography informed by post-structuralist theory (not a biography of the "heroic ego" or the "instrumental body"). He calls it Johnsonian. His coolly knowing account draws on Gramschi's idea of the traditional intellectual for the basic project and the key term of its subtitle. This is a story of fame very different from that of Leo Braudy. It is pursued as a prolegomenon to a study of "Byronic strong Romanticism."

The thorny subtlety of his work will not be to all tastes. He enjoys putting a finer point on things. Indeed, his method is also his subject, for Hume "practices a career, as he composes the *Treatise*, by making one adjustment after another in a continual labor of perpetual refinement." The account of print logic in his long central chapter "The Commerce of Letters" is highly suggestive.

Like Kernan and Christensen, Leo Braudy is interested both in the implications of printing technology and the shape of literary (as well as other) careers in his wide-ranging *The Frenzy of Renown: Fame and its History*. The title comes from Monk Lewis, but Braudy is remembering Johnson's "fever of renown" as well, an apt allusion, for the ironic side of fame is the vanity of human wishes, and it is fitting that the phrase comes from Johnson's portrait of the scholar. The term "frenzy" sorts well also with the schwärmerei of Johnson's poem and the modern day of the locusts Braudy depicts.

Braudy is aware of what he calls, developing an insight of Clark Gable's, the small print in the contract of the famous. And he knows that to write a big book on fame is itself a bid to be famous. Braudy's chapters on the late seventeenth and eighteenth centuries include the obvious names (that is the point of the exercise). Among the English most space is given to Pope, Swift, and Boswell ("The Advent of the Fan"), but a range of figures from our period keeps reappearing throughout the book. Although one cannot do justice to a book which moves from Alexander the Great to Charles Lindberg in this essay—Braudy may be the only writer ever to connect Alexander Pope (as Milton by Richardson) with Marilyn Monroe (as Harlow by Avedon)—*The Frenzy of Renown* deserves to be well-known.

The ideal of intimacy provides the basis for emphasis and judgment in Bruce Redford's *The Converse of the Pen: Acts of Intimacy in the Eighteenth-Century Familiar Letter*. This is a non-fictional genre whose quotidian significance goes far beyond the attention it receives. Redford's conversation piece gives us six portraits in pairs: Lady Mary Wortley Montagu and Cowper, Gray and Walpole, Boswell and Johnson's correspondence with Mrs. Thrale (this last also includes a comparison with Swift's to Stella). Pope is the odd man out, too public for the argument. And Redford claims that Johnson's "normal" letter "resembles a moral essay that has been cursorily adapted to the identity of its recipient." He is committed to a non-Johnsonian belief, to use Richardson's false etymology, in *cor*respondence. Isobel Grundy's essay on Johnson in Korshin's Johnson collection provides a needed complement to his treatment of Johnson.

Redford is aware of the letter's simultaneous claim to historicity and art. There is some reliance on speech-act theory, as the title suggests, but his theory of the letter is not spelled out. His criteria for great letters include "autonomy, fertility, and versatility." He does not put all his writers through the same paces. Usually he chooses a few themes or techniques for close examination. The third chapter is called "The Allusiveness of Thomas Gray." The Lady Mary chapter, which starts off heavily indebted to other writers, makes too much show of identifying her stoicism and is not convincing enough on her putative Senecan style. In the more effective attention to Cowper he emphasizes the mock-heroic, painterly, and emblematic and finds the letters more successful than the poems in this last respect, though I wish he had made an exception of "The Castaway."

As with his letter writers themselves, Redford recognizes the necessity for tact and "the talents of the miniaturist." Implicitly he realizes the dependence on style to carry the slightness of the burden, and seems wary of breaking butterflies upon his wheel. Typical is his unwillingness to use Freud while invoking him in the Thrale-Johnson relationship. Indeed, though some comments suggest an awareness that the art is pastoral (both Lady Mary and Cowper "take strength from an epistolary microcosm that first prefigures and then mirrors a secluded *hortus conclusus*"), more on the genre's miniaturization, put to particularly good use in his discussion of Cowper, would be welcome. (Pierre Bachelard probably has more to offer him in this regard than Levi-Strauss, whom he quotes). I like the book for its urbane attention to an unfashionable genre.

Redford is also responsible for a different sort of publication, a handsome edition of two Sheridan manuscripts, "The Slanderers," and "Sir Peter Teazle" with facsimiles from Princeton's Taylor collection *en face* under the title *The Origins of "The School for Scandal."*

In *The Nonsense Club: Literature and Popular Culture, 1749-1764*, Lance Bertelsen has written a needed account of the activities of Bonnell Thornton, George Colman, Robert Lloyd, Charles Churchill, and William Cowper, but the promise of the subtitle and the footnotes documenting debts to Gramschi, Foucault, and Bakhtin do not succeed in making the book very different in critical orientation from what it might have been thirty years ago.

He is particularly good in dealing with what might seem overbilled as the "Nonsense Club aesthetic." He makes a convincing case for Churchill's process poetry (with its links to Sterne and Byron) as the expression of Nonsense Club beliefs in speed of composition, spontaneity, "criticism of rules and imitation, its abhorrence of the epithetical style and contrived emotion, and its praise for unconfined, if not uneducated genius." And he demonstrates the way such a position led to Thornton's "To Obscurity," Lloyd's "To Oblivion," and Cowper's ironic praise of the "Modern Ode," attacks on what they perceived as the labored productions of Gray and Mason.

My objections are minor. Although he is aware that Fielding has some importance for Thornton, when praising Thornton's parody of Fielding's *Amelia*, he forgets what Fielding himself had accomplished in *Shamela*. And in quoting Colman's *Polly Honeycomb*, he neglects to mention that the language to which she responds in her novel-reading ("Thou hast seen, perhaps . . . the artificial vermillion on the cheeks of Cleora, or the vermillion of nature on those of Sylvia; thou hast seen—in a word, the lovely face of Emilia was overspread with blushes") is a pastiche of Fielding's introduction of Sophia.

His account of taste is interesting, but misses some of the important elements and influences (such as Addison's *Spectator* no. 409). His description of the meaning of "the town," which had undergone some changes since the Restoration, could be richer in its suggestiveness through drawing on some of those theorists he invokes. The book, however, does not overestimate the literary qualities of the Nonsense Club and related productions, and Bertelsen generally is aware of the connections of the writers he studies. Like the Nonsense Club writers themselves, he usually makes what he does look easy.

James King's *William Cowper: A Biography* is now the best biography of its subject. It is appropriate that an editor of Cowper's letters and his autobiography should have undertaken the labor, which he has intelligently performed. Although pathos is the dominant tone of this life of a poet who lived many years under the impression that he was a castaway from God, King does not slight the early years in the Nonsense Club—a good brief account of Cowper's rakish side and susceptibility to feminine beauty is given—and he even makes convincing claims for its formative influence on Cowper's writing. Readers should be informed, however, that the Cowper who was not fuddled by four or five bottles of claret, drank from small, eighteenth-century bottles.

Generally, he handles the complex problems raised by Cowper's madness plausibly. He attributes them to the early death of Cowper's beloved mother and quotes Freud, Evna Furman, and John Bowlby on the problems of mourning and subsequent depressive breakdown. This is certainly the major line of the most recent medical consideration of Cowper and it convinces. Strangely, however, King has very little to say of a remarkable anecdote told by Cowper in his autobiography of his father's asking him to read a defense of suicide in Montesquieu and to respond to it. When Cowper "argued against it," he took his father's silent response as disagreement. This anecdote is taken as an indication of the usually amiable John Cowper's occasional "excessive morbidity" and as evidence that "unlike his wife, [he] was not an unduly demonstrative parent" (an odd phrase). We might expect that the anecdote, whether it tells us most about William Cowper's early life or his later consciousness, would be linked to Cowper's series of suicide attempts.

On the problem of Cowper's sexuality King defers to Ryskamp whose chapter "The Defect" in his account of Cowper's early life quotes the passage by Charles Greville on a putatively lost letter of John Newton's which claims "He was a Hermaphrodite." The relationship to Newton could be developed, though King's accounts of Mary Unwin, Lady Hesketh, and Cowper's friendships in general are well done. The detailing of the friendships, activities and accomplishments of his life balance the emphasis on the breakdowns.

King's is not a critical biography. The poems, which began as "therapy," are considered as events in the life, as in the account of the translation of Homer, one of Cowper's longer labors. The book is written in a readable, sometimes moving, sometimes genteel prose. (We hear of Cowper's mother's "passing" and his father's "demise.") Surprisingly, Romney's painting of Cowper alone appears, as a small title-page frontispiece. This is certainly the place for the Abbott and Lawrence portraits as well.

Ludmilla Jordanova's *Languages of Nature: Critical Essays on Science and Literature* devotes over half its space to the eighteenth century, mostly the later period. A. E. Pilkington's " 'Nature' as Ethical Norm in the Enlightenment" centers on French fiction as does the editor's "Naturalizing the Family." More directly of interest are James Rodgers's "Sensibility, Sympathy, Benevolence: Physiology and Moral Philosophy in *Tristram Shandy*," and Maureen McNeil's "The Scientific Muse: The Poetry of Erasmus Darwin." The editor also contributes a long introduction and supererogatory introductions to each essay (including her own).

Janet Todd is stronger at specific analysis than in getting some of the key concepts of *Sensibility: An Introduction* straight. Her consideration of the terminology makes some of the necessary distinctions, but they are a bit clotted, a situation perhaps endemic to the subject. This book seems more about sentimentalism than sensibility, though as Todd notes, the two are often treated interchangeably during the period. Sensibility is best thought of as the physiological grounding for the reception of sentiment. Although she treats the topic in drama, poetry, and fiction, she recognizes the preeminence (if that's the right word) of the novel from 1740-1770 and gives it three chapters to one apiece for the other genres. The book concludes with a chapter on the attacks on sensibility and an epilogue. Apart from some shaky sentences and a few errors (she gives us Charlotte Brooke for Frances), the formulations are often to the point:

> The sentimental novel is often said to be the vehicle of a sentimental philosophy positing innate virtue or goodness in all humanity. Nothing could be further from the scene presented in the majority of these novels. A single vulnerable hero is opposed to the expanse of a hostile society, and while the sentimental Humean virtues of benevolence and tender-

> ness [she might add the Shaftesburian and Hutchesonean, as well] are indeed the basis of human worth and fellowship, these virtues on the whole occur defensively and impotently and their possession always creates the victim.

Much of the book provides the useful introduction that the title promises.

Irish Booksellers and English Writers, 1740-1800 deals with what Richard Cargill Cole genteelly calls "the Irish reprinting tradition." He argues that "Irish booksellers through cheap reprints disseminated the works of the major British writers of their time and augmented the audience for these writers not only in Ireland but in Britain and the United States." One can hardly take exception to this thesis, and it is good to see the case argued without heavy moralizing. Because of loopholes in the copyright acts of 1709 and 1739, it was not illegal for the Irish to publish English books for sale in Ireland without paying either the original publishers or the authors. Their defense was either high-minded (poor students would not be able to afford them) or cynical (if they did not do it, the Dutch would), but they subsisted on theft and smuggling. Cole claims that the Irish audience consisted primarily of the landowning and professional classes, though they would be more likely to have their books survive than poor students. At best the Irish reprinters were not the Robin Hoods they claimed to be. Cole's work deals centrally with new books by novelists, historians, Goldsmith, Johnson, and Boswell. Johnson was both the most lucrative author and the subject of the single most reprinted book, Boswell's *Life*. The literary quality of the book can be gauged by the title of one chapter, "Reprinting the Great CHAM and his satellite."

As in Cole's case, John Feather's *The Provincial Book Trade in Eighteenth-Century England* begins with the lapse of the Printing Act in 1695. His lucid and succinct account of the growth of the provincial book trade deals with the market, distribution system, bookselling business, and the printing office. It includes a range of illustrations (maps of newspapers, places of business of a representative bookseller) as well as plates and a series of appendixes listing book and paper stock, printing equipment of selected booksellers, and lists of subscribers to several books.

Deborah Rogers has brought together a good deal of archival material (much from untapped collections at Duke and the New York Historical Society) in *Bookseller as Rogue: John Almon and the Politics of Eighteenth-Century Publishing*. Unfortunately, her concept of relevance is seriously flawed, and the book reads like an unrevised doctoral dissertation. It includes an appendix listing Almon's reprints.

An interesting grouping centers on politics. David Erdman's modestly subtitled *Commerce des Lumières: John Oswald and the British in Paris, 1790-1793* actually gives a biography of the shadowy radical soldier in its first hundred pages, working its way through a confused and uncertain chronology. Oswald served in India, became a hack writer in London and died as a commander fighting for the French Revolution. Erdman gives a close account of political events connected with Oswald, who later became a model for the villain of Wordsworth's *The Borderers.* The cast of characters includes the "Brain-Sucker" William Thomson, some of whose writings are here assigned to Oswald, Walking Stewart, Lord Hamilton, Godwin, Gilray and others. A good deal is conjectural, though reasonable. Erdman has given us another interesting chapter in the history of late eighteenth-century radicalism.

Thomas N. Corns has brought together a group of essays on an unusual topic for such collections in *The Literature of Controversy: Polemical Strategy from Milton to Junius.* Six of the eight are from our period. Hobbes, Marvell, Baxter, Defoe, Swift, and Junius are the subjects, and the essays tend to focus on a single work.

The relationship of Gustave Simonson's manuscript of the 1930s to Simonson and Francesco Cordasco's *Junius and His Works: A History of the Letters of Junius and the Authorship Controversy* is now one of the lesser Junian authorship puzzles. It contains a wide range of necessary information, repetitively presented. Cordasco himself favors Laughlin Macleane over the frontrunner Sir Philip Francis and a host of others. Cordasco's *Junius: A Bibliography* is a valuable listing of the primary and secondary materials which presents a good deal of what is in the companion volume more manageably.

In *Liberty and Poetics in Eighteenth Century England* Michael Meehan takes an excellent theme and works through it author by author from Shaftesbury to Wordsworth. Blackwell, Akenside, Hume, Ferguson, and Johnson get short chapters to themselves; Thomas Sheridan and John Brown share one. His thesis is that "patriotic ideas, founded on . . . optimistic views, reached far beyond the bounds of specifically political verse, and early century panegyric towards a general reshaping of national artistic character." I can easily accept this position and am grateful for the material he has found, but the results strike me as extremely limited. The treatment of the tradition of civic humanism deriving from Shaftesbury is much more richly handled by John Barrell, though Meehan is also indebted to John Pocock and displays an informed, up-to-date knowledge of the historical and political scholarship surrounding the subject. He is aware of the danger of himself writing a new version of the whig interpretation of literary history, but I am not sure that he has avoided it.

He misses some of the key statements and implications. Although his topic is poetics, not poetry, he should notice that the poem on liberty became a virtual genre, and though he considers Wordsworth, he is silent on Blake, whose whole poetic production might be considered a song to liberty, and who is very explicit on the subject. Perhaps more directly chargeable is his missing in his account of Akenside a footnote to Akenside's odes which claims of Pindar, who goes unmentioned by Meehan, that:

> A real historical fact in his life is, that the Thebans imposed a large fine on him on account of the veneration which he expressed in his poems for that heroic spirit, shewn by the people of Athens in defence of the common liberty, which his own fellow-citizens had shamelessly betrayed. And as the argument of this ode implies, that *great poetical talents, and high sentiments of liberty, do reciprocally produce and assist each other*, so Pindar is perhaps the most exemplary proof of this connection, which occurs in history.

Pindar should be explicitly mentioned as a model of the liberty of poets, but the more important point is that to write of liberty helps to make one a poet. We could argue that the proposition is false, and Meehan is only too aware of the dreadful poems turned out in eighteenth-century England in liberty's name, but he fails to see a key element in an important belief of the period that goes back farther. (In connection with the disparity between theory and practice Donald J. Greene's typically astringent " 'Sweet Land of Liberty': Libertarian Rhetoric and Practice in Eighteenth-Century England," in *The American Revolution and Eighteenth-Century Culture*, edited by Paul J. Korshin, makes some necessary observations.)

To take another example, Meehan misses that line of argument from Milton to Blake that insists on a break with rhyme as the condition of freedom and great poetry (often nationalistically conceived). And once Meehan has decided to do a chapter on Wordsworth, it is surprising to find that there is not even a sentence devoted to Shelley's conception of the poet as "the unacknowledged legislator of the world," for the poet as legislator is one of his subthemes, one somewhat lost in the organization by author. Flawed as it may be, however, this book remains a very useful if too short account of an important and neglected topic. His publishers, Croom Helm, have not helped him. This is the ugliest book of the year (apart from a handsome dust jacket), and far more than the margins are unjustified. Hardly a line is printed clean and the small typescript is a horror to read.

John Barrell's *The Political Theory of Painting from Reynolds to Hazlitt: The Body of the Public* is brilliant, original, and strongly argued. Drawing on John Pocock, he distinguishes three political theories: the selfish, which he traces to Mandeville (but would be better chasing back to Hobbes), the social, and the civic. He argues that the discourse of civic humanism, promulgated by Shaftesbury and developed most significantly for art theory by Reynolds (to whom he devotes the longest chapter), Barry, and Fuseli, was lost following the emphasis on individualism in Hazlitt. Civic humanism would emphasize a "republic of taste" (related to the familiar notion of the republic of letters, with which too little has been done), and art's highest calling was to instill public virtues in free citizens.

The social discourse, operative from the middle of the century, continues the discourse of civic humanism in attenuated form. In a commercial society the function of art is to "promote not public but 'social' virtues, whether public or private." Barrell has some telling pages on the "privatization" of society and painting. The return to civic humanist discourse comes with the founding of the Royal Academy, and Reynolds's annual presidential lectures. But if one expects Barrell to dismiss Reynolds as providing upper-class ideology, he will be surprised. Reynolds in this reading is not simply making of the dirty-handed painter a gentleman, though Barrell would stress gentlemen as the primary audience of the lectures, rather than students. Reynolds's central principle "that it is the function of art to create and to confirm a republic, or at least a community, of taste" open to more citizens than Shaftesbury's is for Barrell a vital one, however mystified. Barrell certainly shows that the community of taste in Reynolds, like the political franchise in eighteenth-century England, was distinctly restricted. While I cannot do justice to the subtlety of the argument here, Barrell finds Reynolds's shifts during the course of the lectures from an emphasis on universality to make a place for "custom" correspond to a political change and point to an increased nationalism.

The short account of Blake is the most provocative. His chapter bears the title "A Blake Dictionary" (a very Blakean touch that opposes Barrell's own understanding of some key notions to the contraries represented by authoritative Blake scholarship, and borrows Foster Damon's title to do so). He quite explicitly thinks that Blake was right when he claimed of Reynolds's *Discourses* that "This Whole Book was Written to Serve Political Purposes," but he would add that so was Blake's corpus of ideas on art and those of the other late eighteenth-century theorists he studies. He would do away with Blake as "a founding father of the liberal individualism which has been the prevailing ideology of 'Blake Studies.'" He argues rather that for Blake what "constitutes [the true artist's] originality is the fact that he has access to a vision of the heavenly origin of what it is that art should represent." Therefore, he will be like rather than different from other true artists. This leads to the conclusion that Reynolds and Blake are not opposed as Neo-Classic to Romantic but rather differ about the way in which the discourse of civic humanism is to be used "to enable painting to describe a modern complex society, and to create a public capable of understanding that description and its significance to the conduct of civic life." This will be a highly controversial finding, but it is a powerful, blunt argument. In the context of the book it brings Blake even closer to the Barry we know he admired.

It is Barry's distinction to take the discourse of civic humanism as established by Reynolds and refashion it so that "painting should depict the diversity of a society divided by the division of labour, but in such a way as enables its members to grasp the common ends, political and religious, which their divided labours co-operate to achieve." Barry would democratize the republic of taste, and Barrell points out that Barry's democratic principles were mooted in connection with his expulsion from the Royal Academy. (Not least valuable is Barrell's downplaying of the personal side of the "difficult" Barry and taking his ideas seriously.) The parallel of Barry to David is relegated to a footnote, but would be worthy of further consideration. Yet at the same time Barrell recognizes a possible "sinister" side to Barry's emphasis on physiognomy, which may imply that vice and virtue can be deduced from physique, and that men are classed in "immutable" categories. Barrell, inquiring closely, finds this troublesome but inconclusive. What he decides is that for Barry all citizens must display some character-type: "However many uniforms may be kept in the stores, and even if we can choose which one to wear, no one is allowed to wear mufti." (The shift from body to clothes metaphor is worth noting.) Fuseli is treated in shorter scope as a pessimistic historian of art who speaks with "the voice of the stoic guardian of public virtue." But he also speaks in a "milder voice" which recognizes his own unprivileged historical position. The darker side of art theory appears with William Hazlitt, who stresses individual response, and Benjamin Haydon, who fills the position of Romantic vacated by Blake.

This book should also be distinguished from what it is not. It is not a history of art, and the illustrations only sometimes (especially in the case of Barry) seem important. It is also not a typical history of art theory. Barrell's emphasis on political discourse leads him to be somewhat less concerned with forerunners of these theorists in art and literary theory (the centrality of civic humanism makes this a pragmatic or affective theory), though he certainly comments on some of them and is aware of traditions going back to Plato and Renaissance attacks on Plato's rejection of the poet from the commonwealth (which he might identify in part as neoplatonic). He does not, for example, treat Reynolds's *Discourses,* as W. J. Bate does, as "the most representative single embodiment in English of eighteenth-century critical principles." He links Johnson to Reynolds in terms of the political pamphlets as well as the criticism, though he takes Imlac as more of a straight representative of Johnson than I would. In passing he has some incisive observations on other theorists, such as his comparison of the image of the road in Reynolds and Edward Young. I have some minor quarrels, but the book is an extraordinary achievement, and I doubt we will read eighteenth-century art criticism in the same way any longer.

Some of what Barrell has to say about Blake as copyist was anticipated in the essay "Blake and Reynolds" by Edgar Wind. It is good at last to have Wind's *Hume and the Heroic Portrait: Studies in Eighteenth-Century Imagery* collected, and his long, important title essay Englished. It argues the importance of differing philosophical traditions and conceptions of human nature behind the portraiture of Reynolds and Gainsborough. The rest of the dozen essays are mainly short. Wind was among the most erudite and subtle of an extraordinarily learned group. The slight literary piece, "Johnson and Demonax," provides grist for Donald Greene's mill in arguing that the Johnson of Boswell's *Life* has been tricked out in joke-book and proverb lore, but it may equally prove that Johnson was not above adapting or deploying the jokes or wisdom of others, hardly an action inconsistent with his beliefs.

Finally, I will quickly consider a few more books on art with strong implications for literary studies. Ann Uhry Abrams's *The Valiant Hero: Benjamin West and Grand-Style History Painting* gives a summary of the career of the prolific West. Morton Paley presents a Burke-centered account of sublimity in *The Apocalyptic Sublime* with chapters on West, Loutherbourg, and Blake as well as nineteenth-century figures. W. J. T. Mitchell's *Iconology* contains a chapter on "Eye and Ear: Burke's Politics of Sensibility." Ann Bermingham pays particular attention to Gainsborough and the picturesque in the eighteenth-century part of her excellent *Landscape and Ideology: The English Rustic Tradition, 1740-1860.*

All ages are ages of transition, but the period 1660-1800 is even more so. Although this necessarily synchronic consideration of the year's scholarship is unlikely to spot trends (except for how widespread the practice is of having dust jacket blurbs written by the dissertation director of the author), one might notice a Shaftesbury boomlet (Barrell, Meehan, Marshall) and the number of books that explicitly or implicitly consider the consequences of secularization (McKeon, Zimbardo, Weber, Erickson, and—I would argue—Castle). It could also well be a major focus for a biography of Sir Samuel Garth. I would also note that as a whole eighteenth-century studies have been resistant to recent theory, but as some of the best books this year show, the joining of the traditional strength in history to contemporary methods may lead to excellent work.

BOOKS RECEIVED

Abrams, Ann Uhry. *The Valiant Hero: Benjamin West and Grand-Style History Painting.* Washington : Smithsonian Institute Press, 1985. Pp. 256. $39.95 cloth. $19.95 paper. ISBN 0-87474-206-4, cloth. ISBN 0-87474-206-2, paper.

[Amory, Hugh.] *New Books by Fielding: Commentary toward an Exhibition.* Cambridge, Mass.: Houghton Library, 1987. Pp. 56. ISBN 0-91463-001-6.

[Arrowsmith, Joseph.] *The Reformation of Comedy.* Los Angeles: William Andrews Clark Memorial Library, Univ. of California, 1986. Pp, xii +80.

Backscheider, Paula R. *Daniel Defoe: Ambition and Innovation.* Lexington: Univ. Press of Kentucky, 1986. Pp. ix +299. $25.00. ISBN 0-8131-1596-5.

Barrell, John. *The Political Theory of Painting from Reynolds to Hazlitt: The Body of the Public.* New Haven and London: Yale Univ. Press, 1986. Pp. ix +366. $30.00. ISBN 0-300-03720-1.

Behn, Aphra. *Love-Letters Between a Nobleman and his Sister.* New York: Penguin Books, 1987. Pp. xvii +461. $7.95. ISBN 0-14-016-160-0.

Bermingham, Ann. *Landscape and Ideology: The English Rustic Tradition, 1740-1860.* Berkeley and Los Angeles: Univ. of California Press, 1986. Pp. xviii +254. $35.00. ISBN 0-520-05287-0.

Bertelsen, Lance. *The Nonsense Club: Literature and Popular Culture, 1749-1764.* Oxford and New York: Oxford Univ. Press, 1986. Pp. xi +322. $45.00. ISBN 0-19-812859-2.

Borck, Jim Springer. *The Eighteenth Century: A Current Bibliography*, n.s. 8

(1981). New York: AMS Press, Pp. 603. $67.50. ISBN 0-404-62213-5.

Bourgeois, Susan. *Nervous Juyces and the Feeling Heart: The Growth of Sensibility in the Novels of Tobias Smollett.* American Univ. Studies: Series 4, English Language and Literature, vol. 35. New York and Berne: Peter Lang, 1986. Pp. 188. ISBN 0-8024-0273-7.

Brady, Frank. *Mickle, Boswell, Garrick, and "The Siege of Marseilles". Transactions: The Connecticut Academy of Arts and Sciences, vol. 46. Hamden, Conn.: Archon Books, 1987. Pp. 235-97. $12.50. ISBN 0-208-02131-0.*

Braudy, Leo. The Frenzy of Renown: Fame and its History. New York and Oxford: Oxford Univ. Press, 1986. Pp. xiii +649. $27.50. ISBN 0-19-504003-1.

Bronson, Bertrand H., and O'Meara, Jean M., eds. *Selections from Johnson on Shakespeare.* New Haven and London: Yale Univ. Press, 1986. Pp. xxxvii +373. $40.00, cloth. ISBN 0-300-03707-4. $12.95, paper. ISBN 0-300-3708-2.

Bunyan, John. *The Barren Fig-Tree, The Strait Gate, and the Heavenly Foot-Man.* Ed. Graham Midgley. *The Miscellaneous Works of John Bunyan*, vol. 5. Oxford and New York: Clarendon Press, 1986. Pp. lii +194. $59.00. ISBN 0-19-812733-2.

Burney, Fanny. *Cecilia, or, Memoirs of an Heiress.* New York: Viking Penguin, 1986. Pp. xiii +919. $7.95. ISBN 0-14-016-136-8.

Cash, Arthur H. *Laurence Sterne: The Later Years.* London and New York: Methuen, 1986. Pp. xxiv +390. $49.95. ISBN 0-416-32930-6.

Castle, Terry. *Masquerade and Civilization: The Carnivalesque in Eighteenth-Century English Culture and Fiction.* Stanford: Stanford Univ. Press, 1986. Pp. x +395. $37.50. ISBN 0-8047-1313-8.

Chambers, Sir Robert. *A Course of Lectures on the English Law: Delivered at the University of Oxford, 1767-1773.* Ed. Thomas M. Curley. Madison: Univ. of Wisconsin Press, 1987. Vol. 1 : Pp. xix +483. Vol. 2 : Pp. xv +445. $60.00 for both volumes. Vol. 1: ISBN 0-299-10011-1. Vol. 2: ISBN 0-299-10012-X.

Christensen, Jerome. *Practising Enlightenment: Hume and the Formation of a Literary Career.* Madison: Univ. Wisconsin Press, 1987. Pp. xi +284. $17.50 paper. ISBN 0-299-10754-X. $40.00 cloth. ISBN 0-299-10750-7.

Clark, Constance. *Three Augustan Women Playwrights.* American Univ. Studies: Series 4, English Language and Literature, vol. 40. New York and Berne: Peter Lang, 1986. Pp. 355. $35.00. ISBN 0-8204-0309-1.

Cole, Richard Cargill. *Irish Booksellers and English Writers, 1740-1800.* London: Mansell Publishing, and Atlantic Highlands, N. J.: Humanities Press, 1986. Pp. xv +266. $39.95. ISBN 0-391-03432-4.

Cordasco, Francesco. *Junius: A Bibliography of the Letters of Junius with a Checklist of Junian Scholarship and Related Studies.* Fairview, N. J., and London: Junius-Vaughn Press, 1986. Pp. viii +278. $30.00. ISBN 0-940198-04-5.

Cordasco, Francesco, and Simonson, Gustave. *Junius and his Works: A History of the Letters of Junius and the Authorship Controversy.* Fairview and London: Junius-Vaughn Press, 1986. Pp. xx +454. $42.00. ISBN 0940-198-05-7.

Corns, Thomas N., ed. *The Literature of Controvery: Polemical Strategy from Milton to Junius.* Totowa, N.J.: Frank Cass, 1987. Pp. viii +176. $25.00.

ISBN 0-7146-3292-9.

Curran, Stuart. *Poetic Form and British Romanticism*. Oxford and New York: Oxford Univ. Press, 1986. Pp. 265. $29.95. ISBN 0-19-504019-8.

DeMaria, Robert Jr., ed. *Johnson's Dictionary and the Language of Learning*. Chapel Hill and London: Univ. of North Carolina Press, 1986. Pp. xii +303. $25.00. ISBN 0-8078-1713-9.

Eighteenth Century Life.10, n.s. 1 (January 1986). Ed. Robert P. Maccubbin. Williamsburg: College of William and Mary, 1986. Pp. 104. ISSN 0098-2601.

Enright, D. J. *The Alluring Problem: An Essay on Irony*. Oxford and New York: Oxford Univ. Press, 1986. Pp. vii +178. $19.95. ISBN 0-19-212253-3.

Erdman, David V. *Commerce de Lumières: John Oswald and the British in Paris, 1790-1793*. Columbia: Univ. of Missouri Press, 1986. Pp. xii +338. $39.00. ISBN 0-8262-0607-7.

Erickson, Robert A. *Mother Midnight: Birth, Sex and Fate in Eighteenth-Century Fiction (Defoe, Richardson, and Sterne)*. New York: AMS Press, 1987. Pp. xiv +326. $39.50. ISBN 0-404-61476-0.

Farquhar, George. *The Recruiting Officer*. Ed. Peter Dixon. Manchester: Manchester Univ. Press, 1986. Pp. xiii +207. $42.00. ISBN 0-7190-1534-0.

Feather, John. *The Provincial Book Trade in Eighteenth-Century England*. Cambridge and London: Cambridge Univ. Press, 1985. Pp. xvi +176. $39.50. ISBN 0-521-30334-6.

Ferguson, Rebecca. *The Unbalanced Mind: Pope and the Rule of Passion*. Philadelphia: Univ. of Pennsylvania Press, 1986. Pp. xvi +205. $26.95. ISBN 0-8122-7885-2.

Fielding, Henry. *The History of Our Own Times*. (Facsimile.) Notes by Thomas Lockwood. Delmar, N.Y.: Scholar's Fascimiles and Reprints, 1986. Pp. 69+122. ISBN 0-8201-1409-X.

Fielding, Henry, *An Institute of the Pleas of the Crown*. Ed. Hugh Amory. Cambridge, Mass.: Houghton Library, 1987. Pp. 30. ISBN 0-914630-02-4.

Flynn, Elizabeth A., and Schweickart, Patrocinio P., eds. *Gender and Reading: Essays on Readers, Texts and Contexts*. Baltimore and London: Johns Hopkins Univ. Press, 1986. Pp. xxx +306. $27.00 cloth. $10.95 paper. ISBN 0-8018-2907-0.

Goldsmith, M. M. *Private Vices, Public Benefits: Bernard Mandeville's Social Thought*. Cambridge and New York: Cambridge Univ. Press, 1985. Pp. x + 183. $29.95. ISBN 0-521-30036-3.

Griffin, Dustin. *Regaining Paradise: Milton and the Eighteenth Century*. Cambridge and New York: Cambridge Univ. Press, 1986. Pp. xi +299. $29.95. ISBN 0-521-30913-1.

Griswold, Wendy. *Renaissance Revivals: City Comedy and Revenge Tragedy in the London Theatre, 1576-1980*. Chicago and London: Univ. of Chicago Press, 1986. Pp. xviii +288. $24.95. ISBN 0-226-30923-1.

Grundy, Isobel. *Samuel Johnson and the Scale of Greatness*. Athens: Univ. of Georgia Press, 1986. Pp. viii +278. $30.00. ISBN 0-8203-0867-6.

Hammond, Brean S. *Pope*. Atlantic Highlands, N. J. : Humanities Press, 1986. Pp. xi +218. $25.00. ISBN 0-391-03421-9.

Harp, Richard L., ed. *Dr. Johnson's Critical Vocabulary: A Selection from His Dictionary*. Lanham and London: Univ. Press of America, 1986. Pp. xlv +268. $15.75. ISBN 0-8191-5473-3.

[Haywood, Eliza.] *Bath Intrigues: In Four Letters to a Friend in London*. Augustan Reprint Society no. 236. Intro. Simon Varey. Los Angeles: Williams Andrews Clark Memorial Library, Univ. of California, 1986. Pp. x +51.

Hemlow, Joyce. *The History Of Fanny Burney*. Oxford: Clarendon Press, 1986. Pp. xvi +528. $39.95. ISBN 0-19-811549-0.

Hill, Bridget, ed. *The First English Feminist: "Reflections Upon Marriage" and Other Writings by Mary Astell*. New York: St. Martin's Press, 1986. Pp. vii +235. $29.95. ISBN 0-312-29232-5.

Hopkins, David. *John Dryden*. Cambridge and New York: Cambridge Univ. Press, 1986. Pp. viii +216. $39.50 cloth. ISBN 0-521-30901-X. $13.95 paper. ISBN 0-521-31379-1.

Ingram, Allan. *Intricate Laughter in the Satire of Swift and Pope*. New York: St. Martin's Press, 1986. Pp. x +206. $25.00. ISBN 0-312-42540-6.

Jordanova, Ludmilla, ed. *Languages of Nature: Critical Essays on Science and Literature*. New Brunswick: Rutgers Univ. Press, 1986. Pp. 351. $30.00. ISBN 0-8135-1194-1.

Kaminski, Thomas. *The Early Career of Samuel Johnson*. Oxford and New York: Oxford Univ. Press, 1987. Pp. ix +268. $24.96. ISBN 0-19-504114-3.

Kauffman, Linda S. *Discourses of Desire: Gender, Genre and Epistolary Fictions*. Ithaca and London: Cornell Univ. Press, 1986. Pp. 331. $24.95. ISBN 0-8014-1853-4.

Kenshur, Oscar. *Open Form and the Shape of Ideas: Literary Structures as Representations of Philosophical Concepts in the Seventeenth and Eighteenth Centuries*. Cranbury: Bucknell Univ. Press, 1986. Pp. 140. $23.50. ISBN 0-8387-5081-8.

Kernan, Alvin. *Printing Technology, Letters and Samuel Johnson*. Princeton : Princeton Univ. Press, 1987. Pp. 357. $29.50. ISBN 0-691-06692-2.

King, James. *William Cowper: A Biography*. Durham: Duke Univ. Press, 1986. Pp. xiii +340. $35.00. ISBN 0-8223-0513-5.

Korshin, Paul J. *The American Revolution and Eighteenth-Century Culture*. New York: AMS Press, 1986. Pp. xiv +271. $39.50. ISBN 0-404-61471-X.

Korshin, Paul J., ed. *Johnson After Two Hundred Years*. Philadelphia: Univ. of Pennsylvania Press, 1986. Pp. xix +253. $35.00. IBSN 0-8122-8016-4.

Kupersmith, William. *Roman Satirists in Seventeenth-Century England*. Lincoln: Univ. of Nebraska Press, 1985. Pp. xii +193. $19.95. ISBN 0-8032-2710-8.

Land, Stephen K. *The Philosophy of Language in Britain: Major Theories from Hobbes to Thomas Reid*. New York: AMS Press, 1986. Pp. vii +255. $37.50. ISBN 0-404-61722-0.

Leites, Edward. *The Puritan Conscience and Modern Sexuality.* New Haven and London: Yale Univ. Press, 1986. Pp. xi +196. $17.50. ISBN 0-300-03490-3.

Lennox, Charlotte. *The Female Quixote.* London and Boston: Pandora Press, 1986. Pp. xv +423. $7.95. ISBN 0-86358-080-7.

Levine, Joseph M. *Humanism and History: Origins of Modern English Historiography.* Ithaca and London: Cornell Univ. Press, 1987. Pp. 297. $29.95. ISBN 0-8014-1885-2.

Lonsdale, Roger, ed. *Thomas Gray and William Collins: Poetical Works.* Oxford and New York: Oxford Univ. Press, 1986. Pp. xxiii +232. $13.50, ISBN 0-19-281169-X.

Lynch, James J. *Henry Fielding and the Heliodoran Novel: Romance, Epic, and Fielding's New Province of Writing.* Rutherford: Fairleigh Dickenson Univ. Press, and London and Toronto: Associated Univ. Presses, 1986. Pp. 128. $19.50. ISBN 0-8386-3268-8.

Marks, Sylvia Kasey. *Sir Charles Grandison: The Compleat Conduct Book.* Lewisburg: Bucknell Univ. Press, and London and Toronto: Associated Univ. Presses, 1986. Pp. 173. $27.50. ISBN 0-8387-5090-7.

Marshall, David. *The Figure of Theater: Shaftesbury, Defoe, Adam Smith, and George Eliot.* New York: Columbia Univ. Press, 1986. Pp. 269. $27.00. ISBN 0-231-06084-X.

McHenry, Robert W., Jr., ed. *Absalom and Achitophel.* Hamden: Archon Books, 1986. Pp. xiv +283. $29.50. ISBN 0-208-01845-X.

McKeon, Michael. *The Origins of the English Novel, 1600-1740.* Baltimore : Johns Hopkins Univ. Press, 1987. Pp. xi +529. $29.95. ISBN 0-8018-3291-8.

McIntosh, Carey. *Common and Courtly Language: The Stylistics of Social Class in 18th-Century Literature.* Philadelphia: Univ. of Pennsylvania Press, 1986. Pp. vii +167. $20.00. ISBN 0-8122-7998-0.

Meehan, Michael. *Liberty and Poetics in Eighteenth Century England.* London and Dover: Croom Helm, 1986. Pp. 190. $31.00. ISBN 0-7099-4623-6.

Messenger, Ann. *His and Hers: Essays in Restoration and Eighteenth Century Literature.* Lexington: Univ. Press of Kentucky, 1986. Pp. ix +271. $26.00. ISBN 0-8131-1575-2.

Mitchell, W. J. T. *Iconology: Image, Text, Ideology.* Chicago: Univ. of Chicago Press, 1986. Pp. x +226. $20.00. ISBN 0-226-53228-3.

Myer, Valerie Grosvenor, ed. *Samuel Richardson: Passion and Prudence.* Totowa, N. J. : Barnes and Noble, 1986. Pp. 184. $28.50. ISBN 0-389-20650-4.

Myers, William, ed. *Restoration and Revolution.* London and Dover: Croom Helm, 1986. Pp. 248. $20.50. ISBN 0-7099-3558-7.

Neubauer, John. *The Emancipation of Music from Language: Departure from Mimesis in Eighteenth-Century Aesthetics.* New Haven and London: Yale Univ. Press, 1986. Pp. ix +249. $21.50. ISBN 0-300-03577-2.

Paley, Morton D. *The Apocalyptic Sublime.* New Haven and London: Yale Univ. Press, 1986. Pp. xii +196. $35.00. ISBN 0-300-03674-4.

Patey, Douglas Lane, and Keegan, Timothy, eds. *Augustan Studies: Essays in*

Honor of Irvin Ehrenpreis. Newark: Univ. of Delaware Press, 1985. Pp. 270. $35.00. ISBN 0-87413-272-X.

Perry, Ruth. *The Celebrated Mary Astell: An Early English Feminist.* Chicago and London: Univ. of Chicago Press, 1986. Pp. xiv +549. $45.00 cloth, ISBN 0-226-66093-1. $19.95 paper, ISBN 0-226-66095-8.

Person, James E., Jr., ed. *Literature Criticism from 1400 to 1800.* Detroit: Gale Research, 1986. Pp. 567. $85.00. ISBN 0-8103-6103-5.

Pope, Alexander. *The Prose Works*, vol 2. Ed. Rosemary Cowler. Hamden : Archon Books, and Oxford: Basil Blackwell, 1986. Pp. xv +529. $47.50. ISBN 0-208-02059-4.

Real, Hermann J., and Vienken, Heinz J., eds. *The Proceedings of the First Münster Symposium on Jonathan Swift.* Munich: Wilhelm Fink, 1985. Pp. 396. DM 98,00. ISBN 3-7705-2300-8.

Redford, Bruce. *The Converse of the Pen: Acts of Intimacy in the Eighteenth-Century Familiar Letter.* Chicago and London: Univ. of Chicago Press, 1986. Pp. ix +252. $11.95. ISBN 0-226-70679-6.

Redford Bruce, ed. *The Origins of "The School for Scandal": "The Slanderers" and "Sir Peter Teazle."* Princeton: Princeton Univ. Library, 1986. Pp. 168, 72 plates. $30.00. ISBN 0-87811-027-5.

Richardson, Samuel. *Clarissa, or, The History of a Young Lady.* Ed. Angus Ross. Harmondsworth, Middlesex: Penguin Books, 1985. Pp. 1533. $12.95. ISBN 0-14-043215-9.

Rogers, Deborah D. *Bookseller as Rogue: John Almon and the Politics of Eighteenth-Century Publishing.* American Univ. Studies: Series 4, English Language and Literature, vol. 28. Berne and New York: Peter Lang, 1986. Pp. xviii +151. ISBN 0-8024-0221-4.

Roosen, William. *Daniel Defoe and Diplomacy.* Selinsgrove, Pa.: Susquehana Univ. Press, and London and Toronto: Associated Univ. Presses, 1986. Pp. 144. $23.50. ISBN 0-941-664-12-0.

Roussel, Roy. *The Conversation of the Sexes: Seduction and Equality in Selected Seventeenth- and Eighteenth-Century Texts.* New York and Oxford: Oxford Univ. Press, 1986. Pp. 178. $15.95. ISBN 0-19-503659-X.

Schofield, Mary Anne, and Macheski, Cecilia. *Fetter'd or Free? British Women Novelists, 1670-1815.* Athens and London: Ohio Univ. Press, 1986. Pp. xvii +441. $38.50. ISBN 0-8214-0799-6.

Schulz Max F. *Paradise Preserved: Recreations of Eden in Eighteenth- and Nineteenth-Century England.* Cambridge: Cambridge Univ. Press, 1986. Pp. xv +368. $39.50. ISBN 0-521-30173-4.

Scott, Sarah. *Millenium Hall.* New York: Viking Penguin, 1986. Pp. xvi +207. $6.95. ISBN 0-14-016-135-X.

See and Seem Blind: Or, a Critical Dissertation on the Publick Diversions, &c. [1732]. Intro. Robert D. Hume. Los Angeles: William Andrews Clark Memorial Library, Univ. of California, 1986. Pp. xii +30.

Sena, John F. *The Best-Natured Man: Sir Samuel Garth, Physician and Poet.* New York: AMS Press, 1986. Pp. xii +215. $34.50. ISBN 0-404-61475-2.

Seidel, Michael. *Exile and the Narrative Imagination*. New Haven and London: Yale Univ. Press, 1986. Pp. xiv +234. $18.50. ISBN 0-300-03498-9.

Simpson, K. G., ed. *Henry Fielding: Justice Observed*. Totowa, N. J. Barnes and Noble, 1985. Pp. 205. $28.50. ISBN 0-389-20591-5.

Smyth, John Vignaux. *A Question of Eros: Irony in Sterne, Kierkegaard and Postmodernism*. Tallahassee and Gainesville: Univ. Presses of Florida, 1986. Pp. xv +415. $29.95. ISBN 0-8130-0834-4.

Spencer, Jane. *The Rise of the Woman Novelist: From Aphra Behn to Jane Austen*. Oxford and New York: Basil Blackwell, 1986. Pp. xii +225. $14.95. ISBN 0-631-13916-8.

Spender, Dale. *Mothers of the Novel : 100 Good Women Writers Before Jane Austen*. London and New York: Pandora, 1986. Pp. x +357. $25.00. ISBN 0-86358-081-5.

Stallybrass, Peter, and White, Allon. *The Politics and Poetics of Transgression*. Ithaca : Cornell Univ. 1986. Pp. ix +228. $29.95 cloth, ISBN 0-8014-1893-3. $12.95 paper, ISBN 0-8014-9382-X.

Studies in Eighteenth-Century Culture 16. Ed. Brack, 0 M, Jr. Madison: Univ. of Wisconsin Press, 1986. Pp. ix +309. $25.00. ISBN 0-299-10940-2.

Styan, J. L. *Restoration Comedy in Performance*. Cambridge and New York: Cambridge Univ. Press, 1986. Pp. xiv +271. $39.50 cloth, ISBN 521-25405-1. $12.95 paper, ISBN 0-521-27421-4.

Sutherland, James. *The Restoration Newspaper and its Development*. Cambridge and New York: Cambridge Univ. Press, 1986. Pp. ix +262. $39.50. ISBN 0-521-32613-3.

Swift, Temple and the Du Cros Affair. Intro. David L. T. Wooley. Los Angeles: William Andrews Clark Memorial Library, Univ. of California, 1986. Pp. xvii +72.

Todd, Janet. *Sensibility: An Introduction*. London and New York: Metheun, 1986. Pp. 169. $27.50 cloth, ISBN 0-416-37710-6. $9.95 paper, ISBN 0-416-37720-3.

Turner, Thomas. *The Diary of Thomas Turner, 1754-1765*. Ed. David Vaisey. New York: Oxford Univ. Press, 1985. Pp. xxxix +386. $8.95. ISBN 0-19-281899-6.

Varey, Simon. *Henry Fielding*. Cambridge and New York: Cambridge Univ. Press, 1986. Pp. x +153. $34.50 cloth. ISBN 0-521-26244-5. $11.95. paper. ISBN 0-521-27876-7.

Wahba, Magdi. *Samuel Johnson: Commemorative Lectures Delivered at Pembroke College, Oxford*. Beirut: Librarie de Liban and Longman, 1986. Pp. 78.

Wagner, Peter. *Lust & Liebe in Rokoko (Lust and Love in the Rococo Period)*. Norlingen: Greno Verlag, 1986. Pp. 238. DM 48,00. ISBN 3-89190-607-2.

Wasserman, George. *Samuel Butler and the Earl of Rochester: A Reference Guide*. Boston: G.K. Hall, 1986. Pp. xx +176. $45.00. ISBN 0-8161-8625-1.

Weber, Harold. *The Restoration Rake-Hero: Transformations in Sexual Understanding in Seventeenth-Century England*. Madison: Univ. of

Wisconsin Press, 1986. Pp. x +253. $27.50. ISBN 0-299-10690-X.

Wind, Edgar. *Hume and the Heroic Portrait: Studies in Eighteenth-Century Imagery*. Ed. Jaynie Anderson. Oxford and New York: Oxford Univ. Press, 1986. Pp. xv +139, 124 plates. $62.00. ISBN 0-19-817371-7.

Wood, Nigel. *Swift*. Atlantic Highlands, N.J. : Humanities Press, 1986. Pp. xiv +153. $25.50. ISBN 0-391-03416-2.

Zimbardo, Rose A. *A Mirror to Nature: Transformations in Drama and Aesthetics 1660-1732*. Lexington: Univ. Press of Kentucky, 1986. Pp. viii +248. $25.00. ISBN 0-8131-1590-6.

SEL

Studies in ENGLISH LITERATURE 1500-1900

The Nineteenth Century

VOLUME 27 AUTUMN 1987 NUMBER 4

Studies in English Literature
1500 - 1900

VOLUME 27 AUTUMN 1987 NUMBER 4

PUBLISHED BY RICE UNIVERSITY

CONTENTS

Blake's Antifoundationalist Poetics — Karen Shabetai — 555

The May-Day Celebration in Wordsworth's Immortality Ode — Clarence H. Miller — 571

"Sport of Transmutations": The Evolution of Wordsworth's "To Lycoris" — Douglass H. Thomson — 581

Personal Identity in *Mansfield Park*: Forms, Fictions, Role-Play, and Reality — C. Knatchbull Bevan — 595

Lionel Trilling and *Mansfield Park* — Paul Pickrel — 609

Tennyson's "The Epic": An Experiment in Perspective — Mary Ann Klein — 623

"A Yorkshire burr": Language in *Shirley* — Susan Belasco Smith — 637

Trollope and James: The "Germ" Within — Henry N. Rogers III — 647

On Heroes and Their Demise: Critical Liberalism in *Beauchamp's Career* — Gary Handwerk — 663

Recent Studies in the Nineteenth Century — Peter J. and Sylvia Manning — 683

Studies in English Literature
1500 - 1900

PUBLISHED BY RICE UNIVERSITY

Studies in English Literature is a quarterly journal of historical and critical studies. Each issue will be devoted to one of four fields:

WINTER: The English Renaissance
SPRING: Elizabethan and Jacobean Drama
SUMMER: Restoration and Eighteenth Century
AUTUMN: The Nineteenth Century

SEL: Studies in English Literature, 1500–1900 (ISSN: 0039-3657) is published quarterly (February, May, August, and November) at $15.00 per year for individuals, $20.00 per year for U.S. institutions, $25.00 per year for foreign institutions, and $6.00 per single issue, by Rice University, 6100 South Main Street, P.O. Box 1892, Houston, Texas 77251. Second-class postage paid at Houston, Texas. **Postmaster:** Send address changes to the Business Manager, *SEL,* Rice University, P.O. Box 1892, Houston, TX 77251.

Studies in English Literature invites historical and critical essays of moderate length (ten to twenty-five pages) that contribute significantly to the understanding of English Literature, 1500-1900. Typescripts should be double-spaced throughout and prepared in conformity with the Chicago Manual of Style. Clean photocopy on uncoated paper is acceptable in place of the ribbon copy. We will not consider articles being simultaneously submitted elsewhere, nor will we print essays to appear in a book published within a year of scheduled publication of *SEL*. Those wishing to omit their identities from manuscripts may do so, but should include a covering letter.

Manuscripts submitted for publication should be addressed to the Editor, *Studies in English Literature,* Rice University, P.O. Box 1892, Houston, TX 77251. They must be accompanied by a sufficient number of unattached stamps for return. Receipt of manuscripts will be acknowledged by postcard. Editorial decisions usually take a minimum of three months.

Annual subscription rates: $15.00 for individuals, $20.00 for U. S. institutions, $25.00 for foreign institutions, $6.00 per issue for partial subscriptions and single copies. Regular subscriptions may be obtained for any or all quarterly issues. Remittance should accompany subscription requests. Notice of non-receipt of an issue must be made within ninety (90) days following the publication of that issue. No refunds or cancellations. Business communications should be addressed to Business Manager, *Studies in English Literature,* Rice University, P. O. Box 1892, Houston, TX 77251.

Microfilms of previous volumes (Vols. 1-26) may be obtained from University Microfilms, Inc., 300 N. Zeeb Road, Ann Arbor, Michigan 48106; xerox copies of individual articles may be ordered by calling (800) 521-0600 (toll free). Copies of articles are also available from ISI's The Genuine Article service, 3501 Market Street, Philadelphia, PA 19104; phone (800) 523-1850; telex 84-5305; electronic mail through CLASS; or facsimile transmission via FAXPAX.

Volumes 1 through 3 and 5 through 10 of *Studies in English Literature* are available from Johnson Reprint Corporation, 111 Fifth Avenue, New York, N. Y. 10003, or Berkeley Square House, London W. 1, England.

SEL 27 (1987)
ISSN 0039-3657

Blake's Antifoundationalist Poetics

KAREN SHABETAI

"Platonic Philosophy . . . blinds the Eye of Imagination The Real Man"[1]

Recent debates about the uses of theory imply that such inquiries raise new questions about interpretation, questions that, though enriched by analytic philosophy, are the special domain of literary criticism.[2] The participants in the debate appear to share a faith in the currently popular antifoundationalist position, a position that is, in part, a product of the recent discussions challenging the prominence of foundationalist epistemology in philosophical tradition: the project to provide self-certifying, or indubitable foundations for inquiry.[3] Antifoundationalism claims that such foundations cannot exist, or if they were to we would have no direct cognitive access to them. Antifoundationalists question the notion of grounded truth; they reject such notions as Plato's Forms, Descartes's *Cogito* and Kant's thing-in-itself—all of which depend on outside foundations. Most important, I think, is antifoundationalism's recognition that there is no outside space, some neutral ground from which to offer interpretation.[4]

Something like a pragmatic or an antifoundationalist position has appealed to thinkers who have had to contend with a philosophical tradition that searches for "an all-embracing ahistorical context" by which to understand the world.[5] Certain of Blake's positions anticipate those of the traditional, as well as the "new," pragmatists, because like them he was responding to a philosophical tradition that was at an epistemological impasse. He shares certain affinities with the antifoundationalists and especially with Richard Rorty because he saw the problem of the Platonic tradition as epistemological; Blake's approach is similar to Rorty's but also superior

Karen Shabetai, who teaches English literature and writing at the University of Washington, is working on a book on philosophical contexts of Blake and Keats.

to it because Blake avoids Rorty's relativism by appealing to internal standards of critical evaluation. Charles Taylor argues for the value of "recovering previous articulations" of a philosophical position in order to achieve "successful articulation" and "an adequate understanding of" that position;[6] Blake's anti-foundationalism can be viewed as an illuminating formulation of the current problem in theoretical discourse; an examination of his articulation can elucidate the positions in the current debate and offer a reply to the charge about the negativity of such a position.[7]

Blake's attacks on Platonism, then, situate him in a tradition that has culminated in recent years in the various antifoundationalist movements in philosophy and literary theory. These movements, according to Rorty, "deny that there are foundations to serve as common ground for adjudicating knowledge-claims."[8] It would appear, though, that Blake exposes the inadequacies of his foundationalist predecessors only to promote his belief in creative imagination. Blake, in the end, may not appear to be an antifoundationationalist; he would urge that there is knowledge with "special status," and he believed in certain unchanging Truths: "Error is Created Truth is Eternal" ("A Vision of the Last Judgment," p. 565). I would argue, however, that all antifoundationalists are in the end foundationalists of sorts; antifoundationalism can hardly be a consistent stance. Still "antifoundationalists" depend on fewer foundations or on shifting ones; the Creative Imatination in which Blake has faith is a faculty that depends on contexts and particulars. Blake asserts in "A Vision of the Last Judgment," "This world of Imagination is the World of Eternity," and although "The Nature of Visionary Fancy or Imagination . . . & the Eternal nature & permanence of its ever Existent Images" "is very little Known," its source is "contemplative Thought" (p. 555). In other words, although Blake believed in "Eternal Things" (p. 561, he complicates their foundationalist status by making their source human; that which depends on human thought cannot be eternal in the Platonic sense.

Blake explicitly sought knowledge that modern antifoundationalists reject, but he held that the way to that knowledge required abandoning foundations. He always, despite his belief in truth, remained alert to the hazards of a foundationalist position. An episode in *Jerusalem* which involves the misuse of a foundationalist position illustrates this point. In Chapter 2 Albion constructs a perspective from which to "punish[ ] & judge." He has made "his secret seat" out of the "hills & valleys" that, because they "are accursed witnesses of Sin," he has "condense[d] into solid rocks, stedfast! A foundation and certainty and demonstrative truth." From his firm seat he sacrifices his sons to "Justice" and "Truth" (p. 174). These are not the truth and justice in which Blake had faith, but perversions of these principles, a consequence of Albion's "solid" perspective. Los, in Chapter 4, contends that "General Forms have their vitality in Particulars"; he calls for the organization of "Minute Particulars" (p. 251). Acts of creative genius or imagination allow the organization of the world into contraries, and the dialectical force of contrariety allows the progress called for in *The Marriage of Heaven and Hell.*[9] These notions resemble foundationalism (as the upper case letters suggest), but Blake's insistence on action and particularity evince an effort to avoid such a position: "Active Evil is better than Passive Good" (p. 592).

Blake's example illustrates that the consequences of antifoundationalism need not be as threatening as the tone of the current debate suggests; almost two hundred years ago, Blake was confronting a similar set of philosophical problems, but he concluded that one could indeed make *use* of what was essentially an antifoundationalist position, that what for him functioned as a theory could govern a reading of the philosophical tradition with which he was contending. I am claiming then that Blake should not merely be situated within a tradition that is manifest in the current debate, but that a proper appreciation of Blake's subtlety could actually change the terms of that debate. Blake shows that antifoundationalism need not lead to relativism, as it seems to in Rorty. What is highly distinctive about Blake's position is that it overcomes what Skinner calls the "foundationalist urges of epistemology" while maintaining its confidence in discovering principles of knowledge (*Return of Grand Theory*, p. 51).

Blake's attack on antinomies is at once pragmatic and anticipatory of deconstruction. Rorty recognizes the natural alliance of Pragmatists and Derrideans, but he questions the usefulness of either position: "there is no natural priority of one strategy over the other . . . if we ever did get rid of all the jargon of the tradition, we should not even be able to state the realist's position, much less argue against it."[10] And Derrida's self-critique preempts the charge of his critics that *his* practice could "always in a certain way [fall] prey to its own work."[11] The priority may not be "natural," but one need not conclude then that there is no priority at all. I would agree with Habermas that Derrida's stance is irresponsible.[12] To my mind, what is wrong with the projects of the various antifoundationalists is their inability to state a positive position, a weakness that Blake doesn't share. When a positive position is detected in an antifoundationalist, a charge of inconsistency follows. As David Hoy notes in a discussion of Derrida and "Grand Theory," Derrida shows that "in the absence of a clear alternative to the grand tradition and its eternal problems, theories that supposedly avoid metaphysics tend to remain trapped in the old vocabulary and dilemmas" (p. 45). Whether or not by intention, antifoundationalists offer theories that end up being grand theories in their own right.[13] I would argue that this charge is not a negative one. Antifoundationalism has been used mainly as a negative stance, by its critics as well as its advocates; Blake achieves a positive stance through antifoundationalist means. As I note above, Blake's discussion about the "Nature" of "Creative Imagination" in "A Vision of The Last Judgment" turns into a discussion about "Eternal Things." He uses Platonic language to refute Plato; the source of those Things Eternal is "Contemplative Thought and Divine Humanity."

Derrida's language of destruction is characteristic of the various programs of deconstruction as well as other antifoundationalist "theoretical discourses."[14] His early remarks on his enterprise acknowledge his purpose: "The movements of deconstruction do not destroy structures from the outside. They are not possible and effective, nor can they take accurate aim, except by inhabiting those structures" (*Of Grammatology*, p. 24). But if indeed the aim is accurate and we get rid of these structures (that such discourses tell us weren't supported by any "real" foundation anyway), what are we left with? Blake anticipates Donald Davidson's commonsensical solution; Davidson holds that a philosophical attack depends on underlying agreement about basic beliefs. According to Davidson, this is a *sine qua non* of philosophical discourse: "without a vast common ground, there is no place for disputants to have their quarrel." "Much mutuality" is necessary for agreement as well as disagreement.[15] Blake offers a possible model for a productive quarrel with the authority of foundationalism, one that doesn't proceed from deconstruction to relativism. For instance, when he attacks an antinomic philosophical system, he does so from the "inside"; but when he turns negations into contraries, he is making use of the system—it is not destroyed, but "re-presented." He challenges the fixed dogmas of philosophy that produce negations and calls for contraries that are supported not by a claim for some outside authority but by the very "difference" between their elements; the tension between contraries constitutes their power.

Foucault speaks of the necessary relationship between power and "freedom's refusal to submit" as one of "permanent provocation."[16] This notion of power reveals how the *non-positions* of antifoundationalism can be practices that work as positions. By this I mean that it is the tension of power relationships that functions *as* a position, though of course the position is not grounded in anything at all and is constantly shifting with the dynamics of the power relationship. In Blake, this would be the relations of power in contraries. Foucault has emphasized the reversibility and the potential instability of power relations. This is the notion of power behind Blake's contraries; they both incorporate the weapons of deconstruction and go beyond them. Contrariety attacks the authority of a supposedly architectonic and all-inclusive position using a method that is both diacritical and "sense-making": "without contraries is no progress," Blake insisted. His method reveals the role of the diacritical in allowing progress, at the same time as exposing the dangers of a position of authority as the congealed, mystified projection of a single perspective masquerading as totality. He rejects the authority that philosophical systems have awarded certain antinomies by challenging the notion that there can exist such a privileged position from which to assign such authority. "With youthful audacity," Bataille observes, "the poet confronted every antinomy."[17] His system governs thought at the level of particulars, not generalizations; Blake provides an answer to the hostility that antifoundationalism provokes by justifying certain aspects of it, and by illustrating that contrariety allows progress. In Blake's words, "General Knowledge is Remote Knowledge it is in Particulars that Wisdom consists & Happiness too" (p. 560).

Blake's (non-) position is his system of contraries, a system that depends on tension and "permanent provocation" (to use Foucault's language, p. 790) between its elements. He will not use traditional antinomies because (as Derrida will make clear) opposing one notion to another results in a relationship of domination. Blake sought, as Foucault did more recently, to avoid fixed positions in order to avoid the consequences of the antinomic relationship. His system of contraries was a direct response to what he saw as the tyranny of such a relationship. The provocation gives the system power that isn't based on authority: such power, according to Foucault, assumes mutuality (though perhaps never stable or equal); whereas authority requires a fixed position. In other words, authority is power which is justified; antifoundationalists attack the authority of external justification itself. Blake's system of contraries doesn't depend on external justification—contraries aren't grounded at all. The contraries resemble a system but are antisystematic in that they can constantly shift—they are contextually determined: "things are good or bad according to circumstances."[18] For instance, as W. J. T. Mitchell illustrates, the devil is favored over the angel in that set of contraries in *The Marriage* "because he sees the history of his culture as the deification of the angelic virtues of rational passivity and self-restraint."[19] In Chapter 1 of *Jerusalem*, Blake describes how contraries are turned into negations:

> They take Two Contraries which are calld Qualities, with which
> Every Substance is clothed, they name them Good & Evil
> From them they make an Abstract, which is a Negation
> Not only of the Substance from which it is derived
> A murderer of its own Body: but also a murderer
> Of every Divine Member: it is the Reasoning Power.
> (pp. 152-53)

When contraries are decontextualized (made into abstractions), they become negations; negations destroy any chance of progress because they are not relational—they preclude activity, or the play of contrariety. But the antifoundationalist quality of contrariety that is disturbing is its seeming relativism; how can a system governed by context, that allows no inherent priorities, be used as a system of value? Blake's solution to this problem can be illuminated by a consideration of such issues in current philosophical debate.

Antifoundationalist theoretical discourse has evoked hostility principally because, it seems, it can have no "use"—how can a "non-position" constitute a position? Most antifoundationalists don't mind such a charge; Rorty does mind, though he finds no solution. Davidson views such a realization as liberating. In an essay on the usefulness of conceptual schemes, he urges that we abandon our faith in them, but that in so doing we would not be giving up the "notion of objective truth." He persuasively argues that we cannot know or use some "space" outside the "world," some "uninterpreted reality," a notion of a conceptual scheme—one that, it seems, would fit Knapp and Michaels's narrow definition of "theory" (Knapp and Michaels, p. 11). But unlike Knapp and Michaels, Davidson urges that giving up such a notion is merely relinquishing a dogma, and not "relinquishing objective truth."[20]

Blake constructs texts using principles of interpretation very much in keeping with Davidson's position; his success (though it usually isn't complete) depends on a conscious destruction of positions of authority, and the "non-position" that remains can be "used." I am not making a claim that Blake could be said to have had a theory (according to Knapp and Michaels's definition)—something outside historical contexts—a notion that analytic philosophers as well as Knapp and Michaels have, I think, convincingly shown to be meaningless; rather, though he was concerned with language and interpretation in strikingly modern ways, he never seemed to wish to step outside his own system of belief, or to appeal "to an account of interpretation in general" (Knapp and Michaels, p. 11). Blake's position anticipates what Rorty calls "the recent purifying move from talk of ideas to talk of meanings," which, he claims, "dissipated the epistemological skepticism which motivated much of past philosophy."[21] Though he borrowed arguments from the empiricists to construct his epistemology, he could not accept their conclusions, as he makes clear in his early philosophical works. In *There is No Natural Religion*, he remarks: "Mans perceptions are not bounded by organs of perception. he percieves more than sense (tho' ever so acute) can discover" (p. 2). In *ALL RELIGIONS are ONE*, he acknowledges the power of desire and what he calls "Poetic Genius" to account for knowledge and experience that empiricism, which depends on "the confined nature of bodily sensation," cannot accommodate (p. 1).[22] His position, finally, combines premises from opposing philosophical traditions; though he holds that there is unchanging "Truth," he suspends his commitment to the grounding of knowledge when he creates his system of contraries which, with their contextual shifting, preclude the need for external justification.

Blake's purpose resembles the "new Pragmatists' " in certain important ways, especially in his distrust of Western metaphysics and his rejection of externally justified systems of authority. Rorty, speaking for the pragmatists, calls for a "narrative philosophy," which should not "degenerate into inquiry" (*Philosophy and the Mirror of Nature*, p. 372). Both recognize that they cannot (and do not wish to) answer questions asked by what Rorty calls Philosophy, the inquiry into the nature of such "normative notions" as "Truth," "Rationality" and "Goodness" "in the hope of better obeying such norms." Derrida celebrates the power of play he discovers in his nonposition, and Rorty is happy enough to dispense with such questions as "What is the meaning of a text?" and "How do you know?" Hoy describes the movement away from epistemology to a kind of hermeneutics as an attempt to reject "the idea that the primary task of philosophy is to supply foundations and guarantee certainty" (p. 51). Rather, Rorty urges, philosophers should participate in "conversations," and abandon, as Derrida too demands, their faith in the Platonic tradition. Blake wanted something more than such conversations; he hoped for productive discourse: "The

Four Living Creatures Chariots of Humanity Divine," at the end of *Jerusalem*, "conversed together in Visionary forms dramatic which bright / Redounded from their Tongues in thunderous majesty" (p. 257). For such an end, a "deconstruction" of the Platonic tradition was necessary, though of course Blake's program of action had to consist of a different vocabulary: in Jerusalem, Los "built the stubborn structure of language" (p. 183) which, at the end of the poem, culminates in "thunderous" discourse (pp. 257-58).

Blake's solution to the problem of Plato, or to the problem of Western philosophy as he perceived it, was to construct a poetic system that would depend for its authority on shifting contexts, on the creative perception of the subject (subjects in his poems, his readers as well as himself). Blake's critics generally agree that his work will not often allow the reader a position of authority from which to seek meaning. This feature of Blake's approach appears in various aspects of his work: many of his lyrical poems insist on ambiguity as part of their "meaning" (a stance similar to Davidson's Wittgensteinian critique of meaning as an intrinsic property or essence to be discovered as opposed to being part of the whole speech practice[23]); central passages in the prophecies will not allow a character a firm place from which to view a situation; an underlying principle of the longer prophecies is a resistance to linear narrative structures.

Such features of his work are in part a consequence of his emphasis on creative perception. Theories of perception are central to Romantic poetry in general, but Blake's radical rejection of the external world, which for him must include authoritative systems, makes his particular theory exceptional. Earl R. Wasserman, in an essay on the epistemology of the English Romantics, finds Wordsworth's, Coleridge's, Keats's, and Shelley's concern to discover a "meaningful relationship" between "subject and object" to be a response to the eighteenth century's "revolutionary epistemological speculation."[24] Wasserman understands this concern as particularly Romantic. Blake, however, while contending with the same philosophical issues as the other Romantics, rejected such attempts by his contemporaries, as he makes clear in his attack on Wordsworth's propositions about the intimate relationship between mind and nature. What other English Romantic poet denies the positive (at least potentially positive) influences of nature? ("Natural Objects always did & now do Weaken deaden & obliterate Imagination in Me Wordsworth must know that what he Writes Valuable is Not to be found in Nature," Blake responds to Wordsworth's comments about the good effects of nature on imagination [p. 665].) While Blake's emphasis on psychology in his theory of perception reveals his eighteenth-century preoccupations, it also reveals his need to find an exclusively internal source of stimuli. While the mind and imagination are central to all the Romantics, Blake has to make them everything: "One Power alone makes a Poet.—Imagination The Divine Vision," he asserts in his annotations to Wordsworth's *Poems* (p. 665).

Blake's rejection of the outside world resembles what Rorty calls Derrida's creation of "a new thing for writing to be about." Derrida writes about "not the world, but texts," as if our only standpoint of appraisal were a correspondence of internal representations and external presence. Derrida claims, according to Rorty, that "we should stop trying to test texts for accuracy of representation."[25] Derrida also questions, as Hoy demonstrates, "philosophical belief in immediate, indubitable features of mental life like ideas or sense data, intentions or perceptions" (p. 52). Blake makes the "mental life" central, but he makes its ruling feature imagination; to make way for the imagination and its creative capacity, Blake denies an objective external world: "Where is the Existence Out of Mind or Thought Where is it but in the Mind of a Fool" ("A Vision of the Last Judgment," p. 565).

His rejection of the outside world (with the retention of the importance of sense impressions) is a move that combines features of Locke's, Berkeley's, and Hume's epistemologies; he emphasizes the importance of experience, sense perceptions, and imagination as a creative faculty. Despite Blake's debts to these philosophers, he has no kind words for them. While he would applaud Hume's demonstration of the inadequacy of reason to explain our belief in the outside world, he likewise had to deal with the problem of skepticism that such a displacement of reason sanctioned. Kant, who had to deal with the same philosophical situation, sought foundations in order to characterize knowledge in terms of certainty rather than understanding. Blake was perhaps motivated by the same fear of skepticism, but he followed a different path; he finds the source of our belief in the outside world to be independent of the understanding, and like Hume he attributed the source to the imagination, for Blake "creative" imagination. If the imagination is creative, a belief in an independent external world loses meaning: "I assert for My self that I do not behold the Outward Creation & that to me it is Hindrance & not Action it is as the Dirt upon my feet No part of Me" ("A Vision of the Last Judgment," p. 565). Blake seems to follow Berkeley in making the external world depend on our perceptions ("Mental Things are alone Real" [p. 565]), but he swerves from such a stance when he turns Berkeley's "God" into imagination, a human faculty. Blake uses skeptical arguments only "to clear ground" for his belief in creative imagination (as in *There is No Natural Religion*).[26] Blake's radical move is in making imagination the basis of an epistemology, the source of all perception. His position combines antifoundationalism with faith in creative imagination. But such a stance gets him into trouble in his imagery.

The imagery of a poet who dismisses nature yet insists on the importance of the body, who embraces the basic premises of idealism yet abhors generalizations, is bound to appear inconsistent. The center of his imagery, and what yields seeming inconsistencies, is his theory of perception. For this discussion, I am interested in his perception theory in so far as it demonstrates his antifoundationalist stance. What I wish to explore are the effects of deliberate ambiguity on an imagistic system; what happens to the imagery of a poet/artist whose work depends on the psychology of perception?

In the next section of this paper, I will examine the role of perception in the printing house allegory in *The Marriage of Heaven and Hell*; I will argue that Blake uses perception as a language to destroy the "Platonic myth" that he held responsible for the damaging metaphysics of his age. Blake rejected the notion that Rorty claims "holds traditional philosophy captive," that the mind is a great mirror of nature (*Philosophy and the Mirror of Nature*, p. 12). In fact, Blake's radical rejection of nature demonstrates his conscious rejection of such a notion. He uses his theory of creative perception to illustrate the fallacy of projects that depend on nature; he does so by investing certain images with ambiguity and creating seeming inconsistencies to separate himself from a tradition of fixed meaning.

Now Blake's purpose is not exactly what we today call deconstructionist, antifoundationalist, or even pragmatic. He was profoundly attached to the pursuit of Truth and Goodness, quests happily (though perhaps not successfully) abandoned by Derrida, Rorty, and company. Programs like Derrida's or Knapp and Michaels's would be strange and unattractive to Blake, though he shares some of their aims. But my claim is that there can be no pure antifoundationalist position; Blake makes use of something like antifoundationalism to make room for his own sense-producing system. He never abandons faith or belief; in fact, they are necessary to him. He is hopeful and optimistic about the power of art: he believes that his program has consequences. As he remarks in a famous letter to a critic, it "rouzes the faculties to act."[27] Creative perception or imagination, according to Blake, depends on the assumptions of detachment from outside structures or foundations. But a claim that value is the product of creative perception presents special problems when dealing with imagery; how can an image be coherent when reality "alters" with the altering psychology of the subject? But perhaps this articulation of the problem over-emphasizes subjectivity. The issue is more centrally the language of re-presentation; if part of a text's meaning lies in ambiguity, how can the reader evaluate a particular feature of the text? The reader must ask with Urizen in *The Four Zoas*, "Where shall we take our stand to view the infinite and unbounded?"

Images of enclosure are especially significant for Blake because of the emphasis he places on the importance of looking inward (understanding the self) on the one hand, and on the dangers of restriction and confinement, on the other. In a more abstract sense, one can connect consequences of containment with the closure of foundationalist rhetoric; to a thinker like Blake, containment like foundationalism has its attraction, but the dangers require a shifting of valuation. Unfallen man contains the world within his own breast: yet, images of containment are usually symptoms of error in Blake's system. Likewise, movements away from enclosures are ambiguous. The fallen world is created by looking outward; fallen man perceives division and separation. In the tradition of poetic topography, enclosures have often represented tombs, the body as cavern, a female place such as a womb or a place of self-knowledge such as the psyche. The English Romantics employed the topos in order to explore and test the conclusions of their predecessors as part of a more general revision of the uses of images taken from the natural world. A voyage into a cave, for instance in Shelley's *Alastor* or *Prometheus Unbound*, may be a descent into the self, a quest for self-knowledge, as well as a return to the womb, a place of origins—and the voyage may find Nature's caves a "cradle or a sepulchre" (*Alastor*, line 430).

Caves have different meanings in such poets as Shelley, but the images used are drawn from the external world and they in part are used to test the uses of nature. Caves and other images of enclosure in Blake are difficult to make sense of. He appears to follow the poets who, traditionally, have used descents into enclosures to create an image for such things as a quest for knowledge or a movement into a tomb. With equal force, Blake makes entering a cave preclude a productive quest *and* he makes it the very condition for one; for him, both "descent" and "cave" can denote an escape away from or into restriction. While the epic hero could descend into the underworld as part of a process of gaining knowledge, part of a positive movement, a Blakean hero may not be so fortunate. Most often the rich caves of tradition become, in Blake, poisonous wombs, religious shrines of tyrannical religion, or tombs of inactivity and death. It is nothing new to portray caves in these various ways; it was common enough among Blake's contemporaries. But Blake employs these uses with a difference; Mitchell correctly notes that "the very subject of Blake's [visual] art is [the] power to transform and reshape visual imagery";[28] likewise, I would add that this power, the power of creative perception— the power that challenges external positions of authority— is the very subject of such shifting images. Blake is rejecting the entire tradition of Western philosophy that is worried about knowing and representing the outside world.

The Marriage of Heaven and Hell is one of the first works in which Blake invests caves with significance. The poem offers two very different kinds of caves, and it can be used to demonstrate Blake's attack upon the Platonic tradition. His method anticipates deconstruction, but goes beyond it when he makes his contextually based meaning productive of sense. In Plate 14, he follows the Platonic tradition when he images the body as a cavern: "For man has closed himself up, till he sees all things thro' chinks of his cavern" (p. 39). And he swerves from this tradition in the same plate when he describes the error that has led to this cavernous limitation: the body/soul dualism: "The notion that man has a body distinct from his soul, is to be expunged." Blake had offered in Plate 4 a clear attack on this dualism: "Man has no Body distinct from his Soul for that called Body is a portion of Soul discernd by the five senses, the chief outlets of Soul in this age" (p. 34). Blake makes Plato's own premises responsible for the condition that Plato criticizes. Blake proposes to correct this error, by "melting apparent surfaces away" (Plate 14). The cavernous body, then, is only a product of erroneous perception; the body is only an "apparent" surface. And then Blake does something that is startling. He uses the same image, the cavernous enclosure, as the locus of creative activity.

In Plate 15, he reverses the meaning of enclosures, demonstrating their contrariety; the cave image becomes an allegory of printing, of creative intellect and imagination. Their meanings are marked by potential instability and reversibility, as Foucault describes power relations (p. 794). Enclosures—caves, chambers, and palaces—become infinite spaces. He makes enclosures in *The Marriage* into utopian regions (that is, outside space) created by the intellect; the controlling, limiting spaces of tradition become their opposite, a release from the fallen world's "space to which time is added" (p. 107). Blake is rejecting the Platonists and the empiricists for what he saw as their common error (an error that philosophers have noticed and are worrying about today); both accounts of things assumed a fixed reality, a position of authority. Blake saw the body/soul dualism of the Platonists as analogous to the space/time "reality" of the empiricists. What are called "Unnam'd forms," the product of creative imagination, then "took forms of books & were arranged in libraries." This seemingly inconsistent use of enclosures as limiting and limitless spaces does not constitute a contradiction; Blake considers two kinds of movements into enclosures, one confining and one expanding. The former depends on the outside world; the latter depends on its rejection. In *The Marriage*, with its printing house allegory (for Blake's solution is usually an aesthetic one), he offers perhaps his best argument for the supremacy of the creative genius—a foundation-free discourse. (And such a belief in creative genius marks the important difference between Blake and the antifoundationalists.) It transforms limiting spaces and, using images drawn from the material world, demonstrates the mind's control over matter.

Blake's use of the cave in *The Marriage* is part of his program to destroy or "melt away" the delusive foundations of the metaphysics of his age. He makes enclosures demonstrate the power of perception, his vocabulary for his attack on positions of authority. When Blake describes his quest in the company of an angel in *The Marriage* to see their "eternal lot," the vision of the horrors of the "infinite Abyss" with its spiders and Leviathan is replaced by a "pleasant bank beside a river by moon light" with a "harper who sang to the harp" (pp. 41-42). The difference in the two scenes, the enlightened "I" of the poem explains to the bewildered angel, is "owing to your metaphysics."

NOTES

I am grateful to Fred Randel, David Simpson, and Jerome McGann for their helpful suggestions at various stages of this article.

[1]William Blake, "Annotations to Berkeley's *Siris*." *The Complete Poetry and Prose of William Blake*, ed. David V. Erdman, comm. Harold Bloom; rev. edn. (Garden City: Anchor-Doubleday, 1982), p. 664. All quotations from Blake will be from this edition and will appear parenthetically in the text by page number.

[2]I am referring to the debate stimulated by Stephen Knapp and Walter Michaels's article, "Against Theory." The debate, which was recorded in *CritI*, is now collected in *Against Theory: Literary Studies and the New Pragmatism*, ed. W. J. T. Mitchell (Chicago: Univ. of Chicago Press, 1985). My references will be from that edition and will appear in the text.

[3]In *Philosophy and the Mirror of Nature* (Princeton: Princeton Univ. Press, 1979) and *Consequences of Pragmatism* (*Essays: 1972-1980*) (Minneapolis: Univ. of Minnesota Press, 1982), Richard Rorty calls for a new program in philosophy that would involve a recovery of the pragmatist's project; he shows how philosophy as invented by Plato has led to a perhaps arbitrary concern for epistemology. He blames Kant and Descartes for making philosophy "epistemology-centered." Page references to these works will appear in the text. For replies to Rorty's arguments, see the special issue of *The Journal of Philosophy* devoted to *Philosophy and the Mirror of Nature, 77* (October 1980).

[4]Though to some extent this claim must also qualify the conclusions of antifoundationalists; there can be no true foundationless discourse. For some useful articulations of this position, see Rorty, *Philosophy and the Mirror of Nature*, p. 330, and Quentin Skinner, ed., *The Return of Grand Theory in the Human Sciences* (Cambridge and New York: Cambridge Univ. Press, 1985), p. 13. Skinner refers to Rorty's discussion and they both refer to Foucault. Also see Christopher Norris, *Contest of Faculties; Philosophy and Theory after Deconstruction*, especially the chapter "On Not Going Relativist (Where It Counts): Deconstruction and 'Convention T' " (London and New York: Methuen, 1985), pp. 193-217.

[5]This is what Rorty calls the Kantian assumption in "Pragmatism, Relativism, and Irrationalism" (*Consequences of Pragmatism*, p. 160). See also Richard J. Bernstein, for a lucid discussion of Habermas's important contribution to this debate, *Philosophical Profiles: Essays in a Pragmatic Mode* (Philadelphia: Univ. of Pennsylvania Press, 1986), pp. 58-93.

[6]See Charles Taylor's essay, "Philosophy and Its History," in *Philosophy in History: Essays on the Historiography of Philosophy*, ed. Richard Rorty, J. B. Schneewind, and Quentin Skinner (Cambridge: Cambridge Univ. Press, 1984), pp. 17-30.

[7]To try to force a philosophical system out of Blake's poetry may appear a dubious undertaking. He insists on certain philosophical positions only to assert their opposite with almost equal fervor, such as when he makes claims about the reliability of sense perceptions. In such cases one cannot trace a development and a refinement of a position so much as a willingness to sacrifice consistency to some greater purpose. When annotating Swedenborg, for instance, Blake willingly denounces "demonstration by the senses" in order to expose the error of a belief in an "invisible God," though more often he affirms the importance of sense perceptions, especially to explain the workings of imagination. On this particular issue see Stephen D. Cox's discussion of Blake

in *"The Stranger Within Thee": Concepts of the Self in Late-Eighteenth-Century Literature* (Pittsburgh: Univ. of Pittsburgh Press, 1980) pp. 127-56. One can see the marks on Blake's thought of the empiricists and other philosophers, though his work could never be reduced to a simple affirmation, rejection, or even revision of these philosophers. Blake's work is first an imaginative system, but he also offers many philosophical insights that can illuminate current discussions.

[8]*Philosophy and the Mirror of Nature,* p. 317.

[9]As Jerome McGann argues, Blake is not skeptical of his own method in *The Marriage* (1790-93), as he will become in his later prophecies. McGann correctly notes the "unusual confidence in the mutually constructive powers of imagination and criticism when both operate dialectically"—*The Romantic Ideology: A Critical Investigation* (Chicago and London: Univ. of Chicago Press, 1983), p. 108. As I take most of my examples of Blake's method from *The Marriage,* I risk presenting an overly positive Blake. But I wish to generalize about Blake's "confidence" in his methodology, despite his later skepticism, in order to contrast him to the current articulations of antifoundationalism. Though more careful and self-critical, as McGann notes, Blake retains in his later works the basic tenets of his methodology that I deal with in this paper.

[10]"Philosophy Without Principles," in *Against Theory,* p. 135.

[11]Jacques Derrida, *Of Grammatology,* trans. Gayatri Chakravorty Spivak (Baltimore: Johns Hopkins Univ. Press, 1976), p. 24, as quoted by David Simpson in "Reading Blake and Derrida—Our Caesars Neither Praised nor Buried," in *Unnam'd Forms: Blake and Textuality,* ed. Nelson Hilton and Thomas A. Vogler (Berkeley and Los Angeles: Univ. of California Press, 1986), p. 19.

[12]See Jurgen Habermas, "Modernity Versus Postmodernity," *NGC* 22 (1981):13; Hoy refers to this discussion in his essay, "Jacques Derrida," in *The Return of Grand Theory,* p. 61. Future references to Hoy' s essay will appear in the text.

[13]See Skinner, *The Return of Grand Theory,* pp. 12-13.

[14]It is perhaps not accurate to speak of deconstruction and the various antifoundationalist programs in analytic or Anglo-American philosophy as if they were the same thing. There are of course important differences, differences that are expressed in the current division between continental and analytic philosophy. Rorty's position, in some ways, falls between these two schools (which is convenient for my project). For the purpose of this paper, I exaggerate the similarities. In any event, I think that the prophetic tone of those engaged in literary discourse is unwarranted if one considers that similar discussions have been going on among philosophers without the tone of crisis. For a discussion of the possible "reconciliation between traditional Anglo-American philosophy and contemporary French deconstruction," see A. J. Cascardi's "Skepticism and Deconstruction," *P&L* 8 (1984):1-14.

[15]Donald Davidson, "The Method of Truth in Metaphysics" in *Inquiries into Truth and Interpretation* (Oxford and New York: Oxford Univ. Press, 1984), p. 200. "We can make sense of difference," Davidson writes, "but only against a background of shared belief."

[16]Michel Foucault, "The Subject and Power," *CritI* 8 (Summer 1982):790. Further references to this work will appear in the text.

[17]George Bataille, *Literature and Evil,* trans. Alastair Hamilton (New York: Urizen Books, 1973), p. 71.

[18]I am quoting Northrop Frye' s phrase from his discussion of contrariety in *Fearful Symmetry: A Study of William Blake* (Princeton: Princeton Univ. Press, 1947), p. 189.

[19]W. J. T. Mitchell, *Blake's Composite Art: A Study of the Illuminated Poetry* (Princeton: Princeton Univ. Press, 1978), p. 11. Stanley Fish notes that antifoundationalism is always historicist: "its strategy is always . . . to demonstrate that the norms and standards and rules that foundationalist theory would oppose to history, convention, and local practice are in every instance a function or extension of history, convention, and local practice" ("Consequences" in *Against Theory*, p. 112). Blake's contention that the social and the natural worlds are products of the human intellect aligns him with the historicists.

[20]Donald Davidson, "On the Very Idea of Conceptual Scheme" in *Inquiries into Truth and Interpretation*, p. 198. Davidson argues that conceptual relativism is a notion that comes out of the dogma of the dualism, scheme and reality, and that once we dispense with that dogma, the notion of conceptual relativism becomes meaningless. Subsequent references will appear in the text.

[21]Richard Rorty, "Philosophy as a Kind of Writing," *Consequences of Pragmatism*, p. 91.

[22]See *There is No Natural Religion* (a and b), and *All Religions are One*.

[23]See Davidson, "Truth and Meaning," in *Truth and Interpretation*, pp. 17-36.

[24]Earl R. Wasserman, "The English Romantics: The Grounds of Knowledge" *SIR* 4 (1964):17-34, 22.

[25]"Philosophy as a Kind of Writing," p. 95.

[26]Skinner points to a curious combination of "Grand Theory" and skepticism in such thinkers as Derrida and Foucault; I see Blake as a precursor of such a position, though he wouldn't have attempted to avoid such a charge as have Derrida and Foucault. I would hold that there can be no true antifoundationalist position for the same reason that there can be no true skeptical one, or at least no useful one—true antifoundationalism, like true skepticism, would be incurable, as Hume says of Cartesian doubt.

[27]To Rev. Trusler, 23 August 1799 (p. 702).

[28]*Blake's Composite Art*, p. 37.

SEL 27 (1987)
ISSN 0039-3657

The May-Day Celebration in Wordsworth's Immortality Ode

CLARENCE H. MILLER

It is clear, though apparently not obvious, that Wordsworth's "Ode. Intimations of Immortality from Recollections of Early Childhood" is a May-day poem. I say it is not obvious because I can discover no commentator or critic who has ever mentioned the fact. Once mentioned, it will be clear simply from reading the pertinent lines:

Now, while the Birds thus sing a joyous song,
And while the young Lambs bound
As to the tabor's sound,
To me alone there came a thought of grief:
A timely utterance gave that thought relief,
And I again am strong.
The Cataracts blow their trumpets from the steep,
No more shall grief of mine the season wrong;
I hear the Echoes through the mountains throng,
The Winds come to me from the fields of sleep,
And all the earth is gay,
Land and sea
Give themselves up to jollity,
And with the heart of May
Doth every Beast keep holiday,
Thou Child of Joy,

Clarence H. Miller, who is Dorothy Orthwein Professor of English at St. Louis University, is the Executive Editor of the Yale Edition of the Complete Works of St. Thomas More and has edited or coedited five volumes in that series. Apart from various articles on English poets, he has edited the Latin text of Erasmus's *Praise of Folly* for the Amsterdam *Opera omnia* and translated it into English (New Haven and London: Yale Univ. Press, 1979). He is presently engaged in translating Erasmus's Latin poems for the Toronto Collected Works of Erasmus.

Shout round me, let me hear thy shouts, thou happy
Shepherd Boy!

Ye blessed Creatures, I have heard the call
Ye to each other make; I see
The heavens laugh with you in your jubilee;
My heart is at your festival,
My head hath it's coronal,
The fullness of your bliss, I feel—I feel it all.
Oh evil day! if I were sullen
While the Earth herself is adorning,
This sweet May-morning,
And the Children are pulling,
On every side,
In a thousand vallies far and wide,
Fresh flowers.

(lines 19-48)[1]

There is ample evidence that the poet imagines himself seeing and hearing a traditional celebration of May Day: "tabor's sound,"[2] "heart of May,"[3] "keep holiday," "jubilee," "festival," "coronal," "sweet May-morning," "Children . . . pulling . . . Fresh flowers." And yet this scene bears strangely little resemblance to what we might expect in a May-day poem—what we find, for example in the supreme poem of the genre, Herrick's "Corinna's Going a Maying."[4] It lacks the predawn excursion into the woods, the hawthorn boughs brought back to decorate the house doors and church pillars, dancing around the maypole, the May king and queen, above all the erotic overtones that derive ultimately from fertility rites.[5]

Wordsworth knew of such details and mentions them in other poems.[6] In particular he lamented their disappearance in Book 8 of the 1805 *Prelude*. The shepherds he knew in his boyhood, he says, were not like those of Arcadia or those in Shakespeare's plays,

Nor such as Spenser fabled. True it is,
That I had heard (what he perhaps had seen)
Of Maids at sunrise bringing in from far
Their May-bush, and along the Streets, in flocks,
Parading with a Song of taunting Rhymes,
Aim'd at the Laggards slumbering within doors;
Had also heard, from those who yet remember'd,
Tales of the May-pole Dance, and flowers that deck'd
The posts and the Kirk-pillars, and of Youths,
That each one with his Maid, at break of day,
By annual custom issued forth in troops,
To drink the waters of some favorite well,

And Hang it round with garlands. This alas!
Was but a dream.[7]

The mention of Spenser refers to a description of May-day festivities in the May eclogue of *The Shepheardes Calender*, which may well have suggested many of the elements of the scene in the Ode:

Sicker this morrowe, ne lenger agoe,
I sawe a shole of shepeheardes outgoe,
With *singing*, and *shouting*, and *iolly* chere:
Before them yode a lusty *Tabrere*,
That to the many a Horne *pype playd*,
Whereto they dauncen eche one with his mayd.
To see those folkes make such *iouysaunce*,
Made my *heart* after the *pype* to daunce.
Tho to the greene Wood they speeden hem all,
To fetchen home *May* with their musicall:
And home they bringen in a royall throne,
Crowned as king: and his Queene attone
Was Lady Flora.[8]

But Spenser's vivid vignette, which lends itself to the woodcut (however crude) which precedes the eclogue in the 1579 edition, is quite unlike Wordsworth's expansive, attenuated, and yet animated scene.

Another feature of Wordsworth's scene, the singing birds welcoming May, was a standard element in the treatment of May Day, especially in medieval poems, One need look no further than the pseudo-Chaucerian *The Cuckoo and the Nightingale*, which Wordsworth modernized in December 1801, about three months before he began the Ode. In Wordsworth's modernization the singing birds, described at some length, "Began to honour May with all their powers."[9]

Wordsworth, however, could draw upon other sources besides oral reports and literary depictions of the old-fashioned festivities of May Day, for the holiday was still celebrated during his lifetime. But it was no longer the occasion for the sexual revelry which the Puritans of the sixteenth and seventeenth centuries found so abominable. It had become (and remains to this day) a prepubescent rite celebrated by children.[10] For the purposes of the Ode, the social custom had played right into Wordsworth's hands. About two years earlier he had opened "The Idle Shepherd-Boys or, Dungeon-Ghyll Force, a Pastoral" with a realistic May-day scene based on practices he himself had experienced:

The valley rings with mirth and joy;
Among the hills the echoes play
A never never ending song,
To welcome in the May.
The magpie chatters with delight;
The mountain raven's youngling brood
Have left the mother and the nest;
And they go rambling east and west
In search of their own food;
Or through the glittering vapours dart
In very wantonness of Heart.

Beneath a rock, upon the grass,
Two boys are sitting in the sun;
Their work if any work they have,
Is out of mind—or done.
On pipes of sycamore they play
The fragments of a Christmas Hymn;
Or with that plant which in our dale
We call stag-horn, or fox's tail,
Their rusty hats they trim:
And thus, as happy as the day,
Those Shepherds wear the time away.
Along the river's stony marge
The sand-lark chants a joyous song;
The thrush is busy in the wood,
And carols loud and strong.
A thousand lambs are on the rocks,
All newly born! both earth and sky
Keep jubilee, and, more than all,
Those boys with their green coronal.[11]

These lines present several anticipations of the May-day scene in the Immortality Ode, but on the whole they show what Wordsworth was *not* trying to do in the Ode: he did not wish to present a fully detailed and realistic description. Instead he made the celebration general and universal by excluding details and by widening the perspective to include not merely "earth and sky" but "Land and sea," not merely "The valley" but "a thousand vallies far and wide." No one at one vantage point could see the lambs, the shepherd boy, the cataracts, and sea, all the earth, every beast, and the children in a thousand valleys. The scene includes highly selective realistic details from a May-day festival or holiday, but it has been vastly expanded to form a universal May Day in which all of nature everywhere and even all children are united. Even the realistic details of the scene were not drawn from an immediate experience of a particular May Day: Wordsworth wrote the description at breakfast after a morning walk on 27 March 1802, long before May first and some time before the bounding lambs had even been born.[12] For the purposes of his poem he deliberately fused all nature and all children in the joy of a May-day celebration from which the poet himself is excluded. Like the growing boy of the middle section of the poem, upon whom the shades of the prison house have only begun to close, the shepherd boy and all the May-day children join with nature in a joy unqualified by any inkling of human mortality. This unthinking joy is precariously impermanent, and Cleanth Brooks rightly pointed out that the "somewhat frenetically whipped-up enthusiasm is dramatically quite appropriate."[13] The "strained effect" which he mentions and for which he gives some metrical evidence results not merely from the repeated exclamatory invocations but also from the combination of details from a real May-day festival with a universal May-day celebration that can exist only in the imagination of the observing poet. The unthinking children have no need to imagine a universal May Day; they simply shout, call to one another, wear coronals, pull flowers, pipe, and play. But the poet here displays the imaginative reach that will finally enable him to cope with the experiences of human mortality.

Hence it seems to me that Jonathan Wordsworth is not correct when he speaks of the "determined superficiality" of this scene in the Ode: "It is all very literary, and not very persuasive; few can read 'My heart is at your festival, / My head hath its coronal . . .' without some sense of unease."[14] Literary is precisely what it is not, at least not in the sense of relying too heavily on literary antecedents. Even one of the details singled out for censure, the coronal, is not literary but realistic, as Wordsworth himself staunchly insisted when Southey objected to the "green coronal" in "The Idle Shepherd-Boys" as merely fanciful. Many years later, in a note he dictated on this poem, Wordsworth went out of his way to demonstrate that the "green coronal" worn by the shepherd boys was factual: no sooner had Southey raised his objection than "two boys appeared with the very plant entwined around their hats."[15]

Another line, admired even by Jonathan Wordsworth, presents a remarkable fusion of realistic detail and imaginative projection: "The Cataracts blow their trumpets from the steep." Blowing horns was in fact a well known feature of May-day celebrations before, during, and after Wordsworth's lifetime. John Brand's *Observations on the Antiquities of Great Britian*,[16] written by about 1795, revised and augmented by Sir Henry Ellis, and first published in 1813, gives a wealth of information about May-day practices in Wordworth's time, though unfortunately it gives no examples from Grasmere or the Lake District. Brand confirms that the celebration of May Day had become limited to children, but he also points out several times that blowing horns or trumpets was a regular feature of it. He notes that, according to a report of 1641, young men "on Mayday morning, before day, went into the country to fetch home a Maypole with drumme and trumpet, whereat the neighboring inhabitants were affrighted, supposing some enemies had landed to sack them" (pp. 238-39). He quotes a passage by the eighteenth-century scholar Thomas Hearne which speaks of the old custom of blowing horns on May first so that "the custom of blowing them prevails at this season, even to this day at Oxford" (p. 213). An account in *The Literary Gazette* of May 1847 mentions that on May first choristers sing in the tower of Magdalen College at Oxford, the bells are rung, and "the boys . . . now blow their trumpets lustily, and . . . start off in all directions, and scour the fields and lanes, and make the woods re-echo to their sounds, in search of flowers" (p. 233). The custom is mentioned again toward the end of the nineteenth century: "May Day is ushered in at Penzance by the discordant blowing of large tin horns. At daybreak the boys assemble and perambulate the town blowing their horns and collecting money for a feast."[17] Just as the dancing of the children has been transferred to the bounding lambs, their trumpets have been given over to the cataracts. The cataracts blowing their trumpets combine realistic and imagined features in a startling but totally satisfying way; surely here what Coleridge calls the esemplastic power was at work.[18]

The blend of realism and projection in the children of the May-day scene is quite unlike the seemingly irreconcilable and unfortunate disparity (continually discussed from the time of Coleridge) between the sentimental, realistic vignette of "A four year's Darling of a pigmy size" and the lofty invocation of the same child as "best philosopher, . . . Mighty Prophet! Seer blest!"[19] The disparity between Wordsworth's realistic children and his children in complete harmony with universal nature is penetratingly analyzed by David Perkins, in the Ode and elsewhere, especially in "We Are Seven."[20] To what he says we might add that the May-day children in the opening of the Ode are at one and the same time realistic May revellers and creatures who share effortlessly in the universal joy of nature. The successful fusion in the May-day scene is achieved by the poet's imagination, and though this particular imaginative fusion cannot be sustained because of the intrusion of grief and mortality, the same fusing imagination will make it possible for the poet to emerge from his meditation on mortality with a new blend of realism (this time the grievous fact of mortality) and idealized, universal harmony (the poet's own sober sympathy with natural beauty). The final scene is more circumscribed: not "Cataracts," "mountains," "all the earth," "Land and sea," "every Beast," "the heavens," "a thousand vallies," but rather "Fountains, Meadows, Hills, and Groves," "Brooks which down their channels fret," "The innocent brightness of a new-born day," "The Clouds that gather round the setting sun." The mountains have become hills; the cataracts have become brooks (and fretting brooks at that). Formerly the poet had created the fusion in the May-day scene, though he could not share in it; now he has created another fusion and embodies it in himself.

That is why, when the May-day children return in the conclusion of the poem they are presented only briefly and realistically:

Then, sing ye Birds, sing, sing a joyous song!
  And let the young Lambs bound
  As to the tabor's sound!
We in thought will join your throng,
  Ye that pipe and ye that play,
  Ye that through your hearts to day
  Feel the gladness of the May!

(lines 171-77)[21]

An awareness of this structural function of the May-day children, who reappear so simply in the second-to-last stanza, may go some way toward answering Professor Perkins's objection that "the last two stanzas violate both the tone and the logical scheme of the poem."[22] The children still have a simple joy, but the larger harmony they embodied at the beginning of the poem has disappeared. The final harmony, muted and in a minor key, now belongs to the poet himself. He could not share in theirs; neither can the May-day children share in his.

NOTES

[1]*Poems, in Two Volumes, and Other Poems, 1800-1807*, ed. Jared Curtis (Ithaca: Cornell Univ. Press, 1983), 271-72.

[2]"As to the tabor's sound" is not a simile, It means "as if the young lambs were bounding to the tabor's sound," not "as if there were a tabor to which they were bounding." The tabor is a real part of the scene, as are the pipes at line 175.

[3]Not "the middle of May" but "the inner joy associated with the first day of May."

[4]Herrick's poem had been echoed in Thomson's *Seasons* ("Spring," lines 480-93) some 75 years before Wordsworth wrote the Immortality Ode. David Garrick's ballad opera *May Day*, presented at Drury Lane in 1775, is a lighthearted presentation of sexual and satirical shenanigans, complete with gipsies; see *The Poetical Works of David Garrick*, 2 vols. (London: George Kearsley, 1785; rpt. New York: Benjamin Blom, 1968), 1:465-77.

[5]Sir James G. Frazer, *The Golden Bough*: *A Study in Magic and Religion*, 3rd edn., 12 vols. (New York: Macmillan, 1935), pt. 1, vol. 2, pp. 59-96.

[6]*Poetical Works*, ed. Thomas Hutchinson, rev. Ernest de Selincourt (London: Oxford Univ. Press, 1936; rpt. Oxford, New York, Toronto, and Melbourne: Oxford Univ. Press, 1981), pp. 130, 233, 354, 397, 604, 663.

[7]*The Prelude or Growth of a Poet's Mind*, ed. Ernest de Selincourt, rev. Helen Darbishire (Oxford: Clarendon Press, 1959), p. 274.

[8]*The Poetical Works of Edmund Spenser*, ed. J. C. Smith and Ernest de Selincourt (London and New York: Oxford Univ. Press, 1912), p. 436. I have italicized the words Wordsworth seems to echo. Some of them occur in a later passage in the Ode when Wordsworth returns to the May-day scene (lines 171-77). The later passage was written early in 1804; see Mark L. Reed, *Wordsworth*: *The Chronology of the Middle Years, 1800-1815* (Cambridge, Mass.: Harvard Univ. Press, 1975), pp. 13, 27.

[9]*Poetical Works*, ed. Hutchinson, rev. de Selincourt, p. 437.

[10]See Peter H. Ditchfield, *Old English Customs Extant at the Present Time* (London: Methuen, 1896; rpt. Detroit: Singing Tree Press, 1968), pp. 98-102, 106-07, 109, and Laurence Whistler, *The English Festivals* (London: W. Heinemann, 1947), pp. 146-48.

[11]*Poetical Works*, ed. Hutchinson, rev. de Selincourt, pp. 66-67.

[12]Mary Moorman, *William Wordsworth, A Biography*, 2 vols. (Oxford: Clarendon Press, 1957), 1:527, 530-31. I have not been able to find any clue as to why Wordsworth should have thought of May Day on March 27. But it is not surprising that this poem, like many of his best poems, should be based on recollected details.

[13]Cleanth Brooks, *The Well Wrought Urn*: *Studies in the Structure of Poetry* (New York: Harcourt, Brace, and World, 1956), p. 135.

[14]Jonathan Wordsworth, *William Wordsworth: The Borders of Vision* (Oxford: Clarendon Press, 1982), p. 157.

[15]*The Poetical Works of William Wordsworth*, ed. Ernest de Selincourt and Helen Darbishire, 5 vols. (Oxford: Clarendon Press, 1940-1949), 1:362.

[16]Three volumes (London: G. Bell and Sons, 1877-1882). I cite this edition by giving the page numbers of volume 1 in parentheses.

[17]Ditchfield, *Old English Customs*, pp. 105-106.

[18]Perhaps the context of May Day can help us to understand the puzzling but highly suggestive line "The Winds come to me from the fields of sleep." May-day revels began in the dark before dawn. Wordsworth wrote the first four

stanzas of the Ode at breakfast after an early morning walk (Moorman, 1:527). The line seems to describe the winds which had been sleeping in the fields but awaken like the revellers and begin to blow at dawn. One is reminded of the dawn wind in Dante's *Purgatorio* (canto 1, lines 15-17) or Tennyson's *In Memoriam* (No. 95, lines 53-61.

[19]That Wordsworth was perhaps aware of this disparity is suggested by the original epigraph he placed before the poem, "Paulo majora canamus," from the first line of Virgil's "messianic" fourth eclogue. The primary reason, of course, was that Wordsworth, like Virgil, was rising to a higher style, but there is a less obvious similarity: as in Wordsworth's Ode, the high and the low seem to be in playful but somewhat uncomfortable proximity in Virgil's poem, in which the helpless, smiling babe ushers in a new great expanse of golden centuries.

[20]David Perkins, *The Quest for Permanence: The Symbolism of Wordsworth, Shelley, and Keats* (Cambridge, Mass.: Harvard Univ. Press, 1959), pp. 69-80.

[21]*Poems, In Two Volumes*, ed. Curtis, p. 276.

[22]*The Quest for Permanence*, p. 80.

SEL 27 (1987)
ISSN 0039-3657

"Sport of Transmutations": The Evolution of Wordsworth's "To Lycoris"

DOUGLASS H. THOMSON

In "Tintern Abbey" Dorothy plays a powerful yet simple and moving role in Wordsworth's recovery of his faith in Nature and himself. Appearing as a reinforcement to the faith "taught" (113)[1] to him by this special place in nature and the memories it evokes, she provides the poet another link to his being of the past:

> in thy voice I catch
> The language of my former heart, and read
> My former pleasures in the shooting lights
> Of thy wild eyes. Oh! yet a little while
> May I behold in thee what I was once,
> My dear, dear Sister!
>
> (116-21)

Beyond this moment of unity and affirmation loom many difficulties in our understanding of Dorothy's role in her brother's poetry—problems such as the degree to which biography and psychology can determine that understanding, her role as a symbol of nature and memory, and her relation to the mysterious Lucy, to name only a big few. A relatively neglected poem which Wordsworth developed through various manuscript stages touches upon these issues at the

Douglass H. Thomson, who received his Ph.D. from the University of Rochester, is an Assistant Professor of English at Georgia Southern College. He has written about Romantic poetry and contemporary criticism in such journals as *Studies in Romanticism*, *Studies in The Novel*, and (forthcoming) *Philosophy and Rhetoric*, among others.

same time its imagery and mode of address provide an extension of the poetics of memory found in "Tintern Abbey." Finally published as the ending to the sequel of the "Ode to Lycoris" (1820),[2] the verses reach back to Wordsworth's work on the poem "Nutting" (1798) and include a version as an independent lyric ("This is the Spot") which Dorothy read to her brother the night preceding his completion of "Resolution and Independence" (1802). As De Selincourt remarked in his "Notes" on "To Lycoris," these lines "seem to have haunted Wordsworth's mind for nearly twenty years" (*PW* 2:423).[3] A study of Wordsworth's development of this address to Dorothy provides us with what no interpretation of any one of the so-called Dorothy poems can give: an *evolving* conception of the role she assumes in his poetry. Throughout these revisions she remains, as in "Tintern Abbey," a medium for Wordsworth's reflections on his past, and these verses provide us a special context in which to trace the poet's developing attitude toward this "dearest" of his audiences.

The verses underlying the ending of "To Lycoris" appear in various editions of William's and Dorothy's writings (*PW* 4:96 and 423; Moorman, pp. 120-121; *PW* 2:504-506). Let us bring them together for closer inspection:

Nutting

Ah! what a crash was that! with gentle hand
Touch these fair hazels—My beloved Friend!
Though 'tis a sight invisible to thee
From such rude intercourse the woods all shrink
As at the blowing of Astolpho's horn.
Thou, Lucy, art a maiden "inland bred"
And thou hast known "some nurture"; but in truth
If I had met thee here with that keen look
Half cruel in its eagerness, those cheeks
Thus ( ) flushed with a tempestuous bloom,
I might have almost deem'd that I had pass'd
A houseless being in a human shape,
An enemy of nature, hither sent
From regions far beyond the Indian hills—
Come rest on this light bed of purple heath,
And let me see thee sink into a dream
Of gentle thoughts, protracted till thine eye
Be calm as water when the winds are gone
And no one can tell whither.

(1-19)

This is the Spot

This is the spot:—how mildly does the sun
Shine in between the fading leaves! the air
In the habitual silence of this wood
Is more than silent; and this bed of heath—
Where shall we find so sweet a resting-place?
Come, let me see thee sink into a dream
Of quiet thoughts, protracted till thine eye
Be calm as water when the winds are gone
And no one can tell whither. My sweet Friend,
We two have had such happy hours together
That my heart melts in me to think of it.

To Lycoris

Shutting up thyself within thyself,
There let me see thee sink into a mood
Of gentler thought, protracted till thine eye
Be calm as water when the winds are gone
And no one can tell whither. Dearest Friend!
We two have known such happy hours together
That, were power granted to replace them (fetched
From out the pensive shadows where they lie)
In the first warmth of their original sunshine,
Loth should I be to use it: passing sweet
Are the domains of tender memory!

(41-51)

One immediately can note many interesting variants in Wordsworth's invitation to rest, but all three share two important features that link its listener to the one of "Tintern Abbey": first, the reference to Dorothy as a special or dearest "Friend"; second, the emphasis on that dearest Friend's eyes. Although less obvious in the "Nutting" manuscript, all three occasion Wordsworth's reflections on the past, especially as memory relates that past to this privileged audience. The poet's desire to calm those "wild eyes"—in which he once could "catch . . . these gleams / Of past existence" ("Tintern Abbey," 148-49)—signals a change in Wordsworth's understanding of the language of his former heart; this change helps explain why he would be "Loth to use" a certain "power" if granted him in "To Lycoris." To define Wordsworth's change toward both Dorothy as an audience and the "power" of memory associated with her, we must first recover the texts and contexts from which this poetry comes.

Dove Cottage Manuscript 15 contains the earliest drafts of poetry that would eventually lead to the ending of "To Lycoris." In its heavily emended passage and the other, more finalized version from the Goslar period (MS 16), Wordsworth's invitation to rest does not exist as an independent lyric but comprises a section of what have been traditionally referred to as "overflow passages" of "Nutting." In them, Wordsworth experiments with a frame for the narrative of his childhood memory. He begins by directly addressing a Lucy—"with gentle hand / Touch those fair hazels, my beloved Maid" (MS 16, 1-2). Her early appearance in longer versions of "Nutting" solves one riddle that has long troubled critics: the abrupt concluding address to a "dearest Maiden" in the published version. With an audience firmly established at the beginning of the poem and the "dearest Maiden" named, Wordsworth's longer version frames the telling of his boyhood pillage of the hazel trees, and the poem achieves a greater moral coherence. The narrative of the boy's "ravage" of the trees and his vague chastisement becomes a lesson drawn for the Friend's benefit in the present; in the Goslar beginnings, she is even considered, conditionally, an "enemy of nature" to underscore the need for her chastisement and instruction.

The passage before us, with its gentle invitation to Lucy to come rest, contains many fascinating features: the direct address to Lucy, rare in poems concerning her; the allusions to Ariosto and Shakespeare's *As You Like It*; the depiction of the usually sympathetic Friend possessing a "keen look / Half cruel in its eagerness" (MS 16, 8-9). This opening to the frame has also achieved a kind of notoriety in Wordsworth criticism, for Bateson used it to identify Lucy as Dorothy, a basis for his still controversial reading of the Lucy poems.[4] But the key feature in understanding this as a poem concerning the power and effect of memory (the unifying link in the three passages above) is, as Bateson and others[5] have also noted, the confounding of the schoolboy ravisher with the potentially cruel Friend, the subject of the extended poem with its audience. (Bateson goes so far as to say they are "*interchangeable.* In writing about her he was writing about himself, and *vice versa*" [p. 153].) This doubling characterizes Wordsworth's most radical imaginative identification with his past and offers an intensification of the union affirmed in "Tintern Abbey" between himself and his past as figured in Dorothy.

However, this poetry from Goslar also sharply differs from the ideals of "Tintern Abbey." In this instance, the close alignment between poet and friend, an alignment based on their potential for cruelty, disrupts the moral pattern Wordsworth seeks to formulate for his narrative of the past. The problems caused by this confusion between listener and former self probably explain why Wordsworth abandoned his otherwise perfectly coherent frame for the poem. The poetry that survives this attempt, the invitation to "come rest," thus begins with real ambiguity. On the one hand, the poet's desire to calm that "keen look / Half cruel in its eagerness" (MS 16, 8-9) serves as an attempt to prepare his friend for his education of her. On the other hand, Wordsworth's lullaby-like address can be read as an attempt to negate the disturbing implications of *his* close identification with the threat to nature she poses. The Friend does fade from the poem after this address, as Wordsworth turns to a different audience in an expansive apostrophe to "the gentle stewards" and "Powers" of Nature. While appearing to transcend (or ignore) the maiden, the apostrophe actually helps explain what motivates Wordsworth's desire to see the Friend "sink into a dream / Of gentle thoughts" (16-17). The poet extols "powers"

> whose general ministry it is
> To interpose the covert of these shades,
> Even as sleep, betwixt the heart of man
> And the uneasy world, 'twixt man himself,
> Not seldom, and his own unquiet heart,
> Oh! that I had a music and a voice
> Harmonious as your own, to tell the world
> What ye have done for me.[6]

This quieting of self-consciousness, described in a contemporaneous Lucy poem as "Kind Nature's gentlest boon" ("Strange Fits of Passion," 18), resembles the dreamworld designed to calm the "tempestuous" maiden. She is in this one instance an emblem of his "unquiet heart." With his invitation to come rest, Wordsworth appropriates the "music and voice" of nature to sublimate the threat she poses—and one part of himself represents—to his familiar vision of a sympathetic and harmonious Nature.

In "Tintern Abbey," Dorothy's role as a medium of past existence had supported her brother's delicate and "cheerful faith," that "all which we behold / Is full of blessings" (133-34)—a faith built not upon traditional religious assurances but upon a mythopoetics of Nature, a sympathetic "she" who can "inform / The mind within us" (125-26). In the overflow passages of "Nutting," one sees just how delicate and conditional is this faith built upon nature and memory, the two forces constantly associated with Dorothy. The "wild eyes" of "Tintern Abbey" can possess at times a "keen look / Half cruel in its eagerness" (MS 16, 8-9); memory can offer a challenge to the whole idea of "natural piety." In subsequent reworkings of the invitation to rest, we find Wordsworth revising his understanding of the direction provided by this guide to his moral being.

The second version of Wordsworth's address to his special Friend leaves far behind the complexities and irresolutions of "Nutting." The poem provides another example of "interchange" between speaker and listener but of a simpler kind. Dorothy reports in her journal that she read the poem to her brother the night of 4 May 1802 to help ease anxiety occasioned by his composition of the "Leech-Gatherer" (the previous night "he went to bed nervous and jaded in the extreme"): "We soon went to bed. I repeated verses to William while he was in bed—he was soothed and I left him. 'This is the Spot' over and over again" (Moorman, p. 121). Certainly, in this case, we have an example of Wordsworth hearing the language of his former heart in the voice of his friend. As an independent lyric, the invitation to "sink into a dream / Of quiet thoughts" takes the form of a lullaby. The dreamworld of "Nutting" had led to an abrupt awakening and the assertion of a "spirit in the woods"; the "habitual silence" of the wood in "This is the Spot" offers instead a "resting-place," a soothing pause in which the poet and his "sweet Friend" gratefully acknowledge the legacy of heartfelt emotion. Its strangely localized spot leads to a general memory of "happy hours together," so unlike the more detailed narrative character of a true "spot of time." Although "This is the Spot" offers the simpler consolation, it seems to address the same anxiety represented in "Resolution and Independence": the reversals of time ("We Poets in our youth begin in gladness; / But thereof come in the end despondency and madness" [48-49]). Appearing to the poet "Like one whom I had met with in a dream" (110), the Leech-Gatherer provides the troubled poet with an example of perseverence in the face of inevitably "slow decay" (125). The very repetition of his tale (told three times) serves to counteract the future. Dorothy's reading of "This is the Spot" ("over and over again") probably served the same purpose. The fitful "spirit" that hauntingly concludes "Nutting" has given way to the surer consolation of the heart.

Although "This is the Spot" deletes the troubled spirit of "Nutting," a knowledge of both these textual sources proves crucial in understanding the final poem of the group, "To Lycoris." One strong link in the group is provided by Wordsworth's increasingly insistent affirmation of the heart and of deeply felt emotion, especially as understood by the Friend:

> Then, dearest Maiden, move along these shades
> In gentleness of heart; with gentle hand
> Touch—for there is a spirit in the woods.
> ("Nutting," *PW* II, 212:54-56)

> My sweet friend,
> We two have known such happy hours together
> That my heart melts in me to think of it.
> ("This is the Spot," 9-11)

> —Oh, tis the *heart* that magnifies this life,
> Making a truth and beauty of her own.
> ("To Lycoris," 12-13; Wordsworth's emphasis)

But "To Lycoris" is actually more a poem of renunciation than of affirmation. In singing his praise for the "humbler cravings of the heart" (*The Excursion*, IV, 354), Wordsworth not only renounces the "steep and rough" ground trod by "Ambition" but his earlier, visionary (or "apocalyptic," in Hartman's terms) attitude toward nature. This elaborate renunciation in "To Lycoris" explains why Wordsworth tells Dorothy he should be "loth" to use a certain power if granted him; it also signals the final change in his attitude toward the "language of [his] former heart" ("Tintern Abbey," 117).

Dove Cottage Manuscript 67 preserves Wordsworth's penultimate reworking of these verses, "Here let us rest," which leads directly to the conclusion of "To Lycoris." The manuscript passage also anticipates a change in the way the poet views nature that will provide the major themes of the later poem to Lycoris-Dorothy:

> Come let us venture to exchange the pomp
> Of wide-spread landscape for the internal wealth
> Of quiet thought—protracted till thine eye
> Be calm as water when the winds are gone.[7]

Wordsworth's exchange of a sweeping natural panorama for the quiet, meditative calm signals a key development in his invitation to rest. In this passage, he does not humanize nature, as he had in "Nutting" and the Lucy poems;[8] he disregards it. Why does he now see "pomp" in a "widespread landscape," of all things? A discarded manuscript passage from "To Lycoris" provides the answers:

> Oh! tis the heart that magnifies this life
> Making a truth and beauty of her own;
> And moss-grown alleys, circumscribing shades,
> Such as do now surround us, aid her more
> In the blest work than tower'd Palace high
> Far blazing as if built of fire: or *pomp*
> Of sea and land contending for regard
> Of the lone Shepherd on the mountain top
> While he perchance following some humble quest
> Of both is heedless. Rather would I gaze
> On a small flower, retaining at my feet
> Its long-loved aspect, than become the sport
> Of transmutations, taking more away
> Than they can give in recompense. Rest here
> And let me see thee sink into a dream.
>
> (my emphasis)[9]

Wordsworth forswears the "pomp / Of widespread landscape"—the kind of natural vision one would have from a mountain top—because such landscape offers the eye a contentious variety of changing perspectives. He prefers the localized and earth-bound flower to the widespread and mutable vista: the painter of natural scenery here exchanges the "transmutations" that characterize the sublime for the solace of the still-life. Such transmutations—"Fallings from us, vanishings; / Blank misgivings of a Creature / Moving about in worlds not realised" ("Immortality Ode," 143-45)—inevitably recall the younger Wordsworth's own mountain ascents, especially Snowden, in which sky and sea "contend" and the clouds metamorphose into a "still ocean" (*The Prelude*, XI, 45) through the agency of the moon. These had been moments when Wordsworth asserted the primacy of perception, when "The mind is lord and master—outward sense / The obedient servant of her will" (*The Prelude*, XII, 222-23). Now the poet applauds the Shepherd's heedless attitude, as he fears that such visionary changes take "more away / Than they can give in recompense." The solitary traveller of

"Nightpiece" and *The Prelude* would now prefer to keep his "unobserving eye / Bent earthward" ("Nightpiece," 10-11 and cf. *The Prelude*, XIII, 28-29).

We shall see very soon how Wordsworth's decision to publish his invitation to rest in "To Lycoris" complements this forswearing of the visionary landscape. The poem develops in a highly mythopoetic way the contrast between ascent (ambition) and acquiescence (humility). In the first lines of the poem, Wordsworth abandons the ascent—"Enough of climbing toil" (1)—which we find is an underlying metaphor for "Ambition." His description of nature echoes the underlying manuscript passage: he terms the "empire" of the clouds "fickle," and they promise only a "Most uncertain recompense" (4). Wordsworth specifies what troubles him about ambition's ascent:

> Each weary step, dwarfing the world below,
> Induces, for its old familiar sights,
> Unacceptable feelings of contempt,
> With wonder mixed—that Man could e'er be tied,
> In anxious bondage, to such nice array
> And formal fellowship of petty things!
>
> (6-11)

The poet finds he cannot tolerate the overreacher's contempt for "old familiar sights." Yet wonder is "mixed" with this haughty disregard, for the climber who mounts ambition's "steep and rough" path can assert his singularity and reject his "anxious bondage" with a world literally and figuratively below him.

Such freedom Wordsworth often finds exhilarating in *The Prelude*, and even such a relatively late passage as the Wanderer's attempt to rouse the Solitary sings praise for transcendent yearnings:

> Ambition reigns
> In the wilderness: the Soul ascends,
> Drawn towards her native firmament of heaven,
> When the fresh eagle, in the month of May,
> Upborne, at evening, on replenished wing,
> This shaded valley leaves; and leaves the dark
> Empurpled hills, conspicuously renewing
> A proud communication with the sun
> Low sunk beneath the horizon.
>
> (*The Excursion*, IV, 394-402)

But the Wanderer's "proud communication" troubles the persona of *The Excursion,* who doubts such a vision will help one already disappointed with the world. He instead argues for "humbler cravings of the heart" (IV, 354), and this therapy aligns him precisely with the poet of "To Lycoris": "Oh! 'tis the *heart* that magnifies this life" (12; Wordsworth's emphasis). Wordsworth, when mountain climbing, had once asserted that

> Our destiny, our being's *heart* and home
> Is with infinitude, and only there;
> With hope it is, hope that can never die,
> Effort and expectation, and desire,
> And something evermore about to be.
> (*The Prelude,* VI, 605-609, my emphasis)

But "To Lycoris" shows that he has come to mistrust the visionary ascent and its thirst for "something evermore about to be." The poet's emphasis on the heart has shifted to "this life," and his insistence that humbler cravings replace ambition recalls many Christian contexts critical of the overreacher. Yes, this conservatism signals the later, more orthodox Wordsworth. But in his criticism of ambition, Wordsworth also revises an integral part of his earlier thought about creativity. Where he once could rejoice in the fact that men "from their native selves can send abroad" mutations "kindred" to those of natural forces (*The Prelude,* XII, 93-94), he now sees the visionary as prey to contending forces, as a mere "sport of transmutations."

Wordsworth turns to his "Dearest Friend" at the very end of "To Lycoris" to offer a still, quiet respite from the fitful changes that characterize visionary ambition:

> Shutting up thyself within thyself,
> There let me see thee sink into a mood
> Of gentler thought, protracted till thine eye
> Be calm as water when the winds are gone
> And no one can tell whither.
> (41-45)

This turn to Dorothy so late in a poem is not unexpected in Wordsworth's poetry: the audience of "Tintern Abbey" and the published "Nutting" also only emerges toward the conclusion. The key point is that Wordsworth's address to Dorothy does not interrupt but continues the subjects of the meditations and apostrophes preceding it. His renunciation of a visionary poetic in "To Lycoris" leads directly to his rejection of a closely related power:

> Dearest Friend!
> We two have known such happy hours together
> That, were power granted to replace them (fetched
> From out the pensive shadows where they lie)
> In the first warmth of their original sunshine,
> Loth should I be to use it: passing sweet
> Are the domains of tender memory!
>
> (45-51)

Wordsworth does not forswear the object of memory—he would not "replace" the hours with others—but the immediacy ("first warmth") of remembered experience. Even if "granted," he would deny the power that can place again those hours in their "original sunshine." Earlier, Wordsworth had gloried in the merging of memory and imaginative illumination, praising

> Those recollected hours that have the charm
> Of visionary things, those lovely forms
> And sweet sensations that throw back our life,
> And almost make remotest infancy
> A visible scene, on which the sun is shining.
>
> (*The Prelude,* I, 632-36)

In "To Lycoris," Wordsworth declines use of this "power" of radical reflection (as a philosopher might put it, the power to make reflection emulate the unreflective life of consciousness). He instead distinguishes another kind of memory, more like nostalgia, in which he and his Friend can "shut" themselves up, at a distance from the troubles of the world. Within these "passing sweet" domains, the poet and his dear companion can "soften objects" and "smooth forgone distress," powers which Wordsworth attributes to "Memory" in a later poem of that name (8-10). But the charm and light that once illumined those "pensive shadows" of the past (the kind of memory work we see at its best in the "spots of time") have faded.

As the many painstaking revisions of these verses attest, what aligns Wordsworth's denial of this "power" with his forswearing of "visionary things" is that such radical reflection also can make man "the sport of transmutations." In "Nutting" the dreamworld into which the Friend slips leads to a violent reversal, the "crash / And merciless ravage" (44-45) of a boy at odds with the dream of nature's "general ministry" (MS 16, 45). The language of the former heart does not always vindicate that of the present heart, as it had in "Tintern Abbey." The three key developments of the invitation to the friend can be well understood in terms of Wordsworth's classifications for his poems: the first version dates from a "poem of the imagination," its dream designed to calm and sublimate the radical assertiveness of a consciousness realized in opposition to nature; the second, "This is the Spot," resembles a poem of reflection and sentiment, in which "happy hours" spent together reassure the poet; the third, included in "Poems of Sentiment and Reflection," continues the consolation and reassurance of "This is the Spot" but includes a renunciation of the very kinds of transmutations that characterize the poems of the imagination. Dorothy remains throughout a figure who prompts the poet's meditations on his former heart. But she and Wordsworth's address to her are also subject to the "sport of transmutations," as his memory discovers various beings of the past—and as the poet comes to revise his understanding of the moral value and reliability of memory in his poetry.

NOTES

[1]All citations of Wordsworth's poetry (except *The Prelude*) refer to Ernest De Selincourt's *The Poetical Works of William Wordsworth*, 5 vols. (Oxford: Clarendon Press, 1947), hereafter referred to as *PW*, and are noted by line number in my study. For *The Prelude* and its variants, I use *The Prelude: 1799, 1805, 1850*, ed. Jonathan Wordsworth and Stephen Gill (New York: Norton, 1979), cited by book and line.

[2]Hereafter referred to as "To Lycoris." The original title of the poem, "To the Same," follows Wordsworth's "Ode to Lycoris," but the blank verse of the sequel bears more similarities to the verse pattern of "Tintern Abbey'" than to his odes, which are characteristically English in their use of intricate rhyme schemes. Yet one remembers that while Wordsworth did not "venture to call ['Tintern Abbey'] an Ode," he wrote it with the "hope that in the transitions, and the impassioned music of the versification, would be found the principal requisites of that species of composition" (see *PW*, 2:517). "To Lycoris" shares these characteristics, especially in its "transition" from discussion of ambition to "humbler cravings of the heart."

[3]Six versions date from 1798 to 1820. The first three appear in Wordsworth's work on a "beginning" to "Nutting," preserved in Dove Cottage MS 15 (the "Christabel Notebook"), DC MS 16, and a loose sheet in the handwriting of Mary Hutchinson (a sheet recently included in DC MS 24). As there exist no really significant variants in these three versions, my study of this early form of

these verses concentrates on the DC MS 16 copy, long available to scholars in *The Poetical Works*, 2:504-506. (James Butler's forthcoming edition of the *Lyrical Ballads* for *The Cornell Wordsworth* will include the other two "Nutting" MSS.) The fourth version is the independent lyric "This is the Spot" referred to by Dorothy in her journal; it can be found in the *Journals of Dorothy Wordsworth*, edited by Mary Moorman (Oxford: Clarendon Press, 1971), pp. 120-21. DC MS 41 ("Sara's Poets") preserves Sara Hutchinson's transcription of this poem, with a new title, "Travelling." The fifth reworking of the lullaby, "Here let us rest," dates from 1816-May 1817 and can be found in Dove Cottage MSS verse 67 (old DC listing). The published sequel to the "Ode to Lycoris," "To the Same," includes the sixth and final version of these lines (41-51).

[4] F. W. Bateson, *Wordsworth: A Reinterpretation* (London: Longmans, 1954), p. 152, hereafter referred to by page number.

[5] Roger N. Murray in *Wordsworth's Style: Figures and Themes in the Lyrical Ballads of 1800* (Lincoln: Univ. of Nebraska Press, 1967) also notes the confusion between audience and speaker in the poem: "in the overflow portions of 'Nutting' . . . Wordsworth comes very close to describing himself at the moment of breaking the bough" (p. 67).

[6] MS 16 "Nutting," 45-52. A version of "Nutting" similar to the one published in *The Lyrical Ballads* begins with the completion of this line ("It seems a day").

[7] *PW,* 4:424, lines 8-11.

[8] "The subject of 'Nutting' is not the life in nature, or its secret manifestation, but how the child's willful consciousness matures into the sympathetic imagination. Nature's activity . . . is related primarily to this end." Geoffrey Hartman, *Wordsworth's Poetry: 1787-1814* (New Haven: Yale Univ. Press, 1964), p. 75.

[9] See De Selincourt's *apparatus criticus* in *PW*, 4:96-97.

SEL 27 (1987)
ISSN 0039-3657

Personal Identity in *Mansfield Park*: Forms, Fictions, Role-Play, and Reality

C. KNATCHBULL BEVAN

Two papers which deal pertinently with acting as a rhetorically crucial theme in *Mansfield Park* are those by Lionel Trilling and Thomas R. Edwards.[1] Of these, Lionel Trilling's seminal essay fails to observe the pervasiveness of the theme of role-play in the novel as a whole. Professor Edwards, though he deals cogently with the whole question of acting and its relationship to emotional reality in *Mansfield Park*, tends to focus his attention almost exclusively on the personal relationships explored and developed through the novel, and to ignore the wider significance of such relationships placed as they are within a broad thematic context of personal identity in its relation to a reality which includes but goes beyond the emotional to embrace phenomena, language, and art.

This paper sets out to examine the importance of acting, and of fiction-making, as themes in *Mansfield Park*. It will be argued that acting is used both as an illustration of, and as a metaphor for, invalid attempts to express and define the self. Such attempts are shown to be invalid because, ultimately, they deny the self they seek to create. They deny, also, important realities of the external world in which the self must exist, substituting for them forms, fictions, and material values. To this false art of life, exemplified at its most extreme by the Crawfords, is opposed a true art of life, consisting in a harmonious relationship between the perceiver and all that is perceived, where the objects of perception are the self, others, natural phenomena, and artefacts. The exemplar of this true art of life is

Until recently a Senior Lecturer at the National University of Singapore, C. Knatchbull Bevan has published on Henry Fielding, Dr. Johnson, and Keith Douglas. He is currently working on the rhetoric of syntax in Jane Austen's novels.

Fanny Price. Her creative tools are two personal qualities, delicacy and associative memory, and these qualities are opposed throughout *Mansfield Park* to the fictions, forms, and role-play by means of which the Crawfords, and others, seek to create their own reality.

At the time of the rehearsals for *Lovers' Vows* Fanny makes a revealing statement. Tom has asked her to act Cottager's wife. She replies: "Indeed you must excuse me. I could not act anything if you were to give me the world. No, indeed, I cannot act" (p. 145). Again, a little later, she explains: "It is not that I am afraid of learning by heart but I really cannot act" (pp. 145-46). This would seem to be a crucial comment by Fanny upon herself, for we are made strongly aware from the first that Fanny, unlike almost all those by whom she finds herself ignored or patronised at Mansfield, is incapable either of creating fictions or of performing in them. Furthermore, as is so often the case in Jane Austen,[2] the performing arts, acting and music, are opposed negatively, in *Mansfield Park,* to nature and to rational conversation. At one point Fanny, left alone with Edmund at the drawing-room window, turns to the scene outside and observes the brilliant unclouded night and the contrasting colour of the woods. " 'Here's harmony!' said she, 'Here's repose! Here's what may leave all painting and all music behind, and what poetry only can attempt to describe' " (p. 113).

Nature provides the truest and best art, all else is imitation. Those who have been taught to "*think* and *feel* on the subject" (italics mine) have been well taught. But having himself acknowledged the value of Nature, Edmund moves towards the fortepiano, away from nature and from rational conversation to performance and the rendering of applause. What he has done is to follow with his person what he has already followed admiringly with his eyes, the appeal of artifice in appearance, whether the appearance in question be an attractively composed woman or musical glee. "She [Mary Crawford] tripped off to the instrument, leaving Edmund looking after her in an ecstasy of admiration of all her many virtues, from her obliging manners down to her light and graceful tread" (p. 112).

That Fanny "cannot act" is seen as the expression of her contact with nature both human and phenomenal. When she first arrives at Mansfield we are told, by the author-commentator, that "Her feelings were very acute." It is a result of her education at Edmund's hands that these "feelings" are developed in the direction of the understanding of herself and others so that they become "sympathetically" acute. It is just this "sympathetic acuteness of feeling," or delicacy that is missing from Fanny's treatment by the Mansfield relations, by all of whom Fanny is viewed less as a person than as one who must fulfil a preordained role. To Mrs. Norris, Fanny is a poor relation who is to be used. To Sir Thomas it is, not altogether improperly, Fanny's household and social roles that matter. To Maria and Julia, Fanny is to be judged by her possessions and her lack of accomplishments, while to Lady Bertram Fanny has one role only, that of helper. What all these attitudes reveal is the absence of a sympathy which arises from feeling and seeks knowledge. Fanny's emotional reality is denied by people who themselves habitually cast others, as they cast themselves, in roles. Role-casting is presented as the polar opposite, and as the inhibitor, of that "sympathetic acuteness of feeling" of which Fanny, as the result of Edmund's educational care, is to become the exemplar. A term used frequently in *Mansfield Park* to describe this quality is "delicacy," and it is in terms of their lack of delicacy that the human incompleteness of other characters is often expressed. Thus Mr. Yates is "without discernment or diffidence, or delicacy, or discretion enough" to understand that Sir Thomas had rather leave the topic of theatricals alone. Henry Crawford's unwelcome perseverance with Fanny's affections is regarded by her as "a want of delicacy and regard for others." Fanny considers that Sir Thomas, "He who had married a daughter to Mr Rushworth," can have no "romantic delicacy" which might enable him to see beyond merely factual information, into her real feelings concerning Crawford. The term "delicacy," then, would seem to connote sympathetic discernment, of the kind demonstrated by Edmund when he finds the child Fanny crying on the stairs, and of the kind shown by Fanny in her constant concern with the workings of the minds and feelings of others, and of herself. It is a measure of Edmund's falling off from excellence, during his pursuit of Mary Crawford, that he allows his prepossession in favor of her brother Henry to blunt the delicacy of his perceptions. Having assured Fanny "you did not love him—nothing could have justified your accepting him," he immediately exhorts her,

> "But (with an affectionate smile), let him succeed at last, Fanny, let him succeed at last. You have proved yourself upright and disinterested, prove yourself grateful and tender-hearted; and then you will be the perfect model of a woman, which I have always believed you born for."
>
> (p. 347)

Edmund is here asking Fanny to dispose her emotional reactions to Henry Crawford much as she is in the habit of disposing her active life in the service of others. But Fanny, in pursuing her life of service, is being emotionally true to herself. She cannot, and herein lies Edmund's lack of delicacy, assume emotional roles, because to do so would mean being untrue to the grounds of feeling within her. She "cannot act."

What Fanny demonstrates, in direct contradistinction to the Crawfords, and to the other role-players and role-imposers, is a state of being grounded in feeling, not in role-play, in actual, not in imagined experience. This state of being consists in a harmonious relationship between the inner and the outer life, and between self and others. Thus she is constantly engaged in the effort to see both herself and others as they really are in terms of motive, feeling, and moral intention, not as she would have them be. When Fanny and Edmund are in conversation, or when Fanny is employed in speculative meditation, one notices frequent evaluations which are themselves the subject of doubt and enquiry. In an early discussion of Mary Crawford (p. 63) moral judgments are qualified by such expressions of doubt as "I think," "I do not know that," "It must be difficult," "I do not pretend to know," "Do not you think." Fanny, whose "own thoughts and reflections were habitually her best companions," tries to exercise them in honest enquiry even when her own pride is under attack as, from a distance, she observes Mary Crawford's competent horsemanship and Edmund's apparently eager attentions. "She saw it, or the imagination supplied what the eye could not reach. She must not wonder at all this; what could be more natural than that Edmund should be making himself useful, and proving his good-nature by any one?" (p. 67). Fanny's approach to all experience is to question it and, she hopes, to discover meanings. Inferences are recognized for what they are and are qualified by reasonable doubt.

Unlike Fanny, Mary Crawford deals with experience not by trying, through sympathetic feeling, to understand it. Instead she creates out of it fictional anecdotes, and her language is characterized not by doubt and enquiry but by assertion and by a conscious pattern-making designed to delight the listener and to distort the truth. The devotional life of the Rushworth forebears, the wilderness at Sotherton, the Owen girls, the sensation that Fanny's marriage to Crawford is to make in the fashionable world, are all entertaining fictions which satisfy Mary Crawford's urge to create rather than to know. What her brother's plans for radical improvement are to Sotherton, so Mary Crawford's fictional renderings of reality are to reality itself; imposed re-creations. They are not developments of what is in fact there, but falsifications. This disjunction between reality and the Crawford fictions receives expression in the language

Mary Crawford uses. Frequently we observe an incompatibility between the syntactic forms she employs and the semantic function these forms actually perform. Most typical of her speech is her use of the attributive clause.[3] Thus when she declares clergymen to be motivated by "indolence and love of ease—a want of all laudable ambition, of taste for good company, or of inclination to take the trouble of being agreeable," the qualities she attributes to clergymen are, clearly, not factual but merely expressions of her own feeling. Underlying the formal syntactic realization here is a function which should appropriately be expressed in a reactive clause. She uses language, in short, to manipulate truth and to falsify it, not, after the fashion of Fanny and Edmund, in order to discover it.

The relationship of Fanny to reality is, then, harmonious, for she is always seen trying to come to terms with it by discovering it. That of the Crawfords is disharmonious, for they are shown always to recreate it and thereby to falsify it.

Fanny's harmonious relationship to reality receives further expression, and rhetorical reinforcement, in frequent accounts of the importance to Fanny of people, places, and possessions, and in the nature of their operation upon her memory. At Sotherton, while Mrs. Rushworth is lecturing Fanny and Mary Crawford on the ancestral pictures, Mary Crawford had, we are told, "only the appearance of civilly listening," while Fanny listened eagerly, "delighted to connect any thing with history already known." Her pleasure at William's visit is thus accounted for:

> All the evil and good of their earliest years could be gone over again, and every former united pain and pleasure retraced with the fondest recollection. An advantage this, a strengthener of love, in which even the conjugal tie is beneath the fraternal. Children of the same family, the same blood, with the same associations and habits, have some means of enjoyment in their power, which no subsequent connections can supply.
>
> (pp. 234-35)

Earlier, after she has been upset by Tom's insistence that she act, Fanny goes off alone to her east room.

> The comfort of it in her hours of leisure was extreme. She could go there after any thing unpleasant below, and find immediate consolation in some pursuit, or some train of thought at hand. —Her plants, her books—of which she had been a collector, from the first hour of her commanding a

> shilling—her writing desk, and her works of charity and ingenuity, were all within her reach . . . she could scarcely see an object in that room which had not an interesting remembrance connected with it.—Everything was a friend, or bore her thoughts to a friend.
>
> (pp. 151-52)

The function of memory here is to blend together events, people, possessions, and emotional experience, into a totality of harmonious association. Through memory, Fanny's loved ones and her possessions become a part of the self, inseparable from it. Upon them her self depends, and from them it receives definition. In contrast the Crawfords are, to use a term often employed in *Mansfield Park*, "unfixed," having no attachment to people, places, or things. Thus, "To any thing like permanence of abode, or limitation of society, Henry Crawford had, unluckily, a great dislike" (p. 41). He is "every thing to every body and seemed to find no-one essential to him" (p. 306). That his sister's predicament is identical with his is demonstrated at the time when Fanny and Mary are together in the parsonage shrubbery. Fanny observes:

> "Every time I come into this shrubbery I am more struck with its growth and beauty. Three years ago, this was nothing but a rough hedgerow along the upper side of the field, never thought of as any thing, or capable of becoming any thing; and now it is converted into a walk, and it would be difficult to say whether most valuable as a convenience or an ornament. . . . How wonderful, how very wonderful the operations of time, and the changes of the human mind. . . . If any one faculty of our nature may be called *more* wonderful than the rest, I do think it is memory."
>
> (p. 208)

Memory at once locates in time and links in time, links the shrubbery as it was to the shrubbery as it is, and links also the human perceiver to the inanimate objects that are perceived. Mary Crawford, however, who is without fixed location and thus without the associative capability that felt memory provides, "untouched and inattentive, had nothing to say." Shortly afterwards she remarks, "I see no wonder in the shrubbery equal to seeing myself in it." There is surely more to this than a bald revelation of egotism. What her remark reveals, more importantly, is her isolation from the phenomena which, through the action of memory, give people communal roots in experience. To be free, as Mary Crawford and her brother are, is to be alone. It is an important irony in *Mansfield Park*, perhaps the most important, that it is the Crawfords, who appear to be the most socially adept of all the characters, who are in reality the most alone, whereas Fanny, the most socially isolated, is in other and crucial senses the most fully integrated. The isolating nature of the Crawfords' freedom is revealed in another incident. Mary Crawford expresses surprise at the difficulty of hiring a horse and cart to convey her harp from Northampton to Mansfield. Being unrooted in a community, she cannot see that horses and carts have their necessary function in the seasonal rhythms upon which the Mansfield community must depend (it is the time of the hay harvest), and that the London maxim "every thing is to be got with money" substitutes artificial and material for natural bonds. Again, in the discussion on Sotherton and improvement, Edmund counters Henry Crawford's radical suggestions with the remark "I would rather have an inferior degree of beauty of my own choice, and acquired progressively." Here change, as in Fanny's observations on the shrubbery, is viewed as developmental not radical, progressive not sudden.

What the Crawfords are being shown to lack, and Fanny to possess, are delicacy and seminal memory. Of these two qualities, delicacy, or sympathetically concerned interdependence between people, creates harmony on the personal level. Seminal memory further establishes that harmony, as in the case of Fanny's love for her brother William, and extends it to comprehend both the natural phenomena upon which communities depend, and the possessions which, by association, link past with present feeling into a unified whole. It is these qualities of delicacy and memory which anchor Fanny in the real world. Their absence from the Crawfords' experience unfixes both from necessary links with people, places, and phenomena and, consequently, from any community of felt experience. It is for this reason that, having but slender links with reality, they live by fictions.

But the Crawfords are not fiction-makers only, they are performers also, interpreters, that is to say, of those fictions by which they aim to manipulate reality into the form most appealing to their creative imaginations. In the parsonage shrubbery, Mary Crawford addresses Fanny who has suggested that Mansfield and its environs are perhaps too quiet for Mary. " 'I should have thought so *theoretically* myself, but' —and her eyes brightened as she spoke— 'take it all in all, I never spent so happy a summer. —But then' —with a more thoughtful air and lowered voice— 'there is no saying what it may lead to' " (p. 210). Speech and gesture are here represented in the manner of stage dialogue, with gesture expressed as stage directions. These directions are emphasized by their placing, for when they occur they break, each time, a syntactic unit. This emphasis draws the reader's attention to them and thus to Mary Crawford's communication as an exercise in studied elegance, a means of enabling the speaker to fulfil an assumed role, in this case that of hopeful lover. A similar technique is used a little later with some utterances of Henry Crawford. He is talking of Rushworth and Maria, and his aim is to impress Fanny.

> "Poor Rushworth and his two-and-forty speeches!" continued Crawford. "Nobody can ever forget them. Poor fellow! —I see him now; —his toil and his despair. Well, I am much mistaken if his lovely Maria will ever want him to make two-and-forty speeches to her"—adding, with a momentary seriousness, "She is too good for him—much too good." And then changing his tone again to one of gentle gallantry, and addressing Fanny, he said, "You were Mr. Rushworth's best friend."
>
> (p. 224)

Stage-directions are used again to suggest the staginess of the speaker, whose tonal gestures are shown to be successively manufactured with a view to creating conversational effects, rather than as a means of expressing genuine feeling.

The Crawfords are actors who invent and perform their own dramas as a substitute for the reality of which they have, ultimately owing to a faulty education,[4] been deprived. Jane Austen cleverly reduces the art they practice to triviality in a single episode in volume one, when Mary Crawford is ready to play on her harp to a receptive audience.

> A young woman, pretty, lively, with a harp as elegant as herself; and both placed near a window, cut down to the ground, and opening on a little lawn, surrounded by shrubs in the rich foliage of summer, was enough to catch any man's heart. The season, the scene, the air, were all favourable to tenderness and sentiment. Mrs Grant and her tambour frame were not without their use; it was all in harmony; and as every thing will turn to account when love is once set going, even the sandwich tray, and Dr Grant doing the honours of it, were worth looking at.
>
> (p. 65)

Such conscious patterning in such an emphatically homely context is delightfully absurd. In this comic little arrangement of people and setting, people are indistinguishable in function from place, for both are important only insofar as they contribute to the harmonious visual impact of the scene. Mary Crawford is, with rhetorical appropriateness, first deindividualized, becoming merely "a young woman," and then dehumanized, as elegant as—her harp. The entire description presents an epitome, which is at the same time a *reductio ad absurdum*, of the Crawford world view, in which people exist merely as objects to be disposed to the most agreeable, and convenient, advantage.

The Crawfords, then, are creative artists, actors, and producers. They are creative artists in that they invent the fictions by which, and in which, they choose to live; they are actors in that they exercise their skill in order to present these fictions persuasively, and they are producers in that they aim to regulate the reactions of others to conform with the roles they envisage for them in the Crawford drama. Thus, for Henry Crawford, people, like landscapes, are assessed on the grounds of their capabilities. Of Fanny we learn that "he was no longer in doubt of the capabilities of her heart" (p. 235).

I have earlier observed how it is that Mary Crawford falsifies reality by manipulating language. Language too has "capabilities," and her use of it must be further considered, for there is more than one feature of her language use that exemplifies what is for her, as for her brother, the primacy of rendition over truth. First there is her use of the modal auxiliary *must*. This she uses, as an attributive intensifier, simultaneously to express prediction, obligation, and, often, logical necessity. Tom *must* be preferred to Edmund; it *must* be the case that almost everybody is taken in when they marry; she *must* "look down upon any thing contented with obscurity when it might rise to distinction." Here, as frequently elsewhere in Mary Crawford's speech, language is chosen and arranged so as to suggest the certain accuracy of the fictions she invents. Her style has other functions, all wittily inventive and falsifying. She may aim to give a comic elegance, and hence an appeal, to the morally unjustifiable. Alternatively she may invest the trivial with a spurious dignity. Two of her aphorisms, both of which have a marked Wildean quality, may be adduced as examples of the first category of linguistic creation. 1. "Selfishness must always be forgiven, you know, because there is no hope of a cure" (p. 68). 2. "I am very strong. Nothing ever fatigues me but doing what I do not like"(p. 68). In both these cases the inventive wit, and the appeal, reside in linguistic falsification. In the first, "selfishness" is given an additional selectional feature

(+ disease), and in the second, "fatigue" is given two simultaneous features (+ physical and + boredom), which, in orthodox usage, it may possess only separately depending upon whether the term is used literally or figuratively. The wit lies, in other words, in skilled semantic trickery. It is this that, incidentally, seems to distinguish Mary Crawford's speech from that of Elizabeth Bennet in *Pride and Prejudice*.[5] Unlike Elizabeth, Mary Crawford consistently exploits the falsifying surface of language in order to communicate fictions which, through the choice and organization of the language in which they are presented, give appeal to untruth. But, in the case of Mary Crawford, Jane Austen ensures that although rhetoric aims at concealment within the action, it simultaneously highlights for the reader those truths it aims to hide. The conversation in the shrubbery between Mary and Fanny provides a case in point. Mary begins to elaborate upon the pleasures offered by country residence:

> "I am conscious of being far better reconciled to a country residence than I had ever expected to be. I can even suppose it pleasant to spend *half* the year in the country, under certain circumstances—very pleasant. An elegant, moderate-sized house in the centre of family connections—continual engagements among them—commanding the first society in the neighbourhood—looked-up to perhaps as leading it even more than those of larger fortune, and turning from the cheerful round of such amusements to nothing worse than a tete-a-tete with the person one feels most agreeable in the world."
>
> (p. 210)

In this case, the trivial is dignified by a syntactic arrangement of parallel post-modifying phrases and clauses, which magnifies triviality into dignity through the emphasis of repetition. At the same time the evident contrast between emphasis and moral meaning, form and content, highlights the shallow insignificance of the speaker's views. Edmund's appearance very soon afterwards is used in order to place Mary Crawford's views in negative contrast with Fanny's. To Mary, the name Edmund, signalling that its owner is a younger brother, is pitiful. For Fanny, it is Mr. Bertram that is "cold and nothing-meaning," and Edmund which has "nobleness," being "a name of heroism and renown—of king's, princes, and knights; and seems to breathe the spirit of chivalry and warm affections." The difference between the two young women is located in the kind and quality of association made by each. Fanny's words function in such a way as to draw attention to the large areas of emotional experience that Mary Crawford's judgment excludes. To judge people, as Mary Crawford does, by the standard of social position is, of course, to judge by form. Her language, like her judgments, is formally conceived with a view to appearance, not substance.

To the organic patterning of Fanny's emotional and moral life is contrasted patterning of a purely social and linguistic kind. The contrast may be seen as one between two opposed conceptions of art. In the one, that embodied in Fanny Price, order is created by the sympathetic imagination, controlled by moral principle, which responds to and thereby coheres the animate and inanimate world by which it is confronted and through which it lives. In the other, that embodied in the Crawfords, order is created by an imposition of the will upon reality. The world is, as it were, reshaped, and its real constituents ignored at the wishes of the "improver." Such an aesthetic cannot, and in the case of the Crawfords does not, take into account the emotional life of others, for to view experience with "sympathetic acuteness of feeling" would be to lay one's art of life open to modification by external and unpredictable forces. The creative will would no longer be free. The Crawford art of life is as unreal in the artificiality of its patterning as the invented world of Millamant, whose hair must be pinned up with love letters in verse, never with those in prose.[6] Like Millamant, the Crawfords invent their own alternative to reality, and similarly delightful in its outrageous patterning it often is. But such invention, appropriate though it is to comic art, is inappropriate to life, for comedy demands emotional distance and, with the Crawfords, emotional distance becomes emotional impoverishment, a debility far more crippling than Fanny's merely physical frailty.

The Crawfords' emotional impoverishment is a consequence and an expression of their lack of involvement with people and places, of their unwillingness to "fix" themselves. Their threat to Mansfield lies in their encouragement of these selfsame destructive forces, all of which are shown to exist at Mansfield already, before they arrive. Thus Tom, like Henry Crawford, is unfixed both in place and in his affections. Sir Thomas, after his return, perceives as we have already perceived, that Rushworth is "as ignorant in business as in books, with opinions in general unfixed, and without seeming much aware of it himself" (p. 200). Maria and Julia are likewise unfixed in moral principle and in emotional contact with their family. In consequence they follow the formal constraints and expectations their society imposes without being capable of giving felt consent to these constraints. Thus Julia, at precisely the permitted time in her life, "was quite ready to be fallen in love with" (p. 44). Mr. Rushworth "was from the first struck with the beauty of Miss Bertram, and being inclined to marry, soon fancied himself in love" (p. 38). To Maria, as to Rushworth, marriage is merely a proper step in life's pre-ordained ritual. "Being now in her twenty-first year, Maria Bertram was beginning to think matrimony a duty."

In these cases, formal expectation decrees that feeling be fabricated; there are no emotional realities, only ritual procedures. That this is so is shown to be in great part the fault of Sir Thomas who, man of principle though he be, is damagingly unable to move beyond form to feeling: "and would he only have smiled upon her and called her 'my dear Fanny' while he said it, every former frown or cold address might have been forgotten." His immediate reaction to Rushworth is also revealing. "There was nothing disagreeable in Mr. Rushworth's appearance, and Sir Thomas was liking him already." Even his newly awakened concern over Fanny, after his return from Antigua, seems to arise only from her improved physical looks. Sir Thomas unwittingly begins what the Crawfords deliberately continue when they provide those formal conditions, the theatricals, which function as the sanction for unprincipled conduct. Where forms, not felt principles, are the springs from which behavior arises, then morality becomes dependent upon formal conditions alone.

The Crawfords' preference for fiction-making and for linguistic patterning over enquiry and the search for truth is exemplified in Mrs. Norris, whose foolishness functions as an oblique evaluation of these qualities in the Crawfords. It is through language manipulation, though of a naive kind, that Mrs. Norris creates the world she clearly does not, in reality, inhabit. In Mrs. Norris's case, self-concern masquerades as concern for others. Linguistically, this contrast between role and reality is, typically, given simultaneous expression. Role is projected through hyperbole—*excessively, vast, every thing, prodigious, always* (pp. 53-54). These hyperbolic terms suggest the intense, though notional, activity to which Sotherton inspires Mrs. Norris. Reality is conveyed in the structure of her discourse. Its movement from Sotherton to Mrs. Norris in her parsonage reveals her egocentricity, and its lack of ordered cohesion her foolishness.

It is not, of course, that Jane Austen meant to persuade readers that a life lived according to forms is necessarily less than fully human. At Portsmouth we see a combination of formlessness and egotism that makes Fanny reflect with longing upon the formality of Mansfield life, where "there would have been a consideration of times and seasons, a regulation of subject, a propriety, an attention towards every body which there was not here" (p. 383). It is simply that formal regulations should be informed by conscious moral principle rooted in feeling. Without such moral principle, forms, so the action of *Mansfield Park* demonstrates, may become divorced from feeling, and function as the weapons of pretense and self-seeking in the armory of the emotionally and morally isolated self. Thus it is that the selfishness of the Crawfords, disastrous practically though its consequences are, is primarily significant as a contradiction of true, integrated selfhood. The self, without contact through sympathetic feeling with others, without those roots in place nurtured by memory through association, becomes an empty shell seeking substance through those forms, fictions, and invented patterns which, ironically, display its emptiness.

If this is so, then the Mansfield theatricals must be regarded as thematically central. The point is not that acting itself is morally wrong. Professional actors, whose performances may be considered "good hardened real acting" are in control. For the "hardened" actor the self is forgotten in the role but remains intact to be later resumed. But the Mansfield actors, encouraged by the Crawfords, conflate role and self, so that the role becomes the self. The theatricals are thus an exercise in deracination, cutting away those values which root the characters, morally and emotionally, in their community. In displacing their father's furniture they are devaluing associations, the formative importance of which is made clear in Fanny's reflections on her own possessions in the east room. In allowing her allotted role to give free rein to her desire for Henry Crawford, Maria is moving even further away than her misguided education has already placed her from the harmonious life in which social forms, moral principle, and feeling are conjoined. In compromising his moral principles by agreeing to act, Edmund is allowing appearances to supercede moral realities, as he has already begun to do as a result of his attraction to Mary Crawford. In allowing the desire for display to displace feeling for each other, to displace delicacy, in a word, the entire company is denying harmony. "Every body had a part either too long or too short—nobody would attend as they ought, nobody would remember on which side they were to come in—nobody but the complainer would observe any directions" (p. 165). This harmony, the denial of which the Crawfords exemplify and encourage, is presented throughout *Mansfield Park* as a harmony of nature, not of artifice. It is principle that is the harmonizing force, linking the self to other people, to places, and to possessions.

Much of the importance of the theatricals lies, then, in their figurative relationship to the novel as a whole. In theater, what is required is effective rendition, not personal sincerity or feeling; fiction not fact; role not reality; form or effect, not truth. The

Crawfords bring to Mansfield a manner of personal living in which the self is lost in the role, and truth in fiction and rhetoric. The only major character undamaged by them is Fanny Price, and Fanny "cannot act."

NOTES

All quotations from *Mansfield Park* are taken from the edition edited by R. W. Chapman (Oxford: Oxford Univ. Press, 1923).

[1]Lionel Trilling, *The Opposing Self* (New York: Viking, 1955), pp. 207-30. Thomas R. Edwards, Jr., "The Difficult Beauty of *Mansfield Park;*" *NCF* 20 (1965):51-67.

[2]See *Pride and Prejudice*, ed. R. W. Chapman (London: Oxford Univ. Press, n.d.), p. 25.

[3]See M. A. K. Halliday, "Types of Process" in his *System and Function in Language* (Oxford: Oxford Univ. Press, 1976), pp. 159-73. Halliday distinguishes three clause types, those of *action*, of *mental process* and of *relation*. The attributive clause is a clause of *relation* containing two terms joined usually by the verb *to be*, as in the clause, "*Goldsmith was vain.*" In this attributive clause, as in all attributive clauses, the relation between the two terms, here *Goldsmith* and *vain*, is one of class inclusion. The reactive clause is one of *mental process*, consisting, as in the clause, "Mary Crawford likes music," of *processor* (Mary Crawford), *phenomenon* (music), and a *verb of reaction* (likes).

[4]The crucial importance of education as a means of handing down, and thus of maintaining, values whose existence is objective and divinely validated, is implied throughout A. M. Duckworth, *The Improvement of the Estate* (Baltimore: John Hopkins Univ. Press, 1971).

[5]See Lionel Trilling, p. 213. Of Mary Crawford, Trilling observes, "Irony is her natural mode, and we are drawn to think of her voice as being as nearly the author's own as Elizabeth Bennet's is."

[6]William Congreve, *The Way of the World*, II.ii.

SEL 27 (1987)
ISSN 0039-3657

Lionel Trilling and *Mansfield Park*

PAUL PICKREL

Lionel Trilling's essay on *Emma* is better known than his essay on *Mansfield Park* chiefly because it stands as the introduction to the very widely used Riverside edition, though no doubt the greater popularity of its subject has something to do with its larger reputation. Yet the essay on *Mansfield Park* has occupied a central position in the criticism of the novel for a generation (it first appeared in 1954 and was collected in the volume called *The Opposing Self* the following year),[1] and its preeminence seems to be in no danger of diminution even now. For instance, in his recent magisterial study of character in fiction, *Forms of Life*,[2] as judicious a critic as Martin Price calls it "a bold and forceful" reading of the novel and warns the critic that he had better not dissent unless he can come up with something even bolder.

Some irony, perhaps self-reflexive, seems to tinge this otherwise sternly Kuhnian view of the critical enterprise, but even so its warning probably should be enough to silence disagreement from one who has nothing as vivid as Trilling's reading to offer, especially one who for a long time simply assumed total congruence between that reading and the text. Yet with rereading the incongruities have gathered, and simply to acknowledge that they are there may be the first step toward readings that fit the text better.

The kernel of Trilling's interpretation (the word *indictment* would not be wholly inappropriate) occurs in a few sentences:

Paul Pickrel, Professor Emeritus of English at Smith College, was formerly Managing Editor of *The Yale Review* (1949-66) and Chief Book Reviewer of *Harper's Magazine* (1954-62). He is currently working on two series of essays—one on novels in English and the other on problems in language.

> No other great novel has so anxiously asserted the need to find security, to establish, in fixity and enclosure, a refuge from the dangers of openness and chance. . . . Most troubling of all is [the novel's] preference for rest over motion [, for dealing] with the world by condemning it, by withdrawing from it and shutting it out, by making oneself and one's mode and principles of life the very center of existence and [living] the round of one's days in the stasis and peace thus contrived. . . . Its praise is not for social freedom but for social stasis. It takes full notice of spiritedness, vivacity, celerity, and lightness, but only to reject them as having nothing to do with virtue and happiness, as being, indeed, deterrents to the good life.[3]

This is bold and vigorous all right, but it is also a bit misleading. Trilling offers no evidence in support of his conviction that the book is all for fixity and stasis and enclosure against freedom and openness, perhaps because the evidence seems to be on the other side. In every Jane Austen novel a major function of the plot is to regroup the insiders and the outsiders, to replace a community based upon consanguinity and contiguity by a community of shared feelings and values, and in no other of the novels is that regrouping so radical, in none is change so pervasive. Consider: the woman who at the beginning of the story dominates life in Mansfield Park (Mrs. Norris) by the end has been banished thence forever. The brilliant prospects of her darlings, the two daughters of the house, end in exile of varying degrees of severity for both. The eldest son is changed by illness and his sisters' fate from a life of frivolity to responsibility and seriousness. Even Lady Bertram's almost impenetrable placidity is finally disturbed enough to awaken her to the troubles that have overtaken her children; and her husband, the very keystone of the Mansfield moral arch, has to acknowledge that he has erred in the rearing of his children. Except for Edmund there is no important character whose status is not seriously altered in the course of the story; for several of the characters alteration amounts to reversal. And all these changes occur with the author's obvious approval: the fall of Mrs. Norris, for instance, has no hint of tragedy about it; it is richly deserved and unlamented, except, many years later, by Kingsley Amis.

Trilling has a particularly hard time in getting the Bertrams right. He speaks of Lady Bertram as one of the "middle-aged, stupid, maternal persons" who are "favorite butts for Jane Austen" (p. 227), apparently grouping her with someone like Mrs. Musgrove in *Persuasion*. But the characterization is inaccurate. Maternal Lady

Bertram most decidedly is not: "thinking more of her pug than of her children,"[4] the text says. Whether she is middle-aged depends no doubt on the reader's perspective. Probably she is in her middle thirties when the story opens: her oldest child is seventeen; we know that Sir Thomas believes in early marriage where means permit; and when beauty is the only trump, as in Lady Bertram's case, it is best played early in the game. (Not that her looks are gone; Jane Austen says that she has always been a beauty, and the aspect of the verb indicates that she still is.) Whether Lady Bertram is stupid is more of a question. Henry Crawford thinks so because she fails (or declines) to master a trivial card game that they play at the Grants', but she manages to get life on her own terms more than most of us do, and if that is what stupidity will do for you it may deserve a better press than it usually gets. In her dealings with Mrs. Norris, a chief insurer of her life of ease, she shows occasional glints of shrewdness that suggest an accurate enough appraisal of her sister. When, for instance, Mrs. Norris declares that she *must* live on her income and "lay by a little at the end of the year," Lady Bertram calmly says, "You always do, don't you?" She hasn't been asleep on that sofa all the time.

Trilling's misreading of Sir Thomas's character is more consequential. "Maria's sin and Julia's bad disposition," he writes, "are blamed directly on [Sir Thomas's] lack of intelligence and sensibility" (p. 226). But that is not what the text says: "He had sacrificed the right to the expedient" is what we read there. The formality of manner that has distanced him from his children is blamed too, but his intelligence never. The most curious thing about the picture of Sir Thomas that Trilling draws is the determined effort to make him responsible for a certain line of objection to the theatricals at Mansfield, when in fact Sir Thomas never expresses any objection to the theatricals on those grounds or any other.

> What is decisive [in the objection to the theatricals, Trilling writes,] is a traditional, almost primitive, feeling about dramatic impersonation. . . . It is the fear that the impersonation of a bad or inferior character will have a harmful effect upon the impersonator, that, indeed, the impersonation of any other self will diminish the integrity of the real self. . . . It is [Sir Thomas] who identifies the objections to the theatricals as being specifically that of impersonation.
>
> (pp. 218, 224)

That is fanciful. Edmund, not his father, makes the only remarks that could possibly be interpreted as having any bearing on the subject of impersonation, and they lend little support to Trilling's reading. On one occasion, when his sister Julia reminds Edmund that in spite of his objections to their home theatricals he really loves the theater, he replies, "True, [I would go far] to see real acting, good hardened real acting; but I would hardly walk from this room to the next to look at the raw efforts of those who have not been bred to the trade,—a set of gentlemen and ladies, who have all the disadvantages of education and decorum to struggle through" (p. 95). The objection here is to incompetence and amateurism, not to impersonation. Later, when it is suggested to Edmund that he should play the role of a clergyman in the play because he is himself about to be ordained he makes the only other remark in the book that can be read as bearing on the subject: "the man who chooses the profession himself, is, perhaps, one of the last who would wish to represent it on the stage." No one would want to hang much of an argument on those words, but the objection seems to be not to impersonation as such but to the very opposite, to the *lack* of distance between role and player; it recalls the rule of the puppet theater that the one part a puppet must never play is that of a doll. Henry Crawford's willingness to take any part, and his skill in doing so, might be adduced as an argument against impersonation in the novel, but the plasticity of Henry's temperament is a symptom of what is wrong with him, not the cause. The universal commendation that greets Mrs. Grant when she assumes the part that Fanny declines hardly supports those who find a prejudice against impersonation in the book, but they may derive a little comfort from the fact that she turns out to be a very poor actress.

II

In remarking that *Mansfield Park* "takes full notice of spiritedness, vivacity, celerity, and lightness, . . . only to reject them," Trilling can only be thinking of the Crawfords, and in fact the Crawfords are the test case of his reading. He sees a problem here: he speaks of Mary Crawford as "all pungency and wit, . . . downright, open, intelligent, impatient" (p. 213); then a few pages later he changes his tune: "although on a first reading . . . Mary Crawford's speeches are all delightful, they diminish in charm as we read the novel a second time. We begin to hear something disagreeable in their intonation: it is the peculiar modern bad quality which Jane Austen was the first to represent—insincerity . . . as we become inured to the charms of her performance we see through the moral impersonation" (p. 220).

Trilling makes no effort to reconcile these contradictions, and given his view of the novel as essentially celebrating stasis, there is no way he could do it. The central fact about the Crawfords is that they change, change dramatically, not once but twice, and their change is less a matter of status, like Mrs. Norris's, than a matter of moral nature, like Tom Bertram's. When the Crawfords arrive at Mansfield they are a pair of jaded Londoners, premature worldlings brought up by a corrupt uncle and aunt now dead. No one, even on first reading, could find "spiritedness, vivacity, celerity, and lightness" in Mary's studiedly cynical remarks about marriage, picked up in the cheap and flashy London circles she has just left, or in her tiresome worrying of the question whether Fanny is "in" or "out." Then, under the influence of Mansfield, the Crawfords slowly improve: they begin to recognize and to share and to value authentic feelings until there are moments when Mary is indeed a young woman of great charm, though she never deserves all of Trilling's praise: her spirit and vivacity are never sufficient to obscure her view of the main chance, and she is never really "open," as the incident of the chain she gives Fanny proves. (Here she is "false as a woman" as well as a friend, and how much Jane Austen believes women owe each other can hardly be exaggerated.) Henry is more of a chameleon than his sister and improves even more, or seems to: the young man we see on his visit to Portsmouth—finely bred, manly, tactful and engaging, a conscientious landowner and devoted friend—is worthy of even such a bride as Fanny. Then they leave Mansfield and the moral pall of London descends upon them again; Mary becomes capable of writing the unfeeling, self-seeking letters we read, and Henry betrays the hospitality of Mansfield and his love of Fanny by running away with Maria Bertram, whom he doesn't even like very much.

There may be problems in narration here of course; that is quite a different matter. It is a good deal for a writer to expect us to believe that characters change once; to expect us to believe that they change twice may be too much. Yet there is a good deal of continuity in the Crawfords; Mansfield lifts them above themselves for a little bit and then, back in London, they revert to their old natures. A more serious problem is that the second change takes place entirely off-stage; we never see either Crawford after it occurs, though of course we hear about Henry and read Mary's letters. The last time the Crawfords actually appear on the stage of the novel, the last time we see them for ourselves as it were, they are almost pleasing enough to deserve Trilling's kindest words; but those are not the Crawfords on whom the book passes its final moral judgment. That is passed on the two as recorrupted by London. And the judgment does not say that charm has nothing to do with virtue and happiness or deters its possessors from the good life. At most it says that there are other things more important than charm for those who would lead the good life; more certainly it says that those who turn their backs on the good life cease to be charming, as the Crawfords most resoundingly do.

To miss the changes in the Crawfords is to miss a central concern of the novel: its deep involvement with the question of how nature and nurture are involved in the development of character. Jane Austen spent her life among three generations of a large, vigorous, highly gifted, and extremely various family. Two of her brothers became admirals; one was knighted and lived to be ninety-one. Another came into very considerable wealth; she was living in a cottage on the grounds of one of the splendid estates he inherited when she wrote the novel. Still another brother "was never able to take his place in the family"; he may have been congenitally deaf—Jane Austen knew sign language. No person of her intelligence could have watched the unfolding of such variation among the offspring of the same stock without pondering its mystery; no woman, at a time when the rearing of children was woman's chief concern, could refrain from asking herself how it could best be done and what difference it made.

In many ways Mary Crawford and Fanny Price are mirror-images of each other. Mary seems to have all the advantages of nature: born with health, looks, energy, charm, fortune; but in nurture she has all the disadvantages. Both girls are brought up in the houses of uncles, but one uncle is vicious where the other, though ponderous and distant, is cultivated and just. One girl has her wits and her ambitions sharpened by life in London; the spirit of the other is gently nourished by the continued contact with nature that country life affords. Each has as her chief companion a brother or brother-figure, but Henry Crawford for all his charm can only heap presents on Mary where Edmund Bertram guides Fanny's taste and corrects her judgment. Mary knows nothing of the trials and deprivation, the feelings of inconsequence, that play so large a part in shaping Fanny's character; "spoilt! spoilt!" is Edmund's final judgment on her; but the night that Sir Thomas watches Fanny lead out the ball he is proud to think that "education and manners she owed to him."

The moral categories that Trilling uses in placing the Crawfords are too simple to be useful without further examination. Take "celerity"—does the book really take "full notice" of it only to reject it, and does this make *Mansfield Park* different from the other novels? There does seem to be a marked distrust of speed in this book, but so is there in all of them. *Pride and Prejudice,* described by its author herself as "too light, and bright, and sparkling," was nevertheless originally called *First Impressions*, a title that can only have meant that impressions *hastily* formed are not to be trusted; the word *prejudice* in the present title carries much the same suggestion. One of the absurdities of Mr. Collins's proposal is that it happens so fast; Elizabeth Bennet's friendship with Mr. Wickham is to be questioned on the same grounds. In *Emma*, the other book that seems swiftest in action, Mr. Woodhouse's fear of haste is made comic to be sure, but the only marriage that takes place quickly is the Eltons', and its speed is a major symptom of the vacancy of character in its principals. Mary Crawford's "celerity" can be a form of impatience both tiresome and rude. She has so much to say about how slow everything in Mansfield is that Mrs. Grant, the best-natured character in the book, her devoted half-sister and hostess, speaks to her rather pointedly on the subject. And before we conclude with Trilling that the book makes an unqualified case for slowness, shows a uniform "preference for rest over motion," we must consider the character of Lady Bertram, whose immobility and languor deprive her of any moral consequence whatever.

III

In many ways Fanny Price is unique among Jane Austen's heroines. She is the only outsider—all the others are daughters of the main family who live in the big house. Hers is the only story that begins in childhood—all the others begin as the heroines reach marriageable age. She is the only heroine who changes social class, indeed the only character in Jane Austen who certainly does. All the other heroines except Emma do rather better in the matrimonial marketplace than their economic qualifications alone should have led them to expect, but there is little or no social disparity in their marriages: they are daughters of gentlemen marrying gentlemen. Fanny is not. She traverses a vast social distance (that, presumably, is the reason her story must begin so early): at the outset she is a frightened, inconsequential little stranger, the crude product of a grim lower-middle-class life in Portsmouth who cries herself to sleep every night; at the end she is the bride of Mansfield's worthiest son, the daughter Sir Thomas has always wanted, the spiritual center of the great house itself. She is a very odd heroine for a novel whose "praise is . . . for social stasis."[5]

Trilling acknowledges Fanny's development as a person, but in a curiously backhanded way. "At a certain point," he says, "the author . . . sees to it that Fanny becomes taller, prettier, and more energetic." The idiom manages to make the process of growing up sound unnatural, though most of us increase our stature between the ages of ten and eighteen without authorial intervention or novelistic fraud.

Jane Austen is merely showing nurture coming to the aid of nature—the good food and air of Mansfield, the horsebackriding and so on, are helping to develop the shy little thing of the novel's opening pages into an attractive young woman.

The increase in Fanny's physical size and social standing is matched by an increase in her moral authority. Each of the first two of the three books that make up *Mansfield Park* ends with enormous pressure being brought to bear upon her to do something that she is quite sure is wrong for her to do—first, pressure to appear in the play the other young people are putting on, and second, pressure to marry Henry Crawford. The two situations have similarities (both are isolating in their effect), but they are carefully graded in importance and in the kind of strength that they require of Fanny. Appearance in the play is obviously much less permanent in its consequences than marrying Henry Crawford; besides, just as the pressure to appear reaches its strongest, Sir Thomas returns and the whole project is shelved; there is no such lucky relief in the second situation; it goes all the way.

Since both of Fanny's decisions are refusals they may be misread as signs of passivity, but remember that she is in no position to initiate actions: she is a woman, an outsider, a person of no economic or social importance. Yet the actions she takes are at least as decisive, and their consequences at least as far reaching, as the actions of any other Jane Austen heroine. Consider comparable situations: when Elizabeth Bennet refuses Mr. Collins she stirs up a momentary ripple in the family but it is soon forgotten; when Emma Woodhouse refuses Mr. Elton she is truly ashamed of having encouraged Harriet Smith to look in that direction for a husband but there are absolutely no public consequences; but when Fanny Price refuses Henry Crawford her whole known world is shaken and for a time falls apart. She deeply offends Sir Thomas, her protector and surrogate father; she turns the dislike of one aunt (Mrs. Norris) into positive hatred and forfeits the new-found respect of another aunt (Lady Bertram); she surrenders a chance to increase the esteem of the man she cares about most (her cousin Edward) as well as a chance to score against his sisters, who have never treated her very well; she offends a man (Henry Crawford) who has already signally aided her beloved brother William and who stands in a position to help her younger sister Susan almost as much. Ultimately she pays the price of banishment from Mansfield Park, seat of every grace and dignity she knows, and has to go back to Portsmouth. This last consequence she could not have foreseen, but all the rest she could have and there is no reason to doubt that she did.

No other Jane Austen heroine goes anything like as far as Fanny in defying her society; no other lives in a society so malleable, subject to such sweeping changes, attaching so much importance to environment and rearing. It is an open world, a world in process, where the consequences we see are not inevitable. We cannot imagine any circumstances in which Mr. Elton would finally have won Emma's hand or Mr. Collins Elizabeth Bennet's, but if Henry Crawford had not "indulged in the freaks of coldblooded vanity a little too long . . . there would have been every probability of success and felicity for him." He, not Edmund Bertram, would have been Fanny's husband. Things need not have turned out the way they did.

IV

Nearly two decades after he published his essay on *Mansfield Park* Trilling returned to the subject in the Charles Eliot Norton Lectures, *Sincerity and Authenticity*.[6] This time he put his argument somewhat differently: "*Mansfield Park* ruthlessly rejects the dialectical mode. . . . It does not confirm our characteristic modern intuition that the enlightened and generous mind can discern right and wrong and good and bad only under the aspect of process and development, of futurity and the interplay and resolution of contradictions. . . . It is antipathetic to the temporality of the dialectical mode; the only moment of judgement it acknowledges is *now*" (pp. 79-80). In denying that there are process and development in the novel Trilling is merely rephrasing his early assertion that it is fixed and static and closed, but in his discovery that the book "ruthlessly rejects the dialectic mode" he seems to introduce a new basis for judgment.

But there is a chance that Trilling fails to find dialectical movement in *Mansfield Park* because he looks for it in the wrong place. Whatever may be the situation in our own lives, it is doubtful that in novels such a movement reconciles good and evil, right and wrong; certainly it does not in the novels of Jane Austen. There the interplay lies between two modes of being or two moral qualities both of which are desirable in themselves but each of which is insufficient for a good life if it is taken alone, and difficult to reconcile with the other if they are taken together.

In *Pride and Prejudice* and *Emma* the dialectical movement is much the same. In both novels the heroine represents energy, vitality, a fresh and vigorous and inventive way of looking at things. Elizabeth Bennet may trust her perception too much and Emma Woodhouse may trust her imagination too much, but it is a significant part of the value of both of them that they are genuinely perceptive and alert. The men they marry represent something like order; the marriage that ends each book is a reconciliation of exuberance and control; society is revitalized by its ability to incorporate the very psychic abundance that seemed to threaten it.

In *Mansfield Park* the contraries to be reconciled are very different. They first emerge in the choice the novel makes between the Crawfords on the one hand and Fanny Price and Edmund Bertram on the other, and there they seem irreconcilable; but in the more inclusive pattern of the book they emerge in the relation between the heroine and her adoptive home, where reconciliation is achieved. Mansfield makes Fanny worthy of being its spiritual heir at the same time that she makes it worth inheriting. Under its influence the little outsider grows up to be the daughter Sir Thomas has always wanted and under her influence the great house becomes as good as it has always been beautiful. Each assimilates the other without losing what is essential in its own nature. When Henry Crawford watches Fanny with her brother William, Jane Austen says that he has enough "moral taste" to appreciate the scene. The phrase neatly encapsulates the reconciliation of the moral and the aesthetic modes which is the dialectic of the book.

It would be easy to imagine an autobiographical basis for this dialectic. *Mansfield Park* seems to celebrate the author's solemn joy in finding once more a settled home on her brother's beautiful estate after the years of wandering occasioned by her father's retirement and death, and it is not difficult to understand a nature that would take the occasion to scrutinize its own worthiness of such a felicitous outcome of past uncertainties. At the same time *Mansfield Park* is the first new novel that Jane Austen had been able to complete in more than a decade; in it she resumes in sober middle age a career that had begun in youthful high spirits, and in doing so she must have been concerned to reconcile her gifts as an artist with her duty as a Christian.

V

Some readers who will grant inaccuracies in Trilling's reading will nevertheless argue that it has some kind of psychological truth to it; it may not correspond at every point with the text but it certainly corresponds with the way they feel when they read the text. This quite understandable opinion results, I think, less from the narrative than from the narration, the way the story is told.

Jane Austen's three sunny novels, *Northanger Abbey, Pride and Prejudice*, and *Emma* (the books that are most popular with modern readers), have one narrative strategy in common: in all of them we see the story largely from the point of view of a herione who is essentially wrong about what is going on, and this strategy has a lot to do with the reader's enjoyment of the books. For one thing, what leads the heroines astray is central both to their charm and to their value: at its most general it is a shared capacity to see the world as more wonderful and exciting and challenging than it is. For another thing, their mistaken point of view, in combination with the usually more subdued narrative voice in the background, gives us a binocularity of vision that lends depth to what we see; it keeps us guessing; it gives to the book the fun of a puzzle; we receive enough misleading or conflicting cues to create suspense by keeping us in doubt about what is really going on. But most important perhaps, a point-of-view character who sees things wrong is very reassuring, very unthreatening. For many of us such a character goes far to confirm what we have always suspected about other people's way of looking at the world anyway.

Now the unforgivable thing about Fanny Price is that she is always right. The recent study by Martin Price (no relative) mentioned at the outset argues convincingly that there is a good deal more of Jane Austen's gentle irony playing around Fanny than some of us were earlier ready to grant, but at most the irony calls attention to a certain naivety or angularity or singleness of mind with which our heroine pursues virtue; it never suggests, as the irony that surrounds Emma does, that she may be headed in the wrong direction. When we see a story from the point of view of a character whose appraisal of what is going on is essentially correct, obviously we do not have to wait to get the true view; this diminishes suspense and is responsible, I think, for the effect that Trilling describes when he says "the only moment of judgement is *now*." As the example of the Crawfords shows, judgment can be delayed, but it is likely to be delayed less than when we have to wait for the point-of-view character to be enlightened.

Another thing: although Fanny is not (as it were) personally passive, in that she makes decisions that require great strength of character and that carry consequences of considerable danger to herself, the book ultimately casts her in a passive role, and many readers find that uncongenial. Where the heroines of the three sunny novels just mentioned break through their misconceptions to make the central discoveries of their novels, the central discovery of *Mansfield Park* is made *about* Fanny. The story-sentence of *Emma*, for instance, goes something like this: "In the course of trying to make matches with one another for several of her acquaintances Emma *discovers* that there is one man for whom she wants to make a match with no one but herself"; but the story-sentence of *Mansfield Park* goes something like this: "As a consequence of making a series of decisions that seem to push her farther and farther toward the fringes of Mansfield Park society Fanny *is discovered* to belong at its very center." It is a curious complication of voice: by acting she becomes acted upon. Because Fanny has always seen things pretty much as they are there is no big discovery left for her to make, and the big discovery must be made by others about her.

Probably we prefer heroines in whom energy and virtue are less ambiguously united. For all her love of nature and Scott and Cowper, Fanny looks to the past of literary history, not to the future. In character she strikingly resembles that other Christian heroine, Clarissa, whose fate is so different, and hardly at all resembles Jane Eyre, whose story bears so many similarities to hers. If a reader thinks that Fanny should be more like Jane Eyre, there is plenty of room for that opinion, as well as many others. All that I have meant to suggest here is that there can be a responsible reading of the text quite different from Trilling's, and that the limits within which responsible readings of the text can occur may be somewhat different from those he tried to establish.

NOTES

[1]The essay first appeared under the title "Mansfield Park" in *Partisan Review* 21, 5 (September-October 1954):492-511. *The Opposing Self* was published by Viking in New York.

[2]*Forms of Life: Character and Moral Imagination in the Novel* (New Haven: Yale Univ. Press, 1983).

[3]*The Opposing Self*, pp. 210-11.

[4]The text of *Mansfield Park* as prepared by R. W. Chapman in the Riverside Edition (Boston: Houghton Mifflin, 1965) is the one cited here and throughout. This quotation occurs on p. 16.

[5]There is a tradition of reading *Mansfield Park* very different from Trilling's; it not only acknowledges the presence of change in the novel but makes it central to the meaning. This tradition may take its departure from "Jane Austen and the Peerage" by Donald J. Greene, *PMLA* (1953):1017-31; it finds its fullest elaboration in *A Reading of "Mansfield Park": An Essay in Critical Synthesis* by Avrom Fleishman (Minneapolis: Univ. of Minnesota Press, 1967) and a briefer recapitulation in *Jane Austen's Novels: Social Change and Literary Form* by Julia Prewitt Brown (Cambridge, Mass.: Harvard Univ. Press, 1979). But these writers are so intent on finding a social message in the novel that they allegorize some parts of the narrative to the neglect of others. Fleishman, for instance, says that the emphasis of the novel falls "on the correction of the gentry's way of life" (p. 33). But the way of life of the lower-middle-class Prices in Portsmouth exhibits much the same faults as the way of life of the more favorably placed Bertrams at Mansfield Park: in both instances the parents are insufficiently attentive to their children with the consequence that the children are getting out of hand. Since the Portsmouth household suffers further from "the greatest misery of all . . . [the lack of] elegance, propriety, regularity, harmony . . . peace and tranquility" (ch. 39), the reader might more reasonably conclude that the emphasis of the novel falls on the notion that since misconduct is much the same in all social classes it is best endured in comfortable surroundings. Mrs. Brown for her part argues: "Marriage is the highest form of self-fulfillment in Jane Austen, yet the debasement of this most primal hope is revealed in the three marriages described in the opening of the novel. From its economic to its spiritual condition, the world of *Mansfield Park* is a world in transition and decline" (p. 86). But the point is that the marriage that *ends* the story (Fanny's marriage to Edmund) is a vast improvement over "the three marriages described in the opening" (her mother's and two aunts'). In order to find *Mansfield Park* describing "a world in . . . decline" Mrs. Brown has to read the novel backward.

[6]*Sincerity and Authenticity* (Cambridge, Mass.: Harvard Univ. Press, 1972).

SEL 27 (1987)
ISSN 0039-3657

Tennyson's "The Epic": An Experiment in Perspective

MARY ANN KLEIN

In 1886, as Tennyson neared the completion of the *Idylls of the King*, he stated his purpose in creating a nineteenth-century Arthuriad: "to teach men . . . the need of the ideal."[1] Tennyson's phrasing suggests that a mere delineation of the ideal is not enough at a time when new value systems are being stridently urged by many of his contemporaries and just as stridently attacked by many others as illegitimate transvaluations. Men and women, Tennyson implies, must above all be convinced of the need for ideals, rather than directed to specific sources of authority and faith. But from the beginning of his work with Arthurian material Tennyson knew that transmitting the "need of the ideal" was fraught with problems, as I will show in this study of "The Epic,"[2] a critical early stage in the development of the imagination which eventually brought forth the *Idylls*.

As Tennyson begins to work with Arthurian material in "The Epic," he seems to face two major problems: how to determine the content of the ideal and how to develop a form that can confront readers with their own modes of perceiving that ideal. In this prototype Tennyson experiments with the content of the ideal. He invokes ideals corresponding to and contrary to the culture's values. He even invokes dead or dying systems of value which might still produce the resonance of idealism in his readers. He moreover seems bent on anticipating his readers' reservations, challenges, and conflicts and building them into the poem, thus inviting his readers to find their own perspectives dramatically rendered and placed in

Mary Ann Klein is Professor of English at Quincy College in Quincy, Illinois. She is currently working on an article on Tennyson's 1859 idylls, part of a book on the compositional stages of the *Idylls of the King*.

conflict with other perspectives. He creates a complex network of characters, actions, scenes, settings, and imagery to dramatize various modes of perception. Thus "The Epic" is an important experiment in multiple perspective, the technique Tennyson will perfect in the *Idylls*.

"The Epic" consists of three parts, one preceding and one following the "Morte" and the "Morte" itself. The frame provides a contemporary setting for the reading of the "Morte," calling attention to it as an artistic creation[3] and thereby distancing the world of the ideal from Tennyson's readers. In the first part of the frame, the narrator sketches in the scene: Francis Allen and his guests are gathered on Christmas eve around a half-empty wassail bowl after somewhat shopworn rituals have been perfunctorily performed, "The game of forfeits done—the girls all kissed / Beneath the sacred bush and past away."[4] The unromantic lethargy of this scene of nineteenth-century life, a contrast to the spirited revelry usually accompanying such rituals in past ages and in past literature, sets the tone for the rest of the frame. Responsible for the muted tone are Francis Allen's guests: Everard Hall, a poet; Holmes, a parson; and the narrator, an awkward skater. The narrator charts the currents of conversation. He begins with a commonly shared lament about dying Christmas traditions, "How all the old honor had from Christmas gone, / Or gone, or dwindled down to some odd games / In some odd nooks like this" (7-9). Next he reports Parson Holmes's strident complaints about contemporary events threatening his position and function as clergyman:

> Now harping on the church-commissioners,
> Now hawking at Geology and schism;
> Until I woke, and found him settled down
> Upon the general decay of faith
> Right through the world, "at home was little left,
> And none abroad: there was no anchor, none,
> To hold by."
>
> (15-21)

Last he moves to Francis Allen's hearty countering pledge of trust in the poet and friend, Everard Hall, who wrote an epic, "his King Arthur" (28), but doubting its value, destroyed all but one of his twelve books, that one salvaged by Francis Allen. Through the narrator's setting of scene and placement of characters in that scene, Tennyson deals with the first of his problems. What has been deftly sketched is a world where shifting values force people to assume stances, as they struggle to determine the source of problems and solutions, even while the ground shifts beneath them.

Tennyson then builds into the poem some possible reservations his readers might have about formulators of problems and solutions. He first explores reservations about religious formulators. Holmes, like a number of ineffectual religious figures in the *Idylls,* is unable to provide enlightenment. He is a muddled man who flails about trying to pinpoint the cause of his anguish. He is replaced by the poet, Hall, as a potential authority or "anchor," but Hall is hesitant to view himself in that role or to claim that function for his poetry. Tennyson also builds in some reservations about the form the poet might choose. Critics who see Tennyson as the too self-conscious poet here have sometimes singled out these reservations about form, neglecting the context in which Tennyson has articulated them. Hall is the chief source of these reservations. The host reports Hall's disclaimers:

> He thought that nothing new was said, or else
> Something so said 'twas nothing—that a truth
> Looks freshest in the fashion of the day:
> God knows: he has a mint of reasons: ask,
>
> (30-33)

and then Hall himself elaborates on his doubts:

> 'Why take the style of those heroic times?
> For nature brings not back the Mastodon,
> Nor we those times; and why should any man
> Remodel models? these twelve books of mine
> Were faint Homeric echoes, nothing-worth,
> Mere chaff and draff, much better burnt.'
>
> (35-40)

These reservations reveal the poet's sensitivity to those fashionable critical dicta he is violating: the preference for the topical subject, for modern forms rather than classical models. The host, urging the reading of the "Morte," speaks against these fashionable dicta and defends the epic, saying, "it pleased *me* well enough" (34). Yet he voices his own reservation about the salvaged book. The host's solemnly intoned proverbial "keep a thing, its use will come" (42) reveals his embarrassed sentimental attachment to the poem disguised as a utilitarian or pragmatic assessment of it. Both his attachment and his assessment are undercut by "I hoard it as a sugar-plum for

Holmes" (43), a comic view of the poem as a sentimental sop to ease Holmes's pain with no mention of its serving a like but crucial function for the host. The final reservation and the most important one in the frame is that of the narrator, initially styled as a rather disinterested and detached observer of the entire scene, who rouses himself from a half-waking state to participate in the conversation. It is he who ultimately asks the poet to read the "Morte." The narrator's superficial reason for the request is his recollection of Everard's college fame as a poet. A more subtle reason, foreshadowing his final response to the "Morte" in the second half of the frame, is suggested by the image the narrator chooses to describe himself: "I, though sleepy, like a horse / That hears the corn-bin open, pricked my ears" (44-45). In spite of himself and because of an interior hunger he longs to hear what promises enlightenment. This image assumes even greater significance when one recalls that it echoes a scene in *The Tempest* where Ariel reports to Prospero that his music charmed Caliban, Trinculo, and Stephano:

> like unback'd colts they prick'd their ears,
> Advanced their eyelids, lifted up their noses
> As they smelt music. So I charmed their ears.
>
> (IV.i.176-78)

Ariel's music here becomes the music of the poet who must appeal to his readers' senses to lead them to contemplate ideals which will draw them from their lesser selves. The narrator then readies himself to consider the poem and the poet as potential sources of transformation. The poet has been given the chance to be elevated to the position of priest of the new religion, poetry, but is not yet so situated.[5]

The first part of the frame ends with the group settling back to hear the poet read his poem, the "Morte." The "Morte's" opening scene is analogous to the frame poem's opening scene: it dramatizes the collapse of Arthur's order, his ideal way of life. The poem begins with a description of the Lyonnesse battlefield, strewn with Arthur's fallen knights, and of a wounded Arthur, guarded by his last knight, Bedivere. The setting underscores the notion of collapse as does Bedivere's initial action:

> The bold Sir Bedivere uplifted him,
> Sir Bedivere, the last of all his knights,
> And bore him to a chapel nigh the field,

A broken chancel with a broken cross,
That stood on a dark strait of barren land.

(6-10)

The visual images here suggest fragmentation, disintegration, and deterioration and provide a poignant backdrop to the image of Arthur and Bedivere shrinking in stature as they cross this waste and sterile landscape which threatens to overpower them.

Just as the function of the setting in the "Morte" is analogous to that of the frame's setting, so too is the function of Arthur and Bedivere analogous to that of the characters in the frame. At times Arthur and Bedivere seem to catch up the concerns of the characters in the frame. Like the guests at Francis Allen's who mourn the collapse of their traditions, both Arthur and Bedivere mourn the collapse of Arthur's order and search for causes of the collapse and solutions to the problems spawned by it. Arthur's reactions are varied. At first he, like Holmes, feels intense chagrin at the untimely closing of his era. Then he wistfully regrets that the joys of knightly companionship are past:

Such a sleep
They sleep—the men I loved. I think that we
Shall never more, at any future time,
Delight our souls with talk of knightly deeds,
Walking about the gardens and the halls
Of Camelot, as in the days that were.

(16-21)

He takes feeble comfort from Merlin's pledge that he "should come again / To rule once more" (23-24), but that comfort is dispelled by his own most unsettling realization, "I perish by this people which I made" (22). He does, however, allow himself the comfort of a memory, his receiving Excalibur from the Lady of the Lake in "those old days" (29). Finally, he clings to the hope that "wheresoever I am sung or told / In aftertime, this also shall be known" (34-35). Arthur's trust in the song or the poem to touch men even in the "aftertime" is like that of the poet and the host in the frame who want to trust in the efficacy of the poem. Arthur is searching for ways to understand what he has accomplished and what he has been. Anxious to validate himself in the midst of the ruin of his order, Arthur sends Bedivere to perform a ritual—the casting of Excalibur into the "middle mere" (37). Shaken by seeing his order reduced to a single knight, Arthur only imperfectly understands the ritual but believes it will produce signs verifying his identity and function. He trusts in the ritual and trusts that accompanying signs will become an integral part of the legend he will become. In the same way Francis Allen and some of his guests trust to the ritual, the reading of the "Morte," to reveal the poet's and the poem's function. Tennyson, through these analogies, establishes the integral relationship between the frame poem and the imbedded poem.

Consumed by his own anguish, Bedivere does not share Arthur's. Neither does he share Arthur's trust in the song or tale to preserve his memory as the shaper of "The goodliest fellowship of famous knights / Whereof this world holds record" (15-16). Indeed, he is determined to save Excalibur as a "record" (98) or "relic" (98), proof against his fears that Arthur will be remembered only as an "empty breath / And rumours of a doubt" (99-100). Bedivere's fears are supported by the setting against which his thoughts are placed; he carries Excalibur through

> the place of tombs,
> Where lay the mighty bones of ancient men,
> Old knights, and over them the sea-wind sang
> Shrill, chill, with flakes of foam.
>
> (46-49)

Bedivere fears that Arthur will become like those nameless and forgotten "ancient men," mourned only by the sea wind. He betrays the fragility of Arthur as ideal for he wishes to retain a palpable object, a sword to verify Arthur as ideal, to preserve a witness to his existence. Bedivere's mode of perception, shared at times by Arthur here, by Francis Allen and Holmes in the frame, Leodogran in "The Coming of Arthur" and Balin in "Balin and Balan," is such that he needs objective, tangible signs to maintain his belief. Francis Allen, for example, needs to cling to the salvaged manuscript of the "Morte" in order to bolster his belief. While betraying the fragility of Arthur as ideal, Bedivere also evinces his own strong need for the ideal, if only as something useful to himself. He is anxious to secure respect for himself, to gain for himself a function and a place of authority as the guardian of Arthur's memory. He wants to become the living record: "So might some old man speak in the aftertime / To all the people, winning reverence" (107-108).

While Bedivere believes that holding on to Excalibur is necessary for his future role and identity, Arthur believes that his own future role and identity depend on letting Excalibur go. Arthur drives for verification that he did exist as witness to the value of the ideal. Trusting Bedivere's faithfulness to the virtues he has instilled in his knights, Arthur exhorts Bedivere to perform the ritualistic action. Bedivere's reluctance and ultimately his deception are yet another test of Arthur's faith in himself. Arthur charges Bedivere with being "miserable and unkind, untrue, / Unknightly, traitor-hearted" (119-20) and finally is reduced to threatening him with death to force compliance. Finding thus no human verification of his identity, Arthur strains and insists on magical, mystical verification. The sword is thrown; the signs appear; Bedivere and Arthur are restored to a measure of belief.[6]

At this point in the "Morte," Arthur begins to swell to his full identity as an ideal, but an ideal in the most abstract sense. While the reader is to believe that Arthur represents the perfection of man's nature because of his dedication to values such as honor, courage, trust, and faithfulness, those values are only intoned, not fully delineated, since Arthur is only sketchily linked with the "goodliest fellowship of knights," a romantic code automatically associated with idealism. Precisely how Arthur is to function and precisely what he is to represent are unclear. In the last scene of the "Morte," for example, Arthur is drawn as a figure evoking pity rather than one representing knightly valor. Here Bedivere completes the ritual of bearing Arthur to the mysterious barge apparently launched with the casting of Excalibur.[7] Arthur reclining in the barge is thus described:

> So like a shattered column lay the King;
> Not like that Arthur who, with lance in rest,
> From spur to plume a star of tournament,
> Shot through the lists at Camelot, and charged
> Before the eyes of ladies and of kings.
>
> (221-25)

This description shows Arthur as fallen ideal. Bedivere, however, restores his stature when he expresses his fears at seeing Arthur received by the three queens aboard the black-draped barge:

> "For now I see the true old times are dead,
> When every morning brought a noble chance,
> And every chance brought out a noble knight.
> Such times have been not since the light that led
> The holy Elders with the gift of myrrh.
> But now the whole ROUND TABLE is dissolved
> Which was an image of the mighty world;
> And I, the last, go forth companionless,
> And the days darken round me, and the years,
> Among new men, strange faces, other minds."
>
> (229-38)

Bedivere's lament works in several ways: it grants to Arthur and his order validity, for it refers to the "true old times"; it places Arthur firmly in that romantic world of chivalry informed by the value, nobility; and it links Arthur with Christ, without equating them, by referring to the coming of the magi.

Beneath Bedivere's lament is the desire to believe that Arthur is the ideal and the doubt that he is not. Bedivere also fears that he who has believed will not be able to deal with a world foreign to him. Bedivere thus reveals fully the source of his anguish: not being able to sustain the ideals Arthur represented and yet not being able to abandon them completely. Thus it is clear that Bedivere, like Arthur, is designed to reflect stances taken by characters in the frame.

Arthur attempts to comfort Bedivere by placing his order in a larger historical and cultural perspective. Arthur addresses Bedivere from the barge:

> "The old order changeth, yielding place to new,
> And God fulfils Himself in many ways,
> Lest one good custom should corrupt the world.
> Comfort thyself: what comfort is in me?
> I have lived my life, and that which I have done
> May He within Himself make pure!"
>
> (240-45)

While this statement is meant to comfort Bedivere, it may disquiet him, for Arthur reveals his inability to define himself.[8] He must trust to God to reveal what his life has meant. If his tone suggests resigned confidence, his subsequent farewell speech does not. Arthur is uncertain about his fate,[9] but he permits himself to entertain paradisial visions with distinct Homeric echoes:

> "But now farewell. I am going a long way
> With these thou seest—if indeed I go—
> (For all my mind is clouded with a doubt)
> To the island-valley of Avilion;
> Where falls not hail, or rain, or any snow,
> Nor ever wind blows loudly; but it lies
> Deep-meadowed, happy, fair with orchard-lawns
> And bowery hollows crowned with summer sea,
> Where I will heal me of my grievous wound."
>
> (256-64)

Arthur's fate seems less uncertain when the image of the barge he sails on is studied:

So said he, and the barge with oar and sail
Moved from the brink, like some full-breasted swan
That, fluting a wild carol, ere her death,
Ruffles her pure cold plume, and takes the flood
With swarthy webs.

(265-69)

Arthur, like Tennyson's Arthur Hallam and Ulysses, seems bound toward death.[10] Yet Bedivere provides no interpretation of Arthur's final words or of the removal of the figure he clung to in desperation. Bedivere is fixed in the indeterminate stance[11] of one

Revolving many memories, till the hull
Looked one black dot against the verge of dawn,
And on the mere the wailing died away.

(270-72)

The "Morte" ends then with these two inconclusive portraits of Arthur and Bedivere who have been locked in a struggle to define their own identities and functions and their relationships to one another. Each of them operates out of a different mode of perception which prevents him from understanding or embracing the perspective of the other.

The "Morte" is then followed by the second part of the frame poem. A sober profundity of tone provides continuity between the ending of the "Morte" and the beginning of the frame. Just as Bedivere is transfixed by his memories and the fading of the barge from his sight and the wailing from his hearing, so too are the listeners transfixed by the "Morte" which has ended. The conclusion of Hall's poem brings another dying, the dying of the light the poet read by: "Here ended Hall, and our last light, that long / Had winked and threatened darkness, flared and fell" (273-74). The progress of the light is like that of Arthur's barge and like that of the poem itself. The flaring out of the light occurs as the "Morte" ends with the fading of Arthur's way of life. The events and images join to create a charged moment. The "light that threatened darkness" is Arthur, is the poet, and is the poem. The complex relationship between the frame and the "Morte" and the importance of the strategy Tennyson is using become apparent.

Ironically, the parson who longed for an "anchor" fails to respond to the "light that threatened darkness," and does not participate in this charged moment. He has fallen asleep during the reading and awakens to assess the poem vaguely as "Good" (276). Because of his insistence on religious formulations, he has locked out the poetic formulation and consequently learns nothing from the poem.[12] The sympathetic host and the skeptical narrator, however, sit "rapt"(277). The host finds his judgment about the poem's great worth substantiated and reasserts his conviction in an ironic and understated way, " 'There now—that's nothing' " (285). The narrator, no longer disinterested, is confused and unsure why the poem has succeeded in moving them, but he speculates that

> it was the tone with which he read—
> Perhaps some modern touches here and there
> Redeemed it from the charge of nothingness—
> Or else we loved the man, and prized his work;
> I know not.
>
> (277-81)

The once disinterested narrator is haunted by the "Morte" and finds King Arthur invading his dreams and remaining there when "dreams / Begin to feel the truth and stir of day" (290-91). The narrator is able in the first stages of his dreaming to perceive Arthur as represented in the poem. He, unlike Bedivere and Holmes, is able "To sail with Arthur under looming shores, / Point after point" (289-90). Yet even while the narrator embraces Arthur as an ideal, the nature of that ideal remains shadowy and undefined. The narrator, however, is able to extend the image of Arthur. Through his dream, in which Arthur is recreated as a contemporary, the narrator assumes the poet's role: to create a medium in which the ideal can be contemplated. In that stage of dreaming dreams that image inchoate truth he brings him back from Avilion healed of his wound and transformed into "a modern gentleman" (294), to be greeted by a crowd which includes the narrator and which eventually becomes a whole people pledging complete faith in Arthur and embracing him as ideal:

> To me, methought, who waited with a crowd,
> There came a bark that, blowing forward, bore
> King Arthur, like a modern gentleman
> Of stateliest port; and all the people cried,
> "Arthur is come again: he cannot die."
> Then those that stood upon the hills behind
> Repeated—"Come again, and thrice as fair";
> And, further inland, voices echoed—"Come
> With all good things, and war shall be no more."
> At this a hundred bells began to peal.
>
> (292-301)

The narrator finds his dreams merging with his waking state when he hears bells ringing: "That with the sound I woke, and heard indeed / The clear church-bells ring in the Christmas-morn"(302-303). The merging of the bells welcoming Arthur the "modern gentleman" with the bells heralding Christmas morning suggests a further linking of Arthur and his way of life with the tradition of Christmas. The ritual of the bells has acquired, perhaps by association, new vitality; and Christmas, as in *In Memoriam*, has been recharged with meaning. But while the vitality is clear the meaning is still vague.

As the poem ends, the narrator shows the poet's power to capture him, to move him so deeply that Arthur and all he represents inform not only his dreams but also his waking state. Arthur as image has the power to steady the narrator, the awkward skater troubled with keeping his balance on the slippery surface of life. Most important, the narrator has been moved to participate in the poet's task of creating "his King Arthur." Yet even at the poem's end, the ideals Arthur represents and the exact qualities restored to the Christmas tradition are not clear.[13] They are only vaguely suggested by the line from the narrator's dream: "Come / With all good things, and war shall be no more"(300). As the poem ends the reader is to believe that the narrator has learned much from the "Morte" which will spill over into his life. More important, the reader sees the narrator being stirred not by any of those causes he speculates about in his waking moments, but by the imaginative experience of the poem penetrating his being so deeply that he becomes a man consumed. The narrator's mode of perception is only suggested here but is not fleshed out. It is, however, the mode of perception most fully explored in the frame poem and one to be more completely developed in later stages of Tennyson's work such as "The Coming of Arthur."

In this early handling of Arthurian material, Tennyson addressed his first problem: how to handle the content of the ideal. His uncertainty about possible solutions shows in his vague treatment of Arthur's way of life and Arthur's function.[14] At this stage of Tennyson's thinking, he has not fixed the plan for the *Idylls*. He has not determined, for example, where the "Morte" will finally appear in the series of idylls or that Bedivere will eventually be the narrator of the "Morte," when it becomes the core of "The Passing of Arthur." Tennyson also worked on his second problem: how to develop a form suitable to readers with varying modes of perception. Clearly Tennyson is experimenting with strategies he will later perfect: the use of the dream as the medium in which the ideal can be contemplated; the use of the passage of a character from waking to dreaming states; the use of the repeated scene to show changes; the use of a frame and imbedded poem to establish correspondences and to reinforce one another. Most important, he has dramatized various modes of perception and played them against one another.[15] He will expand on the modes of perception sketched out in the frame and the "Morte," those of Arthur, Bedivere, the poet, the parson, the hearty host, and the narrator. He will elaborate and create variations on each of these and add many more as he expands the range of his characters and the number of episodes in later *Idylls*. But it is here in "The Epic" that Tennyson begins to discover a form wherein "to teach men the need of the ideal."

NOTES

[1]Hallam Tennyson, *Alfred Lord Tennyson: A Memoir*, 2 vols. in 1 (New York: Greenwood Press, 1969), 2:337.

[2]"The Epic" is usually dealt with only sketchily by Tennyson's critics. Among those who comment on it briefly are: Jerome Buckley, *Tennyson: The Growth of a Poet* (Cambridge Mass.: Harvard Univ. Press, 1960), pp. 80-81; Kathleen Tillotson, "Tennyson's Serial Poem," in Geoffrey and Kathleen Tillotson, *Mid-Victorian Studies* (London: Univ. of London; Athlone Press, 1965), pp. 86-88; Clyde de L. Ryals, *From the Great Deep* (Athens: Ohio Univ. Press, 1967), pp. 18-19, 21; John R. Reed, *Perception and Design in Tennyson's "Idylls of the King"* (Athens: Ohio Univ. Press, 1969), pp. 109-12; J. Phillip Eggers, *King Arthur's Laureate: A Study of Tennyson's "Idylls of the King"* (New York: New York Univ. Press, 1971), p. 224; Ward Hellstrom, *On the Poems of Tennyson* (Gainesville: Univ. of Florida Press, 1972), pp. 89-90; Christopher B. Ricks, *Tennyson* (New York: Macmillan, 1972), p. 265; John D. Rosenberg, *The Fall of Camelot* (Cambridge, Mass.: Belknap Press of Harvard Univ. Press, 1973), p. 150; Paul Turner, *Tennyson* (London: Routledge & Kegan Paul, 1976), pp. 77-80; Henry Kozicki, *Tennyson and Clio: History in the Major Poems* (Baltimore: Johns Hopkins Univ. Press, 1979), pp. 39-44, 114; Robert Pattison, *Tennyson and Tradition* (Cambridge, Mass.: Harvard Univ. Press, 1979), pp. 64-66, 93: J. M. Gray, *Tho' the Vision of the Night: A Study of Source, Evolution, and Structure in Tennyson's Idylls of the King* (Montreal: McGill-Queens Univ. Press, 1980), pp. 10-12; Donald S. Hair, *Domestic and Heroic in Tennyson's Poetry* (Toronto: Univ. of Toronto Press, 1981), pp. 43, 64, 122-26, 207, 228; F. B. Pinion, *A Tennyson Companion* (London: Macmillan, New York: St. Martin's Press, 1984), pp. 99, 104-105, 172.

[3]A. Dwight Culler in *The Poetry of Tennyson* (New Haven: Yale Univ. Press, 1977), pp. 99-109, provides one of the fuller, although uneven, discussions of "The Epic." He particularly focuses on the relationship between the frame poem and the "Morte." While I argue that Tennyson is very tentative in "The Epic," Culler asserts that the poem provides clear solutions, namely, "through prayer, labor, and imagination to prepare for the new" (p. 107).

[4]*The Poems of Tennyson*, ed. Christopher Ricks (New York: W. W. Norton, 1972), p. 583, lines 2-3. All quotations from Tennyson's published work are taken from this edition. Line numbers are given in the text.

[5]Culler sees both the host and the narrator clearly recognizing poetry as "the true source of . . . spiritual nourishment" (p. 107). I find Tennyson far more tentative in his presentation of their stances on the matter.

[6]For an alternative reading of Bedivere and Arthur's roles in this scene, see Culler, pp. 102-103. I must disagree with Culler when he maintains that Bedivere has learned "to see spiritually" (p. 103).

[7]For an alternative reading of this scene, see Culler, pp. 103-104. I disagree with Culler's assertion that Bedivere is the protagonist of the "Morte." He seems to deemphasize the role of Arthur in this scene, perhaps anticipating the change in Bedivere's role in "The Passing of Arthur" when he becomes the narrator of the idyll.

[8]David Staines, in *Tennyson's Camelot: The Idylls of the King and Its Medieval Sources* (Waterloo, Ontario, Canada: Wilfrid Laurier Univ. Press, 1982), p. 46, maintains that Tennyson's "dependence upon Malory and his uncertainty about the proper treatment of Arthurian material do not allow him to move inside what remains a distinguished but one-sided portrait of the King."

[9]Marcia C. Culver in "The Death and Birth of an Epic: Tennyson's 'Morte d'Arthur,' " *VP* 1 (Spring 1982): 51-61, provides an excellent discussion of the evolution of the "Morte" by tracing manuscript changes. She demonstrates the poet's tentativeness about his conception of Arthur but she maintains that the poem finally shows that Tennyson "achieved restrained consolation and weary peace" (p. 55) and that the poem "ended in hope and a new beginning" (p. 60). Another fine article which discusses Tennyson's evolution as a poet is Joyce Green's "Tennyson's Development During the 'Ten Years' Silence,' " *PMLA* 66 (September 1951): 662-97.

[10]For another reading of this scene see Culver, pp. 54-57.

[11]See Culler, p. 159, for a different reading of Bedivere's stance.

[12]I cannot agree with Culler's interpretation of the parson's sleeping during the reading, namely, that it "is a compliment rather than the reverse" (p. 106).

[13]For an alternative reading of this scene see Culler, p. 106.

[14]See also Staines, p. 22.

[15]J. S. Lawry in "Tennyson's 'The Epic': A Gesture of Recovered Faith," *MLN* 74 (May 1959):400-403, does not deal with Tennyson's experimentation with many perspectives; hence he judges the poem to be clearly an "affirmation of faith in Christ, in human greatness, and in poetry" (p. 403), not the tentative and speculative piece I propose it is. Neither can I agree with H. A. Mason in "The First Setting of Tennyson's 'Morte d' Arthur,' " *English Association Essays and Studies* 31 (1978):98-114, who maintains that the poem's central focus is a "sense of nightmare, of utter collapse" (p. 111). Walter Nash, in "Tennyson: 'The Epic' and 'The Old "Morte," ' " *CQ* 6 (1975):326-49, provides an extremely fine reading of Tennyson's "The Epic" and rightly calls attention to its importance. When he explores the relationship between the frame poem and the imbedded poem, he focuses on Holmes and his troubled perspective. He therefore reads the "Morte" as an affirmative answer to this character's anguish alone. Because Nash singles out Holmes's perspective, as if there were no other characters in the frame, and because he interprets the "Morte" from this perspective, perhaps forgetting that Holmes sleeps through the reading of the "Morte," he does not deal with the uneasy relationship between Arthur and Bedivere, tortured and uncertain about their own identities and roles. Nash argues that the poem "becomes an elegiac tribute to the personal 'sun king,' an expression of grief at the loss of one whose confidence gave meaning to life, a profession of faith in the consolatory and constructive power of prayer (p. 342).

Nash does not see Tennyson in these early stages of his work with Arthurian material as experimenting with what Arthur will represent, but rather sees Tennyson presenting a fully realized Arthur. Most important, Nash (like Lawry) does not deal with the fragmentation of perspectives as an indication of the poet's tentativeness and speculation.

SEL 27 (1987)
ISSN 0039-3657

"A Yorkshire burr": Language in *Shirley*

SUSAN BELASCO SMITH

In writing *Shirley*, Charlotte Brontë moved from the personal issues of *Jane Eyre* to a consideration of the larger issues of her day. Although *Shirley* is no *Uncle Tom's Cabin* (a novel that Brontë admired very much), there is, in *Shirley*, an underlying concern about societies that isolate and degrade individuals who are socially, economically, and politically disenfranchised. *Shirley* was written in 1848, the year of European revolutions, and as Asa Briggs has clearly demonstrated, the novel is based on the fierce 1812 Luddite protests against the introduction of machinery into the textile mills, an innovation that had threatened many jobs held by working-class men.[1] Brontë researched the background of *Shirley* by studying the files of *The Leeds Mercury* at the time of the riots. Still, as a life-long resident of Yorkshire, she already knew the roots of the story and was quite familiar with the problems of working-class, unskilled laborers in an age of increasing technology. Among the large cast of characters in *Shirley* are uneducated working-class men such as the machine breakers, as well as their children, and an assortment of friendless women, desperate governesses and tutors, and overworked mothers and wives. All of these groups are at the mercy of middle class entrepreneurs determined to put the new technology to work. Language acts as the central marker of the acute divisions separating these groups. Brontë's clear and carefully offered variations of dialect and her comments on language help to undergird her central theme of society's inhumanity to the powerless.

Shirley is also striking in relying on language as an indicator of character, as a mark of regional pride, and as a sign of Brontë's

Susan Belasco Smith, who recently completed her Ph.D. in English at Texas A&M University, is currently Assistant Professor of English and Director of Composition at Allegheny College.

growing uneasiness with a rigid class system, marked so clearly by language in England. Dialect, in particular, allows Brontë to delineate her characters and, simultaneously, to call attention to those barriers established by a society that discriminates against its less powerful members. Nevertheless, *Shirley* is ultimately a novel about the breakdown of social barriers. Here, tutors marry heiresses, mill owners marry the nieces of clergymen, and speakers of broad Yorkshire dialect have fine collections of Italian art in their homes.

The various dialects and attitudes toward language thus reveal Brontë's attitudes toward class. Like Caroline Helstone of her novel, Brontë, as a clergyman's daughter, could freely circulate among different social strata and was therefore in a unique position from which to observe the changing class structure of mid-Victorian England. Although she was no avowed social reformer, her abiding theme is the supremacy of the world of feeling over the world of thought, and in *Shirley*, this theme is underscored by the use of language, especially that of the bidialectal character Hiram Yorke who can speak with a "Yorkshire burr"[2] as well as with an educated, middle-class accent. A symbol of the breakdown of social classes, Yorke also exemplifies the new man Brontë envisions for England: he is sensitive to the plight of the displaced workers but proud of his Yorkshire roots. Brontë's careful presentation of Yorke's bidialectal facility is a literary device designed to heighten the reader's awareness of his symbolic function.

Superficially, the characters of *Shirley* can be easily grouped according to the particular kind of dialect they use. There are minor characters like Mr. Malone and Mr. Donne, whose accents suggest a provincialism that sets them apart as outsiders who cannot come to terms with the idiosyncracies of Yorkshire society. A second group, primarily made up of native Yorkshire speakers, uses a broad West Yorkshire dialect that reflects their honest, hard-working approach to life. A third group is composed of middle-class characters whose dialect is not consistently represented orthographically; frequently the narrator offers us commentary about the sound of their voices and their style of language. A fourth group is bidialectal. These characters, like Mr. Hall and Mr. Yorke, speak Yorkshire when the occasion demands it, but use a generalized middle-class dialect when placed with middle-class peers. The narrator belongs to this last group, and as such, she crosses all of the dialect boundaries of the novel. By turns, she uses Yorkshire words and phrases, French expressions, and of course, her educated middle-class voice.

When Brontë wishes to convey a character's insensitivity, she has him speak in an affected way. The two characters who are most pretentious are the English Mr. Donne and the Irish Mr. Malone, two of the "abundant shower of curates [which] has fallen upon the north of England" (p. 7). As the honest, impoverished William Farren says to Shirley, " 'Ay, *I am* proud, and so are ye; but your pride and mine is t'raight mak'—what we call i'Yorkshire "clean pride," —sich as Mr. Malone and Mr. Donne knows nought about: theirs is mucky pride' " (p. 365). And the language of Donne and Malone clearly demonstrates what Farren means.

Donne, the curate from the south of England who has some deluded hope of wooing Shirley, uses speech that is full of the epenthesis of [r] at the end of words like "idea," syllable deletions as in "fam'ly," "reg'la," and "pos'tively," and the omission of a final [r] on words like "propa." As Mr. Donne attempts to captivate Shirley, the narrator snidely tells us that "You must excuse Mr. Donne's pronunciation, reader; it was very choice; he considered it genteel, and prided himself on his southern accent; northern ears received with singular sensations his utterance of certain words" (p. 322). Mr. Donne's affected accent is an orthographic representation of his affected character, and he is one of the least attractive characters in the book.

Likewise, Mr. Malone's Irish expressions like "shindy" for "fight," his pronunciation of [m] so that "firm," "helm," and "storm," are pronounced as the dysyllabic "firrum," "hellum," and "storrum," and the substitution of [θ] for [t] as in "counthrey" for "country" betray his Irish ancestry and make him an object of scorn not only because of his Irish background (Brontë's father was after all an Irishman), but mainly because his own unfeeling attitude to the working classes is very much like that of the pretentious Mr. Donne.

Opposed to those speakers of English who cause Yorkshiremen to wince are the characters who speak in the broad West Yorkshire dialect still heard in the north of England today. In *Shirley*, this dialect has the status of received pronunciation; as Mr. Yorke says, " 'A Yorkshire burr . . . was as much better than a Cockney's lisp, as a bull's bellow than a ratton's squeak' " (p. 58). A large group of characters in the novel are working-class people among whom Brontë had numerous friends and acquaintances. Brontë represents the speech of this group of Yorkshire speakers in a very detailed orthography.[3] By mid-century, dialect literature was flourishing in Yorkshire, and the poems of Ben Preston (1819-1902) were particularly popular. Preston was born in Bradford (close enough to Haworth for the Brontë sisters to walk there and back occasionally) and worked in the woolen trade. Many of his best poems were concerned with the struggles of the working classes. Preston and other poets before him established a tradition using the Yorkshire dialect, and part of the appeal of *Shirley* to Yorkshire readers was Brontë's use of native speech. In fact the reception of *Shirley* was more favorable in Yorkshire than in other areas of England. The dialect speakers in *Shirley* speak as G. L. Brook says of dialect generally, of "homely things in a homely way."[4] Brontë's use of the local dialect thus also allowed her to appeal to a wider readership who might value its directness and unpretentiousness.

Brontë recreates the Yorkshire dialect by using unique lexical forms and by respelling words to indicate vowel differences, assimilations, and substitutions. For example, all of the dialect speakers use "miln" for "mill," which was a common pronunciation; in fact, in his *English Dialect Dictionary*, Joseph Wright uses the superscription of the warning note addressed to Robert Moore, "the Divil of Hollows-miln," as an example of this West Yorkshire usage.[5] Other distinct lexical items in *Shirley*, cited by Joseph Wright as major examples in his *Dictionary*, include Joe Scott's description of Yorkshire girls as being "some o't'bonniest and mimmest-looking," meaning pretty and demure; William Farren's description of Shirley's eyes as having a "gleg light," meaning a bright light; and Farren's statement that he has had to sell his wife's "set o'cheeney," which Wright cites as a West Yorkshire form for "china." In addition, the general West Yorkshire words like "fairish" for "fairy," "shivered" for "shattered," "middling" for "average," and "childer" and "bairn" as synonyms for "children" lend realism and vitality to the speech of the dialect speakers.[6]

But on another level, the plain speech of these Yorkshire characters reflects their attitudes and position in the novel: they are homely, honest, and occasionally desperate men who are fighting for their livelihood and a way of life that was fast disappearing from the Yorkshire dales.

A homely aphorism like Joe Scott's "I can tell cheese fro' chalk" (p. 69) nicely captures the way in which such characters assess the affectation of the social classes that seek to oppress them. Scott tells Robert Moore that " 'We allus speak our minds i' this country; and then young parsons and grand folk fro' London is shocked at wer 'incivility,' and we like weel enow to gi'e 'em summat to be shocked at, 'cause it's sport to us to watch 'em turn up the whites o' their een, and spreed out their bits o'hands, like as they're flayed wi' bogards, and then to hear 'em say, nipping off their words short, like—'Dear! dear! Whet seveges! How very corse!' " (p. 68). By relying on his Yorkshire dialect to mimic his perception of a London accent, Scott not only reveals his sense of pride but also underscores the peculiarly English sensitivity to language as a marker of social class. In the same way, Mrs. Gale, who serves the curates in the opening scene of the novel, is disgusted with their affected ways and says that they "set everybody beneath their 'fit' " (p. 10). The narrator tells us that the curates " 'are always speaking against Yorkshire ways and Yorkshire folk,' and by that very token, Mrs. Gale does not believe one of them to be a real gentleman, or come of gentle kin" (p. 11).

But not only the minor characters are sensitive to the linguistic expression of class pretensions. Shirley, too, whom Tom Winnifrith has called "the nearest approach in Charlotte Brontë's novels to the advocate of a classless society," becomes outraged with Mr. Donne's denunciation of Yorkshire.[7] Donne complains to Shirley: " 'Wretched place—this Yorkshire,' " and " 'you scarsley ever see a fam'ly where a propa carriage or a reg'la butla is kep' " (p. 322). Shirley orders him from her house: " 'Walk through . . . and pretty quickly, and set foot on this pavement no more.' " When Donne shows no immediate response, Shirley exclaims, " 'Rid me of you instantly—instantly!' " (p. 323). The contrast between Donne's pretentious pronunciation with his dropped "r's" and Shirley's use of the Yorkshire imperative construction is striking. As with all the cultural confrontations depicted in the novel, the first indicator of the event is language that emphasizes the contrast between Yorkshire dialect and middle-class accents.

Often Brontë does not orthographically represent the speech of the middle-class characters. Instead, the narrator prefers to comment directly on their language and speech. Mrs. Pryor, who, in the grand tradition of coincidence in the Victorian novel, turns out to be Caroline Helstone's real mother, has the voice that is most closely scrutinized. She is shy and refined, not eager for the company of others. The narrator explains: "The lady had the clearest voice imaginable: infinitely softer and more tuneful than could have been reasonably expected from forty years, and a form decidedly inclined to embonpoint. This voice Caroline liked; it atoned for the formal, if correct, accent and language" (p. 219). Mrs. Pryor's strongest asset was her private conversation: "In dialogue, she was a good converser: her language, always a little formal, was well chosen; her sentiments were just; her information was varied and correct" (p. 247). Mrs. Pryor becomes the anchor of Caroline's frail life. Her voice and her language indicate a character whose strength and power are the crucial elements in the recovery that Caroline makes from her near-fatal illness. Although opposite in every way from the reticent Mrs. Pryor, Shirley actually says very little in the course of the novel. Few commments are made about her language, but two remarks are significant. Caroline says to Moore, "You know she can be eloquent: I yet feel in fancy the glow of the language in which her opinion was conveyed" (p. 686). And Moore himself describes Shirley's enunciation to Yorke: "She pronounced it herself in the most musical of her many musical tones" (p. 605). The "glow" of Shirley's language is a key to her personality, which was probably modeled on that of Emily Brontë; Charlotte Brontë has a clear preference for Shirley's lively, headstrong manner.

Some of the middle-class characters understand the usefulness of bidialectalism. Characters who must move back and forth among social groups know the importance of speaking the same language, especially in a novel about the breaking down of social barriers. For example, Caroline, in her dealings with Martin Yorke as a go-between for herself and Moore, is careful to ask him, " 'Are your father and mother well?' " The narrator parenthetically comments, "it was lucky she did not say *papa* and *mama*: that would have undone all"(p. 648). By saying "father" and "mother," Caroline uses Martin's own terminology and thus establishes rapport with him. The point is that dialect and accent are social markers that Caroline understands very well. She adopts Martin's vocabulary in order to minimize the difference between herself and him.

No character, however, understands this point better than Hiram Yorke. Hardly a central figure in the novel, he is certainly the most enigmatic. His very name announces his special status in the novel: the plain, work-a-day "Hiram" is coupled with a respelling of the important Yorkshire city of York, once the capital of Roman Britain. But our first actual introduction to Yorke is his report of the discovery of Robert Moore's men lying in a ditch after being attacked by the machine breakers. Mr. Yorke announces himself in a Yorkshire dialect that Moore immediately recognizes. As Yorke talks with Moore, however, his language changes, and the narrator comments, "It will have been remarked that Mr. Yorke varied a little in his phraseology; now he spoke broad Yorkshire, and anon he expressed himself in very pure English. His manner seemed liable to equal alternations; he could be polite and affable, and he could be blunt and rough. His station then you could not easily determine by his speech or demeanour; perhaps the appearance of his residence may decide it" (p. 50). Here the narrator conducts the reader on a tour through Yorke's front parlor which is filled with Italian art such that "a connoisseur had selected them; they were genuine and valuable" (p. 50). And indeed the significant point is that Brontë shows us a man whose station is not easily detected by his language. Indeed, no character understands the utility of adjusting language to fit social expectation better than Mr. Yorke. In other words, while language may be generally perceived as an indicator of social *worth* in England, Mr. Yorke explodes this perception through his bidialectal maneuvering. *His* dialect—or lack of it—has little to do with his true character.

The bidialectal characters in *Shirley* therefore serve an important function. These characters are subtle reminders that the social system is not fixed and unchanging. While single dialect speakers show the assumed rigidity of the class system, bidialectal characters undermine those underlying assumptions and subvert the system through their control of language. This phenomenon is explicit in the character of Yorke, who raises knowledgable children, gives sound advice to Moore, has little patience with the affected curates, and is a genuine, honest, and admirable character. In one sense, Yorke is the epitome of the ideal Yorkshire man; his roots are clear, but he has refinement and grace that one must look for beyond his language. The narrator says of him: "His manners, when he liked, were those of a finished gentleman of the old school; his conversation, when he was disposed to please, was singularly interesting and original; and if he usually expressed himself in the Yorkshire dialect, it was because he chose to do so, preferring his native Doric to a more refined vocabulary" (p. 58). Yorke's "Yorkshire burr" exactly suited Brontë's desire to present a figure whose facility with language transcends prescribed social classes.

Brontë's language in *Shirley*, then, provides a contrapuntal commentary on the action of the novel. Although *Shirley* undoubtedly has defects of plot and characterization, Brontë's subtle but extremely skillful handling of dialect in the novel highlights her theme. Her careful execution of language begins with the "shower of curates" and their stilted accents and Latinate phrasing. Just as their expressions are out of place in the Yorkshire dales, so will their efforts become useless in solving the problems created by mill-owners and the anonymous machine breakers whose Yorkshire voices we hear as if from a Greek chorus. *Shirley* ends, not with the middle-class accents of the curates, but with the Yorkshire voice of the old servant Martha, describing what the hollow was like before the mill and before the advent of the machines: " 'A lonesome spot it was—and a bonnie spot—full of oak trees and nut trees. It is altered now' "(p. 740).

Bracketed by the dialects of the protagonists who have contributed to this alteration of Yorkshire is the bidialectal Hiram Yorke who emerges inviolate from the conflict: he understands the utility of language sufficiently to move effectively in the rising middle-class world but has no desire to give up his Yorkshire roots. As the narrator says of him:

> Mr. Yorke . . . is proud of his race. Yorkshire has such families here and there amongst her hills and wolds—peculiar, racy, vigorous; of good blood and strong brain; turbulent somewhat in the pride of their strength, and intractable in the force of their native powers; wanting polish, wanting consideration, wanting docility, but sound, spirited, and true-bred as the eagle on the cliff or the steed in the steppe.
>
> (p. 170)

This "peculiar, racy, vigorous" Yorkshire character finally transcends rigid social structure. Charlotte Brontë's use of language as an indicator for the breaking down of social barriers is a subtle but effective reinforcement of her concern about the dangers inherent in a rigid class system.

NOTES

[1]Asa Briggs,"Private and Social Themes in *Shirley*," *Brontë Society Transactions* 13 (1958):208-209.

[2]Charlotte Brontë, *Shirley*, ed. Herbert Rosengarten and Margaret Smith (Oxford: Clarendon Press, 1979), p. 58. All subsequent references to *Shirley* are from this edition and will be cited in the text.

[3]Brontë was a cautious and careful crafter of dialect; when she edited the second edition of Emily's *Wuthering Heights*, she wrote to W. S. Williams that "I should wish to revise the proofs, if it be not too great an inconvenience to send them. It seems to me advisable to modify the orthography of the old servant Joseph's speeches; for though as it stands it exactly renders the Yorkshire dialect to a Yorkshire ear, yet I am sure Southerners must find it unintelligible; and thus one of the most graphic characters in the book is lost on them" ("To W. S. Williams," 29 September 1850, Letter 606, *The Brontës: Their Lives, Friendships, and Correspondence*, ed. Thomas J. Wise, 4 vols. (1933; rpt. Philadelphia: Porcupine Press, 1980), 3:165). Charlotte Brontë had no such difficulty in revising her own *Shirley* for publication. Her representation of the Yorkshire dialect is clear and careful, and orthographically modified so that even a southerner can understand the language.

[4]G. L. Brook, *English Dialects* (London: Andre Deutsch, 1963), p. 191.

[5]Joseph Wright, ed., *The English Dialect Dictionary*, 6 vols. (London: Oxford Univ, Press. 1961).

[6]Apart from the lexical differences, Brontë also uses the grammatical forms peculiar to this dialect. "Mun" is the present tense form of "must"; "weesen" is the possesive form of "ourselves," and when William Farren asks plaintively if "Mun we say, whist! and lig us down and dee?", he is using "lig" as the present tense of "lie." The characteristically Yorkshire forms of "summat," "nobbut," and "dunnat" are used for "somewhat," "nothing," and "do not but," and the indeclinable "that" is used in place of the more modern, specialized, relative pronouns.

Additionally, Brontë represents the pronunciation by respellings of a variety of words. In general, the "i" of "iver," "divil," "niver," "mich," and "sich" is pronounced [I]. The double "e" of "greet," "weel," and "teed," is meant to be [i]. Consonant deletions are an important part of the representation, and Brontë deletes medial "k" in words like "mista'n" and often indicates elisions like "o'your," "i'peace," and "wi'your." Eye dialect is also occasionally used for emphasis and for humor as in the case of Moses Barraclough who exclaims "Looard! Looard!" when startled, Sugden who says "febewerry," and Joe Scott who calls a fool a "fooil."

[7]Tom Winnifrith, *The Brontës and Their Background: Romance and Reality* (London: Macmillan, 1973), p. 176.

SEL 27 (1987)
ISSN 0039-3657

Trollope and James: The "Germ" Within

HENRY N. ROGERS III

It seems more often true than otherwise that in literary matters "comparisons is odious." Student efforts tend to begin with the confident assertion that "Hemingway and Faulkner are both writers" and end with the remarkable discovery that "both men are now dead." And too often we professional critics produce a version of the standard "these writers are alike in some ways and different in others." Nevertheless, one is sometimes led to attempt a valid and meaningful comparison, especially when it involves an author undergoing the critical reevaluation now being accorded Anthony Trollope. In this case the effort seems worthwhile, for it stimulates a fresh and, I think, valuable look at the literary relationship of Trollope and Henry James and, more particularly, at the nature of Trollope's artistry.

The "germ" for this essay lies in Trollope's short story, "*The Panjandrum.*" Trollope's short fiction is generally not well known, and it has as yet received little critical attention.[1] James Kincaid' s attitude is not atypical: "Trollope's short stories . . . are, without exception, of little interest to us, to Trollope's contemporaries, or to Trollope himself."[2] Fortunately Professor Kincaid's judgment is inaccurate, first because the stories are always competent and often of excellent quality, and secondly because of the opportunity for critical insight which they provide. "*The Panjandrum*" is among Trollope's best stories, one of several drawn from his own experiences as a writer and editor. In *An Autobiograpy*, he notes that "in my own early days there was a struggle over an abortive periodical which was intended to be the best thing ever done."[3] Thus "*The Panjandrum*"

Henry N. Rogers III is Professor of English at the University of Central Arkansas. He has published essays on Defoe, Dickens, Thackeray, and Trollope.

is the account of a small group of literary aspirants—five men and a woman—who, fired with varying degrees of idealism, egotism, and ambition, attempt to found a new and of course unique periodical. Narrated by a potential contributor and would-be editor, the tale is fascinating in its intimate presentation of the literary world Trollope knew so well, particularly as it is embodied in the hopes, dreams, and disappointments of the narrator himself. Its chief interest here, however, lies in the detailed depiction of this young man's humorous, anguished, and ultimately successful efforts to write.

The popular and still widely accepted perception of Trollope as a writing machine, grinding steadily on with little regard for situation or inspiration, is well known. Fostered by Trollope's observable writing practices and his explicit, controversial statements on composition in *An Autobiography*, this image of the "cobbler" novelist has been so perpetuated, by James among others, that it has often seemed set in granite. Recent critical studies have begun to alter many enduring views of Trollope and his fiction, but that which sees him as essentially a disciplined drudge has proven especially longlived. Yet the creative process so vividly dramatized in "*The Panjandrum,*" that "means" by which the struggling narrator finally produces his story, can only be described as both spontaneous and organic.

The anxious and hopeful narrator, faced with a deadline for his initial contribution to the periodical, approaches his task with proper Trollopian method. The results, however, are far from satisfactory. After much thought, a search for advice, and several false starts, he finds that he cannot even choose a subject: "Three days, three out of the fourteen, passed by, and I could think of no fitting subject on which to begin."[4] As time passes, his trepidation and the reader's amusement grow: "The twenty-one pages loomed before me as a wilderness . . . which I could never traverse" (*Panj.,*" p. 77). A general discipline continues to govern his efforts, but their forms become increasingly irrational: "The sixth and seventh days I passed altogether within my room, . . . I drank green tea. I ate meat very slightly cooked. I debarred myself from food for several hours. . . . I sat up one night, nearly till daybreak, with a wet towel around my head" ("*Panj.,*" p. 78). These, of course, produce the appropriate results: "On the morning of the eighth day I was still without a subject." His dismay and insecurity gather momentum: "A horrid idea came to me that I was struck, as it were, with sudden idiocy" ("*Panj.,*" p. 78). On Sunday he thinks of excuses, and on Monday he thinks he is ill. In desperation he turns to exercise, hoping that inspiration might come "if I could divest myself from all effort in searching for it" (*"Panj.,"* p. 80). And as he walks, inspiration does come, unexpected and unbidden.

During his journey through Regent's Park, he encounters a small girl and her nurse. The meeting is brief—only long enough for a close look and to hear the child's words: " 'Oh, Anne, I do so wonder what he's like!' " (*"Panj.,"* p. 81). The impression, however, is strong enough to trigger a creative response, one which the narrator explicitly describes: "Gradually, as the unforced imagination came to play upon the matter, a little picture fashioned itself in my mind" (*"Panj.,"* p. 82). That picture evolves swiftly into a full fledged story. The little girl becomes a young woman, the narrator's long-lost sister, whom he finds, loves, and loses, gladly and sadly, to a friend. Indeed, the tale develops so rapidly that it is essentially complete when the narrator finishes his walk. Only then, because "I had made this castle for myself" (*"Panj.,"* p. 82), does he think of *The Panjandrum.* All that remains is to place his creation on paper, and now that he has "a thing to say," he doubts "whether any five days in my life were ever happier than those which were devoted to this piece of work" (*"Panj.,"* p. 82).

This episode is immediately striking in two repects. Most startling is what appears an almost complete contradiction between the spontaneous workings of the narrator's "unforced imagination" and Trollope's most familiar statements concerning the writing process. In *An Autobiography* he clearly states his belief in a disciplined, methodical approach to writing and expresses his scorn for those "who think that the man who works with his imagination should allow himself to wait—till inspiration moves him" (*Auto.*, p. 121). He much prefers, he says, the industry of the shoemaker: "I certainly believe in the cobbler's wax much more than the inspiration" (*Auto.*, p. 121). Yet the young author in "*The Panjandrum*" finds industry and method utterly fruitless. Only when he decides, almost in despair, to "divest myself from all effort in searching for it (inspiration)," does he discover the stimulus that enables him to write. The creative process so described and dramatized is authenticated within Trollope's story by the tale it produces and by that tale's inherent merit; although *The Panjandrum* is stillborn, the young writer's work is later published elsewhere. It should be noted here that the suggestiveness of the apparent discrepancy between Trollope's stated precepts and this fictional treatment of the creative experience does not depend upon an exact identification of Trollope with his unnamed narrator; indeed, such an author/narrator identification is never absolute in a work of fiction. The all too common insistence upon it is naive and unnecessary, and denial of it does not preclude a narrator's being endowed with so much of his creator as that creator chooses.

The "creative episode" of "*The Panjandrum*" elicits simultaneously a perhaps equally provocative impression. If it seems to dramatize an inconsistency in Trollope's own theory and practice, it also appears a remarkable embodiment of some of Henry James's most significant artistic concepts. Although Trollope's story was first published in 1870 and James's "The Art of Fiction" in 1884—and his prefaces much later—the similarities between the narrator's experience and James's later minutely delineated creative processes and critical theories are immediately evident. The theory of the "germ," for example, drawn from Turgenev, is a Jamesian commonplace. As he describes it in the preface to *The Spoils of Poynton,* a "germ," is a "single small seed,"[5] "minute and wind-blown," a word, a suggestion, a "merest grain" which pricks the writer's imagination like a needle and "communicates the virus of suggestion." And for James, a germ is always a germ for a story. A more exact description of the young narrator's response to his chance encounter with the little girl could scarcely be imagined. And as that response, that "castle in the air," evolves from and is constructed around the incident, so is it organic. The "he" of the child's words becomes the narrator himself, she becomes his sister, a young woman who comes to love his friend, etc., until the building is perfected. So James, who also began with "seeds," "had to find for them the right relations, those that would most bring them out"[6]—in short, to construct an "architecture" founded on a "single small cornerstone." Trollope's narrator, distanced from his adventure by many years, speaks of "these wondrous castles in the air" from a larger perspective: "It is when they come uncalled for that they stand erect and strong before the mind's eye, with every mullioned window perfect, the rounded walls all there, the embrasures cut, the fosse dug, and the drawbridge down" ("*Panj.*," p. 82). Metaphorically as well as theoretically this is a startling anticipation of the James who in *The Portrait of a Lady* would construct "a square and spacious house," would "build large—in fine embossed vaults and painted arches."[7]

Clearly, then, the narrator's creative experience in "*The Panjandrum*" is a provocative one. The specific similarities implied between Trollope and James, so unexpected in light of many seldom questioned ideas concerning the two men, suggest the need for reexamination of the writers and their literary relationship. The most striking feature of the episode, the ironic dichotomy between Trollope's best known critical pronouncements and this fictional treatment of the writing process, compels a particularly close and comprehensive scrutiny of what Trollope actually said and did, and why. Realization of how much critical opinion of Trollope's literary methods and achievements has been shaped by James's attitude toward them makes the need to look directly at Trollope himself even more imperative.

James's views concerning Trollope were widely published and are generally well known. They were unfavorable in many respects. Trollope's use of the intrusive third-person narrator made him James's most famous example of the "nonserious" novelist, one who deliberately destroyed his created illusion of life. In his contemporary reviews of Trollope's fiction, James is not only critical but often sarcastic and vituperative. "'Miss Mackenzie,'" he says "begets upon the reader the very disagreeable impression that not only no imagination was required for the work before him, but that a man of imagination could not possibly have written it."[8] James asserts that *Can You Forgive Her?* is essentially the same as all of Trollope's earlier novels; choose any of them, and "It is neither better nor worse than the tale which you will select."[9] The essay in *Partial Portraits*[10] presents James's most comprehensive and persuasive criticism of Trollope. More mature and balanced than the earlier reviews, it is also on the whole more favorable. James praises Trollope for his "complete appreciation of the usual," his "great appreciation of the real," his "extreme interest in character," and his ability to bring all these to life, to make his "people stand on their feet." James even acknowledged that the older writer did possess imagination, though he abused it with the rapidity of his writing. Unlike Dickens and Thackeray—of all people—Trollope did not allow a "period of gestation" or "wait for inspiration," and his novel writing finally became "a perceptibly mechanical process." James labelled Trollope an "unconscious" author who lacked theory and avoided form; he just told his story in "heavy-footed prose." "With Trollope we were always safe; there were sure to be no new experiments" (*P. P.*, p. 100). James also faulted Trollope for endowing characters with "fantastic" names such as Quiverful, Sentiment, and Neversay Die. This minor criticism, from the progenitor of Stackpole, Fanny Assingham, and the Pococks, could almost in itself induce skepticism concerning his other critical judgments.

Such skepticism would in fact be eminently justified, for James's portrayal of Trollope is hardly disinterested. James Kincaid in *The Novels of Anthony Trollope* argues that James's writings are not criticism at all but "terribly effective propaganda." "It is myth-making."[11] Vivien Jones feels that "His [critical] preconceptions . . . blind him to the different merits in Trollope."[12] To delineate and argue for his own methods and aesthetics, James created an opposing symbol of the "dead" novelistic tradition he wished to reject. "He called this symbol Trollope."[13] Whether or not James's motives were so exclusively propagandistic is problematic, but certainly a major result of his critical comments was the transformation of Trollope into just such an image. This was accomplished primarily by the sometimes laudatory but often subtly deceptive evaluation in *Partial Portraits*. James finds considerable value in Trollope's literary achievement, his more obvious criticisms sound objective and reasonable, yet he undercuts apparently warm praise with surprising consistency: "with his extraordinary gift [imagination], there was always in him a certain infusion of the common" (*P. P.*, p. 99). In this fashion Trollope is frozen into a safe, unthinking, pedestrian realist who at best belongs to the second rank of English novelists. The fact that this account of him may have little if anything to do with Trollope or his fiction has proven almost irrelevant. As Kincaid points out, "the power of that symbol is undeniable, controlling as it has virtually all commentary on Trollope, both from friend and foe,"[14] until the last fifteen years. This view of James's treatment of Trollope is strongly supported by recent studies which are drastically altering opinions of Trollope's novels. The works are seen as more ironic, complex, dramatic, even more experimental than previously realized. Thus the striking similarities between the methods of the two novelists suggested in "*The Panjandrum*" seem dramatically illustrative of what much recent criticism implies—that Trollope is more like James than the latter knew or chose to acknowledge and is perhaps far different from the Trollopian image of the writing mechanic who, James said, "never troubled his head . . . about the nature of his business" (*P. P.*, p. 100). It is not only illuminating but fair to turn the tables and use the comparison to obtain a more accurate picture of Trollope's literary principles and practices, a comparison with James's "symbolic" Trollope as much as with James himself. Indeed, it is in many respects the same thing, for the deficiencies James discerns in Trollope are by implication suggestive of his own strengths. As the comparison evolves from the embryonic episode in "*The Panjandrum*," a more careful and serious artist, a more creative, "inspired" writer emerges from behind the Trollopian facade.

The primary source for the image of Trollope the writing machine is Trollope himself, of course. His self-depiction as a common workman—disciplined, indefatigable, scornful of inspiration, and somewhat deficient of genius—is a prominent feature of *An Autobiography*. James, who made an Atlantic crossing with the elder novelist, had witnessed and in his fashion admired Trollope's ability to write under any and all circumstances. It is this Trollope, initially self-characterized and finally embalmed with James's aid, who seems to have presented in "*The Panjandrum*" a creative writing process unequivocally at odds with his own. The apparent paradox arises not from Trollopian inconsistency, however, but from acceptance of a form of critical metonomy—taking the part for the whole. There is truth in this view of Trollope the unstoppable, but it is hardly all the truth. The discoveries engendered by the catalytic episode in "*The Panjandrum*" reveal a more complex and enigmatic figure who transcends such comfortable over-simplification.

As we have seen, the narrator's principal difficulty is his want of a subject. He has no subject because he is inexperienced—he doesn't know enough. When he considers writing about "the ballot," he discovers "that I didn't exactly know how to say anything about it" ("*Panj.*," p. 77). After all his frantic efforts, he finds his subject only when he decides to walk "and employ my mind, simply, in observing the world around me" ("*Panj.*," p. 80). In so doing he encounters the girl and her nurse, an experience which becomes his inspiration, a "germ" upon which his imagination can build. He is the very model of one who learns the hard way the validity of James's injunction to "write from experience and experience only."[15] Indeed, if not from experience, the narrator cannot write at all. As *An Autobiography* reveals, Trollope himself certainly did not. In the chapter "On Novels and the Art of Writing Them," he describes exactly the dilemma faced by his narrator: "He cudgels his brain, not always successfully, and sits down to write, not because he has something which he burns to tell, but because he feels it to be incumbent upon him to be telling something" (*Auto.*, p. 230). The obstacle can be surmounted when "some series of events, or some development of character, will have presented itself to his imagination,—and this he feels so strongly that he thinks he can present his picture . . . to others" (*Auto.*, p. 229). Trollope's commentary is still more comprehensive and explicit about the necessity of experience for imaginative creation. The writer must "unceasingly" give his mind to that work of observation and reception from which comes his power "which work should be going on . . . in all his walks abroad, in all his movements through the world, in all his intercourse with his fellow creatures" (*Auto.*, p. 231). He can never stop, "because in those walks abroad he has, unconsciously for the most part, been drawing in matter from all that he has seen and heard" (*Auto.*, p. 231). As "*The Panjandrum*" narrator's experience demonstrates, a writer cannot anticipate which matter of all he may observe will prove the spur to imagination. As James quotes Turgenev in the preface to *Portrait of a Lady*, "As for the origins of one's wind-blown germs themselves, who shall say . . . where *they* come from? . . . They are so . . . floated into our minds by the current of life."[16] Faced always with such uncertainty concerning his source of inspiration, a writer could never rest from the observation and reception "without which," Trollope says, "his power cannot be continued" (*Auto.*, p. 231). It is monumentally true that *he* never paused. "*The Panjandrum*" narrator is a novice in his youth; Trollope, with his ceaseless travelling and irrepressible vigor of body and mind, was in many respects a mature epitome of James's ideal—"one of the people upon whom nothing is lost."[17]

Novice he may be, but the narrator's "unforced imagination" is instantaneously galvanized by the germ thrown before him by the "current of life." From that "seed" derives his castle, an edifice growing from the "little picture" to "stand erect and strong before the mind's eye" ("*Panj.*," p. 82). As he later comes to know, it does so because it comes "uncalled for." "These wondrous castles in the air never get themselves well built, when the mind, with premeditated skill and labour, sets itself to work to build them" ("*Panj.*," p. 82). Even as the castle is made, however, there comes into play that faculty which James maintained that Trollope lacked: "that sustained action of the imagination . . . which would intensify and animate his first concept."[18] The young narrator "walked the whole round of Regent's Park, perfecting the building—and I did perfect it" ("*Panj.*," p. 83). Essentially complete, the tale is not finally so until his five happy days of writing are over. Although the actual writing becomes largely a matter of transcription, the story remains alive to his imagination and critical judgment so long as it remains under his pen: "While I was walking, eating, or reading, I was still thinking of my story" ("*Panj.*," p. 84).

The most self-conscious of writers, James experienced and analyzed the creative act in much the same fashion. The workings of an "inspired" imagination, even James's, are ultimately at some point indefinable. Certainly those necessary "acquisitions" for the portrait of Isabel Archer came unbidden and untraceable from within James's consciousness: "I seem to myself to have waked up one morning in possession of them."[19] Called into existence by his "sense of a single character," "It was as if they had simply, by an impulse of their own, floated into my ken." So possessed, they became the pieces of his puzzle, the bricks with which his own sustained action of the imagination built the architecture which "does" Isabel, his initial conception.

For Trollope himself, the art of castle building was not only a literary activity, it was literally a way of life. As *An Autobiography* discloses, the wretchedness of his childhood and early manhood forced him into an inner life so necessary that "I was always going about with some castles in the air firmly built within my mind" (*Auto.*, p. 42). These tales are remarkable testimony to Trollope's capacity, even need for sustained imaginative action: "For weeks, for months, . . . I would carry on the same tale, binding myself down to certain laws, to certain proportions, and proprieties, and unities " (*Auto.*, p. 42). It was a creative labor from which Trollope not only never desisted—"In after years I have done the same" (*Auto.*, p. 43)—it was one he deliberately cultivated. In "A Walk in a Wood,"[20] an essay of 1879, he speaks with more explicitness than in *An Autobiography* of the crucial role of imagination, even, by implication, of inspiration, in his creative process. Trollope here describes the necessity of a setting—ideally a walk in a wood—which enables him to escape those things "altogether destructive of fancy" and thus allow fancy, imagination, what he calls his "Ariel," to work. He is aware that, as his "*Panjandrum*" narrator discovers, what he seeks may be difficult to summon: "It may be that your spirit should on occasion be as obedient as Ariel, but that will not be often" ("Walk," p. 5). Yet Ariel must come, imagination must work freely in its place and then must be bound carefully to the "circumstances of the world"—or there will be no story. Indeed, without what Susan Humphreys calls Trollope's "lifelong tendency to plunge into an imaginary world"[21]—a creative practice consciously developed and refined—"I have often doubted whether . . . I should ever have written a novel" (*Auto.*, p. 43).

The manner in which Trollope wrote is also embodied in the narrator's experience. Well aware of criticism of the rapidity of his writing, he steadfastly maintained that "the work which has been done quickest has been done the best" (*Auto.*, p. 175). It came swiftly and well when "I have been impregnated with my own creation til it has been my only excitement to sit with the pen in my hand, and drive the team before me" (*Auto.*, p. 176). Like the narrator's, Trollope's composing was largely done internally, so in similar fashion much of his writing was essentially transcription. His organic conceptions were not so deliberately or comprehensively developed as were James's, which often encompassed whole novels. He claimed that the construction of an entire plot was "a huge difficulty," one that he generally found "altogether beyond my power of accomplishment" ("Walk," p. 1). But as Andrew Wright has pointed out, Trollope did have what he called "plotlings"—

small blocks of a novel—thoroughly worked out before he picked up his pen.[22] Indeed, "thoroughly worked out" seems an understatement, for Trollope asserts that a creative walk is not complete until every scene is so minutely developed that even "the proper words may be spoken and the fitting effect produced" ("Walk," p. 6). And in fact his concern with the larger shape of his works was greater and more thoughtful than is generally realized. As Humphreys points out, his working papers reveal "that Trollope was very sensitive to the form of a novel, both in space and time."[23] And despite the speed of his work, what James referred to as the "sober second thought"[24] was clearly an integral element in Trollope's creative process. His writings stayed within his mind and then beneath his hand long enough for self-criticism: "It has been my practice to read everything four times at least—thrice in manuscript and once in print" (*Auto.*, p. 178). Wright indicates that manuscript evidence reveals Trollope as a careful if not an extensive revisor, a serious author concerned about the quality of his work. Given this concern, what becomes significant are the remarkably few revisions which Trollope found necessary. In Wright's words, "page after page, indeed chapter after chapter, of his novels are as neat as fair copies."[25] Such consistent satisfaction with his initial effort is further evidence that Trollope's actual writing was indeed little more than transcription, that he seldom set pen to paper until the creative process—his "castle building"—was finished.

Thus far this comparison of Trollope and James has brought several matters into a clearer light. The initial striking similarity between "*The Panjandrum*" narrator's creative experience and James's theories of composition proves not illusory but actual—and often remarkably pronounced. While that resemblance is real, the apparently startling dichotomy between Trollope and his fictional creation is not. The seeming discrepancy vanishes along with the largely mythical conception of Trollope the methodical and mindless word processor. What emerges from the comparison with James is a figure in many ways far more like James and far different from the longlived Trollopian image than generally imagined. The discrepancy which "*The Panjandrum*" does reveal is the one between that image and Trollope himself. The novice writer's experience is in fact a dramatization of Trollope's own literary theories and imaginative processes, and in this respect at least, he himself becomes a fictional projection—a persona—of Trollope. With this realization the "germ" pricks the mind once more, for it again provokes the question of the relationship of creator and creation. If the fallacy of their absolute identification is avoided, the answers are illuminating and significant. The relationship of "*The Panjandrum*" narrator to his tale, "The New Inmate," indicates much about Trollope's relationship to his literary art.

The narrator's creative experience dramatizes the way Trollope wrote, how he composed. It also, more subtly but no less persuasively, suggests his motives, the *why* of his writing. Though desperate for a literary composition, the would-be author does not compose to meet that need but because, when inspiration comes, he has no conscious choice. His "unforced imagination" works until he discovers "I had made this castle for myself" ("*Panj.*," p. 82). He does not even compose the story primarily to be written, for the castle is perfected before it occurs to him "that I might use the thing." He can then write it because "I had a thing to say, and I would say it." But he has created that "thing"—his tale—for other reasons. Those reasons are never articulated, for the narrator, even in looking back on the incident after many years, neither comments explicitly on the matter nor provides any personal information which might illuminate it. This is hardly surprising, both because the entire occurrence is only a part of the larger concerns of *The Panjandrum*, and because such a question of motive may become a highly personal and private issue. The story he tells indicates that this is indeed the case, even as it suggests the general nature of his motives by its contents and his response to them.

The narrator's most immediate and unpremeditated response to the little girl in Regent's Park is to make her his sister. From this initial conception evolves a familial relationship in which he himself plays the major role, that of a loving, protective, self-sacrificing brother. His characters and story become so real to him that when he finally marries his sister to his best friend, "I could hardly write it for my tears" ("*Panj.*, p. 84). The story "came to me to be a matter that admitted of no doubt." Much later, the narrator tells us, "To this moment I can distinguish the voice in which she spoke to me" ("*Panj.*," p. 85). His imaginative world is finally more real than the actual one, and preferable to it: "What need is there of a sister or a friend in the flesh—a sister or a friend with probably so many faults—when by a little exercise of the mind they may be there, at your elbow, faultless?" ("*Panj.*," p. 85). If the narrator, distanced by time, offers no explanation for the nature of his story nor for his own powerful reaction to it, he is certainly aware of the extremity, even the possible abnormality of his response: "When one thinks of it, the reality of it all is appalling" ("*Panj.*," p. 85). The implications of the tale suggest that his motives arise from emotional and psychological needs so internalized as to be largely unconscious. The content of the narrator's story and its heightened realism and perhaps inordinate importance to him seem powerful manifestations of an acute need for love, for a sense of family, for a world better than the real one he must inhabit. The unmistakable inference is that he does not sufficiently possess those things; he therefore creates and thus possesses them, and his work becomes a form of compensation—it is therapeutic.

In *An Autobiography* Trollope reveals much about the misery and suffering of his life from its beginning until early manhood. The causes were various: poverty, parental failures, brutal schools, his own youthful weaknesses. Their combined effect was undeniable: "My boyhood was, I think, as unhappy as that of a young gentleman could well be" (*Auto.*, p. 2). The pain and deprivation were primarily emotional and psychological. His feelings at fifteen characterize those of many other years: "I not only had no friends, but was despised by all my companions" (*Auto.*, p. 11). As such an existence created in Trollope a sense of failure and inadequacy and an almost incessant "craving" for love, it also generated his "inner life," that endless creation of characters and stories which comprised a better world for him to inhabit. Like the narrator of "*The Panjandrum*," Trollope was his own hero, in fact precisely the same kind of hero: "beautiful young women used to be fond of me. And I strove to be kind of heart, and open of hand, and noble in thought" (*Auto.*, p. 43). His characters too were so real that he could "hate them" and "love them"—in other words, live with them. As A. L. Rowse asserts, this passionate internal life of the imagination was for Trollope therapeutic, a form of psychological compensation, a process of escape from one world through the creation of another.[26] The practice never ceased entirely, and if it enabled him eventually to write his novels, it first enabled him to live, made the outer world endurable. If in part he wrote for money and reputation as he claimed, he was, like "*The Panjandrum*" narrator, largely compelled to compose.

At the outset of *An Autobiography* Trollope declares, "it will not be so much my intention to speak of the little details of my private life" (*Auto.*, p. 1). At its conclusion he reiterates what his purpose was not: "It will not, I trust, be supposed by any reader that I have intended in this so-called autobiography to give a record of my inner life" (*Auto.*, p. 65). This is hardly an inconsistent attitude for one whom N. John Hall describes as so shy and deeply insecure that in public life he continually played roles and adopted masks to protect his private self.[27] Numerous contemporary accounts attest to the bluff, hearty, vigorous, workman-like manner which he presented to the world. W. P. Frith's is a single example: "It would be impossible to imagine anything less like his novels than the author of them. The books, full of gentleness, grace, and refinement; the writer of them, bluff, loud, stormy, and contentious."[28] As Hall points out, the more deeply embedded the personal features "threatened," the more zealously they were guarded. Trollope was more publically forthcoming about many matters, including private ones, in *An Autobiography* than ever before, in part because "what I now write will certainly never be read till I am dead" (*Auto.*, p. 39). But what is most private is often most indirectly revealed because, in P. D. Edwards's words, "Trollope tells us exactly what and exactly as much as he wishes us to know."[29] With his carefully controlled mixture of frankness and reticence, in *An Autobiography* he creates a persona much as he did in everyday life, one which is "only a fragment of his true self."[30] On the other hand, the parallels between "*The Panjandrum*" narrator's creative experience and Trollope's own suggest that in his narrator he creates a persona which is in some ways a more intimate revelation of himself than the "hero" of the *Autobiography*.

In *An Autobiography* Trollope of course speaks of himself; in "*The Panjandrum*" he does not. However similar the narrator and his creator appear to be, they are by definition not the same. Well aware of the immediacy and potentially confessional nature of a first person perspective,[31] Trollope makes the narrator very much like himself. The creative experience seems an amazing reflection of Trollope's own, yet his personal identity is granted a measure of protection because the story and narrator are fiction. The narrative structure within the story furnishes him still more insulation, for it implies progressively greater distance between Trollope and the narrator as the latter's experience becomes more immediate and internal. Trollope is closest to the older narrator who is himself separated by time from the incident he recounts and comments upon. From that youthful adventure, then, which dramatizes those aspects of the creative process too personal, perhaps too difficult of definition for interpretation, Trollope is himself twice distanced. The narrator's own story implicitly but convincingly suggests the most intimate, least accessible elements of his creative act. From the intensely personal psychological and emotional implications discerned in the narrator's own tale, a fiction within a fiction, Trollope is therefore thrice removed. As the narrator's creative experience appears to lead ever closer to the deepest sources of Trollope's art, the narrative structure operates to dissociate Trollope the author from the meaning of his fictional persona. This dissociative effect is not nearly so strong as the similarities between Trollope and "*The Panjandrum*" narrator, but its influence serves as a counterbalance to those identifying forces and so insures a degree of protection for Trollope's own identity.

Thus guarded by his fiction, Trollope reveals more about his own creative processes and his relationship to his literary art in "*The Panjandrum*" than perhaps anywhere else in his canon. As James knew well, each writer has "a manner best known to himself. His manner is his secret, not necessarily a jealous one. He cannot disclose it as a general thing if he would; he would be at a loss to teach it to others."[32] If Trollope would not and could not disclose his "secret manner" explicitly, he could and did reveal it through recreating the thing itself as a dramatic fictional experience, the kind fully understood only when shared. He may have revealed more than he intended. Trollope was observant, perceptive, sensitive—but he was not as a rule introspective or self-analytic. As Edwards says, "he kept the inner citadel of his emotional life inaccessible—perhaps even to his own conscious mind."[33] But in the psychological nuances of the narrator's tale Trollope exposes more than he consciously knew about how his fiction was shaped by his inner life. The nature and influence of those feelings implied by "The New Inmate" are powerfully indicative of the deepest wellsprings of Trollope's art.

The "germ" within "*The Panjandrum*" has therefore proven provocative and meaningful. Small seed that it is, it has led to a clearer perception of both writers, particularly Trollope, a perception which effectually removes the mask largely placed upon him by James himself. Without minimizing their differences, the Trollope who emerges is much more like James, especially in regard to the fundamental nature of creative experience, than James cared to admit. As the "mythic" Trollope fades, a more realistic figure appears, one whose features reveal the consistency of the narrator's experience and Trollope's own theory and practice. And, when the comparison of James and Trollope has brought the latter's literary methods into sharper focus, the more profound significance of the narrator's authorship can be seen. The full implications, artistic and psychological, of the young writer's creative activity and its fictional presentation provide remarkable insight into the nature of Trollope's relationship to his art. They are strongly suggestive of the most carefully hidden, perhaps in part unconscious sources of his imaginative world.

Thus in the creative experience it presents, "*The Panjandrum*" furnishes a very specific fictional situation and a unique critical opportunity, and so the notable insight it gives is particularly valuable. From a more general perspective, the meanings of the narrator's experience and its manner of presentation urge a careful reevaluation of the nature, function, and implications of the narrative presence throughout Trollope's fiction. Of course, as James said and the "germ" of "*The Panjandrum*" seems to bear out, relations end nowhere. The striking anticipation in concept and metaphor by Trollope's "wondrous castles" and "square cut gems" of James's later theoretical writings suggests the potential value of a look from another window—from Trollope toward James. "But that *is* another matter."[34]

NOTES

[1]A useful general essay is by Donald D. Stone, "Trollope as a Short Story Writer," *NCF* 31 (1976): 26-47.

[2]James R. Kincaid, *The Novels of Anthony Trollope* (Oxford: Clarendon Press, 1977), p. 25.

[3]Anthony Trollope, *An Autobiography* (Oxford: Oxford Univ. Press, 1980), p. 337. Page references will be noted in the text, cited as *Auto.*

[4]Anthony Trollope, "*The Panjandrum,*" in *Editors and Writers*, vol. 3 of *Anthony Trollope: The Complete Short Stories*, ed. Betty Jane Slemp Bryer, 5 vols. (Fort Worth: Texas Christian Univ. Press, 1979), p. 76. Future references will be noted in the text, cited as "*Panj.*"

[5]Henry James, preface to *The Spoils of Poynton*, in *The Art of the Novel* (New York: Scribner's, 1934), p. 119.

[6]Henry James, preface to *The Portrait of a Lady*, in *The Art of the Novel* (New York: Scribner's, 1934). p. 43.

[7]Ibid., p. 52.

[8]Henry James, review of "Miss Mackenzie," *The Nation*, 13 July 1865; rpt. in *Notes on Novelists* (Cambridge, Mass.: Dunster House, 1921; rpt. Freeport: Books for Libraries Press, 1968), p. 72.

[9]Henry James, review of *Can You Forgive Her?*, *The Nation*, 28 September 1865; rpt. in *Notes on Novelists* (Cambridge, Mass.: Dunster House, 1921; rpt. Freeport: Books for Libraries Press, 1968), p. 84.

[10]Henry James, "Anthony Trollope," in *Partial Portraits* (London: Macmillan, 1888; rpt. Westport, Conn.: Greenwood, 1970), pp. 97-133. Future references will be cited in the text as *P.P.* The essay first appeared as an obituary article in the *Century Magazine*, July 1883.

[11]Kincaid, p. 7.

[12]Vivien Jones, "James and Trollope," *RES* n.s. 33, 131 (August 1982):284.

[13]Kincaid, p. 7.

[14]Kincaid, p. 8.

[15]James, "The Art of Fiction," *Longman's Magazine*, 1884, rpt. in *P.P.*, p. 389.

[16]James, preface to *Portrait of a Lady*, p. 43.

[17]James, "Art of Fiction" p. 390.

[18]James, review of *Can You Forgive Her?*, pp. 87, 88.

[19]James, preface to *Portrait of a Lady*, p. 53.

[20]Trollope, "A Walk in a Wood," *Good Words*, September 1879; rpt. in *Miscellaneous Essays and Reviews* (New York: Arno Press, 1981). The volume contains no pagination. References to "A Walk" will be to the page of the essay. Future references will be noted in the text as "Walk." Trollope suggested in a letter to his publisher, William Isbister, in May 1879 that the essay might be titled, "How we write our books."

[21]Susan L. Humphreys, "Order—Method: Trollope Learns to Write," *DSA* 8 (1980):261.

[22]Andrew Wright, "Trollope Revises Trollope," In *Trollope Centenary Essays*, ed. John Halperin (New York: St. Martin's Press, 1982), p. 113, hereafter cited as *Centenary Essays*.

[23]Humphreys, p. 267.

[24]James, review of *Can You Forgive Her?*, p. 87

[25]Wright, p. 114.

[26]A. L. Rowse, "Trollope's *Autobiography*," in *Centenary Essays*, p. 137.

[27]N. John Hall, "Trollope the Person," in *Centenary Essays*, p. 178.

[28]W. P. Frith, *My Autobiography and Reminiscences*, 2 vols. (New York: Harper, 1888), p. 496, rpt. by N. John Hall, "Trollope the Person," in *Centenary Essays*, p. 163.

[29]P. D. Edwards, introduction to *An Autobiography* (Oxford Univ. Press, 1980), p. xiii.

[30]Edwards, p. xvi.

[31]Humphreys points out that Trollope fundamentally disliked the first person perspective for these very reasons—he found it dangerously egotistical. Thus his usual third person narration is in part a means of personal protection (p. 257).

[32]James, "The Art of Fiction," p. 385.

[33]Edwards, p. xiii.

[34]James, preface to *Portrait of a Lady*, p. 58.

SEL 27 (1987)
ISSN 0039-3657

On Heroes and Their Demise: Critical Liberalism in *Beauchamp's Career*

GARY HANDWERK

> I am not countenancing the sort of "hero-worship" which applauds the strong man of genius for forcibly seizing on the government of the world and making it do his bidding in spite of itself. All he can claim is, freedom to point out the way. The power of compelling others into it, is not only inconsistent with the freedom and development of all the rest, but corrupting to the strong man himself.
>
> (J. S. Mill, *On Liberty*)

> Ni espoir, ni crainte, mais point de déceptions. Lumière. Ce sont les ténèbres qui tuent.
>
> (*Beauchamp's Career*, 2:258)

I

Although it has provoked relatively little critical interest, Meredith's *Beauchamp's Career* is one of the most outstanding examples of the nineteenth-century political novel. For unlike many other authors, who use politics essentially to provide backdrop or atmosphere, Meredith takes the status of political fiction seriously. His concern with how fiction can be self-consciously political in any meaningful way allows us to study closely the premises and dynamics of this narrative subgenre. In addition, the rigor of Meredith's presentation makes it possible to use interpretation of this text as a way of approaching the larger question of how politics

Gary Handwerk is Assistant Professor of English at the University of Washington, Seattle. Author of *Irony and Ethics in Narrative*, he is currently at work on the relations between aesthetics and politics in nineteenth-century political fiction.

and literature are related, especially what the role of the literary text might be in helping to shape political values.[1]

In treating political fiction, perhaps the most crucial question is where one chooses to locate the ideological focus of a given text, whether in explicit authorial statements or in the allegorical background or in the formal structures of the text. Interpreting any political novel should involve more than extracting an author's personal opinions, more even than extracting a possibly unconscious authorial ideology that lies beneath them. For the value of political novels resides not only in their mimetic representation of political life, but even more in their explicit posing of the question of what literature can contribute to political thought by reflecting on as well as simply reflecting ideology. *Beauchamp's Career* provides an ideal instance of this possibility, for Meredith recognizes the temptation of reducing one level of his text—its political themes or domestic plot—to the other, yet refrains from doing so. He allows us to ask, then, whether the novel, as a genre focusing on personal relationships, can serve to test political theory, whether its function can be anything beyond a more or less complexly mimetic one.

The ideological status of Meredith's text can usefully be focused around three prominent interpretive questions. Most obvious is the exact relation of this novel to Carlyle, especially the Carlyle of *On Heroes*. Several critics have dealt with this aspect of the text, yet without going back to Carlyle's essay, an essential step if we expect to ascertain its precise resonance in *Beauchamp's Career*. Equally crucial for interpreting the novel is the question of why politics gives way to an essentially domestic plot as the narrative progresses, a shift seen as anomalous and diminishing even by certain characters in the text. The curious squeezing of politics out of the text has ideological implications that can further clarify Meredith's relation to Carlyle. The final and perhaps most difficult question is why Beauchamp is made to die at the end as he does, a solitary hero drowning in a failed attempt to rescue a drowning child. This conclusion colors the political atmosphere of the whole text and has been seen by critics as "arbitrary," as "sour and bleak," as "cruel."[2] The very difficulty of resolving the end into anything other than an emotional response suggests its importance for the ideological issues raised by the novel. As I hope to show, this conclusion crystallizes a logic of heroism that needs to be elaborated fully if one is to perceive the inner necessity of Meredith's argument.

Beauchamp's Career insists that it be read in ideological terms as a meditation on Carlyle's romantic conservatism.[3] The narrative probes in a variety of ways the ideological foundation of heroes and hero-worship. "Heroism" has multiple senses in the novel, ranging from the chivalric to the martial, yet its overriding emphasis must be understood as Carlylean. The distinction is important, because Meredith's question is less one of historical timeliness, whether heroism is *possible* in the modern age, than whether heroism can be in any form *advisable* in the present.[4] Particularly because the likelihood of any hero arising depends on our receptivity to that possibility, Meredith is concerned most with the ethical effect that a hero is likely to have on others. This is, of course, Carlyle's key question, too. He insists that the hero's influence is undoubted and wholly positive; the hero serves as a pattern for all and as the basis of social order. "Society is founded on Hero-worship."[5]

For Meredith, however, this idealization of the hero has become extremely problematic. From his perspective, the very elevation of the hero has inevitably corrosive effects on the intellectual and ethical sensibilities of others, and eventually on the hero as well, regardless of how well-intentioned, regardless of how "right" in any sense of the word a hero might be. Not his irrelevance, but the actual political possibility of the hero in Victorian England, makes heroism and hero-worship extraordinarily dangerous. Carlyle's heroic ideal installs a model of human subjectivity that Meredith is at pains to reject throughout his work.

Beauchamp's Career, like much else in Meredith's writing, is a critique of the inherently anti-liberal effects of hero-worship, of its resuscitated patriarchalism. Meredith's own ideology, however, differs greatly from utilitarian liberalism with its assumption of independent, even isolated, subjects. Meredith articulates instead a communal liberal ideal, based upon a positive and progressive interdependence of all subjects in the acquisition of that self-knowledge that makes rational self-direction possible. The destruction of the hero, of our hero, Beauchamp, must be seen not as a sign of his untimeliness, but as a judgment on heroism itself. However consciously or unconsciously, Meredith anticipates a historical necessity that goes far beyond the fate of Beauchamp as an individual character. Like ostracism in the city-state, Beauchamp's exclusion provides a necessary, if lamentable, reaffirmation of the integrity of the community.

II

Meredith invokes Carlyle early in *Beauchamp's Career*, in a way that leaves no doubt about his importance for the ideological questions in the text. Seen through the eyes of Rosamund, worshipper of Beauchamp and housekeeper for his uncle-guardian, *On Heroes* is cited as having a powerful formative influence on the youthful Beauchamp, articulating and directing his unformed political sensibilities.

> His favourite author was one writing of Heroes, in (so she esteemed it) a style resembling either early architecture or utter dilapidation, so loose and rough it seemed; a wind-in-the-orchard style, that tumbled down here and there an appreciable fruit with uncouth bluster; sentences without commencements running to abrupt endings and smoke, like waves against a sea-wall, learned dictionary words giving a hand to street-slang, and accents falling on them haphazard, like slant rays from driving clouds; all the pages in a breeze, the whole book producing a kind of electrical agitation in the mind and the joints. This was its effect on the lady. To her the incomprehensible was the abominable, for she had our country's high critical feeling; but he, while admitting that he could not quite master it, liked it. He had dug the book out of a bookseller's shop in Malta, captivated by its title, and had, since the day of his purchase, gone at it again and again, getting nibbles of golden meaning by instalments, as with a solitary pick in a very dark mine, until the illumination of an idea struck him that there was a great deal more in the book than there was in himself. This was sufficient to secure the devoted attachment of young Mr. Beauchamp.
>
> (1:22-23)

Besides imitating Carlyle's own style in its metaphoric and blustery quality, this passage hints at the deeper effect of Carlyle's ideological framework, the "electrical agitation" that results from his insistent polarization of issues and persons. Carlyle typically creates and enforces absolute distinctions in *On Heroes*, charging political matters and all others alike with moral significance. "In Kings, and in all human Authorities, and relations that men god-created can form among each other, there is verily either a Divine Right or else a Diabolic Wrong" (p. 198).

This rhetorical deluge is very troubling to Rosamund's conventional sensibilities. She objects primarily to its incomprehensibility, an evasive reaction since Carlyle's prose is all too comprehensible as a threat to bourgeois values and their idolatry of comfort. Her incomprehension indicates her resistance to its message of abolishing a public-private split and respiritualizing existence more than any inherent difficulty of the text.

On Heroes revolves around an insistence that politics and life need to be more than an interplay of material interests. "I esteem the modern error, that all goes by self-interest and the checking and balancing of greedy knaveries, and that, in short, there is nothing divine whatever in the association of men, a still more despicable error . . . than that of a 'divine right' in people *called* Kings" (p. 199). For Carlyle, the preferable alternative mode of human activity begins with a Fichtean model of subjectivity. Who we are and what we are to do depend on the place in which we originally find ourselves, as subjects before the universe. "This universe, ah me—what could the wild man know of it; what can we yet know? That it is a Force, and thousandfold Complexity of Forces; a Force which is *not we*. That is all; it is not we, it is altogether different from *us*" (p. 8). This Fichtean contrast of subject and alien otherness is not, however, recuperated as in Fichte by reasserting the primacy of the subject and its own positing or generation of the not-subject. Instead, Carlyle regularly attempts to accommodate the subject to a preregulated universe. "A man must conform himself to Nature's laws, *be* verily in communion with Nature and the truth of things, or Nature will answer him, No, not at all" (p. 44). "It has ever been held the highest wisdom for a man not merely to submit to Necessity,—Necessity will make him submit,—but to know and believe well that the stern thing which Necessity had ordered was the wisest, the best, the thing wanted there" (p. 56).

Carlyle's hero is defined by his exceptional capacity to apprehend intuitively those things that constitute his universe, a trait Carlyle sums up as "sincerity." "A Hero, as I repeat, has this first distinction . . .That he looks through the shows of things into *things*" (p. 55). Vision must also be supplemented by conviction, the internal assurance of the validity of this essentially personal insight. "Belief I define to be the healthy act of a man's mind. It is a mysterious indescribable process, that of getting to believe. . . . We have our mind given us, not that it may cavil and argue, but that it may see into something, give us clear belief and understanding about something, whereon we are then to proceed to act" (pp. 173-74). These qualities are confirmed by their passage into speech, where the semi-mystical experience takes on social meaning and force. "The *word* that will describe the thing, follows of itself from such clear intense sight of the thing" (p. 104). Individual subjects confronting and eagerly conforming to the shapes of things—such is the framework of Carlyle's romantic epistemology and objectifying terminology.

Beauchamp's first stab at heroism indicates how strongly Meredith refuses Carlyle's rhetorical fusion of public and private, his easy conversion of personal vision into public guidance. The young Beauchamp takes the diplomatic rhetoric of France towards England at this period as a personal insult, to which he responds by the quintessentially personal gesture of challenging the entire French royal guard to a duel. His heroic aims are in sharply comic disproportion to real political possibilities, completely detached from the practical world of politics. Meredith's very first use of any form of "hero" makes the term problematic from the start, when he styles Beauchamp's behavior here "heroical-nonsensical" (1:10). Beauchamp attempts to reduce public questions to the shape and size of personal ones, thus immediately disarming his heroic pretensions.[6] This scene, to be sure, does not even begin to resolve the link between public and private spheres, but it already indicates Meredith's refusal to short-circuit the disjunction, as Carlyle does. The question of heroism remains more serious than this comic introduction to the topic might suggest.

The same issues are later taken up by Dr. Shrapnel, Beauchamp's political mentor, in a Radical critique of English society which parallels Carlyle's analysis at many key points. Beauchamp explicitly associates the two figures. "He cited his old favourite, the black and bright lecturer on Heroes. 'You have read him, I know, Cecilia. Well, Dr. Shrapnel is another, who writes in his own style, not the leading-article style or modern pulpit stuff' " (2:94). Shrapnel's main theoretical points are set out in a letter near the center of the text, where he focuses his barrage on the politics of interests, which in a bourgeois society produces an idolatry of comfort.[7] "The religion of this vast English middle-class ruling the land is Comfort. It is their central thought; their idea of necessity; their sole aim. Whatsoever ministers to Comfort—seems to belong to it—pretends to support it, they yield their passive worship to. Whatsoever alarms it they join to crush. There you get at their point of unity" (2:7). This desire for comfort springs from that vice to which Meredith is particularly hostile—egoism. What remains in other Meredith texts (such as *Sandra Belloni* or *The Egoist*) a diagnosis of individual psychology, however, here becomes the germ of all political ills. Even the family, as Shrapnel perceptively remarks, is nothing but a veil for such egoism. "The family view of a man's fit conduct is the weak point of the country. It is no other view than, 'Better thy condition for our sakes.' Ha! In this way we breed sheep. . . . The family view is everlastingly the shopkeeper's" (1:116-17).

In opposition to this ideology, Shrapnel sounds a distinctly Carlylean note. "The soul only is life" (2:11). Meredith himself doubtless agrees here, having earlier insisted, "the ideas of men, which are—it is policy to be emphatic upon truisms—are actually the motives of men in a greater degree than their appetites: these are my theme" (1:7). Yet it makes all the difference *how* one chooses to go beyond the world of appetites and interests. Shrapnel's critique of utilitarian liberalism, like Carlyle's, insists that given these constraints the simple promulgation of individual liberty can never provide an adequately positive basis for community. Mere liberty is nothing but a recipe for social indifference and political fragmentation. As Beauchamp says, "Their [the English] idea of liberty is, an evasion of public duty" (2:156). According to Carlyle, mere political liberty is "for the Working Millions a liberty to die by want of food; for the Idle Thousands and Units, alas, a still more fatal liberty to live in want of work."[8]

Yet Shrapnel's proposed solution to these problems is distinctly un-Carlylean. He advocates the dispersal of ego rather than focusing it in the hero, presumed in some sense to be above ego. "Anyhow, with numbers there is rough nature's wisdom and justice. With numbers ego is inter-dependent and dispersed; it is universalized" (2:12). His democratic sentiments respond directly and in a characteristically liberal way to the issues that Carlyle would prefer to transcend. Shrapnel explicitly denounces the hero, coupling him with the blandishments of Catholicism. "The helpless poor and the uneasy rich are alike open to the seductions of Romish priests and intoxicated ranters" (2:10). His final appeal is to society as a whole, a social totality that, as in much political theorizing, remains tantalizingly vague. "Society is our one tangible gain, our one roofing and flooring in a world of most uncertain structures built on morasses. . . . Rebellion against Society, and advocacy of Humanity, run counter" (2:12-13). All of this, however, remains at best half of a solution, for Shrapnel fails to provide any supplementary answer as to what *can* constitute that sense of community that he sees as lacking. Dispersal of ego is at most a negative guarantee against any premature imposition of heroic or not-so-heroic forms upon society. Most curious of all, the political thread of the novel breaks off here, never to regain the intensity of discussion in this chapter even though half the novel still remains. If any further answers to Carlyle's and Shrapnel's laments are to be found, they must be uncovered elsewhere than in the overt political texture of the text.

III

With the text thus poised between romantic conservatism and an ill-defined alternative, Meredith chose in the immediately succeeding chapter to shift radically the direction of the narrative. Political theory and practice henceforth give way to an essentially domestic drama, a conflict between Beauchamp and his Uncle Romfrey, whose presumed heir he is. The sense of loss or diminishment that results is not the reader's alone, but is explicitly articulated as such by the narrator. "His indifferent England refused [a conceivable epic] to him. . . . The greater power of the two, she seems, with a quiet derision that does not belie her amiable passivity, to have reduced in Beauchamp's career the boldest readiness for public action, and some good stout effort besides, to the flat result of an optically discernible influence of our hero's character in the domestic circle; perhaps a faintly-outlined circle or two beyond it" (1:40). Although the stress here seems to be on how *England* falls short of fostering heroism, the issues run deeper than this. For the novel itself seems to fall short as well, to be unable to sustain the level of political seriousness with which it began or to connect those issues directly to the personal relationships in the text. Seen in these terms alone, Beauchamp's failure would also be Meredith's, as well as a comment on the ideological limits of the genre of the novel, locked into a model of subjectivity that renders it unable to articulate any political relevance for the subject.

Yet to represent political issues through the lens of a domestic drama need not mean that the political dimension is thereby discarded. Rather than excluding politics, the second half of *Beauchamp's Career* begins a more subtle transformation of politics into questions of human relationships and intersubjectivity that make the text an unusually powerful political narrative. It works in this way toward a broader, more coherent political vision than the explicitly political scenes of the first half of the novel ever attain.

The incident that governs the remainder of the text is Romfrey's horse-whipping of Shrapnel, for which Beauchamp pursues his uncle incessantly in demand of a formal apology. The whipping has its source far back in the text, in a misunderstanding that leads us to important links between the political and domestic layers of the text. Put as concisely as possible, Romfrey is avenging what he understood Rosamund had given him to understand that she had understood as an insult by Shrapnel to her virtue (based on her somewhat ambiguous position as the bachelor Romfrey's unmarried, but eminently marriageable, housekeeper). This typically Meredithian interpretive tangle lies at the heart of his meditation on heroism, for only in its light do we begin to perceive the consequences and costs of hero-worship. On one level, this incident seems almost too blatantly a symbol for the political alignments of the text—Tory force being used to repress Radical dissent, all veiled by a hypocritical evocation of moral issues—but the Carlylean elements of these events complicate this overly simple analysis. In any case, the shift to this domestic drama denotes neither the loss of political questions nor their reductively symbolic rearticulation, but instead their conversion into ethical questions, a juncture of levels of discourse that the novel as genre is particularly well-suited to articulate. For Meredith, the worth of any political ideology can be measured by its practical effects, both ethical and intellectual, on its adherents. These effects are what the second half of *Beauchamp's Career* can measure more closely than the overtly political sections of the novel, burdened as they are with the effects of rhetoric and caricature.

To judge Beauchamp's behavior in relation to this particular incident, however, we need first to see the larger role he plays in the text and his specific species of heroism. Beauchamp is, from the first, thoroughly at home in the ideological atmosphere of hero-worship. "Veneration of heroes, living and dead, kept down his conceit. He worshipped devotedly. . . . Not to love his hero was to be strangely in error, to be in need of conversion, and he proselytized with the ardour of the Moslem" (1:12). More importantly, Beauchamp himself serves as focal point for the worshipping gazes of others; he is himself as much a hero as contemporary English society can allow. Explicitly differentiated from the Byronic, Beauchamp's heroism is characterized by its explicitly political, Carlylean quality. "But Nevil was for a plan, a system, immediate action; the descending among the people, and taking an initiative, LEADING them, insisting on their following, not standing aloof and shrugging" (1:29). Just as with Carlyle, this heroism emphasizes articulation as the main task for and test of the vision and sincerity that identify a hero. "The value he put upon speaking, urging his views, was really fanatical" (1:174).[9] Beauchamp's life can therefore serve to test the consequences of establishing a hero as center of a text that endeavors to take the political implications of the hero as seriously as the narrative ones.

The substance of hero-worship here becomes most evident in Beauchamp's relationships with women.[10] His ties to Rosamund, to Cecilia, and to Jenny reveal different aspects of the heroic pattern, but all converge on a common result. Consistently and forcefully, Meredith demonstrates how the dynamics of heroism produce an ethical and intellectual diminishing of worshippers and hero alike.

As his first and most ardent worshipper, Rosamund displays most strongly the possessive strains of hero-worship. Her attachment to Beauchamp remains complex and ambiguous, a mixture of maternal, erotic, and sisterly elements that even she cannot disentangle. Her unwavering worship of Beauchamp's heroic qualities makes her a seemingly ideal case for the merging of wills that Carlyle takes as the sign of hero-worship. "The Commander over Men; he to whose will our wills are to be subordinated, and loyally surrender themselves, and find their welfare in doing so, may be reckoned the most important of Great Men" (p. 196). Whether Beauchamp's own aspirations run in this direction or not, Rosamund's aspirations for him certainly do. Yet this hero-worship does not foster their mutual welfare; instead the repression of differences between them becomes ruinous, promoting subterfuge and deceit.

In Meredith's analysis, two mutually reinforcing reasons almost guarantee such ruin. First, hero-worship never operates unalloyed; the merging of wills is never complete. The worshipper always interprets her or his hero idiosyncratically, with an inmixture of private interest and personal subjectivity. The flaws of egoism that Carlyle believes heroism would elide are only displaced. Rosamund always renders Beauchamp into her own terms, confident that she knows what is best for him. She proceeds to act without consulting him, yet has her own capacity for action distorted because she tries to operate from within two divergent perspectives simultaneously, as when she tries to conceive Beauchamp's view of Shrapnel: "Rosamund strained her mental sight to gain a conception of [Beauchamp's] prodigious horror of the treatment of Dr. Shrapnel, that she might think him sane: and to retain a vestige of comfort in her bosom she tried to moderate and make light of as much as she could conceive. Between these two efforts she had no sense but that of helplessness" (2:87). Torn between her mind and Beauchamp's, yet unable to admit the divergence, Rosamund loses any power to act independently, eventually even to act at all, with her inaction proving almost fatal to her, to Shrapnel, and to Beauchamp.

By promoting such repressions, hero-worship corrupts the interpretive acuteness and judgment of the worshipper. Such idolatry creates just those psychological conditions conducive to self-deception and deception of others. For by creating unresolved tensions from which the mind turns away, hero-worship creates a space in discourse where an excessive free play of imaginary comparisons can thrive. Meredith always concedes the inevitable and invaluable presence of imagistic components in discourse, yet he remains troubled by how these can act as terminal points for thought, markers of a refusal to think through a particular judgment or decision. "It is the tricksy heart which sets up that balance, to jump into it on one side or the other. Comparisons come of a secret leaning that is sure to play rogue under its mien of honest dealer" (1:252).

Rosamund falls prey to such temptation repeatedly—from her encounter with Renée to her contacts with Jenny. Its worst fruit is borne by her meeting with Shrapnel, where her private notion of worship for Beauchamp and her repressed motives make her unable either to express herself or to comprehend Shrapnel. "How strange, besides hateful, it was to her to hear her darling spoken of by a stranger who not only pretended to appreciate but to possess him. . . . Of course she could have shot a rejoinder, to confute him with all the force of her indignation, save that the words were tumbling about in her head like a world in disruption, which made her feel a weakness at the same time that she gloated on her capacity, as though she had an enormous army, quite overwhelming if it could but be got to move in advance" (1:117-18). Unable to confront her own motives, unable to speak lest she unwittingly reveal them, Rosamund takes refuge in a comparison that plants the seed for the whipping, an image in which hero-worship reveals its reactionary roots. "What champion was she to look to? . . . It was with a spasm of delighted reflection that she hit on Mr. Romfrey. . . . With his strength and skill, his robust common sense and rough shrewd wit, his prompt comparisons, his chivalry, his love of combat, his old knightly blood, was he not a match, and an overmatch, for the ramping Radical who had tangled Nevil in his rough snares? . . . Could she but once draw these two giants into collision in Nevil's presence, she was sure it would save him. The method of doing it she did not stop to consider: she enjoyed her triumph in the idea" (1:118). The collision, of course, does come to pass, subconsciously abetted by Rosamund's self-concealing mind. Her zeal on Nevil's behalf, coupled with her own half-conscious motives, generates a rhetoric with fairy-tale, biblical, and chivalric echoes where even her passivity can be validated by her status as a maiden in distress. She allows Romfrey to misinterpret her reaction, to assume that Shrapnel had insulted her, and to build his own imagistic drama in which Shrapnel, "a tall man," plays the evil giant.

Rosamund's failure here, as elsewhere, is an interpretive one. With her mind made hesitant by her worship of Beauchamp, she proves unable to act in a world where success often depends on "the delicate chance for an understanding" (1:74). Hero-worship increases the force of egoism, precisely because it displaces and represses it. She retreats into a self-inflicted blindness that is the contrary of Carlyle's empowering vision. "She could not bear to think of her part in the mischief. She was not bound to think of it, knowing actually nothing of the occurrence" (2:59-60). As Beauchamp sowed in demanding veneration, so he reaps a harvest of incomprehension traceable to his taste for Carlyle.

Beauchamp's own involvement with and responsibility for hero-worship are even more clearly evident in his relationship with Cecilia, a Tory heiress whom his uncle would prefer to see him marry. Meredith depicts the mutual corruption of hero and worshipper as Beauchamp uses his charisma to blunt the reflective self-consciousness of another, to repress her judgment. Beauchamp's pursuit of Cecilia is, as far as he can see, scrupulous to a fault. The very utility of her wealth to his cause makes him reluctant to propose. He aims not to separate private and political motives, however, but to make one the basis of the other. Beauchamp wants first to convert Cecilia, to gain her political allegiance, then her hand.

Sincerity, however, proves much more complex than Beauchamp or Carlyle had estimated, a point on which Meredith always insists. "Up to the extent of his knowledge of himself, the man was fairly sincere" (2:127). That extent in Beauchamp, unfortunately, is rather less than Meredith considers acceptable, precisely because of his being enmeshed in the structures of heroism. Carlyle himself provides no standard for gauging sincerity, except that only the sincere can ascertain its presence, a hopelessly circular criterion.

Beneath Beauchamp's apparent respect of Cecilia's independence lies the subjugating impulse latent in hero-worship. Carlyle's idea of voluntary, whole-hearted acquiescence in the guidance of a self-evident hero cannot be normative in a world of much more diverse aims, so that heroic ideals can only be surrendered or imposed. Whereas Rosamund seems to make herself into a victim, Beauchamp clearly acts to make Cecilia his victim. The quality of his pursuit is neatly captured by the metaphors in terms of which he thinks of her. "That element of the barbarous which went largely to form his emotional nature was overjoyed in wresting such a woman from the enemy, and subduing her personally. She was a prize. She was a splendid prize, cut out from under the guns of the fort" (1:239). As so often in Meredith's fiction, language enters to trip us up precisely where something like hero-worship dulls our pursuit of reflective self-consciousness. By choosing to play the heroic role with Cecilia, Beauchamp reveals its repressive substratum and its corrupting influence wherever he becomes convinced of his own heroic mission. "He gazed at [London]—a place conquerable yet, with the proper appliances for subjugating it: the starting of his daily newspaper, THE DAWN, say, as a commencement. It began to seem a possible enterprise. It soon seemed a proximate one. If Cecilia!—He left the exclamation a blank, but not an empty dash in the brain; rather like the shroud of night on a vast and gloriously imagined land" (2:184). Just as with Rosamund, Beauchamp's refusal to concede any difference between himself and another produces an image that seems to resolve a tension it has only elided.

Regardless of his rectitude, Beauchamp's approximation of the hero here displays his proximity to the tyrant. Unable to submit, unable not to worship, Cecilia feels herself reduced to impotence. "With a heart subdued, she had still a mind whose habit of independent judgment was not to be constrained, and while she felt that it was only by siding with Nevil submissively and blindly in this lamentable case that she could hope for happiness, she foresaw the likelihood of her not being able to do so as much as he would desire and demand" (2:51). Like Rosamund, the demands and constraints of hero-worship undermine Cecilia's capacities for judgment and for action, inhibiting the emergence of latent tensions and differences which might promote their resolution.

Rather than perpetuating her subjection, Cecilia steers for the only port where it appears likely that her desire for freedom can be satisfied—marriage to the Tory ideologue, Tuckham. When Beauchamp does finally propose, "All she could feel was a harsh joy to have struck off her tyrant's fetters, with a determination to cherish it passionately lest she should presently be hating herself: for the shadow of such a possibility fell within the narrow circle of her strung sensations" (2:219). Her ideological conversion to Radical values is ironically what makes marriage to the exponent of those values, Beauchamp, impossible. Her choice of spouse illuminates harshly the gap that Beauchamp has opened up, but fails to see, between his theory and his practice. Ideological commitment to Radical values cannot be made compatible with the practice of Carlylean heroism. Nor is the neutral guarantee of equality and liberty adequate in itself. Cecilia attempts to choose freedom, but instead reveals the latent unfairness in the liberal reliance on persuasion, which assumes the existence of an ideal equality of persuasive powers that can instead be used as a screen for coercion and force.[11] Most crucially, however, it is Beauchamp's heroic traits that allow Cecilia's egoism to triumph (2:231). Hero-worship intensifies the social ills that it was supposed to remedy.

The final female character, Jenny (Shrapnel's ward), seems to be an exception to this pattern. Rather than worshipping Beauchamp, she often disagrees with his most earnest (and often most short-sighted) proposals. She counters his appeal to polarized moral alternatives, the opposition of reason and its enemies, with this admonition. "If we can be sure that we ourselves are using reason rightly, Nevil!—not prejudice" (2:306). Moreover, Beauchamp significantly courts her in a way that he never did with Rosamund or Cecilia, whose worship he took for granted.

Yet Jenny's status remains troubling as well and indicative of deeper social pressures. She is manipulated into marriage by Beauchamp's and Shrapnel's insistence that she needs to be taken care of; her submission results from her inability to control Beauchamp and leaves her "broken and sobbing, senseless" and "grovelling" (2:293-94). Although theoretically an equal voice with theirs, "She was a faltering unit against an ardent and imperative two in the council" (2:305). The residual power of linguistic and social structures remains in force as Beauchamp exerts all his male prerogatives. Although this reference is to a single incident, its ominous overtones are inevitable for any reader attentive to the novel's indictment of hero-worship. "He put his legal right in force to shut her mouth. . . . While practising this mastery, he assured her he would always listen to her" (2:307). Meredith balances this passage with a reiteration of their dialogic engagement to each other, yet Beauchamp cannot shed the air of being an unregenerate and unreformed hero.

IV

Having analyzed Beauchamp's status as a hero, we can better understand the force and significance of the second half of the novel and its redirection of political energies into domestic drama. In one sense, Beauchamp's insistence on an apology is a very Carlylean act. It reduces political questions to moral ones, abstracting from the greater complexity of the former. It dramatizes the inescapable danger of the hero, his temptation and ability to turn the political arena into a personal crusade. The domestic triumph attained by Beauchamp in getting Romfrey to apologize is therefore many-edged. Not only Romfrey, but we as readers, are tempted to overestimate its significance, partly because no comparable political triumph appears in the novel. Yet even when read as a symbolic resolution, reinforced later by Shrapnel's and Romfrey's mutual support in their grief at Beauchamp's death, it seems insufficient. For the contest between Romfrey and Beauchamp has finally been more on Romfrey's terms, a regression into the feudal past where force, whether of arms or conviction, was decisive.

This process, however, is also a measure of the success of Meredith's text as political fiction. The unsettling qualities of the conclusion are essential if Meredith is to convey successfully his claim that heroism is inherently and irremediably flawed. The cult of the hero fosters blindness; rather than being an antidote to liberalism's flaws, it exacerbates its worst characteristics. Hero-worship allows self-interest to abide undetected in the mask of sincerity, precisely because that sincerity is never called on to examine itself. "The Great Man's sincerity is of the kind he cannot speak of, is not conscious of" (*Heroes*, p. 45). These traits suffice to rouse Meredith's concern against fanatical adherence to any single person, idea, or truth. "[A single idea] is at once a devouring dragon, and an intractable steam-force; it is a tyrant that has eaten up a senate, and a prophet with a message. Inspired of solitariness and gigantic size, it claims divine origin. The world can have no peace for it" (2:110). Meredith's judgment on Carlyle (and on so much else in modern history) focuses on the lack of self-awareness that the ideology of the hero perpetuates and validates. To need a single moral standard and to take one person as its measure are for Meredith irrecoverable errors. "It is not so difficult to be right against the world when the heart is really active; but the world is our book of humanity, and before insisting that *his* handwriting shall occupy the next blank page of it, the noble rebel is bound for the sake of his aim to ask himself how much of a giant he is, lest he fall like a blot on the page, instead of inscribing intelligible characters there" (2:120-21). No one can write for all; no one can write alone. Not only is there a potential for abuse of hero-worship, Meredith insists, such abuse is inherent in its ideological premises.

The novel as genre may itself seem complicitous with this ideology in its proclivity for one or a few "heroes." Even *Beauchamp's Career* allows the political dimension of community to seem to recede and an individual hero to become its center. So one might finally recall the question of whether Meredith provides any answers to the political problems that he asserts the hero cannot resolve. Although no complete response can be found in the text, Meredith does suggest a possible reshaping of liberalism, especially its analysis of the problem of divergent self-interests. Rather than focusing only on the negative aspects of liberal theory—dispersal of ego and tolerance—Meredith supplements it with an obligation of civic political education. Restriction of political reform to institutional changes will fall short of creating or defining any genuine political community, which must instead be based on a rethinking of the subject that acknowledges its fundamentally social identity.

Meredith's position echoes Mill's *On Liberty*, where "individuality is the same thing with development."[12] The key section of the essay in this regard is "Of the Liberty of Thought and Discussion," rather than the more frequently cited "Of Individuality," for in the former part Mill stresses the vital interdependence among particularized subjectivities. "The only way in which a human being can make some approach to knowing the whole of a subject is by hearing what can be said about it by persons of every variety of opinion, and studying all modes in which it can be looked at by every character of mind. No wise man ever acquired his wisdom in any mode but this; nor is it in the nature of human intellect to become wise in any other manner" (p. 232). This necessarily involves an increase in self-knowledge commensurate with knowledge of other things. "If the cultivation of the understanding consists in one thing more than in another, it is surely in learning the grounds of one's own opinions" (p. 244). The ebb and flow of engagement with others is the first element that Meredith opposes to the one-directional flow of hero-worship.

Yet Meredith goes further, pushing beyond the rational individualism of Mill. Mill asserts that, "with respect to his own feelings and circumstances, the most ordinary man or woman has means of knowledge immeasurably surpassing those that can be possessed by anyone else" (p. 277). Just this privileged self-access, whether attributed to the hero or to all persons alike, is what Meredith would deny. His characters do not know themselves better than they know others; in general they know themselves far worse. Instead they *come* to self-awareness through the displacement from self that characterizes an intersubjective understanding, the partly intuitive apprehension of the otherness of another's position that allows one to recognize one's own status much more consciously and explicitly.

This is the reverse side of Romfrey's apology, the element that keeps it from being just a regression to a feudal past. Beauchamp's near-fatal illness sparks the mental leap that he has been trying to force his uncle to make, a leap that lets him re-image the condition of England and his complicity with that condition. Romfrey overhears workmen waiting for news of Beauchamp mispronounce their names, which "pushed him to reflections on the madness of Nevil in endeavoring to lift them up and brush them up; and a curious tenderness for Nevil's madness worked in his breast as he contrasted this much-abused nephew of his with our general English" (2:261). Although born of emotional attachment, Romfrey's response is far from hero-worship in that it never obliterates the differences between himself and Nevil. His apology is not a submission, but a positive reestimation of those differences. Nor could it result from a purely sympathetic or emotional attunement to others; it requires a heightened linguistic awareness that cannot be unmediated or one-sided.

For Meredith, the rational self-direction of liberalism requires this constant unearthing of the unconscious sources of speech and action, both personal and political, in the misapprehensions and anomalies of discourse. Even imprecision and indirection can contribute to this process, as when Beauchamp directs Renée's attention to a gourd reflected on the river. "Very strangely, the ridiculous thing, in the shape of an over-stretched likeness, that she never would have seen had he indicated it directly, became transfused from his mind to hers by his abstract, half-amused observation of the great dancing gourd. . . . Her senses imagined the impressions agitating Beauchamp's, and exaggerated them beyond limit" (1:278). Hero-worship, insofar as it blurs differences and hinders this interpretive growth, can never be acceptable.

Not incidentally, Meredith's liberalism would also leave a space for a distinctively literary contribution to political discussion. His fiction goes beyond Shrapnel's prescription for dispersing ego by trying to demonstrate the necessary interdependence of ego, the profound reliance of every individual subject on all others—at a minimal level even in its rational pursuit of its own self-interest, but maximally even more completely in its positive commitment to its own development. Meredith thus shares the Romantic awareness that the subject can never perceive all facets of itself, so that only another subject can effectively supplement it in an infinitely progressive development.

All of this remains admittedly ideal in a text that gives us only hints of how to achieve such social and political interchange, the more so since its moments of achievement in the text are often accidental. Meredith's fiction aims first to depict the labyrinth of self-development and the multitude of dead ends in the process—of which Beauchamp is one. But it also demands that its readers exercise their critical faculties, expanding them to include more than pure reason. Gillian Beer has noted how *Beauchamp's Career* is radical above all in seeking to create active readers, by using as modes of self-presentation the same linguistic devices on which its characters necessarily rely. Yet its own claims are not finally heroic, with all the hubris and self-deception that might entail. The image that governs the close of the novel articulates a conscious renunciation of any overly personal investment in political affairs. To Beauchamp's lament that he had not even managed directly to bring about Romfrey's apology (caused by his illness), Shrapnel opposes a fable of sowing seed, of trusting in the efficacy of one's actions rather than demanding an immediate harvest of them in praise or worship. Shrapnel succeeds in abolishing the obsessiveness of the apology not only from the mind of Beauchamp and from its dominant position in the second half of the novel, but one hopes from the reader's mind as well. "I spoke of seed sown. I spoke of the fruits of energy and resolution. Cared I for an apology? I took the blows as I take hail from the clouds" (2:288).

Yet one more thing remains to be done. Shrapnel's blessing cannot finally absolve Beauchamp from his Carlylean taint or his propensity for heroism. Meredith therefore steps in with a conclusion that is at once political and cautionary, abrupt to be sure, but an essential termination to the logic of hero-worship. Only the death of Beauchamp can suffice as a final denial of the cult of the hero. Beauchamp's drowning, as he endeavors to save a boy whose brother he had already saved, draws him back into an indispensable equivalence with his fellow citizens, while shifting the obligation for action from him to us. Meredith here insists upon heroism's relevance being only to a narrower, moral world that remains detached from political and ethical complexities. Heroism is better not erected into a political doctrine, not because of its irrelevance to that world, but because of its obsessive absorption and consequent degradation of that world.

Meredith's final point is doubtless directed to us as readers in need of heroes. Beauchamp's death should cause us to reflect on our own tendencies to hero-worship, our own submission to certain habits of reading. Meredith's fiction never quite becomes radically experimental; his choice is always for reform rather than revolution. But his call to reform, from the grounds up, is no less insistent for that.

NOTES

[1]The novelty of Meredith's undertaking, or at least the rigor with which he pursued it, was already evident to contemporary reviewers, such as J. C. Carr (*Saturday Review*, 13 May 1876), cited in Ioan Williams, *Meredith: The Critical Heritage* (London: Routledge & Kegan Paul, 1971), pp. 182-87. All quotations from *Beauchamp's Career* refer to the American Memorial Edition, 27 vols: (New York: Charles Scribner's Sons, 1909-10), and will be cited in the text by volume and page number.

[2]The first assessment is from Arnold Kettle, "*Beauchamp's Career*," in *Meredith Now: Some Critical Essays*, Ian Fletcher, ed: (New York: Barnes & Noble, 1971), p. 199. The latter two are from Gillian Beer, *Meredith: A Change of Masks: A Study of the Novels* (London: Athlone Press, 1970), pp. 76-77. In contrast, David Howard's valuable essay on Meredith's political novels sees this same event as "brilliantly minimal" and a "triumphant" transfer of worth from Beauchamp to the boy. David Howard, "George Meredith: 'Delicate' and 'Epical' Fiction," in *Literature and Politics in the Nineteenth Century: Essays*, John Lucas, ed. (London: Methuen, 1971), p. 170.

[3]This focus differs from that of Beer or Howard, whose studies are the most far-reaching analyses of the text. Both critics take Beauchamp largely as he presents himself—as a Radical—rather than exploring the validity of joining Radicalism and heroism. Yet these Radical impulses are grounded on a

problematic Carlylean element that dramatically alters how we can read the ideology of the text.

[4]Beer's essay adopts the first stance. See especially pp. 74 and 103.

[5]Thomas Carlyle, *On Heroes, Hero-Worship and the Heroic in History*, Carl Niemeyer, ed. (Lincoln: Univ. of Nebraska Press, 1966), p. 12. All further citations from *Heroes* will be by page number in the text.

[6]The character of Renée, a young French woman whom Beauchamp tries to save from an arranged marriage and who repeatedly returns as a romantic interest, represents this same temptation for him throughout the novel. His relationship with her invites him to turn politics into a sphere for the gratification of his ego, to make society conform to the shape of his desires. Since the kind of heroism relevant here is chivalric rather than Carlylean, her role is quite different from those other female characters whom I will examine later.

[7]This letter, like many of the important political statements in the novel, is presented in a curiously roundabout way. See Howard, p. 160, for a useful discussion of this mode of presentation.

[8]Thomas Carlyle, *Past and Present* (New York: Charles Scribner's Sons, 1903), p. 219.

[9]This trait suggests one important link between Beauchamp's demand for an apology and the larger political questions it seems to displace. The verbal debate between Beauchamp and his uncle serves as an epitome of the political act par excellence. "Lay on to his uncle as he would, that wrestler shook him off. And here was one man whom he could not move! How move a nation?" (2:111).

[10]Howard, pp. 166-71, provides a fine analysis of how women come to be equated with the people because of their marginal, powerless status.

[11]Meredith's sensitivity to this problem in liberalism finds even more vigorous expression in *One of Our Conquerors*, where the personal situation of Nataly, lover-companion of another such hero-conqueror as Beauchamp, Victor Radnor, brings out the political resonances of heroism and language. See, for instance, pp. 122-23 in the Memorial Edition.

[12]John Stuart Mill, *Collected Works*, 25 vols. (Toronto: Univ. of Toronto Press, 1977), 18:267.

SEL 27 (1987)
ISSN 0039-3657

Recent Studies in the Nineteenth Century

PETER J. MANNING AND SYLVIA MANNING

When we first contemplated this review we fantasized each reading every book, thinking that two heads were likely to be more just than one and that divergent responses would mirror the continuing methodological variety of the discipline (about which more in a moment). That notion collapsed under the sheer number of works forwarded to us; the appended list of "Books Received" is the ghostly record of a substantial reality. We began where our interests lay, hoping eventually to crisscross our way through the entire territory, but the trails we marked in a year's reading do not map the whole terrain. Eventually, all system gave way to the deadline upon us. Charles Lamb wrote to another Manning that "Nothing puzzles me more than time and space, and yet nothing puzzles me less, for I never think of them": reviewers, less fortunate, must yield to both constraints. In consequence, absences from the following discussion do not indicate adverse verdicts or even decisions that a work is omissible; many of the books we have not mentioned deserve, and no doubt will obtain, notice elsewhere. A second regret arising from the effort to characterize in limited space a year's work in a fertile field is that praise will seem inadequately grounded, and reservations capricious; the summary judgment, keenly visible to readers as well as authors (and every reader of this enterprise is at least a potential

Sylvia Manning is a member of the Department of English and Vice-Provost at the University of Southern California; she is the author of *Dickens as Satirist*, of *Hard Times: An Annotated Bibliography*, and of essays on Victorian fiction.

Peter J. Manning is chair of the Department of English at the University of Southern California; he is the author of *Byron and His Fictions* and of essays on Romantic poetry.

author), seems conclusive but is only the reduced sign of a lengthy process of engagement and reflection.

Even more notable than the quantity of material submitted for review are its internal divisions. Advanced critical essays arrived in the same carton as elementary introductions; monographs that wouldn't stoop to recognize so low a thing as an author emerged next to old-fashioned surveys of life-and-works. It briefly seemed possible to align the difference in critical assumptions, practices, and languages with that between commercial and university presses, but although the distinction remains significant the fit is not perfect. The range from explanatory, paraphrasing guides at one end of the spectrum to metacomment and cultural critique at the other is broad, and the audiences projected by the various volumes are largely discontinuous, perhaps even mutually incomprehending. The more daring formulations initially arouse excitement and unfairly cast into shade achievements built on familiar plans, but as the year progressed our tolerance for slipshod brilliance declined. Too many of the more audacious studies depend on unfaithful accounts of the texts they analyze, or on prose alternately so loosely constructed or clottedly abstract that argument itself evanesces. At such moments one begins to suspect that meaning is only a meaning-effect, produced by sentences that yield no definable content even to prolonged contemplation. Our respect for reliable scholarship and lucid expression rose proportionally.

Deconstruction endures, most often as a healthy force animating careful attention to the instabilities of language within other critical approaches, most purely perhaps in Cynthia Chase's collection of reprinted essays, *Decomposing Figures: Rhetorical Readings in the Romantic Tradition,* spanning from Rousseau and Wordsworth to Baudelaire and Freud, with a chapter on Paul de Man, *fons et origo.* In *The Ethics of Reading*, J. Hillis Miller approaches the relationship of literature to social responsibility by examining the ethical obligations incurred in the act of reading. Studying moments of self-reading in Kant, de Man, George Eliot, Trollope, James, and Benjamin, Miller narrates again the familiar scene of the unreadability of the text, arguing now that the reader's effort to reach the matter behind the text generates further narratives and further acts of doomed understanding. The suggestion that there is a matter to seek draws back from the most radical deconstructive pronouncements of recent years, but the *mise en abîme* of the text reappears in the conception of society Miller engenders. Miller's elegant demonstration of the differing fault lines of his specimen texts disproves the charge that deconstruction always already reaches the same end, but one may doubt whether this narrowly focused inquiry will repel the challenges by which Miller evidently feels himself beset, from conservative humanists on the right and materialists on the left.

That debate is joined in *Romanticism and Contemporary Criticism*, edited by Morris Eaves and Michael Fischer. The contributors, participants in a lecture series at the University of New Mexico, include Northrop Frye on the survival of Eros in poetry and W. J. T. Mitchell, who offers a compact, informative essay on Blake's "visible language." At the heart of the volume are M. H. Abrams and J. Hillis Miller, whose comments on each other's positions are amplified in provoking question-and-answer sessions. The final piece, Stanley Cavell's "In Quest of The Ordinary: Texts of Recovery," is a remarkable, characteristically Cavellian rumination conducted by way of Kant and Heidegger, the Intimations Ode, and "The Rime of the Ancient Mariner." Groping and circuitous, this meditation on skepticism and connection to the world often converges with *The Ethics of Reading*, but breathes an altogether ampler air.

The most ambitious poststructuralist project in the work we received may be Robert Siegle's in *The Politics of Reflexivity: Narrative and the Constitutive Poetics of Culture*: "to extend the reflexive frame of reference to all narrative and to make the corresponding revisions in narrative poetics that such an extension would enable." In typical deconstructionist moves he investigates the ideology not merely of narrative but of criticism of narrative and argues the case for a constitutive rather than mimetic poetics. His concern is more with literary or cultural ideology than with their social or political roots. Despite the short introduction's obligatory debunking of the delusion of literary history, the remainder of the book is divided by periods, only the first of which is within the scope of this essay. That chapter, largely on *Vanity Fair* but supported by briefer discussions of other novels and novelists, is a fine instance of the revelatory power of Derridean methods at their best: especially because the point of view and narrative stance of *Vanity Fair* have always posed a crux, one enjoys repeatedly the sense that at last someone is being fully true to the experience of reading the novel.

If productive power is a test of criticism, then New Historicism has earned its polemic confidence. In *The Romantic Fragment Poem* Marjorie Levinson subjects such typically sly broken forms as "Christabel," "Kubla Khan," *The Giaour*, and "Julian and Maddalo" to a fearsome critical machine. Situating the works within the conditions of their production, and pursuing their reception in contemporary criticism, Levinson elaborates a materialist history of an exemplary Romantic mode. Often, as in a discussion proceeding from the Victorian error of believing that Keats composed "The Fall of Hyperion" before "Hyperion," she forces one to think through the critical maneuvers fictions of irresolution generate. More often Levinson's discourse blankets the poems, which are seldom quoted; abstractions, nominalizations, and the use of nouns and nominative phrases as adjectives abound: "a dramatic monologue scenario," "contextuality interests." There is a good deal of "problematizing" and "ideology," reading becomes a matter of "activat[ing] a mechanism," "protocols" and "reception acts" reign, and the poems themselves are reified into "the RFP." Byron's obsessively but cavalierly expanded *Giaour* puzzles her earnestness: Levinson ascribes to Byron the model of Herodotean historical narrative and then rather belabors the poem for failing to achieve it. Sobersidedness weakens the treatment of "Julian and Maddalo" too. Levinson notes that at its close Maddalo is reported to be off in the mountains of Armenia, without registering Shelley's allusion to Byron's Armenian studies; ignoring the wit and friendship the private joke suggests, she takes the dreadful loneliness the poem proclaims as an impasse of history uncomplicated by the social gesture the poem itself makes. One grumbles because Levinson is plainly a powerful intelligence, and the irritable reaching after system and theory and the tendency to extract what poems seem to state rather than to consider the elusive bearings of their words which mar *The Romantic Fragment Poem* are symptomatic of literary studies today; one wants to counter with Hillis Miller: "Deconstruction is nothing more or less than good reading as such." Much better is Levinson's second book, *Wordsworth's Great Period Poems*, discussed below.

Jon Klancher's *The Making of English Reading Audiences, 1790-1832* is a slender, sinewy, important history of its topic. A conceptually self-conscious grasp of social theory informs Klancher's examination of historical audiences; indeed, because he sees "audience" itself as a social formation mediating between class consciousness and an idealized classless humanity Klancher never loses the dynamic, mutually shaping exchanges of writers and readers as together they map a social text. His account of the evolution of the periodicals from their eighteenth-century origins as mirrors and bonds of a stable society through the explosions of the 1790s is first-rate social history, scrutiny of stylistic features going hand-in-hand with recovery of the ideological worlds they image. He ranges from Paine and Cobbett and the minor radical journals that only patient archival work can recover to the great quarterlies, *Blackwood's* and the *Edinburgh Review*. Wordsworth's despairing imagination of an ideal "people" in which the class distinctions of the "public" would be effaced, and Coleridge's remedy of an unpresentable clerisy—the reading public conceived as ideal institution—Klancher sets forth in the final chapter, "Romantic Theory and English Reading Audiences," as symbolic recourses required by the failure to reshape the audience attempted years before by the *Lyrical Ballads.* Solidly grounded, adventurous, and intelligently discriminating, *The Making of English Reading Audiences* vivifies our sense of the cultural situation in which the Romantics found themselves and the strains with which their fictions contend.

A very different focus on contemporary readership is achieved, not apparently as the primary goal, in Ann H. Jones's *Ideas and Innovations: Best Sellers of Jane Austen's Age.* Essentially this book is a mapping of terrain in traditional terms, historicist rather than new historicist, filling in a gap in the history of the novel during the first two decades of the nineteenth century. Jones is concerned with who wrote the best sellers and what they were like, and the authors who get a chapter each are chosen accordingly: Elizabeth Hamilton, Amelia Opie, Mary Balfour Brunton, Jane Porter, Anna Maria Porter, Thomas Skinner Surr, Sydney Owenson (Lady Morgan), and Charlotte Dacre. These chapters offer résumé and broad analysis of theme, style, characterization, plotting, and tone, with refreshing restraint in assertions of merit or social significance, while making good on Jones's claim to challenge our sense of literary history, of who was influenced by what. But the work's major contribution is that it allows a sampling of popular taste while sparing us the doubtful pleasure of the extensive reading that Jones had to do for it. Against this context we come newly to understand Austen's very modest popular success, and the usefulness of the contrast legitimates the otherwise curious elevation of Austen to the subtitle.

Richard Altick's *Deadly Encounters* provides a considerably less conventional and more playful entry into popular taste half a century later, though it too eschews new-historicist critique. The central and longest part of this book is a detailed newspapers'-eye-view account of two "sensational" cases of 1861, the attack of the Baron de Vidil upon his son and the encounter between William Roberts and Major Murray in Northumberland Street. There follows a discussion of the press philosophizing on the significance of these cases and a brief relating of these "sensations" to the "sensation drama" and the "sensation novel" of the 1860s. Although the latter should be our main interest, the draw of the book is in the narrative of the two cases (which are interwoven with each other, but marked off by headings that we are invited to follow if we prefer consecutive accounts), its genius in the use of lengthy quotation from the newspapers. Like the fiction the book describes, one cannot put it down.

For sharp contrast in the treatment of a lode of historical material we can turn to what is surely the most thoroughgoing Marxism of the year's collection, N. N. Feltes's *Modes of Production of Victorian Novels.* Its statement of purpose is characteristically succinct and awkward: "This book argues the importance of such details as format as being the concrete mediations of the historical in the production of novels, determining in complex ways the actual production of a particular novel and tracing themselves in its text and its own production of ideology." The style is not improved by a penchant for quotation, out of which on occasion an entire argument is constructed, as though the critic mistrusted his own language. But perhaps the effect of authority gained from relentless citation is related to the authoritativeness of manner in the book as a whole, a thin book for whose slender physique virtually all evidence to support theory has been sacrificed. For example, to the statement that we need to see how *Pickwick Papers* "encodes within itself its own ideology of how, by whom and for whom it was produced," we get only one demonstration, the urbanization of its setting. Racked though it is by endless changes on its own dozen pet phrases and the promulgation of key distinctions, such as between commodity-book and commodity-text (the former a petty-commodity production, the latter full-blown capitalist production) the terms of which are never fully convincing, *Modes of Production of Victorian Novels* has the virtue of being consistently interesting on matters related to the material means of production and controversies such as the Booksellers' Question of 1852. We may remain disappointed with its relation of that material to any novel chosen for discussion, but we have been informed in a matter too generally neglected in literary history.

The range possible within essentially Marxist criticism might be demonstrated by comparing Feltes with Lennard J. Davis's *Resisting Novels.* In an utterly engaging personal style Davis advocates "political resistance" to novels so as to "open the possibility for understanding the historical origins of novel-reading defenses, the present function of such defenses, and the ability to save ourselves as a culture from the passive and crippling effects of fiction as an obsession"—this from a self-confessed novel-addict. The second chapter traces the development of the concept of ideology from de Tracy through Jameson and then announces that "It will be the burden of the rest of this book to show in what formal and structural [that is, *not* thematic] ways novels are moulded in the image of the ideological." Unlike the vast majority who attempt such avoidance of the thematic, Davis succeeds; he looks at location, character, dialogue, and plot, *per se*. The method is Marxist/Freudian, more Marxist on location, more Freudian on character and narrators. He raises effectively fundamental questions, such as why we "believe" in characters and why we accept narratorial authority. He argues that plots suggest order and change but novelistic plots keep the focus on individual, not social, change. He not only reminds us of the divergence between real-life conversation and dialogue, but points out that the latter creates a linguistic elite outside class, of which the reader is part. Sometimes the argument relies on too broad an historical generalization, such as the statement that under feudalism land "was in effect not owned and therefore could not be transferred or sold," and sometimes the statements are too facile. But those statements are provisional and the book is as provocative as it is open-ended. It looks at novels with a good deal more point than most theoretical discussions muster and it even achieves its announced purpose, to arouse in us some powers of resistance. This is a short book to which résumé hardly does justice.

Feminism continues to enlarge the canon and to drive reinterpretation of familiar works. In *Bearing the Word* Margaret Homans argues that the dominant myth of language makes women into the silent or vanished object of male quest, incapable themselves of acts of representation. Faced with a culture in which the figurative was reserved to men, Homans asserts, women writers responded by exploiting the literal to which they were consigned. Homans identifies the dominant myth of language as Lacanian, an elevation which will give most psycholinguists pause, rather than seeing that Lacan's structures are deeply informed by Romantic myths. For Homans the dilemma of the nineteenth-century woman writer is to find herself the bearer of the prior Romantic word which denies her place, but the lack of perspective on Lacan means that Homans's own framework repeats Romantic categories. The unresolved difference between "Romantic" and "dominant" entails another, between "Romantic" and "male." A critique of Romanticism, a particular school, is not the same as the critique of culture as a whole to which the book aspires, but Homans moves from one to the other without the broad differential analysis which would authorize the move. Because the only male author discussed at length is Wordsworth, the considerable objections to the will to power of the Romantic imagination both from within (it was Keats who pinned on Wordsworth the label "egotistical sublime") and from without (think of Jeffrey's reviews) are occluded, and a uniform male tradition consolidated. A number of women writers (Anna Seward, Charlotte Smith, Henrietta Maria Williams, not to mention Mme. de

Stael, Maria Edgeworth, Jane Austen, and other novelists such as those discussed by Jones) whose practice and success might have complicated Homans's account of language are also omitted. Even within Homans's own terms there are difficulties: the argument requires that she identify the intuitive communication between mother and child which she initially defines as the "presymbolic" with the "literal," and this elision remains dubious. Moreover, the very notion of a "literal" language women may employ is self-contradictory; within the Lacanian scheme *all* language is figurative. The examples of "literal" language Homans quotes may be non-Romantic or may actualize Romantic tropes, but they do not cease to be figurative. *Bearing the Word* is nonetheless a steadily interesting examination of the representation of women's experience by women: Dorothy Wordsworth, Mary Shelley, the Brontës, Elizabeth Gaskell, and George Eliot. The larger theoretical claims of the book remain debatable, but they have empowered a series of illuminating readings.

A similar insecurity of fit between theory and evidence hampers Helena Michie's *The Flesh Made Word.* The first chapter, for instance, discovers within its strongly demonstrated configuration of feminine weakness, anorexia, and male dominance the following paradox: "the hourglass figure which, in effect, prescribes that women live in two bodies at the same time: they must have the breasts and hips of a sensuous woman and the waistline of a schoolgirl. The same culture that advocated padding the bust, shoulders, and back demanded that women wear corsets." But the paradox is examined no further, despite its apparent challenge to the central argument of the chapter. Or a contrast is drawn between Oliver Twist's ability to "assert his desire" for more gruel and Jane Eyre's need to "sneak to Miss Temple's room" for a light tea, without regard for the contexts in which Oliver is not only the mere emissary who has drawn the short straw but is whipped for his effort and in which Jane, Miss Temple, and Helen enjoy all the delights of an unauthorized meal taken among kindred souls. The power of Michie's argument is in its range, not in what it offers to our apprehension of individual texts; that her ideology can limit as much as it enables entry into specific work can be seen from a comparison of her discussion of Dante Gabriel Rossetti's "Jenny" with John P. McGowan's in *Representation and Revelation* (discussed below). The final chapter, however, examines the engagement of contemporary feminist poetry with "Victorianism" and the poetry's struggle to "reach beyond phallic discourse." One might define this book teleogenically (the term is adapted from Lennard Davis on plot) as a contemporary feminist discourse on women, women's bodies, work, sex, and representation, with a more rhetorical and less heuristic purpose to its analysis. In these terms it becomes more compelling.

Not all the significant work of the year is propelled by avowed social commitments. Stuart Curran describes *Poetic Form and British Romanticism* as a history of British Romantic poetry; it is also evidence of the recent renewed vitality of genre study. Curran depicts British Romanticism not as a period of self-expression and generic breakdown but as an era deeply penetrated by generic conceptions and intensely engaged with its own past. Chapters on the sonnet, the hymn and ode, the pastoral, the romance, and the epic make good the argument, and lead to the penultimate chapter, which aptly borrows Wordsworth's 1815 term, "composite orders," to describe the multiplication of generic signals which characterize the Romantics' great extended works, *Don Juan, The Prelude,* and *Prometheus Unbound.* Curran demonstrates that these works make their meaning by playing formerly self-contained codes against one another and thereby calling attention to their own inclusiveness. Readers who assent to the premise that the structural syntax, as it were, of Romantic poetry is genre, may nonetheless resist the conclusion that the works are serenely balanced. From this formalist perspective what others have seen as fruitfully problematic tensions appear as "generic impasses," and even this recognition is contained. For Curran *The Prelude* moves toward oneness of personality, and though he acknowledges that many have been troubled by the withdrawal of Prometheus and Asia he asserts that recognition of the intricate generic complexity of *Prometheus Unbound* repudiates such misinterpretation. When treatment of individual works is as concise as the impressive range of the book requires, however, disagreements are inevitable, and matter less than the wealth of knowledge Curran commands. *Poetic Form and British Romanticism* substantially broadens our understanding of the contexts in which the canonical figures wrote: to be asked to see Shelley's *Queen Mab* in conjunction with Joel Barlow's *Columbiad,* or to approach Wordsworth's sonnets through the women writers whose influence on him Wordsworth minimized in order to advance his Miltonic heritage, or to find serious discussion of Southey as literary innovator, is to recover a sense of the age's variety and energy. The book is elegantly written and generous in spirit.

Similar qualities grace George P. Landow's *Elegant Jeremiahs: The Sage from Carlyle to Mailer,* which offers a "generic description of the works of the sage" with the purpose of "ascertain[ing] the proper way to read" his writings. The chapters are organized by characteristics clearly defined at the start and illustrated from the full range of writers, which include Carlyle, Ruskin, Thoreau, Arnold, Lawrence, Mailer, Didion, and, less frequently, several other twentieth-century figures such as Germaine Greer and Tom Wolfe. Victorian sages, Landow asserts, employ "the full prophetic structure" of the Old Testament and their writings are marked by "the sage's contentious attitude toward his audience, his alternation of satire and vision, and his use of discontinuous literary structure." The eccentricity of his message is essential and leads to the characteristics shared by Victorian and twentieth-century sages, which Landow enumerates. Stated thus the approach seems rigid, but it has many virtues. Lucidity as well as system make the argument a pleasure to read, even if one remains unpersuadable to the axioms of genre that Landow sees as justifying the enterprise. In fact, the enterprise is justified by its steady illumination, both local and reaching across the range of instances he works with. At the end he allows that providing a taxonomy is more important to him than convincing us that there is a single genre spanning two centuries of work, but the span is part of what is satisfying in this book.

Modes of pastoral in Romantic poetry form the subject of Lore Metzger's *One Foot In Eden*. Metzger takes her model of pastoral from Schiller and moves fluidly between enlarging philosophical category and formal description. Approaching Wordsworth's "Michael," *Home at Grasmere*, and *The Prelude*, Blake's songs, and Keats's *Hyperion* and odes through the German tradition smooths some of the difficult quiddities of the works, but Metzger displays a sure touch in placing pastoral *topoi* or interludes as moments within structures that contest their aspirations, and her sense of the precarious achievements of pastoral rhetoric, bringing man and nature briefly into a harmony under increasing challenge as the period progressed, reasserts the values to which her poets were pledged. Pastoral differently conceived underlies *Paradise Preserved*, by Max Schulz, an examination, as its subtitle announces, of "re-creations of Eden in eighteenth- and nineteenth-century England." Intentionally not concerned with exclusionary theoretical rigor, Schulz traces instead the hold of the idea of Eden on the imagination and the multiform attempts at realization it has inspired. Here is Schulz's plenty: eighteenth-century landscape gardening, the various blissful retreats of Romantic poetry, the technological sublime of the Victorians (from actual bridges to Turner's paintings to the Crystal Palace), Tennyson's Camelot, the pre-Raphaelites, Whistler, and more. The book has the enthusiastic appetite of the century to which it is chiefly devoted, and that Cambridge should price this large, well illustrated, handsomely produced volume at no more than it asks for the thin, jacketless, hardbound versions of its introductory critical series—$39.50—is an index of the current book trade one would like Feltes to analyze.

In *The Self as Mind: Vision and Identity in Wordsworth, Coleridge, and Keats* Charles Rzepka follows a phenomenology that might itself be characterized as Romantic, but he is by no means unaware of the cultural contexts in which his authors were situated. Rzepka focuses on the penalties entailed by "visionary solipsism," as he names it, neatly laying out the disembodiment of the self and loss of the other consequent upon the Romantic valorization of a transcendental imagination. For Rzepka, to be present is to be present for others, and he pursues the foundations of identity into the paradoxes of theatricality with deft clarity. He is particularly good on the passionate mirroring of Porphyro and Madeline in "The Eve of St. Agnes," advancing discussion of that poem at last beyond the oppositions of idealism and debunking set by Wasserman and Stillinger. In demonstrating the Romantics' acknowledgment that the self is constituted through others Rzepka makes a welcome, dialectical corrective to still-prevailing views. Rzepka has learned from Ricoeur and Lacan as well as from Perkins and Bate, and he synthesizes these diverse traditions into an excellent study.

The distinction Keats drew between Wordsworth's egotistical sublime and his own camelionic manner has long defined the poles of English Romantic poetry. In her ambitious and accomplished work, *The Questioning Presence*, Susan Wolfson thinks through the distinction to show that the very different manners of questioning and self-questioning in Wordsworth and Keats exemplify a defining interrogative mode among the Romantics, cutting across conventional generic boundaries. Examining Wordsworth's career from the *Lyrical Ballads* to *The Excursion* and that of Keats—his evolution a running critique of his elder—from the 1817 volume to *The Fall of Hyperion*, Wolfson reveals the doubts and the speculative energies which shape their contrasting innovations in lyric, narrative, and epic. Her attentiveness to the windings of language has evident affinities to the New, and newer, criticism, but she respects intention, and tellingly interprets the circumstances—personal, social, historical—in which poems come into being. Wolfson relishes complexity and play, and is preternaturally alert to syntactic effects and the implications of discontinuities, but she never condescends to her authors. Her title nicely catches the balance of her method: while subtly showing how texts elude or subvert their announced programs, she illuminates the authorial presence they figure. Capacious, drawing effortlessly on letters, journals, and the details of compositional history, steadily amplifying its argument by adducing the other Romantics, humane in its dialogue with fellow critics and beautifully written, *The Questioning Presence* makes a major contribution to understanding of the period.

The patterns of Romantic prose also attracted careful attention this year. John Nabholtz long since put all students of English Romantic essayists in his debt with convenient editions of Lamb and Hazlitt. In "*My Reader My Fellow-Labourer*" he offers confessedly not a comprehensive study of Romantic prose expression but scrutiny of the various strategies through which Lamb, Hazlitt, Wordsworth, and Coleridge sought to arouse the participation of their readers. Nabholtz concentrates on the reader projected by the prose, forgoing the opportunity to strengthen formal analysis by considering the tension between this creation and the actual audience of which the writers were keenly aware; in this respect Jon Klancher's book, discussed above, is a necessary complement. The differentiation of the nondiscursive playing with possibilities which characterizes Hazlitt's expression from the classical rhetorical traditions which underlie Coleridge's manner illustrates that within his chosen restrictions Nabholtz has much to teach. He presents Wordsworth's preface to the *Lyrical Ballads* as a rhetorical document seeking to establish the credibility of the author rather than as the systematic poetics others have wished to make of it, and rewardingly repays some of the attention Wordsworth lavished upon *The Convention of Cintra*.

As usual, the largest number of books received were monographs. The critical activity inspired by Wordsworth attests his continued centrality to our formulation of Romanticism. Marjorie Levinson's *Wordsworth's Great Period Poems* proceeds from the assumption that representation is always a displacement of an unresolvable historical contradiction. Levinson's mode is what in discussing Freud Ricoeur calls a mode of suspicion, and her view of history is solely one-way: the later critic discerns the author's limitations, untroubled by wondering whether Wordsworth might have had access to an order of meaning now lost. The weakness to which such work is prone is that when its assertions are put in their strong form—the "single Field" of the Intimations Ode is the Champ de Mars—they are at worst false to the overdetermination of poetic language and at best unverifiable, and when put in their weaker form—the light lost in the Ode is revolutionary hope—they are scarcely startling. But, as with psychoanalytic criticism, the asserted specificity enables impressively dense and detailed accounts of the verbal surface, and Levinson's analyses of the procedures set in motion by the skirting of history in "Tintern Abbey," the economics sublimed into vision in "Michael," the transformation of political question into abstraction in the Intimations Ode, and, richest of all, the compromises underlying the smooth facade of "Peele Castle," make this book invigorating. The admirably succinct handling of the four representative poems yields a compelling account of the great decade.

Paul Hamilton's *Wordsworth*, a volume in the Harvester series New Readings, grows from beliefs kin to Levinson's. Hamilton argues that Wordsworth knew the imagination to construct nature from language that is inevitably historically invested, and so came to recognize society as an analogous construction: love of nature leads to love of man because they are interimplicated. Hamilton is lucid and informed, and his book is filled with shrewd commentary on the unsettling irresolution of Wordsworth's verse and the self it figures. He covers the period from the 1790s through *The Excursion*, and though his conclusion, that religious consolation substituted for commitment to social change, is not new, even experienced readers of the poet will find Hamilton's account of the tensions that led Wordsworth to this end provocative. And therein lies the question: readers who know Wordsworth will fill out Hamilton's remarks from their own knowledge, whereas the beginning students for whom this volume is intended may be merely puzzled by the unsupported assertions and rapid connections which the restricted format imposes. As noted below, other contributions to this series suffer from the same problem.

Hugh Sykes Davies's *Wordsworth and the Worth of Words* is very different from the foregoing studies, a record of a lifetime's engagement with the poet, deeply personal and within the range of its concerns powerfully illuminating. Sykes Davies begins with linguistic pattern, drawing into focus those recurrent words and combinations of words that define Wordsworth's idiolect. Behind verbal surface for him stand those perplexed combinations of thoughts, feelings, and concrete objects in Wordsworth's experience which he describes by DeQuincey's term "involutes." His Wordsworth is the poet of the "naked," "bare," and "single," one who works through the picturesque tradition he inherited to recover an authentic sense of man's place as "inmate" of nature. *Wordsworth and the Worth of Words* is at once intellectual history and literary criticism, linguistic analysis and spiritual autobiography. Even in disagreement the book moves one as criticism rarely does, because its special qualities depend on circumstances unlikely to recur: childhood vacations in the Lakes when Wordsworthianism was a living presence, and an academic career apparently insulated from critical fashion. The book unfolds as it were from within: free from antithetical impulse, it could only have been written by someone saturated in the poetry. Left unfinished at Sykes Davies's death in 1984, *Wordsworth and the Worth of Words* was edited by Jonathan Wordsworth and John Kerrigan, to whom Romanticists owe a debt of gratitude.

Happily rather than elegiacally difficult to place is Jeffrey Robinson's *Radical Literary Education: A Classroom Experiment with Wordsworth's "Ode."* Robinson recounts a course devoted to tracing the filiations radiating from the Intimations Ode, but the poem is the occasion of the course, not its self-contained subject. *Radical Literary Education* sets against a humanism Robinson sees as encouraging the passive reception of tradition a critical consciousness which upholds explicit confrontation with the ideological bases of the works preserved by the academy. His book is in part a comment on the design of curricula and a demonstration of pedagogical strategies, and in part a contextualization of Wordsworth's poem in the ode tradition, fuller than previous more conventional studies. And it is simultaneously a continuing conversation between a teacher meditating at mid-career on his life and training, and students encountering through Wordsworth their own adolescent crises and political uncertainties. *Radical Literary Education* is a model of how reader-response criticism and psychoanalytic insight can focus rather than flatten both texts and readers; it is a tribute to Robinson's tact and dramatic skills that all involved retain their integrity, and that the power of the Ode to disturb through its very acts of consolation is recovered.

Two studies of Coleridge contrast in manner but reach mutually reinforcing conclusions. Anya Taylor describes the aim of *Coleridge's Defense of the Human* as straightforwardly reconstructive. In the labyrinth of Coleridge's interests Taylor pursues the thread of his concern to maintain "the sacred distinction between persons and things," now defending identity as the self's creative construction of itself and deriving a social theory from the respect due others, now insisting that science is imaginative, an outering of man's spiritual truths, now arguing the proof of God from man's desire to conceive beyond himself. At the outset there are a few unneeded gestures toward contemporary relevance and the level seems that of a very good undergraduate lecture, but the book gains strength as it proceeds. Taylor's command even of unpublished material requires respect, and her sense of Coleridge's continuous intellectual struggle to find the mediation between opposing oversimplifications in whatever field is impressive. The Coleridge who emerges from these pages, always on the borders, willing himself to leap over the voids of which he is conscious, is a multifaceted seminal figure.

Coleridge's Philosophy of Language is more narrowly focused, but James McKusick's tracing of Coleridge's lifelong reflections on the relation of language and thought establishes the linguistic underpinnings of Coleridge's poetic practice, literary criticism, and philosophy. McKusick concisely situates Coleridge within language theory since Plato, locating the influence of the German philologists whom Coleridge encountered at Göttingen as the force which enabled him to move beyond Tooke's noun-based etymologies to a dynamic conception of language as evolving function, thinking as opposed to thing-ing. The process of desynonymization was for Coleridge the key to understanding language as produced by the accumulating willed choices of speakers, a vehicle for expression rather than a prison-house. If in placing Coleridge McKusick gives a somewhat partial view of the English linguistic tradition, and if he scants Wordsworth in demonstrating why Coleridge believed his formulation that natural language, however complex, is appropriate language (so that even Shakespeare's language may be said to be "natural"), to be superior to Wordsworth's, these do not detract greatly from a knowledgeable, subtle, tightly organized argument. A revisionary reading of the still little-known *Logic* in the final chapter shows Coleridge giving Kant a linguistic turn and transforming a philosophy of absolutes into a grammar of cultural progress. *Coleridge's Philosophy of Language* is a work to read and reread.

In *Social Relations in Byron's Eastern Tales* Daniel Watkins argues that the dilemmas which shape the plots of Byron's exotic narratives are those of the social world Byron knew. Like the other new historical studies covered in this review, the approach has the advantage of recovering the contemporary force of works which in this instance have often seemed either manifestations of timeless metaphysical gloom or lurid bids for best-sellerdom. Watkins goes to the heart of the matter by suggesting that the works' popularity arises from their mirroring of cultural impasses: far from being unique, the Byronic hero typifies the isolation of bourgeois individualism, his flamboyant alienation the mark not of separation from society but of society's own alienating abstractions. So far so good, yet the argument rests on analogy, or homology, between the plots of the tales and diagnosis of the culture at large, and to be persuasive the parallels must be both thick and supply conceived; too often Watkins lets down his hypothesis by thinly supported schematizing, and thus lapses into exactly the kind of abstraction the book stigmatizes. Still, to choose one example, Watkins shrewdly demonstrates that the passivity of Zuleika in *The Bride of Abydos* is not a sign of innocence but of her implication in oppressive class structures, and at moments like these his book suggests the potential fruitfulness of his method.

The specificity lacking in Watkins is to be found in Malcolm Kelsall's *Byron's Politics*. Kelsall's term for Byron is "Whig," not "Romantic," and he demonstrates how thoroughly Byron's political position represents the diminished end of the liberal tradition which he sought to join. The threat to property raised by the French Revolution ended the aristocratic world Whig egalitarianism inhabited; frightened at the shapes liberty assumed from the 1790s on, the Whigs were left with an empty rhetoric, echoed, Kelsall reveals, everywhere in Byron. Kelsall inscribes the poet's despair as the futility of an outmoded politics, and he brilliantly specifies the conservative allegiances that underwrite Byron's satire. The *entente* between Tory Michael and Whig Satan in "The Vision of Judgment" Kelsall takes to betray that they have more in common with each other than either with proletarian radicals: opposition, as he wittily observes, exists to sustain the system, not to transform it. He is equally canny in suggesting that Byron's attack on the *ancien régime* in *Don Juan* is a safe displacement from the current political situation, and in naming Lord Henry as the Whig aristocrat Byron might have become Kelsall puts his finger on the unease that runs through the English cantos. Method, Gerald Bruns has wisely remarked, is what we turn to when our knowledge fails us; Kelsall, without any grandiose theoretical gestures, has written a permanently valuable study, to be kept next to the new editions of Byron noted below.

In this company Mark Storey's *Byron and the Eye of Appetite* pales. Storey is an alert close reader, and his meditations on the recurrent images and figures (such as the gaze and the tableau) which passion takes in *Childe Harold* and *Don Juan* produce rewarding local insights, but he reads the poetry *in vacuo*, indifferent to the work of the last decade and to the kind of contextual force it has shown Byron's verse to possess, and his structure is so loosely associative that the book can scarcely be said to develop an argument. *The Calculating Passion of Ada Byron*, by Joan Baum, ascribes greater mathematical ability to Byron's daughter than does Dorothy Stein's recent study, but it too is slight.

Three studies of Shelley follow quite different paths. *Shelley's Venomed Melody*, by Nora Crook and Derek Guiton, seeks beneath the numerous sexually alluring but malign women and the pervasive images of plague in Shelley's poetry the reality of syphilis, the disease likely to have been the root also of what the Bible and later tradition understood as leprosy. The authors waver between ascribing to Shelley a specific infectious encounter and pointing to the similarity between his language and the discourse of venereal plague. Their learning compasses Shelley's medical and scientific knowledge, and his vegetarianism and chemical experiments look less odd when placed in the context of contemporary prescriptions. This effort to find a material base for Shelley's imagery, however, has the effect of making Shelley seem tediously obsessive and hypochondriac, and so it is perhaps fortunate that the verdict must be Not Proved.

Andrew Welburn comes to Shelley from Steiner, Barfield, and the Gnostics, and this heritage serves him and Shelley well in *Power and Self-Consciousness in the Poetry of Shelley*. The dualisms of Welburn's Zoroastrian vocabulary are peculiarly appropriate to delineate the suspended tensions of Shelley's poetry, but a flourish of diagrams at the close of the book betrays the distance between discursive intellectual analysis and the complex mediations of Shelley's fictions.

Ronald Tetreault's *The Poetry of Life: Shelley and Literary Form* is a chronological survey of Shelley's career. Its premise, that the constituent oppositions of Shelley's universe are not skepticism and certainty or truth and beauty, but desire and anxiety, power and authority, provides a revealing perspective on the canon. Tetreault depicts Shelley as working towards open forms that encourage play and participation, generating mental activity and self-consciousness in the reader by their own indeterminacy. Others may be less troubled by Tetreault's employment of a deconstructive terminology to describe effects within an old-fashioned author-centered account of a growth in artistic mastery, but an undeniable consequence of the strategy is the deemphasis of Shelley's substance. Tetreault's informative discussion of Shelley's interest in opera tends in the same direction: to think of *Prometheus Unbound* as a "poetic ballet" raises fresh formal possibilities, but devalues the particular way words mean. In Tetreault's account the Rousseau of The *Triumph of Life* seems only a character, unrelated to any historical original. To conclude on that note, however, would be unfair to a book which steadily illuminates Shelley's variety and rhetorical skill.

The decisive voice heard in the opening sentence of John Barnard's *John Keats* distinguishes the study throughout: "Keats is a poet of exclusion, perpetually longing for admission to an imagined other world." As he proceeds Barnard succinctly conveys the difficulties posed by the world Keats confronted: the importance of class, the divisions of politics, the changing audience for poetry. Barnard's characterization of Keats's work is wonderfully concentrated: he needs only a phrase to contrast the "yeasty, ardent and diffuse" *Endymion* with the "cold, bright . . . unsettled and unsettling *Lamia*." Yet quotation does not reveal the knowledge that the style distills: few critics move with equal surefootedness through the publishing history of Keats's medieval narratives and the sexual fantasies which they embody. Barnard is a judicious critic, but his judiciousness has the excitement of measured argument rather than the blandness of compromise. He establishes the central lines of Keats's development without sentimentalizing the poet, or idealizing his achievement; if he concludes of "To Autumn" that "Fictions, as well as telling untruths, tell truths," he is also willing to concede in the conclusion the constriction of Keats's formal style in comparison to his letters or to the colloquial urbanity of Byron and Shelley. Students and specialists will profit from this model brief introduction; only the latter will appreciate the mastery of the genre.

It must be an author's nightmare which brings R. S. White's *Keats as a Reader of Shakespeare* and Jonathan Bate's *Shakespeare and the English Romantic Imagination* within a month of each other; in the event, the two studies complement each other satisfyingly. White is restricted in aim and low key in manner, but as he moves through Keats's responses to Shakespeare's comedies and tragedies he brings out the experiential complexities which drew Keats to Shakespeare, catching the incorporative, exploratory quality of a style his contemporaries dismissed as barbarously innovative. Bate is more ambitious, casting his net through Wordsworth, Blake, Coleridge, Byron, and Shelley, as well as Keats, in order to address the general question of poetic influence. Paired chapters surveying first the poets' comments on Shakespeare and then their transformation of the legacy make good Bate's claim against Bloom that encounter with a great predecessor can be empowering. Bate writes crisply, and his sense that the Romantics ground their individuality through their varying difference from Shakespeare enables him to illuminate both terms of his comparison.

We have three monographs on Jane Austen, one, Margaret Kirkham's *Jane Austen, Feminism and Fiction*, the American issue of a 1983 British publication. One wonders why the book was not revised to take into account the intervening work by Mary Poovey and on eighteenth-century feminism, a major topic for Kirkham, but the failure is of a piece with a general disregard for criticism since Trilling and even for the work of 1970s American feminists

(Auerbach is the exception, but Gilbert and Gubar are ignored). Kirkham sets out to "relate Austen as literary artist and innovator to her declared position as feminist moralist and critic of fictional tradition." She places her firmly in the line back through Wollstonecraft to Mary Astell but deals less successfully with the problem of Austen's political conservatism. We may be made uneasy with the degree of reliance on what "must have" been, which appears even in the most interesting theme of the book, when the revelation of Austen's mode of significant burlesque verges upon tactics reminiscent of the *roman à clef*. But this theme is important: Kirkham develops, for example, *Emma*'s allusions to Kotzebue's *Die Vershonung* (through Thomas Dibdin's *The Birthday*) and Eaton Stannard Barrett's *The Heroine, or Adventures of Cherubina* and traces through Austen's novels her reversals "of the burlesque schema in which a romantic heroine learns sense and comes to adopt the viewpoint of her pastors and masters."

Even less wholly a 1986-87 book is Tony Tanner's *Jane Austen*, the chapters of which, we are told, were written between 1966 and 1985. Three, on *Sense and Sensibility, Pride and Prejudice,* and *Mansfield Park*, are "somewhat altered" reprints of Penguin introductions. Tanner too wishes to de-emphasize Austen's conservatism, arguing that her canvas is wider that the stereotype allows and less ideologically bound: "Jane Austen's novels do not 'perennialise' society: they problematise it." In the introduction he establishes themes of property, education, and language, the latter two vitally connected with the first (Austen's language, for instance, is "that of a person who feels engaged with and embattled on behalf of the values of a particular class in a particular phase of history"), and he carries these themes, loosely, through the chapters-per-novel that follow. He also allows himself numerous digressions to the novel more broadly considered, never without relevance. The book is lively reading for someone familiar with Austen and looking for an intelligent, conversational discourse. The most interesting of the threads is the theme of the "break up" of "English society" as Austen sees it, in which Tanner discerns a change in the later works from "confidence to defensiveness."

Michael Williams in *Jane Austen: Six Novels and Their Methods* announces a tauter methodology than Tanner's—viewing the novels from Iser's "dialectic relationship between text, reader, and their interaction," looking at technique but avoiding his predecessors' fragmentation of the novels into techniques—but whether he in fact achieves more is doubtful. Interested in practical application rather than theory, he decides not to bother with Iser's notion of the "implied reader." He takes each novel separately and intends to show them dealing less "in truths and certainties, but . . . rather . . . investigating and testing propositions and situations." He considers other, mainly eighteenth-century, novelists, and looks some at social and historical context. But the chapter on *Northanger Abbey* is mainly intent on proving that the novel is a "complex whole"; the reader has little role until the end, when we come to the irresolution of the issues of the relation between fiction and reality and of Catherine's education. The method shows no more clearly in the chapter on *Emma*—neither as method nor in results. Williams rather overdoes the uncertainty of *Emma*; he also discusses such matters as the general absence in this novel of literary causation (in the manner of *Don Quixote* or *Northanger Abbey*), the issue of imagination, the mystification of the reader, and first vs. second readings—all well enough, but also perhaps explaining why the introduction so defensively justifies his eclecticism. When all is done, the book is much in the same mode as Tanner's, but not as elegant or probing.

We received seven books on Dickens, excluding the Clarendon *Pickwick*. Four are introductory texts, three of them upon a single novel. One may appreciate whatever concatenations of events have led to critics of the standing of Bert Hornback and Graham Storey to produce such texts (Hornback's *"Great Expectations": A Novel of Friendship* is a Twayne series book, Storey's *Charles Dickens: "Bleak House"* is for Landmarks of World Literature): they are readable, reliable, and traditional in the best sense. It seems right that both have avoided what Hornback calls " 'critical jargon' and all that stuff called theory of criticism," but one might have asked nonetheless for some more recent references in the bibliographies at the end of each book: the latest work cited by Hornback is 1979 and Storey has only one later than that, 1982. Kate Flint's *Dickens*, for the Harvester New Readings, suffers the same problem as Hamilton's in this series (see above). It appears to be written to a student audience that knows nothing about Dickens but can tolerate numerous casual references to and quotations from the novels—as well as numerous typographical errors. The determination to introduce critical method while avoiding accepted terminology—the series aims to offer handbooks informed by the range of current criticism—also creates frequent awkwardness. Flint prefers thematic to chronological arrangement, but in consequence it is often difficult to tell what a particular chapter is about, at least until one finds the thesis statement waiting in the final paragraph.

The problem of introducing students to the contemporary ferment of criticism is central to another series, called *The Critics Debate*.

Jeremy Hawthorn's volume is on *Bleak House* and within the flexibility offered by the general editors he chooses to present the first part, the critical survey, thematically rather than by "schools" of criticism. Although the required brevity makes this section unavoidably superficial, it is deft and readable and it does manage to address a reader who is both a neophyte Dickensian and intelligent. It also makes the debate sound interesting, perhaps because it takes the difficult choice to limit discussion to a small number of critical writings. The second part of the *Critics Debate* books is the authors' own appraisals of the texts. Here Hawthorn is less successful, his essay suffering from confinement of space, the need to keep to an introductory level, and the choice to break into short subsections ordered not to shape an argument but to cover a number of topics.

Badri Raina's *Dickens and the Dialectic of Growth* responds to this welter of critical approach with a brief theoretical outline designed, he winningly asserts, to "clear space." Raina presents a Dickens not unfamiliar: the dialectic is the "one central contradiction of [Dickens'] career, that which involves his simultaneous roles as aspiring, successful, and disgusted Victorian." The special gambit of this readable account is to root the anagnorisis of *Great Expectations* in *Oliver Twist* and the sacrificial figure of Dick. As Raina traces Dick through his later avatars in Smike, Nell, and Paul Dombey he finds that "the martyred self becomes an increasingly more sophisticated and distanced critique of the culture." One may wonder, though: Raina assumes that in *Oliver Twist* and *Nicholas Nickleby* the oppressors are criticized for their material values, but perhaps it is only that they will not share their material goods. Thus Raina's fine argument on *Dombey and Son* rather depends on his ignoring both Toots and the conclusion. In the "dark" novels Raina finds a relentless exploration of the culture and in *Great Expectations* a deconstruction of the entire oeuvre, especially *David Copperfield.* Again, this is not an original reading, but it is well presented. Raina's claim that we must read his footnotes, however, is nonsense, except in so far that by not doing so we will miss some rather charming jibes at other critics.

A very different—and more innovative to Dickens studies—dialectic orders Dirk den Hartog's *Dickens and Romantic Psychology.* Starting from the phrase "the experience of modernity" taken from Marshal Berman to indicate ambiguity of response to the "possibility of freedom and expansion," "both delight *and* fear . . . embracing it as liberation whilst shrinking from its threat of *anomie,*" he looks at that dialectic in nineteenth-century writing: "the conflict of Romantically legitimated freedom and traditionally authorised restraint," out of which authority becomes moral and internal, a part of the self. In Wordsworth—and den Hartog argues well his relevance for Dickens—the core of selfhood is developed in early childhood. But Dickens is both a Wordsworthian conservative and Promethean, sentimental, and demonic, a duality that den Hartog ties to the "fierce determination with which he mastered the trauma" of the blacking warehouse. Dickens displaces the drive for "individuation" (as opposed to Wordsworthian "symbiosis") "into the demonic grotesques," thus at once expressing and disowning it. The chapters on *Dombey and Son*, *Little Dorrit*, and *Great Expectations* are each better than the other. The chapter on *Great Expectations* is the trickiest, meshing intrapsychic and social reading with highly provocative and energizing results; in some degree den Hartog carries the argument by acknowledging its difficulties, pre-empting any charge that he is being "wilfully speculative." One is annoyed by a critical climate in which den Hartog feels obliged to apologize in the preface for centering the author and to assure us that he knows that what is in the work depends upon "conflicting ideologies and sundry anterior textual 'presences' by which Dickens and his artistic expression in general terms are constituted." The only things really wrong with this book are a free-wheeling use of pronouns that sent this reader reeling from a plethora of *it's* and *this's* desperately (and usually fruitlessly) hunting antecedents and enough typographical errors to disconcert those of us who expect conventionality in the use of *s* for plurals and apostrophes for possessives.

Whatever the pleasures of Raina or den Hartog, the prize of the collection—not just the Dickens collection but perhaps the year's—for reviewers remunerated in books is surely Harry Stone's *Dickens' Working Notes for His Novels*. This is not a monograph, but we discuss it here to keep it alongside the work on Dickens. This magnificent volume collects Dickens's extant plans and notes for the novels. Each sheet is reproduced in actual size and on the facing page is transcribed in typographic facsimile. Other illustrations include portraits, wrappers, occasional illustrations to the novels, and ms. pages. There are an extensive general introduction and introductions to each novel: *The Old Curiosity Shop, Martin Chuzzlewit, Dombey and Son, Bleak House, Hard Times, Little Dorrit, Great Expectations, Our Mutual Friend,* and *The Mystery of Edwin Drood.* The general introduction reviews Dickens's comments on his work and our sources for understanding the process of his writing; describes in detail the format of the number plans; illustrates how the notes can be used to study naming in the novels, as indicators of intentionality, as evidence of deliberate structuring; and discusses at length Dickens's use of the word "picture." The individual introductions present the compositional and printing history for each novel. The reproductions are excellent, the typographical transcriptions are a blessing, and the commentary is erudite, elegant, and committed. It is worth considering that Chicago is offering the book at $74.95, less than the cost of a mere pair of the slimmest, minimally produced books we received.

Of the three books on George Eliot, only Gillian Beer's *George Eliot* takes a feminist perspective. The book is filled with insight that comes literally in flashes. Sustained argument or thesis is hard to find and often the very paragraphs seem to follow each other in mysterious sequence, but the nuggets encountered in passing are often brilliant. Especially satisfying is the setting of *Middlemarch* in the context of contemporary debate on women's education and work.

Simon Dentith's *George Eliot* is another Harvester New Reading, but it handles the difficulties of the series better than Hamilton and Flint do. Dentith proposes a "defence of George Eliot as a realist writer" that will allow structuralist, deconstructionist, and Marxist readings to influence it, but not explicitly. He follows two themes, the idea of "extension of sympathy" and the novels' formal organization. From a background sketch of intellectual history (with a smidgeon of social history) he moves to a discussion of George Eliot and class and then to the typicality of her characters and archtypicality of her heroes and heroines. He is suggestive on how the moral axis obscures continuing material differences and how Eliot's "own class and historical position set limits to her artistic project . . . that lead her to make her characteristic humanist move in piercing through the surface of the historically specific to the humanly general." In a social, realist reading of Eliot's work, he traces a plausible line of development with sympathy and periodic illumination.

Mary Wilson Carpenter's *George Eliot and the Landscape of Time* is a problematic book. It is well written and it marshals a wealth of material; it could be persuasive if it did not fail to argue its premises nor yield to the temptation of excessive speculation upon shreds of evidence. What is difficult to decide is when we have crossed the boundary from erudite exegesis to numerology out of control. Carpenter begins from Eliot's early interest in prophecy ("continuous historical" exegesis) and her recognition that "every history maps the landscape of time by imposing an imaginary line on an otherwise inchoate mass." Good enough. But we hesitate before the numerological labor that follows in the decoding of *Adam Bede*. Carpenter's reading of the novel is based on the lessons of the lectionary for the dates specified in the story. There are two problems here: one is that we have no direct evidence that Eliot plotted any of this; the other is that we learn nothing from it that is not otherwise available in the narrative. Carpenter asserts that the "hidden hermeneutic structure of *Adam Bede* deconstructs its conventional narrative," but in fact, in the very terms she uses, the narrative deconstructs itself overtly: its "traditional happy ending" is thoroughly questioned. When we reach *Middlemarch* and find the central notion of the "key" taking on the role of apocalyptic allusion and numerology in the other novels and being vital because it unlocks a secret, we may reflect back on the entire procedure of this book as one motivated by a compulsion to uncover secrets in a text. At the same time, a good deal of the material brought to bear on the novels does have relevance, as is most convincingly demonstrated in the chapter on *Daniel Deronda*, and throughout the display of learning ranges from impressive to dazzling.

Tessa Brodetsky's *Elizabeth Gaskell* may be explained by its place in the Berg Women's Series, which treats both literary figures and others. It seems to be an introductory description for a non-specialist audience, perhaps for high school students. A biographical sketch displays Gaskell "as a woman of great energy and many interests, the foremost being the welfare of her family" and the chapters on the novels display a similar moral tone. Brodetsky concludes that "There is no contradiction between the principles and standards which Elizabeth Gaskell followed in her life and those which she extolled in her writing"; perhaps that is why this book is so dull.

Equally disappointing is Terence Wright's *Critics Debate* on "*Tess of the d'Urbervilles*," which refers to no criticism later than 1979. There are four works cited from 1975, one from 1974, one from 1970, and the rest from the 1960s and back. The more recent works are the least discussed; earlier criticism is worthwhile, but this choice seems out of phase with the intention of the series. The "approaches" by which Part I is organized are so thoroughly mediated by Wright that one misses the sense of debate that Hawthorn achieves around *Bleak House*. Part II offers an "affective" (as opposed to "causative") reading of the tragedy that is neither reproachable nor exciting.

An unoriginal thesis within a much more lively text is to be found in Daniel Albright's *Tennyson: The Muses' Tug-of-War*. The tug is between the "earthly" and "celestial" muses, between the commonplace and the sublime. Albright seems to see himself as refining upon the work of Kincaid and Culler, but what he adds to them may be primarily stylistic. He has a penchant for rich triplets (a scene is "slack, disembowelled, neutralized"; we hear of the "hasty sketching, shading, scumbling of a pencil" and of "mannered, virtuosic, overgorgeous stuff") and a knack for statements that sound concrete but are wholly abstract and undemonstrable, such as this: "a symbol . . . might provide a model for the ideal poetic act in which the celestial and the earthly muses join hands and dance. . . . Tennyson is rarely able to sustain the requisite focus, and the symbolic mode fractures into a headache of double vision" (headache is a frequent metaphor in this book). One more example should demonstrate how Albright's writing is forceful, metaphoric, affective, but problematic at the literal level. What is meant by an assertion such as: "Tennyson [in *Maud*, *In Memoriam*, and *The Princess*] explores the possibilities of giving artistic shape to speakers and speeches that defy all but the most complicated and extenuated kinds of definition: each poem presents an assault on the inexpressible, and in each Tennyson is lead [sic] to bizarre aesthetic compromises because of the intractability of his material, the small size of the human mouth, that balks at being forced to utter certain monstrosities"—especially the last phrases? If one spends an inordinate amount of space upon the style of this book, that is because the style is its substance. Beyond that it pursues the chestnut of Tennyson's division between the need to become part of human action and the need to remain an artist. Yet Albright looks steadily through a specific lens that sometimes offers odd, and therefore interesting, perceptions.

There is considerable contrast between the linguistic exuberance of Albright and the competent, sober formalism of Linda K. Hughes's *The Manyfacèd Glass: Tennyson's Dramatic Monologues*. Using biography, casual psychology, and formal analysis, she defines the Tennysonian dramatic monologue (in particular against Browning's) and proceeds to a chronological survey intended "to see how varied, numerous, and . . . successful were Tennyson's ventures in this form" and to provide "a key to understanding his poems written in other forms." The product measures up to the promise. Hughes manages to take *The Devil and the Lady* seriously as poetry, to include a long essay on *In Memoriam* on the grounds that in it Tennyson drew on the techniques of his dramatic monologues and reflected the speaker's consciousness ("rendering of consciousness," as opposed to Browning's display of personality, is a useful and key distinction), and to brave the late poetry while acknowledging its defects. Her standards are the perfection of various criteria for the monologue, notably the "feint" (the "fusion of the pole of fiction with the poet's 'I' ") and achieved "objectivity," but there are no clear procedures for such judgments and the method seldom leads us to more interesting or novel readings of the poems. Hughes's interpretations, based on "gaps" in the texts, are very sure, and her book does what it sets out to do.

The third monograph on Tennyson is the least inspiring. To his credit, Alastair W. Thomson declares at the outset of *The Poetry of Tennyson* that he does not seek a "radical revision of generally accepted opinions about Tennyson." He offers a survey of the poetry, arranged chronologically and working relentlessly through a very large number of the poems, intended to steer between the faults of undue hostility and over-enthusiasm. Aspects of the poetry ranging from theme and characterization to imagery and prosody come in for varying degrees of discussion in the various poems. The chapters have the unfocused quality of a set of introductory lectures, and as such the book is pleasant enough, benefitting most of all from Thomson's very good ear and his willingness to judge by it.

The most satisfying feminist writing in the collection is Dolores Rosenblum's *Christina Rossetti: The Poetry of Endurance.* Rosenblum generates the concept of the "poetry of endurance," in which "repetitions and stylizations are survival strategies," from Sandra Gilbert's "aesthetic of renunciation," which remains central to Rosenblum's analysis. She notes that endurance means both to bear and to outlast, and argues that Rossetti's poems are about "the power to will that which has been foreordained and to overturn that which has been enforced." Rosenblum examines Rossetti's "power to generate a consistent and authentic female myth" by studying a series of models, the "exemplary female figure who, in various guises, testifies both to her alienation and to her transfiguration." A densely argued introduction gives way to more expansive writing in the chapters that follow. Rosenblum calls her method "roughly psychological-phenomenological"; for this reader, she is far more successful in the latter half than the former. Fine synchronic readings of the poetry are less finely supported by biographical speculation; when she gets to the portraits of Rossetti, Rosenblum indulges in confessed fantasy. Neither the psychobiographical support nor the doctrinaire axioms (all women must suffer and feel alienated from their culture; a woman thinking is not an erotic object) are necessary to the persuasive and powerful understanding of the poetry and the compelling figure of Rossetti that emerge from Rosenblum's consistently engaged and engaging prose.

Catherine Peters's *Thackeray's Universe* deserves praise if only for one sentence: "Thackeray's novels are not so much loose baggy monsters as parcels that have come untied in the post." The book is a biography-cum-discussion of the writings, with greatest emphasis on the relation between the life and the work. More attention is therefore given to the journalism than one usually gets. The book is lively and intelligent, accessible to the educated layman and enjoyable for the scholar. There is neither theory nor an axiom for the hypotheses, but the picture of Thackeray it paints is complex, as is the relation of that picture to the work. The illustrations are generous and well chosen.

Regenia Gagnier's idea of studying the contradictions of Oscar Wilde through the audiences to whom he vaunted his indifference was a good one, but *Idylls of the Marketplace: Oscar Wilde and the Victorian Public* is disappointing. Gagnier focuses on Wilde as the marketer of his own image as aesthete, rendering himself a commercial item even as he criticized the society which lionized him, and she locates the success of his dramas in the images they mirrored to a specular society. Gagnier commands a wealth of interesting sociological material, but she juxtaposes rather than integrates it with Wilde's work, and she does not observe the distinction between "class" and "audience" Klancher draws. The result is that interpretations of individual texts are flatly repetitive, thin displacements of a diagrammatic class analysis.

Wilde figures in Linda Dowling's *Language and Decadence in the Victorian Fin de Siècle*, a study arguing the origin of decadence in fears, spawned by the triumph of scientific philology, that language was not the bearer of civilization's highest values but an autonomous force. In developing the dimensions of this crisis Dowling moves gracefully from the history of linguistics to the sociology of knowledge, setting Pater in the midst of Oxford debates over language, and on to stylistic and thematic analysis of Pater, Wilde, Machen, Symons, Davidson, and Yeats. Though the intellectual history Dowling compellingly narrates is not an exhaustive explanation of decadence—consider the economic shifts Gagnier emphasizes—hers is rich criticism, recovering the subversive force of writers still seen as marginal, and written with flair.

Language and Decadence joins Taylor's and McKusick's books to form a valuable subset of works on nineteenth-century theory of language, to which should be added Stephen Prickett's *Words and The Word: Language, Poetics and Biblical Interpretation*. Prickett's study of biblical hermeneutics and literary criticism in their common concern with figurative language reaches back to Vico, Herder, and Eichhorn and forward to Ricoeur; the focus of this volume, however, is less germane to readers of this journal than Prickett's earlier *Coleridge and Wordsworth: the Poetry of Growth* and *Romanticism and Religion: the Tradition of Coleridge and Wordsworth in the Victorian Church*, which the new book frequently cites.

Several of this year's books that range beyond a single author deal in one way or another with description. Lori Hope Lefkovitz chooses to examine *The Character of Beauty in the Victorian Novel* because "novelists promote those cultural values that the idealized figures embody, and description is a significant way in which sexual difference is encoded in literature and enforced by society." Her principal focus is on three major oppositions: art and nature, birth and breeding, delicacy and strength. She covers a lot of ground and inevitably has not enough space, with the result that one is conscious of rapid survey, a technique of skim and dip, that at times leaves an argument less thoroughly worked through than one would like. At the same time, her always interesting expositions of biblical allusion through midrash are not always clearly connected to the literary tradition that is the focus here. This book sets terms for further study and is most provocative from the fourth chapter on, when Lefkovitz begins to look in specific texts for the "dichotomies" of oppositional traits in the hero and heroine and "the qualities that reconcile them." With *Middlemarch*, for example, she traces the opening jewels back to biblical tradition and then forward, looking as well at Scott and Thackeray, and finally suggests that in Dorothea a concept of "Hebrew beauty" is recovered for Christianity. Perhaps most original is her development of the notion of health as a trait of beauty, which she traces through *The Scarlet Letter, Adam Bede, Odd Women*, and *Jude the Obscure.*

In *The Literature of Images:. Narrative Landscape in the Novel from "Julie" to "Jane Eyre"* Doris Y. Kadish undertakes what she describes as a semiotic reading of landscape set into deeper and fuller relation with the surrounding texts than the method usually displays. She argues for a "relational reading," which is described in contrast to "pictorial reading" as the reading of landscape description "in relation to narrative point of view, . . . to the novel's other parallel or contrasting descriptive passages, and . . . to the sociopolitical outlook that underlies the novel." Though she makes a greater fuss about the method, implying a greater radicalness, than it warrants, she displays it adeptly and it works well. Most of the book is on French writers (Rousseau, Bernardin de Saint-Pierre, Chateaubriand, Balzac, Flaubert), but chapter 4 is on Radcliffe and Mary Shelley and chapter 7 on *Jane Eyre.* In chapter 4 she analyzes *The Mysteries of Udolpho* and *Frankenstein*, following Jameson, by applying Greimas's "semiotic square" to the characters and then showing how descriptions of nature carry the necessary features of opposition. Landscape also becomes the vehicle for coding liberation from the oppositional structure. The grid Kadish applies is rigid but remarkably effective in establishing the semiotic valences of sublime and beautiful, masculine and feminine. Her essay on *Jane Eyre* is also provocative, though her equation of landscape-describing with woman's work and her thematizing of landscape-describing as activity seem tenuous. And Kadish also seems to become rather protective of Brontë, allowing full play to Terry Eagleton's and Jina Politi's critiques of the novel's ideology without succeeding in answering them as well as she thinks. All told, Kadish seems more powerful as a semiotician than as a feminist. The local readings of landscape in *Jane Eyre* are convincing and they enrich our sense of interplay within the text.

Rhoda L. Flaxman adapts the "aesthetic categories from Erwin Panofsky's *Studies in Iconology* to a generally semiotic methodology" for *Victorian Word-Painting and Narrative: Toward a Blending of Genres.* She defines word-painting as "extended passages of visually oriented descriptions whose techniques emulate pictorial methods" and enumerates its features at maturity. By the end of the book one is very weary of the phrase "visually oriented description." Flaxman traces its development in both novelists and poets, beginning with Radcliffe as the first to "elevate extended, visually oriented description . . . to a position of prominence in English fiction" and compares Scott unfavorably. The chapter on Dickens shows his progressive integration of narrative, dramatic, and descriptive modes through *Barnaby Rudge*, *David Copperfield*, and *Little Dorrit.* The ideal held up is a full fusion of description with narrative and drama. When she turns to poetry Flaxman focuses on Wordsworth and Tennyson; here her approach seems less innovative than with the novels, where description has been more neglected. In contrast to Thomson's, Wordsworth's word-paintings, she argues, "participate actively in the narrative impulse of his long poems." And Tennyson, like Dickens, "increasingly integrates descriptive with narrative materials." The book's achievement lies in a real attention to description and a sense of its varieties and development, but it does not quite meet the scale of its claims: it does very little with painting as an analogue and offers less than we are led to expect of the question of genre. The subject is admittedly a tough one, and future work in this area may benefit from Ann Bermingham's *Landscape and Ideology: The English Rustic Tradition, 1740-1860.* This book is about painting and gardens (and conduct-books), not literature, but may set literary studies a model for clarity of argument and complexity of approach in deeply socio-historical semiology. It is also beautifully illustrated. Future students of literary landscape may also seek to integrate examination of landscape description with its manifestation in minor writers: Ann H. Jones offers a brief discussion of Jane Porter's nature that raises questions about Kadish's and Flaxman's exclusive regard to major figures (*Ideas and Innovations*: see above).

Roger Sale's *Closer to Home: Writers and Places in England, 1780-1830* may perhaps belong with this group, though it is a quite different sort of book. Sale concentrates on the importance of locale to five writers—Crabbe, Austen, Cobbett, Clare, and Wordsworth—drawing out their sense of lives shaped by limited environments. Sale has a keen eye for the strengths and constraints of what Wordsworth called "localised affection," and it makes him a sympathetic but discriminating commentator. Engaged and evaluative rather than scholarly, *Closer to Home* is a pleasure for that too rarely considered creature, the common reader.

The fitting conclusion to the group is Karl Kroeber's *British Romantic Art*, a work that one would pronounce magisterial were that not the wrong adjective for its greatest virtue, Kroeber's delight in the maximalist aesthetic of the Romantics, their self-querying, reflective, polymorphous artistry. In the reshaping of the relations between the artwork and its audience Kroeber finds a common goal, and not the least lesson of this rich book is its proof that socio-historical analysis can be performed with the tact of an essay. The title conveys the directness and inclusiveness of Kroeber's vision, for he treats visual and literary art together, but from other angles it is inadequate, because Kroeber's concern with the Romantics' historical consciousness leads to such unexpected comparisons as that between Scott and von Clausewitz, and because he situates the innovative "efficacious indeterminacy" of the Romantics against Hogarth at one end and the pre-Raphaelites, George Eliot, Dickens, and Conrad at the other. The larger arguments persuade, as when Kroeber aligns the fluidity of Turner with revision in *The Prelude* as kindred instances of pluralizing visions, engaging the beholder and implementing a notion of identity as participative. And Kroeber often clinches a formal point with an apt phrase, as when a chapter on narrative infolding and unfolding springs the characterization of *Don Juan* as "open-sided," responsive to the world around; Byron, so long the odd man out in critical formulations of Romanticism, here recovers his representative importance. Kroeber concludes on the perception that the endless interpretability disclosed by current criticism is Romantic energy with the sign reversed, a clue to this study's wiser understanding of its subject. *British Romantic Art* is a book to savor; to do anything like justice to it would take space far exceeding the limits of an omnibus review.

The Novel in the Victorian Age: A Modern Introduction by Robin Gilmour surveys the novel and its context from Bulwer-Lytton and Disraeli through Thackeray, Kingsley, Gaskell, the Brontës, Dickens, Collins, Trollope, Eliot, Meredith, James, Stevenson, Hardy, Moore,

Gissing, Butler, and Ward. Untroubled by epistemological doubt or methodological self-consciousness, Gilmour tells in characteristically graceful prose "the story of the novelists' attempt to interpret their changing world, and to hold on to a hopeful vision of the future until the pressure of pessimistic insight at the end of the period could no longer be contained within the reconciling mixed form." This book meets a real need.

Raymond Chapman's *The Sense of the Past in Victorian Literature* does not present itself as an introductory work but it confines its quotations to the most widely known set texts and offers sentences such as: "The work of Walter Scott stands of course not only in the vanguard of the historical novel, but also as a part of the vigorous but amorphous area of literature known as the Romantic Movement." From a discussion of general Victorian attitudes toward history and historiography he moves to a series of chapters on periods from the middle ages to the immediate past of the Victorians, seeking the ways in which they derived "both judgemental and constructive commentary on their own time." Because Chapman never quite offers what the title promises—we do not get inside the literature, but only to the opinions of various writers—the book is informative, but disappointing.

Other broad-ranging discussions select a particular theme. In *Sacred Tears* Fred Kaplan attempts "to encourage a more informed and tolerant understanding and to stimulate more discussion of Victorian sentimentality by providing a brief introduction and a speculative theory that places Victorian sentimentality in the context of the history of ideas." From the eighteenth-century distinction between sentimentality and sensibility Kaplan moves to Dickens and Thackeray, for whom he argues the control of moral vision over aesthetic choices that we might assume were mere pandering to popular taste. Carlyle, Kaplan's third major figure, demonstrates a greater tolerance for sentimentality "in fact than his principles would seem to permit." Kaplan intends to raise questions rather than provide answers and he clarifies well the issues and their terms. His conclusion is profoundly humanist: the Victorian sentimentalists "affirmed a fragile hope that human beings, in their instinctive natures, innately know right from wrong, and that at the level of innate response they take pleasure in the triumph of goodness and the defeat of evil in literature and in life."

A much more concrete issue occupies Barbara Weiss in *The Hell of the English: Bankruptcy and the Victorian Novel*. From a review of the "reality" of bankruptcy in Victorian England and its reflections in popular art, including painting, theater, and popular fiction, where the emphasis falls on bankruptcy's effect on the family, Weiss moves to the major novelists to whom it was left "to examine not only its effect upon the domestic hearth, but also its implications for the character of individuals, and its meaning in a wider social context as well." Ultimately bankruptcy "becomes a metaphorical upheaval that exposes a crisis of economic, social, sexual, and religious values that threatens to annihilate the very existence of the individual self." Heroes, even chastened ones such as Dombey, remained well off at the end so long as writers were able to believe "that industrialism would allow man to master his fate." But with the development of corporate capitalism (and Weiss discusses in some detail the Limited Liability Act), bankruptcy becomes a metaphor for social apocalypse (*Little Dorrit*, *The Way We Live Now*), appropriate for a crisis that originated in materialism. Innocent of problems of representation and ideology, this book is informative in its history, interesting in its critical chapters, and always readable.

In contrast to Lennard Davis's challenge to the genre of the novel itself, Michael Ragussis's *Acts of Naming: The Family Plot in Fiction* valorizes the novel as that which "responds to a critical disjunction in Enlightenment culture: the neglect of the proper name within Enlightenment philosophy versus the new value of the proper name within the domain of the eighteenth-century family." Ragussis remains within the ideology of the genre in so far as he presents individual identity as paramount, so much so that even the family is a threat, let alone the social group. There are flaws to this book. A clever decoding of the name of Mrs. Thing*m*ummy in *Oliver Twist* suffers from the fact that the character's name is only "Thingummy." A very solemn reading of the names that children go by in Tom-all-Alone's never takes into account the machismo of such naming among adolescent boys. The prose chimes with first-person references ("I recall," "I do," "I mean," "I call," "I refer") and Ragussis insistently totalizes his thesis into a full history of the novel, without any demonstration of how this thesis comes to be granted such priority. But that thesis is often compelling and the book is powerful. It is well worth reading both for its larger theme and for its discussions of *Oliver Twist*, *Bleak House*, *The Mill on the Floss*, and above all *Tess of the d'Urbervilles*. There are also chapters on *Pierre*, *The Scarlet Letter*, and, for the entire third part, *Lolita*.

W. David Shaw in *The Lucid Veil* sets out to do for the Victorians what M. H. Abrams's *The Mirror and the Lamp* did for the Romantics. In the preface he expresses the hope that the scholars and critics to whom this book is indebted "will not . . . think it unscholarly or ungenerous to have omitted reference to them here or in the notes"; others of us may suggest that it is not merely unscholarly and ungenerous, but also bad manners and lazy. Shaw argues that "Because a wide and rough but genuine consistency of outlooks is manifest equally in the poetry, the science, and the philosophy of the Victorian period, it is rewarding to see what changes in one field coincide with similar changes in another." This promises well, but in the text we see little of science, not a great deal of poetry, and a cartload of philosophy. Nor is the book always lucid, suffering from the result of what Shaw seems to defend: he cut not only scholarly references but most illustrations, "a painful process" whose "result may seem skeletal and austere [but is a] desirable feature of all theoretical argument." Perhaps so, especially for readers who prefer the abstruse paths of cognitive philosophy to the material swamps of poetry; those who do will find such exposition well done here, but it seems unlikely to energize the reading of poetry as Abrams did.

Issues in philosophy, epistemological and linguistic, are applied to literature much more trenchantly in John P. McGowan's *Representation and Revelation,* in which McGowan bases his approach on a distinction between "two fundamental sources of knowledge: representation and revelation." His chapters on Rossetti, Carlyle, and Ruskin are more successful than those on the novels because in the latter he has to create an argument based on extrapolation from the fiction. For example, in his analysis of *David Copperfield* he attempts to move from Dickens's terms "fancy" and "real" as they are worked through in the narrative to the plane of "representation" and "revelation" on which the earlier chapters have developed, a transformation that does not quite work although his approach yields an interesting reading of both this and later Dickens novels. There is similar difficulty in the slide from moral to epistemological in the discussion of *The Mill on the Floss.* But McGowan's treatments of the novels are in themselves valuable, especially for *Daniel Deronda.* His method is excellent for Browning. He traces in all these figures the post-Lockean struggle to define a relation between mind and a prior and independent reality and the writers' changing—sometimes dual—conceptions of both the reality and the possibilities for knowing it.

The year brought many editions, several of them further volumes in series, such as the third installment of Wilfred Dowden's restoration of Tom Moore's enlighteningly gossipy *Journal.* Most editions we have had to confine to the list of books received; a few demand comment. *Don Juan* is the latest addition to the splendid

Clarendon Byron, edited by Jerome McGann, who confidently begins his introduction: "*Don Juan* is the most important poem published in England between 1667 (when *Paradise Lost* was issued) and 1850 (when *The Prelude* finally appeared in print)." How times have changed since a Yale graduate student contemporary with McGann, asked on his doctoral orals "What is the most important long poem of the nineteenth century?" and answering "*Don Juan*," was brusquely told by his examiners: "Think again." McGann presents the manuscript evolution and production history of the poem more thoroughly than ever before, and makes numerous adjustments in the text. The wealth of annotation serves the argument that as the poem evolved Byron made it into a deliberate double history of his times, setting the narrative of Juan's career in the 1790s amidst his reflections on the ideological situation of the restored monarchies of the Europe of 1819-1824. Byron's renewed importance has been accomplished largely through McGann's labors in the last decade and a half, initiated with *Fiery Dust* in 1968, and this edition is their crown.

We are grateful for two other appearances in Clarendon series: *Pickwick Papers*, edited by the late James Kinsley, and *Middlemarch*, by David Carroll. Both conform to the high standards we have come to expect. Because only about forty-five manuscript leaves and no proofs of *Pickwick* survive and there were only about a thousand variants in the three subsequent lifetime editions, the annotations are relatively light, but we are no less gratified by a fine text, sharply printed illustrations, and a full history of the work's composition and printing. For *Middlemarch* the copy-text is the cheap edition of 1874, with full listings of variants in the manuscript, first and third editions, and proofs to the first and second editions. The introduction is comprehensive, and the modest addition of explanatory footnotes (a feature of this series) welcome.

A manuscript of *Beppo* and new information about his life in Venice, including notes from his mistresses, makes Byron the highlight also of volumes 7 and 8 of *Shelley and His Circle*, directed by Donald Reiman. At the other extreme from the sumptuous presentation of this series are McGann's one-volume selection from Byron in the Oxford Authors series, the classroom text with *Childe Harold* and *Don Juan* complete for which we have been waiting, and Alun Jones's convenient paperbound edition of Wordsworth's *Poems* of 1807.

These scrupulous editions and the generations of sloppy printers that their editors have had to deal with lead us to the matter of current editorial standards. Circumstantial evidence might suggest that for some prolonged period between 1984 and 1986 there was an industry-wide strike of proofreaders—which perhaps in some mysterious way also accounted for the contemporaneous rise in the cost of books. Less facetiously, we wish to call attention to the apparently growing practice among publishers of forgoing the services of copy-editors. Copy-editors, as those of us who have enjoyed their services can attest, save authors not only from the inconsistencies to which human weakness leads, but from their worst deliberate flubs. They require us to murder our darlings, they prod us kindly out of clumsiness and gaff.

Surely, if he is herein described correctly, the cofounder of the London Mathematical Society, Augustus De Morgan, has taken several proverbial turns at being pronounced "De Morg*o*n, [who] was known to be fasti*t*ious about detail." We found innumerable less comic typographical errors, and authorial errors ranging from the spelling "super*c*ede" to singular verbs for plural subjects and all the other dreary usage errors at which we weary in Freshman Composition. Perhaps professors of English should never make such mistakes, but we do. Our favorite is the following: "Perched as she is in the ever-shifting center of the series of paradoxes that frame the depiction of women's bodies and Victorian representation in general, Lily's body and its entrances . . .": does one perch *in* a center? does a linear series make up a frame? shouldn't the pronoun for "body" be "it"? could somebody please block our metaphors?

A book turned to throughout the year when such vexations soured our task is Leo Braudy's *The Frenzy of Renown: Fame and Its History*. Historians of ideas would have found themselves at home with Braudy's tracing of a unitary topic, but few of them had Professsor Braudy's immersion in the periods he animates, from antiquity to the present, and his grasp of the odd, paradigmatic anecdote, of high culture and low, and of the innumerable particular forms of life in which the lure of fame at any given moment has its existence. Braudy touches down on the nineteenth century to examine the mythologizing of Byron and Napoleon, and if the rest of our reading was an indulgence out of period, the combination of scholarship, gusto, and subtle reflection made quitting impossible.

BOOKS RECEIVED

Abbey, Cherie D., ed. *Nineteenth-Century Literature Criticism*, vol. 13. Detroit: Gale Research, 1986. Pp. 531. $88.00. ISBN 0-8103-5813-1.

Abbey, Cherie D., ed. *Nineteenth-Century Literature Criticism*, vol. 14. Detroit: Gale Research, 1977. Pp. 559. $90.00. ISBN 0-8103-5814-X.

Albright, Daniel. *Tennyson: The Muses' Tug-of War*. Charlottesville: Univ. Press of Virginia, 1986. Pp. x + 304. $24.95. ISBN 0-8139-1100-1.

Altick, Richard. *Deadly Encounters: Two Victorian Sensations*. Philadelphia: Univ. of Pennsylvania Press, 1986. Pp. vii + 164. $13.95. ISBN 0-8122-1227-4.

Aske, Martin. *Keats and Hellenism: An Essay*. Cambridge and New York: Cambridge Univ. Press, 1987. Pp. xii + 193. $32.50. ISBN 0-521-30561-6.

Aubrey, Bryan. *Watchmen of Eternity: Blake's Debt to Jacob Boehme*. Lanham, MD, and London: Univ. Press of America, 1986. Pp. xiii + 193. $27.00, cloth, ISBN 0-8191-5220-X. $13.25, paper, ISBN 0-8191-5221-8.

Barker, Francis, et al., eds. *Literature, Politics and Theory: Papers from the Essex Conference 1976-84*. London and New York: Methuen, 1987. Pp. xix + 259. $11.95.

Barnard, John. *John Keats*. Cambridge: Cambridge Univ. Press, 1987. Pp. xi -172. $39.50. ISBN 0-521-26691-2.

Bate, Jonathan. *Shakespeare and the English Romantic Imagination*. Oxford: Clarendon Press, 1986. Pp. xiv + 276. $39.00. ISBN 0-19-812848-7.

Bate, W. Jackson. *Coleridge*. Cambridge, MA., and London: Harvard Univ. Press, 1987. Pp. xii + 244. $10.95. ISBN 0-674-13680-2.

Baum, Joan. *The Calculating Passion of Ada Byron*. Hamden: Archon Books, 1986. Pp. xix + 133. $21.50. ISBN 0-208-02119-1.

Beer, Frances, ed. *The Juvenilia of Jane Austen and Charlotte Bronte*. New York: Penguin, 1986. Pp. 389. $5.95. ISBN 0-14-043267-1.

Beer, Gillian. *George Eliot*. Key Women Writers. Bloomington: Indiana Univ. Press, 1986. Pp. xii + 246. $27.50, cloth, ISBN 0-253-30100-9. $7.95, paper, ISBN 0-253-254507.

Bermingham, Ann. *Landscape and Ideology: The English Rustic Tradition 1740-1860*. Berkeley and London: Univ. of California Press, 1986. Pp. xviii + 254. $35.00. ISBN 0-52-05287-0.

Braddon, Mary E. *Lady Audley's Secret*. New York: Viking Penguin, 1987. Pp. xix + 376. $6.95. ISBN 0-14-016185-6.

Braudy, Leo. *The Frenzy of Renown: Fame and Its History*. New York and Oxford: Oxford Univ. Press, 1986. Pp. ix + 649. $27.50. ISBN 0-19-504003-1.

Brodetsky, Tessa. *Elizabeth Gaskell*. New York: St. Martin's Press, 1987. Pp. vii + 113. $6.95. ISBN 0-907582-83-4.

Brooks, Michael W. *John Ruskin and Victorian Architecture*. New Brunswick and London: Rutgers Univ. Press, 1987. Pp. xi + 364. $28.00. ISBN 0-8135-1205-0.

Browning Institute Studies, vol. 13. Ed. Adrienne Auslander Munich. New York: Browning Institute, 1985. Pp. xvi + 234. ISBN 0-930252-18-7. ISSN 0092-4725.

Brunton, Mary. *Discipline.* London: Pandora Press of Routledge & Kegan Paul, and New York: Methuen, 1987. Pp. vii + 375. $8.95. ISBN 0-86358-105-6.

Brunton, Mary. *Self-Control.* Mothers of the Novel. London and New York: Pandora, 1986. Pp. xi + 437. $7.95. ISBN 0-86358-084-X.

Buckler, William E. *Walter Pater: Three Major Texts.* New York and London: New York Univ. Press, 1986. Pp. vii + 550. $50.00. ISBN 0-8147-1088-3.

Buckley, Jerome H., ed. *The Pre-Raphaelites.* Chicago: Academy Chicago, 1987. Pp. xii + 514. $10.95. ISBN 0-89733-237-7.

Byron, George Gordon, Lord. *Lord Byron: The Complete Poetical Works*, vol. 5, *Don Juan.* Ed. Jerome J. McGann. Oxford: Clarendon Press, 1986. Pp. xxiv + 771. $110.00. ISBN 0-19-812757-X.

Byron, ed. Jerome J. McGann. Oxford: Clarendon Press, 1986. Pp. xxvii + 1080. ISBN 0-19-254184-6.

Cambridge, Ada. *The Three Miss Kings.* New York: Viking Penguin, 1987. Pp. xvi + 314. $6.95. ISBN 0-14-016164-3.

Carpenter, Mary Wilson. *George Eliot and the Landscape of Time.* Chapel Hill and London: Univ. of North Carolina Press, 1986. Pp. xvi + 246. $25.00. ISBN 0-8-78-1681-7.

Chapman, Raymond. *The Sense of the Past in Victorian Literature.* New York: St. Martin's Press, 1986. Pp. 212. $27.50. ISBN 0-312-71301-0.

Chapple, J. A. V. *Science and Literature in the Nineteenth Century.* London and New York: Macmillan, 1986. Pp. xi + 192. $29.95, cloth, ISBN 0-333-37586-6. $9.95, paper, ISBN 0-333-37587-4.

Chase, Cynthia. *Decomposing Figures: Rhetorical Readings in the Romantic Tradition.* Baltimore and London: Johns Hopkins Univ. Press, 1986. Pp. ix + 234. $25.00. ISBN 0-8018-3136-9.

Chilcott, Tim. *"A Real World and Doubting Mind." A Critical Study of the Poetry of John Clare.* Hull: Hull Univ. Press, and Atlantic Highlands: Humanities Press, 1986. Pp. xxi + 292. $25.00. ISBN 0-85958-446-1.

Chitham, Edward, and Winnifrith, Tom, eds. *Selected Brontë Poems.* Oxford and New York: Basil Blackwell, 1985. Pp. xxxi + 262. $34.95 cloth, ISBN 0-631-14564-8. $8.95 paper, ISBN 0-631-14565-6.

Clare, John. *John Clare's Autobiographical Writings*, ed. Eric Robinson. Oxford and New York: Oxford Univ. Press, 1986. Pp. xix + 185. $5.95. ISBN 0-19-281923-2.

Clare, John. *The Parish: A Satire.* New York: Viking Penguin, 1986. Pp. 96. $5.95. ISBN 0-14-043242-6.

Cohen, Morton N., and Gandolfo, Anita, eds. *Lewis Carroll and the House of Macmillan.* Cambridge and New York: Cambridge Univ. Press, 1987. Pp. ix + 384. $59.50. ISBN 0-621-25602-X.

Collins, Wilkie. *Blind Love.* New York: Dover, 1986. Pp. 312. $6.95. ISBN 0-486-25189-6.

Cotsell, Michael. *The Companion to "Our Mutual Friend".* London and Winchester: Allen and Unwin, 1986. Pp. xvi + 316. $34.95. ISBN 0-04-80035-3.

Cox, Michael, and Gilbert, R. A., eds. *The Oxford Book of English Ghost Stories.* Oxford and New York: Oxford Univ. Press, 1986. Pp. xvii + 504. $18.95. ISBN 0-19-214163-5.

Crook, Nora, and Guiton, Derek. *Shelley's Venomed Melody.* Cambridge and New York: Cambridge Univ. Press, 1986. Pp. xii + 273. $39.50. ISBN 0-521-32084-4.

Crump, R. W. *Charlotte and Emily Brontë, 1955-1983: A Reference Guide,* Boston: G. K. Hall, 1986. Pp. xviii + 319. $35.00. ISBN 0-8161-7953-0.

Curran, Stuart. *Poetic Form and British Romanticism.* New York and Oxford: Oxford Univ. Press, 1986. Pp. ix + 265. $29.95. ISBN 0-19-504019-8.

Dahl, Erhard. *Die Entstehung der Phantastischen Kinder-und Jugenderzahlung in England.* Paderborn: Schoningh, 1986. Pp. 192. DM 37. ISBN 3-506-78454-4.

Darwin, Charles. *The Correspondence of Charles Darwin,* ed. Frederick Burkhardt and Sydney Smith. Vol. 2: 1837-1843. Cambridge and New York: Cambridge Univ. Press, 1987. Pp. xxxiii + 603. $37.50. ISBN 0-521-25588-0.

Davies, Hugh Sykes. *Wordsworth and the Worth of Words.* Cambridge and New York: Cambridge Univ. Press, 1987. Pp. xii + 324. $49.50. ISBN 0-521-30909-3.

Davis, Lennard J. *Resisting Novels: Ideology and Fiction.* New York and London: Methuen, 1987. Pp. x + 262. $12.95. ISBN 0-416-37830-7.

Dentith, Simon. *George Eliot.* Harvester New Readings. Atlantic Highlands, NJ: Humanities Press, 1986. Pp. x + 150. $22.50. ISBN 0-391-03418-9.

Dickens, Charles. *The Pickwick Papers.* Ed. James Kinsley. Oxford: Clarendon Press, 1986. Pp. civ + 901. $110.00. ISBN 0-19-812631-X.

Dowling, Linda. *Language and Decadence in the Victorian Fin de Siecle.* Princeton: Princeton Univ. Press, 1986. Pp. xvi + 294. $32.50. ISBN 0-691-06690-6.

Duthie, Enid L. *The Brontës and Nature.* New York: St. Martin's Press, 1986. Pp. x + 273. $27.50. ISBN 0-312-10599-1.

Eagleton, Mary. *Feminist Literary Theory: A Reader.* Oxford and New York: Basil Blackwell, 1986. Pp. xiv + 237. $14.95. ISBN 0-631-14805-1.

Eaves, Morris, and Fischer, Michael, eds. *Romanticism and Contemporary Criticism.* Ithaca and London: Cornell Univ. Press, 1986. Pp. 246. $8.95. ISBN 0-8014-9352-8.

Edgeworth, Maria. *Helen.* London: Pandora Press of Routledge & Kegan Paul, and New York: Methuen, 1987. Pp. xii + 444. $8.95. ISBN 0-86358-104-8.

Edgeworth, Maria. *Patronage.* London and New York: Pandora Press, 1986. Pp. xi + 631. $25.00. ISBN 0-86358-106-4.

Eliot, George. *Middlemarch*. Ed. David Carroll. Oxford: Clarendon Press, 1986. Pp. lxxvv + 825. $115.00. ISBN 0-19-813558-5.

Ellsberg, Margaret R. *Created to Praise: The Language of Gerard Manley Hopkins*. New York and Oxford: Oxford Univ. Press, 1987. Pp. 145. $15.95. ISBN 0-19-504098-8.

Emeljanow, Victor. *Victorian Popular Dramatists*. Twayne's English Authors Series. Boston: Twayne, 1987. Pp. 181. $24.95. ISBN 0-8057-6935-8.

Etudes Anglaises 39, 3 (July-September 1986). Paris: Didier Érudition. Pp. 257-382. 379 FF overseas. ISSN 0014-195X.

Feltes, N. N. *Modes of Production of Victorian Novels*. Chicago and London: Univ. of Chicago Press, 1986. Pp. xiii + 125. $18.95. ISBN 0-226-24117-3.

Fitch, Raymond E. *The Poison Sky: Myth and Apocalypse in Ruskin*. Athens and London: Ohio Univ. Press, 1986. Pp. xii + 722. $18.95. ISBN 0-8214-0642-6.

Flaxman, Rhoda L. *Victorian Word-Painting and Narrative: Toward the Blending of Genres*. Ann Arbor: UMI Research Press, 1987. Pp. ix + 150. $39.95. ISBN 0-8457-1787-6.

Flint, Kate. *Dickens*. Atlantic Highlands, NJ: Humanities Press, 1986. Pp. xi + 159. $19.95. ISBN 0-391-03419-7.

Frank, Frederick S. *The First Gothics: A Critical Guide to the English Gothic Novel*. New York: Garland, 1987. Pp. xxxi + 496. $50.00. ISBN 0-8240-8501-9.

Fraser, Hilary. *Beauty and Belief: Aesthetics and Religion in Victorian Literature*. Cambridge and New York: Cambridge Univ. Press, 1987. Pp. xii + 287. $34.50. ISBN 0-521-30767-8.

Gagnier, Regenia. *Idylls of the Marketplace: Oscar Wilde and the Victorian Public*. Stanford: Stanford Univ. Press, 1986. Pp. 255. $29.50. ISBN 0-8047-1334-0.

Gardner, Stanley. *Blake's "Innocence and Experience" Retraced*. London: Athlone; New York: St. Martin's Press. 1986. Pp. xvii + 211. $27.50. ISBN 0-312-08354-8.

Gertzman, Jay A. *Fantasy, Fashion and Affection. Editions of Robert Herrick's Poetry for the Common Reader, 1810-1968*. Bowling Green: Bowling Green State Univ. Popular Press, 1986. Pp. 240. $25.95, cloth, ISBN 0-87972-349-1. $13.95, paper, ISBN 0-87972-350-5.

Gilmour, Robin. *The Novel in the Victorian Age: A Modern Introduction*. London: Edward Arnold, 1986. Pp. 221. $14.95. ISBN 0-7131-6468-9.

Grylls, David. *The Paradox of Gissing*. London: Allen & Unwin, 1986. Pp. xiii + 226. $29.95. ISBN 0-04-800081-7.

Hagstrum, Jean H. *The Romantic Body: Love and Sexuality in Keats, Wordsworth, and Blake*. Knoxville: Univ. of Tennessee Press, 1986. Pp. xvi 177. $4.95. ISBN 0-87049-482-1.

Hamer, Mary. *Writing By Numbers: Trollope's Serial Fiction.* Cambridge and New York: Cambridge Univ. Press, 1987. Pp. xiv + 199. Price not set. ISBN 0-521-32528-5.

Hamilton, Paul. *Wordsworth.* Atlantic Highlands, NJ: Humanities Press, 1986. Pp. xii + 159. $22.50. ISBN 0-391-03417-0.

Hardy, Thomas. *A Pair of Blue Eyes.* Ed. Roger Ebbatson. New York: Viking Penguin, 1986. Pp. 480. $4.95. ISBN 0-14-043266-3.

Harris, Laurie Lanzen, and Abbey, Cherie D., eds. *Nineteenth Century Literature Criticism,* vol. 12. Detroit: Gale Research, 1976. Pp. 576. $88.00. ISBN 0-8103-5812-3.

Hartog, Dirk den. *Dickens and Romantic Psychology: The Self in Time in Nineteenth-Century Literature.* New York: St. Martin's Press, 1987. Pp. xi + 177. $27.50. ISBN 0-312-19989-9.

Harvey, Geoffrey. *The Romantic Tradition in Modern English Poetry: Rhetoric and Experience.* New York: St. Martin's Press, 1986. Pp. + xi 134. $25.00. ISBN 0-312-69188-2.

Harwell, Thomas Meade, ed. *The English Gothic Novel: A Miscellany in Four Volumes.* Vols. 1, 2, 3, and 4. Salzburg: Univ. Salzburg, 1986. Pp. 341, 353, 241, and 317.

Hawthorn, Jeremy. *Bleak House.* Atlantic Highlands, NJ: Humanities Press, 1987. Pp. 93. Cloth, ISBN 0-391-03425-1; $7.95 paper. ISBN 0-391-03424-3,

Hawthorn, Jeremy, ed. *Nineteenth-Century British Novel.* Stratford -upon-Avon Studies, Second Series. London: Edward Arnold, 1986. Pp. viii + 175. $19.95. ISBN 0-7131-6470-0.

Herbert, Christopher. *Trollope and Comic Pleasure.* Chicago and London: Univ. of Chicago Press, 1987. Pp. x 245. $24.00. ISBN 0-226-32741-8.

Hilton, Nelson, ed. *Essential Articles for the Study of William Blake,* 1970-1984. Hamden, CT: Archon Books, 1986. Pp. x + 333. $35.00. ISBN 0-208-02091-8.

Hinde, Wendy. *Richard Cobden: Victorian Outsider.* New Haven and London: Yale Univ. Press, 1987. Pp. xi + 367. $30.00. ISBN 0-300-03880-1.

Homans, Margaret. *Bearing the Word: Language and Female Experience in Nineteenth-Century Women's Writing.* Chicago and London: Univ. of Chicago Press, 1986. Pp. xiv + 326. $22.00. ISBN 0-226-35107-6.

Hornback, Bert G. *"Great Expectations": A Novel of Friendship.* Boston: G.K. Hall, 1987. Pp. xii + 152. ISBN 0-8057-7956-6.

Hughes, Linda K. *The Manyfacéd Glass: Tennyson's Dramatic Monologues.* Athens and London: Ohio Univ. Press, 1986. Pp. x + 311. $27.95. ISBN 0-8214-0853-4.

Jacobson, Wendy S. *The Companion to "The Mystery of Edwin Drood".* London and Winchester: Allen and Unwin, 1986. Pp. 209. $29.95. ISBN 0-04-80063-9.

Jaki, Stanley, L. *Chesterton, A Seer of Science.* Chicago: Univ. of Illinois Press, 1987. Pp. x + 164. $12.50. ISBN 0-252-01283-6.

Jay, Elisabeth. *Faith and Doubt in Victorian Britain.* London: Macmillan, and Atlantic Highlands, NJ: Humanities Press, 1986. Pp. xi + 136. $9.95. ISBN 0-333-37657-5.

Jekel, Pamela L. *Thomas Hardy's Heroines: A Chorus of Priorities.* Troy: Whitston, 1986. Pp. 233. $22.50. ISBN 0-87875-309-5.

Johnston, John H. *The Poet and the City: A Study in Urban Perspectives.* Athens, GA: Univ. of Georgia Press, 1987. Pp. xx + 275. $25.00. ISBN 0-8203-0714-9.

Jones, Alun R. *Wordsworth's Poems of 1807.* Atlantic Highlands, NJ: Humanities Press, 1987. Pp. xxvii + 192. $15.00. ISBN 0-391-03500-2.

Jones, Ann H. *Ideas and Innovations: Best Sellers of Jane Austen's Age.* New York: AMS Press, 1987. Pp. ix + 361. $42.50. ISBN 0-404-61482-5.

Jordanova, L. J., ed. *Languages of Nature: Critical Essays on Science and Literature.* New Brunswick, NJ: Rutgers Univ. Press, 1986. Pp. 351. $30.00. ISBN 0-8135-1194-1.

Kadish, Doris Y. *The Literature of Images: Narrative Landscape in the Novel from "Julie" to "Jane Eyre."* New Brunswick, NJ: Rutgers Univ. Press, 1987. Pp. vii + 211. $32.00. ISBN 0-8135-1183-6.

Kalikoff, Beth. *Murder and Moral Decay in Victorian Popular Literature.* Ann Arbor: UMI Research Press, 1986. Pp. 193. $39.95. ISBN 0-8357-1762-3.

Kaplan, Fred. *Sacred Tears: Sentimentality in Victorian Literature.* Princeton: Princeton Univ. Press. 1987. Pp. xi + 156. $19.50. ISBN 0-691-06700-7.

Kelley, Philip, and Hudson, Ronald, eds. *The Brownings' Correspondence,* vol. 4. Winfield, KS: Wedgestone Press, 1986. Pp. xiv + 451. $47.50. ISBN 0-911459-09-X

Kelsall, Malcolm. *Byron's Politics.* Brighton, Sussex: Harvester Press, and Totowa, NJ: Barnes & Noble, 1987. Pp. viii + 211. $28.50. ISBN 0-7108-0692-2.

Kipperman, Mark. *Beyond Enchantment: German Idealism and English Romantic Poetry.* Philadelphia: Univ. of Pennsylvania Press, 1986. Pp. xii + 242. $27.95. ISBN 0-8122-8024-5.

Kirkham, Margaret. *Jane Austen, Feminism and Fiction.* New York: Methuen, 1986. Pp. xvii + 186. $10.95. ISBN 0-416-01181-0.

Klancher, Jon P. *The Making of English Reading Audiences, 1790-1832.* Madison and London: Univ. of Wisconsin Press, 1987. Pp. xi + 210. $25.00 ISBN 0-299-10780-9.

Kloesel, Christian J. W., comp. *English Novel Explication.* Supplement III. Hamden, CT: The Shoe String Press, 1986. Pp. vi + 533. $42.50. ISBN 0-208-01464-0.

Kroeber, Karl. *British Romantic Art.* Berkeley and London: Univ. of California Press, 1986. Pp. xi + 278. $35.00. ISBN 0-520-0584-9.

Landow, George P. *Elegant Jeremiahs: The Sage from Carlyle to Mailer.* Ithaca and London: Cornell Univ. Press, 1986. Pp. 198. $17.50. ISBN 0-8014-1905-0.

Lane, Maggie. *Jane Austen's England.* New York: St. Martin's Press, 1987. Pp. 224. $19.95. ISBN 0-312-00366-8.

Layton, Lynne, and Schapiro, Barbara Ann. *Narcissism and the Text: Studies in Literature and the Psychology of Self.* New York and London: New York Univ. Press, 1986. Pp. xvi + 295. $42.50. ISBN 0-8147-5020-6.

Lefkovitz, Lori Hope. *The Character of Beauty in the Victorian Novel.* Ann Arbor, MI: UMI Research Press, 1987. Pp. viii + 243. $39.95. ISBN 0-8357-1755-0.

Levinson, Marjorie. *The Romantic Fragment Poem: A Critique of a Form.* Chapel Hill and London: Univ. of North Carolina Press, 1986. Pp. x + 268. $29.00. ISBN 0-8078-1684-1.

Levinson, Marjorie. *Wordsworth's Great Period Poems: Four Essays.* Cambridge and New York: Cambridge Univ. Press, 1986. Pp. x + 170. $32.50. ISBN 0-521-30829-1.

Lister, Raymond. *The Paintings of William Blake.* Cambridge: Univ. Press, 1986. Pp. 176. $29.95 cloth, ISBN 0-a521-30538-1. Paper, ISBN 0-521-31557-3.

Loesberg, Jonathan. *Fictions of Consciousness: Mill, Newman, and the Reading of Victorian Prose.* New Brunswick and London: Rutgers Univ. Press, 1986. Pp. ix + 380. $18.00. ISBN 0-8135-1173-9.

Luhmann, Niklas. *Love as Passion: The Codification of Intimacy.* Trans. Jeremy Gaines and Doris L. Jones. Cambridge, MA: Harvard Univ. Press, 1986. Pp. 247. $27.50. ISNB 0-674-53923-0.

Lynch, Tony. *Dickens's England.* New York and Oxford: Facts On File, 1986. Pp. 200. $16.95. ISBN 0-8160-1533-3.

MacDonald, Susan Peck. *Anthony Trollope.* Boston: G. K. Hall, 1987. Pp. 138. $17.95. ISBN 0-8057-6945-5.

McGowan, John P. *Representation and Revelation: Victorian Realism from Carlyle to Yeats.* Columbia: Univ. of Missouri Press, 1986. Pp. vi + 206. $26.00. ISBN 0-8262-0492-9.

McGrath, F. C. *The Sensible Spirit: Walter Pater and the Modernist Paradigm.* Tampa: Univ. of South Florida Press, 1986. Pp. xi + 299. $25.00. ISBN 0-8130-0829-8.

Machin, Robert, and Norris, Christopher, eds. *Post-Structualist Readings in English Poetry.* Cambridge and New York: Cambridge Univ. Press, 1987. Pp. x + 406. $49.50. ISBN 0-521-30605-1.

McKusick, James C. *Coleridge's Philosophy of Language.* New Haven and London: Yale Univ. Press, 1986. $15.95. Pp. xiii + 175. ISBN 0-300-03667-1.

McMaster, R. D. *Trollope and the Law.* New York: St. Martin's Press, 1986. Pp. xii + 179. $25.00. ISNB 0-312-81891-2.

Melada, Ivan. *Sheridan Le Fanu.* Boston: Twayne, G. K. Hall, 1987. Pp. 142. $21.95. ISBN 0-8057-69374.

Meltzer, Francoise. *Salome and the Dance of Writing.* Chicago and London: Univ. of Chicago Press, 1987. Pp. x + 226. $24.95. ISBN 0-226-51971-6.

Meredith, Michael. *Meeting the Brownings.* Waco: Baylor Univ., 1986. Pp. 128. $17.50. ISBN 0-930252-19-5.

Metzger, Lore. *One Foot in Eden: Modes of Pastoral in Romantic Poetry.* Chapel Hill and London: Univ. of North Carolina Press, 1986. Pp. xv + 274. $25.00. ISBN 0-8078-1678-7.

Michie, Helena. *The Flesh Made Word.* New York and Oxford: Oxford Univ. Press, 1987. Pp. 179. $16.95. ISBN 0-19-504107-0.

Miller, J. Hillis. *The Ethics of Reading: Kant, de Man, Eliot, Trollope, James, and Benjamin.* New York: Columbia Univ. Press, 1987. Pp. xi + 138. $20.00. ISBN 0-231-06334-2.

Miller, Robert Keith. *Carlyle's Life of John Sterling.* Ann Arbor: UMI Research Press, 1987., Pp. 103. ISBN 0-8357-1782-8.

Minor British Poets 1789-1918. Part Three: The Later Victorian Period 1870-1899. Davis: The Library, Univ. of California, 1986. Pp. 315.

Moore, Thomas. *The Journal of Thomas Moore,* vol. 3: 1826-1830, ed. Wilfred S. Dowden. Newark: Univ. of Delaware Press, and London and Toronto: Associated Univ. Presses, 1986. Pp. 895-1360. $60.00. ISBN 0-87413-255-X.

Morgan, Lady. *The Wild Irish Girl.* London: Routledge & Kegan Paul, and New York: Methuen, 1987. Pp. xi + 255. $7.95. ISBN 0-86358-097-1.

Myers, Robin, and Harris, Michael, eds. *Economics of the British Booktrade, 1605-1939.* Alexandria, Va: Chadwyck-Healey, 1985. Pp. xiii + 231. ISBN 0-85964-169-4.

Myers, Robin, and Harris, Michael, eds. *Bibliophily.* Alexandria: Chadwyck-Healey, 1986. Pp. x + 172. $35.00. ISBN 0-85964-186-4.

Nabholtz, John R. *"My Reader My Fellow-Labourer": A Study of English Romantic Prose.* Columbia: Univ. of Missouri Press, 1986. Pp. viii + 135. $22.00. ISBN 0-8262-0491-0.

Oliphant, Mrs. *The Perpetual Curate.* New York: Viking Penguin, 1987. Pp. xiv + 540. $7.95. ISBN 0-14-016-161-0.

Ong, Walter J. *Hopkins, the Self, and God.* Toronto: Univ. of Toronto Press, 1986. Pp. 180. $20.00. ISBN 0-8020-5688-1.

Opie, Mrs. *Adelina Mowbray, or, The Mother and Daughter.* London and Boston: Pandora, 1986. Pp. viii + 275. $4.95. ISBN 0-86358-085-8.

Orel, Harold. *The Victorian Short Story.* London and New York: Cambridge Univ. Press, 1986. Pp. x + 213. $29.95. ISBN 0-521-25899-5.

Pater, Walter. *Appreciations: With an Essay on Style.* Evanston, IL: Northwestern Univ. Press, 1987. Pp. 261. $11.95. ISBN 0-8101-0747-3.

Peckham, Morse. *The Birth of Romanticism 1790-1815*. Greenwood, FL: Penkevill, 1986. Pp. ix + 413. $32.50. ISBN 0-913283-08-8.

Peters, Catherine. *Thackeray's Universe: Shifting Worlds of Imagination and Reality*. New York: Oxford Univ. Press, 1987. Pp. xi + 292. $29.95. ISBN 0-19-504855-5.

Prickett, Stephen. *Words and The Word: Language, Poetics and Biblical Interpretation*. Cambridge and New York: Cambridge Univ. Press, 1986. Pp. xii + 305. $39.50. ISBN 0-521-32248- 0.

Proust, Marcel. *On Reading Ruskin*. Trans. and ed. Jean Autret, William Burford, and Phillip J. Wolfe. New Haven and London: Yale Univ. Press, 1987. Pp. liii + 173. $18.50 ISBN 0-300-03513-6.

Radford, Jean, ed. *The Progress of Romance: The Politics of Popular Fiction*. London and New York: Routledge & Kegan Paul, 1987. Pp. x + 238. $11.95. ISBN 0-7102-0963-0.

Ragussis, Michael. *Acts of Naming: The Family Plot in Fiction*. New York and Oxford: Oxford Univ. Press, 1986. Pp. 268. $22.50. ISBN 0-19-504070-8.

Raina, Badri. *Dickens and the Dialectic of Growth*. Madison: Univ. of Wisconsin Press, 1986. Pp. xiii + 172. $27.50. ISBN 0-299-10610-1.

Reade, Charles. *Plays*. Ed. Michael Hammet. British and American Playwrights 1750-1920. Cambridge and London: Cambridge Univ. Press, 1986. Pp. xii + 170. $44.50 cloth, ISBN 0-521-24361-0. $14.95, paper, ISBN 0-521-28627-1.

Reiman, Donald H., ed. *Shelley and His Circle 1773-1822*. Cambridge MA: Harvard Univ. Press, 1986. Vol. 7, pp. xlvii + 609. Vol. 8, pp. xiii + 611-1228. Two vols. $90.00. ISBN 0-674-80613-1.

Rigaud, N.J., ed. *L'Angleterre et le monde Mediterranean*. Aix en Provence: Univ. de Provence, 1987. Pp. vii + 91. 50 F. ISBN 2-85399-152-0.

Robinson, Jeffrey. *Radical Literary Education: A Classroom Experiment with Wordsworth's "Ode."* Madison: Univ. of Wisconsin Press, 1987. xix + 201. $13.95. ISBN 0-299-11064-8.

Rose, Jonathan. *The Edwardian Temperament: 1895-1919*. Athens and London: Ohio Univ. Press, 1986. Pp. xiv + 275. $26.95. ISBN 0-8214-0821-6.

Rosenbaum, S. P. *Victorian Bloomsbury: The Early Literary History of the Bloomsbury Group*. Vol 1. New York: St. Martin's Press, 1987. Pp. xvi + 316. $24.95. ISBN 0-312-84051-9.

Rosenblum, Dolores. *Christina Rossetti: The Poetry of Endurance*. Carbondale: Southern Illinois Univ. Press, 1987. Pp. xvii + 247. $23.95. ISBN 0-8093-1269-7.

Rzepka, Charles J. *The Self as Mind: Vision and Identity in Wordsworth, Coleridge, and Keats*. Cambridge, MA, and London: Harvard Univ. Press, 1986. Pp. viii + 286. $27.50. ISBN 0-674-80085-0.

Sadrin, Anny. *L'Etre et L'Avoir dans les Romans de Charles Dickens*. Paris: Didier Érudition, 1985. Pp. 800. ISBN 2-86460-069-2.

Sale, Roger. *Closer to Home: Writers and Places in England, 1780-1830*. Cambridge, MA, and London: Harvard Univ. Press, 1986. Pp. 153. $15.95. ISBN 0-674-13625-X.

Salomon, Roger B. *Desperate Storytelling: Post-Romantic Elaborations of the Mock-Heroic Mode*. Athens and London: Univ. of Georgia Press, 1987. Pp. x + 302. $32.50. ISBN 0-8203-0895-1.

Sanders, Valerie. *Reason Over Passion: Harriet Martineau and the Victorian Novel*. Brighton, Sussex: Harvester Press, and New York: St. Martin's Press, 1986. Pp. 236. $32.50. U.K. ISBN 0-7108-1018-0. U.S. 0-312-66533-4.

Schulz, Max F. *Paradise Preserved: Recreations of Eden in Eighteenth- and Nineteenth-Century England*. Cambridge and London: Cambridge Univ. Press, 1986. Pp. xv + 368. $39.50. ISBN 0-521-30173-4.

Seiberling, Grace. *Amateurs, Photography, and the Mid-Victorian Imagination*. Chicago and London: Univ. of Chicago Press, 1986. Pp. x + 195. $34.95. ISBN 0-226-74498-1.

Shatto, Susan. *Tennyson's Maud*. Norman and London: Univ. of Oklahoma Press, 1986. Pp. xxi + 295. $39.50. ISBN 0-8061-1986-1

Shaw, W. David. *The Lucid Veil: Poetic Truth in the Victorian Age*. Madison: Univ. of Wisconsin Press, 1987. Pp. xix + 311. $26.50. ISBN 0-299-11210-1.

Siegle, Robert. *The Politics of Reflexivity: Narrative and the Constitutive Poetics of Culture*. Baltimore and London: Johns Hopkins Univ. Press, 1986. Pp. ix + 271. $27.50. ISBN 0-8018-3334-5

Simon, Richard Keller. *The Labyrinth of the Comic: Theory and Practice from Fielding to Freud*. Tallahassee: Florida State Univ. Press, 1986. Pp. x + 260. $27.95. ISBN 0-8130-0831-X.

Sloan, Barry. *The Pioneers of Anglo-Irish Fiction 1800-1850*. Totowa, NJ: Barnes and Noble, 1987. Pp. xxxvi + 277. $28.50. ISBN 0-389-20662-8.

Steinhoff, Stephen T., ed. *Keats's Endymion: A Critical Edition*. Troy: Whitston, 1987. Pp. 300. $30.00. ISBN 0-87875-236-6.

Stone, Harry. *Dickens' Working Notes for His Novels*. Chicago and London: Univ. of Chicago Press, 1987. Pp. xxxv + 375. $74.95. ISBN 0-226-14590-5.

Storey, Graham. *Charles Dickens: "Bleak House."* Cambridge and New York: Cambridge Univ. Press, 1987. Pp. 110. $5.95. ISBN 0-521-31691-X.

Storey, Mark. *Byron and the Eye of Appetite*. New York: St. Martin's Press, 1986. Pp. ix + 229. $25.00. ISBN 0-312-11124-X.

Sultana, Donald. *The Journey of Sir Walter Scott to Malta*. New York: St. Martin's Press, 1986. Pp. xvi + 190. $25.00. ISBN 0-312-44504-0.

Tanner, Tony. *Jane Austen*. Cambridge, MA: Harvard Univ. Press, 1986. Pp. x + 291. $20.00 cloth, ISBN 0-674-47173-3.

Taylor, Anya. *Coleridge's Defense of the Human*. Columbus: Ohio State Univ. Press, 1986. Pp. xii + 223. $20.00. ISBN 0-8142-0413-9.

Taylor, Beverly. *Francis Thompson*. Boston: G. K. Hall, 1987. Pp. 158. $22.95. ISBN 0-8057-6930-7. $8.95 paper, ISBN 0-674-47174-1.

Tetreault, Ronald. *The Poetry of Life: Shelley and Literary Form*. Toronto and London: Univ. of Toronto Press, 1987. Pp. xi + 290. $35.00. ISBN 0-8020-5696-2.

Thackeray, William Makepeace. *The History of Pendennis*. Ed. Donald Hawes. Harmondsworth, Middlesex, and New York: Penguin Books, 1986, 1972. Pp. 810. $5.95. ISBN 0-14-043076-8.

Thesing, William B., ed. *Victorian Prose Writers Before 1867. Dictionary of Literary Biography*, vol. 55. Detroit: Gale Research, 1987. Pp. xiii + 379. $90.00. ISBN 0-8103-1733-8.

Thomson, Alastair W. *The Poetry of Tennyson*. London and New York: Routlege & Kegan Paul, 1986. Pp. x + 278. $55.00. ISBN 0-7102-0716-6.

Timko, Michael, Kaplan, Fred, and Guiliano, Edward, eds. *Dickens Studies Annual*. New York: AMS Press, 1986. Pp. xiv + 438. $25.00. ISBN 0-404-18535-5.

Trollope, Anthony. *The Bertrams*. New York: Dover, 1986. Pp. 487. $8.95. ISBN 0-486-25119-5.

Trollope, Anthony. *Harry Heathcote of Gangoil*. New York: Dover Publications, 1987. Pp. 159. $3.95. ISBN 0-486-25317-1.

Trollope, Anthony. *Miss Mackenzie*. New York: Dover, 1986. Pp. 388. $7.95. ISBN 0-486-25201-9.

Twitchell, James B. *Forbidden Partners: The Incest Taboo in Modern Culture*. New York: Columbia Univ. Press, 1987. Pp. xiv + 311. $24.95. ISBN 0-231-06412-8.

Wallace, Robert K. *Emily Brontë and Beethoven: Romantic Equilibrium in Fiction and Music*. Athens: Univ. of Georgia Press, 1986. Pp. ix + 237. $30.00. ISBN 0-8203-0813-7.

Waller, John O. *A Circle of Friends: The Tennysons and the Lushingtons of Park House*. Columbus: Ohio State Univ. Press, 1987. Pp. xvi + 290. $29.50. ISBN 0-8142-0424-4.

Watkins, Daniel P. *Social Relations in Byron's Eastern Tales*. Rutherford: Fairleigh Dickinson Univ. Press, 1987. Pp. 163. $24.50. ISBN 0-8386-3287-4.

Weiss, Barbara. *The Hell of the English: Bankruptcy and the Victorian Novel*. Lewisburg: Bucknell Univ. Press, and London and Toronto: Associated Univ. Presses, 1986. Pp. 208. $29.50. ISBN 08387-5099-0.

Welburn, Andrew J. *Power and Self-Consciousness in the Poetry of Shelley*. New York: St. Martin's Press, 1986. Pp. xiv + 234. $25.00. ISBN 0-312-63371-8.

Welsh, Alexander. *The City of Dickens*. Cambridge, MA, and London: Harvard Univ. Press, 1971. Pp. xi + 232. $8.95. ISBN 0-674-13185-1.

White, R. S. *Keats as a Reader of Shakespeare*. Norman and London: Univ. of Oklahoma Press, 1986. Pp. 250. $24.95. ISBN 0-8061-2053-3.

Wilkes, G.A. ed. *Essays & Studies 1986*. London: John Murray; Atlantic Highlands, NJ: Humanities Press, 1986. Pp. 120. $29.95. ISBN 0-391-03404-9.

Wilks, Brian. *The Illustrated Brontës of Haworth*. New York and Oxford: Facts on File, 1986. Pp. 224. $21.95. ISBN 0-8160-1399-3.

Williams, Meg Harris. *A Strange Way of Killing: The Poetic Structure of "Wuthering Heights"*. Oxford: Clunie Press, 1987. Pp. xii + 243. ISBN 0-902065-23-9.

Williams, Michael. *Jane Austen: Six Novels and Their Methods.* New York: St. Martin's Press, 1986. Pp. viii + 214. $25.00. ISBN 0-312-43989-X.

Witke, Joanne. *William Blake's Epic: Imagination Unbound.* New York: St. Martin's Press, 1986. Pp. 231. $27.50. ISBN 0-312-88024-3.

Wolfson, Susan J. *The Questioning Presence: Wordsworth, Keats, and the Interrogative Mode in Romantic Poetry.* Ithaca and London: Cornell Univ. Press, 1986. Pp. 392. $29.95. ISBN 0-8014-1909-3.

Wright, Andrew. *Fictional Discourse and Historical Space.* New York: St. Martin's Press, 1987. Pp. 116. $27.50 ISBN 0-312-28816-6.

Wright, Terence. "*Tess of the D'Urbervilles.*" London: Macmillan, and Atlantic Highlands, NJ: Humanities Press, 1987. Pp. xii + 84. $7.95. ISBN 0-391-03451-0.

Yost, George. *Pieracci and Shelley: An Italian "Ur-Cenci."* Scripta Humanistica 19. Potomac: Scripta Humanistica, 1986. Pp. ix + 141. $27.50. ISBN 0-916379-33-7.

Zipes, Jack, ed. *Victorian Fairy Tales: The Revolt of the Fairies and Elves.* New York and London: Methuen, 1987. Pp. xxiv + 381. $24.95. ISBN 0-416-42080-X.

Studies in English Literature 1500-1900

VOLUME 27, 1987

CONTENTS

Archer, Mark, The Meaning of "Grace" and "Courtesy": Book Six of *The Faerie Queene* 17

Armistead, J. M., Dryden's Poetry and the Language of Magic 381

Bailey, Vicki Sapp, Pope and Antithesis: "Law and War With Words" 437

Bevan, C. Knatchbull, Personal Identity in *Mansfield Park*: Forms, Fictions, Role-Play, and Reality 595

Comensoli, Viviana, Play-making, Domestic Conduct, and the Multiple Plot in *The Roaring Girl* 249

Corse, Taylor, "Heaven's Last Best Work": Pope's "Epistle to a Lady" 413

Cubeta, Paul M., Falstaff and the Art of Dying 197

Dawson, Anthony, *Women Beware Women* and the Economy of Rape 303

DeNeef, A. Leigh, Recent Studies in the English Renaissance 141

Duncan, Douglas, *Gammer Gurton's Needle* and the Concept of Humanist Parody 177

Finkelpearl, Philip J., John Fletcher as Spenserian Playwright: *The Faithful Shepherdess* and *The Island Princess* 285

Folkenflik, Robert, Recent Studies in the Restoration and Eighteenth Century 503

Goldsmith, Steven, The Muting of Satan: Language and Redemption in *Paradise Regained* 125

Handwerk, Gary, On Heroes and Their Demise: Critical Liberalism in *Beauchamp's Career* 663

Howard, Jean E., Recent Studies in Elizabethan and Jacobean Drama 321

Hunt, John, Allusive Coherence in Sidney's *Apology for Poetry* 1

Hunt, Maurice, Comfort in *Measure for Measure* 213

Klein, Mary Ann, Tennyson's "The Epic": An Experiment in Perspective 623

Luckyj, Christina, "Great Women of Pleasure": Main Plot and Subplot in *The Duchess of Malfi* 267

Lull, Janis, Expanding "The Poem Itself": Reading George Herbert's Revisions 71

Manning, Peter J., and Sylvia, Recent Studies in the Nineteenth Century 683

Marshall, W. G., The Presence of "the Word" in Cowper's *The Task* 475

Matar, N. I., Milton and the Idea of the Restoration of the Jews 109

Miller, Clarence H., The May-Day Celebration in Wordworth's Immortality Ode 571

Novak, Maximillian E., *A Vindication of the Press* and the Defoe Canon 399

Pickrel, Paul, Lionel Trilling and *Mansfield Park* 609

Riddell, James A., The Arrangement of Ben Jonson's *Epigrammes* 53

Rogers, Henry N. III, Trollope and James: The "Germ" Within 647

Ross, Deborah, Mirror, Mirror: The Didactic Dilemma of *The Female Quixote* 455

Rothenberg, Molly Anne, Blake Reads "The Bard": Contextual Displacement, and Conditions of Readibility in *Jerusalem* 489

Shabetai, Karen, Blake's Antifoundationalist Poetics 555

Skulsky, Harold, The Fellowship of the Mystery: Emergent and Exploratory Metaphor in Vaughan 89

Smith, Molly, The Mythical Implications in Pope's "Epistle to a Lady" 427

Smith, Susan B., "A Yorkshire burr": Language in *Shirley* 637

Stillman, Robert E., "Words cannot knytt": Language and Desire in Ralegh's *The Ocean to Cynthia* 35

Strout, Nathaniel, Jonson's Jacobean Masques and the Moral Imagination 233

Thomson, Douglass H., "Sport of Transmutations": The Evolution of Wordsworth's "To Lycoris" 581